Cognitive-Behavioral Therapies for Trauma

Cognitive-Behavioral Therapies for Trauma

EDITED BY

Victoria M. Follette
Josef I. Ruzek
Francis R. Abueg

THE GUILFORD PRESS
New York   London

© 1998 The Guilford Press
A Division of Guilford Publications, Inc.
72 Spring Street, New York, NY 10012
http://www.guilford.com

Printed in the United States of America

This book is printed on acid-free paper.

Last digit is print number: 9 8 7 6 5 4 3 2 1

Library of Congress Cataloging-in-Publication Data

Cognitive-behavioral therapies for trauma / edited by Victoria M.
  Follette, Josef I. Ruzek, Francis R. Abueg
     p. cm.
   Includes bibliographical references and index.
   ISBN 1-57230-400-6 (hardcover)
   1. Post-traumatic stress disorder—Treatment. 2. Cognitive therapy.
I. Follette, Victoria M. II. Ruzek, Josef I. III. Abueg, Francis R.
RC552.P67C65   1998
616.85′210651—dc21   98-37114
                                                              CIP

Contributors

Francis R. Abueg, PhD, Trauma Resource Consulting, Inc., Cupertino, CA

Dudley David Blake, PhD, Evaluation and Brief Treatment PTSD Unit, Boise Department of Veterans Affairs Medical Center, Boise, ID

Claude M. Chemtob, PhD, Stress Disorders Laboratory, Veterans Administration Research, Honolulu, HI

Marylene Cloitre, PhD, Payne Whitney Clinic, New York Hospital–Cornell Medical Center, New York, NY

Jill Serafin Compton, PhD, Duke University Medical Center, Durham, NC

Ann Elliott, PhD, Department of Psychology, Emory and Henry College, Emory, VA

Matthew Fanetti, MA, Department of Psychology, University of Nevada, Reno, Reno, NV

William F. Flack, Jr., PhD, Department of Psychology, Indiana University of Pennsylvania, Indiana, PA

Edna B. Foa, PhD, Center for the Treatment and Study of Anxiety, Department of Psychiatry, Allegheny University of the Health Sciences, Philadelphia, PA

Victoria M. Follette, PhD, Department of Psychology, University of Nevada, Reno, Reno, NV

William C. Follette, PhD, Department of Psychology, University of Nevada, Reno, Reno, NV

Steven C. Hayes, PhD, Department of Psychology, University of Nevada, Reno, Reno, NV

Lee Hyer, PhD, University of Medicine and Dentistry of New Jersey, Edison, NJ

Terence M. Keane, PhD, Psychology Service, Boston Veterans Affairs Medical Center, Boston, MA

Robert J. Kohlenberg, PhD, Department of Psychology, University of Washington, Seattle, WA

Edward S. Kubany, PhD, ABPP, National Center for PTSD, Pacific Islands Division, Department of Veterans Affairs, Honolulu, HI

Marsha M. Linehan, PhD, Department of Psychology, University of Washington, Seattle, WA

Brett T. Litz, PhD, Psychology Service, Boston Veterans Affairs Medical Center, Boston, MA

Elizabeth A. Meadows, PhD, Department of Psychology, Central Michigan University, Mt. Pleasant, MI

Amy E. Naugle, BA, Department of Psychology, University of Nevada, Reno, Reno, NV

Raymond W. Novaco, PhD, Department of Psychology and Social Behavior, University of California, Irvine, Irvine, CA

William O'Donohue, PhD, Department of Psychology, University of Nevada, Reno, Reno, NV

Melissa A. Polusny, PhD, Department of Psychology, Mankato State University, Mankato, MN

Josef I. Ruzek, PhD, National Center for PTSD, Veterans Affairs Palo Alto Health Care System, Palo Alto, CA

Richard T. Sonnenberg, PhD, Evaluation and Brief Treatment PTSD Unit, Boise Department of Veterans Affairs Medical Center, Boise, ID

Mavis Tsai, PhD, Private Practice, Seattle, WA

Amy Wagner, PhD, Department of Psychology, University of Wyoming, Laramie, WY

Robyn D. Walser, MA, Department of Psychology, Weber State University, Ogden, UT

M. G. Woods, MS, Family Connection, Medical College of Georgia, Augusta, GA

Preface

The simple and complex act of living one's life is sufficient to put one at risk for exposure to traumatic experiences. The symptoms associated with combat trauma, referred to over the years by terms such as "war neuroses" and "battle fatigue," have been recognized throughout history. However, in the 1970s a new awareness emerged of the effects of trauma symptoms resulting from other types of stresses (van der Kolk, Weisaeth, & ver der Hart, 1996). In addition to combat experiences, interpersonal victimization, natural and accidental disasters, medical experiences, and internment are among the precipitants that have been associated with the development of stress reactions. An ever-increasing interest in trauma has captivated not only mental health providers, but also members of the culture at large. While this blossoming of interest has had a number of important benefits, such as an emphasis on laboratory and clinical research investigating trauma, it has also resulted in some negative outcomes. For example, interest in trauma has come to be seen as faddish and lacking in scientific rigor. Some worry that we have become a society of victims, with individuals no longer taking responsibility for their lives. Despite some of the negative impacts of these perspectives, such criticisms have also had a positive impact. Attention to these issues has served a regulatory function, actually enhancing the quality of the work aimed at understanding trauma. We believe that the investigation of trauma and its effects has entered a new level of maturity and will continue to grow as a recognized and valid area of scientific inquiry.

This book is intended to provide the reader with a detailed accounting of the current state of cognitive-behavioral treatments of trauma symptoms. After our overview chapter, two introductory chapters provide a foundation for the text. The first, by Blake and Sonnenberg, presents current data on cognitive-behavioral outcome research with trauma populations. Naugle and Follette follow with a chapter describing a functional analytic approach to determining the treatment focus for clients with a trauma history. Their chapter lays the groundwork for the remainder of the book. Rather than presenting a treatment package for the various types of trauma experiences, the text presents treatment strategies that address symptoms, or constellations of symptoms, that have been found across trauma experiences. Thus, the chapters that follow address issues such as intrusion and arousal, with Flack, Litz, and Keane focusing on combat trauma and Meadows and Foa examining these issues in relation to sexual trauma. Kubany examines the problem of guilt, a relatively new target for trauma therapists. While anger has been a focus of treatment for cognitive-behavioral therapists for many years, Novaco and Chemtob provide a new perspective on this problem in relation to trauma. Ruzek, Polusny, and Abueg have tailored established elements of substance abuse treatment to meet the special needs of trauma survivors. Similarly, Walser and Hayes have adapted their discussion of acceptance and commitment to the dilemmas confronting clients exposed to trauma experiences. Dissociation has not been extensively examined in the cognitive-behavioral tradition; however, the relationship of this phenomena to trauma experiences is generally accepted. Wagner and Linehan provide a unique analysis of dissociation that remains consistent with a cognitive-behavioral paradigm. Cloitre's discussion of the difficult issue of revictimization further elaborates treatment targets traditionally addressed by cognitive-behavioral therapy. Additionally, we are concerned with the role of the interpersonal context in treatment and recovery. These issues are discussed in chapters on the therapeutic relationship by Kohlenberg and Tsai and couple treatment by Serafin and Follette. Finally, in order to encourage attention to the developmental matters, we have included chapters focusing on the treatment of children (O'Donohue, Fanetti, & Elliott) and elders (Hyer & Woods). Each chapter describes the relevance of behavioral theory to the problem being addressed, a brief description of empirical research, and extended discussion of clinical applications. The book includes several features:

- A focus on a variety of traumatic experiences (e.g., combat, rape and child sexual assault, domestic violence) with the goal of bridging the gap between various trauma literatures.
- A grounding in theory and empirical research, so that treatment design is informed by the current state of knowledge regarding trauma.
- Extended attention to the pragmatics of treatment to help translate theory and research into usable, clinician-friendly, therapeutic practices.

We hope that this book will function as a practical tool for clinicians interested in trauma work, and as a textbook for use in instructional settings. We have therefore attempted to bring together, within one volume, extended practical discussions of the treatment options related to a variety of symptoms associated with trauma. One tenet of cognitive-behavioral therapy is that clinical practices be embedded in developed theory and subjected to empirical scrutiny, and we have asked contributing authors to ensure that the practices recommended in this volume are theory-driven and supported by (or at least consistent with) current empirical evidence.

REFERENCE

van der kolk, B. A., Weisaeth, L., & van der Hart, O. (1996). History of trauma in psychiatry. In B. A. van der Kolk, A. C. McFarlane, & L. Weisaeth (Eds.), *Traumatic stress: The effects of overwhelming experience on mind, body, and society* (pp. 47–74). New York: Guilford Press.

Contents

Cognitive-Behavioral Therapies for Trauma

P A R T O N E

THEORY AND EMPIRICAL FOUNDATIONS

A Contextual Analysis of Trauma
THEORETICAL CONSIDERATIONS

VICTORIA M. FOLLETTE
JOSEF I. RUZEK
FRANCIS R. ABUEG

While trauma researchers have emerged from a variety of psychological para-digms, behaviorists have played an important role in defining the field. Behavioral therapy (BT) is particularly well suited to the treatment of stress reactions. Many of its treatment methods were originally fashioned as a response to problems of fear and anxiety. The theoretical underpinnings of BT were developed, in part, through the application of models of classical conditioning and operant learning to situations in which exposure to aversive stimuli generated fear, escape, and avoidance responses. With a tradition of careful attention to anxiety and its disorders, it is natural that behavioral practitioners and researchers have increas-ingly brought to bear their clinical and theoretical insights on the domain of trauma and its consequences.

The chapters that make up this volume describe a range of behavioral and cognitive-behavioral approaches to problems associated with traumatization. They represent the views of a diverse group of practitioners and researchers who concern themselves with different survivor populations. While there are some differences in the authors' conceptualizations of the behavioral models and treat-ment methods, there are a number of common factors that unite this work. While it is not our goal to provide a unitary definition of cognitive-behavioral therapy, we are interested in highlighting the similarities of the points of view of the authors in this text. There remain many misconceptions associated with more current behavioral theory. For example, contemporary forms of BT incorporate both observable behaviors and private events such as thoughts and feelings. In order to be clear that the work described here includes both private and observable behaviors, we use the term "cognitive-behavioral therapy" (CBT) to describe the treatments presented in this text. This is also consistent with other contemporary behavioral approaches (e.g., Linehan, 1993; Hayes, Wilson, Gifford, Follette, & Strosahl, 1996). Additionally, we argue for an ecological approach to trauma and its consequences that encompasses developing contextual forms of CBT. Finally, we raise several issues of importance for future research. The importance of the recursive loop connecting science and practice is a long tradition in behavioral therapies. While this text focuses on current aspects of applied work with trauma survivors, the interplay of science and practice continues to move the technology forward.

There are a number of principles and philosophical assumptions associated with a contextual behavioral approach (Hayes, Follette, & Follette, 1995). However, of primary importance is the idea that behavior is best understood in terms of its function rather than its form. This concept is more fully elaborated in the Naugle and Follette chapter that describes a functional analytic approach to treating problems associated with trauma. While many of the chapters in this text are consistent with a traditional syndromal classification, typically posttraumatic stress disorder (PTSD), our conceptualization moves beyond that construct. Syndromal classification has provided some direction for treatment development, particularly with regard to anxiety disorders. However, a contextual behavioral approach moves away from traditional classification, in order to more fully understand the behaviors in their context. We argue that an analysis of the issues bringing any client to treatment should include both distal and proximal variables. For example, in the case of childhood trauma, it is important to investigate a wide range of childhood experiences (physical and sexual abuse, family environment, and positive support) as well as current stressors (couples' problems or job stress) that may have an impact on current functioning (Polusny & Follette, 1995). Thus, the treatment proposed in this text emphasizes an inclusive approach, with attention to not only the trauma, but also to a number of variables that may mediate or moderate adult outcomes.

THEORETICAL ISSUES IN COGNITIVE-BEHAVIORAL APPROACHES TO TRAUMA

Multiple Theoretical Perspectives on Trauma

As the field of behavioral therapy has evolved, it has generated a large number of both broad and specific theories (O'Donohue & Krasner, 1995) that sometimes complement one another and sometimes compete for explanatory relevance. Indeed, there has been much debate about whether such a range of theoretical formulations can or should be accommodated under a single rubric of "behavioral therapy" or "cognitive-behavioral therapy," when alternative formulations sometimes do violence to the core assumptions and conceptual underpinnings of one another. With the growth in trauma-related cognitive-behavioral research and treatment, these same controversies are present. However, we believe there is some movement toward a rapprochement among these differing perspectives.

Learning Theory

Theories of classical and operant learning provide important conceptual grounding for clinical scientists working in the trauma area. Behavioral treatments have developed from learning theory, with two traditions evolving from the basic discipline. While applied behavior analysts and behavioral therapists shared a belief in a number of basic principles, they also became part of traditions that increasingly diverged in both theory and practice (Hayes et al., 1995). However their interest in the science of behavior based on learning principles held them together under the basic umbrella of the BT movement.

Models of classical conditioning have provided the central idea that stimuli associated with traumatic events can, through learning, come to elicit responses similar to those shown during exposure to trauma itself. Trauma-related behaviors and symptoms—for example, intrusive thoughts and images, fear-related physiological changes, aggression, hypervigilance, or problematic interpersonal behaviors—may then occur in situations in which no further traumatic exposure occurs. Through this mechanism, then, the spread of traumatic reactions to the domains of ordinary life can be explained. This fundamental understanding of trauma and learning has led to a central tenet of much of the therapy discussed in this text—the importance of exposure in treating trauma.

Theories of operant learning direct attention to the factors that maintain apparently maladaptive responding, and the processes of reinforcement that continue to affect behavior. According to this way of thinking, many of the behaviors shown by trauma survivors—avoidance, social isolation, aggression, dissociative responding—are in part maintained by their emotional, social, and environmental consequences. Treatment implications include the need to alter the consequences of problematic behaviors, teach different ways of achieving desired outcomes, and arrange for reinforcement of alternative responses.

Mowrer's (1960) two-factor theory as it relates to problems associated with anxiety provides a strong foundation for understanding trauma symptoms. The theory suggests that classical conditioning explains basic fear acquisition and that avoidance behavior is maintained through operant conditioning. This integration of the two learning paradigms provides a more comprehensive explanation of trauma-related symptoms. The pairing of of the aversive or unconditioned stimulus (UCS) with the neutral (condtioned) stimulus (CS) will elicit fear responses. For example, some survivors of sexual abuse report that the perpetrator smelled of alcohol during the abuse experiences and that now the smell of acohol elicits a fear response. Fears are maintained through avoidance, which is negatively reinforced. This lack of exposure to the CS prevents new learning from taking place, hence the fears are maintained. One example of this mechanism observed in abuse survivors is avoidance of intimate relationships. This analysis of anxiety disorders led to the proposal that exposure therapies be used for trauma survivors. The exposure principle is a recurrent theme in this text and continues to provide a foundation for BT and CBT.

Cognitive Perspectives

In the 1960s, cognitive science emerged as an important discipline in experimental psychology and set the stage for significant transitions in behavioral therapy. These approaches were less concerned with external environmental influences on behavior, and more focused on reaching inside the "black box" to describe and label internal processes, using constructs such as "belief," "attitude," "memory," "schema," and "semantic network." A variety of mediators were identified that were used in creating connections between the organism and the environment.

One type of cognitive approach is concerned with identification of common negative beliefs or "self-talk." This cognitive content-oriented approach emphasizes the role of negative beliefs in causing distress and helping to maintain symptoms, with anxiety disorders as a primary exemplar of this process. Beliefs emphasized include those related to personal safety or vulnerability, dangerousness of the world, lessened trust in others, loss of confidence in the fairness and benevolence of the world, self-blame and guilt, low self-efficacy or perceived self-competence, negative future outcome expectancies, low self-worth or esteem, and loss of spiritual beliefs. One practical outgrowth of this orientation is the application of cognitive restructuring methods to challenge overly negative or distorted interpretations of traumatic experiences.

A second conceptual stream applies the semantic network model of internal memory structure to traumatization (Lang, 1979; Foa, Steketee, & Rothbaum, 1989; Foa & Rothbaum, 1998). According to these accounts, traumatic experiences lead to the development of fear structures in memory, which require therapeutic modification. In order for this modification to occur, two conditions must be met: Fear structures must be "activated," and new information must be incorporated. This model directs attention to the importance of actively accessing trauma-related cognitive processes if they are to be changed. It has been used to provide a theoretical understanding of the utility of treatment via direct therapeutic exposure, and to conceptualize factors that disrupt "emotional processing" (Foa, Riggs, Massie, & Yarczower, 1995).

A third view focuses on the personal accounts that individuals give of their experience and its consequences: their trauma "narratives" (Meichenbaum & Fong, 1993). Rather than focusing attention on single classes of negative thoughts, it draws attention to the importance of the narrative as a whole, and to narrative change across repeated tellings. Importantly, it is also beginning to prompt development of a set of novel measures of therapeutic change. Recently, it has been shown that changes in narrative structure are correlated with PTSD symptom change (Foa, Molnar, & Cashman, 1995; Foa, 1997).

Finally, the experimental psychological methodologies and models of "cognitive science" have increasingly been brought to bear on the phenomena of traumatization. Researchers have studied processes of attention (e.g., Thrasher, Dalgleish, & Yule, 1994) and subliminal processing of threat cues (e.g., McNally, Amir, & Lipke, 1996). A variety of aspects of memory in trauma survivors has begun to receive research attention, including autobiographical memory (McNally, Litz, Prassas, Shin, & Weathers, 1994), implicit and explicit memory (e.g., McNally, 1997), performance on "directed forgetting" tasks (e.g., Cloitre, Cancienne, Brodsky, Dulit, & Perry, 1996), and source monitoring (e.g., Golier, Harvey, Steiner, & Yehuda, 1997). Some of this work has implications for the understanding of processes responsible for effective and ineffective treatment using behavioral methods. For example, Brewin, Dalgleish, and Joseph (1996) used recent models of memory and emotion processing to conceptualize three types of outcome resulting from efforts to cope with traumatic memories and emotions: completion/integration, chronic emotional processing, and premature inhibition of processing. So far, these approaches have had more impact on theory than on treatment design and effectiveness. However, they offer the promise of development of relatively "nonreactive" trauma-related assessment tools, methods of measuring PTSD that do not rely solely on self-reported symptoms and therefore are less subject to effects of mood, motivation, and malingering or compensation seeking. They provide novel, methodologically sound assessment technologies linked with larger bodies of cognitive sciences research. And they link the psychology of trauma with current developments in experimental psychology.

The working models of most cognitive-behavioral theoreticians would incorporate multiple aspects of the various learning and cognitive conceptualizations outlined here. For instance, the cognitive reprocessing treatment designed by Resick and her colleagues (Resick & Schnicke, 1993) incorporates learning theoretical conceptualizations and cognitive restructuring methods. As the emotion processing model developed by Foa and her colleagues has evolved, it has embraced elements of learning theory, internal memory structures, cognitive content specific to PTSD, and the narrative perspective (Foa, Molnar, & Cashman, 1995).

Behavioral Analysis and Cognitive-Behavioral Therapy

We hope that one unique contribution of this book is to help increase the mutual influence of behavior analysis and mainstream BT. With the "cognitivization" of BT, there has been an increased awareness of the influence of cognitive processes on behavior, and the development of treatment methods with a distinctly cognitive focus. Within the various approaches to trauma treatment, practitioners and theorists have paid more attention to the "inner" world of their client, to the subjective meanings of traumatization, to internal "fear structures" (Foa, Steketee, & Rothbaum, 1989), to schemas, beliefs, and attitudinal "stuck points" (Resick & Schnicke, 1993). By contrast, behavior analysts have traditionally directed attention to the external influences on behavior, to the social influences on symptoms, and attempts at coping. They remind us that the people with whom survivors interact—their "significant others," families, peers, coworkers, treatment providers, and their culture—combine to help shape responses to trauma. The behavioral analytic framework also teaches that, as with other complex sets of behaviors, the sequelae of traumatization are many and varied, differing across individuals and in their relationships to one another. It challenges the very concept of "syndrome" (Krasner, 1992), and indeed, of "posttraumatic stress disorder." PTSD as a syndrome of trauma is seen as a classification imposed by human observers. Syndromal classification in DSM-IV is viewed as an analytic approach with distinct limitations. For example, the link between disorders and differential treatment is weak (Hayes, Nelson, & Jarrett, 1987), and problems subsumed under the same category (e.g., depression) may be caused or maintained by very different variables (Naugle & Follette, Chapter 3, this volume). Thus, the inclusion of the behavioral analytic approach elaborates and strengthens a repertoire for evaluating the various responses to trauma.

TOWARD A CONTEXTUAL–ECOLOGICAL PERSPECTIVE ON TRAUMA

Although a perusal of the contents of this text reflects a focus on the intrapersonal sequelae associated with traumatic experiences, we believe that the symptoms and problems discussed must be considered in terms of the broader contexts in which they occur. Bronfenbrenner (1979) has described an ecological approach to human development that is useful in explicating the many interconnected systems in which the individual is embedded. A consideration of these systems leads to a more thorough understanding not only of the reasons for the development and maintenance of symptomatic behaviors, but also identification of targets for intervention.

Our perspective includes a contextual analysis of both observable and nonobservable behaviors (Hayes, Follette, & Follette, 1991). In this analysis, behaviors are conceptualized in terms of their functions and not simply their topographies. These functions are assessed in terms of both historical and situational factors, with a concurrent examination of multiple layers of systems. Both systems with which the individual is in direct contact and those that are outside of the individual's direct contact are assessed. This analysis includes distal and proximal variables from a number of contexts. Thus, the trauma survivor who is having difficulties in an intimate relationship is considered not only in terms of intrapersonal behavioral deficits, such as intimacy-avoidant behaviors, but also in terms of the context of variables in the couple relationship. Relationships are considered as a reciprocal interchange of behaviors that can only be clearly understood using a contextual analysis. Moreover, extrafamilial systems, such as work environment, treatment facilities, and friendship networks also impact upon the traumatized individual. At yet a higher level of analysis is the sociocultural context in which all of the other systems are embedded. Using this framework, dysfunction is examined not only within the individual, but also between and within other systems at other levels.

Interpersonal Contexts of Traumatization

As noted earlier, the people with whom trauma survivors interact influence them. Social situations provide many of the "trauma reminders" or stimuli that elicit or prompt symptoms and problem behaviors. It is in social environments that traumatized persons attempt to cope with the effects of their experience by talking with family or friends, participating in support groups, or seeking professional help from physicians or mental health professionals. Cognitions about trauma and its implications are usually expressed in interpersonal contexts, through the descriptions given to helpers and significant others in conversation and to researchers via self-report measures. Disclosure of traumatic experience, which has been hypothesized to engender healing processes of exposure, cognitive restructuring, and social support, also is an essentially interpersonal event.

Understanding environmental factors, particularly those of "invalidating environments" (Linehan, 1993), provides a broader terrain for the completion of the functional analysis. As described by Linehan an invalidating environment is one in which an individual's expression of his or her private experience is responded to with "erratic, inappropriate, and extreme responses" (p. 49). For example, a sexual abuse survivor may disclose aspects of her abuse experiences to her significant other in an attempt to seek validation and understanding. If her partner vacillates between expressions of sadness and anger, becomes frustrated with his lack of ability to remedy the situation, and tells her "Just forget it" and get on with her life, this reaction could lead to continuing avoidance of closeness with the partner. It could also lead to increasing emotional avoidance at both an internal and public level. Trauma survivors with such experiences may invalidate their own interpretations of experience and become more distrustful not only of their environment, but also of themselves. In the clinical situation described here, an attention to the posttrauma interpersonal context suggests targets for change and intervention strategies distinct from those emerging from an exclusive focus on the symptoms, thoughts, and feelings of the survivor.

Larger Environmental Contexts of Traumatization

Invalidation need not occur only at an interpersonal level. Vietnam War veterans who would now be considered to be suffering from symptoms of PTSD often had punishing experiences when seeking help in hospitals: They were considered psychotic, placed on inappropriate medications, or even suspected of malingering. Many veterans were denied or had great difficulty in qualifying for compensation in the days before PTSD became a formal psychiatric diagnosis included in the DSM. These experiences confirmed for some veterans their more broad distrust of all government agencies, based on experiences in the military. On yet another front, as veterans can well describe, a significant part of the pain for many of them was related to the anger and hostility they experienced upon coming home. The nation's strong ambivalent feelings about the war were often directed at the veterans themselves, thereby exacerbating the strangeness of returning to civilian life.

Issues of gender, ethnic minority membership, and aging have become important considerations in the developing literature on trauma, and the field of clinical behavior therapy has not ignored these large-scale influences on the treatment experiences offered trauma survivors. As mentioned earlier, Linehan and Foa and colleagues have attempted to incorporate the broad social environment into their models dealing with repeated victimization of women. Insidious traumatization—everyday slights, discrimination, and even explicit epithets—appear to arise from simply occupying a lower social class, having less power or status, characteristic of American minorities and women. These chronic stressors have a broad demoralizing effect upon the trauma victim, and each small instance, though often unnoticed or unmeasured, takes its psychological toll on the individual. A practical, behavioral stance in therapy might require sharing a philosophical approach with the patients (e.g., a "wise mind" would take into account the offense through a balanced understanding of the emotional hurt along with the rational "weighing" of its meaning). In combination with the more familiar strategies of assertiveness training and increasing positive activities, authors herein discuss explicit efficacy and control-enhancing interventions.

As yet another example, the mass media, with their depiction of traumatic events and the experiences of survivors, may also be an important larger context for the understanding of traumatization and its consequences. For example, violent injury is an all-too-common fixture of television programming. However, injured parties usually adapt instantly to their wounding with no apparent psychological effects. Actors, despite exposure to life-threatening events—shootings, stabbings, attempted kidnappings and assaults, natural disasters—routinely carry on as if normal response to such events includes only brief distress and few implications for the future. Such coverage distorts public awareness of the consequences of violence and other forms of tramatization. In so doing, it helps create a social climate in which victims are surprised by the intensity of their reactions, families may lack sympathy for a member with chronic problems, and health care systems may fail to routinely address the psychosocial needs of injured patients (Ruzek & Garay, 1996).

The Contexts of Treatment

One of the consequences of a contextual or ecological perspective is an increased awareness that both theories of traumatization and therapist behaviors (and, indeed, treatment systems themselves) are part of the larger environment in which a trauma survivor must adapt. Kohlenberg and Tsai (Chapter 12, this volume) bring this issue to the forefront. Their examination of clinically relevant behaviors occurring in the session provides a unique addition to a behavioral approach to treatment. Additionally, it is important to realize that treatment is almost without exception conducted in the context of a "medical model" of human difficulties and service delivery (Krasner, 1992). Within this context, posttrauma problems are conceptualized as medical "disorders" that are treated by "mental health" specialists, often in hospitals or other medical settings. We are so thoroughly embedded in this context that it is sometimes difficult to recognize it as such, and to remember that many alternative models are in fact possible. Nonetheless, the model has consequences, including the stigmatization that may be associated with the seeking of "treatment" for a "mental health" problem, the reification of the posttrauma problems into a posttraumatic stress "disorder," and the pragmatic constraints on treatment delivery imposed by the model itself. For example, treatment is often (rather unreflectively) delivered in 50-minute blocks, in an environment far removed from that normally encountered by the client. This mode of service delivery is unlikely to be optimal for change.

The notion that alcoholism is a "disease" has been held to reduce the stigma associated with entry into treatment. Similarly, PTSD has been much described as a "normal response to abnormal circumstances," partly with the intention of directing attention to the primacy of extreme stress and not individual differences in determining response. However, research indicates that many people do not in fact develop PTSD following trauma exposure, and therefore PTSD is not "normal" (Yehuda & McFarlane, 1995). Will increased public and professional awareness of this finding create a different societal situation for the trauma survivor, in which the likelihood of viewing posttrauma problems as psychopathologies of the individual ("blaming the victim") increases? Rather, we hope that a dialectic emerges that encompasses both healthy, adaptive responses and more symptomatic responses to trauma as normal.

SOME FUTURE PRIORITIES FOR TRAUMA-RELATED COGNITIVE-BEHAVIORAL THERAPY

Consistent with its history of empirical evaluation, cognitive-behavioral treatment methods for stress-related responses to trauma and other consequences of traumatization have been tested in more controlled outcome studies than other treatment procedures (Foa & Meadows, 1997). As treatments for survivors of trauma develop, it will be important to increasingly target specific problems, which have as yet received little attention. Often, the syndrome of responding called PTSD has been targeted globally. Intervention is delivered and changes in aggregate levels of symptomatology are measured. One strength of a cognitive-behavioral perspective has been its specificity of intent; with treatment elements that have been designed to affect specific aspects of responding. Future studies should tackle problems that have been difficult to change, such as emotional numbing (Litz, 1992). They should investigate and measure clinically significant behaviors that have not been included in outcome studies. They should target trauma-related problems that have been largely ignored by cognitive-behavioral practitioners and theorists.

Second, there is a clear need for increased effort to develop prevention and early intervention services targeted at recently traumatized populations. Foa, Hearst-Ikeda, and Perry (1995) provided a demonstration that a cognitive-behavioral early intervention service comprised of education, stress management, direct therapeutic exposure, and cognitive restructuring could prevent development of chronic PTSD in rape victims. Similar efforts targeted at other trauma populations are much needed.

Finally, there is a dearth of empirically tested cognitive-behavioral treatments designed for traumatized children. CBT methods have much to offer in the development of preventive interventions and treatments for traumatized children (e.g., Peterson & Brown, 1994; Peterson, Gable, Doyle, & Ewigman, 1997), but to date, their contribution remains largely unrealized. An important early step is the treatment approach developed and tested by Deblinger and Heflin (1996) for sexually abused children and their nonoffending parents.

Finally, we are very optimistic regarding the contributions of behavioral therapies to the general field of trauma research and therapy. A behavioral approach has the advantage of focussing on a number of responses to trauma, with the understanding that no symptoms are pathognomonic of a trauma history. Symptoms are best understood in terms of their current functions, rather than solely as a consequence of events of the distant past. Behavioral analyses of responses to trauma have yet another advantage. Behavioral responses to trauma are seen as perfectly understandable when analyzed functionally. Thus, a behavioral approach is inherently respectful of people, with a nonblaming approach applied to the analyses of behavioral repertoires. In closing, we would propose that the analyses of problems associated with trauma histories should not just occur at the level of the individual. Instead, as scientists and practitioners, it is incumbent upon us to intervene at higher systems levels. While trauma will never be eliminated from the human experience, the incidence of some types of trauma (i.e., perpetration of violence against particularly vulnerable groups such as women and children) can be greatly reduced with the implementation of prevention strategies.

REFERENCES

Brewin, C. R., Dalgleish, T., & Joseph, S. (1996). A dual representation theory of posttraumatic stress disorder. *Psychological Review, 103,* 670–686.

Bronfenbrenner, U. (1979). *The ecology of human development: Experiments by nature and design.* Cambridge, MA: Harvard University Press.

Cloitre, M., Cancienne, J., Brodsky, B., Dulit, R., & Perry, S. W. (1996). Memory performance among women with parental abuse histories: Enhanced directed forgetting or directed remembering? *Journal of Abnormal Psychology, 105,* 204–211.

Deblinger, E., & Heflin, A. H. (1996). *Treating sexually abused children and their nonoffending parents.* Thousand Oaks, CA: Sage.

Foa, E. B. (1997). Psychological processes related to recovery from a trauma and an effective treatment for PTSD. *Annals of the New York Academy of Sciences, 821,* 410–424.

Foa, E. B., Hearst-Ikeda, D. E., & Perry, K. J. (1995). Evaluation of a brief cognitive-behavioral program for the prevention of chronic PTSD in recent assault victims. *Journal of Consulting and Clinical Psychology, 63,* 948–955.

Foa, E. B., & Meadows, E. A. (1997). Psychosocial treatments for posttraumatic stress disorder: A critical review. *Annual Review of Psychology, 48,* 449–480.

Foa, E. B., Molnar, C., & Cashman, L. (1995). Change in rape narratives during exposure therapy for PTSD. *Journal of Traumatic Stress, 8,* 675–690.

Foa, E. B., Riggs, D. S., Massie, E. D., & Yarczower, M. (1995). The impact of fear activation and anger on the efficacy of exposure treatment for PTSD. *Behavior Therapy, 26,* 487–499.

Foa, E. B., & Rothbaum, B. O. (1998). *Treating the trauma of rape: Cognitive-behavioral therapy for PTSD.* New York: Guilford Press.

Foa, E. B., Steketee, G., & Rothbaum, B. O. (1989). Behavioral/cognitive conceptualization of posttraumatic stress disorder. *Behavior Therapy, 20,* 155–176.

Golier, J., Harvey, P., Steiner, A., & Yehuda, R. (1997). Source monitoring in PTSD. *Annals of the New York Academy of Sciences, 821,* 472–475.

Hayes, S. C., Follette, W. C., & Follette, V. M. (1995). Behavior therapy: A contextual approach. In A. S. Gurman & S. B. Messer (Eds.), *Essential psychotherapies: Theory and practice* (pp. 128–181). New York: Guilford Press.

Hayes, S. C., Nelson, R. O., & Jarrett, R. (1987). Treatment utility of assessment: A functional approach to evaluating the quality of assessment. *American Psychologist, 42,* 963–974.

Hayes, S. C., Wilson, K. G., Gifford, E. V., Follette, V. M., & Strosahl, K. (1996). Emotional avoidance and behavioral disorders: A functional dimensional approach to diagnosis and treatment. *Journal of Consulting and Clinical Psychology, 64,* 1152–1168.

Krasner, L. (1992). The concepts of syndrome and functional analysis: Compatible or incompatible. *Behavioral Assessment, 14,* 307–321.

Lang, P. J. (1979). A bio-informational theory of emotional imagery. *Psychophysiology, 6,* 495–511.

Linehan (1993). *Cognitive-behavioral treatment of borderline personality disorder.* New York: Guilford Press.

Litz, B. T. (1992). Emotional numbing in combat-related post-traumatic stress disorder: A critical review and reformulation. *Clinical Psychology Review, 12,* 417–432.

McNally, R. J. (1997). Implicit and explicit memory for trauma-related information in PTSD. *Annals of the New York Academy of Sciences, 821,* 219–224.

McNally, R. J., Amir, N., & Lipke, H. J. (1996). Subliminal processing of threat cues in posttraumatic stress disorder? *Journal of Anxiety Disorders, 10,* 115–128.

McNally, R. J., Litz, B. T., Prassas, A., Shin, L. M., & Weathers, F. W. (1994). Emotional priming of autobiographical memory in post-traumatic stress disorder. *Cognition and Emotion, 8,* 351–368.

Meichenbaum, D., & Fong, G. (1993). How individuals control their own minds: A constructive narrative perspective. In D. M. Wegner & J. W. Pennebaker (Eds.), *Handbook of mental control* (pp. 473–489). New York: Prentice-Hall.

Mowrer, O. H. (1960). *Learning theory and behavior.* New York: Wiley.

O'Donohue, W., & Krasner, L. (Eds.). (1995). *Theories of behavior therapy: Exploring behavior change.* Washington, DC: American Psychological Association.

Peterson, L., & Brown, D. (1994). Integrating child injury and abuse/neglect research: Common histories, etiologies, and solutions. *Psychological Bulletin, 116,* 293–315.

Peterson, L., Gable, S., Doyle, C., & Ewigman, B. (1997). Beyond parenting skills: Battling barriers and building bonds to prevent child abuse and neglect. *Cognitive and Behavioral Practice, 4,* 53–74.

Polusny, M. A., & Follette, V. M. (1995). Long-term correlates of child sexual abuse: Theory and review of the empirical literature. *Applied and Preventive Psychology, 4,* 143–166.

Resick, P. A., & Schnicke, M. K. (1993). *Cognitive processing therapy for rape victims: A treatment manual.* Newbury Park, CA: Sage.

Ruzek, J. I., & Garay, K. (1996). Hospital trauma care and management of trauma-related psychological problems. *National Center for Post-Traumatic Stress Disorder Clinical Quarterly, 6,* 87–90.

Thrasher, S. M., Dalgleish, T., & Yule, W. (1994). Information processing in posttraumatic stress disorder. *Behaviour Research and Therapy, 32,* 247–254.

Yehuda, R., & McFarlane, A. C. (1995). Conflict between current knowledge about PTSD and its original conceptual basis. *American Journal of Psychiatry, 152,* 1705–1713.

CHAPTER TWO

Outcome Research on Behavioral and Cognitive-Behavioral Treatments for Trauma Survivors

DUDLEY DAVID BLAKE
RICHARD T. SONNENBERG

Although posttraumatic stress disorder (PTSD) has had a brief life as a formally recognized mental disorder (American Psychiatric Association, 1980), the body of information about it has grown rapidly (Blake, Albano, & Keane, 1992; Saigh, 1992). This growth of information has included an evolving literature on PTSD treatment. A range of such treatments has been employed and studied, including anger management training (McWhirter & Liebman, 1988), eye movement desensitization and reprocessing (Montgomery & Ayllon, 1994; Shapiro, 1995, 1991, 1989a, 1989b; Wolpe & Abrams, 1991), hypnosis (Kingsbury, 1988; Venn, 1988), implosive therapy (Black & Keane, 1982; Fairbank & Keane, 1982; Keane, Fairbank, Caddell, & Zimering, 1989; Keane & Kaloupek, 1982; Mueser, Yarnold, & Foy, 1991; Rychtarik, Silverman, Van Landingham, & Prue, 1984), music therapy (Burt, 1995), relaxation and biofeedback (Blanchard & Abel, 1976; Hickling, Sison, & Vanderploeg, 1986; Peniston, 1986), stress inoculation training (Pearson, Poquette, & Wasden, 1983), systematic desensitization (Bowen & Lambert, 1986; Kushner, 1965; Saul, Rome, & Leuser, 1946; Schindler, 1980; Wolff, 1977), Thought Field Therapy (Callahan, 1995), transcendental meditation (Brooks & Sarano, 1985), and trauma focus therapy (Rozynko & Dondershine, 1991; Scurfield, Corker, Gongla, & Richard, 1984).

Perhaps the most exciting and promising additions to the world of PTSD treatment are the *behavioral* and *cognitive-behavioral therapies*. These treatment approaches appear to address directly many of the common sequelae of trauma exposure. Moreover, the behavioral and cognitive-behavioral approaches derive from a solid base of theoretical and conceptual writings from which to direct their study (e.g., Fairbank & Brown, 1987; Chemtob, Roitblat, Hamada, Carlson, & Twentyman, 1988; Creamer, Burgess, & Pattison, 1992; Keane, Zimering, & Caddell, 1985; Holmes & St. Lawrence, 1983; Foa, Steketee, & Rothbaum, 1989; Joseph, Yule, & Williams, 1995; Kreitler & Kreitler, 1988; Litz, 1992; Litz & Keane, 1989; McCann & Pearlman, 1990; Rychtarik et al., 1984).

It is important to note at the outset of this chapter that a considerable amount of confusion and controversy exists regarding what respectively comprises "behavioral therapy" and "cognitive-behavioral therapy." Some behavioral therapists maintain a conviction that all behavioral therapy strategies involve cognitive aspects, and thus the term "cognitive-behavioral therapy" is superordinate and encompasses all of behavioral therapy (e.g., witness the recent [but unsuccessful] proposal to change the name of the Association for Advancement of Behavior Therapy [AABT] to the Association for the Advancement of Cognitive-Behavioral Therapy [AACBT]). Others steadfastly maintain that *behavioral therapy* is conceptually and historically the superordinate label and that cognitive-behavioral therapy is largely a division and offshoot of the "parent" field, behavioral therapy. In this chapter, we bypass this controversy and, in order to maintain conceptual clarity, use the term "behavioral therapy" to describe the strategies that have a primarily *behavioral* focus and whose principles can be traced more directly to operant and classical conditioning, and use the term "cognitive-behavioral therapy" to describe the strategies that have a primarily *cognitive* focus and whose principles can be traced more directly to cognitive theories.

In this chapter, we review the current status of behavioral and cognitive-behavioral treatments in the professional literature on PTSD. First, we describe these treatments and their application with trauma survivors. Next, we outline the empirical foundation for behavioral and cognitive-behavioral therapy, and include a discussion of why behaviors and cognitions are necessary and vital treatment foci in work with trauma survivors. Following that section, we review and critique the extant treatment outcome literature in which behavioral and cognitive-behavioral therapy was applied to the treatment of trauma survivors, and propose areas for further study. Finally, we discuss issues related to the current and future use and evaluation of behavioral therapy and cognitive-behavioral therapy in PTSD treatment.

BEHAVIORAL AND COGNITIVE-BEHAVIORAL THERAPY FOR TRAUMA SURVIVORS

Behavioral therapy for trauma survivors comprises an ensemble of therapeutic techniques that includes systematic desensitization, flooding or implosive therapy, and eye movement desensitization and reprocessing (EMDR). These treatments make up the bulk of behavioral treatments used with trauma survivors, and, although they share many conceptual and pragmatic features, they differ in their form and method of application.

Systematic desensitization (Wolpe, 1958) generally involves first establishing a desirable behavior (usually a state of relaxation) that is incompatible with the undesired fear or anxiety responses. The individual is then gradually exposed to a hierarchy of feared stimuli or images so that he or she can ultimately tolerate full exposure to the entire range of (real or imagined) fear stimuli. Thus, the individual learns to remain relaxed while imagining/remembering increasingly greater amounts of the feared/traumatic imagery, effectively replacing reactive distress with relative sangfroid.

In flooding and implosive therapy (Stampfl & Levis, 1967), the therapist directs the individual repeatedly and systematically to imagine all (sensory, imaginal, thematic) aspects of the traumatic incident(s). The treated individual is often encouraged to recall the event as vividly as he or she can and to involve as many senses (visual, auditory, gustatory, olfactory, tactile) as possible during the imagery (Lyons & Keane, 1989). In contrast to systematic desensitization and EMDR, implosive therapy involves encouraging the individual actually to experience the undesired conditioned (fear) responses that are associated with the fear-provoking stimuli. The fear responses are deliberately maintained until they are eliminated via the natural extinction process. The individual eventually becomes less fearful since, unlike during the traumatic event, the trauma and its tragic accompaniments do not occur.

EMDR (Shapiro, 1991, 1989a, 1989b) and its precursor, eye movement desensitization (EMD), involve having the patient engage in saccadic (back and forth) eye movements while conjuring up images of the event or stimulus that makes him or her uncomfortable, unhappy, or anxious. As a treatment for trauma survivors, EMDR involves "(1) exposure to trauma related visual imagery, (2) exposure to aversive trauma-related (negative) cognitions, (3) rehearsal of adaptive (positive) cognitions, (4) rapid eye movements, (5) active visual attention on an object (moving finger), (6) thought and image stopping, and (7) a deep breath at the end of each set" (Renfrey & Spates, 1994, p. 233). The trauma survivor identifies a traumatic event on which he or she wants to work, provides a SUDs rating (a 0–10 or 0–100, *from least to most,* of subjective units of discomfort or distress) to indicate how much discomfort he or she feels while recalling the event creates, articulates positive and negative self-statements related to the event, provides a "validity of cognition" (VoC) rating for how strongly he or she believes each of the two self-statements, and describes a "safe place" where he or she can return to mentally at the end of the session. With his or her head held still, the survivor conjures up thoughts and images related to the traumatic event(s) and is instructed to visually track the therapist's pen or finger for 15–20 waves. A number of trials or sets of this treatment are provided and, when the therapist is assured that the traumatic event has become significantly less upsetting (assessed through periodic SUD ratings), the therapist helps the survivor to mentally journey to the "safe place." The therapist again solicits SUD and VoC ratings related to the traumatic event and the positive and negative self-statements.

The typical scenario for these behavioral therapy treatments is an individual treatment setting in which the trauma survivor sits in a comfortable chair and actively participates in the treatment procedure. The individual receiving the treatment provides detailed information related to the traumatic event(s) to the behavioral therapist in preparation for the graduated or sustained exposure/extinction trials to follow. The individual then typically assumes a comfortable position, and either closes his or her eyes, or focuses them on a waving hand, to commence the treatment.

Cognitive-behavioral treatments can be delivered in both group and individual contexts but tend to have more of a pedagogical/educative flavor. Treatment often involves providing information to the survivor about the trauma (e.g., sexual assault victims may be given information about the national incidence of rape, or Vietnam veterans are sometimes educated about the history of the Vietnam War) as well as information about PTSD, its theories, and its treatment. These educative therapy efforts add to the patient's *knowledge* about trauma and his or her PTSD symptoms. The treatment may involve educating the survivor about learning theory or about how cognitions affect mood and behavior. The trauma survivor is often taught how to monitor and record information about his or her thoughts and behavior. Due in large part to this information-based nature, cognitive-behavioral therapy can easily be delivered in a classroom-like setting. In both group and individual settings, therapists can augment the treatment with handouts, audiotapes, videotapes, role-play exercises, behavioral rehearsal, and between-session "homework."

Two approaches have been employed in cognitive-behavioral therapy with trauma survivors. The first approach involves helping the individual identify and replace cognitive *distortions* (e.g., Beck, 1976; Burns, 1992) or *irrational beliefs* (Ellis, 1994; Ellis & Grieger, 1986). The second approach involves helping the individual identify *themes, constructions* ("stories"), or *narrative memories* and persuading them in some fashion to adopt more flexible and less punitive ones (e.g., Meichenbaum, 1994). It is important to note, however, that there is probably *no* cognitive-behavioral treatment for PTSD that completely adheres to either the distortion/irrational belief or the constructivist narrative approach. In practice, cognitive-behavioral therapy treatment is almost always a blend of these interventions; separating them is thus somewhat artificial, but it is helpful to do so in order to better understand the active elements of these forms of therapy.

BEHAVIORAL AND COGNITIVE CHANGE: NECESSARY COMPONENTS IN PTSD TREATMENT

Behavioral change appears to be essential for successful trauma treatment. Indeed, trauma survivors who benefit from treatment *behave differently* from how they behaved before treatment. One illustrative example of this behavioral change can be seen in the avoidance and social withdrawal behavior that is typically seen in PTSD patients. Arguably, PTSD treatment will only be effective with these patients if it leads to a cessation and reversal of avoidant/withdrawal behavior. Similarly, the coping skills literature provides uniform support for behavioral or problem-focused methods (vs. emotion-focused methods) being associated with favorable outcomes with trauma survivors.

It is also likely that *all* of the effective treatments for trauma survivors contain the core elements found in behavioral therapy. For example, the trauma revivification employed in psychodynamic treatment, critical for tension-release, catharsis, and corrective emotional experiences, may in fact be the same process that must occur in successful desensitization and flooding/implosive therapy treatments. Behavioral therapy is effective in large part *because* it promotes the trauma survivors' exposure to (i.e., reexperiencing of) the trauma; once the trauma is reexperienced, the individual can work toward attenuating (extinguishing) its adverse impact. If the trauma is *not* reexperienced, the individual (and the therapist) is left largely to adopt a less effective, intellectualizing perspective from which to view, appraise, and evaluate the trauma(s) and its impact.

Cognitive change in trauma survivors is also important for at least two reasons. First, exposure to trauma typically leads to changes in cognitive processes and content (Bryant & Harvey, 1995; Cassidy, McNally, & Zeitlin, 1992; Hiley-Young, 1990; Joseph, Williams, & Yule, 1993; Kaspi, McNally, & Amir, 1995; McNally, English, & Lipke, 1993; Muran & Motta, 1993). Indeed, memories and cognitions related to the traumatic event(s) may be pathognomonic of PTSD. Furthermore, the menu of PTSD phenomenology includes numerous symptoms that clearly have a cognitive component, such as when the trauma survivor experiences upsetting recollections of the traumatic event (i.e., the PTSD reexperiencing symptoms). Accordingly, at least one trauma survivor has called PTSD "the syndrome of memory" (Norman, 1989, p. 241).

Trauma survivors also typically experience other symptoms that involve internal experiences, including irritability and anger, concentration difficulties, sleep problems and upsetting dreams, and a sense of a foreshortened future. For example, trauma survivors with sleep problems often cannot routinely attain or sustain sleep because of ruminative thoughts stemming from or related to their trauma experience; waking in the middle of the night or early in the morning is often preceded and accompanied by thoughts about the trauma and its implications. Since so much of the PTSD complex includes symptoms that rely on the person's *thinking* in order to experience and be disturbed by them, it is logical that PTSD treatments should, in some fashion, direct their efforts at changing these disturbing thoughts.

Second, nearly all behavioral treatments for PTSD (and, likely, all psychological treatments) have cognitive elements that are a vital, albeit secondary, part of the intervention. In implosive therapy, for example, the PTSD patient is encouraged to adopt a more clinical and objective cognitive set in which imaging the traumatizing event(s) allows him or her to cognitively "reframe," emotionally process, or "extinguish" the event and the related symptoms. Indeed, many trauma survivors who report reduced PTSD symptoms after receiving a behavioral treatment also report a concomitant "insight" or revised opinion about the trauma, themselves, and the world around them.

EMPIRICAL AND THEORETICAL FOUNDATIONS OF BEHAVIORAL AND COGNITIVE-BEHAVIORAL TREATMENT

One strength of behavioral therapy is its reliance on reproducible data in determining the direction of treatment and research (e.g., if a "reinforcer" is not shown to increase the frequency of a behavior, then it is *not* a reinforcer). Behavioral therapy strategies typically rely on empirically verifiable or measurable information about the process and content of both the disorder and its treatment. This aspect of behavioral therapy enhances our understanding about trauma and increases the therapist's ability to monitor and reliably implement treatment. When a treatment is not working, the behavioral therapist can alter his or her strategies accordingly. Pretreatment and posttreatment checklists, SUD ratings, and behavioral recordings are invaluable aids in the efforts to reproduce successful treatment outcomes. The confidence that clinicians, educators, parents, administrators, and researchers have in behavioral therapy can be traced to its reliance on this empirical tradition.

Behavioral therapy approaches to treating trauma survivors are conceptually founded on the two-factor learning theory (Mowrer, 1960), which involves both classical and operant conditioning paradigms. In the trauma version of this theory, a highly stressful event occurs (the unconditioned stimulus, UCS), leading to stress and other reactions (the unconditioned responses, or UCRs). The UCS is nearly always coincident with other, neutrally valenced stimuli. This coincidental pairing or association leads to conditioning in which the previously neutral stimuli (the conditioned stimuli, or CSs) can soon elicit responses on their own (called conditioned responses, CRs). For example, a victim of a terrorist bombing may become extremely anxious, fearful, or horrified. The bombing and the co-occurring death and destruction (UCSs) are coincident and paired with previously neutral stimuli (CSs) such as the physical characteristics of area in which the trauma survivor was present prior to and during the bombing, muffled yells and screams, the smoke and darkness that descended immediately after the explosion, and so on, and these stimuli also come to elicit the arousal, anxiety, fear, and horror (the CRs) that the bombing itself produced. Later, the individual may experience these adverse feelings when in the presence of bombing-associated sights, sounds, and smells, such as the ground rumbling when heavy vehicles drive by, the sound of people crying, yelling, or speaking excitedly, smoke or dust, or sudden darkness (e.g., ceiling or street lights turning off).

Often, the trauma survivor will engage in instrumental behavior to escape or avoid the CSs or to avoid or escape the elicitation of the CRs. When the escape/avoidance is successful, the behavior is more likely to occur again in the future (i.e., it is *reinforced*). Examples of this behavior with trauma survivors are the excessive use of alcohol and drugs, expressions of anger and rage, and social isolation, all of which serve to take the survivor away from exposure to the aversive CSs and CRs. This sequence, together with the classical conditioning process that preceded it, is called two-factor learning and provides a useful explanatory model for viewing PTSD phenomenology.

Cognitive-behavioral therapy arose in part because of perceived deficiencies of a strictly behavioral therapy approach. Many clinicians and clinician researchers were uncomfortable with ignoring or avoiding "mental phenomena" and felt that including them would *add* to their ability to understand, predict, and control human behavior. Cognitive-behavioral therapy nevertheless retained the strong empirical tradition of behavioral therapy. Although of more recent origin, it is likely that cognitive-behavioral PTSD treatment has generated more research than all of the noncognitive, nonbehavioral PTSD treatments combined.

Cognitive-behavioral therapy focuses more directly on the private events known as cognitions (Beck, 1976; Burns, 1992; Ellis, 1994; Ellis & Grieger, 1986; Meichenbaum, 1994). In this focus, the patient's "distorted" cognitions develop from being exposed to extreme events, in part because they are adaptive for understanding the event or for preventing the event(s) from recurring. For example, the pejorative expression, "The only good 'Gook' is a dead one," despite the clear overgeneralization and labeling, may have served to have survival value to the person by dehumanizing members of the ethnic group that (at an earlier point) represented the greatest threat to life and limb (i.e., Korean or Vietnamese enemy combatants). Similarly, the belief, "All men are sexual perverts" may help a rape victim avoid company with males, who clearly pose the greatest risk of a repeated sexual assault. Unfortunately, these cognitive distortions also serve as barriers to more desirable outcomes (e.g., learning about people from other cultures, benefiting from an intimate opposite-gender relationship, etc.). Also, people exposed to extreme trauma may have had their beliefs and assumptions about the world and other people shattered when they were victimized or otherwise exposed to stressors outside the range of usual human experience. For example, one's sense of safety about automobile travel can be upset by being involved in a serious car accident, whether caused by an errant or intoxicated driver, an unexplained vehicle parts failure, and so on. Not only may automobile travel become inordinately uncomfortable, but broader assumptions (e.g., about safety and trust) may be affected.

STATUS OF THE BEHAVIOR THERAPY
OUTCOME RESEARCH ON PTSD

A considerable quantity of empirical research has accrued in the professional literature on behavioral and cognitive-behavioral treatments for trauma survivors. Three general classes of research can be found: case studies and single-subject research, group pretreatment–posttreatment research, and controlled outcome research.

Most of the research reports on behavioral therapy (i.e., systematic desensitization, implosive therapy, flooding, EMDR) for trauma survivors involve descriptive cases studies or single-subject designs. Only the group and controlled treatment outcome studies on behavioral therapy are reviewed here. The case studies, single-subject research, and reports of less rigorously controlled research are summarized in detail elsewhere (e.g., Blake, Abueg, Woodward, & Keane, 1993; Frueh, Turner, & Beidell, 1995; Solomon, Gerrity, & Muff, 1992) and in other chapters found in this book (e.g., Flack, Litz, & Keane, Chapter 4; Meadows & Foa, Chapter 5).

Desensitization and Flooding Treatments

We found nine studies of systematic desensitization and implosive therapy/flooding treatments that relied on group pretreatment–posttreatment or controlled outcome methodologies (Table 2.1). These provide insights about the utility of behavioral treatments with trauma survivors.

In 1986, Bowen and Lambert employed systematic desensitization in treating 10 "highly symptomatic" military veterans. The veterans were first taught progressive muscle relaxation, then received approximately 12 sessions of desensitization over a 6-month period. The treatment significantly reduced reactive stress, heart rate, and forehead muscle tension. While the study lends support for the effectiveness of systematic desensitization in treating traumatized veterans, it contains a number of methodological limitations, including the use of a small sample size, failure to employ a control group (despite likely treatment confounds, such as concurrent group therapy and pharmacotherapy), and providing no follow-up assessment.

Peniston (1986) applied electromyographic (EMG) biofeedback-assisted systematic desensitization in the treatment of 8 Vietnam War combat-veteran inpatients diagnosed with PTSD. As compared to a no-treatment group ($n = 8$), the treated veterans showed significant reductions in forehead tension and reported reduced nightmares and flashbacks. While none of the treated veterans required rehospitalization in the 2 years following behavior therapy, 5 of the untreated veterans did. Furthermore, the treated group reported a cessation of flashbacks and nightmares following their treatment. However, it is important to note that the treated group received 48 sessions and no credible control condition

TABLE 2.1. Outcome Research Involving Flooding and Desensitization Treatments with Trauma Survivors

Author(s)	Target population	Research design	n	Form of treatment	Length and no. of sessions	Findings	F/U
Boudewyns, Hyer, Woods, Harrison, & McCranie (1990)	Vietnam combat veteran inpatients	Post hoc controlled outcome	58	Inpatient PTSD treatment with either flooding or "conventional" psychotherapy	10–12 individual sessions	Significantly more inpatient treatment successes received flooding therapy; significantly more failures did not.	n/a
Boudewyns & Hyer (1990)	Vietnam combat-veteran inpatients	Controlled outcome (random assignment)	38	Inpatient PTSD treatment with either flooding or "conventional" psychotherapy	10–12 individual sessions	Flooding subjects showed reduced heart-rate reactivity, and greater gains; global index of symptoms and adjustment at 3 months posttreatment; no differences between the groups on self-rated anxiety.	3 months
Bowen & Lambert (1986)	Traumatized combat (9) and noncombat (1) military veterans	One-group pretest–posttest design	10	Systematic desensitization	Every 2 weeks for an average of 6 months	Desensitization significantly reduced reactive stress, heart rate, and frontalis muscle tension.	None
Brom, Kleber, & Defares (1989)	Male and female adult outpatients diagnosed with PTSD (violent crime, traffic accidents, violent or tragic loss of loved ones)	Controlled outcome (random assignment)	29 29 31 23	Psychodynamic psychotherapy, hypnotherapy, desensitization, wait-list control	14–19 individual sessions	All treatments significantly reduced psychometrically assessed symptoms (SCL-90-R, IES). Desensitization and hypnotherapy led to greater decreases in intrusive symptomatology; treatment dropouts spread evenly across conditions.	3 months
Cooper & Clum (1989)	Vietnam combat-veteran outpatients	Controlled outcome (matched groups)	7 7	"Standard" PTSD treatment, "standard" PTSD treatment plus imaginal flooding	6–14 individual 90-minute sessions	Flooding group showed gains in sleep disturbance, nightmares, state anxiety, and discomfort during a behavioral avoidance task.	3 months

(continued)

23

TABLE 2.1. (*continued*)

Author(s)	Target population	Research design	n	Form of treatment	Length and no. of sessions	Findings	F/U
Frueh, Turner, Beidel, Mirabella, & Jones (1996)	Vietnam combat-veteran outpatients	One-group pretest–posttest design	11	Trauma management therapy (TMT; flooding and social–emotional rehabilitation)	29 group and individual sessions (over 17 weeks)	Significant reduction in PTSD symptoms (including elevated heart rate and nightmares) and anxiety; significant increase in sleep and social activities; no change in experience and expression of anger; four TMT treatment dropouts.	None
Keane, Fairbank, Caddell, & Zimering (1989)	Vietnam combat-veteran inpatients and outpatients	Controlled outcome (random assignment)	11 / 13	Implosive therapy (flooding), wait-list control	14 individual sessions	Treatment group showed significant reduction in PTSD (particularly reexperiencing and hyperarousal symptoms) and associated symptoms (depression, anxiety, fear); no change in social adjustment.	6 months
Peniston (1986)	Vietnam combat-veteran inpatients and outpatients	Controlled outcome (random assignment)	8 / 8	Biofeedback-assisted systematic desensitization versus no treatment	48 30-minute individual sessions None	Treatment led to significant reductions in EMG frontalis tension, nightmares, and flashbacks; gains were maintained at 2-year follow-up.	2 year
Vaughan & Tarrier (1992)	Male and female adult outpatients diagnosed with PTSD (robbery and violent crime, sexual assault, combat, torture)	One-group pretest-posttest design	10	Image habituation training (IHT; exposure to audiotaped narrations of the trauma)	10 individual sessions	IHT treatment lead to significant reductions in self-rated problem severity, scores on depression, PTSD, and anxiety scales; significant increase in self-rated sense of control over their lives.	At least 6 months

24

(other than "no-treatment") was provided. This study nevertheless provides an early glimpse of the effectiveness of behavioral therapy in reducing the arousal/anxiety symptoms typically reported by trauma survivors.

Cooper and Clum (1989) compared 7 Vietnam War combat veterans diagnosed with PTSD who received "standard" individual and group treatment with 7 veterans who received this same treatment *plus* imaginal flooding. While no significant changes were seen in the standard treatment group, veterans in the flooding group showed significant improvements in sleep disturbance, nightmares, state anxiety, and reactive discomfort. Most of these improvements were maintained at a 3-month follow-up assessment. This report serves as an impressive demonstration of the efficacy of exposure-based treatment with trauma survivors, particularly with regard to reducing reexperiencing and hyperarousal symptoms. It is noteworthy (and troubling), however, that the flooding condition led to a nearly 50% attrition rate. While this treatment appears to reduce PTSD symptoms, can trauma survivors tolerate it long enough to benefit?

In an early controlled test of behavioral therapy with trauma survivors, Keane et al. (1989) randomly assigned 24 Vietnam War veterans to implosive therapy or to a wait-list control condition. Veterans in the treatment condition showed clear gain in therapist ratings of PTSD and on self-report questionnaires (PTSD, anxiety, depression, fear). They also experienced the greatest improvement in the *reexperiencing* dimension of their PTSD symptomatology (e.g., reductions in startle responses, memory and concentration problems, and irritability). No significant changes were seen in the veterans' social adjustment. The treatment effects were maintained at 6-month follow-up. Despite not employing a credible control condition (i.e., the wait-list participants were doing just that, *waiting for treatment,* and hence may have experienced a demand that they were *not supposed to* change), the study provides a compelling demonstration of the robust treatment effects of behavioral therapy with trauma survivors.

Brom, Kleber, and Defares (1989) reported a randomized treatment outcome study comparing three different PTSD interventions (psychodynamic psychotherapy, hypnotherapy, and desensitization) with a wait-list control treatment in the treatment of 112 adult outpatients who carried a diagnosis of PTSD (with traumatic bereavement, criminal violence, illness, and vehicular accidents as the stressor events). Participants in the treatment groups received 14–19 individual sessions with a therapist trained in his or her respective treatment modality. The treated participants showed significant symptom reduction. Desensitization and hypnotherapy appeared to reduce intrusion symptoms and psychodynamic therapy was found to have a greater effect on the avoidance symptoms. Furthermore, the treated participants, particularly those in the psychotherapy group, showed gains in several trait–personality indices. The investigators reported that all of the treatments, including desensitization, were effective in treating trauma survivors, and suggested that the similarity in outcomes across treatment modalities can be attributed to similarities in the behavior of the therapists in all three groups.

Boudewyns and Hyer (1990) randomly assigned 38 Vietnam War veteran PTSD inpatients to either direct therapeutic exposure (flooding) or "conventional" (but not behavioral) psychotherapy treatment conditions. All of the veterans participated in 10–12 individual sessions, and daily groups and inpatient milieu treatment. The veterans in the flooding condition showed decreased physiological reactivity, particularly heart rate, and significant gains on a global index of anxiety/depression, alienation, vigor, and confidence in skills at 3 months posttreatment. This study provides a well-controlled "real-world" (inpatient PTSD treatment context) test of a behavioral treatment. Unfortunately, the fact that more time and attention were spent with the flooded veterans (i.e., without a comparable activity for the unflooded veterans) dilutes the confidence one can have in the study's conclusions.

To study the efficacy of flooding therapy, Boudewyns, Hyer, Woods, Harrison, and McCranie (1990) examined 58 Vietnam War combat veterans who had successfully completed an inpatient PTSD program. These PTSD program inpatients were randomly assigned to either a conventional inpatient treatment or to conventional treatment *and* flooding. Calculating residual gains scores on measures of social adjustment, the highest 15 patients were categorized as "successes" and the bottom 15 as "failures." A significantly greater number of treatment successes (10 of 15) had received flooding treatment, whereas the failures (12 of 15) were primarily from the conventional treatment condition. Unfortunately, the post hoc method used by the investigators (i.e., using success vs. failure as a grouping variable instead of flooding–no flooding) is a curious way to examine the effects of the treatment, obscuring the effect size obtained, and limiting the study's comparability to other research.

Vaughan and Tarrier (1992) reported on the successful use of an innovative flooding-like treatment, called image habituation training (IHT). In this treatment, each traumatized individual audiotaped six descriptions of the recurrent (trauma) images he or she reexperienced. During a treatment session, the trauma survivor listened to each audiotaped narration, followed by a 30-second silent period in which to visualize the images evoked by the narration, before going on to the next narration. He or she was then instructed to listen to the tape on his or her own for 1 hour each day. Ten PTSD-diagnosed trauma survivors (robbery and violent crime, sexual assault, and torture victims, and a combat veteran) received 10 individual sessions of IHT, which led to significant reductions in self-rated problem severity, depression, PTSD, and anxiety. The survivors also evidenced an increased sense of control over their lives. These gains were maintained at 6-months follow-up. This report demonstrates once again that behavioral therapy reliably reduces PTSD symptomatology in trauma survivors. A notable advantage of this treatment is its economy, since much of the treatment is audiotaped and self-administered.

In light of numerous reports suggesting that the reexperiencing and hyperarousal PTSD symptoms, but not avoidance/numbing symptoms, are reduced by exposure-based behavior therapy (e.g., systematic desensitization, flooding, implosive therapy), these latter symptoms may be best ameliorated through more traditional psychotherapy and psychosocial rehabilitation treatments (e.g., social skills training, assertiveness training, etc.). Comprehensive PTSD treatment may require both behavioral and psychosocial elements. Following this logic, Frueh, Turner, Beidel, Mirabella, and Jones (1996) treated 11 Vietnam War combat veterans (4 others dropped out of the treatment) with multicomponent trauma management therapy (TMT), which included individually tailored flooding sessions and group sessions of social and emotional rehabilitation (SER; social skills, anger management, and issues management training). TMT was found to be as effective as the investigators reasoned it would be: Both the arousal and avoidance/numbing symptoms were significantly reduced. Furthermore, arousal symptoms (sleep problems and elevated heart rate) decreased when flooding was administered, and avoidance/numbing symptoms (e.g., level of social activity) improved when the veterans received the SER treatment. Unfortunately, the 4 veterans who dropped out before finishing the treatment raise concern about both the treatment (i.e., the 4 who dropped out conceivably were having less success with the treatment) and whether the 29-session treatment is sufficiently tolerable for widespread application. The Frueh et al. findings nevertheless highlight the dual or multifaceted nature of trauma sequelae and suggest that combined treatments are essential for effecting meaningful clinical change with trauma survivors.

The reports reviewed here and detailed in Table 2.1 support the use of systematic desensitization, flooding, and implosive therapy for trauma survivors, particularly Vietnam War combat veterans. One observation is that behavioral therapy, as reported, tends to require much effort—the exposure-based treatments may be upsetting to the individuals who must revivify their trauma—and many treatment sessions (e.g., Peniston, 1986) or sessions of lengthy duration (Keane et al., 1989) are frequently employed. This concern about behavioral therapy is offset somewhat, however, by the promising findings of IHT (Vaughan & Tarrier, 1992) in which much of the treatment is implemented by the trauma survivor him- or herself and can be conducted outside the therapist's office. As a whole, the behavioral therapy treatments appear particularly effective in reducing heart rate, forehead tension, intrusive memories, sleep disturbance, nightmares, anxiety, and fear. When these treatments are supplemented with the hospital milieu, psychotherapy, or psychosocial intervention programs, however, the effects tend to become more general and extend to the avoidance and emotional numbing symptoms seen in trauma survivors.

Eye Movement Desensitization and Reprocessing

Dozens of case studies and single-subject studies of EMDR with trauma survivors have been published, nearly all of which provide support for the effectiveness of the procedure. These research efforts are useful in the early stages of treatment development, but do not possess the methodological rigor to test adequately the treatment's efficacy (for thoughtful critiques, see DeBell & Jones, 1997, and Herbert & Mueser, 1992). A number of clinical researchers, however, have recently risen to the challenge of vigorously examining the effectiveness of EMDR. Eleven studies of this promising treatment are described here and outlined in Table 2.2.

Randomly assigning 22 participants to either a treatment or placebo/delayed treatment condition, Shapiro (1989) tested the effectiveness of a single session of EMD treatment. The placebo condition was a "modified flooding procedure" in which the participants were asked to describe their traumatic event and provide SUDs ratings every 1 to 1½ minutes (about the same rate as in EMD). Dependent measures were the participants' presenting problem, and their SUDs and VoC ratings related to the traumatic imagery and cognition. As expected, the EMD participants, but not the placebo participants, showed significant gains in all of the dependent measures. After receiving their modified flooding treatment, the control participants were given the EMD treatment and they, too, showed dramatic improvement. Follow-up assessments 1- and 3-months posttreatment indicated that these effects endured over time.

Sanderson and Carpenter (1992) treated 58 "phobics," including 8 cases of traumatic phobia (i.e., their phobia began after trauma exposure), using EMD in an effort to reduce traumatic imagery. The investigators compared EMD to "image confrontation" (IC), in which participants were instructed to remember the traumatic/phobic image but to keep their eye gaze fixed (vs. making saccadic movements). Using a single-session crossover design, in which all of the participants received one session of both treatments in randomized order, the IC procedure proved to be as effective as EMD at reducing imagery-induced distress (i.e., SUDs). However, the traumatic phobics, who most closely parallel trauma survivors, showed the most pronounced SUDs change from EMD. While this study suggests that for most individuals the saccadic eye movement portion of EMD/EMDR treatment is not necessary (and that it may be the imaginal exposure that is essential), it may be essential for persons with trauma imagery.

Oswalt, Anderson, Hagstrom, and Berkowitz (1993) followed Shapiro's (1989) research methodology in their one-session EMDR treatment of 5 hospital inpatients and 3 college students who reported having at least one "traumatic memory." Shapiro's favorable outcomes were not replicated: Only three of the participants showed improvement (the college students) and 8 (the hospital inpatients) either did not improve or became more symptomatic. This study is interesting and raises important concerns about EMDR, but it contains many obvious methodological problems (e.g., failure to employ standardized measures, no control group, no specification of therapist training) that call into question its controversial findings.

Boudewyns, Stwertka, Hyer, Albrecht, and Sperr (1993) randomly assigned 20 Vietnam combat veteran inpatients to EMD ($n = 9$), exposure control ($n = 6$), and control (inpatient milieu only, $n = 5$) conditions. After participating in two

TABLE 2.2. Empirical Research Involving Eye Movement Desensitization and Reprocessing with Trauma Survivors

Author(s)	Target population	Research design	n	Form of treatment	Length and no. of sessions	Findings	F/U
Boudewyns, Stwertka, Hyer, Albrecht, & Sperr (1993)	Vietnam combat-veteran inpatients	Controlled outcome (random assignment)	9 6 5	EMD, exposure control, control (milieu only)	2 individual sessions (approximately 1 week apart)	EMD group evidenced the greatest reduction in anxiety (SUDs) associated with combat imagery; no significant change in psychophysiological or PTSD measures.	None
Forbes, Creamer, & Rycroft (1994)	Male and female outpatients recruited from treatment providers	One-group pretest–posttest design	8	EMDR	4 individual sessions	Participants showed significant reductions in PTSD symptomatology, depression, and symptom distress; gains were maintained at follow-up.	3 months
Jensen (1994)	Vietnam combat-veteran outpatients	Controlled outcome (random assignment)	13 12	EMDR, control group	3 individual sessions (occurring within 10 days)	Neither EMDR nor control subjects improved on PTSD, cognition, or goal attainment measures; EMDR group evidenced reduced in-session anxiety associated with combat imagery.	None
Oswalt, Anderson, Hagstrom, & Berkowitz (1993)	Traumatized hospital inpatients (5) and college students (3)	One-group pretest–posttest design	8	EMDR	1 individual session	College students showed gains on SUDs; inpatients failed to show gains.	None
Renfrey & Spates (1994)	University psychology clinic outpatients previously exposed to trauma (21 diagnosed with PTSD)	Pretest–posttest comparison (random assignment)	8 8 7	EMD, auto-EMD, fixed gaze	2–6 individual sessions	All participants made gains in HR, SUDs, VoC (positive) at posttreatment and at follow-up; no significant differences among the treatments.	4 months
Sanderson & Carpenter (1992)	58 phobics, including 8 with trauma exposure	Single-session crossover trial (quasi-experimental)	58	EMD, image confrontation (IC)	1 individual session per condition	EMD and IC were equally effective in reducing SUDs levels; EMD appeared to produce greatest gains with traumatic phobics.	1 month

(continued)

TABLE 2.2. (*continued*)

Author(s)	Target population	Research design	n	Form of treatment	Length and no. of sessions	Findings	F/U
Shapiro (1989)	Adult male and female survivors of combat, sexual assault, incest, and emotional abuse	Controlled outcome (random assignment)	22	EMD, control (placebo-delayed treatment)	1 individual session	All participants evidenced significant gains in presenting problem, SUDs, and VoC ratings following EMD treatment.	1 and 3 months
Silver, Brooks, & Obenchain (1995)	Vietnam combat-veteran inpatients	Uncontrolled post hoc pretest–posttest	55 13 9 6	Inpatient (I) only, I + EMD-R, I + relaxation training, I + biofeedback	At least 1 EMDR session, 3 or more relaxation biofeedback sessions	I + EMDR participants did significantly better than the other groups on five of eight subscales of a self-report measure of problems.	None
Vaughan, Armstrong, Gold, O'Connor, Jenneke, & Tarrier (1994)	Male and female outpatients exposed to traumatic events	Controlled outcome (random assignment)	12 13 11	EMD, image habituation training (IHT), applied muscle relaxation (AMR), versus wait list	3–5 individual sessions over 2–3 weeks	Compared to wait list, all treatment groups showed significant gains in Criteria C and D PTSD symptoms; no consistent superiority for any single treatment, but EMD led to significantly fewer intrusive symptoms, nightmares, and flashbacks.	3 months
Wilson, Becker, & Tinker (1995)	Male and female outpatients who reported traumatic memories	Controlled outcome (random assignment) crossover design	80	EMD-R (immediate vs. delayed treatment)	Three 90-minute individual sessions	EMDR led to within-session SUDs reductions and VoC increases, and significant posttreatment gains in STAI state and trait anxiety, IES intrusion and avoidance, and on all nine SCL-90-R clinical scales.	90 days
Vaughan, Wiese, Gold, & Tarrier (1994)	Male and female outpatients exposed to traumatic events	One-group pretest–posttest design	10	EMD	1–6 individual sessions (M = 3.3)	SUDs ratings and mean scores for all three symptoms groups showed significant reduction, especially reexperiencing symptoms.	8–12 weeks following start of treatment

individual sessions, scheduled a week apart, the EMD group showed the greatest reduction in combat image-related anxiety (SUDs); however, no significant changes were found in psychophysiological reactivity or the measures of PTSD symptomatology. Unfortunately, it is unclear why, given random assignment, the group sizes among the conditions varied so much; the discrepancy in group sizes raises concern about whether the EMD group size might have been inflated in some systematic fashion (e.g., patient symptom status, motivation, or preference) that might also explain the study's findings.

In an uncontrolled test, Vaughan, Wiese, Gold, and Tarrier (1994) provided an average of three sessions of EMD to 3 male and 7 female outpatients who had been exposed to various traumas (armed robberies and violent crime, vehicle accidents, a devastating storm, incest, a gassing accident). The treatment proved to be highly effective, with significant reductions in SUDs ratings and mean ratings of all three PTSD symptom clusters (reexperiencing, avoidance/numbing, hyperarousal). The treatment appeared to be especially effective in reducing the reexperiencing symptoms. These gains were maintained at follow-up scheduled 8–12 weeks from the beginning of treatment.

In part to address criticisms that research on EMD/EMDR relies on nonstandardized measures of outcome (i.e., using subjectively rated SUDs or VoCs), Forbes, Creamer, and Rycroft (1994) used an assortment of standardized psychological measures and interviews, and psychophysiological assessment (forehead EMG). Eight participants recruited for the study were administered four EMD sessions. One week after the final treatment, the participants were retested on the dependent measures. The participants showed significant reductions in PTSD symptoms, depression, and distress. Unfortunately, no control group was used, so the treatment's effects independent of history, maturation, and other threats to internal validity, is not known.

Jensen (1994) randomly assigned 25 Vietnam combat-veteran outpatients to either EMDR ($n = 13$) or a no-treatment control group ($n = 12$). The EMDR was delivered in three individual sessions, scheduled across a 10-day period. Results of the study showed that neither the EMDR nor the Control Group participants improved on PTSD, cognition, or goal attainment measures. However, the EMDR group reported significantly reduced in-session anxiety associated with combat imagery. Unfortunately, the study's results may be due in part to demand characteristics, given that the participants in the no treatment condition did not receive a credible control experience.

Renfrey and Spates (1994) treated 23 outpatient trauma survivors (domestic violence, incest, sexual assault, motor vehicle accidents, combat, etc.) comparing 2–6 sessions of EMDR with two other treatments containing visual components (mechanically induced saccadic eye movements and a fixed-gaze format). Like Sanderson and Carpenter (1992), the investigators were interested in determining whether saccadic eye movements were essential for EMDR. All three treatments led to reduced reactive heart rate and trauma-related SUDs, and increased VoC ratings for positive cognition. No significant differences were found between the treatment conditions, casting doubt on the necessity of saccadic eye movements for successful EMDR. Curiously, the investigators referred to a number of PTSD and associated symptom measures as dependent variables and, although they state that "there was a significant change on all dependent variables between pretreatment and the second assessment" (p. 237), no data on these measures are presented. Furthermore, the investigation also did not include a no-treatment control condition, so it is not clear how well the participants might have fared without treatment.

Vaughan, Armstrong, et al. (1994) compared EMD, IHT, and applied muscle relaxation (AMR) with a wait-list condition in the treatment of 36 male and female trauma survivors (violent crimes, rape, child abuse, and vehicle accidents). Assigning the participants to one of the three conditions, treatment was also staggered in order to include wait/no-wait conditions. Participants in the no-wait treatment conditions showed significantly greater gains in PTSD Criterion C (Avoidance) and D (Hyperarousal) symptoms; an inspection of the data suggested that the treatments did not produce significant benefit in Criterion B (Reexperiencing) symptoms, likely attributable to the little change observed in the IHT group. EMD led to significant posttreatment change in decreased flashbacks and nightmares, and reduced intrusive symptoms (as measured by the Impact of Event Scale). These effects were maintained at 3 months follow-up. The data provide support for all three treatments but suggest that EMD produced the greatest effects. Impressively, EMD was the *least* time-consuming for the trauma survivors (IHT and AMR required an additional 40–60 minutes between sessions).

In an effort to gauge the additive effects of EMDR, Silver, Brooks, and Obenchain (1995) reviewed the records of 93 graduates of their inpatient PTSD treatment program. Thirteen graduates had received the standard inpatient treatment plus at least one EMDR session, 9 had received the inpatient treatment plus relaxation training, and 6 others had received the inpatient treatment plus three or more biofeedback (type not described) sessions. The EMDR participants showed the greatest improvement in psychiatric symptoms and adjustment problems. The investigators concluded that these data provide compelling support for EMDR as an adjunct to inpatient PTSD treatment. Unfortunately, the study was uncontrolled and was analyzed *after the fact*, leaving the results vulnerable to selection factors (e.g., the EMDR participants might have been unwittingly selected on the basis of motivation or suggestibility, making them more likely to benefit from *any* treatment). Furthermore, no follow-up data were reported, shedding no light on treatment durability (i.e., EMDR might have short-lived effects).

Wilson, Becker, and Tinker (1995) assessed the effects of three sessions of EMDR on 80 individuals who reported memories of trauma (physical or mental abuse, death of significant other, rape and sexual molestation, relationship crisis, health crisis, phobic memory, and combat). Equal numbers of males and females were assigned to either immediate or delayed treatment conditions. Both the process (SUDs, VoC) and outcome (all nine clinical scales of the Symptom Checklist 90—Revised [SCL-90-R; Derogatis, 1992], the Impact of Event Scale [IES; Horowitz, Wilner, & Alvarez, 1979], and the State–Trait Anxiety Inventory [STAI; Spielberger, Gorsuch, Lushene, Vagg, & Jacobs, 1983]) measures showed that the EMDR led to significant change. The effects of EMDR were equivalent for PTSD-diagnosed and non-PTSD-diagnosed participants, and these gains were maintained at 90-day follow-up assessment. These findings support those of Shapiro (1989), showing EMDR to be a robust treatment for individuals exposed to a wide variety of traumas.

What does EMDR promise to deliver? The controlled outcome research (as opposed to the PTSD treatment literature's abundant single-case reports) indicates that EMDR effectively reduces the PTSD symptomatology, maladaptive cognitive ideation (VoC), and subjectively rated discomfort of trauma survivors (SUDs). Clearly, these are not trivial gains. If trauma survivors feel better, it is highly likely that their life quality will be enhanced and posttrauma sequelae are more likely to shift into the background of their experiential world. Along these lines, Sharpley, Montgomery, and Scalzo (1996) applied EMDR to a nonclinical sample and found that it reduced the vividness of troubling images. If this is the active ingredient of EMDR, it is likely that the treatment works, at least in part, by reducing the intensity of feared and horrific images that the survivor conjures up as part of the PTSD complex (i.e., the reexperiencing of symptoms).

Not all of the studies reviewed showed EMDR to be effective, or, at least, to be any more effective that other traditional behavior therapy treatment. Furthermore, two studies raise concern that the saccadic eye movement element of EMDR, which is clearly its hallmark, may not be necessary. This contention points to other factors, such as exposure/extinction and cognitive restructuring, to explain EMDR's effects.

One consistent finding is the astonishingly few EMDR sessions employed to accomplish the gains reported. Logically, a treatment that delivers measurable improvement in the span of a few sessions (e.g., the one-session treatment reported by Shapiro, 1989, and the two-session treatment reported by Boudewyns et al., 1993) is preferable to a treatment regimen that delivers an equivalent outcome over many sessions.

COGNITIVE-BEHAVIORAL THERAPY FOR PTSD

We were able to locate a total of nine studies involving cognitive-behavioral treatments with trauma survivors. These studies fell in the three identified classes of research, and are summarized in Table 2.3. Please note that we reviewed only explicitly cognitive behavior therapy interventions, and did not examine interven-

TABLE 2.3. Empirical Research Involving Cognitive-Behavioral Therapy with PTSD Patients

Author(s)	Target population	Research design	n	Form of treatment	Length and no. of sessions	Findings	F/U
Clarke & Llewelyn (1994)	Adult survivors of childhood and adult sexual and self abuse	One-group pretest–posttest design	7	Cognitive analytic therapy	8–16 individual sessions, weekly	Significant decrease in BDI and SCL-90 General Symptom Index; increased correlation between real and ideal self; increased distinction between father–offender construals and decreased distinction between offender 1 and offender 2 construals	3 months
Foa, Hearst-Ikeda, & Perry (1995)	Female survivors of sexual and nonsexual assault	Controlled (matched subjects) treatment outcome	10 10	Combined education, imaginal exposure, and *in vivo* exposure, and cognitive restructuring versus assessment control	4 individual sessions, weekly	Treated subjects showed accelerated reductions in depression and PTSD at posttreatment and at follow-up.	5½ months postassault
Foa, Rothbaum, Riggs, & Murdock (1991)	Sexual assault survivors	Controlled treatment outcome (random assignment)	17 14 14 10	Stress inoculation training (with CBT), versus prolonged exposure, supportive counseling, and wait-list control	9 individual sessions, biweekly (over 4½ weeks)	All treatment conditions demonstrated significant PTSD reduction at posttreatment and at follow-up; stress inoculation superior to supportive counseling and wait-list control at posttreatment; prolonged exposure superior to other conditions at follow-up.	3½ months

Study	Population	Design	N	Treatment	Procedure	Findings	Follow-up
Frank, Anderson, Stewart, Dancu, Hughes, & West (1988)	Sexual assault survivors	Controlled treatment outcome	36 48	Systematic desensitization versus cognitive–behavioral therapy	14 individual sessions, weekly	Treatments equally effective, both for "early" and "late" seekers of treatment in reducing psychometrically assessed depression, anxiety, fear, and feelings of inadequacy.	3–4 and 6 months postassault
Lawson (1995)	Vietnam combat veteran	Description; case report	1	"Schema"-based CBT model	8 months of individual sessions, weekly	Decreased avoidance of trauma reminders; decreased flashbacks, more "balanced" schemas; increased frustration tolerance; increased involvement with family.	None reported
McCormack (1985)	Vietnam combat veteran	Case report	1	Cognitive therapy	20 individual sessions, weekly	Decreased frequency and severity of intrusive recollections and depressive episodes, increased ability to control anger and to communicate with wife and children.	None reported
Nishith, Hearst, Mueser, & Foa (1995)	Sexual assault survivor	Single-subject (repeated measures design)	1	Education, relaxation, imaginal exposure, cognitive–behavioral therapy	24 individual sessions, weekly	Significant decrease in PTSD, reduction in RAST, BDI, and DES scores; outcomes dramatically improved by adding six imaginal or *in vivo* exposure sessions.	1 and 3 months
Resick & Schnicke (1992)	Sexual assault survivors	Controlled treatment outcome	19 20	Cognitive processing therapy versus wait-list control	12 individual sessions, weekly	Treated patients evidenced less PTSD and depression at treatment and follow-up.	6 months
Sharpe, Tarrier, & Rotundo (1994)	Sexual assault survivors	Case study	1	Behavioral and cognitive–behavioral therapy		Decreased depersonalization and PTSD symptoms.	None reported

tions that one might surmise had cognitive components, such as interventions involving anger management and assertiveness training.

Case Studies and Single-Subject Research

McCormack (1985) applied a Beck-style (1976) treatment to a Vietnam War combat veteran in what may be the first published report about cognitive-behavioral therapy with trauma survivors. Identifying cognitions that led to the development and maintenance of maladaptive behaviors, the investigator conducted 20 counseling sessions over a 5-month period. The participant reported a decrease in the frequency and severity of his intrusive recollections, an increased ability to communicate with his family, and a decrease in the frequency and severity of his depression.

More recently, Sharpe, Tarrier, and Rotundo (1994) employed a cognitive-behavioral treatment with a female sexual assault survivor who had been diagnosed with PTSD. An idiographic analysis of her problems and other behaviors (e.g., assessment of behaviors related to her sleep disturbance), was conducted prior to the initiation of the treatment. The investigators were particularly interested in the depersonalization aspects to her presentation. Most of her PTSD symptoms, as well as the depersonalization, were completely eliminated with treatment.

Lawson (1995) employed schema-based (cf. McCann, Sakheim, & Abrahamson, 1988) cognitive-behavioral therapy with a male Vietnam War veteran. The veteran was troubled by a range of core PTSD symptoms and clinical depression. Triggers (symptom-eliciting situations) that disrupted his day-to-day functioning situations were first identified. The veteran and therapist then charted and discussed these trigger situations and the emotions they elicited. Thoughts associated with these situations were determined, and alternative interpretations were explored. The thematic issues that surfaced for this veteran established that *trust, safety,* and *power* were paramount. These themes became the primary focus of the veteran's subsequent treatment. After 5 months of counseling, the veteran exhibited decreased flashbacks, increased frustration tolerance and self-esteem, and greater participation in family activities.

Nishith, Hearst, Mueser, and Foa (1995) treated an adult woman with assault-related PTSD for 18 weeks using cognitive-behavioral treatment. Improvement, reflected by score changes on various symptom indices, was noted, but these changes did not achieve statistical significance. Exposure-based treatment (a variant of flooding) was then instituted, and the woman improved significantly. These gains were maintained at 1- and 3-month follow-up. Here, cognitive-behavioral therapy proved to not be as effective as exposure-based treatment. However, these findings might instead be due to threats to internal validity (History, Treatment Order Effects) or to a failure to use measures that adequately reflect the changes that take place.

Group Pretreatment–Posttreatment Research

Clarke and Llewelyn (1994) treated 7 female childhood sexual assault survivors using cognitive analytic therapy (CAT). Unfortunately, CAT was not well described, so it is not clear how closely this treatment compares to other forms of cognitive-behavioral therapy. While PTSD symptoms were targeted for change, the main goal of treatment was the "view of self" adopted by the participants. Although significant symptom reduction was noted, no appreciable change in the "construed self" of the participants was demonstrated. The investigators concluded that a pathogenic self-image from abuse is a core component in trauma-related maladaptive behaviors.

Controlled Outcome Research

Frank et al. (1988) compared cognitive-behavioral therapy (CBT) and systematic desensitization (SD) in the treatment of rape trauma. First, a comparison of treatment-seeking participants and non-treatment-seeking controls (who had also experienced a sexual assault) showed both groups benefited: Both treatments produced improvements in anxiety, depression, and fear. Second, in comparison with late treatment seekers (i.e., individuals who sought out treatment 3–4 months after the rape), immediate treatment seekers exhibited comparable treatment success. Whether employing CBT or SD, or beginning treatment immediately after the sexual assault (when symptoms tend to be most severe), or within 3 to 4 months, those participants manifesting "high" levels of distress showed significantly reduced anxiety. Finally, posttreatment results revealed no difference between the treatments.

Foa, Rothbaum, Riggs, and Murdock (1991) randomly assigned 45 rape victims to one of four treatment conditions: (1) prolonged exposure (PE; $n = 14$), (2) stress inoculation training (SIT; $n = 17$), (3) supportive counseling (SC; $n = 14$), and (4) wait-list control (WL; $n = 10$). Although SIT is not formally a cognitive-behavioral treatment, it includes many explicitly cognitive elements (e.g., sessions devoted to thought stopping, cognitive restructuring, and covert modeling). All of the treatment conditions led to significantly decreased PTSD, anxiety, and depression. However, SIT produced the greatest PTSD reductions. PE led to the most impressive overall gains and showed continued decreases at 3-month follow-up. A lower (but not statistically significant) percentage of SIT participants (17.6%) dropped out of treatment than PE (28.6%) or SC (21.4%) participants. There are two potential implications of these attrition data. First, it is reasonable to assume that participants who benefited most remained in their respective treatment condition and those who failed dropped out; the greater attrition in the PE and SC conditions may have thus served to artifactually inflate their success rates (i.e., and appearing more effective than they were). Second, these data suggest that SIT, the treatment with the clear cognitive-behavioral elements, may be less aversive or more credible than the other treatments, leading a larger proportion of its recipients to complete the full regimen.

Resick and Schnicke (1992) provided 12 weeks of group cognitive processing therapy (CPT) to 19 sexual assault survivors, compared to 20 survivors in a wait-list condition. The CPT included two sessions specifically devoted to imaginal exposure. Thus, the relative contribution of cognitive-behavioral therapy versus exposure-based treatment could not be established. The CPT participants showed significant reductions in PTSD and depression symptoms. Seventeen CPT participants met PTSD diagnostic criteria at pretreatment, but none of them met the full criteria following the treatment. These positive gains were maintained at 3- and 6-month follow-up assessments (though 2 CPT participants met PTSD criteria at the 3-month interval).

Foa, Hearst-Ikeda, and Perry (1995) compared the impact of a brief cognitive-behavioral prevention program with no treatment on a group of female sexual and nonsexual assault survivors. At the end of treatment, significant differences between the groups were noted in PTSD but not depression. While most all of the participants improved, those receiving cognitive-behavioral therapy improved quicker, and had achieved superior adjustment by 5½ months postassault, although statistically significant differences occurred only with the areas of reexperiencing symptoms *and* depression.

The cognitive-behavioral therapy research provides further promise for this treatment with trauma survivors. Individuals who receive this form of treatment clearly benefit; it is not so clear, however, whether cognitive-behavioral therapy is more effective than alternatives. More controlled research will be needed to answer this question.

SUMMARY

The 29 studies reviewed here provide compelling evidence that PTSD symptoms can be ameliorated using behavioral and cognitive-behavioral therapy. These treatments appear to most reliably reduce the anxiety- and arousal-based symptoms (i.e., reexperiencing and hyperarousal symptoms). One implication of the finding is that adjunctive treatments, such as *social and emotional rehabilitation,* leisure skills and assertiveness training, and insight-oriented psychotherapy, may be necessary to ameliorate the avoidance and numbing symptoms.

The outcome research on the behavioral and cognitive-behavioral treatments for PTSD is quite impressive, particularly for such an early point in the "life" of the field (first two decades). A range of theory-based treatments has been developed, and efforts to systematically evaluate these treatments are well underway. Unfortunately, the existing research contains a number of clear shortcomings, limitations that future researchers will need to overcome. First, only four of the behavioral therapy studies (Brom et al., 1989; Cooper & Clum, 1989; Keane et al., 1989; Peniston, 1986), five of the EMDR studies (Boudewyns et al., 1993;

Jensen, 1994; Shapiro, 1989; Vaughan, Wiese, et al., 1994; Wilson et al., 1995), and three of the cognitive-behavioral therapy studies (Foa et al., 1991; Frank et al. 1988; Resick & Schnicke, 1992) employed *a priori* random assignment of participants. Clearly, studies controlled in this fashion reduce many sources of error (e.g., History, Maturation, Selection, etc.) and more confidence can be placed on the investigators' explanations of their findings. Second, a good portion of the studies either employed an unsuitable, noncredible control condition or failed to use one at all. It is not enough to say that one group of participants received "treatment *X*" and a second group received no treatment or were instructed to wait for treatment. Clearly, this situation is fertile ground for demand characteristics (i.e., the wait-list or no-treatment participants may resist change to correspond with someone not receiving any treatment, overriding nontreatment [and potentially "curative"] influences such as maturation, regression toward the mean, and history).

One other point about the studies reviewed is the length of follow-up period. Ten treatment studies reported *no* follow-up assessment, and all but four included follow-up intervals of *less than 6 months*. Although follow-ups extend the life of the study for the investigator and can make the work seem interminable, information about the durability of the treatment, particularly for a disorder involving symptoms that chronically wax and wane, is extremely important. Also, as PTSD treatments become more brief, the danger may increase that their effects will be less durable. Researchers, and perhaps more importantly, grant reviewers, journal editors, and journal reviewers, should be encouraged to support efforts that endeavor to update the scientific public about the treated survivors years, and even decades, after their treatment.

Most of the behavioral therapy research has been conducted with combat veterans, while the cognitive-behavioral therapy research has primarily involved adult survivors of adult and child sexual assault. Restricting the populations to a particular population (or two) limits our ability to generalize the treatment to other trauma survivors. Extending the treatments to other populations will greatly advance our understanding of the generalizability of these treatments to all trauma survivor populations. Most of the published research is also restricted to treatments delivered on an *individual* basis. As mentioned earlier, the behavioral treatments are viable (and can be delivered efficiently) using a *group* format; however, it has not been established whether the promising effects of these treatments can also be obtained in the group setting. Likewise, it is important to establish whether a *combined* individual–group treatment effort produces an even greater therapeutic impact than either alone.

Future Directions for Outcome Research on Behavioral Therapy and Cognitive-Behavioral Therapy

Controlled research, using randomization and credible control conditions, is vital for establishing the efficacy of any treatment. In these efforts, trauma researchers might compare existing treatments, for example, cognitive-behavioral therapy *versus* traditional behavioral therapy (systematic desensitization, flooding, implosive therapy), or *versus* psychodynamic approaches (process-oriented psychotherapy, object relations therapy). In addition, many of the past studies of behavioral therapy and cognitive-behavioral therapy have included or have been obscured by other potent treatments (e.g., anger management training and deliberate therapeutic exposure, etc.); the specific effects of a treatment can only be established by separating out other known treatment components (i.e., dismantling research designs). This concern may be especially true for EMDR, which includes at least two potent interventions: imaginal exposure and cognitive restructuring.

Another important concern about the research pertains to the selection of dependent measures. A core set of reliable instruments used across studies will help make the treatments and their effects more comparable. This concern is especially relevant to the studies of EMDR, which often relies on SUDs and VoC as main dependent variables; these two indices are neither reliable nor standardized. Ideally, a measurement package should be used that includes interview, self-report (i.e., psychometric instruments as well as self-ratings), and psychophysiological indices. The measurement should be comprehensive (i.e., sample broadly across the PTSD spectrum) but not unwieldy. For example, researchers could use a standard package comprised of the widely used Clinician Administered PTSD Scale (CAPS; Blake et al., 1995), Impact of Event Scale (Horowitz et al., 1979), SUDs ratings, and heart-rate measurement. Other measures can be added to this standard package according to the study's purpose and the interests of the investigator.

A related measurement shortcoming pertains to the research on cognitive-behavioral therapy. Only a handful of the reports employed a validated cognitive measure, and instead relied on measures of PTSD, anxiety, depression, and so on. While it is important to assess the predominant symptom cluster for the population being treated and studied (e.g., depression, fear), it is also critical to utilize measures that more closely correspond to the variables that are being targeted. Interventions aimed at changing cognitive distortions and cognitive patterns should also include measures that are directly pertinent to these treatment targets, for example, the Automatic Thoughts Questionnaire (Hollon & Kendall, 1980), the Stroop Color-Naming Paradigm (McNally et al., 1993), and the Dysfunctional Attitude Scale (Weissman, 1978, as cited in Burns, 1992). Contextualist or constructive–narrative approaches that target changes in the patient's "schemas," "themes," "scripts," or assumptive world are best measured by psychometric tools that actually assess these dimensions, for example, the World Assumptions Scale (Janoff-Bulman, 1989), the Traumatic Stress Institute Belief Scale (Pearlman, 1994), or the Repertory Grid Analysis (Adams-Webber, 1979).

Future research on behavioral and cognitive behavioral therapy might more closely examine patient–treatment matching (e.g., matching based on patient–

therapist gender, recency of trauma, treatment themes, etc.). McCann et al. (1988), for example, suggest that five cognitive "themes" should be addressed in work with sexual assault victims: Trust, Safety, Power, Self-Esteem, and Intimacy; however, these themes might not be optimal for work with survivors of other types of trauma. By way of contrast, Boehnlein and Sparr (1993) identified themes of Grief, Trust, Mortality, and Socialization in their group treatment of World War II combat-veteran prisoners-of-war. To take this point further, it is likely that each individual will benefit from an ideographic assessment of their themes for optimal treatment effectiveness (cf. Dansky, Roth, & Kronenberger, 1990). Clearly, research on a group versus individual assignment of trauma themes is needed. These and other matching characteristics should be examined in a carefully controlled research climate.

The Practitioner and Behavioral and Cognitive-Behavioral Therapy

The task of determining the efficacy of behavioral and cognitive-behavioral therapy is not solely the responsibility of the researcher. Similarly, clinical trials, which, as the rule more than the exception, seem to be implemented by graduate students and psychology interns rather than more experienced clinicians, may not provide the most "real-world" test of a given treatment approach. To be certain of the viability of a treatment, seasoned clinicians working in applied settings must play a role in outcome research; in many respects, clinicians must become "scientist–practitioners" (Barlow, Hayes, & Nelson, 1984). Clinicians also have obligations to their professional practice, and to their patients, to monitor the effectiveness of the treatment they provide. Measurement before, during, and after treatment is one way to monitor whether the treatment being provided is in fact delivering the desired effect(s), and allowing the clinician to carefully monitor the effectiveness of his or her treatment. Furthermore, clinicians must stay abreast of current research on PTSD treatment and be informed consumers of this research (i.e., developing the basic knowledge about research methodology necessary to interpret research findings adequately).

How should information about efficacious behavioral therapy and cognitive-behavioral therapy approaches be disseminated to the clinician? In the history of psychology and mental health, most of the changes that have occurred on the clinical front lines have been gradual. Clinical researchers develop and field-test a treatment strategy that gradually wends its way to the practitioner through university training, through word of mouth, and from clinician colleagues who conscientiously stay abreast of clinical research. Less commonly, developers of behavioral and cognitive-behavioral treatment follow the lead of pharmaceutical companies: After basic and, ideally, rigorous research has been conducted, the treatment developers initiate marketing efforts aimed directly at the front-line clinician. EMDR is a brilliant example of a PTSD treatment that has been successfully disseminated to clinicians in part through this testing/marketing approach. EMDR is also a good example of how widespread training and credentialing can be accomplished for the other behavioral and cognitive-behavioral treatments for PTSD. It may be that this less traditional and "scholarly" channel is the most realistic and efficient method for transferring behavioral therapy and cognitive-behavioral therapy interventions from the researcher's laboratory (and journals) to the practitioner's office.

In this chapter, we have described the current status of outcome research on behavioral and cognitive-behavioral therapy for PTSD. In this endeavor, we described these treatments and outlined their empirical foundations, providing rationale for their use. We then reviewed and critiqued the existing research and proposed future directions for outcome research. A number of treatments have been developed and have demonstrated their effectiveness. Without question, the future holds much promise for PTSD treatment and for those individuals whose lives have been adversely affected by trauma.

REFERENCES

Adams-Webber, J. (1979). *Personal construct psychology: Concepts and applications.* New York: Wiley.

American Psychiatric Association. (1980). *Diagnostic and statistical manual of mental disorders* (3rd ed.). Washington, DC: Author.

Barlow, D. H., Hayes, S. C., & Nelson, R. O. (1984). *The scientist practitioner: Research and accountability in clinical and educational settings.* New York: Pergamon Press.

Beck, A. T. (1976). *Cognitive therapy and emotional disorders.* New York: International Universities Press.

Black, J. L., & Keane, T. M. (1982). Implosive therapy in the treatment of combat-related fears in a World War II veteran. *Journal of Behavior Therapy and Experimental Psychiatry, 13,* 163–165.

Blake, D. D., Abueg, F. R., Woodward, S. H., & Keane, T. M. (1993). Treatment efficacy in post-traumatic stress disorder. In T. R. Giles (Ed.), *Handbook of effective psychotherapy* (pp. 195–226). New York: Plenum Press.

Blake, D. D., Albano, A. M., & Keane, T. M. (1992). Twenty years of trauma: *Psychology Abstracts* 1970 through 1989. *Journal of Traumatic Stress, 5,* 477–484.

Blake, D. D., Weathers, F., Nagy, L. M., Kaloupek, D. G., Gusman, F., Charney, D. S., & Keane, T. M. (1995). The development of a clinician-administered PTSD scale. *Journal of Traumatic Stress, 8,* 75–90.

Blanchard, E. B., & Abel, G. G. (1976). An experimental case study of the biofeedback treatment of a rape-induced psychophysiological cardiovascular disorder, *Behavior Therapy, 7,* 113–119.

Boehnlein, J. K., & Sparr, L. F. (1993). Group therapy with WWII ex-POW's: Long-term postraumatic adjustment in a geriatric population. *American Journal of Psychotherapy, 47,* 273–282.

Boudewyns, P. A., & Hyer, L. (1990). Physiological response to combat veterans and preliminary treatment outcome in Vietnam veteran PTSD patients treated with direct therapeutic exposure. *Behavior Therapy, 21,* 63–87.

Boudewyns, P. A., Hyer, L., Woods, M. G., Harrison, W. R., & McCranie, E. (1990). PTSD among Vietnam veterans: An early look at treatment outcome with direct therapeutic exposure. *Journal of Traumatic Stress, 3,* 359–368.

Boudewyns, P. A., Stwertka, S. A., Hyer, L., Albrecht, J. W., & Sperr, E. V. (1993). Eye movement desensitization for PTSD of combat: A treatment outcome pilot study. *Behavior Therapist, 16,* 29–33.

Bowen, G. R., & Lambert, J. A. (1986). Systematic desensitization therapy with post-traumatic stress disorder cases. In C. R. Figley (Ed.), *Trauma and its wake* (Vol. II, pp. 281–291). New York: Brunner/Mazel.

Brom, D., Kleber, R. J., & Defares, P. B. (1989). Brief psychotherapy for postraumatic stress disorders. *Journal of Consulting and Clinical Psychology, 57,* 607–612.

Brooks, J. S., & Sarano, T. (1985). Transcendental meditation in the treatment of post-Vietnam adjustment. *Journal of Counseling and Adjustment, 64,* 212–215.

Bryant, R. A., & Harvey, A. G. (1995). Processing threatening information in posttraumatic stress disorder. *Journal of Abnormal Psychology, 104,* 537–541.

Burns, D. D. (1992). *Feeling good: The new mood therapy.* New York: Avon Books.

Burt, J. W. (1995). Distant thundering: Drumming with Vietnam veterans. *Music Therapy Perspectives, 13,* 110–112.

Callahan, R. J. (1995, August). *A Thought Field Therapy (TFT) algorithm for trauma: A reproducible experiment in psychotherapy.* Paper presented at the annual meeting of the American Psychological Association, New York.

Cassidy, K. L., McNally, R. J., & Zeitlin, S. B. (1992). Cognitive processing of trauma cues in rape victims with post-traumatic stress disorder. *Cognitive Therapy and Research, 16,* 283–295.

Chemtob, C., Roitblat, H. L., Hamada, R. S., Carlson, J. G., & Twentyman, C. T. (1988). A cognitive action theory of post-traumatic stress disorder. *Journal of Anxiety Disorders, 2,* 253–275.

Clarke, S., & Llewelyn, S. (1994). Personal constructs of survivors of childhood sexual abuse receiving cognitive analytic therapy. *British Journal of Medical Psychology, 67,* 273–289.

Cooper, N. A., & Clum, G. A. (1989). Imaginal flooding as a supplementary treatment for PTSD in combat veterans: A controlled study. *Behavior Therapy, 20,* 381–391.

Creamer, M., Burgess, P., & Pattison, P. (1992). Reaction to trauma: A cognitive processing model. *Journal of Abnormal Psychology, 101,* 452–459.

Dansky, B. S., Roth, S., & Kronenberger, W. G. (1990). The trauma constellation identification scale: A measure of the psychological impact of a stressful life event. *Journal of Traumatic Stress, 3,* 557–571.

DeBell, C., & Jones, R. D. (1997). As good as it seems?: A review of the EMDR experimental research. *Professional Psychology: Research and Practice, 28,* 153–163.

Derogatis, L. R. (1992). *SCL-90: Administration, scoring, and procedures manual—II.* Baltimore, MD: Clinical Psychometric Research.

Ellis, A. (1994). Post-traumatic stress disorder (PTSD): A rational emotive behavioral theory. *Journal of Rational–Emotive and Cognitive-Behavior Therapy, 12,* 3–25.

Ellis, A., & Grieger, R. (1986). *Handbook of rational–emotive therapy* (Vol. 2). New York: Springer.

Fairbank, J. A., & Brown, T. A. (1987). Current behavioral approaches to the treatment of posttraumatic stress disorder. *Behavior Therapist, 10,* 57–64.

Fairbank, J. A., & Keane, T. M. (1982). Flooding for combat-related stress disorders: Assessment of anxiety reduction across traumatic memories. *Behavior Therapy, 13,* 499–510.

Foa, E. B., Hearst-Ikeda, D., & Perry, K. J. (1995). Evaluation of a brief cognitive-behavioral program for the prevention of chronic PTSD in recent assault victims. *Journal of Consulting and Clinical Psychology, 63,* 948–955.

Foa, E. B., Rothbaum, B. O., Riggs, D. S., & Murdock, T. B. (1991). Treatment of posttraumatic stress disorder in rape victims: A comparison between cognitive-behavioral procedures and counseling. *Journal of Consulting and Clinical Psychology, 59,* 715–723.

Foa, E. B., Steketee, G., & Rothbaum, B. O. (1989). Behavioral/cognitive conceptualizations of post-traumatic stress disorder. *Behavior Therapy, 20,* 155–176.

Forbes, D., Creamer, M., & Rycroft, P. (1994). Eye movement desensitization and reprocessing in post traumatic stress disorder: A pilot study using assessment measures. *Journal of Behavior Therapy and Experimental Psychiatry, 25,* 113–120.

Frank, E., Anderson, B., Stewart, B. D., Dancu, C., Hughes, C., & West, D. (1988). Efficacy of cognitive behavior therapy and systematic desensitization in the treatment of rape trauma. *Behavior Therapy, 19,* 403–420.

Frueh, B. C., Turner, S. M., & Beidel, D. C. (1995). Exposure therapy for combat-related PTSD: A critical review. *Clinical Psychology Review, 15,* 799–817.

Frueh, B. C., Turner, S. M., Beidel, D. C., Mirabella, R. F., & Jones, W. J. (1996). Trauma management therapy: A preliminary evaluation of a multicomponent treatment for chronic combat-related PTSD. *Behaviour Research and Therapy, 34,* 533–543.

Herbert, J. D., & Mueser, K. T. (1992). Eye movement desensitization: A critique of the evidence. *Journal of Behavior Therapy and Experimental Psychiatry, 23,* 169–174.

Hickling, E. J., Sison, G. F. P., Jr., & Vanderploeg, R. D. (1986). Treatment of posttraumatic stress disorder with relaxation and biofeedback training. *Biofeedback and Self-Regulation, 11,* 125–134.

Hiley-Young, B. (1990). Facilitating cognitive-emotional congruence in anxiety disorders during self-determined cognitive change: An integrative model. *Journal of Cognitive Psychotherapy: An International Quarterly, 4,* 225–236.

Hollon, S. D., & Kendall, P. C. (1980). Cognitive self-statements in depression: Development of an Automatic Thoughts Questionnaire. *Cognitive Therapy and Research, 4,* 383–395.

Holmes, M. R., & St. Lawrence, J. S. (1983). Treatment of rape-induced trauma: Proposed behavioral conceptualization and review of the literature. *Clinical Psychology Review, 3,* 417–433.

Horowitz, M. J., Wilner, N., & Alvarez, W. (1979). Impact of Event Scale: A study of subjective stress. *Psychosomatic Medicine, 41*(3), 209–218.

Janoff-Bulman, R. (1989). *The World Assumptions Scale.* (Psychological test available from the author at the Department of Psychology, University of Massachusetts, MA 01003.)

Jensen, J. A. (1994). An investigation of eye movement desensitization and reprocessing (EMD/R) as a treatment of posttraumatic stress disorder (PTSD) symptoms of Vietnam combat veterans. *Behavior Therapy, 25,* 311–325.

Joseph, S., Williams, R., & Yule, W. (1993). Changes in outlook following disaster: The preliminary development of a measure to assess positive and negative responses. *Journal of Traumatic Stress, 6,* 271–279.

Joseph, S., Yule, W., & Williams, R. (1995). Emotional processing in survivors of the Jupiter cruise ship disaster. *Behaviour Research and Therapy, 33,* 187–192.

Kaspi, S. P., McNally, R. J., & Amir, N. (1995). Cognitive processing of emotional information in posttraumatic stress disorder. *Cognitive Therapy and Research, 19,* 433–444.

Keane, T. M., Fairbank, J. A., Caddell, J. M., & Zimering, R. T. (1989). Implosive (flooding) therapy reduces symptoms of PTSD in Vietnam combat veterans. *Behavior Therapy, 20,* 245–260.

Keane, T. M., & Kaloupek, D. G. (1982). Imaginal flooding in the treatment of a post-traumatic stress disorder. *Journal of Consulting and Clinical Psychology, 50,* 138–140.

Keane, T. M., Zimering, R. T., & Caddell, J. M. (1985). A behavioral formulation of post-traumatic stress disorder in combat veterans. *Behavior Therapist, 8,* 9–12.

Kingsbury, S. J. (1988). Hypnosis in the treatment of posttraumatic stress disorder: An isomorphic intervention. *American Journal of Clinical Hypnosis, 31,* 81–90.

Kreitler, S., & Kreitler, H. (1988). Trauma and anxiety: The cognitive approach. *Journal of Traumatic Stress, 1,* 35–56.

Kushner, M. (1965). Desensitization of a post-traumatic phobia. In L. P. Ullmann & L. Krasner (Eds.), *Case studies in behavior modification* (pp. 193–196). New York: Holt, Rinehart & Winston.

Lawson, D. M. (1995). Conceptualization and treatment for Vietnam veterans experiencing posttraumatic stress disorder. *Journal of Mental Health Counseling, 17,* 31–53.

Litz, B. T. (1992). Emotional numbing in combat-related post-traumatic stress disorder: A critical review and reformulation. *Clinical Psychology Review, 12,* 417–432.

Litz, B. T., & Keane, T. M. (1989). Information processing in anxiety disorders: Application to the understanding of post-traumatic stress disorder. *Clinical Psychology Review, 9,* 243–257.

Lyons, J. A., & Keane, T. M. (1989). Implosive therapy for the treatment of combat-related PTSD. *Journal of Traumatic Stress, 2,* 137–152.

McCann, I. L., & Pearlman, L. A. (1990). *Psychological trauma and the adult survivor: Theory, therapy, and transformation.* New York: Brunner/Mazel.

McCann, I. L., Sakheim, K. K., & Abrahamson, D. J. (1988). Trauma and victimization: A model of psychological adaptation. *Counseling Psychologist, 16,* 531–594.

McCormack, N. A. (1985). Cognitive therapy of posttraumatic stress disorder: A case report. *American Mental Health Counselors Association Journal, 7,* 151–155.

McNally, R. J., English, G. E., & Lipke, H. J. (1993). Assessment of intrusive cognition in PTSD: Use of the modified Stroop paradigm. *Journal of Traumatic Stress, 6,* 33–41.

McWhirter, J. J., & Liebman, P. C. (1988). A description of anger-control therapy groups to help Vietnam veterans with PTSD. *Journal for Specialists in Group Work, 13,* 9–16.

Meichenbaum, D. (1994). *A clinical handbook/practical therapist manual for assessing and treating adults with post-traumatic stress disorder (PTSD).* Waterloo, Ontario: Institute Press.

Montgomery, R. W., & Ayllon, T. (1994). Eye movement desensitization across subjects: Subjective and physiological measures of treatment efficacy. *Journal of Behavior Therapy and Experimental Psychiatry, 25,* 217–230.

Mower, O. H. (1960). *Learning theory and behavior.* New York: Wiley.

Mueser, K. T., Yarnold, P. R., & Foy, D. W. (1991). Statistical analysis for single-case designs: Evaluating outcome of imaginal exposure treatment of chronic PTSD. *Behavior Modification, 15,* 134–155.

Muran, E. M., & Motta R. W. (1993). Cognitive distortions and irrational beliefs in post-traumatic stress, anxiety, and depressive disorders. *Journal of Clinical Psychology, 49,* 166–176.

Nishith, P., Hearst, D. E., Mueser, K. T., & Foa, E. B. (1995). PTSD and major depression: Methodological and treatment considerations in a single case design. *Behavior Therapy, 26,* 319–335.

Norman, M. (1989). *These good men.* New York: Crown.

Oswalt, R., Anderson, M., Hagstrom, K., & Berkowitz, B. (1993). Evaluation of the one-session eye-movement desensitization reprocessing procedure for eliminating traumatic memories. *Psychological Reports, 73,* 99.

Pearlman, L. A. (1994). *TSI Belief Scale.* (Instrument available from the author at The Traumatic Stress Institute, 22 Morgan Farms Drive, South Windsor, CT 06074.)

Pearson, N. A., Poquette, B. N., & Wasden, R. E. (1983). Stress inoculation and the treatment of post-rape trauma. *Behavior Therapist, 6,* 58–59.

Peniston, E. G. (1986). EMG biofeedback-assisted desensitization treatment for Vietnam combat veterans post-traumatic stress disorder. *Clinical Biofeedback and Health, 9,* 35–41.

Renfrey, G., & Spates, C. R. (1994). Eye movement desensitization: A partial dismantling study. *Journal of Behavior Therapy and Experimental Psychiatry, 25,* 231–239.

Resick, P. A., & Schnicke, M. K. (1992). Cognitive processing therapy for sexual assault victims. *Journal of Consulting and Clinical Psychology, 60,* 748–756.

Rozynko, V., & Dondershine, H. E. (1991). Trauma focus group therapy for Vietnam veterans with PTSD. *Psychotherapy, 28,* 157–161.

Rychtarik, R., Silverman, W., Van Landingham, W., & Prue, D. (1984). Treatment of an incest victim with implosive therapy: A case study. *Behavior Therapy, 15,* 410–420.

Saigh, P. A. (1992). *Posttraumatic stress disorder: A behavioral approach to assessment and treatment.* Boston, MA: Allyn & Bacon.

Sanderson, A., & Carpenter, R. (1992). Eye movement desensitization versus image confrontation: A single session cross-over study of 58 phobic subjects. *Journal of Behavior Therapy and Experimental Psychiatry, 23,* 269–275.

Saul, L. J., Rome, H., & Leuser, E. (1946). Desensitization of combat fatigue patients. *American Journal of Psychiatry, 102,* 476–478.

Schindler, F. E. (1980). Treatment by systematic desensitization of a recurring nightmare of a real life trauma. *Journal of Behavior Therapy and Experimental Psychiatry, 11,* 53–54.

Scurfield, R. M., Corker, T. M., Gongla, P. A., & Richard L. (1984). Three post-Vietnam "rap/therapy" groups: An analysis. *Group, 8,* 3–21.

Shapiro, F. (1995). *Eye movement desensitization and reprocessing: Basic principles, protocols, and procedures.* New York: Guilford Press.

Shapiro, F. (1991). Eye movement desensitization and reprocessing procedure: From EMD to EMD/R—a new treatment model for anxiety and related traumata. *Behavior Therapist, 14,* 128, 133–135.

Shapiro, F. (1989a). Efficacy of eye movement desensitization procedure in the treatment of traumatic memories. *Journal of Traumatic Stress, 2,* 199–223.

Shapiro, F. (1989b). Eye movement desensitization: A new treatment for post-traumatic stress disorder. *Journal of Behavior Therapy and Experimental Psychiatry, 20,* 211–217.

Sharpe, L., Tarrier, N., & Rotundo, N. (1994). Treatment of delayed post-traumatic stress disorder following sexual abuse: A case example. *Behavioural and Cognitive Psychotherapy, 22,* 233–242.

Sharpley, C. F., Montgomery, I. M., & Scalzo, L. A. (1996). Comparative efficacy of EMDR and alternative procedures in reducing the vividness of mental images. *Scandinavian Journal of Behaviour Therapy, 25,* 37–42.

Silver, S. M., Brooks, A., & Obenchain, J. (1995). Treatment of Vietnam War veterans with PTSD: A comparison of eye movement desensitization and reprocessing, biofeedback, and relaxation training. *Journal of Traumatic Stress, 8,* 337–342.

Solomon, S. D., Gerrity, E. T., & Muff, A. M. (1992). Efficacy of treatments for posttraumatic stress disorder. *Journal of the American Medical Association, 268,* 633–638.

Spielberger, C. D., Gorsuch, R. L., Lushene, R. D., Vagg, P. R., & Jacobs, G. A. (1983) *Manual for the State-Trait Anxiety Inventory.* Palo Alto, CA: Consulting Psychologists Press.

Stampfl, T. G., & Levis, D. J. (1967). Essentials of implosive therapy: A learning-theory-based psychodynamic behavioral therapy. *Journal of Abnormal Psychology, 72,* 157–163.

Vaughan, K., Armstrong, M. S., Gold, R., O'Connor, N., Jenneke, W., & Tarrier, N. (1994). A trial of eye movement desensitization compared to image habituation training and applied muscle relaxation in post-traumatic stress disorder. *Journal of Behavior Therapy and Experimental Psychiatry, 25,* 283–291.

Vaughan, K., & Tarrier, N. (1992). The use of image habituation training with post-traumatic stress disorder. *British Journal of Psychiatry, 161,* 658–664.

Vaughan, K., Wiese, M., Gold, R., & Tarrier, N. (1994). Eye movement desensitisation: Symptom change in post-traumatic stress disorder. *British Journal of Psychiatry, 164,* 533–541.

Venn, J. (1988). Hypnotic intervention in accident victims during acute phase of posttraumatic adjustment. *American Journal of Clinical Hypnosis, 31,* 114–117.

Wilson, S. A., Becker, L. A., & Tinker, R. H. (1995). Eye movement desensitization and reprocessing (EMDR) treatment for psychologically traumatized individuals. *Journal of Consulting and Clinical Psychology, 63,* 928–937.

Wolff, R. (1977). Systematic desensitization and negative practice to alter the aftereffects of a rape attempt. *Journal of Behavior Therapy and Experimental Psychiatry, 8,* 423–425.

Wolpe, J. (1958). *Psychotherapy by reciprocal inhibition.* Stanford, CA: Stanford University Press.

Wolpe, J., & Abrams, J. (1991). Post-traumatic stress disorder overcome by eye movement desensitization: A case report. *Journal of Behavior Therapy and Experimental Psychiatry, 22,* 39–43.

A Functional Analysis of Trauma Symptoms

AMY E. NAUGLE
WILLIAM C. FOLLETTE

The clinician who assesses and treats individuals with a history of trauma faces a difficult challenge. The clinical presentation of clients who have trauma histories includes one or more of the following: general psychological distress, depression, anxiety, suicidal behavior, marital and interpersonal difficulties, substance abuse, borderline personality features, anger, emotional numbness, nightmares, and a variety of other symptoms. In addition, some who present after a particular episode of trauma may turn out to have had multiple traumatic experiences. Sometimes the traumatic event occurred recently, and at other times in the distant past, and decades of new history may have occurred before a client presents for therapy. So far, there is no pathognomonic symptom or symptom constellation that always results from a trauma history. There is also no evidence that there are not some people who experience traumatic events and do not manifest any of the aforementioned symptoms.

The clinician faces a real dilemma. How does one make sense of client problems when a client presents with a trauma history? How does one know the relevance of the trauma as a controlling variable in the current presentation of symptoms? How does one know whether or how a traumatic history, as painful as it might have been, is the important issue that affects a client now? How does one develop a treatment plan for such a varied set of symptoms?

In addition to these problems, clinicians have to choose from very different assessment strategies to help with their case planning. One form, referred to as a structuralist approach, emphasizes the correct classification of the form of behavior (Sturmey, 1996). It includes diagnoses and personality characteristics as foci of attention. The alternative approach, and the one emphasized in this chapter, attends to the importance of environmental factors in the initial causation and current controlling and maintaining functions of clinical problems (Haynes & O'Brien, 1990).

In this chapter, we describe a strategy that addresses some of these issues. The goals of this chapter are to (1) define the role of assessment in treating clients with a trauma history; (2) distinguish between traditional assessment strategies and those that we think may be more relevant given the above complexities; (3) describe some clinical principles that should help the clinician make useful treatment choices; and (4) make the clinician aware of inferential errors that may lead to inappropriate or incomplete treatment plans.

THE ROLE OF ASSESSMENT

Conducting a thorough pretreatment behavioral assessment is important in case conceptualization and treatment planning. In traditional approaches to assessment, once the clinical problems have been identified, the clinician attempts to specify the etiology of the psychological symptoms (Barrios & Hartmann, 1986). One possible etiological explanation is that a history of trauma is responsible for the development of the client's current difficulties. Indeed, posttraumatic stress disorder (PTSD) is one of the few diagnostic categories in DSM-IV that identify a specific etiology within the definition. In the case where the trauma is recent and the person was well-functioning prior to the trauma, identifying the trauma as the primary etiology of the problem could be sufficient for implementing an intervention. Such cases would probably respond to exposure and desensitization at a high enough rate to call into question the need for very involved assessment, other than that sufficient to confirm that the dysfunction resulted only from the recent trauma, and that the trauma was not the result of a maladaptive behavioral excess (e.g., drinking) or deficit (e.g., assertion or discrimination of danger).

However, in other cases, the clinician may mistakenly guide his or her intervention based on a *presumed* etiology and fail to appreciate additional or more proximal controlling variables for psychological distress. By this, we mean that even though trauma may have been an important factor in the onset of some initial symptoms, there are other problem behaviors that are the result of the attempts to manage the trauma-related distress. These coping behaviors can then come under the control of more current situational contingencies and become functionally autonomous (i.e., behaviors that occurred as the result of one antecedent are maintained because of other current factors even after those initial conditions no longer exist). In such instances, addressing the initial causal variable (i.e., the trauma) may not affect these current maladaptive responses.

One assessment goal of clinicians treating clients who report a history of trauma is to identify if or to what degree the psychological effects of the traumatic experience are fundamentally important to address; that is, the clinician can reasonably hypothesize that the traumatic experience has had a significant impact on the individual's psychological functioning and explore possible domains of impairment. The task is to be able to modify one's case conceptualization to offer the best possible intervention for a particular client when new assessment information suggests other important factors are clinically relevant. The clinician may utilize a number of different assessment methods to do so, including clinical interviews and trauma-specific self-report instruments. While standardized instruments that identify trauma-related symptoms and assess the details of the client's traumatic experiences offer useful information with regard to generating clinical hypotheses for understanding the client's current difficulties, relying exclusively on this assessment strategy is not sufficient.

A second, related goal of assessment with trauma survivors is to determine whether the fact that a client meets the diagnostic criteria for PTSD is a necessary and sufficient assessment finding. One needs to be protective against assuming that anyone who reports a history of trauma should be treated as a member of a homogenous population without regard for the unique individual and environmental characteristics of a particular client.

One of the points we wish to emphasize in this chapter is that the functional analytic approach to assessment that we advocate can help avoid an important error in case conceptualization that can occur otherwise. Specifically, traditional assessment often emphasizes the symptoms themselves to be targeted for intervention without adequate regard to the purpose those symptoms serve. In technical parlance, assessment based on identifying and counting symptoms attends primarily to the form or topography of symptoms, while we think that it is crucial to attend to the function of the presenting problems, because the same behavior may be under the control of very different environmental factors. Failing to appreciate that the same behavior in two different individuals may have completely different psychological functions can lead to inappropriate treatment or the attribution that a client is "resistant" when, in fact, the treatment is based on inappropriate or incomplete case conceptualization.

WHAT IS FUNCTIONAL ANALYSIS?

Functional analysis is an assessment approach that emphasizes the purposes that behavior serves for the person. The current environment is examined to assess what part it plays in causing and maintaining behavior (Goldiamond, 1974, 1975). Why is this approach appealing? First, such a perspective allows the clinician to examine those factors that he or she actually has the opportunity to analyze and change. This approach also has as part of its philosophical roots the notion that target behaviors are not treated directly, but one goal is to increase functionally equivalent alternative behaviors. This has been referred to as a constructional approach to therapy. It seeks to build on the person's existing behavioral repertoire and encourage the strengthening of the behaviors that work for the person better than those he or she currently exhibits. The task is not to get rid of problem behaviors directly, but rather to replace them with more effective behaviors. This is particularly useful in treating persons with trauma histories, since they cannot change historical aspects of the experience, but can certainly alter how they respond more usefully to the current consequences of the trauma experience.

Another feature of functional analysis is that one of its goals is to identify important relationships between variables that can affect client functioning. However, it is not assumed that the relationships between two variables preclude the identification of other variables that may affect functioning. A functional analysis is an iterative process that requires that a reasonable understanding of the variables controlling the currently identified clinical problems be sufficiently well developed to begin treatment. However, it is not assumed that the assessment be complete or, indeed, even correct. What is required is that the clinician engage in ongoing assessment throughout therapy, refining the analysis until satisfactory clinical outcomes are obtained. If a treatment based on a functional analysis is not producing the desired results, the functional analysis is presumed to be incorrect, inadequate, or incomplete, rather than the problem being that the client is resistant (Hayes & Follette, 1992).

A functional analytic assessment strategy implies that if the assessment is to have treatment utility, the focus must be on understanding the clinical problems of the individual client. Functional analysis is by its nature idiographic. A functional analytic assessment involves identifying the unique situational variables responsible for the development and maintenance of behavior for a given individual and recognizes that these controlling variables vary across individuals and time. Nomothetic strategies, on the other hand, are based on the assumption that there are universal principles that can be applied across clients, and that identifying causal factors for behavior shared across clients is sufficient (Cone, 1986).

There are strengths to both idiographic and nomothetic approaches to assessment, and pragmatically, a functional analysis utilizes a combination of strategies. Cone (1986) suggests that while an individualized understanding of a client's problems is an essential goal of behavioral assessment, we can apply nomothetic principles to guide the individual analysis. In conducting a functional analytic assessment, the clinician selects target behaviors and identifies controlling variables with the assumption that all clinical problems can be understood using behavioral principles. However, a functional analysis does not presume that similar target problems across individuals are under the control of the same historical or current environmental variables.

Trauma-specific assessment measures are standardized across individuals who report trauma experiences that share similar features. These instruments provide a number of common symptoms that individuals with a trauma history may experience. As we suggested earlier, trauma-specific instruments or other standardized symptom inventories may be useful resources for identifying clinically relevant behavior and generating hypotheses. However, the clinician cannot assume that similar target behaviors are maintained by the same variables.

Definition and Goals of Functional Analysis

Definition

Functional analysis is defined differently within behavior therapy. Among other definitions, functional analysis is understood in some cases simply as the process of identifying target behaviors, and in others as the manipulation of variables that are presumed to control a behavior (see Haynes & O'Brien, 1990; Sturmey, 1996). For our purposes, functional analysis involves the identification and specification of functional relationships among variables, indicating how change in one variable impacts change in another (Haynes & O'Brien, 1990; Sturmey, 1996). It is not necessary in a functional analytic assessment to specify the relationship among all variables, only those antecedents and consequences of behaviors that are changeable and that result in modification of the targeted problem behavior (Owens & Ashcroft, 1982). Haynes and O'Brien (1990) propose the following definition of functional analysis "the identification of important, controllable, causal functional relationships applicable to a specified set of target behaviors for an individual client" (p. 654).

The functional relationship between the important controlling variables and the target behavior is understood and stated as a probabilistic causal relationship. Pragmatically, it is not possible to specify all of the relevant factors that can alter the functional relationships among variables most pertinent to our analysis. Therefore, we can only state the probability of the relationship based on the environmental conditions that are known. Functional relationships can change over time. The same factors that contributed to the development of a specific behavior are not necessarily the same variables that maintain the behavior currently. Developing a thorough understanding of a clinical problem, therefore, involves understanding the function of the behavior historically as well as currently (Hayes, Follette, & Follette, 1995).

Specifying causal relationships among variables is often a complex process (Evans, 1985; Nelson & Hayes, 1986). Behaviors may have multiple causes, and the causes may interact with one another and vary based on subtle shifts in other environmental factors (Haynes & O'Brien, 1990). Identifying a relationship among variables does not necessarily illuminate the direction of the relationship. Causal relationships may be bidirectional. This is illustrated using the example of the high rate of substance abuse that is associated with a history of childhood sexual abuse (Polusny & Follette, 1995). It is speculated that increased substance use is a risk factor for revictimization in women who were sexually abused as children (Polusny, 1998). Alcohol use may impair a woman's judgment and place her at risk for being sexually revictimized. It may also be the case that child sexual abuse or sexual assault experiences as an adult may lead to the development of increased alcohol use to escape negative thoughts and feelings related to a previous rape.

Goals

Hayes and Follette (1992) provide a structure for what is entailed in conducting a thorough functional analytic assessment that has treatment utility.

Step 1: Identify potentially relevant characteristics of the individual client, his or her behavior, and the context in which it occurs via broad assessment. The first step in formulating a functional analytic case conceptualization entails gathering a large amount of information about the client and the nature of the presenting concerns. In large part, the clinician uses this broad-based information to begin generating clinical hypotheses. The process of narrowing the focus in Steps 2 and 3 is characterized by Hawkins's (1979, 1986) reference to a "behavioral assessment funnel." As the scope of the assessment narrows, the intervention options narrow as well. This initial, broad-based case formulation can be accomplished using any number of assessment methods, including clinical interviews and self-report questionnaires. Although these traditional assessment methods may not be sufficient in and of themselves, they are useful tools for gathering detailed information about the client's presenting complaints to begin a more thorough case conceptualization. The clinician can then begin identifying the important environmental variables that precede and maintain the specific behaviors. In addition, more direct assessment methods such as self-monitoring, role plays, and naturalistic observation (Barrios, 1988) provide more ecologically valid information regarding the client's behavior and potential controlling variables as they occur outside the psychotherapy environment.

Step 2: Organize the information gathered in Step 1 into a preliminary analysis of the client's difficulties in terms of behavioral principles (e.g., reinforcement, stimulus control) so as to identify important causal relationships that might be changed. Step 2 involves narrowing the conceptualization and prioritizing the focus of the analysis. For each working hypothesis, the client's problems are described using behavioral principles. Controlling variables that account for the greatest amount of variance in the target behavior are selected (Haynes & O'Brien, 1990). The clinician identifies the antecedents that occasion or precede the target behavior, as well as the reinforcement contingencies that maintain the behavior. It is from this refined, principle-based functional analysis that treatment alternatives are designed.

Step 3: Gather additional information based on Step 2 and finalize the conceptual analysis. At this stage of the assessment process, the understanding of the case becomes more concentrated. The clinician may implement additional assessment procedures to clarify the preliminary analyses. For example, the clinician may use the direct assessment methods introduced in Step 1 to more carefully examine relevant controlling variables. In addition, the clinician establishes objective, behaviorally specific criteria for measuring change in the target variables, so that treatment progress is monitored and modified as necessary.

Step 4: Devise an intervention based on Step 3. An important feature of behavioral assessment is the close link between the conceptualization of clinical problems and treatment (Barrios, 1988). As a functional analysis of a clinical problem develops, the suggestions for treatment and the criteria for measuring outcome follow (Kanfer & Saslow, 1969). Once the clinician applies behavioral principles to understanding the client's problem, functional classes of clinical problems emerge that have specific treatment implications. The reader is referred to Hayes et al. (1995) for an overview of examples of clinical problems and feasible interventions from a behavior therapy perspective.

Step 5: Implement treatment and assess change. Within behavior therapy, assessment is viewed as an ongoing process. A functional analysis of behavior is continually evaluated with regard to its treatment utility (Hayes, Nelson, & Jarrett, 1987). Given that the clinician has established behaviorally specific criteria for measuring change, the goal of this step is to determine whether change has occurred, and whether the change is of sufficient magnitude given the dosage of the intervention. It is in this sense that functional analysis is a self-correcting and iterative process. Feedback loops are an integral part of a functional analysis and assist in determining the appropriateness or utility of the case conceptualization (Owens & Ashcroft, 1982).

Step 6: If the outcome is unacceptable, recycle back to Step 2 or 3. The clinician may determine in the process of evaluating outcome that the treatment has not resulted in a desired outcome. Generally, an unacceptable outcome suggests a flaw in the functional analysis (Hayes & Follette, 1992). Therefore, this calls for some modification in the conceptualization. The clinician may be able to make minor changes in the analysis, or it may involve returning to the information gathered in Step 1 and formulating entirely different clinical hypotheses.

Controlling Variables: An Operant Analysis

In this section, we provide a brief overview of basic behavioral principles before providing a description of specific functional domains of clinical problems. The reader is referred elsewhere for a more detailed description of behavior analysis and behavioral concepts (e.g., see Baum, 1994, and Catania, 1992).

Identifying the Target Behavior

An important aspect of functional analysis involves selecting the behavior for the focus of the intervention. The behavior must be operationally defined, and the relevant dimensions of the behavior, such as frequency and severity, should also be noted. However, the scope of potential target behaviors is vast. Historically, behaviorism has been criticized for being rigid and overly simplistic in its application to complex phenomena. The belief that overt, observable behaviors are the only legitimate target for behavioral assessment and treatment persists. However, these are goals of a long-rejected mechanistic stimulus–response (S-R) behavioral psychology. Contextual or radical behaviorism does not exclude private events as legitimate subject matter of a functional analysis. Therefore, thoughts, feelings, and physiological states are included in the domain of possible target behaviors. In working with trauma survivors, intrusive images, flashbacks, stomachaches, or negative thoughts about one's self-worth may all be potential target behaviors. After specifying the target behaviors, observable or unobservable, the task is to identify the controlling variables that precede and maintain the behavior.

In addition to identifying the target behaviors, it is also important for the clinician to identify functionally equivalent behaviors or other aspects of the individual's repertoire that can be supported or increased over the course of treatment. This approach is called a "constructional approach" and focuses on strengthening areas of the client's functioning that currently are effective (Goldiamond, 1974).

Antecedents and Stimulus Control

As environmental conditions change, so do behaviors. Antecedents are those environmental stimuli that precede the behavior. Generally, antecedent stimuli that exert control over the behavior occur in relative temporal proximity to the behavior itself. An environmental event that signals the reinforcement of a particular response is referred to as a "discriminative stimulus." Stimulus control is an operation that determines and signals the conditions under which behavior is likely to be reinforced. The phenomenon of dissociation can be understood as a problem of stimulus control. Physical closeness operates as a discriminative stimulus for dissociative behavior. As a child, dissociating was an effective escape strategy when the child was being sexually abused. However, as an adult, dissociating whenever physical contact is initiated by another person is probably a maladaptive behavior in most circumstances.

Contingencies of Reinforcement

Reinforcing stimuli are those stimuli that follow the behavior and increase the probability of its occurrence. Positive reinforcement is the delivery of a stimulus that strengthens behavior and increases the probability of occurrence. This can explain the development of overly compliant behavior in children who are sexually abused. In order to maintain secrecy and continue sexually abusing a child, the perpetrator may provide the child with gifts or other reinforcers when the child complies with the perpetrator's advances. The compliant behavior is strengthened, and it is more likely that the child will continue to keep quiet and acquiesce to future demands of the perpetrator.

Negative reinforcement is the removal of an aversive stimulus that also strengthens the behavior. Both escape of aversive stimulation and avoidance of negative events are examples of negative reinforcement. For example, a woman who has been raped may report increased physiological arousal and intrusive images of the rape only when she is exposed to particular cues, such as when she is driving in her car alone. So, the woman avoids driving alone and attempts to have a passenger whenever she travels anywhere. Driving with other people in this case is negatively reinforced. The probability of driving with others increases through the avoidance of negative consequences (i.e., physiological arousal and intrusive thoughts).

Punishment, on the other hand, decreases the probability of occurrence of a behavior through the delivery of an aversive stimulus. Physical abuse inflicted by parents in order to decrease child misbehavior is an example of punishment. In order to stop a child's tantrum behavior, a parent may hit or yell at the child. The hitting and yelling are punishing stimuli if the child discontinues the tantrum.

In addition to specifying the contingencies that maintain problematic behavior, an adequate functional analysis should also identify the environmental contingencies that have not supported more effective behavior (Sturmey, 1996). It is possible that effective or desirable behavior was never learned, that such behavior was never adequately reinforced, or that punishing contingencies diminished the strength of the behavior. In simple terms, this means that a person may not have a sufficiently developed behavioral repertoire to take advantage of opportunities that could lead to important personal benefits.

Establishing Operations

Establishing or motivational operations are distinct from stimulus control operations (Michael, 1982, 1994). Discriminative stimuli are those stimuli that directly precede the reinforcement contingent on a particular response. Establishing stimuli are the environmental conditions such as deprivation, satiation, aversive stimulation, or other physiological processes that establish a stimulus as a reinforcer or punisher. In addition, establishing stimuli can change the relative value of the reinforcing or punishing stimulus. Alcohol intoxication is one example of an establishing operation that is relevant to working with clients who have a history of trauma. The level of alcohol intoxication may alter the effectiveness of a reinforcer. For example, alcohol may potentiate the reinforcing effects of social interactions for an individual who reports anxiety in certain social contexts. Engaging others in conversation may be strengthened under these conditions.

The Role of Private Events

We previously introduced the idea that private events such as thoughts, feelings, and physiological responses are legitimate target behaviors within a functional analysis. Private events might serve as antecedent stimuli or consequences within a functional analysis as well. For example, a feeling of anger might be an antecedent to hitting one's spouse. Or the removal of the angry feeling after the aggressive act could be understood as a consequence in a functional analysis of the general problem of spousal abuse. One must be careful, however, in stating that a thought or feeling causes behavior. Thinking and feeling do not cause behavior. Hayes and Brownstein (1986) refer to this problematic analysis of the status of private events as a behavior–behavior relationship. Saying that one behavior causes another behavior is an incomplete analysis, because one cannot change a behavior directly, but rather only the conditions before or after it. For the sake of maintaining maximum utility in an analysis, one looks for changeable initial conditions on which to intervene, instead of merely describing behavior–behavior relationships. We also must understand the environmental contingencies that gave rise to the "causal" behavior in the first place.

Rule-Governed Behavior

To this point, we primarily have included examples of how nonverbal stimuli control behavior. However, behavior may also be controlled by verbal stimuli or by verbal rules. Behavior under the control of verbally stated instructions is called rule-governed behavior and differs from behavior shaped by direct contingencies (Hayes, 1989; Hayes, Brownstein, Zettle, Rosenfarb, & Korn, 1986). For example, rule-governed behavior is less sensitive to changes in nonverbal contingencies than behavior that is directly under the control of those contingencies (Shimoff, Catania, & Matthews, 1981).

Verbal Behavior and Verbal Relations

Skinner (1957) defined "verbal behavior" as behavior that is reinforced and shaped through the mediation of a social–verbal community. Verbal behavior, like any other operant behavior, can be understood with regard to its relationship to a set of contingencies. The variables that are pertinent to a behavioral analysis of verbal events include antecedents of the behavior (i.e., stimulus control), states of deprivation (i.e., establishing operations), and consequential stimuli (i.e., environmental events that function as reinforcers or punishers). By understanding the variables that control verbal responding, we can better under the function, or purpose, that the verbal behavior serves (see Hamilton, 1988, for a behavioral formulation of verbal behavior in psychotherapy). For example, a careful analysis of variables that control a client's verbal repertoire may provide an understanding of why a client with a trauma history may be overly cautious about disclosing personal information about him- or herself even in situations where it is appropriate and intimacy-enhancing to do so. Personal disclosures indeed enhance the level of intimacy in the client's relationships, but also lead to emotional responses that the client attempts to avoid. Likewise, another client may disclose personal information indiscriminately as a way to enhance intimacy. Such a client, a man, for example, tells coworkers detailed information about his trauma history and lacks insight about why it is that people in the work environment avoid him. In this case, the disclosing functions to distance people rather than to build intimacy.

FUNCTIONAL DOMAINS FOR TRAUMA SYMPTOMS

We have given an elementary overview of some of the behavioral principles that may be useful in analyzing the problem behavior of clients. To help better organize these ideas, let us consider a few specific examples. Table 3.1 and the following descriptions of functional domains provided in the text are adopted from the examples of clinical problems and interventions outlined by Hayes, Follette, and Follette (1995).

Antecedents

Inappropriate Stimulus Control

A clinical problem that occurs as the result of inappropriate stimulus control is not problematic because of the form of the response. In fact, the response may be

TABLE 3.1. Functional Domains of Clinical Problems

Functional problem	Description	Specific example
Inappropriate stimulus control	Response is appropriate but occurs under the wrong conditions.	Shares information about trauma history too early in relationships
Inappropriate self-generated stimulus control	Self-generated descriptions lead to ineffective outcomes.	Disturbances of the self, inability to describe one's private experiences
Behavioral excesses	Behavior is excessive in frequency or duration.	Frequent sexual activity with multiple partners
Behavioral deficits	Lacks behaviors or skills that lead to reinforcement	Deficient social or interpersonal repertoire
Experiential avoidance	Avoidance of undesirable thoughts, feelings, and bodily states	Substance abuse, parasuicidal behavior
Lack of available reinforcers	Limited access to reinforcement that will support desired behavior	Depression
Aversive control	Overly punitive environment	Overly compliant behavior, lack of assertiveness

effective and appropriate under some environmental conditions. One might understand the overly affectionate behavior of a child as a problem of inappropriate stimulus control. A mother presented for psychotherapy with her 6-year-old daughter. The girl had been repeatedly sexually abused by her grandfather over a period of 18 months. One of the problematic behaviors identified by the child's mother was a high frequency of affectionate behavior with adult males whom the child did not know well. The child would crawl into the laps of men she had just been introduced to and would hug and kiss them. While hugging and kissing are appropriate behavior under certain conditions (i.e., with nonoffending family members), the child's affectionate behavior in this case was under the control of an inappropriate set of contingencies. Therefore, the goal of therapy would not be to reduce affectionate behavior, but to bring the behavior under the exclusive control of the appropriate contingencies.

Inappropriate Self-Generated Stimulus Control

Issues of the self and the development of self-concept among individuals who experienced sexual abuse in childhood are areas that are given increasing attention in the child sexual abuse literature (Cloitre, Scarvalone, & Difede, 1997). A behavioral interpretation of problems of the self can be understood largely as a problem of self-generated, or private, stimulus control (see Kohlenberg & Tsai, 1991, 1995, and Koerner, Kohlenberg, & Parker, 1996). Development of the self is understood as the process of identifying and describing one's experiences, in large part, one's private experiences. The experience of self is learned early in life and is shaped by the environment. In normal development of the self, a child initially is taught through modeling and direct reinforcement to label experiences (what Kohlenberg and colleagues label "self-referents") based on what is deemed appropriate by the child's social–verbal community (Skinner, 1945). Eventually, describing one's experiences of the world (i.e., "I want," "I feel," "I think") comes under the control of private stimuli.

Problems or disturbances of the self occur along a continuum and are generally the result of inappropriate self-generated stimulus control (Kohlenberg & Tsai, 1991, Chapter 6); that is, self-referents remain largely under the control of public stimuli. Some less severe examples of self-disturbances using this model include clients who have a difficult time stating their preferences or whose behavior is impacted to a large degree by the opinions of others. A more extreme example of a self-disturbance is characteristic of individuals who meet the DSM-IV criteria for borderline personality disorder. Linehan (1993) describes how an invalidating environment in childhood restricts the ability of individuals to talk about emotions, particularly feelings with negative valence. In some cases, a child may be severely punished for expressing feelings or describing other private experiences. Therefore, self-referents under the control of private stimuli are not reinforced. This becomes a real problem when, for example, persons cannot tell others how they feel about how they are being treated. This can result in a series of failed relationships, where neither party in the relationship "knows" why things went wrong.

Rigid Rule-Governed Behavior

Verbally stated rules exert their control over behavior essentially as a discriminative stimulus. A client behavior that is excessively controlled by rules is not impacted by changes in the environmental contingencies; that is, the client does not actually experience the impact of natural consequences on his or her behavior. For example, a young female college student was raped by a man that she had been dating for 8 weeks. The dating relationship was the first serious relationship in which the young woman had been involved. Following the rape, the woman developed an intense mistrust of men. She repeatedly declined dating propositions and would avoid even engaging men in conversations. At the beginning of therapy, the client explicitly stated, "If I trust a man, I will be hurt." This statement illustrates the rigid control the rule exerted over the client's behavior. The client limited her social interactions and declined opportunities that may have had a favorable outcome.

Responses and Behavioral Repertoires

Behavioral Excesses

Behavioral excesses include examples in which the client's behavior is excessive in either frequency or duration and interferes with functioning. Many of the anxiety symptoms reported by trauma survivors can be conceptualized as behavioral excesses. Extreme anxiety interferes with a client's functioning and prohibits him or her from taking advantage of opportunities where alternative behavior may be reinforced or that the client might ultimately find rewarding. Another example of a behavioral excess is the high rate of sexual activity noted in the literature on long-term correlates of childhood sexual abuse (Briere & Runtz, 1993; Polusny & Follette, 1995). Frequent sexual activity with multiple partners is a risk factor for contraction of HIV infection (Allers, Benjack, White, & Rousey, 1993) and may be a risk factor for sexual victimization (Naugle, Follette, & Follette, 1995). Sexual activity is considered a behavioral excess in this example because of the potential interference with a client's functioning.

Some behavior may be labeled as an excess because it is aversive to others. Physically aggressive behavior, regardless of its frequency, may be considered a behavioral excess in that it has negative consequences for others. Aggressive behavior is identified as a behavioral problem that is exhibited by physically and sexually abused children (Deblinger, McLeer, Atkins, Ralphe, & Foa, 1989). High rates of aggression with a spouse or with others have also been reported in samples of male Vietnam War veterans (e.g., Dutton, 1995; Hiley-Young, Blake, Abueg, Rozynko, & Gusman, 1995).

Behavioral Deficits

In some cases, the client's behavioral repertoire may be inadequate; that is, the individual does not emit behaviors that will be subsequently reinforced. The most general example of behavior deficits includes a lack of social or interpersonal skills that might be associated with history of trauma. One feature of intimate interpersonal relationships is the occurrence of self-disclosure in the relationship. Telling another person about your interests, thoughts, feelings, and reactions serves to enhance intimacy within a relationship (Fruzzetti, 1996). A history in which such disclosure was punished may have resulted in a behavioral deficit in this area, therefore restricting a client's ability to initiate and sustain important interpersonal relationships.

Deficient Tacting of Private Experiences

"Alexithymia" is the term used to describe the inability to label one's private experiences, particularly feelings (see Cloitre, Chapter 11, this volume). Labeling is called a "tact." It is a verbal response that is under the control of a discriminative stimulus. Therefore, tacting a feeling is under the control of a bodily state or private event, and labeling the feeling aloud is established and maintained through delivery of reinforcement of the social–verbal community. Said another way, labeling is supported by people around us understanding something about our experience. Expressing feelings is another example of intimacy-enhancing behavior. In addition, expressing feelings may be a strategy for getting one's needs met in a relationship (Kohlenberg & Tsai, 1991). Some individuals as result of their experiences in childhood, may not learn to discriminate effectively and talk about their feelings, because such "I feel" statements have not come under the private control of bodily changes. Some parental environments may effectively punish emotional responding. The strength of the behavior (talking about feelings) is diminished, and the client's repertoire for expressing how he or she feels may be inadequate.

Experiential Avoidance

Experiential avoidance may be understood as a functional class in which avoidance of undesirable thoughts, feelings, and physiological states is negatively reinforced. The form of the behaviors that function to avoid aversive private experience is varied. Self-harming behaviors including substance abuse, and parasuicidal behaviors such as suicidal gestures and self-mutilation may be examples of experiential avoidance. Clients may engage in these behaviors to escape or avoid negative emotional experiences such as extreme anxiety, anger, and sadness (see Walser & Hayes, Chapter 10, for a more thorough discussion).

Conditioned Emotional Responses

Conditioned emotional responses are responses that are elicited through a classically conditioned paradigm. The reexperiencing phenomena characteristic of a PTSD diagnosis are examples of responses that have been classically conditioned and cause problems for the individual. When a person is experiencing flashbacks or is reacting physiologically to environmental stimuli associated with the trauma, it is imperative that the clinician establish the specific contextual variables that elicit the excessive fear or phobic response and present those situations while making sure that the dangerous consequences associated with those situations do not occur. A startle response to a loud noise can be extinguished if the startle-inducing conditions can be presented without corresponding bad consequences.

Contingencies of Reinforcement

Lack of Available Reinforcers

Some client behavior may be influenced by the availability of reinforcement. A man presents for therapy complaining of depression. He is sleeping more than usual, reports depressed mood, and lack of energy. In addition, he indicates that he is socially isolated and has few friends. The clinician discovers that 6 months earlier, the client has moved to a small town from a larger metropolitan area. The small town does not provide the same opportunities for social stimulation and activities that the client previously found reinforcing. The man enjoys visiting the theater and discussing politics, in addition to other social activities. The client's current social network in the small town does not afford the same opportunities. The clinician may therefore work with the client to increase alternative sources of reinforcement that are available in the client's current environment.

Ineffective Reinforcement

Ineffective reinforcement is a functional domain in which normal reinforcement contingencies do not adequately control behavior. Antisocial behavior is a common example of how the delivery of punishing consequences does not sufficiently restrict behavior. Ineffective reinforcement may also unnecessarily sustain behavior. For example, trauma survivors frequently report feelings of guilt associated with the traumatic event. While guilt may indeed be an appropriate label for the individual's private experiences, it may be that talking about guilt is maintained through secondary gain; that is, clients avoid having to take responsibility for their current behavior and evoke sympathy from others as they talk about their feelings of guilt. Overt displays of guilt may function to reduce criticism or negative evaluation from others and to increase social support.

Inappropriate Contingent Control

At times, behavior may be under the control of reinforcers that are viewed as socially unacceptable or that result in additional negative outcomes. Pedophilia is conceptualized as sexual behavior that is under inappropriate contingent control (Wulfert, Greenway, & Dougher, 1996).

Aversive Control

Oftentimes, individuals who have experienced interpersonal victimization be-come overly cautious in their interactions and restrict their behavior in order to avoid punitive consequences. Such individuals are overly compliant in interper-sonal relationships and become overly attentive to subtle changes in the behavior of others. This is problematic when the individual misattributes the actions of others and adjusts his or her own behavior based on the misattribution. For example, a woman who was in a physically abusive relationship for 15 years may be especially attentive to changes in her new partner's mood. When her partner becomes angry, she may assume that she is at risk for being hit or verbally berated. The woman may clean the house on a daily basis, prepare her partner's favorite meal, and send the children to a neighbor's house in order to avoid escalating the situation or prevent physical abuse from occurring, even though her current partner has never been physically or verbally abusive toward her. This may also be an example of inappropriate discriminative control, since the woman fails to recognize that her current partner and past relationships do not signal the same outcomes for a particular behavior. The point here is that there are often multiple ways to conceptualize a clinical problem.

DISTINCTION BETWEEN TOPOGRAPHY AND FUNCTION

In the previous section, we provided an overview of functional analysis and how it can be applied to assessment and treatment of trauma survivors. In order to implement these principles most effectively, it is important to understand the distinction that is made between the topography and the function of psychological problems. The primary tenet of functional analysis is that behavior is understood according to its function, or what purpose it serves, rather than by its formal features. The function of behavior is determined by examining the relevant controlling variables of an objectively defined behavior, including the antece-dents, consequences, and establishing operations. Distinguishing the topography or mere form of the behavior from its function is important for the reasons that are outlined here.

The same stimulus conditions can lead to different topographical expressions of behavior. Individuals who have similar historical experiences or who even experience the same event may be impacted differently. To illustrate this point, consider a family with two children that presents for psychotherapy following a fire that destroyed their home. The parents report that their 7-year-old son has displayed a number of problems since the fire. He has frequent nightmares, complains of stomachaches, and becomes tearful when separated from his parents. The parents report that their 8½-year-old son is relatively asymptomatic except for an occasional increase in aggressive behavior (i.e., hitting his brother). Both children report having been awakened during the night to escape the fire and describe similar details with respect to watching the house burn. Neither child experienced any physical injuries. In this example, both children were exposed to the same event, yet the topographical expressions of behavior in response to the event were appreciably different. What is called for is a more comprehensive analysis of the environment, since something about the fire or what the children experienced in the aftermath led to the emergence of these differing behaviors.

Different etiological conditions can lead to similar topographical behavior. Likewise, the development of behaviors that appear similar based on topographical or formal features may have very different causes. This is illustrated by the multitude of different experiences that can lead to the development of PTSD symptoms. DSM-IV outlines the possible traumatic stressors that can lead to the development of PTSD symptoms.

> Traumatic events that are experienced directly include, but are not limited to, military combat, violent personal assault (sexual assault, physical attack, robbery, mugging), being kidnapped, being taken hostage, terrorist attack, torture, incarceration as a prisoner of war or in a concentration camp, natural or manmade disasters, severe automobile accidents, or being diagnosed with a life-threatening illness. For children, sexually traumatic events may include developmentally inappropriate sexual experiences without threatened or actual violence or injury. Witnessed events include, but are not limited to, observing the serious injury or unnatural death of another person due to violent assault, accident, war, or disaster or unexpectedly witnessing a dead body or body parts. Events experienced by others that are learned about include, but are not limited to, violent personal assault, serious accident, or serious injury experienced by a family member or a close friend; learning about the sudden, unexpected death of a family member or a close friend; or learning that one's child has a life-threatening disease. (American Psychiatric Association, 1994, p. 424)

Two clients may present for therapy and display the same constellation of symptoms that meet the DSM-IV criteria for PTSD. However, these can result through very different trauma histories. The variability in trauma history may not be particularly problematic for clinicians who have an understanding of the impact of trauma that crosses different types of trauma. The treatment implications may be the same regardless of the etiology of the trauma symptoms. Most trauma-related interventions utilize exposure-based strategies.

The example of depression illustrates the point of this section more clearly. The trauma literature suggests that depressive behavior is often a consequence of traumatic experiences (e.g., Polusny & Follette, 1995; Resick, 1990). However, depression is one of the most common problems reported by clients who present for psychotherapy, and the development of depressive symptoms can be explained by a number of causal factors. The presence of a trauma history is only one among many explanatory models (e.g., Beck, 1967; Lewinsohn & Arconad, 1981). So, while the clinical presentation may *look* similar, the variety of possible contributing factors for a clinical problem has different treatment implications.

Same topographical behaviors can have different functions. The distinction between topography and function is particularly important in analyzing specific behaviors. Traditional approaches to diagnosis and treatment focus primarily on identifying symptoms and treating those symptoms regardless of their function. However, the same topographical behaviors can have very different functions, or be under the control of different sets of environmental contingencies. Consider, for example, the high rate of substance abuse that is associated with a history of trauma (see Ruzek, Polusny, & Abueg, Chapter 9, this volume). Two individual trauma survivors, Client *X* and Client *Y*, report similar amounts and frequencies of alcohol consumption. However, their drinking behavior could be under the control of entirely different sets of contingencies. Wulfert et al. (1996) describe a functional classification system for pathological drinking behavior. In their model, they make a primary distinction between positively reinforced drinking behavior (Type P drinking behavior) and drinking behavior that is negatively reinforced (Type N drinking behavior). While drinking behavior for the same individual may be maintained by either type of reinforcement condition depending on additional contingencies (i.e., in different contexts, under different motivational conditions), we will illustrate the functional distinction by comparing the controlling variables for Client *X* with those for Client *Y*.

Client *X* drinks primarily in social contexts, and the consequence of drinking in such situations is a feeling of euphoria and enjoyable social interactions. Client *X*'s drinking behavior can be understood fundamentally as Type P drinking using the model proposed by Wulfert and colleagues. This understanding of the function of Client *X*'s drinking behavior suggests treatment strategies such as cue exposure or relapse prevention. Client *Y*, on the other hand, reports symptoms of anxiety, and when Client *Y* drinks, physiological arousal, physical tension, and catastrophic thoughts abate. This is referred to as Type N drinking, that is, drinking behavior maintained through principles of negative reinforcement.

Drinking behavior under these circumstances may be best modified using exposure strategies, cognitive restructuring techniques, or acceptance and commitment therapy (ACT) directed at the corresponding anxiety behaviors.

From a clinical standpoint, it is important to be aware of how the same response functions differently even within the therapy context. For example, consider a 32-year-old client who as a child was severely beaten for performing poorly at school and answering incorrectly when asked questions, and who was repeatedly told she was stupid. As a child, the client became fearful, overly compliant, withdrew from interactions, and stopped emitting behavior that might be punished. Subsequently, her interpersonal repertoire was limited, her social skills were poorly developed, and she lacked appropriate assertiveness skills. The client presents for therapy complaining of social isolation and the desire to establish relationships. In the interactions between the client and the therapist, the client often responds to the therapist's questions with the response "I don't know." Although "I don't know" is a frequent response, the contingencies under which it is emitted differ. For example, when the therapist queries "What are you feeling?" the response "I don't know" functions to describe a behavioral deficit. As a result of the client's punishing environment as a child, she does not have a repertoire for tacting (Skinner, 1957) or labeling her private experiences. However, when the therapist is working with the client to generate problem-solving strategies for an ongoing problem in the client's work environment, the client also responds with "I don't know" when the therapist asks the client if she has any ideas. The function of "I don't know" in this context is avoidance of negative evaluation or punishment for giving a "wrong" answer.

Different topographical behavior can have same function. It is also the case that behaviors that appear different along topographical features can function in the same way. A child, for example, displays a number of topographically different behaviors that are functionally equivalent; that is, they occur under the same set of conditions and are maintained by the same reinforcing contingencies. A 6-year-old child who has an 8:00 P.M. bedtime may utilize a number of behavioral strategies that postpone the scheduled bedtime. He or she might ask for a drink of water, become particularly affectionate, or even cry and whine. All of these behaviors function to delay bedtime for the child.

One goal of a female client who reports a history of domestic violence may be to avoid further physical abuse. While this is certainly a desirable goal, the specific actions of the client function to limit the opportunities for any relationship to develop, even those that are safe, and where the gains outweigh the risks. For example, the client does not initiate conversations with others, particularly men, is sloppy in her appearance, and is often sarcastic in her comments. All of these actions look different, yet function similarly. Each functions to keep people at arms length and hinder the development of intimate relationships in which the client may be at risk for being revictimized.

HEURISTIC ERRORS IN TRAUMA-RELATED ASSESSMENT

When a client presents for psychotherapy reporting a history of trauma, we must all be aware of possible heuristic rules that may impede our ability to accurately assess important influences that affect our client's behavior. "Heuristics" in this case mean the clinical rules of thumb we use to think about and organize information. In this section, we present a number of cautions regarding potential heuristic errors specifically regarding assessment and treatment strategies for individuals with a history of trauma. In addition, we propose suggestions for reducing the biases that occur within clinical practice with clients who have a trauma history.

Parsimony and the Availability Heuristic

One common error that occurs in clinical practice involves an overreliance on the principle of parsimony; that is, we are interested in efficiently identifying a minimal set of simple causal explanations for the symptoms we observe. In describing controlling variables for a client's presenting problem, we often rely on information that is readily available and then fail to search for additional competing hypotheses (Arnoult & Anderson, 1988). When a client reports many psychological problems and also describes a history of trauma, the clinician may assume that the client's difficulties are the result of the traumatic experience. The client's report of a trauma history may satisfy the clinician's pursuit toward identifying the primary controlling variable and may limit the scope of the resulting assessment and intervention.

While a history of trauma may be one or even the important causal variable for a client's current problems, this cannot a priori be known for certain. In addition, trauma is a distal historical event that cannot be undone or changed. Even if the traumatic event reported by the client is the initial causal variable responsible for the development of the client's constellation of symptoms, other more proximal variables may play an important role in the maintenance of those problems. While we favor simple explanations, it should be noted that the law of parsimony specifies the simplest *sufficient* explanation for a stated purpose. Thus, there is nothing inconsistent within a multifactor explanation for a set of clinical issues if they produce a better outcome than a simpler but less effective outcome.

In addition, the parsimony principle, when improperly implemented, precludes clinicians from identifying multiple causes for a particular problem. For example, a client with a history of active duty in the Vietnam War may present for therapy complaining of depressed mood and decreased activity, occasional flashbacks of his war experience, and chronic pain as the result of a back injury that occurred on the job. In this example, the client's current difficulties are likely the result of a combination of experiences. The clinician should be sensitive to assessing the degree to which the experiences in Vietnam, the chronic pain, and other current environmental factors contribute to the symptoms of depression, that is, what function the depressive behavior serves for the client.

Another common error in clinical judgment we make is called the availability heuristic (Turk, Salovey, & Prentice, 1988). We make use of this heuristic when we attempt to estimate the frequency or probability of the relationship between psychological problems and possible controlling variables. For example, we speculate about the probability that a client who presents with an eating disorder was sexually victimized as a child, or similarly hypothesize about the presence of depressive symptoms in a Vietnam veteran who experienced combat trauma. The availability heuristic suggests that we generate these hypotheses by attending to and making use of the most available information. One strategy for minimizing the biases introduced by using the availability heuristic is to rely heavily on base-rate information. How often does the relationship between trauma and an eating disorder occur? What is the rate of depression in Vietnam veterans, and does it differ from the population as a whole? Would it be more effective to understand the depression differently than as a long-term consequence of the war trauma?

It is more often the case that information that guides our case conceptualization is most available to us, not because of base-rate information, but because of the vividness or saliency of the information. One risk for clinicians who primarily treat individuals with a history of trauma is that the availability heuristic prevents them from entertaining additional causal hypotheses. A history of trauma is a salient event, both for the clinician and the client. This saliency may promote the view that traumatic events are the sole or most important causes of current psychological distress and strongly guide the conceptualization of a client's problems. A client may overattend to the traumatic experience as an explanation for current distress and inadvertently fail to report additional important information that may alter the clinician's understanding of the client's difficulties. Similarly, a clinician with trauma expertise may selectively attend to the trauma and overdiagnose PTSD without adequately addressing other historical or current factors that have more clinical utility.

Representativeness

The representativeness heuristic suggests that when a clinician is formulating a case conceptualization and implementing an intervention, he or she is likely to disregard base-rate information and make clinical decisions based on pieces of clinical data that are similar to a prototypical view one has of a particular class of events. An example of this occurs when a clinician assumes a particular historical event, given the client's presentation of symptoms, must be causal.

Consider a 24-year-old female client who presents for therapy meeting the DSM-IV criteria for bulimia. A clinician relying on the representativeness heuristic remembers a previous bulimic client who was sexually abused as a young girl and recalls that bulimia is a long-term correlate associated with a history of child sexual abuse (CSA). As treatment begins, the clinician prompts the client to recall experiences from her childhood that maybe interpreted as sexual abuse, even though the client has not offered such information. While the data suggest a high prevalence of eating disorders in clinical samples of women who report CSA, there is not a reciprocally high rate of CSA in women diagnosed with an eating disorder. Indeed, most studies investigating the relationship between CSA and eating disorders report CSA in only about one-third of bulimic subjects (Polusny & Follette, 1995). Clinicians must be cautious in assuming that a specific profile of symptoms is necessarily representative of a particular historical experience. As clinicians, we must utilize base-rate information when it is available, gather as much information as possible, and always entertain multiple, competing hypotheses.

Confirmation Biases

Several empirical studies have identified an extensive list of psychological problems that are correlated with a history of trauma (e.g., Beitchman, Zucker, Hood, DaCosta, & Akman, 1991; Green, 1991; Kulka et al., 1990; Polusny & Follette, 1995; Resick, 1990; Vrana & Lauterbach, 1994). The description of confirmation biases asserts that we likely overvalue evidence that supports our prior beliefs and undervalue or are overly critical of contradictory evidence. Therefore, when a client describes him- or herself as having a trauma history, confirmation bias prompts clinicians to assume a broader constellation of symptoms than the problems identified by the client. The clinician assumes that a specific trauma experience impacts a client in a particular way and results in a similar clinical presentation across clients.

For example, given the high prevalence of PTSD symptoms among rape victims who present for therapy, a clinician may overattend to specific information reported by a client that confirms or supports a diagnosis of PTSD. Such an assumption results in implementing a treatment plan that disregards the idiographic nature of the individual client's presenting problems. Effective assessment strategies involve more than deducing a symptom profile given information about a client's history. Having information about specific experiences that the client has experienced may provide a useful jumping-off point in terms of generating clinical hypotheses and guiding further assessment. Again, it is important for clinicians to entertain competing hypotheses and alternative explanations for the client's presenting problems. Moreover, clinicians must be willing to gather disconfirming evidence that allows them to discard a hypothesis or revise it as necessary. A functional analysis helps eliminate or reduce the errors that occur when these heuristics are operating, not because functional analysts are immune to heuristics, but because a functional analysis is an iterative and self-correcting process that ends only upon a successful outcome.

CONCLUSION

Functional analysis and contemporary behavior theory offer an alternative strategy for understanding the clinical problems associated with a history of trauma, as well as for identifying appropriate interventions. A functional analysis of clinical problems involves identifying the conditions that give rise to the behavior as well as the consequences that follow. We propose that implementing an effective intervention requires a detailed and idiographic assessment, identifies specific client problems, and specifies unique environmental variables that contribute to the development and maintenance of the target problems. In addition, we introduce a subset of potential functional domains that may guide the assessment and treatment when a clinician is working with clients who report of history of trauma. Finally, it is imperative in our work with trauma survivors that we attend to closely to the rules of thumb that guide our conceptualization and treatment of these populations. We need constantly to attend to the potential risk for inappropriately assigning causality of a client's current difficulties more than is warranted to trauma experiences. Clients present for therapy with complex and extensive histories of learning, in addition to traumatic experiences that may be more important factors in maintaining the problems.

REFERENCES

Allers, C. T., Benjack, K. J., White, J., & Rousey, J. T. (1993). HIV vulnerability and the adult survivor of childhood sexual abuse. *Child Abuse and Neglect, 17,* 291–298.

Arnoult, L. H., & Anderson, C. A. (1988). Identifying and reducing causal reasoning biases in clinical practice. In D. C. Turk & P. Salovey (Eds.), *Reasoning, inference, and judgment in clinical psychology* (pp. 209–232). New York: Free Press.

American Psychiatric Association. (1994). *Diagnostic and statistical manual of mental disorders* (4th ed.). Washington, DC: Author.

Barrios, B. A. (1988). On the changing nature of behavioral assessment. In A. S. Bellack & M. Hersen (Eds.), *Behavioral assessment: A practical handbook* (3rd ed., pp. 3–41). Boston: Allyn & Bacon.

Barrios, B., & Hartmann, D. P. (1986). The contributions of traditional assessment: Concepts, issues, and methodologies. In R. O. Nelson & S. C. Hayes (Eds.), *Conceptual foundations in behavioral assessment* (pp. 81–110). New York: Guilford Press.

Baum, W. M. (1994). *Understanding behaviorism: Science, behavior, and culture.* New York: HarperCollins.

Beck, A. T. (1967). *Depression: Clinical, experimental and theoretical aspects.* New York: Harper & Row.

Beitchman, J. E., Zucker, K. J., Hood, J. E., DaCosta, G. A., & Akman, D. (1991). A review of the short-term effects of child sexual abuse. *Child Abuse and Neglect, 15,* 537–556.

Briere, J., & Runtz, M. (1993). Childhood sexual abuse: Long-term sequelae and implications for psychological assessment. *Journal of Interpersonal Violence, 8,* 312–330.

Catania, A. C. (1992). *Learning* (3rd ed.). Englewood Cliffs, NJ: Prentice-Hall.

Cloitre, M., Scarvalone, P., & Difede, J. (1997). Post-traumatic stress disorder, self and interpersonal dysfunction among sexually revictimized women. *Journal of Traumatic Stress, 10,* 435–450.

Cone, J. D. (1986). Idiographic, nomothetic, and related perspectives in behavioral assessment. In R. O. Nelson & S. C. Hayes (Eds.), *Conceptual foundations in behavioral assessment* (pp. 111–128). New York: Guilford Press.

Deblinger, E., McLeer, S. V., Atkins, M., Ralphe, D., & Foa, E. (1989). Post-traumatic stress in sexually abused, physically abused, and nonabused children. *International Journal of Child Abuse and Neglect, 13,* 403–408.

Dutton, D. G. (1995). Trauma symptoms and PTSD-like profiles in perpetrators of intimate abuse. *Journal of Traumatic Stress, 8,* 299–316.

Evans, I. M. (1985). Building systems models as a strategy for target behavior selection. *Behavioral Assessment, 7,* 21–32.

Fruzzetti, A. E. (1996). Causes and consequences: Individual distress in the context of couple interactions. *Journal of Consulting and Clinical Psychology, 64,* 1192–1201.

Goldiamond, I. (1974). Toward a constructional approach to social problems: Ethical and constitutional issues raised by applied behavior analysis. *Behaviorism, 2,* 1–85.

Goldiamond, I. (1975). Alternate sets as a framework for behavioral formulation and research. *Behaviorism, 3,* 49–86.

Green, B. L. (1991). Evaluating the effects of disasters. *Psychological Assessment, 3,* 538–546.

Hamilton, S. A. (1988). Behavioral formulations of verbal behavior in psychotherapy. *Clinical Psychology Review, 8,* 181–193.

Hawkins, R. P. (1979). The functions of assessment: Implications for selection and development of devices for assessing repertoires in clinical, educational, and other settings. *Journal of Applied Behavior Analysis, 12,* 501–516.

Hawkins, R. P. (1986). Selection of target behaviors. In R. O. Nelson & S. C. Hayes (Eds.), *Conceptual foundations in behavioral assessment* (pp. 331–385). New York: Guilford Press.

Hayes, S. C. (Ed.). (1989). *Rule-governed behavior: Cognition, contingencies, and instructional control.* New York: Plenum.

Hayes, S. C., & Brownstein, A. J. (1986). Mentalism, behavior–behavior relations, and a behavior analytic view of the purposes of science. *Behavior Analyst, 9,* 175–190.

Hayes, S. C., Brownstein, A. J., Zettle, R. D., Rosenfarb, I., & Korn, Z. (1986). Rule-governed behavior and sensitivity to changing consequences of responding. *Journal of the Experimental Analysis of Behavior, 45,* 237–256.

Hayes, S. C., & Follette, W. C. (1992). Can functional analysis provide a substitute for syndromal classification. *Behavioral Assessment, 14,* 345–365.

Hayes, S. C., Follette, W. C., & Follette, V. M. (1995). Behavior therapy: A contextual approach. In A. S. Gurman & S. B. Messer (Eds.), *Essential psychotherapies: Theory and practice* (pp. 128–181). New York: Guilford Press.

Hayes, S. C., Nelson, R. O., & Jarrett, R. B. (1987). The treatment utility of assessment: A functional approach to evaluating assessment quality. *American Psychologist, 42,* 963–974.

Haynes, S. N., & O'Brien, W. H. (1990). Functional analysis in behavior therapy. *Clinical Psychology Review, 10,* 649–668.

Hiley-Young, B., Blake, D. D., Abueg, F. R., Rozynko, V., & Gusman, F. D. (1995).

Warzone violence in Vietnam: An examination of premilitary, military, and postmilitary factors in PTSD in-patients. *Journal of Traumatic Stress, 8,* 125–141.

Kanfer, F. H., & Saslow, G. (1969). Behavioral diagnosis. In C. M. Franks (Ed.), *Behavior therapy: Appraisal and status* (pp. 417–444). New York: McGraw-Hill.

Koerner, K., Kohlenberg, R. J., & Parker, C. (1996). Diagnosis of personality disorder: A radical behavioral alternative. *Journal of Consulting and Clinical Psychology, 64,* 1169–1176.

Kohlenberg, R. J., & Tsai, M. (1991). *Functional analytic psychotherapy: Creating intense and curative therapeutic relationships.* New York: Plenum.

Kohlenberg, R. J., & Tsai, M. (1995). I speak, therefore I am: A behavioral approach to understanding the self. *Behavior Therapist, 18,* 113–116.

Kulka, R. A., Schlenger, W. E., Fairbank, J. A., Hough, R. L. Jordan, B. K., Marmar, C. R., & Weiss, D. S. (1990). *Trauma and the Vietnam War generation: Report of findings from the national Vietnam veterans readjustment study.* New York: Brunner/Mazel.

Lewinsohn, P. M., & Arconad, M. (1981). Behavioral treatment of depression: A social learning approach. In J. F. Clarkin & H. I. Glazer (Eds.), *Depression: Behavioral and directive intervention strategies.* New York: Garland.

Linehan, M. (1993). *Cognitive-behavioral treatment of borderline personality disorder.* New York: Guilford Press.

Michael, J. (1982). Distinguishing between discriminative and motivational functions of stimuli. *Journal of the Experimental Analysis of Behavior, 37,* 149–155.

Michael, J. (1994). Establishing operations. *Behavior Analyst, 16,* 149–155.

Naugle, A. E., Follette, W. C., & Follette, V. M. (1995, November). *Toward the prevention of revictimization in sexual abuse survivors.* Paper presented at the annual meeting of the Association for Advancement of Behavior Therapy, Washington, DC.

Nelson, R. O., & Hayes, S. C. (1986). The nature of behavioral assessment. In R. O. Nelson & S. C. Hayes (Eds.), *Conceptual foundations in behavioral assessment* (pp. 3–41). New York: Guilford Press.

Owens, R. G., & Ashcroft, J. B. (1982). Functional analysis in clinical psychology. *British Journal of Clinical Psychology, 21,* 181–189.

Polusny, M. A. (1998). *Childhood and adult victimization, alcohol abuse, and high risk sexual behavior among female college students: A prospective study.* Unpublished dissertation, University of Nevada, Reno.

Polusny, M. A., & Follette, V. M. (1995). Long-term correlates of child sexual abuse: Theory and review of the empirical literature. *Applied and Preventive Psychology, 4,* 143–166.

Resick, P. A. (1990). Victims of sexual assault. In A. J. Lurigio, W. G. Skogan, & R. C. Davis (Eds.), *Victims of crime: Problems, policies, and programs* (pp. 69–86). Newbury Park, CA: Sage.

Shimoff, E., Catania, A. C., & Matthews, B. A. (1981). Uninstructed human responding: Sensitivity of low-rate performance to schedule contingencies. *Journal of the Experimental Analysis of Behavior, 36,* 207–220.

Skinner, B. F. (1945). The operational analysis of psychological terms. *Psychological Review, 52,* 270–277.

Skinner, B. F. (1957). *Verbal behavior.* New York: Appleton–Century–Crofts.

Sturmey, P. (1996). *Functional analysis in clinical psychology.* New York: Wiley.

Turk, D. C., Salovey, P., & Prentice, D. A. (1988). Psychotherapy: An information-processing perspective. In D. C. Turk & P. Salovey (Eds.), *Reasoning, inference, and judgment in clinical psychology* (pp. 1–14). New York: Free Press.

Vrana, S., & Lauterbach, D. (1994). Prevalence of traumatic events and post-traumatic psychological symptoms in a nonclinical sample of college students. *Journal of Traumatic Stress, 7*, 289–302.

Wulfert, E., Greenway, D. E., & Dougher, M. J. (1996). A logical functional analysis of reinforcement-based disorders: Alcoholism and pedophilia. *Journal of Consulting and Clinical Psychology, 64*, 1140–1151.

TREATMENT DOMAINS

Cognitive-Behavioral Treatment of War-Zone-Related Posttraumatic Stress Disorder

A FLEXIBLE, HIERARCHICAL APPROACH

WILLIAM F. FLACK, JR.
BRETT T. LITZ
TERENCE M. KEANE

In this chapter, we explicate a cognitive-behavioral approach to the treatment of posttraumatic reactions to the experience of warfare. We begin by describing briefly the prototypical combat veteran who has posttraumatic stress disorder (PTSD), focusing on their military and postmilitary experiences, and tying these experiences to the sorts of posttraumatic reactions most frequently seen in the clinics and hospitals of the Department of Veterans Affairs (DVA). We use veterans of the Vietnam War in our examples, since this is the modal era population seen currently in the DVA. However, we emphasize that many of the issues and characterizations that follow are also applicable to veterans of World War II, the Korean War, and the Persian Gulf War. Next, we summarize a cognitive-behavioral perspective on the origins and sequelae of posttraumatic reactions. The resulting clinical picture in combat veterans is a complex and multifaceted one that requires a systematic and detailed approach to assessment. Following the section on assessment, we discuss our flexible, hierarchical approach to the treatment of combat-related PTSD. The treatment of veterans requires considerable sensitivity to the complexity of their clinical presentation. Our model of treatment offers a range of clinical options that addresses the level of patients' functioning, their personal resources, and both their immediate and long-term needs. Exposure-based treatment is at the center of this cognitive-behavioral model. Thus, we discuss in some detail the boundary conditions of, and clinical guidelines for, this procedure. We end with a case example in order to illustrate the principles and practices described throughout this chapter.

TRAUMA AND THE WAR IN VIETNAM

Although more than 20 years have passed since the end of the Vietnam War, many combat veterans continue to suffer from the consequences of their experiences in the military (Kulka et al., 1990). Phenomenologically, for some, it is often as though they never left Vietnam. For many, they are just now telling their stories for the first time, having lived alone for more than two decades with the memories of repeated, horrifying experiences of the imminent threat and the actual occurrence of destruction, dismemberment, and death. The context within which these experiences occurred was formed by veterans' developmental circumstances (many enlisted in their late teens and early 20s; Kulka et al., 1990), their mode of entry into and exit from Vietnam (both were solitary experiences that lacked the sort of group camaraderie that helps to mitigate anxiety and stress in the military; see Belenky, Noy, & Solomon, 1987; Bion, 1959), and the nature of guerrilla warfare in a jungle environment (for which recruits were unprepared).

Vietnam combat veterans participated in the killing of enemy soldiers, and they were frequently exposed to the threat of death from identified combatants, from unidentifiable civilians who sided with the enemy, and even from infants and children who were sometimes booby-trapped with explosives (Karnow, 1983). And they witnessed, all too often, the horrifying maiming and slaughter of fellow soldiers, those with whom they had formed the most intimate and strongest of bonds. Some veterans also observed terrible acts of unnecessary violence against civilians, while others participated personally in the commission of atrocities. Researchers have shown that those who either committed those acts themselves, or who witnessed but failed to act to prevent atrocities, have a particularly virulent and chronic posttraumatic adjustment (e.g., Gallers, Foy, Donahue, & Goldfarb, 1988).

Women, who were predominantly nurses in the war zone in Vietnam, were also exposed to the horrors of war (Wolfe, Mori, & Krygeris, 1994). They saw many young men wounded grotesquely and dying. Nurses also provided emotional support to the wounded and dying, which had its own psychological legacy. Furthermore, nurses were exposed to the rigors of a war in a foreign country, but were also targets of sexual assault and harassment by their male counterparts (Baker, Menard, & Johns, 1989). As was the case with the male combat veteran, the traumatizing experiences of these nurses and their devastating aftereffects were not given adequate recognition until relatively recently (Leon, Ben-Porath, & Hjemboe, 1990).

Upon their return stateside, veterans found themselves returning abruptly to a society that was increasingly against the war effort and all too often identified

the veteran with those political and military leaders who were ultimately responsible for its continuation. Even fellow veterans of earlier wars shunned soldiers of
the Vietnam War, unfairly blaming them for a losing effort, and preventing their
membership into long-established veterans' organizations. A downturn in the
postwar economy led many Vietnam veterans to find themselves jobless and even
homeless. Small wonder, then, that these veterans found few who were willing to
listen. The result, in many cases, was an unwillingness to disclose their true
feelings about their war-zone experiences, ill-fated attempts to suppress their
traumatic experiences, as well as the unassimilated rage and guilt that often
accompanied them, and, eventually, the development of posttraumatic symptoms. Similar outcomes are seen frequently in veterans of other wars, although
some of the antecedent issues are different.

POSTTRAUMATIC REACTIONS FROM A
COGNITIVE-BEHAVIORAL PERSPECTIVE

Clinicians and researchers continue to debate what they consider to be the
defining features of traumatic life events (Cooper, 1986; Niederland, 1971; Wilson, 1995). Most investigators would agree on the following set of criteria for
defining a traumatic event: (1) an experience that grossly violates fundamental
beliefs and expectations about the self and the world; (2) an event that entails
unconditioned stimulation, including pain, tissue damage, and/or primary affective reactions of helplessness, horror, and disgust; and (3) an event and context
that overwhelms the individual's capacity for coping. Veterans' experiences of
war-zone combat fulfill all of these criteria.

Although little is known about the initial development of posttraumatic
psychopathology, the eventual result of traumatic experience is two basic, competing processes (Horowitz, 1986; Horowitz & Becker, 1971): (1) the extreme ease
of retrieval, or hyperaccessibility, of trauma-related memories (e.g., intrusive
thoughts and feelings about the trauma), and (2) efforts to defend against, or
avoid, these painful unwanted memories (e.g., avoidance of associated cues). Such
memories become overly accessible because the conditioning that occurs as a
result of a traumatic event produces very broad generalization, and over time,
higher order conditioning further expands the range of stimuli, both internal and
external, that activate conditioned emotional reactions (Keane, Zimering, & Caddell, 1985). The conditioned stimuli, along with the responses that they elicit, and
the meanings associated with the event, are thought to be stored in memory in a
complex network (Chemtob, Roitblat, Hamada, Carlson, & Twentyman, 1988;
Foa, Steketee, & Olasov-Rothbaum, 1989). Cognitive processes are also affected
in that, for example, a bias develops toward perceiving ambiguous cues as threatening, thereby taxing the capacity to attend to the world normally (Litz & Keane,
1989). Activation of the trauma network leads to a conditioned emotional re-

sponse that is aversive, and with which the individual attempts to cope through avoidance. Defensive avoidance is negatively reinforced (i.e., strengthened) to the extent that it results in a reduction of the aversive conditioned emotional response (Keane, Zimering, & Caddell, 1985; Mowrer, 1947). In PTSD, defensive reactions are multidimensional and overlearned, and tend, therefore, to be highly resistant to change.

Over time, the repeated occurrence of intrusive, trauma-related memories and defensive responses leads to enduring, trait-like changes in individuals' views of themselves and their world (i.e., schemas). These schemas, or themes, include generalized expectations about self and others that are threatening and pervasively negative. Lebowitz and Newman (1996) recommend focusing on the following as potentially important themes in PTSD: helplessness, fear, rage, loss, self-blame/guilt, shame, legitimacy, isolation/alienation, negative beliefs about the self, negative beliefs about other people, negative beliefs about the world, and the influence of culture. Particularly salient for veterans are schemas regarding trust, self-control, and guilt (e.g., Janoff-Bulman, 1992; Newman, Orsillo, Herman, Niles, & Litz, 1995). These themes can be informed by early premilitary experience (e.g., childhood sexual and physical abuse; Zaidi & Foy, 1994), as well as by postmilitary events (e.g., failure experiences at work). Such schemas lead veterans to expect to be misunderstood and invalidated, to fear loss of agency, to avoid affect or emotion for fear of being overwhelmed, and to feel despair. Suicidal impulses are frequently the result of despair, demoralization, and guilt. Substance abuse is often an attempt to defend against crippling anxiety (Keane & Kaloupek, 1997). Deficits of emotionality, bouts of dysphoria, and outbursts of anger and rage all affect the individual's relationships with others, resulting in problems with communication and intimacy, and leading to disruptions of social interactions at home and at work. If significant others behave in a punitive, rejecting, invalidating, or avoidant manner, the result is a further entrenchment of these beliefs (Carroll, Rueger, Foy, & Donahoe, 1985; Hyer, Woods, & Boudewyns, 1991; Jordan et al., 1992; Keane, Scott, Charoya, Lamparski, & Fairbank, 1985c; Nezu & Carnevale, 1987; Tarrier, 1996).

CLINICAL ASSESSMENT AND TREATMENT PLANNING

The degree of functional impairment, and the complex interrelations among impaired functions noted earlier, are so extensive in war-zone-related PTSD that a detailed and systematic clinical assessment is essential in coming to a comprehensive understanding of the veteran client, and in identifying targets for treatment. The aims of this assessment are (1) to establish the veteran's current condition, including risk for homicidal or suicidal behavior; (2) to determine compensation-seeking status; (3) to evaluate war-zone experiences; (4) to diagnose PTSD and comorbid conditions; (5) to screen for lifespan trauma; (6) to identify areas of functional impairment; (7) to assess personal resources and areas of strength; (8) to prioritize targets for change; and (9) to establish baseline levels of functioning for identified target behaviors. The assessment phase should also be used as a period in which the client can begin to learn about PTSD and available options for treatment, and as a time during which the therapeutic alliance is developed and tested.

We advocate the use of converging methods of assessment and the gathering of multiple sources of information in the evaluation of veterans (see Keane, Newman, & Orsillo, 1997, for a comprehensive review of the literature on the assessment of military-related PTSD; see also Litz, Penk, Gerardi, & Keane, 1992; Litz & Weathers, 1994; Malloy, Fairbank, & Keane, 1983; Newman, Kaloupek, & Keane, 1996). Table 4.1 contains a list of recommended instruments for the comprehensive psychodiagnostic assessment of war-zone-related PTSD.

When evaluating traumatic events in the war zone, clinicians need to gather information about the developmental context, events that occurred just prior to the trauma(s), the traumatic events themselves, including stimuli (sights, sounds, smells), responses (e.g., racing heart), and their meaning (e.g., thoughts of annihilation), the responses of significant others in the war zone, and the aftermath. The context within which any trauma must be understood will include the individual's premorbid history. Important premorbid variables include the individual's early experience with caregivers, histories of abuse, neglect, and brutality, academic and social functioning, dating and sexual relationships, coping responses, and pretrauma beliefs about the self, gender, and expression of emotion (see Litz & Weathers, 1994). Posttrauma variables are also crucial and include the frequency and intensity of PTSD symptoms, both internal and situational triggers of symptoms, coping responses (such as substance use), typical responses to daily stressors, history of responses to previous treatments, and available sources of support.

The end point of this comprehensive assessment is the identification of targets of intervention, and, even more importantly, a prioritization of problems within a hierarchy of clinical need. The clinical decisions about where to start treatment are based on factors such as safety, patient resources (e.g., coping capacity), verbal facility, and current environmental support. These clinical decisions are crucial because the costs of an inappropriate degree or level of treatment are great. Such potential costs include failure and dropping out, with subsequently increasing likelihood of treatment avoidance. The therapist also runs the risk of overwhelming an ill-prepared client, thereby undermining the client's sense of self-control, oversensitizing the client to his or her own aversive emotional states, and exacerbating the current symptom picture. Relapse of comorbid disorders, such as depression and substance abuse, is also possible, and destruction of the therapeutic alliance may occur.

TABLE 4.1. Instruments Used in the NCPTSD for the Assessment of Combat-Related PTSD and Related Conditions

Diagnosis of PTSD and comorbid disorders

1. *Structured Clinical Interview for DSM-IV Axis I Disorders—Patient Edition (SCID-I/P, Version 2.0)* (SCID; First, Gibbons, Spitzer, & Williams, 1996): a structured interview for the evaluation of Axis I disorders.
2. *Clinician Administered PTSD Scale for DSM* (CAPS; Blake et al., 1990): a structured interview for the evaluation of PTSD.
3. *Minnesota Multiphasic Personality Inventory—2* (MMPI-2; Butcher et al., 1989): a paper-and-pencil test for personality functioning and psychopathology; two subscales (Keane et al., 1984; Schlenger & Kulka, 1989) are available for the assessment of PTSD.
4. *Symptom Checklist 90—Revised* (SCL-90-R; Derogatis, 1977): a paper-and-pencil measure of a wide range of psychological problems; two subscales (Saunders et al., 1990; Weathers et al., 1996) are available for the assessment of PTSD.
5. *Beck Depression Inventory—II* (Beck et al., 1996): a paper-and-pencil questionnaire for the assessment of depression.
6. *Beck Anxiety Inventory* (Beck, et al., 1988): a paper-and-pencil questionnaire for the assessment of anxiety.

Evaluation of lifespan trauma

1. *Potential Stressful Events Interview* (PSEI; Falsetti et al., 1994): a comprehensive interview for the assessment of stressful events, including their objective and subjective characteristics.
2. *Evaluation of Lifetime Stressors Questionnaire and Interview* (ELS; Krinsley et al., 1994): a structured interview for the assessment of lifetime exposure to traumatic events.
3. *Traumatic Stress Schedule* (TSS; Norris, 1990): a brief screening instrument for the assessment of traumatic events.

Evaluation of combat experience and trauma

1. *Mississippi Scale for Combat-Related PTSD* (Keane et al., 1988): a paper-and-pencil measure of the severity of PTSD and associated features.
2. *Combat Exposure Scale* (CES; Keane et al., 1989): a paper-and-pencil measure of the degree of combat experienced by the veteran.
3. *PTSD Checklist* (PCL; Weathers et al., 1993): a PTSD questionnaire based on the criteria contained in the *DSM*.

TREATMENT OF COMBAT-RELATED PTSD: A FLEXIBLE, HIERARCHICAL APPROACH

Keane and colleagues (Keane, 1995; Keane, Fisher, Krinsley, & Niles, 1994) have designed an approach to the behavioral psychotherapy of war-zone-related PTSD that is sensitive to the fact that such clients present with a variety of types and degrees of impairment. This approach is an inherently flexible one with respect to matching the level of treatment with the client's current clinical state. It is also hierarchical in nature, in that the utilization of methods in each component of the treatment package presupposes a level of functioning that corresponds to the successful completion of preceding phases. Beginning with methods used during periods of acute crisis, the six components of this treatment approach are stabilization, psychoeducation, stress management, focus on trauma memory, secondary prevention, and aftercare.

Our approach to treatment is designed to address the most pressing concerns within the acute, chronic, and residual phases of combat-related PTSD. Although the steps taken in this treatment approach usually occur in the order presented in this chapter, different clients will present with different sets of needs, requiring more or less time and intensity of treatment in the various phases. For example, some clients who are in crisis and lack basic support systems will need more work on emotional and behavioral stabilization, whereas others who are relatively intact may be able to move more quickly into trauma education and stress management. In general, however, the successful completion of each phase of treatment is a prerequisite for moving on to the next one.

Emotional and Behavioral Stabilization

Clients often present for treatment in an acute phase of PTSD, such that symptoms of reexperiencing, avoidance, and arousal are exacerbated, and even basic levels of psychosocial functioning are compromised. There are three essential goals at this point in treatment. First, issues of safety and basic needs must be addressed initially. Suicidality and homicidality are assessed and, if appropriate, addressed. Obviously, therapy can only be conducted if both client and therapist are safe from the threat of harm. Crises are dismantled, explored, and reduced, if not eliminated, in their intensities. The most elementary needs of the client, sometimes including requirements for food, clothing, and shelter, are addressed. Another goal in this part of treatment is the development of an agreement between therapist and client about the parameters and goals of therapy, and the creation of a positive therapeutic alliance. At this stage, promotion of a positive alliance centers on the issue of trust. Vietnam veterans are likely to demonstrate considerable distrust in others, particularly in the context of a government-based treatment system such as the DVA. The development of trust, therefore, is a slow process that unfolds over time and requires the therapist to be patient and empathic in the face of initially angry, and often very suspicious, presentations. In addition, the client's current strategies for coping are discussed. These strategies often include the use of alcohol and drugs, which must be evaluated and brought under control. Referrals to treatment programs for substance abuse and dependence can be useful adjuncts to PTSD treatment in veterans. Pharmacotherapy, too, may be of considerable help in stabilizing the veteran client, and close consultation with a psychiatrist is highly recommended at this stage in treatment (see Friedman, 1991). Antianxiety medications, such as Ativan and Klonopin, and antidepressant medications, such as Prozac and Zoloft, are typically used. Medications with addictive properties, such as the benzodiazepines, are used less frequently because of the high risk of drug dependence and abuse in this population.

Stabilization and a positive treatment alliance provide a crucial foundation for the remainder of treatment. Clients must be helped to work through the crises that typically drive them into treatment in the first place. The unstable client in the throes of clinical crisis is simply unable to take in or benefit from more taxing therapeutic efforts. Cognitive, behavioral, and emotional resources are drained during periods of acute symptom exacerbation, so that there is little psychological capacity left over to attend to anything else. Therapists' attempts to engage the acutely disturbed client in tasks that are beyond the client's current capacities are likely to meet with failure, dropout, the further exacerbation of symptoms, and a reduced likelihood that the client will seek treatment again in the future. A careful and sympathetic approach taken to the exploration of the client's initial present-ing complaints results in the reduction, if not elimination, of difficulties that are certain to interfere with subsequent treatment. The work of this initial phase of treatment may be best accomplished within the context of a one-on-one relation-ship with the client.

Trauma Education

Once the client is stabilized and adequate supports have been established, efforts can be made to educate the client in more detail about trauma and its effects. The therapist takes a collaborative stance toward the client in this phase of treatment. The therapeutic alliance is aided by the development of a shared therapeutic lexicon about PTSD. The sharing of a common language works both ways in the treatment of combat veterans, since the therapist must also learn a fair amount of military jargon in order to understand adequately the client's traumatic experi-ences of combat. The therapist will learn much of the language of warfare from the client, thus providing the veteran with an opportunity to experience self-effi-cacy during the formation of the treatment alliance. The interpersonal context of life in the military, within which the trauma occurred, must also be fully examined and understood. Thus, the client is taught about the positive (i.e., intrusive thoughts, nightmares, flashbacks) and negative (i.e., anhedonia, numbing, aliena-tion) symptoms of PTSD, common comorbid conditions, and the effects of PTSD on the body, on the sense of self, and on others with whom the client comes into contact. Such information may provide additional relief to the extent that clients are able to assimilate otherwise confusing and overwhelming experiences into a cognitive framework within which they can begin to understand their condition and its impact on others.

PTSD is explained as a normal, natural adaptation to the extreme stress of warfare and its sequelae. Clients are taught that recovery is facilitated by the effective handling of daily stressors, the telling (and retelling) of their story, and the gradual reestablishment of interpersonal ties at home and at work. The work of this second phase is best conducted via a combination of individual therapy, recommended readings and videotapes, and in a psychoeducational group with other combat veterans. The group modality has the added benefit of helping clients to understand that they are not alone in their struggles with PTSD. Psychoeducational approaches can also be used with family members to help them in their efforts to cope with the behavior of the combat veteran and to facilitate the treatment of the individual within the family as a unit.

Stress Management

Once the combat veteran has been given adequate information to understand his condition and its impact on others, the task of helping him to manage everyday stressors can be undertaken. Essentially, the goal of training in stress management is to enable the client to deal more effectively with the behavioral, cognitive, and emotional responses that they tend to have to the typical hassles and stressors of everyday life. Effective coping with such day-to-day stressors is important for a number of reasons. At a theoretical level, a reduction in the client's stress response should lead to a reduction in reexperiencing, since arousal and aversive emotions are powerful sources of memory activation (Litz & Keane, 1989; Litz et al., 1996; McNally, Litz, Prassas, Shin, & Weathers, 1994). In addition, the learning of stress management skills reduces avoidance behavior by enhancing the client's expectancies about coping with a variety of stressful situations. The reduction of avoidance provides opportunities for exposure to corrective information in a variety of domains often associated with the trauma. Furthermore, the likelihood of relapse is reduced when the veteran can effectively call forth healthy coping responses when confronted with stressors.

Various strategies are used in the teaching of positive methods of coping with stress. These include relaxation techniques (Benson, 1975; Jacobson, 1938; Wolpe, 1984), cognitive techniques (Beck, 1972; Kilpatrick, Veronen, & Resick, 1979; Meichenbaum & Jaremko, 1983), and other skills training approaches (e.g., O'Donohue & Krasner, 1994). One of the more frequently used modalities is stress inoculation training (SIT; Meichenbaum, 1985). Typically, SIT consists of a three-pronged approach to the management of stress. First, the client is helped to understand the sources of stress, the stress response itself, and alternative strategies for coping. Second, the client is instructed in the acquisition of specific skills (e.g., problem solving), rehearses these skills, and is given feedback about performance. It is important that the veteran experiences some degree of success in each step in the process of learning how to manage stress. Successful experiences reinforce the veteran's use of these strategies and help to maintain a positive attitude and sufficient motivation when faced with more intense challenges. Third, the client is encouraged to use these skills in real-life situations, and efforts are made to help to maintain these skills and to aid in their generalization. Techniques are available for the treatment of most stress-based difficulties experienced by combat veterans, including anger management (Gerlock, 1996; Novaco, 1996), and many of these skills-based approaches are designed to be conducted in a group format.

Trauma Focus

Assuming that the veteran is stable, and now armed with both an understanding of PTSD and with various means of coping with stress, he or she may be ready for some form of exposure therapy. We emphasize the conditional nature of this statement, because exposure is inappropriate in some cases (e.g., the client is unable to maintain a stable, working therapeutic relationship, continues to lapse into substance abuse, and/or is acutely homicidal or suicidal), or contraindicated at certain points in the trajectory of chronic PTSD (e.g., the client is unable to disclose or identify specific memories of traumatic events; see Litz, Blake, Gerardi, & Keane, 1990).

There is a range of uncovering, or narrative-based psychotherapeutic interventions, both in individual and group modalities, that are also helpful in promoting the sustained direction of attention toward the trauma memory, as well as the elucidation of details of the memory (Fairbank & Brown, 1987). However, direct therapeutic exposure (DTE) is the most efficient, systematic, and well-studied approach to treating traumatic memories and associated conditioned emotional responses. DTE can be employed within a number of formats, including systematic desensitization (Wolpe, 1958), implosive therapy (Stampfl & Levis, 1967), flooding (Rachman, 1966) and, more recently, eye movement desensitization and reprocessing (EMDR; Shapiro, 1995; see Boudewyns & Hyer, 1996; Keane, in press; and Pitman et al., 1996, for a critical discussion of the role of exposure within EMDR). The modal vehicle for exposure therapy of war-zone-related PTSD is imaginal, since the target of the treatment is memory.

At the outset, certain therapist and client factors are viewed as prerequisites to the use of DTE. Therapists must be adequately trained in the modality, including having sufficient sophistication about its theoretical underpinnings and research base (see especially Stampfl & Levis, 1967, and Frueh, Turner, & Beidel, 1995). Such training and knowledge increase therapist confidence in the model. It is vitally important for therapists to be confident in this mode of treatment because, more often than not, clients will look worse before they get better, and they can be quite resistant as a result. In addition, therapists must be able to tolerate not only a great deal of emotional upheaval from their clients during exposure therapy, but they must also manage their own personal affective reactions throughout the course of treating PTSD (see Saakvitne & Pearlman, 1996).

The client should have reasonable sources of support and should be clinically stable, both factors that our treatment approach is designed to facilitate. Many veterans have comorbid conditions and economic hardships that make it difficult for them to engage in any sort of treatment, exposure-based or otherwise. When considering the client's suitability for exposure therapy, therapists need to consider the client's risk for the relapse of comorbid conditions, their living situation (e.g., Do they live in a shelter? On the street?), and problems that interfere with clients' appreciation of their own responsibilities and roles in their care.

Crucial in the preparation of clients for exposure therapy is a careful and considered rationale for the treatment. The therapist begins by giving a simplified account of the two-factor theory of the development and maintenance of the client's reexperiencing symptoms and avoidance problems. It is explained that the horrible events witnessed and survived by the veteran client created very powerful memories that are reactivated very easily by seemingly small and insignificant reminders. When reminded, a traumatized person reexperiences, sometimes only slightly, other times very intensely, painful emotional responses.

Quite naturally, anyone who experiences these painful emotional responses is motivated to avoid the feelings and painful memories that surface. Avoidance behaviors are highly rewarding because they force the painful memories, albeit temporarily, into the background and reduce painful feelings. We emphasize to veteran clients the value of their avoidance behavior while in the military, and in their attempts to adjust to civilian life upon discharge. There are many different ways in which a veteran can avoid both reminders of combat experiences and attendant emotional reactions, and many of these were first learned in the context of life-threatening situations in a war zone. We work with clients to list the various ways in which they avoid reminders or reactions currently, while respecting the prior functional value of these behaviors. Clients learn that avoidance behaviors are, ultimately, counterproductive, and provide only brief relief from pain.

We explain that lasting healing from trauma, within the exposure framework, comes from two sources: careful, patient, and repeatedly sustained exposure to reminders and memories of war-zone experiences, and concurrent prevention of avoidance reactions. Clients are forewarned that they are likely to be quite crafty in the variety of ways that they have come to avoid memories and feelings. Their task is to allow for the exposure to be prolonged sufficiently so that healing can take place. We explain that healing is a natural human process that involves something technically labeled "extinction" (a reduction in emotional reactions to remembering over a period of time). Healing through exposure cannot be prolonged adequately if avoidance behaviors are activated. It is explained that the purpose of imaginal exposure is to provide time within treatment sessions for healing (extinction) to take place. The therapy is designed to provide a safe place for the client to focus on, without avoiding, their traumatic war-zone experiences. The ultimate goal is to reduce, over a period of time, the intensity of the emotional reactions that arise when remembering the traumatic events.

It is vitally important that clients' expectations be accurate about the course of exposure therapy. They are told that, because they have avoided focusing on their memories for so many years, many of those memories have lain dormant. When such memories do surface, it might well be shocking and difficult to cope with the surges of feelings that accompany them. If the therapy is working, clients can expect to feel worse before they improve. We often use the metaphor of a scab that requires healing; when the scab is exposed, the skin is bleeding, raw, and very painful. However, lasting healing can come only from full exposure of the wound. In addition, we forewarn clients that uncovering and sharing their memories of experiences in combat will activate other painful memories of traumatic events, both military-based and otherwise. Some of these memories will come in the form of dreams, while others will emerge in daytime thoughts. There may also be behavioral manifestations of reactivated trauma that are not directly associated with a specific memory.

We instruct veteran clients to monitor the memories that surface as an active coping method, as well as to provide a source of material for subsequent exposure sessions. This typically empowers clients to take an active part in rediscovering what happened to them, and the psychological toll these events have exacted. Such monitoring can facilitate personal distancing from becoming immersed in reexperiencing, and can also reduce the likelihood of avoidance.

Clients are warned about the likelihood that they will have thoughts about quitting, not showing up, or defending against focusing on their memories during the course of exposure therapy. This is quite natural. They are reminded that the trauma is in the past and can do no harm in the present. However, the therapist also communicates an understanding of the extent to which this process is painful, thus normalizing and preempting clients' motivation toward avoidance.

The initial content of exposure sessions is usually provided by the client during the assessment. The therapist should have a general sense of the traumatic memories that the veteran wishes to resolve before beginning exposure therapy. Typically, the therapist will know only the general outlines of a memory or memories, not the minute details. A list of these memories should be made, taking into account both their temporal ordering and their relative aversiveness. In general, it is advisable to start exposure work with the least aversive memories first. The therapist should not feel surprised when memories of traumatic events arise that were not reported by the client during the assessment; in fact, such memories can be expected to surface during the course of exposure treatment. Both therapist and client need to develop a collaboration akin to detective work when uncovering details of the painful past.

A schematic structure for exposure sessions is as follows: (1) the first 10 minutes are devoted to a reporting by the client of his or her attempts to make sense out of military-based memories during the past week, as well as discussion of experiences in carrying out homework exercises, (2) 30 minutes of exposure work, and (3) 10 to 15 minutes of processing the exposure work, as well as other associations and meanings that arise. Homework assignments can be assigned during the last part of sessions.

An exposure session begins with therapist and client collaboratively choosing the memory that will be worked on. The therapist then instructs clients to close their eyes, and to focus on the memory. The therapist behaves like the director of a play, prompting clients to focus on various aspects of a memory. This is done in the context of the here and now, and in the first person. Questions are asked about stimulus elements (e.g., "What do you see?"), response elements (e.g., "What are you feeling?"), and meaning elements (e.g., "What comes to mind as you are feeling _____?") in order to facilitate comprehensive exposure to the memory. Clients' roles are to describe what they see, feel, sense, and think, in the first person, present tense—to relive the event as vividly as possible. Clients often resist or defend against doing this by using the past tense and the third person. The therapist's job is to watch for signs that veterans are accessing a traumatic memory, or a painful aspect of such a memory, and to help veterans focus on what they are seeing and experiencing in those moments. The signals of trauma memory activation are both obvious (rapid breathing, crying) and subtle (slight facial grimace, partial/arrested gesture). Simultaneously, the therapist looks for signs of avoidance behavior. Conditioned emotional reactions triggered by exposure therapy are rarely completely free from the countermanding influences of defensive reactions and other attempts at avoidance. The therapist needs to prompt clients to "stay with" the memory, to remain focused on their feelings, and to share what is occurring to them as they do so. In addition, the therapist hypothesizes constantly about thoughts and feelings that clients may avoid because of their aversive qualities. If all is going well, the therapist eventually recedes into the background, like an empathic, understanding, and patient coach.

During DTE, the therapist assesses the client's emotional state periodically so as to monitor any diminution of conditioned emotional reactions. Scenes are repeated, preferably a number of times within a single session, until the client reports a reduction in anxiety. Once this occurs, the therapist may help the client to return to the relaxed state achieved at the beginning of the session through the use of progressive relaxation exercises. The therapist should also engage the client in a dialogue about the meaning of, beliefs about, and implications of the trauma, in order to help the client integrate further traumatic experiences with his/her current life.

The ideal goal within each session of exposure therapy is to produce a sustained, conditioned emotional reaction, free from the inhibiting influence of avoidance behavior. Such sustained emotional reactions result in the extinction of conditioned emotional responses. This goal is readily attainable when there is a discrete, focal war-zone memory, and when the veteran is not using defensive maneuvers to avoid reexperiencing and sharing emotional reactions. The therapist can reasonably expect some diminution of the conditioned emotional reaction to such a focal traumatic memory. In fact, several sequences of exposure are likely to occur within a given 30-minute session, each followed by some diminution of emotional reaction. The therapist's job is considerably more complicated, however, when there are multiple, intertwining traumatic memories coupled with intricate and overlearned avoidance behaviors.

Typically, 30 minutes of exposure therapy rarely provides sufficient opportunity for full exposure followed by a reduction in emotional reaction. In our experience with veterans, exposure work can be used to "chip away" at painful war-zone memories. It can often be therapeutic for clients to have an intense emotional outpouring in a given session without the dire consequences that they expect to follow. This kind of experiential disconfirmation provides an opportunity for clients to learn, in a vivid and poignant way, that their worst fears (e.g., "I will go crazy," "I will lose control") are unrealized when they focus on their traumas. If the emotional response activated during exposure treatment is particularly intense and stable toward the end of a session, relaxation techniques can be used to help clients to reduce arousal.

It is also important to attend carefully to how veterans handle the aftereffects of exposure treatments, especially when their emotional responses are still moderately intense at the end of a given session. Veterans should be helped and encouraged to take advantage of the opportunities for learning that arise from such emotional episodes. They can learn to allow themselves to feel vulnerable without avoiding, and to cope in healthy ways (e.g., by talking with their partners, writing down their thoughts).

Exposure therapy is both demanding and invasive. It requires a very good therapeutic relationship and considerable resources on the part of both client and therapist. All decisions about when to apply exposure treatment, or even about whether to use it at all, have to be made on a case-by-case basis (see Lyons & Keane, 1989, and Boudewyns & Shipley, 1983, for additional descriptions of this process).

Research on the outcome of treatments for PTSD has been the subject of four recent reviews (Blake & Sonnenberg, Chapter 2, this volume; Frueh et al., 1995; Keane, 1997; Solomon, Gerrity, & Muff, 1992). Frueh et al. (1995) focus specifically on the outcome of exposure therapy for war-zone-related PTSD. The results of controlled and uncontrolled case studies and clinical trials provide sufficient evidence that exposure therapy can be an efficacious treatment for war-zone-related PTSD.

Relapse Prevention

Whether treatment of the combat veteran's traumatic memories is conducted with exposure or with some other type of uncovering psychotherapy, the prevention of relapse is always a concern. In therapeutic work devoted to relapse prevention, the client is encouraged to develop realistic expectations about his or her trauma memories (e.g., they are likely to recur), and about stress reactions (e.g., some associated emotional distress is to be expected). Clients are instructed to take advantage of successful experiences that they have had in treatment so that these experiences can modify their trauma-related schemas. In our treatment approach, the client will have learned a series of coping skills that will assist him or her in planning ahead for life crises and high-risk situations. Nevertheless, the therapist should engage the client in a lengthy discussion of the need to be especially prepared for the inevitable recurrence of painful emotion when the client is reminded of what happened to him or her. The augmentation of social supports and vocational counseling are also aspects of this fifth phase of treatment. Moreover, PTSD is increasingly recognized to be a phasic disorder, with symptoms waxing and waning over time. Perhaps this is due to the strength of the initial conditioning or the complexity of network connections (Bouton, 1993; LeDoux, 1989). Preparing clients for accommodating these recurrent exacerbations may preclude serious decompensations in the future. Since anniversary reactions and cues related to the initial conditioning experiences are unavoidable, teaching clients to anticipate and prepare for their inevitable occurrence is essential.

Aftercare

The prevention of gross symptom exacerbation, a retreat from a health stance to problems that arise, and an avoidant lifestyle is built into the comprehensive treatment that we have described in this chapter. Relapse prevention is less of a "last-phase" of treatment in this regard and more an aspect of care that is reinforced throughout treatment. In fact, if relapse prevention is only attended to at the end of treatment, it is likely not to be taken all that seriously, especially when a client is feeling much better. We recommend that therapists pay particular attention throughout treatment to issues of relapse prevention (see Brownell, Marlatt, Lichtenstein, & Wilson, 1986); that is, when problems arise spontaneously (e.g., problems in relationships, parenting, work, health, etc.), therapists need to attend to the metalevel stance that patients take, as well as to the lessons learned about the client's unique domains of high risk. Ideally, veterans with PTSD need to learn that, by virtue of their war-zone experiences, they are left with the added, lifelong burden of needing to pay attention to their emotional lives and the likelihood of intense reactions to mundane, daily hassles.

Relapse prevention is accomplished when the veteran takes a proactive, problem-solving approach to life's stressors. Veterans need to be aware of the inevitable high-risk challenges that they will face, and to have reasonable expectations about the outcomes of their attempts to deal with problems and their own responses. In addition, they require a multidimensional repertoire of skills that can be brought to bear in their responses to significant life events, especially those that cause them to be reminded of their own traumatic memories. Clients are trained to break problems down into their constituent parts, to perform their own functional analysis of problems, oriented toward coping responses and problem solution.

Aftercare also includes planning for long-term follow-up, and perhaps long-term psychotherapy for the resolution of issues that are not amenable to short-term exposure treatment (e.g., childhood physical, sexual abuse, or neglect).

Proactive involvements such as becoming active in veterans' groups, or volunteering, are encouraged as a means of promoting the client's developing capacity to engage with others and develop new peer groups. Social support systems may be the single most important component to maintaining treatment effects. Identifying individuals, groups, and activities that mobilize and promote the client's sense of interpersonal support and comfort will do much to facilitate generalization of treatment effects over time, people, and places. (The following case example is a composite drawn from multiple clinical cases.)

CASE EXAMPLE

Mr. G. was a 55-year-old, married, African American, Vietnam War combat veteran, father of two, who was self-employed as an accountant. He presented in our clinic for an evaluation for PTSD after a friend, and fellow veteran, suggested that he might be having difficulty in coming to terms with his combat experiences in Vietnam. Mr. G. presented with complaints of chronic nightmares and distressing memories about his experiences in Vietnam, social isolation, sexual problems, sleep disturbance, hypervigilance, and difficulties in concentrating. He reported minimal use of alcohol and marijuana while in the warzone. Pre- and postmilitary social adjustment appeared to be good, although Mr. G. did remark on the "distance" he experienced in his marital relationship. His relationships with his children appeared to be healthy, and one of the few sources of enjoyment he reported.

When asked why he had come to the clinic, Mr. G. responded that he had finally "had enough with the nightmares and memories" and was hoping to find some relief. He reported that these symptoms had begun shortly after his return from Vietnam, where he was the squad leader of an infantry company. Mr. G.'s time in the war zone coincided with the Tet Offensive, a major military campaign undertaken by the North Vietnamese in which many American soldiers were killed or wounded. Mr. G. reported numerous recollections of gruesome events during Tet, although one focal event tended to be the object of his recurrent memories and nightmares. It was during this event, a battle in which he and his company were pinned down by the enemy for 3 days straight, that his closest friend in Vietnam was killed while they were holed up in a bunker together. Mr. G. tried in vain to tend to his friend's wounds and, because of the ongoing battle, was forced to remain in the bunker for another 24 hours before reinforcements arrived, allowing the remainder of the company to retreat.

Mr. G. was not in acute crisis at the time of his presentation at our clinic. His difficulties appeared to be chronic ones, and this observation was borne out by the results of a comprehensive psychodiagnostic evaluation. The results of this evaluation indicated that Mr. G. had been suffering from chronic PTSD and major depression. Although he admitted to some vague thoughts about suicide, Mr. G.

stated flatly that he had never come to a point at which he was in danger of hurting himself, and he denied any history of homicidal thoughts.

The psychologist who evaluated Mr. G. recommended that he begin treatment within a group for trauma education. This began with a psychoeducational group about PTSD, including its symptoms and associated conditions. Mr. G. found helpful the knowledge that he was not alone, coupled with opportunities to talk with others who shared a similar background, and he opted to continue with further treatment. This consisted of a stress management group, which Mr. G. found very useful in coping with both daily hassles and the hyperarousal symptoms of PTSD.

After reviewing the conditions for continuing with this course of treatment, Mr. G. and his psychologist agreed that exposure therapy was indicated. Mr. G. was given a detailed rationale for exposure therapy, so that he would know what to expect about the course of this phase of the treatment. The psychologist forewarned Mr. G. that he was likely to try to avoid these experiences, precisely because they were so painful for him. The psychologist emphasized that Mr. G. now had at his disposal techniques that he could use to manage his stress, and that these would come in handy during this phase of the treatment.

After this preliminary groundwork, Mr. G. and his psychologist then reviewed the memories that were most troubling for him. There were four in all, and they agreed to begin with the least troubling event and end with the focal event described earlier. Subsequent sessions began with identifying the memory to be worked on, followed by therapist-guided imaginal exposure as outlined earlier in this chapter. Predictably, Mr. G. experienced some difficulties from time to time in staying with particular aspects of certain memories, especially when these focused on the event in which his best friend was killed in battle. Mr. G. even missed a few appointments during this period of the therapy, ostensibly for valid reasons, although he had never missed or canceled sessions prior to this time. The psychologist patiently explored the possibility that Mr. G. might be avoiding this difficult and painful work, and Mr. G. agreed that this was the case. After working through this avoidance, he was able to continue and complete the exposure sessions for all four identified memories, a process that entailed twice-weekly sessions for a period of 3 months.

At the end of the exposure phase, Mr. G. reported that his waking memories and nightmares were greatly reduced in frequency and intensity. He expressed surprise at the fact that he was now able to remember most of these events without the intensity of aversive feelings he had previously experienced, although he added that the most troubling memory still made him feel very sad. Mr. G. was considerably more accepting of his feelings of sadness, which he had previously taken great pains to avoid.

Mr. G.'s psychologist had warned him about the possibility of relapse, and the next step in his treatment was focused on its prevention. The psychologist encouraged Mr. G. to focus on his successful experiences, and to apply his newly learned coping skills when faced with stressful experiences. This was to prove especially helpful during the anniversary of the death of Mr. G.'s best friend.

As part of both relapse prevention and aftercare, Mr. G. was then referred to an interpersonally oriented psychotherapy group for combat veterans. His positive experiences in this group helped him to begin to interact with others outside of his family, and he slowly began to expand his social network, including joining the local chapter of a veterans' organization, which was heavily involved in volunteer activities in the community.

AFTERWORD

In this chapter, we have presented a flexible, hierarchical approach to the psychotherapeutic treatment of war-zone-related PTSD. Our approach is based on learning theory principles, and on some of its more recent cognitive-behavioral variations. It is further informed by our clinical experience in treating veterans within the DVA system. There is a need, however, for much more work in the areas of theory development, as well as both basic and applied clinical research with this clinical population. Empirical studies will help us to understand the cognitive mechanisms operative in individuals disabled by PTSD, and instruct us as to how to proceed with the emotional processing necessary for therapy to be successful. Randomized clinical trials to assess outcomes associated with these various interventions will provide pivotal new information on what treatments are working for which clients with what types of traumatic experiences. Such work will be crucial in advancing our understanding and treatment of war-zone-related PTSD.

REFERENCES

Baker, R. R., Menard, S. W., & Johns, L. A. (1989). The military nurse experience in Vietnam: Stress and impact. *Journal of Clinical Psychology, 45*, 736–744.

Beck, A. T. (1972). *Depression: Causes and treatment.* Philadelphia: University of Pennsylvania Press.

Beck, A. T., Epstein, N., Brown, G., & Steer, R. A. (1988). An inventory for measuring clinical anxiety: Psychometric properties. *Journal of Consulting and Clinical Psychology, 56*, 893–897.

Beck, A. T., Steer, R. A., & Brown, G. K. (1996). *Beck Depression Inventory—II.* San Antonio, TX: Psychological Corporation.

Belenky, G. L., Noy, S., & Solomon, Z. (1987). Battle stress, morale, "cohesion," combat effectiveness, heroism, and psychiatric casualties: The Israeli experience. In G. Lucas (Ed.), *Contemporary studies in combat psychiatry.* Westport, CT: Greenwood Press.

Benson, H. (1975). *The relaxation response.* New York: William Morrow.

Bion, W. R. (1959). *Experiences in groups and other papers*. New York: Basic Books.

Blake, D. D., Weathers, F. W., Nagy, L. N., Kaloupek, D. G., Klauminser, G., Charney, D. S., & Keane, T. M. (1990). A clinician rating scale for assessing current and lifetime PTSD: The CAPS-1. *Behavior Therapist, 18*, 187–188.

Boudewyns, P. A., & Hyer, L. (1996). Eye movement desensitization and reprocessing (EMDR) as treatment for post-traumatic stress disorder (PTSD). *Clinical Psychology and Psychotherapy, 3*, 185–195.

Boudewyns, P. A., & Shipley, R. H. (1983). *Flooding and implosive therapy*. New York: Plenum.

Bouton, M. E. (1993). Context, time, and memory retrieval in the interference paradigms of Pavlovian conditioning. *Psychological Bulletin, 114*, 80–99.

Brownell, K. D., Marlatt, G. A., Lichtenstein, E., & Wilson, G. T. (1986). Understanding and preventing relapse. *American Psychologist, 41*, 765–782.

Butcher, J. N., Dahlstrom, W. G., Graham, J. R., Tellegen, A. & Karmmer, B. (1989). *Minnesota Multiphasic Personality Inventory (MMPI-2): Manual for administration and scoring*. Minneapolis: University of Minnesota Press.

Carroll, E. M., Rueger, D. B., Foy, D. W., & Donahoe, C. P. (1985). Vietnam combat veterans with posttraumatic stress disorder: Analysis of marital and cohabiting adjustment. *Journal of Abnormal Psychology, 94*, 329–337.

Chemtob, C., Roitblat, H., Hamada, R., Carlson, J., & Twentyman, C. (1988). A cognitive action theory of post-traumatic stress disorder. *Journal of Anxiety Disorders, 2*, 253–275.

Cooper, A. M. (1986). Toward a limited definition of psychic trauma. In A. Rothstein (Ed.), *The reconstructions of trauma: Its significance in clinical work*. Madison, CT: International Universities Press.

Derogatis, L. R. (1977). *The SCL-90 Manual: 1. Scoring, administration and procedures for the SCL-90*. Baltimore: Johns Hopkins University School of Medicine, Clinical Psychometrics Unit.

Fairbank, J. A., & Brown, T. A. (1987). Current behavioral approaches to the treatment of posttraumatic stress disorder. *Behavior Therapist, 10*, 57–64.

Falsetti, S. A., Resnick, H. S., Kilpatrick, D. G., & Freedy, J. R. (1994). A review of the "Potential Stressful Events Interview": A comprehensive assessment instrument of high and low magnitude stressors. *Behavior Therapist, 17*, 66–67.

First, M. B., Spitzer, R. L., Gibbon, M., & Williams, J. B. W. (1996). *Structured Clinical Interview for DSM-IV Axis I Disorders—Patient Edition (SCID-I/P, version 2. 0)*. New York: Biometrics Research Department.

Foa, E. B., Steketee, G., & Olasov-Rothbaum, B. (1989). Behavioral/cognitive conceptualization of post-traumatic stress disorder. *Behavior Therapy, 20*, 155–176.

Friedman, M. J. (1991). Biological approaches to the diagnosis and treatment of post-traumatic disorder. *Journal of Traumatic Stress, 4*, 67–91.

Frueh, B. C., Turner, S. M., & Beidel, D. C. (1995). Exposure therapy for combat-related PTSD: A critical review. *Clinical Psychology Review, 15*, 799–817.

Gallers, J., Foy, D. W., Donahue, C. P., & Goldfarb, J. (1988). Post-traumatic stress disorder in Vietnam combat veterans: Effects of traumatic violence exposure and military adjustment. *Journal of Traumatic Stress, 1*, 181–192.

Gerlock, A. A. (1996). An anger management intervention model for veterans with PTSD. *National Center for PTSD Quarterly, 6*, 61–64.

Horowitz, M. J. (1986). *Stress response syndromes* (2nd ed.). New York: Aronson.

Horowitz, M. J., & Becker, S. S. (1971). Cognitive response to stressful stimuli. *Archives of General Psychiatry, 25*, 419–428.

Hyer, L. A., Woods, M. G., & Boudewyns, P. A. (1991). PTSD and alexithymia: Importance of emotional clarification in treatment. *Psychotherapy, 28*, 129–139.

Jacobson, E. (1938). *Progressive relaxation.* Chicago: University of Chicago Press.

Janoff-Bulman, R. (1992). *Shattered assumptions: Toward a new psychology of trauma.* New York: Free Press.

Jordan, B. K., Marmar, C. R., Fairbank, J. A., Schlenger, W. E., Kulka, R. A., Hough, R. L., & Weiss, D. S. (1992). Problems in families of male Vietnam veterans with posttraumatic stress disorder. *Journal of Consulting and Clinical Psychology, 60*, 916–926.

Karnow, S. (1983). *Vietnam: A history.* New York: Viking Press.

Keane, T. M. (1997). Psychological and behavioral treatment of posttraumatic stress disorder. In P. Nathan & J. Gorman (Eds.), *Treatments that work.* Oxford, UK: Oxford University Press.

Keane, T. M. (1995). The role of exposure therapy in the psychological treatment of PTSD. *National Center for PTSD Clinical Quarterly, 5*, 1–6.

Keane, T. M., Caddell, J. M., & Taylor, K. L. (1988). Mississippi Scale for Combat-Related Posttraumatic Stress Disorder: Three studies in reliability and validity. *Journal of Consulting and Clinical Psychology, 56*, 85–90.

Keane, T. M., Fairbank, J. A., Caddell, J. M., Zimering, R. T., Taylor, K. L., & Mora, C. A. (1989). Clinical evaluation of a measure to assess combat exposure. *Psychological Assessment: A Journal of Consulting and Clinical Psychology, 1*, 53–55.

Keane, T. M., Fisher, L. M., Krinsley, K. E., & Niles, B. L. (1994). Posttraumatic stress disorder. In M. Hersen & R. T. Ammerman (Eds.), *Handbook of prescriptive treatments for adults.* New York: Plenum.

Keane, T. M., Kaloupek, D. G. (1997). Comorbid psychiatric disorders in PTSD: Implications for research. In R. Yehuda & A. McFarlane (Eds.), *Psychobiology of posttraumatic stress disorder* (pp. 24–34). New York: Annals of the New York Academy of Science.

Keane, T. M., Malloy, P. F., & Fairbank, J. A. (1984). Empirical development of an MMPI subscale for the assessment of combat-related posttraumatic stress disorder. *Journal of Consulting and Clinical Psychology, 52*, 888–891.

Keane, T. M., Newman, E., & Orsillo, S. M. (1997). Assessment of military-related posttraumatic stress disorder. In J. P. Wilson & T. M. Keane (Eds.), *Assessing psychological trauma and PTSD.* New York: Guilford Press.

Keane, T. M., Scott, W. O., Chavoya, G. A., Lamparski, D. M., & Fairbank, J. A. (1985). Social support in Vietnam veterans with posttraumatic stress disorder: A comparative analysis. *Journal of Consulting and Clinical Psychology, 53*, 95–102.

Keane, T. M., Zimering, R. T., & Caddell, J. M. (1985). A behavioral formulation of posttraumatic stress disorder in Vietnam veterans. *Behavior Therapist, 8*, 9–12.

Kilpatrick, D. G., Veronen, L. J., & Resick, P. A. (1979). The aftermath of rape: Recent empirical findings. *American Journal of Orthopsychiatry, 49*, 658–669.

Krinsley, K., Weathers, F., Vielhauer, M., Newman, E., Walker, E., Young, L., & Kimerling, R. (1994). *Evaluation of Lifetime Stressors Questionnaire and Interview.* Unpublished measure.

Kulka, R. A., Schlenger, W. E., Fairbank, J. A., Hough, R. L., Jordan, B. K., Marmar, C. R.,

& Weiss, D. S. (1990). *Trauma and the Vietnam War generation: Report of findings from the National Vietnam Veterans Readjustment Study*. New York: Brunner/Mazel.

Lebowitz, L., & Newman, E. (1996). The role of cognitive–affective themes in the assessment and treatment of trauma reactions. *Clinical Psychology and Psychotherapy, 3*, 196–207.

LeDoux, J. E. (1989). Cognitive–emotional interactions in the brain. *Cognition and Emotion, 3*, 267–289.

Leon, G. R., Ben-Porath, Y. S., & Hjemboe, S. (1990). Coping patterns and current functioning in a group of Vietnam and Vietnam-era nurses. *Journal of Social and Clinical Psychology, 9*, 334–353.

Litz, B. T., Blake, D. D., Gerardi, R. G., & Keane, T. M. (1990). Decision making guidelines for the use of direct therapeutic exposure in the treatment of post-traumatic stress disorder. *Behavior Therapist, 13*, 91–93.

Litz, B. T., & Keane, T. M. (1989). Information processing in anxiety disorders: Application to the understanding of post-traumatic stress disorder. *Clinical Psychology Review, 9*, 243–257.

Litz, B. T., Penk, W. E., Gerardi, R. J., & Keane, T. M. (1992). Assessment of post-traumatic stress disorder. In P. Saigh (Ed.), *Post traumatic stress disorder: A behavioral approach to assessment and treatment*. Boston: Allyn & Bacon.

Litz, B. T., & Roemer, L. (1996). Post-traumatic stress disorder: An overview. *Clinical Psychology and Psychotherapy, 3*, 153–168.

Litz, B. T., & Weathers, F. W. (1994). The diagnosis and assessment of post-traumatic stress disorder in adults. In M. B. Williams & J. F. Sommer (Eds.), *The handbook of post-traumatic therapy*. Westport, CT: Greenwood Press.

Litz, B. T., Weathers, F. W., Monaco, V., Herman, D. S., Wulfsohn, M., Marx, B., & Keane, T. M. (1996). Attention, arousal, and memory in posttraumatic stress disorder. *Journal of Traumatic Stress, 9*, 497–519.

Lyons, J. A., & Keane, T. M. (1989). Implosive therapy for the treatment of combat-related PTSD. *Journal of Traumatic Stress, 2*, 137–152.

Malloy, P. F., Fairbank, J. A., & Keane, T. M. (1983). Validation of a multimethod assessment of posttraumatic stress disorders in Vietnam veterans. *Journal of Consulting and Clinical Psychology, 51*, 488–494.

McNally, R. J., Litz, B. T., Prassus, A., Shin, L. M., & Weathers, F. W. (1994). Emotional priming of autobiographical memory in post-traumatic stress disorder. *Cognition and Emotion, 8*(4), 351–367.

Meichenbaum, D. (1985). *Stress inoculation training*. New York: Pergamon Press.

Meichenbaum, D., & Jaremko, M. E. (1983). *Stress reduction and prevention*. New York: Plenum.

Mowrer, O. H. (1947). On the dual nature of learning: A reinterpretation of "conditioning" and "problem solving." *Harvard Educational Review, 17*, 102–148.

Newman, E., Kaloupek, D. G., & Keane, T. M. (1996). Assessment of posttraumatic stress disorder in clinical and research settings. In B. A. van der Kolk, A. C. McFarlane, & L. Weisaeth (Eds.), *Traumatic stress: The effects of overwhelming experience on mind, body, and society*. New York: Guilford Press.

Newman, E., Orsillo, S. M., Herman, D. S., Niles, B. L., & Litz, B. T. (1995). Clinical presentation of disorders of extreme stress in combat veterans. *Journal of Nervous and Mental Disease, 183*, 628–632.

Nezu, A., & Carnevale, G. (1987). Interpersonal problem solving and coping reactions of Vietnam veterans with posttraumatic stress disorder. *Journal of Abnormal Psychology, 96*, 155–157.

Niederland, W. G. (1971). Introductory notes on the concept, definition, and range of psychic trauma. *International Psychiatry Clinics, 8*, 1–9.

Norris, F. (1990). Screening for traumatic stress: A scale for use in the general population. *Journal of Applied Social Psychology, 20*, 1704–1718.

Novaco, R. W. (1996). Anger treatment and its special challenges. *National Center for PTSD Quarterly, 6*, 56–60.

O'Donohue, W., & Krasner, L. (Eds.). (1994). *Handbook of psychological skills training: Clinical techniques and applications.* Boston: Allyn & Bacon.

Pitman, P. K., Orr, S. P., Altman, B., Longpre, R. E., Poire, R. E., & Macklin, M. L. (1996). Emotional processing during eye movement desensitization and reprocessing therapy of Vietnam veterans with chronic posttraumatic stress disorder. *Comprehensive Psychiatry, 37*, 419–429.

Rachman, S. (1966). Studies in desensitization—II: Flooding. *Behaviour Research and Therapy, 4*, 1–6.

Saakvitne, K. W., & Pearlman, L. A. (1996). *Transforming the pain: A workbook on vicarious traumatization.* New York: Norton.

Saunders, B. E., Mandoki, K. A., & Kilpatrick, D. G. (1990). Development of a crime-related post-traumatic stress disorder scale within the Symptom Checklist-90—Revised. *Journal of Traumatic Stress, 3*, 439–448.

Schlenger, W., & Kulka, R. A. (1989). *PTSD scale development for the MMPI-2.* Research Triangle Park, NC: Research Triangle Park Institute.

Shapiro, F. (1995). *Eye movement desensitization and reprocessing: Basic principles, protocols, and procedures.* New York: Guilford Press.

Solomon, S. D., Gerrity, E. T., & Muff, A. M. (1992). Efficacy of treatments for posttraumatic stress disorder: An empirical review. *Journal of the American Medical Association, 268*, 633–638.

Stampfl, T. G., & Levis, D. J. (1967). Essentials of implosive therapy: A learning-theory-based psychodynamic behavioral therapy. *Journal of Abnormal Psychology, 72*, 496–503.

Tarrier, N. (1996). An application of expressed emotion to the study of PTSD: Preliminary findings. *Clinical Psychology and Psychotherapy, 3*, 220–229.

Weathers, F. W., Litz, B. T., Herman, D. S., Huska, J. A., & Keane, T. M. (1993, October). *The PTSD Checklist (PCL): Reliability, validity, and diagnostic utility.* Paper presented at the annual meeting of the International Society for Traumatic Stress Studies, San Antonio, TX.

Weathers, F. W., Litz, B. T., Keane, T. M., Herman, D. S., Steinberg, H. R., Huska, J. A., & Kraemer, H. C. (1996). The utility of the SCL-90-R for the diagnosis of war-zone-related post-traumatic stress disorder. *Journal of Traumatic Stress, 9*, 111–128.

Wilson, J. P. (1995). The historical evolution of PTSD diagnostic criteria: From Freud to DSM-IV. In G. S. Everly & J. M. Lating (Eds.), *Psychotraumatology: Key papers and core concepts in post-traumatic stress.* New York: Plenum.

Wolfe, J., Mori, D., & Krygeris, S. (1994). Treating trauma in special populations: Lessons from women veterans. *Psychotherapy, 31*, 87–93.

Wolpe, J. (1958). *Psychotherapy by reciprocal inhibition.* Stanford, CA: Stanford University Press.

Wolpe, J. (1984). Deconditioning and ad hoc uses of relaxation: An overview. *Journal of Behavior Therapy and Experimental Psychiatry, 15,* 299–304.

Zaidi, L. Y., & Foy, D. W. (1994). Childhood abuse experiences and combat-related PTSD. *Journal of Traumatic Stress, 7,* 33–42.

Intrusion, Arousal, and Avoidance
SEXUAL TRAUMA SURVIVORS

ELIZABETH A. MEADOWS
EDNA B. FOA

In the United States, the prevalence of assault is alarmingly high. In an epidemiological study of 4,008 women, 12.7% were victims of rape, and 14.3% were victims of other sexual assault (Resnick, Kilpatrick, Dansky, Saunders, & Best, 1993). Prevalence of childhood sexual abuse is similarly high, with one national survey (Finkelhor, Hotaling, Lewis, & Smith, 1990) showing that 27% of women and 16% of men reported having been sexually abused or molested as children. Domestic violence is also very prevalent, with one study indicating that 20–33% of women will be physically assaulted (which may, but does not necessarily, include sexual assault) by a partner or ex-partner in their lifetimes (Frieze & Browne, 1989).

Sexual assault tends to be reported to police less frequently than other crimes (Kilpatrick, Saunders, Veronen, Best, & Von, 1987), and rates of reporting to others vary considerably depending on the wording of the question (Koss, 1993). Thus, these rates, while quite high, may underestimate the actual prevalence of sexual assault. Women appear to be at particular risk for assault, being more likely than men, both in adulthood and in childhood, to be targets of physical violence (Kessler, Sonnega, Bromet, Hughes, & Nelson, 1995). In addition, women are more likely than men to develop posttraumatic stress disorder (PTSD) following a traumatic event (Breslau, Davis, Andresky, & Peterson, 1991; Cottler, Compton, Mager, Spitznagel, & Janca, 1992; Helzer, Robins, & McEvoy, 1987; Norris, 1992; North & Smith, 1992). Because of these gender differences, this chapter will focus primarily on sexual assault in women, although it should be noted that men are also victims of sexual assault and can also suffer from assault-related PTSD.

Sexual assault is associated with a variety of psychological sequelae. Symptoms of PTSD are among the most common, and fall into three clusters. The intrusion cluster includes flashbacks, nightmares, recurrent thoughts, and reactivity to reminders of the trauma. The avoidance cluster includes deliberate efforts to avoid thoughts, feelings, and reminders of the trauma, as well as symptoms of emotional numbing such as detachment from others, loss of interest in activities, and restricted range of affect. Finally, the arousal cluster includes symptoms of sleep and concentration disturbances, hypervigilance, anger and irritability, and increased startle. These symptoms of intrusion, avoidance, and arousal are the focus of the present chapter. However, sexual assault survivors may also experience depression, severe dissociative symptoms, substance abuse, medical problems, or exacerbation of preexisting difficulties, such as personality or psychotic disorders (cf. Dancu & Foa, in press), many of which are the focus of other chapters in this volume.

In a prospective study of female rape victims (Rothbaum, Foa, Riggs, Murdock, & Walsh, 1992), 94% of the women met symptom criteria for PTSD within the 2 weeks following the assault. Over time, rates of PTSD decreased, but 47% continued to meet PTSD criteria 3-months postrape. A retrospective study (Resnick et al., 1993) indicated lifetime and current prevalence rates of 32% and 12.4%, respectively for PTSD in rape victims. Similarly high rates of PTSD were observed in children who had been molested (McLeer, Deblinger, Atkins, Foa, & Ralphe, 1988), as well as in adult women with histories of childhood sexual abuse (Rowan, Foy, Rodriguez, & Ryan, 1994). Thus, it is clear that PTSD in sexual assault survivors is a problem of monumental significance. The scope of this problem clearly underscores the importance of effective treatments for this population. In this chapter, we review cognitive-behavioral treatments that have been used for rape-related PTSD. These include exposure therapy, cognitive therapy, stress inoculation training, and cognitive processing therapy. In discussing each of these treatments, we review their theoretical underpinnings as well as the literature regarding their efficacy. We then describe in some detail implementation of one such treatment: prolonged exposure. Decision making regarding type of treatment are also be discussed, with clinical examples to illustrate implementation of adjunctive treatments or modifications to exposure. Clinical examples throughout the chapter are drawn from real clients but are presented with identifying information disguised and, in some cases, as composites.

REVIEW OF TREATMENTS FOR PTSD

Exposure Therapy

Exposure treatments, in which clients confront their fears in a systematic manner, are rooted in learning theory. The most influential theory in this regard was Mowrer's two-factor theory (1960), in which fear is acquired via classical conditioning and maintained via operant conditioning. For example, a woman raped in a parking lot may develop a fear of this lot. The lot itself is a neutral stimulus that develops anxiety-provoking qualities due to its association with the rape, becoming a conditioned stimulus (CS). As a CS, the parking lot evokes fear in the woman even when no rape is occurring there. Furthermore, higher order conditioning and generalization may occur, so that any parking lot, rather than just the lot in which she was raped, becomes frightening. Other neutral stimuli, such as the type or color of clothing worn during the assault, or physical characteristics of the rapist, may also become conditioned stimuli. The woman then begins to avoid or escape these frightening stimuli, learning through negative reinforcement that this avoidance/escape immediately reduces the anxiety evoked. Thus, the woman in our example avoids the vicinity of that parking lot, maintaining her fear. Within this framework, exposure therapy is thought to work by breaking these associations through the processes of extinction (Stampfl & Levis, 1967) or habituation (Watts, 1979).

More recently, Foa and Kozak (1986) explained the mechanisms underlying exposure therapy by invoking the concept of emotional processing. This theory is informed by Lang's (1979) bioinformational theory of emotion, which views fear as a cognitive structure that is a program for escaping danger and is consistent with Rescorla's (1988) view of conditioning as a change in meaning. According to emotional processing theory, exposure therapy works via activation of the fear structure (by confrontation with feared stimuli) followed by the introduction of corrective information that is incompatible with the pathological elements of this structure. Going back to the earlier example, the parking lot has acquired the faulty meaning of impending danger for the woman in question, leading to her response of fear in its presence. Repeated exposure corrects this erroneous meaning, so that the woman learns that the parking lot itself does not represent immediate, absolute danger. Furthermore, exposure provides the corrective information that remembering the trauma is not the same as reexperiencing it, that anxiety decreases in the presence of feared situations and memories even without avoidance, and that experiencing PTSD symptoms does not lead to a loss of control (Foa & Jaycox, in press).

Systematic desensitization (SD; Wolpe, 1958), was the earliest exposure technique used to treat postrape reactions. In SD, exposure is conducted in a minimally arousing fashion, using short imaginal exposures interrupted by relaxation exercises as anxiety mounts. Case reports and uncontrolled studies (e.g., Frank & Stewart, 1983, 1984) indicated that SD was effective in reducing postrape sequelae, although definitive conclusions cannot be drawn from such studies.

A larger study (Frank et al., 1988) found SD (as well as cognitive restructuring) efficacious in decreasing symptoms in female rape victims when compared with a group of untreated women. The inclusion of recent victims in this sample was noted as a problem by Kilpatrick and Calhoun (1988), because it introduces a possible confound favoring positive outcome as natural recovery would have been perceived as a treatment effect. To examine this, Frank et al. (1988) examined treatment outcome in the subset of women who had delayed treatment seeking, finding again that SD (as well as CR) was effective in reducing symptoms. Another problem lies in the nature of the control group. This untreated group was obtained from studies conducted in other sites rather than randomly derived from the study pool of clients. Thus, the symptom reduction observed following treatment may also be due to extraneous factors such as expectancy. An additional study, although not targeting rape victims as the trauma population, lends further support to the use of SD as a treatment for posttrauma symptoms. This large, controlled study of a sample of mixed trauma victims, including many whose trauma consisted of bereavement, demonstrated that SD significantly reduced self-reported symptoms of intrusion and avoidance (Brom, Kleber, & Defares, 1989).

In recent years, PTSD researchers have focused more on prolonged exposure rather than on SD. This trend away from SD is consistent with the evidence that long exposure is superior to short (e.g., Stern & Marks, 1973) and that real stimuli produces greater change than imagined stimuli (Barlow, Leitenberg, Agras, & Wincze, 1969).

Prolonged exposure (PE) can include imaginal exposure in which the client relives trauma memories, and *in vivo* exposure in which feared situations or activities are confronted. PE has demonstrated efficacy in reducing PTSD symptoms in victims of a variety of traumas. Following the promising initial case reports and uncontrolled studies (e.g., Fairbank & Keane, 1982; Johnson, Gilmore, & Shenoy, 1982; Keane & Kaloupek, 1982), the earliest controlled studies of PE were conducted with combat veterans (e.g., Boudewyns & Hyer, 1990; Boudewyns, Hyer, Woods, Harrison, & McCranie, 1990; Cooper & Clum, 1989; Keane, Fairbank, Caddell, & Zimering, 1989). Although each of these studies suffered from some methodological difficulties, the evidence from them converged to indicate that PE was an effective treatment for combat-related PTSD. Additional evidence for the use of prolonged exposure comes from studies in mixed-trauma groups (e.g., Marks, Lovell, Noshirvani, Livanou, & Thrasher, 1998; Richards, Lovell, & Marks, 1994; Thompson, Charlton, Kerry, Lee, & Turner, 1995).

In the first controlled study of prolonged exposure (PE) for rape-related PTSD, Foa, Rothbaum, Riggs, and Murdock (1991) compared PE, stress inoculation training (SIT), and supportive counseling (SC), as well as a wait list in a sample of female victims of sexual and nonsexual assault. This study fulfilled most of the gold standard criteria of treatment outcome studies outlined in Foa and Meadows (1997), rendering the conclusions from this study quite reliable. At posttreatment, women in both PE and SIT improved on all clusters of PTSD symptoms relative to wait list, with women in SC improving only on the arousal cluster.

A second study conducted by the same research group (Foa et al., in press) further supported the efficacy of PE in treating assault-related PTSD. In this study, which was similar in design to the Foa et al. (1991) study, PE was compared with SIT, a PE–SIT combination, and a wait-list control condition. On all outcome measures, the three active treatments significantly reduced PTSD symptoms relative to wait-list, with PE consistently outperforming both SIT and PE–SIT, although this difference did not always reach statistical significance.

Two studies are currently continuing to examine the efficacy of PE for rape-related PTSD. Foa and her colleagues are comparing PE with PE plus cognitive restructuring (PE–CR), while Resick and her colleagues are comparing PE with cognitive processing therapy (CPT, which is described in more detail later). Preliminary results (Foa, Jaycox, Meadows, Hembree, & Dancu, 1996) indicate that PE continues to be equally or more effective than more complex treatments.

Another form of exposure therapy, eye movement desensitization and reprocessing (EMDR; Shapiro, 1995) has also been employed for PTSD. Most studies of EMDR as a PTSD treatment for various trauma populations have suffered from significant methodological difficulties, rendering their results inconclusive. Rothbaum (1997) conducted a well-controlled study comparing EMDR with a wait-list control for rape-related PTSD, with results indicating that EMDR produced significant improvement both posttreatment and at follow-up. The extent to which the exposure component of EMDR is responsible for this improvement, however, cannot be discerned from this study.

Cognitive Therapy

Both clinical and social–developmental psychology have produced cognitive theories of the etiology and treatment of PTSD. Traditional cognitive therapy was initially developed by Beck (1972; Beck, Rush, Shaw, & Emery, 1979) to treat depression and further developed for the treatment of anxiety disorders (e.g., Beck, Emery, & Greenberg, 1985; Clark, 1986). It is based on the assumption that it is the interpretation of an event, rather than the event itself, that determines emotional states. In this view, dysfunctional thoughts, or thoughts that are inaccurate or too extreme, lead to pathological emotional responses. Cognitive theory posits that different emotions are associated with specific types of thoughts. Specifically, the thoughts associated with anxiety and fear are characterized by danger; those associated with anger are characterized by perceptions of others behaving wrongly; perceptions of oneself behaving wrongly are associated with thoughts of guilt; and perceptions of loss are associated with sadness (cf. Foa & Jaycox, in press).

According to this theory, treatment should aim at changing pathological thoughts. Cognitive restructuring (CR) typically involves several steps. First, clients are taught to identify their dysfunctional thoughts (e.g., thoughts driving intense negative emotional states). Second, they evaluate the validity of these thoughts and challenge erroneous or unhelpful thoughts. Third, they replace such thoughts with more logical or beneficial ones.

To use our earlier example of the woman raped in the parking lot, a dysfunctional thought might be: "If I go back to that mall I will be attacked again." Evidence for the accuracy of this thought would include the fact that she was attacked there once. Evidence against it could include the fact that she had been to that mall dozens of times prior to the assault with no previous difficulties, that thousands of people visit that mall each day without incident, and that she is aware of reasonable precautions such as parking near floodlights that should reduce potential risk. Thus, the evidence for her thoughts of danger is clearly outweighed by the evidence against such thoughts, leading to the rational response: "The mall parking lot is generally pretty safe, and although I was very unlucky the last time I was there, that does not mean I will be in danger if I go back, especially if I take realistic steps to ensure my safety, such as staying away from the farthest reaches of the parking lot in the dark."

CR is a component of several treatments for PTSD, such as SIT. As a stand-alone treatment, CR has not been extensively evaluated in rape victims. The Frank et al. (1988) study reviewed earlier indicated that CR (as well as SD) was effective in reducing postrape symptoms. However, the methodological flaws in this study, such as lack of an adequate control group and the inclusion of recent victims, make it difficult to draw strong conclusions regarding the efficacy of this treatment.

CR is also a component of the PE–CR combination treatment for assault-related PTSD currently being studied by Foa and her colleagues, which was reviewed in the previous section; preliminary results do not indicate an advantage to the inclusion of this component. Similarly, Marks et al. (1998) found that both CR and PE were effective in reducing PTSD in a sample of mixed-trauma victims. Inspection of the means suggests, however, that CR was somewhat inferior to both PE and a PE–CR combination at follow-up.

The efficacy of cognitive therapy for chronic PTSD, especially in rape victims, has not been studied as extensively as has that of exposure. However, there is some support for its use, and at minimum, it may serve as a useful adjunct to exposure treatments, especially in cases where exposure is not well tolerated.

Social and personality theorists (e.g., Epstein, 1989; Janoff-Bulman, 1992; McCann & Pearlman, 1990) have also developed cognitive theories, positing that core schemas are shattered by the experience of trauma, and that this is dealt with via assimilation and accommodation of the new trauma-related information. These theories are discussed in more detail in the section on CPT.

Stress Inoculation Training

Anxiety management techniques were developed from the view that pathological anxiety is a result of skills deficits, and thus they focus on teaching clients specific skills to use when anxious (e.g., Suinn, 1974). A number of strategies, such as self-instruction, biofeedback, and relaxation training, have been used to reduce anxiety, but the anxiety management program that has been studied the most in PTSD patients is stress inoculation training (SIT). SIT was initially developed by Meichenbaum (1974) as a treatment for anxiety, and was modified by Kilpatrick, Veronen, and Resick (1982) for use with rape victims. The modified program included muscle relaxation training, breathing retraining, role playing, covert modeling, guided self-dialog, and thought stopping.

To use our example of the woman raped in the mall parking lot, SIT would be effective by providing the woman with skills she can use to manage the anxiety that arises when she is reminded of the rape, such as returning to that mall. Thus, she might use role playing to rehearse her trip to the mall, relaxation or breathing retraining to calm herself while preparing to go or while there, or thought stopping when she finds herself thinking frightening thoughts such as "I may be attacked again and need to run."

This treatment was examined in case reports and uncontrolled studies (e.g., Kilpatrick et al., 1982; Pearson, Poquette, & Wasden, 1983; Veronen & Kilpatrick, 1982) with promising results, indicating that SIT was effective in reducing rape-related fear and anxiety both posttreatment and at follow-up. Additionally, SIT appeared to be a very palatable treatment for rape victims, who were allowed in the Kilpatrick et al. (1982) study to choose among SIT, SD, and peer counseling: 70% selected SIT.

The first controlled study of SIT in the treatment of rape victims compared it with assertion training, supportive counseling, and a naturally occurring wait list in a quasi-experimental design (Resick, Jordan, Girelli, Hutter, & Marhoefer-Dvorak, 1988). At posttreatment, all three active treatments produced modest improvement in rape-related fear and anxiety relative to the wait list. The largest effect of SIT was observed on self-reported symptoms of intrusion and avoidance. Both of the Foa et al. studies (Foa et al., 1991; Foa et al., in press) described in the earlier section on exposure treatment also examined the efficacy of SIT in reducing PTSD in rape victims. The 1991 study indicated that SIT and PE were equally effective in reducing PTSD symptoms relative to wait list at posttreatment, although there was a tendency for PE to show superiority at follow-up. The second study indicated a similar pattern, with PE, SIT, and the PE–SIT combination all proving effective relative to wait list.

In summary then, SIT appears to be an effective treatment for rape-related PTSD, although perhaps somewhat less so than PE.

Cognitive Processing Therapy

Cognitive processing therapy (CPT) was developed by Resick and Schnicke (1992a) as a treatment specifically geared for rape victims. Incorporating cognitive and information processing theories, CPT includes components of both exposure and cognitive therapy, but these are conducted somewhat differently than in traditional exposure or cognitive therapies.

As noted in the section on cognitive therapy, several theorists have suggested that traumatization results in specific changes in core schemas. The cognitive component in CPT was designed to target five primary themes believed to be disrupted by rape. These themes include safety, trust, power, esteem, and intimacy (McCann & Pearlman, 1990; McCann, Sakheim, & Abrahamson, 1988), with each theme slated for cognitive restructuring at designated sessions. The exposure component in CPT is conducted by having the client write a detailed description of her rape, followed by the client's reading this account.

Two reports have suggested that CPT is effective in treating rape-related PTSD. In the first, Resick and Schnicke (1992a) compared the results of group CPT in 19 rape victims with those of a naturally occurring wait list, finding that the women in the CPT group improved significantly on symptoms of PTSD and depression. A follow-up report (Resick & Schnicke, 1992b) examined a larger sample of 54 women, including the previous 19, with similarly positive results. These studies suggest CPT is an effective treatment for rape-related PTSD. Resick and her colleagues are currently comparing CPT with the more established PE, with preliminary results indicating that both treatments are similarly highly effective. However, it should be noted that the only studies of CPT come from the research group that developed the treatment; stronger conclusions can be drawn if these results are replicated by other research groups.

Summary of Treatment Efficacy Research

A number of treatments have been developed to ameliorate rape-related PTSD. These include PE, CR, SIT, and CPT. All of these have shown some promise to date, but PE currently has the largest number of well-controlled studies to support its efficacy. Several studies comparing PE and other treatments have suggested the superiority of PE; although not all comparisons were statistically significant, there was considerable consistency of the findings across measures. Additionally, PE has fewer components than SIT and CPT, and thus may be more easily disseminated to clinicians (cf. Foa & Meadows, 1997). Given these considerations, we focus for the remainder of this chapter primarily on the clinical implementation of PE. However, as discussed below, PE may not be suitable for all clients, and in some cases, procedural modifications may be warranted (for a review of such instances, see Jaycox & Foa, 1996).

CLINICAL APPLICATION OF PROLONGED EXPOSURE

In this section, we describe the use of the PE treatment developed by Foa and her colleagues (Foa, Hearst-Ikeda, Dancu, Hembree, & Jaycox, 1994) and currently in use at the Center for the Treatment and Study of Anxiety at Allegheny University Hospitals—MCP in Philadelphia. For a full description of the theory underlying PE and instructions regarding its implementation, see Foa and Rothbaum (1998).

The PE treatment program consists of several components, including information gathering, psychoeducation, breathing retraining, imaginal exposure (reliving of the trauma), and *in vivo* exposure (confrontation with trauma reminders). The last two components form the heart of the treatment.

After the therapist has ascertained that the client suffers from PTSD and that PTSD treatment is appropriate, the treatment program is described. This includes the schedule and length of sessions, skills to be learned, and the need for homework practices. Next, the therapist gathers information about the assault and its consequences. This information is used as a springboard for a discussion of common reactions to assault, including symptoms of PTSD and other related difficulties. Breathing retraining is also taught at this initial phase, providing the client quickly with a concrete skill she can use when anxious.

Information Gathering

To gather information about the assault and the client's reactions to it, we use the Standardized Assault Interview (SAI), included in Foa and Rothbaum (1998). Following the client's open-ended description of the assault, specific questions address characteristics of the assault, the client's and others' reactions, medical and legal involvement, and related concerns.

Information gathering serves several purposes. The most obvious is to inform the therapist about what happened to the client during and after the assault. This inquiry promotes therapist–client alliance, and also highlights specific areas that may be especially important to work on during treatment. It also helps the client realize that the therapist can tolerate hearing about the assault, and allows expression of distress.

Most clients do not have difficulties during the information-gathering stage. However, if specific areas are particularly upsetting to a given client, the therapist may decide to postpone those discussions until later. It is important to let clients know that although the sessions are quite directive, they are in control, and their wishes will be respected.

Breathing Retraining

Breathing retraining is a technique that aims at helping the client manage her anxiety. There are two main components in breathing retraining. First, clients are taught to focus on the exhalation that is associated with relaxation, rather than the more commonly thought of inhalation. Second, breathing retraining focuses on taking slower breaths and pausing between breaths, so that the physical arousal stemming from increased breathing gets dampened, leading to a sense of physical calm.

Breathing retraining is taught by having the client inhale to a count of four, then exhale slowly while saying "Calm" to herself. A 4-second pause is placed between breaths, further slowing the breathing process. Initially, the therapist should count and say "Calm" for the client, until a rhythm is established, after which the client may take over. Once the method is learned, clients are instructed to practice the breathing for homework, at least twice daily for 10–20 minutes each time.

It is important to note that although we typically use "calm" as the word paired with relaxation, some clients may object to this, especially if they have been told by others, "Oh, just calm down already." If so, the client should just pick another word that she finds more soothing. Also, many clients have trouble breathing slowly initially, and thus the timing of the cycles may require adjustment, with shorter counts at first and gradually slowing to a count of four.

Common Reactions to Assault

The therapist explains the common reactions to assault in a manner that helps normalize the client's symptoms and experiences, and also provides the groundwork for the rest of treatment. Thus, the discussion of common reactions includes a description of posttrauma symptoms, such as reexperiencing, avoidance, and arousal, as well as anger, depression, guilt, and shame. Many clients enter treatment thinking that their symptoms indicate that they are going crazy or are incapable of taking care of themselves. Provision of information regarding these symptoms can help clients tremendously by alleviating these fears.

In Vivo Exposure

In introducing *in vivo* exposure, the therapist might say:

> "It makes sense that situations reminding you of the trauma, such as going past where it happened or reading about crime in the paper [refer to the client's own situations in this section] are upsetting to you now. And so it also makes sense that you would want to avoid them, because after all, no one wants to do things that upset them. However, we know that although the avoidance can make you feel better in the short-run, it actually keeps you from getting over your fears.
>
> "Because of this, we're going to use the opposite approach, of confronting rather than avoiding the situations that make you afraid. This will let you learn that the situations that remind you of the trauma are not really dangerous, and that your anxiety will eventually decrease even if you don't avoid or leave the situation. Let's start by making a list of situations that you've been avoiding since the assault. We'll rank order these by how much

distress they cause you, so that we end up with a hierarchy of easiest to hardest situations to work on."

Many clients can come up with a fairly long list of avoided situations on their own. For clients who have difficulty, some examples of commonly avoided situations following assault include the site of the assault, going out at night, being near unfamiliar men, reading the newspaper or watching the news, physical contact, and wearing certain clothes or jewelry. Additional situations may be apparent from the client's initial evaluation of PTSD symptoms, or from the discussion of common reactions. Once a number of items have been identified, the client rates these using a SUDs (subjective units of distress) scale, with 0 indicating no distress and 100 indicating extreme distress.

The hierarchy need not include every situation that is avoided; rather, it is a representative list with which the client can begin *in vivo* exposure. Frequently, clients will begin following the session to notice additional situations and activities that can be added to the hierarchy. The most important aspect of the hierarchy is a range of difficulty, so that exposure can begin with moderately distressing (i.e., SUDs of 40 or 50) situations, gradually progressing to more anxiety-provoking ones. For clients who rate all situations as very distressing, introducing additional elements such as presence of a trusted friend or daytime versus nighttime can increase the range.

Safety issues should also be addressed while constructing the hierarchy. Clearly, many situations that are associated with the trauma may be realistically dangerous, and these dangerous situations should not be included on a hierarchy. In some cases, sorting out dangerous and safe situations can be tricky, especially for clients who did not discriminate well between the two even prior to the assault. Some questions that can be used to ascertain danger are "Did this seem dangerous to me before the assault?" and "Do other people see this situation as dangerous also?" For example, one client we saw reported that she had always gone jogging in the evening along a commonly used path. She stated that she had not considered the safety issues before her assault, but that she now believed this to have been an unsafe activity. When she began asking others how they felt, she found that most people viewed the path as fairly safe during the evening as long as they did not jog alone. Thus, her original, preassault views were perhaps not cautious enough, in that she would frequently jog alone at night. Her postassault views, however, were too cautious. Jogging along the path alone during the daytime, and accompanied in the evening, were therefore included on her hierarchy.

Some situations contain a certain degree of danger but are also unavoidable if the client is to function in her daily life. For example, many of our clients live in crime-ridden neighborhoods in which walking from the bus stop to their front door is in fact risky. However, without the means to move to a safer area, the client must either be able to make this walk or remain housebound. Incorporating realistic precautions, such as walking with others, or carrying a whistle at night, can lead to an exposure practice that allows the client to resume her normal functioning while minimizing safety risks.

Once the hierarchy is developed, *in vivo* exposure practices are assigned, beginning with moderately frightening items. Instruct the client to remain in the situation for a minimum of 30 minutes, so that she has a chance to experience a reduction in anxiety and evaluate her beliefs and ideas about the degree of threat involved in confronting them. A good guideline for length of exposure is that the client should remain in the situation until her SUDs decreases by at least 50%. Preparing the client for an initial increase in anxiety can forestall her leaving prematurely, as can an instruction to remind herself of the rationale for exposure at these times, allowing her to stick with the exposure long enough for habituation to occur.

Imaginal Exposure

The thought of reliving the assault in memory is often quite distressing for the clients. This is dealt with in several ways. First, the rationale for imaginal exposure is explained in detail prior to beginning and repeated throughout treatment when warranted. Also, the exposure is conducted somewhat gradually: The client determines the level of detail included in the initial narratives, with increased prompting by the therapist over time. Third, treatment planning is arranged so that the client and the therapist have sufficient time to discuss the experience and, when necessary, use relaxation methods. Finally, the therapist's confidence in this treatment, based on clinical experience and the research evidence, is expressed to the client as is the acknowledgment by the therapist that exposure can be difficult, especially at first.

The rationale for imaginal exposure may be presented as follows:

"Today we're going to spend most of the session doing imaginal exposure, or having you relive the assault in your memory. I know that you think about the assault quite a bit, but in therapy we will confront this memory in a different way. Currently, when you think about the assault you feel upset and therefore try to push the thoughts away. It makes sense that you'd want to avoid thinking about it, since it was such a distressing experience. Unfortunately, as you've already discovered, trying not to think about it doesn't work very well, and it keeps coming back. Some of the symptoms of PTSD, like nightmares, intrusive thoughts, and flashbacks, are signals that you haven't yet dealt with the memories. So in imaginal exposure, you will deliberately confront the thoughts and memories without pushing them away. Reliving the assault in your memory lets you process the experience, so that you can file it away in your mind like any other bad memory, rather than having it be so real for you. It will also show you that you can let yourself think about it and not lose control or go crazy, so that you end up having control over the memories rather than having them control you. You will also learn that the anxiety you experience when you think about the assault eventually decreases, just like it does when you stay in situations you were afraid of."

(*Note*: Although it is uncommon for someone not to avoid traumatic thoughts and memories, if the client does not report such avoidance, this part of the rationale can be modified so as to refer to common strategies of avoidance, or to the client's emotional reaction to such thoughts rather than the avoidance of them.)

Before beginning the exposure practice, the therapist should begin audiotaping so that both the instructions and the exposure itself are on tape, which the client will listen to for homework. Instructions are as follows:

"Get comfortable and close your eyes so you won't be distracted. Begin talking about the assault, and when you talk about it, do so in as much detail as you can. Describe not only what's happening, but also what you're thinking and feeling. Talk about it in the present tense, as if it's happening right now, rather than a story from the past. While you describe it, I want you to visualize it in your head, describing what you're experiencing. We're going to do this for about 45 minutes, so that you have time for the anxiety to decrease, so you may end up telling the story of the assault several times. We'll hold off discussing it until the very end of the exposure rather than at the end of each retelling. Periodically, I'll ask you for SUDs ratings, so I know how you're feeling during this. The rating should be how you feel right now, sitting here, not how you felt at that time during the assault. Before we begin, do you have any questions?"

Once any questions are answered, the exposure begins, with SUDs ratings taken about every 5 minutes. At the end of the allotted time, the client may open her eyes and might be encouraged to use some of the breathing skills. The experience is then discussed, including her reactions to it (i.e., Was it harder or easier than she'd imagined? Was there anything surprising during it?) as well as the therapist's impressions (i.e., She seemed to have difficulty describing certain details of the assault, skipping over some parts).

DECISION MAKING REGARDING TREATMENT APPROACHES

Although PE is currently the most established treatment for PTSD, there are circumstances where it may be preferable to use other approaches either in conjunction with PE or instead of PE. In this section, we will review some of these of these circumstances and provide examples of alternative approaches.

Guilt, Shame, and Anger

The intrusive thoughts most typically observed in PTSD focus on the trauma itself, and the most dominant emotion is the fear experienced at the time of the event. Some clients, however, are more disturbed by thoughts producing guilt or shame. These emotions, unlike anxiety, seem to be less amenable to change by PE alone. On the other hand, CR may be effective in targeting guilt- and shame-producing dysfunctional thoughts, and thus for clients with considerable guilt or shame, the addition of CR seems desirable.

> Maria is a 44-year-old woman who was assaulted outside a bar late at night. When she began treatment, she had significant reexperiencing and avoidance symptoms; these responded well to exposure. However, during each imaginal exposure session, she would interrupt her narrative to castigate herself for having been at the bar in the first place and dwell on her embarrassment at telling others about the assault, for fear they would think badly of her for having been at the bar. The guilt and shame regarding the site of the assault that was elicited by the reliving the trauma was not alleviated by repeated exposure.
>
> Cognitive challenging was initiated shortly after this pattern became apparent. Maria's dysfunctional cognitions included the thoughts that she was a bad person for having been out at a bar and that she should have known that the situation was dangerous, and thus she was to be blamed for the assault.
>
> As evidence in support of her beliefs, Maria asserted that bars are dangerous places at night. As evidence opposing this belief was that she recalled being there previously without incident, and knew many others who had been there without incident as well. Using this evidence, Maria came to the conclusion that she had had no reason to believe that she was in danger by being at that bar, and that she was a victim of bad luck rather than of bad judgment.
>
> Maria's belief that she was a bad person for having been at the bar was more difficult to challenge. She noted that, on the one hand, she enjoyed going out and having a good time, but that she also disapproved of some of her activities. Cognitive challenging focused on evaluating the usefulness of the thought: "I am a terrible person." She arrived at the understanding that she could choose to go to bars if she decided that going to bars was not a bad thing to do. Or, if she truly felt it was an inappropriate activity, she might be better off not to socialize in this manner. What did not make sense was to continue to go to bars and berate herself for it. As a result of CR, Maria came to the conclusion that although she was unsure whether she wanted to go to bars once she completed the exposure (in which she needed to go to bars to combat her fear of them), she would not let her belief that "a good person does not hang out in bars" stop her from telling others about the assault. Interestingly, by the end of treatment, Maria had still not decided how she wanted to resolve the conflict about socializing, but did discuss the assault with friends. She was surprised that no one else seemed to focus on

the fact that it had occurred outside a bar. This absence of external condemnation appeared to alleviate her sense of shame considerably.

Similar to guilt and shame, extreme anger may not be alleviated by PE. In fact, research has shown that anger may hinder the efficacy of PE, by curbing the engagement with the exposure necessary for emotional processing to occur (Foa, Riggs, Massie, & Yarczower, 1995). In many cases, this problem can be overcome by instructing clients to put aside their anger during exposure practices, with reiteration of the rationale for exposure, and thus PE can proceed effectively. Often, once clients begin to respond to the PE, the anger decreases, and there is no need to address it directly. For clients who are unable or unwilling to redirect their focus from their anger, or who have significant anger following other symptom reduction during PE, cognitive therapy is recommended to target this emotion directly.

Richard is a corrections officer who sought treatment for PTSD following an attack by several inmates. Although he was not sexually assaulted during the attack, the inmates made a number of sexual taunts during the episode, and Richard reported having been afraid the physical beating would escalate to a sexual assault as well.

In his initial treatment session, Richard expressed rage directed at his supervisors for placing him in danger. He was also furious that it had taken so long for others to come to his rescue. In addition, Richard was angry that, although he did not wish to return to his position as a corrections officer, he would not be able to find other employment that would provide a similar salary and benefits. Finally, the presence of the PTSD symptoms themselves angered Richard, making him feel he had lost control over his own emotions.

Richard's therapist noticed that his anger seemed to occur each time he began talking about how frightening the attack had been. Thus, although Richard had several legitimate reasons for being angry, the therapist conceptualized some of his anger as a defense against fear. The therapist explained to Richard that by allowing himself to experience the fear that he felt at the time of the assault, he could begin to process the experience and thus to recover. Richard agreed to begin imaginal exposure and to try to focus on his fear.

The first imaginal exposure session was not successful, in that Richard repeatedly erupted in anger and was unable to refocus on the reliving of the assault. The therapist again emphasized the importance of reexperiencing the assault, and shared with Richard her impressions that it was easier for him to tolerate feeling angry than feeling afraid. Richard stated that being afraid made him "feel like a scared little wimp." The therapist acknowledged Richard's feelings, but pointed out that the fear was there anyway, and that pushing it away was keeping him stuck, with both the fear and the anger. Following this discussion, Richard was able to engage in imaginal exposure and to use his anger as a cue to allow himself to experience the fear, so that he could move past all these unpleasant feelings.

Severe Tension

Clients who get extremely distressed by continuous physical tension may object to engaging in prolonged reliving of the traumatic memory because of the initial increase in physical symptoms. For these clients, the muscle relaxation training component of SIT may be especially helpful. Clients who are hesitant to engage in PE may be more willing to do so once they have mastered anxiety management skills, and thus feel more equipped to handle to a temporary increase in symptoms during exposure.

> Allison is a college student who was raped by an acquaintance at a fraternity party. She sought treatment primarily because of difficulty sleeping, due to both insomnia and nightmares. She also reported extensive avoidance that was interfering with her ability to attend classes and keep up with her schoolwork.
>
> Allison was immersed in the psychoeducation component of the PE treatment, and reported reading the handout "Common Reactions to Assault" frequently, with highlighter in hand. The rationale for exposure was received similarly well. However, as imaginal exposure was initiated, Allison began experiencing headaches that made it difficult for her to focus on the trauma reliving. She tried to take slower breaths as she was telling her story, occasionally pausing to focus on her breathing, but the headaches continued.
>
> In discussing the headaches, Allison noted that she frequently got headaches when stressed, and at times when she was very stressed, such as during final exams, her neck and shoulders would ache so much she had to stop studying and take painkillers. To address this complication, the therapist taught Allison progressive muscle relaxation so that she would have a skill with which to alleviate her muscle tension. Furthermore, the relaxation training included learning to discriminate levels of muscle tension, by deliberate tensing her muscles to different degrees in a series of exercises. In this way, Allison learned to notice muscle tension at lower levels so that she could initiate relaxation before the tension built too much. With this skill in place, Allison was able to successfully complete her exposure treatment and recover from the PTSD.

Dissociative Experiences

On occasion, clients may have difficulty titrating their emotions during imaginal exposure, leading to extended flashbacks. This is detrimental to the efficacy of exposure because it prevents the client from realizing that the situation is a safe place, that she is in control, and that remembering that assault is not akin being assaulted again and thus is not dangerous and does not justify extreme anxiety. When the task of reliving the trauma results in a prolonged dissociative experience, the therapist must modify the exposure procedure to help the client stay grounded in the present reality. This can be done in several ways. Clients can be instructed to keep their eyes open rather than closed, making it more difficult to forget their surroundings. The therapist can introduce safety information during exposure, reminding the client that he or she is in the therapist's office and is safe now, and pointing out that the exposure is merely a memory, not an actual reliving of the rape. For clients who respond well to relaxation skills such as the breathing retraining taught prior to beginning PE, or the muscle relaxation training component of SIT, practicing these skills at the beginning of the exposure session may be useful.

Laurie was a 28-year-old woman who was raped by a coworker. Following the assault, she stopped working and did not return to her workplace even to pick up her paycheck. She also made plans to move away from the neighborhood in which the assault had occurred.

Laurie reported frequent reexperiencing symptoms, but only in response to encounters with assault reminders. She did not have untriggered symptoms such as nightmares. PE was presented as a treatment program that would help her confront the situations she had been avoiding as well as facilitate the processing of the assault experience and thereby reduce her continuous high arousal levels. Although she was quite apprehensive about confronting feared situations *in vivo*, she was quite willing to engage in imaginal reliving of the trauma and anticipated no particular difficulties.

In contrast to her expectation, in her first imaginal exposure practice, Laurie became hysterical. She was clearly reliving the assault "as if it was happening now" instead of retaining the perspective that the rape had occurred in the past, and that remembering is not akin to the actual occurrence of the rape. As she narrated the story, her arms flailed as if to fight off the attacker and her voice rose in terror, and then dropped to a whisper. Realizing that Laurie entered a dissociative state, the therapist asked Laurie to open her eyes in order to continue the exposure in a way that would incorporate safety information into the reliving experience. When she opened her eyes, Laurie was clearly shaken by the experience and asked to discontinue the exposure. The remainder of the session focused on discussing her dissociative state and on reassuring Laurie.

Following the session, the therapist and her supervisor discussed ways in which Laurie could be helped to do imaginal exposure without entering a dissociative state. Laurie was asked to keep her eyes open, and the therapist sat close to her with an arm on her chair so that Laurie could reach over to feel the therapist's presence if she wished. The therapist also introduced more reassuring comments during exposure than she had initially, frequently praising Laurie's ability to continue with the reliving, and reminding her it was just a memory.

Laurie's response to imaginal exposure is quite rare. More commonly, clients exhibit difficulty engaging in the rape memory and report feeling emotionally numb when trying to capture the fear that they experienced during the traumatic event. Again, a reiteration of the rationale for exposure, emphasizing the importance of emotional engagement while reliving the trauma, may overcome this problem. Therapists may also use increased prompting during the trauma reliving to enhance the image, or incorporate other cues such as playing music that triggers memories of the assault. Clients who are unable to engage in the imaginal exposure may respond more to *in vivo* exposure, especially if the difficulty lies more in imaginal ability than in ability to engage emotionally, and in these cases focusing more on the *in vivo* exposure may be preferable to continuing imaginal exposure. For clients who cannot engage in either form of exposure, switching to another treatment such as SIT is warranted.

> Loretta is a former police officer who developed PTSD following a rape 3 years prior to treatment. She had to leave the police force shortly after the rape, due to the psychological difficulties that arose. Loretta sought treatment after discovering that leaving the force did not alleviate her symptoms.
>
> In the first exposure session, Loretta engaged well, reporting SUDs levels between 60 and 85. In the next two sessions, however, she was unable to engage emotionally and reported SUDs no higher than 30. Her therapist encouraged her to recount the rape with more detail, and with more attention to her feelings, but she continued to have difficulty engaging.
>
> In the fourth session, the therapist initiated a discussion about Loretta's inability to experience fear during the exposure. Loretta explained her difficulty letting go of her emotions as follows:
>
> "I used to be a very strong person, in the police force, and it was a big part of my personality. I'm afraid to go back there (to the rape) because I don't want to be weak. I'm just starting to feel strong and good about myself again. If I let myself have those feelings, I'll be weak again."
>
> Loretta's belief that fear equals weakness was challenged via cognitive therapy. Loretta substituted this belief with acknowledgment that she had many strengths, and that her ability to face the rape and the associated feelings reflected strength rather than weakness. This cognitive shift enabled Loretta to become more emotionally engaged during exposure, and treatment was quite successful in reducing her PTSD symptoms. (adapted from Jaycox & Foa, 1996.)

OTHER ISSUES IN PTSD TREATMENT DECISION MAKING

Time Elapsed since the Assault

The majority of the studies described throughout this chapter included women treated at least 3 months postassault, who were thus considered to have chronic PTSD. This inclusion criterion allows for greater confidence in the studies' results, as it precludes improvement from being attributed to the natural recovery that often follows assault. However, several researchers have also examined the use of interventions shortly following an assault or other traumatic event; although many crisis intervention programs have been reported on, most have not yet been rigorously studied; thus their efficacy is yet to be determined (cf. Foa & Meadows, 1997). Foa and her colleagues (Foa, Hearst-Ikeda, & Perry, 1995) examined a brief program for women with acute postassault reactions, modeled after their chronic PTSD treatment programs. This program included psychoeducation, breathing retraining, muscle relaxation, imaginal and *in vivo* exposure, and cognitive restructuring. Results of this pilot study were encouraging, and a larger scale study testing this intervention is currently in progress. It should be noted that this brief program was instituted approximately 2 weeks posttrauma, rather than immediately following the event. Foa and Meadows (1997) suggest that such a delay might enhance women's ability to benefit from the intervention, as many assault survivors are in a state of shock immediately postassault and may not be in a position to process information at that time.

PTSD Related to Childhood Sexual Abuse

This chapter focuses primarily on women who have been assaulted in adulthood. However, there is considerable evidence suggesting that many women raped as adults also have histories of childhood sexual abuse (CSA; e.g., Briere & Runtz, 1988; Wyatt, Guthrie, & Notgrass, 1992). This has two implications for the current review. First, many women treated for rape-related PTSD may also be CSA survivors. Second, PTSD may also develop from CSA, and the generalizability of the treatments studied with survivors of adulthood assault to CSA survivors must be examined.

With regard to the first issue, although earlier studies sometimes excluded women with incest histories (e.g., Resick et al., 1988), more recent studies (e.g., Foa et al., 1998) have tended not to do so. Similarly, diagnoses often associated with CSA, such as borderline personality disorder, have also not ruled women out of many recent studies, although acute suicidality would preclude women from participating in most treatment outcome studies for ethical reasons. We recommend that, due to the increased likelihood of CSA history or comorbid diagnoses in a subsample of rape survivors, clinical researchers continue to allow such women into their studies, so that these variables may be more systematically examined. Given the positive outcomes seen in the studies reviewed that have not excluded these women, it seems likely that clinicians need not modify treatment based solely on previous trauma history or comorbid psychopathology, unless these are associated with the other difficulties detailed in the earlier section on decision making.

Dancu, Foa, and Smucker (1993) demonstrated in a pilot study that SIT and PE, shown to be effective for PTSD stemming from adulthood assaults, are also helpful for women with PTSD resulting from CSA.

PE is also being examined as a treatment for CSA-related PTSD in two randomized clinical trials. One study, conducted by Friedman, McDonagh-Coyle, McHugo, and colleagues, is comparing a cognitive behavioral treatment including PE and CR with a "present-centered treatment" that includes psychoeducation and general support and attention but omits specific interventions such as imaginal and *in vivo* exposure. These treatments are also compared with a wait-list control group. No empirical results are available yet, but Friedman (personal communication, September 11, 1997) noted that most of the women in the PE condition appear to tolerate the exposure well.

The second study of CSA-related PTSD treatment has already been reviewed; Foa and colleagues recently expanded their PTSD treatment outcome study (PE, PE–CR, and wait list) to include women with CSA as well as those assaulted as adults. Results are not yet available for the CSA outcomes of the study.

SUMMARY

A number of cognitive-behavioral treatment approaches have been found to alleviate the symptoms of intrusion, avoidance, and arousal commonly seen in individuals who have been sexually assaulted. One of these approaches, PE, has the most evidence for its efficacy, and it seems to be the easiest to learn (Foa & Rothbaum, 1997). SIT has also demonstrated efficacy in several studies; thus, despite its increased complexity relative to PE, it provides a viable alternative for treating rape-related PTSD. Both cognitive therapy and cognitive processing therapy have shown promising results but have fewer well-controlled studies supporting them as yet. However, both these treatments continue to be subjects of PTSD treatment outcome research and may therefore be shown in the future to be valid alternatives to PE. Additionally, these other treatments may be especially useful as adjuncts to PE.

Given this summary, we recommend that PE be the primary treatment for rape-related PTSD. In some circumstances, as outlined in this chapter, the exposure methods may require modification or adjunctive approaches to enhance their efficacy. For clients for whom exposure is not indicated, or for those clients who cannot tolerate the exposure treatment, SIT, CPT, and CR are appropriate alternatives.

REFERENCES

Barlow, D. H., Leitenberg, H., Agras, W. S., & Wincze, J. P. (1969). The transfer gap in systematic desensitization: An analog study. *Behaviour Research and Therapy, 7,* 191–196.

Beck, A. T. (1972). *Depression: Causes and treatment.* Philadelphia: University of Pennsylvania Press.

Beck, A. T., Emery, G., & Greenberg, R. L. (1985). *Anxiety disorders and phobias: A cognitive perspective.* New York: Basic Books.

Beck, A. T., Rush, A. J., Shaw, B. F., & Emery, G. (1979). *Cognitive therapy of depression.* New York: Guilford Press.

Boudewyns, P. A., & Hyer, L. (1990). Physiological response to combat memories and preliminary treatment outcome in Vietnam veteran PTSD patients treated with direct therapeutic exposure. *Behavior Therapy, 21,* 63–87.

Boudewyns, P. A., Hyer, L., Woods, M. G., Harrison, W. R., & McCranie, E. (1990). PTSD among Vietnam veterans: An early look at treatment outcome using direct therapeutic exposure. *Journal of Traumatic Stress, 3,* 359–368.

Breslau, N., Davis, G. C., Andreski, P., & Peterson, E. (1991). Traumatic events and posttraumatic stress disorder in an urban population of young adults. *Archives of General Psychiatry, 48,* 216–222.

Briere, J., & Runtz, M. (1988). Post sexual abuse trauma: Data and implications for clinical practice. *Journal of Interpersonal Violence, 2,* 367–379.

Brom, D., Kleber, R. J., & Defares, P. B. (1989). Brief psychotherapy for posttraumatic stress disorders. *Journal of Consulting and Clinical Psychology, 57,* 607–612.

Clark, D. M. (1986). A cognitive approach to panic. *Behaviour Research and Therapy, 24,* 461–470.

Cooper, N. A., & Clum, G. A. (1989). Imaginal flooding as a supplementary treatment for PTSD in combat veterans: A controlled study. *Behavior Therapy, 20,* 381–391.

Cottler, L. B., Compton, W. M., Mager, D., Spitznagel, E. L., & Janca, A. (1992). Posttraumatic stress disorder among substance users from the general population. *American Journal of Psychiatry, 149,* 664–670.

Dancu, C. V., & Foa, E. B. (in press). Treatment of rape victims. In A. R. Kuczmierczyk (Ed.), *Handbook of Behavioral Obstetrics and Gynecology.* New York: Plenum.

Dancu, C. V., Foa, E. B., & Smucker, M. R. (1993, October). *Cognitive-behavioral treatment of survivors of childhood sexual abuse with PTSD.* Paper presented at the ninth annual meeting of the International Society for Traumatic Stress Studies, San Antonio, TX.

Epstein, R. S. (1989). Posttraumatic stress disorder: A review of diagnostic and treatment issues. *Psychiatric Annals, 19,* 556–563.

Fairbank, J. A., & Keane, T. M. (1982). Flooding for combat-related stress disorders: Assessment of anxiety reduction across traumatic memories. *Behavior Therapy, 13,* 499–510.

Finkelhor, D., Hotaling, G., Lewis, I. A., & Smith, C. (1990). Sexual abuse in a national survey of adult men and women: Prevalence, characteristics, and risk factors. *Child Abuse and Neglect, 14,* 19–28.

Foa, E. B., Dancu, C. V., Hembree, E., Jaycox, L. H., Meadows, E. A., & Street, G. (in press). The efficacy of exposure therapy, stress inoculation training, and their combination in ameliorating PTSD for female victims of assault. *Journal of Consulting and Clinical Psychology.*

Foa, E. B., Hearst-Ikeda, D. E., Dancu, C. V., Hembree, E., & Jaycox, L. H. (1994). *Prolonged exposure manual for assault victims.* Unpublished manual.

Foa, E. B., Hearst-Ikeda, D., & Perry, K. J. (1995). Evaluation of a brief cognitive-behavioral program for the prevention of chronic PTSD in recent assault victims. *Journal of Consulting and Clinical Psychology, 63,* 948–955.

Foa, E. B., & Jaycox, L. H. (in press). Cognitive-behavioral treatment of post-traumatic stress disorder. In D. Spiegel (Ed.), *Psychotherapeutic frontiers: New principles and practices*. Washington, DC: American Psychiatric Association Press.

Foa, E. B., Jaycox, L. H., Meadows, E. A., Hembree, E., & Dancu, C. V. (1996, November). Preliminary efficacy of prolonged exposure (PE) vs. PE and cognitive restructuring for PTSD in female assault victims. In P. Resick (Chair), *Treating sexual assault/sexual abuse pathology: Recent findings*. Paper presented at the annual meeting of the Association for Advancement of Behavior Therapy, New York.

Foa, E. B., & Kozak, M. J. (1986). Emotional processing of fear: Exposure to corrective information. *Psychological Bulletin, 99*, 20–35.

Foa, E. B., & Meadows, E. A. (1997). Psychosocial treatments for post-traumatic stress disorder: A critical review. In J. Spence, J. M. Darley, & D. J. Foss (Eds.), *Annual review of psychology* (Vol. 48, pp. 449–480). Palo Alto, CA: Annual Reviews.

Foa, E. B., Riggs, D. S., Massie, E. D., & Yarczower, M. (1995). The impact of fear activation and anger on the efficacy of exposure treatment for PTSD. *Behavior Therapy, 26*, 487–499.

Foa, E. B., & Rothbaum, B. O. (1998). *Treating the trauma of rape: Cognitive-behavioral therapy for PTSD*. New York: Guilford Press.

Foa, E. B., Rothbaum, B. O., Riggs, D. S., & Murdock, T. B. (1991). Treatment of posttraumatic stress disorder in rape victims: A comparison between cognitive-behavioral procedures and counseling. *Journal of Consulting and Clinical Psychology, 59*, 715–723.

Frank, E., Anderson, B., Stewart, B. D., Dancu, C., Hughes, C., & West, D. (1988). Efficacy of cognitive behavior therapy and systematic desensitization in the treatment of rape trauma. *Behavior Therapy, 19*, 403–420.

Frank, E., & Stewart, B. D. (1983). Physical aggression: Treating the victims. In E. A. Blechman (Ed.), *Behavior modification with women* (pp. 245–272). New York: Guilford Press.

Frank, E., & Stewart, B. D. (1984). Depressive symptoms in rape victims. *Journal of Affective Disorders, 1*, 269–277.

Frieze, I.H., & Browne, A. (1989). Violence in marriage. In L. Ohlin & M. Toney (Eds.), *Family violence. Crime and Justice: A review of the research* (pp. 163–218). Chicago: University of Chicago Press.

Helzer, J. E., Robins, L. N., & McEvoy, L. (1987). Post-traumatic stress disorder in the general population: Findings to the Epidemiologic Catchment Area survey. *New England Journal of Medicine, 317*, 1630–1634.

Janoff-Bulman, R. (1992). *Shattered assumptions: Towards a new psychology of trauma*. New York: Free Press.

Jaycox, L. H., & Foa, E. B. (1996). Obstacles in implementing exposure therapy for PTSD: Case discussions and practical solutions. *Clinical Psychology and Psychotherapy, 3*, 176–184.

Johnson, C. H., Gilmore, J. D., & Shenoy, R. Z. (1982). Use of a feeding procedure in the treatment of a stress-related anxiety disorder. *Journal of Behavior Therapy and Experimental Psychiatry, 13*, 235–237.

Keane, T. M., & Kaloupek, D. G. (1982). Imaginal flooding in the treatment of post-traumatic stress disorder. *Journal of Consulting and Clinical Psychology, 50*, 138–140.

Keane, T. M., Fairbank, J. A., Caddell, J. M., & Zimering, R. T. (1989). Implosive (flooding) therapy reduces symptoms of PTSD in Vietnam combat veterans. *Behavior Therapy, 20*, 245–260.

Kessler, R. C., Sonnega, A., Bromet, E., Hughes, M., & Nelson, C. B. (1995). Posttraumatic stress disorder in the National Comorbidity Survey. *Archives of General Psychiatry, 52*, 1048–1060.

Kilpatrick, D. G., & Calhoun, K. S. (1988). Early behavioral treatment for rape trauma: Efficacy or artifact? *Behavior Therapy, 19*, 421–427.

Kilpatrick, D. G., Saunders, B. E., Veronen, L. J., Best, C. L., & Von, J. M. (1987). Criminal victimization: Lifetime prevalence, reporting to police, and psychological impact. *Crime and Delinquency, 33*, 479–489.

Kilpatrick, D. G., Veronen, L. J., & Resick, P. A. (1982). Psychological sequelae to rape: Assessment and treatment strategies. In D. M. Doleys, R. L. Meredith, & A. R. Ciminero (Eds.), *Behavioral medicine: Assessment and treatment strategies* (pp. 473–497). New York: Plenum.

Koss, M. P. (1993). Detecting the scope of rape: A review of prevalence research methods. *Journal of Interpersonal Violence, 8*, 198–222.

Lang, P. J. (1979). A bio-informational theory of emotional imagery. *Psychophysiology, 6*, 495–511.

Marks, I., Lovell, K., Noshirvani, H., Livanou, M., & Thrasher, S. (1998). Treatment of posttraumatic stress disorder by exposure and/or cognitive restructuring. *Archives of General Psychiatry, 55*, 317–325.

McCann, I. L., & Pearlman, L. A. (1990). *Psychological trauma and the adult survivor: Theory, therapy, and transformation.* New York: Brunner/Mazel.

McCann, I. L., Sakheim, D. K., & Abrahamson, D. J. (1988). Trauma and victimization: A model of psychological adaptation. *Counseling Psychologist, 16*, 531–594.

McLeer, S. V., Deblinger, E., Atkins, M. S., Foa, E. B., & Ralphe, D. L. (1988). Posttraumatic stress disorder in sexually abused children. *Journal of the American Academy of Child and Adolescent Psychiatry, 27*, 650–654.

Meichenbaum, D. (1974). Self-instructional methods. In F. H. Kanfer & A. P. Goldstein (Eds.), *Helping people change* (pp. 357–391). New York: Pergamon Press.

Mowrer, O. A. (1960). *Learning theory and behavior.* New York: Wiley.

Norris, F. H. (1992). Epidemiology of trauma: Frequency and impact of different potentially traumatic events on different demographic groups. *Journal of Consulting and Clinical Psychology, 60*, 409–418.

North, C. S., & Smith, E. M. (1992). Posttraumatic stress disorder among homeless men and women. *Hospital and Community Psychiatry, 43*, 1010–1016.

Pearson, M. A., Poquette, B. M., & Wasden, R. E. (1983). Stress inoculation and the treatment of post-rape trauma: A case report. *Behavior Therapy, 6*, 58–59.

Rescorla, R. A. (1988). Pavlovian conditioning: It's not what you think it is. *American Psychologist, 43*, 151–160.

Resnick, H. S., Kilpatrick, D. G., Dansky, B. S., Saunders, B. E., & Best, C. L. (1993). Prevalence of civilian trauma and posttraumatic stress disorder in a representative national sample of women. *Journal of Consulting and Clinical Psychology, 61*, 984–991.

Resick, P. A., Jordan, C. G., Girelli, S. A., Hutter, C. K., & Marhoefer-Dvorak, S. (1988). A comparative outcome study of group behavioral therapy for sexual assault victims. *Behavior Therapy, 19*, 385–401.

Resick, P. A., & Schnicke, M. K. (1992a). Cognitive processing therapy for sexual assault victims. *Journal of Consulting and Clinical Psychology, 60*, 748–756.

Resick, P. A. & Schnicke, M. K. (1992b, October). Cognitive processing therapy for sexual assault victims. In E. B. Foa (Chair), *Treatment of PTSD: An update*. Paper presented at the eighth annual meeting of the International Society for Traumatic Stress Studies, Los Angeles, CA.

Richards, D. A., Lovell, K., & Marks, I. M. (1994). Post-traumatic stress disorder: Evaluation of a behavioral treatment program. *Journal of Traumatic Stress, 7*, 669–680.

Rothbaum, B. O. (1997). A controlled study of eye movement desensitization and reprocessing in the treatment of posttraumatic stress disordered sexual assault victims. *Bulletin of the Menninger Clinic, 61*, 317–334.

Rothbaum, B. O., Foa, E. B., Murdock, T., Riggs, D. S., & Walsh, W. (1992). A prospective examination of post-traumatic stress disorder in rape victims. *Journal of Traumatic Stress, 5*, 455–475.

Rowan, A. B., Foy, D. W., Rodriguez, N., & Ryan, S. (1994). Posttraumatic stress disorder in a clinical sample of adults sexually abused as children. *Child Abuse and Neglect, 18*, 51–61.

Shapiro, F. (1995). *Eye movement desensitization and reprocessing: Basic principles, protocols, and procedures*. New York: Guilford Press.

Stampfl, T.G., & Levis, D.J. (1967). Essentials of implosive therapy: A learning-theory-based psychodynamic behavioral therapy. *Journal of Abnormal Psychology, 72*, 496–503.

Stern, R. S., & Marks, I. M. (1973). Brief and prolonged flooding: A comparison in agoraphobic patients. *Archives of General Psychiatry, 28*, 270–276.

Suinn, R. (1974). Anxiety management training for general anxiety. In R. Suinn & R. Weigel (Eds.), *The innovative therapy: Critical and creative contributions* (pp. 66–70). New York: Harper & Row.

Thompson, J. A., Charlton, P. F. C., Kerry, R., Lee, D., & Turner, S. W. (1995). An open trial of exposure therapy based on deconditioning for post-traumatic stress disorder. *British Journal of Clinical Psychiatry, 34*, 407–416.

Veronen, L. J., & Kilpatrick, D. G. (1982, November). *Stress innoculation training for victims of rape: Efficacy and differential findings*. Paper presented at the 16th annual convention of the Association for Advancement of Behavior Therapy, Los Angeles, CA.

Watts, F. N. (1979). Habituation model of systematic desensitization. *Psychological Bulletin, 86*, 627–637.

Wolpe, J. (1958). *Psychotherapy by reciprocal inhibition*. Stanford, CA: Stanford University Press.

Wyatt, G. E., Guthrie, D., & Notgrass, C. M. (1992). Differential effects of women's child sexual abuse and subsequent revictimization. *Journal of Consulting and Clinical Psychology, 60*, 167–173.

C H A P T E R   S I X

Cognitive Therapy
for Trauma-Related Guilt

EDWARD S. KUBANY

There is widespread agreement among traumatologists that how trauma survivors intellectually process, judge, or assign meaning to the trauma is an important factor in posttrauma adjustment (Foa, Steketee, & Rothbaum, 1989; Kubany & Manke, 1995; Roth, Liebowitz, & DeRosa, 1997). The role of meaning in trauma has been studied under various labels, including survivor "appraisals," internal and external "attributions" (e.g., Andrews & Brewin, 1990), "maladaptive beliefs" (e.g., Resick & Schnicke, 1993), explanations "why" the trauma occurred (e.g., Frazier & Schauben, 1994), narrative "trauma themes" (Newman, Riggs, & Roth, 1997), "self-blame" (e.g., Miller & Porter, 1983), "behavioral and characterological" self-blame (e.g., Janoff-Bulman, 1985), "assimilation and accommodation" (Resick & Schnicke, 1993), "cognitive schemata" (Dutton, Burghardt, Perrin, Chrestman, & Halle, 1994), "pathogenic schemas" (Smucker & Niederee, 1995), and "errors of logic" and "faulty conclusions" (Kubany & Manke, 1995). Despite this diversity of labels, much of the research on the role of cognition in trauma has focused on survivors' phenomenology of their role in the trauma, much of which relates to guilt and self-blame.

Research reviewed elsewhere shows that trauma-related guilt is a common problem for survivors of many different kinds of traumatic events—including survivors of combat, physical and sexual abuse, technological disasters, and surviving family members of victims of accidents, suicide, homicide, and sudden illness (Kubany et al., 1995; Kubany & Manke, 1995). Our own research, using a recently validated Trauma-Related Guilt Inventory, documents that trauma-related guilt is pervasive both within and across survivor groups (Kubany et al., 1996; Kubany, Haynes, Owens, et al., 1997). In one series of studies, trauma-related guilt was assessed in 74 Vietnam War veterans and 168 treatment-seeking battered women (Kubany et al., 1996). Nearly two-thirds of the veterans reported moderate or greater guilt related to trauma in Vietnam, and almost one-third reported guilt in the considerable to extreme range. Among the battered women, almost half reported moderate or greater guilt related to their abuse, and approximately one in four reported guilt in the considerable to extreme range. Only 6 of 168 women (4%) reported no abuse-related guilt. In a study of treatment-seeking female survivors of rape and incest, 54% of the incest survivors and 68% of the rape survivors reported moderate or greater guilt related to their victimization (Kubany, Haynes, Owens, et al., 1997).

TRAUMA-RELATED GUILT
AND OTHER PSYCHOPATHOLOGY

Research by other investigators indicates that trauma-related guilt is correlated with depression and suicidal ideation among trauma survivors (see Kubany et al., 1995, and Kubany & Manke, 1995, for brief reviews). In our own research with Vietnam War veterans and battered women, trauma-related guilt has been highly positively correlated with posttraumatic stress disorder (PTSD), depression, negative self-esteem, shame, social anxiety and avoidance, and suicidal thoughts (Kubany et al., 1995; Kubany et al., 1996). We have also found significant positive relationships between cognitive aspects of guilt and psychopathology. In studies with 58 Vietnam War veterans and 50 battered women, measures of PTSD and depression were significantly correlated with multiple-choice items assessing beliefs about causal responsibility, justifiability of actions taken, wrongdoing, and preoutcome knowledge (Kubany et al., 1995). In another study with 74 Vietnam veterans and 68 battered women, scores on the Guilt Cognitions scale of the Trauma-Related Guilt Inventory were significantly correlated with measures of depression, PTSD, negative self-esteem, shame, social anxiety and avoidance, and suicidal ideation (Kubany et al., 1996).

Guilt was a core feature of PTSD in DSM-III, but was relegated to associated feature status in DSM-III-R and DSM-IV (American Psychiatric Association, 1994). One of the reasons for this diminished status is that in the DSM, PTSD-related guilt is restricted narrowly to concerns about *survival*. My colleagues and I have noted elsewhere that many important trauma-related guilt issues are unrelated to survival concerns (e.g., Kubany et al., 1996). In light of the pervasiveness and severity of guilt among trauma survivors, we believe that guilt should be considered to be a key feature of PTSD and will be a key feature again when DSM-V is introduced (e.g., Foa, 1993). Furthermore, although needing substantiation in controlled research, it has been my experience that guilt and guilt-related beliefs play an important causal role in the maintenance and perpetuation of posttraumatic stress, depression, and low self-esteem.

A GUIDING CONCEPTUALIZATION OF GUILT

There is widespread agreement that guilt has both affective and cognitive dimensions (Kubany, 1997a; Kubany et al., 1995). My colleagues and I have argued for a conceptualization of guilt in which cognitive elements play an extremely important role. We have identified four cognitive dimensions or components of guilt, which include (1) perceived responsibility for causing a negative outcome, (2) perceived lack of justification for actions taken, (3) perceived wrongdoing or violation of values, and (4) beliefs about preoutcome knowledge (e.g., Fischhoff, 1975; Kubany et al., 1995). Consistent with appraisal theories of emotion (e.g., Ellsworth, 1994), we have defined guilt as *an unpleasant feeling accompanied by a belief (or beliefs) that one should have thought, felt, or acted differently*. This definition has guided our theoretical work on guilt (e.g., Kubany, 1997a; Kubany et al., 1995), our guilt assessment research (e.g., Kubany et al., 1996), and our development of a cognitive therapy model, which is the topic of this chapter.

ERRONEOUS THINKING AMONG TRAUMA SURVIVORS

Faulty Conclusions and Trauma-Related Guilt

Several investigators have observed that many trauma survivors exaggerate or distort the importance of their roles in traumatic events and often experience guilt that has little or no rational basis (see Kubany & Manke, 1995). Kubany and Manke observed that trauma survivors tend to draw four kinds of faulty conclusions concerning their roles in trauma, each of which involves distortion of a cognitive component of guilt. First, many survivors believe they "knew" what was going to happen before it was possible to know, or that they dismissed or overlooked clues that "signaled" what was going to occur (*hindsight bias*; Fischhoff, 1975; Kubany & Manke, 1995). Second, many survivors believe that their trauma-related actions were less justified than would be concluded on the basis of an objective analysis of the facts (*justification distortion*). Third, many survivors accept an inordinate share of responsibility for causing the trauma or related negative outcomes (*responsibility distortion*). Fourth, many survivors believe they violated personal or moral convictions, even though their intentions and actions were consistent with their convictions (*wrongdoing distortion*).

Thinking Errors That Lead to Faulty Conclusions

Kubany and Manke (1995) identified 15 thinking errors that can lead trauma survivors to draw faulty conclusions related to the experience of guilt (also see Kubany, 1997b). Each of these thinking errors is briefly described here.

A Thinking Error That Causes Faulty Beliefs about Preoutcome Knowledge

(PK1) Hindsight-biased thinking. The term "hindsight bias" comes from social psychology and reflects the fact that outcome knowledge tends to bias people's recollections of what they actually knew before events occurred (Fischhoff, 1975; Hawkins & Hastie, 1990). Hindsight bias can lead survivors to conclude that there were signs or clues signaling what was going to happen when signs or clues did not exist or were never perceived; thus, many survivors remember themselves as "knowing" what they did not know. Hindsight-biased thinking is signaled by use of phrases such as, "I should have . . . I could have . . . I saw it coming . . . It was foreseeable." An example is in the following statements by grandparents who lost a grandchild to sudden infant death syndrome (SIDS): "I should have been able to detect a problem . . . I wondered if I could have prevented it" (De Frain, Jacub, & Mendoza, 1992, p. 170).

Seven Thinking Errors That Contribute to Faulty Conclusions about Justification

(J1) Failure to recognize that different decision-making "rules" apply when time is precious than in situations that allow extended contemplation of options. During many traumatic events (e.g., earthquakes, sexual assaults, ambushes during combat), time is precious, and split-second decision making, under extremely stressful conditions, is often required. The quality of decisions having life-and-death implications and made under the pressure of time should not be evaluated against the quality of decisions made after extended contemplation of alternatives.

(J2) Weighing the merits of actions taken against options that only came to mind later. In trying to understand "why" the trauma occurred, many survivors psychologically rehash or replay the trauma over and over. In so doing, they sometimes think of something they "could have" done to prevent or mitigate some tragic outcome—*had it occurred to them prior to or during the trauma.* It is a serious mistake when survivors evaluate their trauma-related actions against "options" that did not perceptually exist when the trauma occurred.

(J3) Weighing the merits of actions taken against ideal or fantasy options that did not exist. Some trauma survivors evaluate their actions during the trauma against idealized (but *unavailable*) "options" that "would have avoided the rape, prevented the beating, stopped the incest, or kept everyone safe and alive" (Kubany & Manke, 1995, p. 38). This thinking error is discussed in a case study later in this chapter of a formerly battered woman who felt guilty about not having left her abusive husband sooner.

(J4) Focusing only on "good" things that might have happened had an alternative action been taken. Sometimes, trauma-related actions that were contemplated but rejected look much better in retrospect than they did when they were

originally considered. For example, some rape victims focus on the possibility that they might have eluded the rape had they fought back and downplay or fail to remember the risks that would have been associated with fighting back. A combat veteran who experienced guilt about withdrawing from an ambush without a missing buddy assumed that he and his platoon could have stayed until they found their buddy *without risk* to everyone else's life (Kubany, 1997c, p. 229).

(J5) Tendency to overlook "benefits" associated with actions taken. Sometimes, trauma survivors validate important values by their trauma-related actions and fail to realize that these values would have been invalidated to some degree had other courses of action been chosen. A Vietnam War veteran who felt guilty about violating "personal, moral, and religious values by taking human lives" argued that he never should put himself in a situation where he would have to choose between killing and getting killed, and should have gone to Canada instead (Kubany, 1997c). In addition to the fact that he did not *know* what he was going to encounter in Vietnam, he also failed to recognize that several important values were validated by his decision to go. For example, he validated central beliefs about himself as a loyal, patriotic American committed to doing his share and serving his country.

(J6) Failure to compare available options in terms of their perceived probabilities of success before outcomes were known. Sometimes, knowledge of outcomes so colors survivors' perceptions about what they think they should have done during the trauma that they completely disregard or "forget" what they thought was likely to happen when they were deciding what to do. For example, during the Vietnam War, many excellent military decisions had adverse consequences because of the operation of unknown factors and chance. This does not mean that choices perceived as having a low probability of success (before outcomes were known) should have been selected.

(J7) Failure to realize that (a) acting on speculative hunches rarely pays off and (b) occurrence of a low probability event is not evidence that one should have "bet" on this outcome before it occurred. Some trauma survivors criticize themselves for not having acted on hunches, intuition, premonitions, or gut feelings— which, if acted upon, might have avoided or lessened the impact of the trauma. For example, a rape survivor recently said to me, "I had a feeling I shouldn't have gone to that party" (where she was assaulted) even though she had absolutely no prior evidence that going to the party posed a danger. People do not ordinarily act on highly speculative hunches, hypotheses, or superstitious thoughts because such ideas do not reliably predict what is going to happen.

Four Thinking Errors That Contribute to Faulty Conclusions about Causal Responsibility

(R1) Hindsight-biased thinking. Hindsight-biased thinking can also lead trauma survivors to conclude that they are to some extent responsible for causing

the trauma because they did not act to prevent an "avoidable" and "foreseeable" outcome. For example, a former client believed that she was completely responsible for exposing her 4-year-old daughter to the trauma of seeing an elephant go on a violent and lethal rampage during a circus performance. Her reasoning was that "I chose to go to the circus at the end of the circus run, when animals are probably tired; trainers are probably tired. Just irresponsible. I was trying to fit it into my schedule."

(R2) Obliviousness to the totality of forces that cause traumatic events. Many trauma survivors appear to be completely unaware of the myriad people, forces, or factors outside of themselves that contribute to the occurrence of traumatic events. For example, an incest survivor who was self-condemning about getting involved in prostitution at age 14 said that she, alone, was responsible for that "choice." This woman completely disregarded a multiplicity of external factors that may have contributed to "her" decision: (a) the incest that lowered her self-esteem and life expectations (e.g., "I'm already damaged goods; what difference does it make?"); (b) the lack of public education about prostitution and sexual abuse; (c) vulnerability associated with homelessness (she had run away to escape the incest); (d) lack of money and (e) lack of social support; (f) pimps; (g) organized crime; (h) inadequate police and judicial enforcement; (i) widespread availability of illicit drugs; and (j) a societal context in which women are sexualized and considered by many as the "less than" gender.

(R3) Equating a belief that one could have done something to prevent a traumatic event with a belief that one caused the event. Although completely illogical, many trauma survivors equate beliefs that they "could have prevented" some tragic outcome with beliefs that they "caused" the outcome. For example, a battered woman who thinks that she provoked or caused her abuse by "talking back" did *not* cause the bruises on her face.

(R4) Confusion between responsibility as accountability (e.g., one's "job") and responsibility as power to cause or control outcomes. Many people believe falsely that when they are given a job or "put in charge," they have complete causal responsibility for negative outcomes associated with that role. For example, just because a Vietnam War army platoon leader was in command, it does not mean that he had the power to keep all of his men alive. Similarly, many parents hold themselves responsible for serious misfortunes that befall their children even though they do not have the superhuman power to foresee and prevent every conceivable bad thing that could happen to their children (e.g., genetic diseases, unforeseeable accidents, random acts of violence; see Rando, 1986).

Three Thinking Errors That Contribute to Faulty Conclusions about Wrongdoing

(W1) Tendency to conclude wrongdoing on the basis of the outcome rather than on the basis of one's intentions (before the outcome was known). When tragic

events occur, some survivors believe they violated their values simply because something bad happened and they were there—*irrespective* of their intentions or inability to influence the outcome. Even when the outcome was unforeseeable and their actions were entirely consistent with their values, some survivors will believe they "should have done more." For example, many innocent incest and rape survivors think they did something "wrong" and feel "dirty," or "ashamed" "just because it happened" and because of religious teachings about purity and sexual behavior.

(W2) *Failure to realize that strong emotional reactions are not under voluntary control (i.e., not a matter of choice or willpower).* Some incest and rape survivors feel "betrayed" by their bodies for being paralyzed with fear or by experiencing sexual arousal during the abuse. Similarly, many combat veterans experience guilt for having had debilitating fear reactions during combat. They may believe they "should have been able to control" their emotions and conclude they violated values by virtue of their failure to adhere to (unattainable) personal standards or expectations. It is important for trauma survivors to know that strong positive and negative emotional reactions are not intellectual "choices." For example, none of the combat veterans wanted to be afraid, and if they had had "choice control" over their emotions, they would chosen *not* to have been afraid.

(W3) *Failure to recognize that when all available options have negative outcomes, the least bad choice is a highly moral choice.* In some traumatic situations, no good choices are available, and no matter what a victim chooses to do, something bad is going to happen. For example, sexual assault victims can fight back and risk being seriously hurt or killed, or they can submit. Faced with such situations, some survivors will believe they violated their values because they deliberately "chose" to cause or "allow" a negative outcome to occur (e.g., "I just lay there and let it happen"). Trauma survivors need to know that if all their choices had negative consequences, their "least bad" choice was a sound and moral choice.

A Thinking Error That Contributes to All of the Faulty Conclusions

Belief that affect associated with a thought or idea is evidence *that the idea is valid or correct.* The presence of this thinking error is usually signaled by the phrase "I feel" in statements about beliefs, such as "I *feel* responsible," "I *feel* that what I did was wrong," or "To think that I shouldn't feel guilty makes me *feel* like I'm trying to squirm out of something." Affect associated with an idea appears to give the idea a ring of "truth" or "untruth"; however, the intensity of feelings associated with an idea is *not* evidence of the accuracy of the idea. Moreover, when feelings are used as evidence for the accuracy of an idea, judgment and objectivity are often impaired. For example, one of the reasons why some battered women make choices that are not in their best interests (e.g., deciding to stay in or return to a lethal situation) is that their decisions are driven by their feelings instead of logic.

OVERVIEW OF COGNITIVE THERAPY
FOR TRAUMA-RELATED GUILT

The goal of cognitive therapy for trauma-related guilt (CT-TRG) is to help clients achieve an objective and accurate appraisal of their roles in trauma. There are three phases in CT-TRG: (1) assessment, (2) guilt incident debriefings, and (3) CT-TRG proper, which involves separate, semistructured procedures for correcting thinking errors that lead to faulty conclusions associated with guilt. Figure 6.1 is a diagrammatic representation of procedures employed in CT-TRG and the order in which they are usually followed. The figure also shows at which stage during CT-TRG each of the thinking errors is most likely to be discussed. The main procedures used in CT-TRG are briefly discussed below. These procedures are described and illustrated in greater detail elsewhere (Kubany; 1997c; Kubany & Manke, 1995), and clinicians who are interested in using CT-TRG are encouraged to examine these other sources.

Guilt Assessment

Assessment is an integral part of the CT-TRG model. My colleagues and I use a structured interview and specially designed questionnaires (1) to identify idiosyncratic sources of trauma-related guilt, (2) to assess clients' faulty thinking patterns, and (3) to evaluate treatment efficacy.

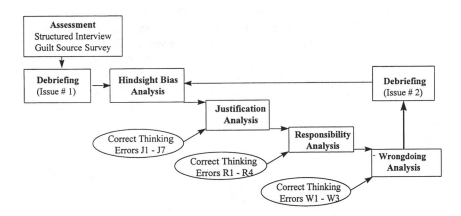

FIGURE 6.1. Procedures and order of procedures in cognitive therapy for trauma-related guilt (CT-TRG).

Sources of Guilt Assessment Interview

We have devised a structured interview to identify important guilt issues across five domains of guilt (Kubany & Manke, 1995). This interview (which also includes follow-up probes) consists of five core questions about the trauma that ask whether respondents feel guilty about (1) anything they *did,* (2) anything they *did not do,* (3) *thoughts or beliefs* they had that they now consider untrue, (4) *feelings* they *had,* and (5) *feelings* they *did not have.*

Sources of Trauma-Related Guilt Surveys

For our work with combat veterans, we have developed a survey that assesses 121 potential sources of guilt from the war zone (Kubany, Abueg, Kilauano, Manke, & Kaplan, 1997). After completing the survey, veteran clients are asked to circle four to six item numbers corresponding to events that are their most significant sources of guilt (e.g., "not being with your unit when casualties occurred"). These events then become treatment targets in CT-TRG.

We have also developed preliminary guilt source surveys for use with battered women (95 items so far), rape victims (80 items so far), and incest survivors (73 items so far) (see Kubany & Manke, 1995; available from Edward Kubany). All of the guilt source surveys can be used instead of, or in conjunction with, the Sources of Guilt Assessment Interview.

Attitudes About Guilt Survey

The Attitudes About Guilt Survey (AAGS; see Appendix) is used to assess the presence and magnitude of guilt components with respect to highly specific guilt issues (Kubany et al., 1995; Kubany & Manke, 1995). The first four items assess the magnitudes of each of the cognitive components of guilt. Clients are asked to fill out a separate AAGS for each guilt issue targeted for intervention, and before each guilt issue is analyzed, they are asked to explain their responses to the guilt cognition items. In addition to its value for initial assessment, the AAGS can be readministered as therapy proceeds to assess progress, lack of progress, or "slippage" (reversion to faulty logic that seemed to have been corrected) and the need for additional work.

Trauma-Related Guilt Inventory

The Trauma-Related Guilt Inventory (TRGI; Kubany et al., 1996) was constructed to assess guilt and cognitive and emotional aspects of guilt associated with specified traumatic events (e.g., combat, physical or sexual abuse). The TRGI includes three scales and three subscales. The scales include a Global Guilt Scale, a Distress Scale, and a Guilt Cognitions Scale, which includes items that comprise the three subscales—Hindsight Bias/Responsibility, Wrongdoing, and Lack of Justification. The TRGI is meant to be used as a molar measure of trauma-related guilt (e.g., combat-related guilt, incest-related guilt) rather than as a measure of more specific guilt issues occurring within the context of the trauma (e.g., guilt about having been afraid or trading places with someone who got killed). The TRGI, which assesses 22 specific trauma-related beliefs, may have considerable utility as a treatment-outcome measure in CT-TRG and other cognitive-behavioral interventions aimed at modifying trauma survivors' beliefs about their role in trauma.

Guilt Incident Debriefings

Prior to CT-TRG proper (with *each* targeted guilt issue), a guilt incident debriefing is conducted. Clients are asked to give a detailed, nonevaluative description of exactly what happened during and immediately preceding the event in question. Clients are asked, "What did you see, hear, feel, and smell? Who did what, who said what, and what thoughts were going through your mind?" After clients describe what happened, they are asked, "What was the worst part of what happened," and what were their "feelings" and their "thoughts" during the worst part?

CT-TRG Proper

CT-TRG proper is a building block or "successive approximations" approach to the treatment of guilt in which guilt issues are addressed one at a time. With each issue, guilt is broken into its component parts, which are also treated one at a time—in isolation from the other components. CT-TRG proper includes considerable psychoeducation, particularly in the early stages of therapy. Much of what happens in later stages of CT-TRG is consistent with Beckian or traditional cognitive therapy (e.g., Beck, Rush, Shaw, & Emery, 1979). The therapist and client are actively involved in assessing the client's beliefs and considering alternative explanations. Much of this process is characterized by a Socratic line of inquiry, during which clients are asked many questions that challenge their logic and noncritical thinking.

After the initial incident debriefing exercise, the therapist discusses the meaning of guilt, its conceptualization as a multidimensional construct, and the various components of guilt. Clients are then given an overview of CT-TRG procedures and goals. They are told that they will be involved in an "intellectual analysis," the goal of which will be "to achieve an appraisal of your role in the trauma that can withstand rational analysis."

The process of correcting thinking errors associated with faulty conclusions is conducted in the context of four semistructured procedures. These four procedures, which are outlined below, were designed to teach clients to distinguish what they knew "then" from what they know now and for analyzing and reappraising perceptions of justification, responsibility, and wrongdoing—in light of what they knew and believed when the trauma occurred.

1. *Probing for and correcting faulty conclusions about preoutcome knowledge (hindsight-bias analysis).* Efforts to correct faulty beliefs about preoutcome knowledge occurs in three overlapping phases or steps. First, clients are given an explanation of hindsight bias, accompanied by examples. The second step is to find out whether clients falsely believe they knew something prior to the trauma that "could have" enabled them to prevent or avoid a negative, trauma-related outcome. The third step is to help clients realize that it is *impossible* for knowledge acquired after an event to guide preoutcome decision making.

2. *Analyzing reasons for actions taken and dispelling faulty conclusions about justification.* Clients are first told that the best (or most justified) choice in *any* situation is the best choice among options actually considered. They are told that options that were ideal, but did not exist, and options that came to mind later should not be included in an analysis of justification. Second, clients are asked to detail their reasons for acting as they did. Third, they are asked what other courses of action they considered but rejected and to describe what they thought *at the time* would have happened had these courses been selected. Finally, clients are asked which choice—of options actually considered—was the most justified choice (knowing only what they knew then); when this is done, the course of action that was taken is almost always selected as the best choice.

3. *Assessing and analyzing external sources of causation and reappraising beliefs about causal responsibility.* There are four steps involved in helping clients achieve an objective assessment of their degree of responsibility for causing trauma-related outcomes. First, clients are made aware of the distinction between causation and blame. For example, the therapist may say, "Causation refers to 'what caused what' without any evaluation of whether what happened is good or bad. Blame implies wrongdoing as well as causation. We'll talk about wrongdoing a little later." Second, clients are assisted in generating a comprehensive listing of people and factors (outside of self) that contributed in some causal way to the outcome. Third, clients are asked to assign a percentage (of responsibility) to each external cause identified. Finally, clients are asked to reappraise their own causal contribution to the outcome.

4. *Correcting faulty conclusions about wrongdoing.* By the time the issue of wrongdoing is discussed, clients' beliefs about the degree to which they violated values are often mitigated in light of altered beliefs about preoutcome knowledge, justification, and responsibility. Clients are told that the label of wrongdoing is most commonly assigned when people intentionally cause harm or *knowingly* violate their values. Clients are asked whether they wanted the tragic outcome to

occur and whether they purposely made it happen. The answers to these questions are often "no," to which the therapist might say:

> "You didn't want it to happen and did not try to make it happen. In addition, you already concluded that there was no possible way that you could have known better, that what you did was the most justified choice, and that you were minimally responsible for causing what happened. How could what you did be wrong in any way?"

When clients experience guilt that stems from situations in which all courses of action had negative consequences, they are helped to realize that the least bad choice is a sound and moral choice.

Self-Monitoring Homework Assignments

Clients are routinely given self-monitoring homework assignments as a way of helping them stop saying or thinking certain kinds of maladaptive statements that may impede recovery from the effects of trauma. Clients are asked to keep track of three types of statements: (1) statements that include the words "should have," "could have," "if only," or "why"; (2) self-put-down statements; and (3) "I feel … " statements that end with words that are not emotions. Homework compliance is promoted by explaining to clients why these statements are maladaptive and why people are better off if they do not use them. They are told that the purpose of the self-monitoring assignment is to increase their awareness of when they make these statements (in thoughts and speech), which will make it easier to stop using them.

1. *Statements that include the words "should have," "could have," "if only," or "why."* Clients may be told that if they never say the words, "should have," "could have," "if only," or "why" ever again, they will be happier. They are told that use of these words and phrases suggest the presence of hindsight bias, which interferes with their ability to think clearly and objectively about their role in trauma. They are also informed that (a) there is evidence that use of "why" statements by trauma survivors is associated with poorer posttrauma adjustment (e.g., Frazier & Schauben, 1994), (b) finding out "why" is not going to make them feel better or change what happened (e.g., "is not going to bring your son back"), and (c) dwelling on "why" and rehashing what happened keeps them "stuck in the past."

2. *Self-put-down statements.* Many trauma survivors are self-deprecating and put themselves down in a variety of ways (e.g., "I'm stupid . . . weak . . . dirty . . . damaged goods . . . gullible . . . a nobody . . . an idiot . . . ugly"). Clients are told that the use of self-put-down statements is not going to make them feel better and is more likely to make them feel depressed and hopeless. The therapist might say:

"What if I said, 'I agree with you. You are stupid, and you're a total mess [self-labels the client used]'? Feel any better? Of course, not. Unfortunately, these words have the same negative effect on you when you say them to yourself as when someone else says them to you. *Nobody* deserves to be talked to that way. You need to start giving *yourself* the same respect that you want to get from others!"

3. *"I feel" statements that end with negative words that are not emotions.* When clients use the phrase, "I feel," with negative words that are not emotions, the feelings associated with the negative words make the statements *seem* more true. Clients are encouraged to use the phrase, "I feel," only with words that signify pure emotions such as happiness, sadness, anxiety, or "good mood" or "bad mood." They are encouraged to stop using the phrase, "I feel," in conjunction with words or phrases that are not emotions (e.g., [I feel] "sorry for him . . . responsible . . . like it's my fault . . . obligated . . . trapped . . . overwhelmed . . . emotionally alone . . . like damaged goods . . . like I'm stuck in a hole," etc.). Clients are told that merging such words with the phrase, "I feel," can produce confusion and impairs their ability to think objectively about themselves and their role in trauma (e.g., "Whether or not you violated your values can be best assessed at an intellectual level. What, if anything, did you do that you *think* was wrong?").

A specially designed self-monitoring form, which clients can use for recording occurrences of the three kinds of statements mentioned earlier is shown in Figure 6.2. Clients are instructed to record (in code, with numbers 1, 2, or 3) *only the first occurrence* of each type of statement *in the interval in which it is observed* to occur (e.g., between 7 and 8 A.M.). If a type of statement does not occur in an interval, nothing is recorded. The total number of observations (for each type of statement) for each day will be the total number out of 18 daily time intervals in which the statement was observed to occur (0 to 18). This type of interval recording procedure is much easier to use and elicits greater compliance than procedures that require clients to record *every* occurrence of a behavior being monitored.

CT-TRG WITH A FORMERLY BATTERED WOMAN

One case study will be described in detail to illustrate the main procedures in CT-TRG proper. The case is that of a middle-aged, formerly battered woman who had multiple sources of abuse-related guilt. The client, Angie, left an abusive family environment before she graduated from high school to marry a man who physically and sexually abused her for several years. Angie experienced guilt for getting involved in an abusive relationship ("out of the frying pan into the fire"), for not leaving the relationship when her children were small, and for not leaving

| Person Observed: _____ | | | | | | | Dates: From _____   To _____ |

Phrases of Concern: 1 = "I should have...could have...If only...Why..."

2 = "I feel..." (with words that are not emotions)

3 = Self-Put-Down Statements

Dates								Comments
	Mon.	Tues.	Wed.	Thurs.	Fri.	Sat.	Sun.	
6 - 7am								
7 – 8								
8 – 9								
9 - 10								
10 - 11								
11 - 12								
12 - 1								
1 - 2								
2 - 3								
3 - 4								
4 - 5								
5 - 6								
6 - 7								
7 - 8								
8 - 9								
9 - 10								
10 - 11								
11 - 6am								
Total "1"s								
Total "2"s								
Total "3"s								

FIGURE 6.2. Self-monitoring recording form.

the relationship later without her children (her husband would have gotten custody). Later, out of the relationship, Angie experienced a resurgence of PTSD and depression symptomatology after finding out that her daughter was being battered by her own boyfriend and her son was involved in illicit drugs. These events exacerbated Angie's guilt for having "allowed" her children to witness domestic violence and for not leaving the relationship sooner. This therapy segment illustrates the practice of CT-TRG proper, in which the main procedures are followed in their usual order—starting with an analysis of hindsight bias, followed by an analysis of justification for actions taken, and then by an analysis of causal responsibility. A wrongdoing analysis, per se, is not included in the segment, but was indirectly included in the other analyses.

In the initial debriefing, which lasted 1½ hours, Angie described in great detail how she had gotten involved with her husband, numerous incidents of abuse, and events leading up to her eventually leaving the relationship. I started CT-TRG proper with Angie by going over her responses on the AAGS about "choosing to get in the relationship and then not leaving." (The therapist–client interactions that follow are based on transcripts of actual therapy sessions.)

Hindsight-Bias Analysis

EK: Item 4 on the AAGS asks, "To what extent should you have known better and could have avoided or prevented the outcome?" This has to do with a concept called *hindsight bias*. It's the belief that we were smarter than we were capable of being when we made certain kinds of decisions, usually decisions with bad outcomes. We seem to think that somehow we could have known how it was going to turn out before it turned out.

A: It's like trying to be a genie.

EK: It's trying to be a person with a crystal ball.

A: I never thought of it that way. It's believing I knew how it was going to turn out before it happened.

EK: Before it happened. That you should have had the wisdom of making the right choice because you should have *somehow* known how it was going to turn out. As if you had information and data that you could draw on that you *did not actually have*.

A: I didn't.

EK: No you didn't. And I want you to know that hindsight bias isn't something that's reserved for crazy people or for trauma survivors. Hindsight bias has been demonstrated with college students in many studies.

A: Then I'm not the only one who does it.

EK: There's a general inclination for people to do it. I'll illustrate with a simple example, the kind of study that has been conducted many times [e.g., Fischhoff, 1975; Hawkins & Hastie, 1990]. Imagine an experiment in which three groups of subjects are asked to predict who is going to win the Superbowl based on statistics given to them about the teams, coaches, and players. The groups are then sequestered in a hotel, and on Monday, the experimenter asks them, "Which team do you think won, Buffalo or Dallas?" One group is "inadvertently" told that Dallas won. The second group is "inadvertently" told that Buffalo won, and the third group is not told who won. There are two interesting outcomes in these kinds of studies. One, if you're given information about the outcome, it's going to bias you in favor of that outcome.

A: So, the ones who were told Dallas won were more likely to predict Dallas.

EK: Right. And more importantly, when they're told that the outcome information biased their predictions, they deny it! They say, "No, no. That's what I would have predicted." And it's something trauma survivors do *all* the time. Now, you did not know 20 years ago what you know now. You knew you were in a hellish situation that you wanted to get away from. You had no idea that you were going to live with years of battering. You had no idea that your children were going to be having the kinds of problems they're having now.

A: Because if I knew, I wouldn't have married him.

EK: You wouldn't have married him.

A: If I knew, there is no way I would've married him.

EK: That's right.

During the previous session, I used an anecdote to illustrate the kind of distorted thinking that is common among trauma survivors. I told Angie about an army medic in Vietnam who unintentionally called a buddy into the line of fire and considered himself 100% responsible for his buddy's death (Kubany & Manke, 1995, p. 36). I make brief reference to this anecdote in my next comment to Angie, which illustrates how psychoeducation early in therapy can be briefly alluded to later to succinctly make an important point.

EK: If the medic I told you about last week had known he was going to be calling his buddy into the line of fire . . .

A: . . . he wouldn't have called him into the line of fire.

EK: But he somehow felt that he could have known. There is no possible way. If we could go back, and I was talking to you at that time [when she got married], you would be telling me all the reasons you thought your life was going to be better.

A: Yeah.

EK: Angie, I would suggest that, unless you know something that I don't know, there is no possible way that you could have known better. One, it would have been impossible for you to tell me how it was going to turn out. And two, had you known, you wouldn't have done what you did.

A: No way, if I knew I was going to be treated like that.

EK: Why would anyone [intentionally] walk into a life like that?

A: Nobody would.

EK: You would have to be crazy, and you're not crazy.

A: Yeah. I wanted to get away from abuse [severe physical abuse from her mother].

EK: Of course. You were motivated to escape pain.

A: It's almost as if I'm punishing myself for nothing.

EK: You can say that again. It's almost as if you're punishing yourself for nothing.

A: Wow.

Justification Analysis

Ruling Out Idealized or Fantasy Choices That Did Not Exist

As we started to explore alternative courses of action that Angie contemplated when trapped in her abusive relationship, she dwelled on a course of action that was ideal but did not exist for her.

A: I thought about leaving when the children were small. I should have somehow gotten my resources together and left. Yeah. Somehow, I should have been able to make it. But, when I sit down, I cannot figure out that somehow. It's like, why wasn't I brave enough to pack up and leave? Why wasn't I the heroine? I used to daydream that I had packed up the kids and was gone to the mainland. And somehow, I had this little apartment, and we were going to make it—just like heroines do. You know? I don't know.

EK: Would you like me to give you an analogy to that?

A: Yeah.

EK: Here's a Vietnam soldier in a terrible situation where it's "kill or be killed." And he has this fantasy of himself on a desert island.

A: So they do the same thing?

EK: Sure. Or a fantasy that somehow, somehow, can't people see the absurdity of this?

A: Everybody wakes up, and nobody gets killed.

EK: Yeah. Let's deal with this like adults. Sometimes, this fantasy-like thinking has some value. But the danger in it is that, if we reify it, make it real, as if those are real options . . .

A: And that's what I did.

EK: It was not an option for that soldier to evaporate and be somewhere else. It was not an option for him to be the mediator and say, "Come on you guys, let's not fight. Let's not kill anyone. No one needs to die." The only options that were available were "kill or be killed." The only options were bad ones. Yes, you had the fantasy of what you would have liked to have happened, but that was not possible.

A: I didn't have any money.

EK: You didn't have any money.

A: I didn't have the money to buy tickets to go. And no resources. It's not like today where people help women get away.

EK: And it's almost as if [had you had gotten away], you would be totally insulated, with no way in the world that he could get to you. As if you had a bubble over your environment. Even if you could have gotten to the mainland, do you really think you would have been safe? Or felt safe? How many battered women have run away from their husbands, and then all of a sudden magically felt safe? What we're talking about here is catch-22.

A: You're damned if you do, and damned if you don't (laughing).

EK: You're damned if you do, and damned if you don't. The reason they experience guilt is that they weigh their alternatives against choices that were not actually available. Let me give you a classic example. This pair of marines in Vietnam had been inserted [by a helicopter] into enemy territory on a secret mission. And now they were trying to make a quick getaway with the enemy in pursuit. They were being hoisted out in harnesses by a hovering helicopter. The veteran's buddy got caught in a tree as they were trying to hoist him out. And the veteran [my client] was faced with the choice of either shooting his partner or allowing him to live and be tortured [with certainty] by the enemy. This man was also caught up with fantasy choices.

A: And he wasn't Rambo who could find a way to get him out (laughing).

EK: Yeah. That's right. And you wanted to see *yourself* as Superwoman.

A: I did!

EK: The veteran said, "I don't know what I could have done, but I should have been able to do *something*."

Comparison of Options When Angie Considered Leaving without the Children

EK: Okay, let's talk about what would have happened if you had left. What would have happened if you had chosen to leave?

A: Then the kids could have visited me. But when I look at that, they would have said that I abandoned them for my own stuff. Then they wouldn't have had any option on how to have been raised because they would have been raised by him. And his values would be the only ones they would ever see. They would never be nurtured emotionally. Now I'm so terrible because I stayed with Dad. But, I probably would have been terrible if I had left [and left them with Dad]. I couldn't win. It's that catch-22 again.

EK: Okay, what else would have happened if you had left?

A: Maybe something that wouldn't happen today but would have happened to a mother 20 years ago. A mother would have been scorned for leaving her children.

EK: So, you would have been subjected to public ridicule.

A: Yes, very much so. The other thing that I would have probably been subjected to is an ousting by the church. And that is a part that is ingrained in my personality or belief system. It's part of who I am—having a spiritual side.

EK: Okay, so you would have had to abandon that.

A: Yeah.

EK: You would have had to give that up—to say you don't really have a spiritual side. "I'm much too much materialistic." If you had decided to leave, and your life unfolded, and we were talking here today, do you think you would feel more guilty or less guilty now?

A: Probably more.

EK: Okay, let's look at your choices. You stayed. Of course, you didn't know what was going to happen because you had no crystal ball. On the other hand, if you had left, the children would not have been nurtured emotionally.

A: No.

EK: They would have been subjected to his sociopathic, narcissistic personality [Angie's characterization of her husband]—to rub off on them. So, any positive influence you could have had on the children would have been eliminated.

A: Totally. Plus, they would have been subject to physical abuse.

EK: That's right. They couldn't be protected.

A: No. Nobody to protect them.

EK: So, he could have mistreated them without any negative consequence whatsoever. And any possible regulation that your presence provided would have been eliminated.

A: Yeah.

EK: You would have been publicly scorned for leaving your children. Probably not only ousted by the church, but have to give up that spiritual side of yourself that you valued. "I've got to turn that in. I don't belong to that club anymore."

A: Yep.

EK: And you would have felt more guilty.

A: Yeah, when I look back at that.

EK: Now, did it make sense for you to have left under those circumstances? Doesn't it sound as if the potential consequences for leaving were worse than those for staying.

A: Yeah, *way more*!

Responsibility Analysis

When the justification analysis was completed, I helped Angie generate a list of all people and factors outside of herself that caused or contributed to her decision to remain in an abusive marriage. After several external sources of causation were identified, Angie was asked to assign a percentage of responsibility to each identified source (without being told that the total had to add up to [only] 100%).

EK: What share of the responsibility did your ex-husband have [for your staying in the relationship and continuing to get abused]? Scientifically, causally, how responsible was he?

A: Now I think more.

EK: More than what?

A: More than I did a few minutes ago.

EK: (*Laughs.*)

A: Strange. I really do. But, even for him I think 70%. How come I can't say 100?

EK: Well, you don't have to. Okay, let's take 70.

A: No. When you say "scientific," it sounds like more than 100%.

EK: Well then, what is it intellectually? This is a scientific question. This is a logic question. This is not an emotional question.

A: If it has nothing to do with emotion and is a scientific question, he's 100% responsible—because I never picked up the thing and hit myself.

EK: (*Laughs.*)

A: That's the bottom line. If you go scientific and [look at] what physically caused it, *he* did it.

EK: Okay. Now, let's go to the police. How much share of the responsibility did the police have for not protecting you and not getting you out of there?

A: Largely responsible. They never did arrest him. Even when he broke temporary restraining orders, he was never arrested. Never.

EK: So, how much responsibility did they share for the perpetuation of the abuse?

A: 100% too, because they kept causing it (*raised voice*)!

EK: So, maybe not in terms of the first time, but in the totality . . .

A: Yeah, because they kept letting him get away with it.

EK: That's right. They might have been able to stop it when they first became involved.

A: Oh yeah, because even when he broke the restraining order with John [her new boyfriend], when I started to date John, [the police dispatcher] kept saying, "They can't catch him. And too bad. They have to see him there."

EK: How about the courts?

A: Oh, the idiotic courts.

EK: How responsible were they for not stopping the abuse and allowing it to continue?

A: They too are another 100%, because of the stupid judges! The social worker was just as largely responsible also [for recommending that her husband be granted custody]. No way I'm gonna leave without my kids. No way I was gonna leave my children to somebody like him. And what about CPS [Child Protective Services]? They also copped out on me.

EK: How about the church or teachings of the church? Teaching you to be a martyr.

A: I don't think that's scientific responsibility.

EK: No, there is a scientific part of it. How much do the religious teachings of the church determine the actions of people in the community?

A: Religious beliefs make up maybe 80% of what we do.

EK: How responsible was your mother for your decision to stick it out?

A: Oh, she's got a large share because, number one, she said, "You can't get a divorce. He's a good provider."

EK: So, she's also giving you *that* propaganda.

A: Oh yeah. "He's a hard worker, and he does this and that." Oh she gave me 10 million reasons how great he was.

EK: I'm going to add up the percentages of everyone you counted, and I'm going to cut the percentages in half. (*Pause to add up the percentages.*) Adding it all up, it comes to 400%. And we haven't even gotten to *you* yet. (*Five-second pause.*) How responsible were *you*?

A: Oh my god. When you break it down, it's real different, isn't it?

EK: How could you have been 75% responsible?

A: I couldn't have.

EK: Not humanly possible.

A: There are so many things playing into it all at once, aren't there?

EK: Remember when I told you about the combat medic last week?

A: That's what I was thinking about. It feels like the soldier. (*Five-second pause.*) He was the one walking around with all the guilt, but he couldn't have stopped everyone else's behavior. I couldn't change the police. I couldn't change the courts. I couldn't teach that social worker. I couldn't help CPS to . . .

EK: You were a twig in a hurricane . . .

A: Oh my god.

EK: . . . that thinks you're responsible for the destruction of the community. You know what I would say? I would say that you were between "no way" and "slightly" responsible. That's what I would say.

A: Me too, now. I would say "slightly" now because I still made a choice.

EK: In a scientific sense, yes.

A: But I didn't make a choice to be abused although my body still had to be there. But, that's all. I did not cause the events that took place.

EK: That's exactly right. Just like the rape victim who says, "I was responsible for the rape because I went to the bar."

A: But there's no way. She might have gone to the bar 10 million times before and never got raped. I've got a lot to think about because of what we did today. I really do. I really do.

SPECIAL TOPIC: DISPUTING FEELINGS AS EVIDENCE FOR THE VALIDITY OF AN IDEA

Anticipation of relief for taking a contemplated course of action can sometimes cause battered women to make decisions that are not in their best interests. For example, one of the reasons that some battered women return to an abusive relationship is to obtain relief (reinforcement) from painful feelings associated with guilt. The following therapy segments are highlights from a session with a battered woman devoted entirely to dissuading her from using feelings as evidence of whether a contemplated decision was a good one. For this woman, anguish associated with her ex-boyfriend's pleadings to "come back," and anticipated relief if she "gave in" and went back, were being used as evidence that she "should go back."

The client, Fran, had been brutally beaten by her live-in boyfriend, Jimmy, on multiple occasions, and had been hospitalized with broken bones more than once. On *the day* Fran left her boyfriend and moved into a shelter for battered women, she had gone to the hospital emergency room more than once following separate incidents of abuse. Shortly before the session from which the therapy segment below was taken, Fran had received a phone call from her ex-boyfriend, pleading with her to come back. When this happened, she had been out of the relationship for almost a year.

F: Jimmy wouldn't take "No" for an answer. He said, "I want to get back together. I want to win you back." I said, "You're still using drugs," and he said, "Just once in awhile. I'll change to have you back. I'm not that bad, am I? I just want to be with you, and that's all I'm going to settle for." No matter how many times I told him "No," he started to cry and said, "I won't ever hit you again. Please. You've ripped my heart out." What really bothers me is what I'm feeling inside. Maybe I should go back and try again. And then I get scared at that feeling and look at everything I have now—my apartment, my car, my credit cards. I think of losing it all over again if I try.

EK: Fran, you've got to remember that you can't allow your feelings to serve as evidence for what decisions you make. When Jimmy says, "Please, please" and starts to cry, you feel bad.

F: I do.

EK: But the fact that you feel bad is not evidence that you should follow a certain course of action. In other words, whether or not it's in your best interests to go back cannot be determined by the intensity of your feelings when you think about going back. You're a very compassionate person, and you have a lot of empathy. And you want relief from feeling bad.

F: Yeah. . . . It just worries me, and he's had a rough time. . . . I don't think I would go back; but, to have those feelings inside . . .

EK: Once again, you're saying you have those feelings inside. You don't have "feelings *to go back.*" You have feelings, and you have thoughts.

F: Yeah.

EK: Don't merge them. . . . Don't use your feelings to guide your decisions. By the way, you have no control over the words that come out of Jimmy's mouth. Remember, words are only sound waves. You're acting like they're hitting you with the impact of huge hammers. They are just sound waves.

F: He knows all the buttons to push.

I explained to Fran that guilt induction can be a very effective way of *influencing* people who are easily made to feel guilty (which Fran definitely was). By "looking" sad or "acting" disappointed, or by sulking, someone can influence a person who has been taught to be guilt-prone to "give in" and do what the other person wants.

EK: Just because he says something doesn't mean it's true, or even that he believes what he's telling you! He is saying those words to influence you. When he says things like, "Please come back," what you want is relief, which is a very powerful reward. You want relief from the way those words make you feel, and going back would be one way to get relief from those feelings—however brief that relief might be.

F: Yeah.

EK: There is no genetic reason why his crying and saying "please" needs to evoke a bad feeling and thoughts that you should do what *he wants* you to do. . . . You need to be able to distinguish your thoughts from your feelings. And don't make decisions based on how you feel because your feelings may change. "I feel good. That means I should stay away. I feel bad. That means I should go back. I feel good. I should stay away." That's what leads to confusion. Neither those good feelings or bad feelings have *anything* to do with whether it's a good idea to stay away or not stay away! You have to remember that.

As the session was drawing to a close, I asked Fran how strongly she believed she would think and react in a specific desired way (which we had set as a goal) the next time Jimmy called.

EK: The next time Jimmy calls, and says something like, "Fran, I love you and miss you so much," how strongly will you believe the following statements: "You are 100% certain it's over. People couldn't drag you back. You might feel sad or bad for a little while, but you will experience zero guilt."

F: The way I'm feeling right at this moment?

EK: Did you hear yourself (*laughs*)? Fran, by saying, "the way I'm *feeling,*" you're allowing feelings to interfere with your judgment about what is in your best interest. Rather than talk about what you "feel you should do," ask yourself, what decision is *in your best interests*?

F: I know it's a good idea to stay away.

Fran decided not to reconcile with her ex-boyfriend, and a few months later, she had a new job and was involved in a romantic relationship with a man who was treating her with respect.

SOME TREATMENT OBSTACLES AND SOLUTIONS

The CT-TRG model incorporates several features that address some of the potential obstacles to the effective treatment of guilt. These particular features, which are discussed below, were incorporated into the CT-TRG model precisely because of obstacles encountered during early efforts to help clients deal with or overcome their guilt.

The Need for Comprehensive Guilt Assessment and the Usual Necessity of Addressing More Than One Guilt Issue

The CT-TRG model emphasizes systematic and thorough assessment. Because many trauma survivors have multiple guilt issues—sometimes related to different traumas and sometimes related to multiple aspects of singular events—treatment of multiple issues may be necessary to effect global and generalized reductions in trauma-related guilt (e.g., Kubany, 1997c). For example, Kubany, Abueg, et al. (1997) suggest that incomplete trauma assessment may be one important reason why PTSD programs for combat veterans have not been very successful (e.g., Johnson et al., 1996). Noting that Vietnam War veterans in their samples reported more than 30 sources of (at least moderate) war-related guilt *on average,* Kubany, Abueg, et al. argue that it may often be necessary to treat multiple guilt issues over multiple sessions in order to produce clinically significant therapeutic benefits.

Comprehensive Trauma History Assessment

Obtaining a comprehensive assessment to lifetime exposure to trauma can sometimes be very important for uncovering all significant sources of trauma-related guilt (e.g., Kubany, Haynes, Leisen, et al., 1997). In fact, in some cases, treatment of guilt related to childhood or earlier traumatic events may be more important than or facilitate treatment related to more recent trauma. Two cases come immediately to mind, and in both cases, the clients accepted an inordinate amount of responsibility for the welfare of others. In the first case, a Vietnam War veteran experienced overwhelming grief and crippling guilt over the death of a buddy, who was next to him when killed by an enemy sniper. This guilt issue was traced back to a "related" childhood event in which a friend died. Snorkeling at the beach, the client and his friend spotted a large school of fish. So, the client suggested that his friend get his fishing pole. On his way to get his pole, the friend fell off a rock jetty and drowned. Treatment of this guilt issue from childhood, which was more encapsulated and perhaps even more irrationally based than the Vietnam issue, seemed to accelerate the process of alleviating the veteran's guilt about the death of his buddy in Vietnam.

In a second case where assessment of lifetime trauma exposure to trauma was considered important, treatment of guilt linked to a childhood trauma seemed to help a formerly battered woman overcome a pervasive tendency to take responsibility for problems in her marriage and abuse by her husband. Even though this woman's presenting complaints revolved around partner abuse, our initial treatment focus was on guilt she experienced about childhood sexual abuse by her brother and a subsequent severe beating her brother received from their father. The theme linking these two sets of events was this woman's tendency to believe that it was her "job" to take care of, protect, and accept responsibility for adverse consequences to anyone with whom she had a close relationship.

The Need to Break Guilt Down into Its Component Parts and Treat One Part at a Time

In its early stages of development, the CT-TRG model did not include an explicit educational component, and distortions of the cognitive components of guilt were not addressed separately, in a stepwise and systematic manner. Cognitive distortions were addressed unsystematically in a piecemeal fashion. When conducting cognitive therapy in this way, I often observed glimpses of insight (e.g., "I never looked at it that way before"), emotional catharses, and expressions of relief at the end of the session. However, by the next session, I also observed frequently that clients had "slipped" back into their old thinking patterns, without appreciable reductions in their original levels of guilt. In the present CT-TRG format, breaking guilt down into its component parts, labeling separate thinking errors, and analyzing the guilt components one at a time seem to facilitate clients' ability to understand their faulty thinking patterns, to understand "why" they were drawing faulty conclusions, and to generalize this understanding to other guilt issues. For example, several CT-TRG clients have commented that they have learned skills or been given "tools" that enable them to understand and work on guilt issues on their own (e.g., Kubany, 1997c).

The Need to Obtain a Detailed Description of the Trauma to Facilitate Expression of Grief or Loss and to Identify Nonobvious Instances of Faulty Logic

As noted by Kubany and Manke (1995), clients' detailed, descriptive retelling of exactly what happened during the trauma can serve as a critical incident stress debriefing (Mitchell & Bray, 1990) that many clients have never had. When clients reexperience their trauma in this way, they often express strong negative affect, such as tearful grieving, and in this respect, the guilt incident debriefing serves as a form of direct exposure that can relieve negative affect associated with the trauma. At the same time, a client's detailed descriptions of events that are sources of guilt can provide invaluable assessment information about distortions in logic.

I partially attribute some of my therapy "failures" in the past to not urging clients to describe their traumatic experiences in great detail. One client whom I did not help much had been deeply in love and was engaged to be married when his fiancée was murdered while on a personal business trip overseas. This man had a demeanor of complete emotional detachment, and he spoke with noticeably flat affect. He came to therapy on the insistence of friends who said he had "changed" since his fiancée's death. When I asked him to tell me about the circumstances surrounding his fiancée's death, he superficially described what happened, and I did not press him to elaborate. After a few sessions, I was at a loss as to how to proceed, and the client dropped out of therapy. In retrospect, I believe that, had I conducted an extensive debriefing of events surrounding the fiancée's death, I might have uncovered important guilt (and anger) issues and also enabled my client to grieve his great loss.

I did not make a similar mistake with Mary, who sought therapy because of an abusive intimate relationship. During our third session, Mary mentioned that she was nearing the first anniversary of the suicide of her much younger brother, with whom she had been very close. I asked her what happened, and she responded, "In a nutshell, he hung himself." I then said, "Tell me—not in a nutshell. Tell me exactly what happened, in detail, and the events that led up to it." For the next several minutes, Mary described—with flat affect—several interactions with her brother, including the last time she saw him alive, when he seemed forlorn and sad. She said, "I asked him, 'What's wrong Tom,' and he said, 'Nothing. I just have a lot on my mind.' " Then, she recalled her brother during happier times. "He was such a happy guy. We went to parties. He was the life of the party. I was dancing next to him, having fun, acting crazy. But when I go to the same parties, it's not the same because my brother isn't there to laugh and have fun and have a good time."

At this point, Mary broke down and cried nonstop for 7 minutes. During these 7 minutes, I continued to conduct therapy, and Mary talked through her tears.

M: I wish he had talked to me—said something so we might have been able to help him.

EK: Had he been capable of telling you.

M: I really wish I pressed harder on that last day I saw him. I wish I had said more. Maybe he would not have died if he felt that somebody could help him.

EK: You *did not know* he was going to kill himself. If you had known he was so desperate, you would have done more.

M: I know that.

EK: You *did not know* that he was going to kill himself.

By the end of this session, Mary was reminiscing positively about her brother. In addition, she reported during subsequent sessions that she was now able to recall the good times with her brother without getting depressed and had no residual guilt regarding his suicide.

Dislodging Hindsight Bias When Clients Insist They "Knew" What Was Going to Happen

It can sometimes be difficult to dislodge hindsight-biased thinking when clients *insist* that they "knew" what was going to happen, especially if they actually entertained or contemplated options that "would have" prevented a traumatic outcome. Under such circumstances, it may be advisable to probe for further details about exactly what happened and determine when the client first knew *with certainty* what was going to happen.

One young woman with whom I worked experienced medical complications on three separate occasions following treatments by her family physician. After the third complication, she almost bled to death, and was left with a permanent disability. This woman experienced guilt about not having switched to another doctor. She said, "I had all the signs and signals that he wasn't a good doctor, and I stayed with him. My life would be profoundly different if I had listened to myself. I should have followed my hunches and got someone else." In probing for hindsight bias, it was clear that this client did not know that the doctor was not taking good care of her until after she almost died. However, she steadfastly maintained that she "knew" she should have switched. I kept asking "*when* did you have first *know* this?" She finally said that she "knew" after the second complication when she had "doubts" (but only doubts as it turned out) about her doctor's competence and actually did consider switching physicians at that time. She told me that she confronted her physician about the quality of care she was receiving, and he took her concerns so lightly that he convinced her that she was worrying for nothing, and "I believed him that nothing was wrong with me." My client then realized that "it didn't make sense" to switch from a doctor who, despite his aloof demeanor, knew her so well, had all her medical records, and whom she believed at the time to be competent.

There is a simple and straightforward Socratic technique that can sometimes effectively dislodge clients' false beliefs that they had knowledge or definitive clues that a tragic outcome was going to occur before it was possible to know. Basically, this technique involves asking clients if they *actually* possessed knowledge that the trauma was going to occur, wouldn't they have done something about it? When clients answer affirmatively, the therapist can respond, "Isn't that proof you didn't know?" For example, a combat veteran who experienced guilt about not saving the life of a friend who was killed by friendly fire (Kubany, 1996) was asked, "If you knew your friend was in danger of being fired on by his own people, don't you think you would have done something about it?"

VET: Of course.

EK: Therefore, isn't that evidence that you had no idea of what the appropriate action was—that you didn't know what was going on?

VET: (*Nods yes.*)

EK: If you *knew* what was about to occur . . .

VET: I would have stopped it.

EK: You would have stopped it, which is evidence that you did *not* know. You found out later—and then you started imagining how you could have known or understand now what you should have done. Because of the outcome, it's *obvious.*

VET: Yeah.

Addressing Guilt of Clients Who Were Attracted to an Abuser Prior to the Abuse (the "Two Movie" Scenario)

Some battered women and many survivors of acquaintance or date rape experience guilt for having liked or been attracted to someone who subsequently abused or assaulted them. A detailed debriefing, starting with when the client first met or went out with the abuser, until the abuse occurred or started, may be indicated in such cases. A good example of this involved a teenage survivor of physical and sexual abuse with whom I worked in another country. Felice had run away from home because of her mother's overrestrictiveness and, while homeless, got involved with drugs. Wanting to escape this lifestyle, and upon the recommendation of her older sister, she went to stay with an older man who subsequently beat her up, raped her, and held her captive. Felice experienced guilt about having been "infatuated" with this man "because I should have known that he was going to hurt me." The following therapy segment occurred after Felice spent 10 minutes describing how she met her abuser, why she liked him, how things changed, and the sequence of events that ended in her getting abused.

EK: When you first met and stayed with him, didn't he seem like a nice guy?

F: Yes.

EK: It didn't seem as if he had the potential to hurt you. You were infatuated with a nice man who treated you well. You saw him as protecting you and helping you get out of a bad life. You enjoyed his company. He was a handsome man. He liked the same kinds of things that you did (e.g., contemporary music). Why not like someone like that? You're remembering yourself as smarter than you actually were. But now, looking back, you think you should have seen some signs. You shouldn't have been so trusting. Looking back, it seems like there were big signals. Flashing red lights. You see, it was really like two different movies. The first movie ended just before he started comparing himself to God. [This was when Felice first got scared and started questioning the man's intentions. Shortly thereafter, he hit her with a broomstick and raped her.] And then, it turned into a horror story. So, the movie theater has two movies. First, it has a love story, and then it has a story about violence. Two different movies. Let me tell you about a similar situation with a woman I am still working with. She was raped by someone she dated. He had been courting her, and on this one occasion they were kissing, and she was getting physically aroused. Then, he started to rape her. And she felt guilty about liking him and getting aroused. It's the same story as yours. Two movies! She did not have the slightest idea that he would abuse her before he abused her. It was inconceivable to her that he would do anything like that. He had been a nice guy, and she was doing something that was consistent with her values by liking him and kissing him. And then, all of a sudden, he took off his mask and started acting like a demon. She had no idea he was going to do that prior to that moment. When she was aroused, she was aroused to a different guy. A different movie. Can you see how that situation is similar to yours.

F: Yes, I can.

(The above interaction also indicates how giving anecdotes about other trauma survivors—who faced situations similar to those faced by the client—may help clients perceive their own situation differently and more clearly.)

Although the "two-movie" analysis seems to apply most often when survivors had positive feelings toward someone who subsequently betrayed and abused them, this analysis is occasionally appropriate in work with survivors of other traumatic events. For example, in Kubany (1997c) I described CT-TRG with a Vietnam War veteran who experienced guilt about firing in the direction of the enemy (because of the possible presence of "friendly forces") and also experienced guilt about not continuing to fire. "A damned-if-you-do and damned-if-you-don't situation, if I ever saw one," the veteran said (p. 233). Prior to our debriefing of this event, he never realized that his first decision (to fire) was based on a different set of "facts" than his second decision (to stop firing).

Getting Sidetracked or Off-Task

Guilt is only one of many problems experienced by trauma survivors, and in the "real world" of therapy, survivors often raise multiple concerns during their therapy sessions. CT-TRG is a very focused, systematic approach for dealing with a highly specific set of problems, and sometimes it is a challenge to keep clients from interrupting the process by getting off-task or bringing up other problems. One way of maintaining the therapeutic focus is to gain upfront agreement from a client that the sole agenda for a session (or series of sessions) will be guilt. Of course, in residential or intensive PTSD treatment programs, it may be practical to include a separate guilt management module as part of a multimodal treatment program.

An off-the-topic issue that comes up frequently in the course of CT-TRG is trauma-related anger. As clients talk about their guilt and their role in the trauma, they sometimes switch the subject and express anger toward someone else about their role in the trauma. For example, when discussing trauma-related guilt, it is not uncommon for incest survivors to precipitously shift the discussion to their anger about being exploited or betrayed or bemoan "why" someone was not there to protect them (e.g., "Why didn't my mother stop the abuse?"). In my experience, clients who have suffered the sudden and untimely loss of loved ones are particularly prone to raise anger issues in the course of addressing their guilt. For example, one client whose wife inexplicably murdered their two small children flip-flopped back and forth between his own guilt and his anger toward his wife, her parents, the police, and the social worker who had not detected his wife's mental illness. When anger issues emerge in the course of CT-TRG, I typically highlight the distinction between guilt and anger and advise clients how I would like to proceed. For example, I may say:

> "Remember, guilt is an unpleasant feeling with associated beliefs about what one should have done differently. Anger is the same unpleasant feeling with associated beliefs about what *someone else* should have done differently. This explains why a person can so easily shift back and forth between guilt and anger. However, we can't treat guilt issues and anger issues at the same time. Let's concentrate on your guilt now. Later, I will help you deal with your anger."

IS CHRONIC GUILT EVER AN "APPROPRIATE" REACTION AND IMPROPER TO TREAT?

It has been suggested that guilt may sometimes be an "appropriate" reaction (as in cases of perpetration, either in war or associated with a history of abuse). It is thought that such guilt may be functional insofar as it leads to prosocial behavior and that treatment of this "appropriate" guilt may be improper, if not unethical. These viewpoints raise a hornet's nest of issues that could easily be the topic of an entire article. Below, I briefly highlight several factors that need to be taken into consideration when examining this complex issue.

First, *transitory* guilt that emerges in the course of everyday life events may often be functional or adaptive because guilt stimulates reparative actions that restore the equilibrium in social relationships (Baumeister, Stillwell, & Heatherton, 1994). However, impulses to make restitution are often thwarted after traumatic events that have irreparable consequences (e.g., death, permanent injuries), and there is little evidence that chronic, trauma-related guilt is adaptive, particularly when it is severe. In fact, there is considerable evidence that trauma-related guilt is very maladaptive. For example, studies cited earlier have found trauma-related guilt to be highly positively correlated with PTSD, depression, negative self-esteem, social anxiety and avoidance, and suicidal ideation. In addition, we have unpublished data that indicate that trauma-related guilt is positively correlated with "hostile ruminations," "desire for drugs or alcohol," "death-wish ruminations," and "isolative depression" (Kubany, 1997d). In many instances, trauma-related guilt may actually be associated with elevations in *dysfunctional* behavior rather than elevations in *prosocial* behavior. Because traumatic events are often considered irreparable and can be extremely painful to remember, *avoidance* reactions may be far more common than *reparative* actions. For example, in structured interviews of the phenemonology of trauma-related guilt with 18 Vietnam War veterans, the most common response to the question, "What do you *do* when you feel guilty about what happened?" was to become socially isolative (Kubany et al., 1996). None of the respondents mentioned efforts to make restitution.

Second, some believe guilt is an appropriate reaction that keeps hostile or antisocial impulses in check. Concerns about whether or not to treat "appropriate" guilt are often predicated on the *assumption* that if someone no longer feels guilty about a perceived transgression, an important social control mechanism—which guilt is presumed to maintain—will collapse. However, there is no *empirical evidence* that alleviation of guilt is associated with a disinhibition of antisocial inclinations (nor has this ever been evidenced in my experience working with many combat veterans and numerous abused women who had also been abusive [e.g., with their children]).

Third, perpetrators whom most people might agree should feel guilty (e.g., rapists, child molesters, batterers, murderers) *do not experience guilt* because they do not get upset when they think about what happened or because they blame their victims instead of themselves. However, it may not be an absence of guilt about *prior* transgressions that causes perpetrators to transgress again, but rather *current deficits* in the capacity to experience empathy. Many professionals emphasize the importance of teaching criminal offenders to experience "anticipatory" *empathetic distress* as a *deterrent to subsequent transgressions* (e.g., to feel badly for a little girl when contemplating molestation rather than to experience sexual arousal [Marshall, Hudson, Jones, & Fernandez, 1995]).

Fourth, when a person believes that someone else deserves to feel guilty, that person casts him- or herself in the role of judge. To express the value that guilt is an appropriate reaction implies that the guilty party should experience *distress* when he or she thinks about what happened (a *necessary* condition for guilt to occur). When this value judgment is made, the question must be asked, "*How badly* should the person feel and for *how long*?" For a perpetrator to continue to experience guilt may be "appropriate" from a societal viewpoint or be functional or serve a useful purpose for the victim (who may want the perpetrator to suffer). However, it may not be in the best interests of or adaptive for the perpetrator to remain guilt-ridden.

In many situations, the real question may not be, "Can perpetrators who feel guilty be taught to experience less guilt?" but rather, "Would clinicians be willing to treat such guilt?" To illustrate, I will give an example of a woman who committed a terrible crime. A couple of years ago, a young South Carolina mother, Susan Smith, murdered her two sons by allowing a car with the boys inside to roll into a lake. I suspect that Ms. Smith could be taught to experience less guilt (*assuming* she feels guilty about what she did) but that many clinicians might be reluctant to treat her guilt because they do not think she deserves treatment.

Fifth, I argued in an earlier article that

> there is a big difference between the belief that "I should have behaved differently" and the belief that "If I had it to do over again and knowing and believing what I do now, I would behave differently." One does not have to feel guilty to have learned from the past and to make enlightened future choices. . . . In addition, it may be all too easy for outsiders to self-righteously pass judgment without fully appreciating the totality of historical and circumstantial forces acting on individuals caught up in a maelstrom of traumatic events. . . . (Kubany, 1994, p. 14)[1]

As a final point, the guilt-related beliefs of the vast majority of trauma survivors with whom I have worked over the years have been so *irrational* that

---

[1]Some readers may be interested in reading about how I addressed a Vietnam veteran's guilt about going against his "personal moral and religious convictions by taking human lives" and about "mutilating enemy dead and taking body parts (ears) as war souvenirs" (Kubany, 1997c).

the ethics of treatment has virtually never been a consideration. However, the issues surrounding the topic of "appropriate" guilt and the conditions under which guilt should be considered adaptive or maladaptive are extremely complex. This important topic certainly merits further discussion and empirical study.

EVALUATION OF TREATMENT AND FUTURE DIRECTIONS

The specific objectives of CT-TRG are very precise and easily measured. For each guilt issue addressed, the objective is to help clients achieve an objective appraisal of their role in the event—in terms of their beliefs about preoutcome knowledge, justification, responsibility, and wrongdoing. Assessing and reassessing these beliefs is an integral part of the process of CT-TRG—as measured by clients' answers to repeatedly asked questions (e.g., "Now how responsible do you think you were for causing . . . ?") and their responses on administrations and readministrations of the AAGS. Thus, therapists practicing CT-TRG will know whether they are making progress toward the specific objectives of CT-TRG as therapy proceeds.

Of course, the broader objectives of CT-TRG—in the larger context of cognitive-behavioral therapy with trauma survivors—are to ameliorate suffering and symptoms of PTSD and posttrauma depression. At present, evidence for the efficacy of CT-TRG is based on client self-reports and client responses on assessment questionnaires administered before and after therapy. Based on my pre–post therapy assessments with individual clients, CT-TRG appears to ameliorate symptoms of PTSD, depression, and negative self-esteem as well as guilt (e.g., Kubany, 1997c). Nonetheless, CT-TRG needs to be evaluated in controlled research before any general claims can be made regarding its efficacy. With that said, the procedures of CT-TRG are firmly grounded in cognitive-behavioral theory and rest on principles that are well established in empirical research.

Importantly, the procedures of CT-TRG are still being refined and elaborated. For example, we have only recently incorporated the systematic use of self-monitoring exercises into the practice of CT-TRG. In addition, we have been developing a cognitive therapy approach for addressing trauma-related anger, which complements CT-TRG. We are also developing a treatment manual and intend to conduct numerous studies to establish the efficacy of CT-TRG—starting with single-subject, multiple baseline, and quasi-experimental designs, culminating eventually in controlled clinical trials.

APPENDIX: Attitudes About Guilt Survey (AAGS; Version All)[2]

Individuals who have experienced traumatic events often experience guilt which is related to these events. They may feel guilty about something they did (or did not do), about beliefs or thoughts that they had (that they now believe to be untrue), or about having had certain feelings (or lack of feelings).

Please take a moment to think about your experience. Briefly describe what happened and what you feel guilty about:

_____

_____

_____

In answering each of the following questions, please circle ONE letter that best reflects or summarizes your view of what happened.

1. To what extent do you think that you should have known better and could have prevented or avoided the outcome?
   a. There is no possible way that I could have known better.
   b. I believe slightly that I should have known better.
   c. I believe moderately that I should have known better.
   d. For the most part I believe that I should have known better.
   e. I absolutely should have known better.

2. How justified was what you did? (i.e., How good were your reasons for what you did?)
   a. What I did was completely justified.
   b. What I did was mostly justified.
   c. What I did was moderately justified.
   d. What I did was slightly justified.
   e. What I did was not justified in any way.

3. How personally responsible were you for causing what happened?
   a. I was in no way responsible for causing what happened.
   b. I was slightly responsible for causing what happened.
   c. I was moderately responsible for causing what happened.
   d. I was largely responsible for causing what happened.
   e. I was completely responsible for causing what happened.
   Your percentage of responsibility _____%

---

[2]Adapted slightly from Kubany and Manke (1995).

4. Did you do something wrong? (i.e., Did you violate personal standards of right and wrong by what you did?)
   a. What I did was extremely wrong.
   b. What I did was very wrong.
   c. What I did was moderately wrong
   d. What I did was slightly wrong.
   e. What I did was not wrong in any way.

5. How distressed do you feel when you think about what happened?
   a. I feel no distress when I think about what happened.
   b. I feel slightly distressed when I think about what happened.
   c. I feel moderately distressed when I think about what happened.
   d. I feel very distressed when I think about what happened.
   e. I feel extremely distressed when I think about what happened.

6. Circle the answer which indicates how often you experience guilt that relates to what happened.
   Never   Seldom   Occasionally   Often   Always

7. Circle the answer which indicates the intensity or severity of guilt that you typically experience about what happened.
   None   Slight   Moderate   Considerable Extreme

REFERENCES

American Psychiatric Association. (1994). *Diagnostic and statistical manual of mental disorders* (4th ed.). Washington, DC: Author.

Andrews, B., & Brewin, C. R. (1990). Attribution of blame for marital violence: A study of antecedents and consequents. *Journal of Marriage and the Family, 52,* 757–767.

Baumeister, R. F., Stillwell, A. M., & Heatherton, T. F. (1994). Guilt: An interpersonal approach. *Psychological Bulletin, 115,* 243–267.

Beck, A. T., Rush, A. J., Shaw, B. F., & Emery, G. (1979). *Cognitive therapy of depression.* New York: Guilford Press.

De Frain, J. D., Jakub, D. K., & Mendoza, B. L. (1992). The psychological effects of sudden infant death syndrome on grandmothers and grandfathers. *Omega, 24,* 165–182.

Dutton, M. A., Burghardt, K. J., Perrin, S. G., Chrestman, K. R., & Halle, P. M. (1994). Battered women's cognitive schemata. *Journal of Traumatic Stress, 7,* 237–255.

Ellsworth, P. C. (1994). Sense, culture, and sensibility. In S. Kitayama & H. R. Markus (Eds.), *Emotion and culture: Empirical studies of social influence* (pp. 23–50). Washington, DC: American Psychological Association Press.

Fischhoff, B. (1975). Hindsight does not equal foresight: The effect of outcome knowledge on judgment under uncertainty. *Journal of Experimental Psychology: Human Perception and Performance, 1,* 288–299.

Foa, E. B. (1993). Reliability and validity of a brief instrument to measure PTSD. In L. A.

King (Chair), *Assessment of PTSD by self-report measures: Implications for construct validity.* Symposium conducted at the 9th Annual Meeting of the International Society for Traumatic Stress Studies, San Antonio, TX.

Foa, E. B., Steketee, G., & Rothbaum, B. O. (1989). Behavioral/cognitive conceptualizations of posttraumatic stress disorder. *Behavior Therapy, 20,* 155–176.

Frazier, P. A., & Schauben, L. (1994). Causal attributions and recovery from rape and other stressful life events. *Journal of Social and Clinical Psychology, 13,* 1–14.

Hawkins, S. A., & Hastie, R. (1990). Hindsight: Biased judgments of past events after outcomes are known. *Psychological Bulletin, 107,* 311–327.

Janoff-Bulman, R. (1985). The aftermath of victimization: Rebuilding shattered assumptions. In C. R. Figley (Ed.), *The study and treatment of post-traumatic stress disorder* (Vol. 1, pp. 15–35). New York: Brunner/Mazel.

Johnson, D. R., Rosenheck, R., Fontana, A., Lubin, H., Charney, D., & Southwick, S. (1996). Outcome of intensive inpatient treatment for combat-related posttraumatic stress disorder. *American Journal of Psychiatry, 153,* 771–777.

Kubany, E. S. (1994). A cognitive model of guilt typology in combat-related PTSD. *Journal of Traumatic Stress, 7,* 3–19.

Kubany, E. S. (1996). *Cognitive therapy for trauma-related guilt with a Gulf War veteran: A training video.* Available from Author.

Kubany, E. S. (1997a). *Guilt: A testable, multidimensional model.* Manuscript submitted for publication.

Kubany, E. S. (1997b). Thinking errors, faulty conclusions, and cognitive therapy for trauma-related guilt. *National Center for Post-Traumatic Stress Disorder Clinical Quarterly, 7,* 6–8.

Kubany, E. S. (1997c). Application of Cognitive Therapy for Trauma-Related Guilt (CT-TRG) with a Vietnam veteran troubled by multiple sources of guilt. *Cognitive and Behavioral Practice, 4,* 213–244.

Kubany, E. S. (1997d). *Factor analyses of the Trauma-Related Guilt Inventory—Part 2 (TRGI-Part 2).* Unpublished raw data.

Kubany, E. S., Abueg, F. R., Brennan, J. M., Owens, J. A, Kaplan, A., & Watson S. (1995). Initial examination of a multidimensional model of trauma-related guilt: Applications to combat veterans and battered women. *Journal of Psychopathology and Behavioral Assessment, 17,* 353–376.

Kubany, E. S., Abueg, F. R., Kilauano, W., Manke, F. P., & Kaplan, A. (1997). Development and validation of the Sources of Trauma-Related Guilt Survey—War-Zone Version. *Journal of Traumatic Stress, 10,* 235–258.

Kubany, E. S., Haynes, S. N., Abueg, F. R., Manke, F. P., Brennan, J. M., & Stahura, C. (1996). Development and validation of the Trauma-Related Guilt Inventory (TRGI). *Psychological Assessment, 8,* 428–444.

Kubany, E. S., Haynes, S. N., Leisen, M. B., Owens, J. A., Kaplan, A. S., Watson, S. B, & Burns, K. (1997). *Development and validation of a comprehensive measure of prior trauma exposure: The Traumatic Life Events Questionnaire (TLEQ).* Manuscript in preparation.

Kubany, E. S., Haynes, S. N., Owens, J. A., Kaplan, A. S., Leisen, M. B., Pavich, E., & Ramelli, A. (1997). *Cross-validation of the Trauma-Related Guilt Inventory with women survivors of incest and rape.* Manuscript in preparation.

Kubany, E. S., & Manke, F. P. (1995). Cognitive therapy for trauma-related guilt: Conceptual bases and treatment outlines. *Cognitive and Behavioral Practice, 2,* 23–61.

Marshall, W. L., Hudson, S. M., Jones, R., & Fernandez, Y. M. (1995). Empathy in sex offenders. *Clinical Psychology Review, 15,* 99–114.

Miller, D., & Porter, C. (1983). Self-blame in victims of violence. *Journal of Social Issues, 39,* 139–152.

Mitchell, J., & Bray, G. (1990). *Emergency services stress.* NJ: Prentice-Hall.

Newman, E., Riggs, D., & Roth, S. (1997). Thematic resolution and PTSD: An empirical investigation of the relationship between meaning and trauma-related diagnosis. *Journal of Traumatic Stress, 10,* 197–214.

Rando, T. A. (Ed.). (1986). *Parental loss of a child.* Champaign, IL: Research Press.

Resick, P. A., & Schnicke, M. K. (1993). *Cognitive processing for rape victims.* Newbury Park, CA: Sage.

Roth, S. Liebowitz, L., & DeRosa, R. R. (1997). Thematic assessment of posttraumatic stress reactions. In J. Wilson & T. M. Keane (Eds.), *Assessing psychological trauma and PTSD* (pp. 512–528). New York: Guilford Press.

Smucker, M. R., & Niederee, J. (1995). Treating incest-related PTSD and pathogenic schemas through imaginal exposure and rescripting. *Cognitive and Behavioral Practice, 2,* 63–93.

CHAPTER SEVEN

Anger and Trauma

CONCEPTUALIZATION, ASSESSMENT, AND TREATMENT

RAYMOND W. NOVACO
CLAUDE M. CHEMTOB

The activation of anger has long been recognized as a feature of clinical disorders that result from trauma, such as dissociative amnesia, dissociated identity, borderline personality, and brain-damage dementia. However, attention to the involvement of anger has occurred most notably with respect to posttraumatic stress disorder (PTSD), for which anger is considered a salient attribute of the arousal symptom cluster. Within the PTSD field, in both clinical and research contexts, concern with anger has occurred primarily in conjunction with combat-related PTSD. Therefore, much of this chapter will pertain to that domain.

The literature pertaining to anger and trauma begins with some classic works in the trauma field. We connect these to contemporary research that points to anger as an important clinical and theoretical variable. We present our own theoretical orientation, which is a regulatory deficits model, and describe types of anger dysregulation. Procedures for anger assessment are discussed, and their congruence with measures of PTSD are highlighted. Anger-focused cognitive-behavioral therapy is an important adjunctive treatment for PTSD, and an approach to anger treatment is presented. A recent, controlled clinical trial that produced significant treatment gains with patients having severe anger and severe PTSD will be discussed. Recommendations are offered for implementing anger treatment, being mindful of the treatment-resistant characteristics of this patient population.

ANGER AS A REACTION TO TRAUMA:
EARLY OBSERVATIONS

Anger has long been identified as a component of traumatic reactions. Freud's writings about affect associated with trauma largely ignored anger. Although he did say some things about retroflected anger in *Mourning and Melancholia,* Freud was preoccupied with fear and anxiety as traumatic affects. However, important historical work in the trauma field, such as Lindeman (1944), Grinker and Spiegel (1945), and Kardiner and Spiegel (1947), offered many observations about anger, hostility, and aggression as trauma-linked responses. The latter two works, which dealt with combat aftereffects, were particularly incisive in describing anger symptom patterns that were given more concerted attention by Vietnam era scholars, such as Bourne (1970), Horowitz and Solomon (1975), and Figley (1978).

Lindeman's analysis of the acute grief observed among patients variously bereaved found irritability and anger to occur along with a disconcerting loss of warmth in personal relationships. He described the hostile reactions as surprising, inexplicable, and disturbing to the patients and perceived by them as "signs of approaching insanity" (p. 142). In addition to these aspects of anger being a regular part of acute grief, he reported that more intense anger occurs in what he termed "distorted reactions" in morbid grief syndromes. There, on top of generalized hostility in social relationships, he found that "furious hostility against specific persons" may emerge, and among the targets for such was the therapist. This latter point is incisive, as anger directed at clinicians indeed represents a significant challenge in anger treatment work.

Early research on combat stress identified anger reactions as central aftereffects. The American soldier drew attention during World War II, because theaters of battle were naturalistic, albeit cruel, domains for the study of psychological trauma and adaptation to extreme environments (Stouffer, 1949). Unmistakably, research on human stress received a key impetus from investigations of psychological functioning in warfare. Grinker and Spiegel (1945) described eruptive anger occurring among flight crewmen reacting to the strains of air combat operations and specified anger and aggression as elements of stress disorder. In the earliest work on psychopathology resulting from combat, Kardiner and Spiegel (1947) described the tendency to aggression and violence as being one of the most common symptoms of traumatic neuroses:

> The aggression may show itself in the tendency to "tempers." Easily aroused to anger, these patients are very prone to motor expression. They either break or tear objects in these fits of temper, or strike the people who happen to be around them. This symptom is subject to wide variations. If the outburst is accompanied by loss of consciousness, the patient is usually dangerous. Often these patients injure themselves unintentionally. . . . The aggressiveness of the traumatic neu-

rotic is not deliberate or premeditated. His aggression is always impulsive. . . .
The sadomasochistic complex is related to the irritability, the incapacity to
analyze stimuli in the environment. (pp. 212–213)

Explosive irritability and unwarranted rage were identified by Kardiner and
Spiegel as a stage in what they saw as a progressive development of incapacitating
breakdowns, beginning with poor appetite and carelessness, then involving irritability and exaggerated reactions of rage, and finally culminating in freezing,
sleep disturbances, and being terrified of one's own artillery. What they describe
in the previous account of anger and aggression fits our own conception of anger
and PTSD developed later in terms of context-inappropriate "survival mode"
functioning.

With the Vietnam war, conceptions of combat stress improved from the
earlier notions of "shell shock" and "combat fatigue." Stressor conditions were
understood to be more than the harsh physical circumstances of war and to
include the psychological ambience of combat. All wars involve immersion in a
hostile atmosphere, but the clandestine nature of the fighting in Indochina
exacerbated the psychological strain. American troops developed "a sense of
helplessness at not being able to confront the enemy in set piece battles. The
specter of being shot at and having friends killed and maimed by virtually
unseen forces generated considerable rage which came to be displaced on anyone or anything available" (DeFazio, 1978, p. 30). Advances in military psychiatry, the general availability of drugs for self-treatment of fear, and the personnel
practice of rotations to relative safety provided for coping with acute stress in
the combat zone; but it was then observed that veterans manifested "delayed
stress responses" (Horowitz & Solomon, 1975), and "indiscriminate rage"
emerged as a common theme. Indeed, it was often the experience of rage and
the fear of one's destructive impulses that prompted veterans to seek treatment.

Early studies with Vietnam veterans highlighted anger dyscontrol. Figley and
Eisenhart (1975) had found that, compared to noncombatant servicemen, combatants got into more verbal fights, more frequently had violent fantasies and
dreams, and had fewer close friends. Similarly, DeFazio, Rustin, and Diamond
(1975), studying a college sample of Vietnam veterans who had been out of service
for an average of 5 years, found that 67% had nightmares and 41% felt themselves
to be short-tempered or hotheads. In addition to these hostile impulses and the
conjoined fear of loss of self-control, the veterans exhibited pervasive distrust of
authority figures, estrangement from society, and considerable contempt for
anything connected with the government (Horowitz & Solomon, 1975). Quite
poignantly, we found these themes to have remained salient in our recent treatment project involving Vietnam veterans with severe PTSD and severe anger
(Chemtob, Novaco, Hamada, & Gross, 1997).

CONTINUING RECOGNITION OF ANGER
IN TRAUMA RESEARCH

The identification of anger as a reaction to trauma has primarily been elaborated in research on veterans, although it has by no means been confined to that population. Nevertheless, the research on combat-related PTSD has been preeminent. Anger has been described as a significant symptom of postwar adjustment difficulties in epidemiological (Boulanger, 1986; Laufer, Yager, Frey-Wouters, & Donnellan, 1981; Kubany, Gino, Denny, & Torigoe, 1994; Kulka et al., 1988), clinical (van der Kolk, Boyd, Krystal, & Greenberg, 1984), and laboratory reports (Chemtob, Hamada, Roitblat, & Muraoka, 1994; Lasko, Gurvits, Kuhne, Orr, & Pitman, 1994).

The laboratory research has served to disentangle alternative explanations for observed anger among veterans. In the Lasko et al. (1994) study, veterans with PTSD were found to be significantly higher in anger, hostility, and aggressiveness than non-PTSD veterans. They also found that the group differences in hostility and aggressiveness were not a function of combat exposure, but they did not analyze combat exposure as a covariate of the *anger* measures. Chemtob et al. (1994), in comparing combat veterans with and without PTSD, matched them on combat exposure and included a group of noncombat veterans. Indexed by a multiple measure anger factor, the combat PTSD veterans were significantly higher in anger. Interestingly, these three groups of veterans did not differ in either cognitive or motor impulsivity, and these factors were independent of anger. Moreover, the relationship of anger to PTSD was found to be independent of trait anxiety. Hence, Chemtob et al. demonstrated that combat exposure, impulsivity, and anxiety did not account for the PTSD–anger relationship.

Clinical research has clearly substantiated the relevance of anger in PTSD patients. Veterans with PTSD report more hostility and aggression toward partners than do non-PTSD veterans (Byrne & Riggs, 1996; Carroll, Rueger, Foy, & Donahoe, 1985) and more anger-related job problems (Knight, Keane, Fairbank, Caddell, & Zimering, 1984). Female partners of veterans with PTSD also report having more violence directed toward them and more relationship problems than do the female partners of veterans without PTSD (Jordan et al., 1992). In addition to the harm to others caused by their violent behavior, this tendency toward hostile responding may also put those men at higher risk for cardiovascular disease. Kubany et al. (1994) found that the hostility scores of veterans with PTSD were one standard deviation higher than the mean for an entire group of 1293 veterans, using the Cook–Medley measure that often has been associated with heart disease incidence and mortality. Overall, it has been widely found that anger is a prominent concern for Vietnam veterans seeking clinical services (Blum, Kelley, Meyer, Carlson, & Hodson, 1984; Scurfield, Corker, & Gongla, 1984; Silver & Iocono, 1984). Thus, it has been amply demonstrated that anger and aggression have wide-ranging impact on veterans, their families, their work settings, and society at large.

The relevance of anger has continued to emerge in trauma research with other populations. Krupnick and Horowitz (1981) found anger to be a major theme in their study groups of trauma cases involving both bereavement and serious personal injury. As evaluated by two clinical judges, "rage at the source" was present in 80% of the bereavement cases and 73% of the personal injury cases. Also "rage at those exempted" was present, respectively, in 40% and 27% of the cases. In terms of the prevalence of the 10 most commonly identified themes, "rage at the source" was second only to "discomfort over vulnerability." In a study by Saunders (1994), involving domestic violence survivors in five states, "irritability and outbursts of anger" occurred as a symptom in 42.5% of the women who obtained help at domestic violence programs and 32.9% of those who obtained help at other types of programs. Indeed, if Saunders's tabled data are examined, "irritability and outbursts of anger" is the fifth highest symptom reported of the 17 symptoms of the DSM-III-R PTSD criteria. Unfortunately, the ordinal position of the anger symptom did not receive comment.

That this relative salience of anger does not receive attention from Saunders is not at all odd, as anger usually has not been a primary investigative concern. In clinical research more generally, anger has typically taken a backseat to depression and anxiety. Thus, it is hardly surprising that the burgeoning research on violence victimization experienced by women standardly ignores anger as a trauma outcome—this can be seen in many studies concerned with domestic violence as a source of PTSD (e.g., Cascardi, O'Leary, Lawrence, & Schlee, 1995; Houscamp & Foy, 1991; Rodriguez, Ryan, Kemp, & Foy, 1997) and in most studies of PTSD as a result of (other) violent crime (e.g., Resnick, Kilpatrick, Dansky, Saunders, & Best, 1993; Resnick, Kilpatrick, & Lipovsky, 1991). Even a superb PTSD treatment study concerning rape victims by Foa, Rothbaum, Riggs, and Murdock (1991) ignored anger as a criterion measure.

In contrast, anger was a quite specific focus of a study by Riggs, Dancu, Gershuny, Greenberg, and Foa (1992) on PTSD among female crime victims. Their investigation concerned 166 victims of violent crime, sexual and nonsexual, and included a comparison group of women who had not been victimized and were matched on age, race, education, and income. The crime victims were further grouped according to PTSD status and were assessed by structured interview and self-report questionnaires (STAXI [State–Trait Anger Expression Inventory] anger and PTSD symptoms) 1 week and 1 month after the assault. While anger was not related to the type of assault (sexual–nonsexual), it was significantly associated with severity of the assault and the victim's responses. Higher anger was found in conjunction with the assailant's use of a weapon and with perceived forcefulness. It was also significantly related to pleading, screaming, or fighting with the assailant. Examining anger as a function of PTSD and victimization, the victim groups had higher state anger than did the nonvictim group, and the victim groups were significantly distinguished by there being higher anger-in scores for the PTSD group. Riggs et al. speculated that intense anger interfered with the recovery from trauma, as holding in anger may block the modification of the traumatic memory due to the overlap between anger and fear structures.

Anger and trauma have an intriguing relationship. We present our conceptualization of their conjunction and of the dynamics of anger in the context of PTSD. Our model asserts that anger occurs in PTSD as a function of regulatory deficits in cognitive, arousal, and behavioral subsystems. The foundations of this conceptualization are compatible models of anger and of PTSD, which we sequentially describe.

ANGER, AGGRESSION, AND ANGER REGULATION

Anger is an emotional state that has both adaptive and maladaptive effects on behavior. As a normal emotion, it has considerable adaptive value for coping with life's adversities, such as enabling perseverance in overcoming obstacles presented by thwartings and injustice. Because anger is a mobilizing mechanism, it can energize corrective action. It provides for personal resilience and is an important guardian of self-worth. However, because anger can activate aggression, anger control is indispensable for aggression control. In addition to the detriments associated with inducing aggression, anger arousal is also problematic because it can interfere with information processing and thereby impair judgment and problem solving.

Anger activates aggression, but aggressive behavior is not an automatic consequence of anger, because aggression is regulated by inhibitory mechanisms engaged by internal and external factors. Regulatory controls of aggressive behavior, such as external restraints, expectations of punishment, empathy, or consideration of consequences in turn can be overridden by disinhibitory influences; that is, the inhibition of aggression can be overcome by facilitating factors, such as heightened arousal, aggressive modeling, lowered probability of punishment, biochemical agents, and environmental cues (Bandura, 1973, 1983). While research and theory on the regulatory control of aggression are well-established, much remains to be articulated with regard to anger, especially concerning its involvement in clinical disorders such as PTSD.

The relationship of anger to aggressive behavior is that it is a significant activator of aggression and is reciprocally influenced by aggression, but it is neither necessary nor sufficient for aggression to occur (Novaco, 1986). With the exception of some theorists, notably Berkowitz (1990, 1993), it is generally agreed that anger is an activator of aggression (Bandura, 1973; Konecni, 1975; Zillmann, 1979). Berkowitz's contrary view is that anger occurs parallel to aggression and that both are produced by "negative affect" induced by unpleasant external events. Were this to be the case, the association between aggression and depression would be roughly equivalent to that between aggression and anger, and there is little to substantiate that deduction.

The concept of anger regulation is not addressed systematically by existing theories of anger and aggression. Neither of the two most prominent theories of aggression, those of Bandura and Berkowitz, provide explicit accounts of anger regulation. While such theories do address processes that regulate aggression, they are quite silent about anger. Bandura (1973) clearly stated that aggressive behavior is regulated by environmental cues, which have response-directing functions through the information they carry concerning response consequences. Also, within his general model, arousal activates prepotent responses; therefore, lowering anger arousal will reduce aggression. Regarding the regulation of anger, as distinguished from aggressive behavior, since Bandura viewed external stimuli as having anger-evoking potency though symbolic conditioning, and since he asserted that anger can be self-generated by provocative thoughts, it can be inferred that changes in cognitive meaning systems and in rumination would be expected to have a regulatory effect on anger. Subsequently, Bandura (1983) conceptualized self-regulation as a product of self-reward and self-punishment through the subsidiary processes of self-observation, judgment, and self-response (contingencies applied to oneself). He understands the disengagement of internal control and disinhibition in terms of the resetting of self-evaluative contingencies, such as self-exoneration.

Similarly, Berkowitz's (1993) attention to regulation and control is virtually all given to aggression, only addressing anger regulation in the context of catharsis. Berkowitz (1990) claimed to address anger regulation (given the title of his article), but said surprisingly little about it, only stating that unwanted feelings activate cognitive activity that searches for coping options; that is, awareness of negative feelings prompts thoughts about causes of those feelings and considerations of how to act. His view of anger is that it is associatively linked with the "negative affect" produced by unpleasant events. He regards anger and fear as processes that only parallel the escape and aggressive motor tendencies evoked by negative affect. For Berkowitz, thought only play a small role in the initial stages of anger evocation, as automatic association processes are dominant and govern the initial reactions. He clearly posits cognitive control of aggressive behavior, as when conscious anticipation of punishment can suppress aggression, but for him, cognition has minimal influence on the activation of anger.

Bandura and Berkowitz have primarily sought to understand aggressive behavior and have treated anger as a secondary phenomenon. In contrast, Averill (1982) took anger as his focus, and his social–constructivist approach to emotion conceives of anger as a transitory social role governed by social rules. As his research has concerned normative patterns of anger, his analysis does not provide for an understanding of anger as a clinical problem or a condition of psychological disturbance; that is, he omits dealing with the dysregulation of anger or internal processes that provide for ongoing monitoring of anger states.

Novaco's (1994a) model of anger pertains to its normal and abnormal forms, conceptualizing anger as entailing three reciprocally connected domains: cognitive, arousal, and behavioral. These domains are also linked to an environmental context. Anger is viewed as a product of (1) the cognitive processing of environmental circumstances, (2) conjoined physiological arousal, and (3) behavioral reactions. Novaco's (1994a) model maps these domains of anger and their subdimensions and stipulates their reciprocal connectedness with each other and with environmental circumstances. However, he left regulatory systems unspecified, stating that regarding "the capacity to regulate anger and aggression . . . much remains to be addressed with regard to psychological deficits in anger control" (p. 53).

Guided by the latter model of anger and by the Chemtob, Roitblat, Hamada, Carlson, and Twentyman (1988) information-processing model of PTSD, which posits "survival mode" functioning as a state of dysregulation, Chemtob, Novaco, Hamada, Gross, and Smith (1997) proposed a new model to account for anger in the context of trauma. This new model construes trauma-induced anger in terms of regulatory deficits in cognitive, arousal, and behavioral systems associated with "survival mode" functioning in PTSD. We recapitulate this model in part here.

TRAUMA, ANGER, AND REGULATORY DEFICITS

In conjunction with trauma, anger is intrusive and is part of a dyscontrol syndrome involving heightened arousal, hostile appraisal, and antagonistic behavior activated as a survival response to severe threat. Maladjustment difficulties obviously occur when the intense anger is activated in the absence of genuine survival threat; that is, the traumatized person fails to regulate covert and overt responses in accordance with situational realities.

Chemtob et al. (1988) conceptualized PTSD symptoms as context-inappropriate activation of "survival mode" functioning, which, in the absence of threat, is usually suppressed by normal cognitive processing. "Survival mode" functioning has a number of important features: (1) It is triggered by perceptions of external, life-threatening events or by expectancies about encountering such threats; importantly, threat perception is not always consciously mediated or "thoughtfully" recognized; (2) once triggered, "survival" mode is peremptory and preemptive of other cognitive processing, because dealing with life threats is a superordinate requirement for the organism; (3) it is characterized by specific cognitive biases, including a tendency to give primacy to pattern matching, to require less evidence of threat to engage action, and to be inclined toward threat confirmation and increased vigilance that leads to more efficient recognition of the presence of threat; (4) it entails a substantial load on the organism's capacity to regulate optimally its arousal level, which may lead to impairment in this capacity; and (5) its peremptory quality entails a loss of self-monitoring (i.e., one does not always recognized the shift into a different mode).

In PTSD patients, "survival mode" functioning becomes maladaptive because its activation is routinely incongruent with the state of affairs confronting the individual. This activation can result from several causes, and frequently from dynamic, interrelated causes. For example, associative reminders can serve to provoke cognitive processing into "survival mode." Once this processing is activated, a positive feedback loop and "confirmation bias" (cf. Chemtob et al., 1988) tend to validate the engagement of "survival mode" through the identification of threat-confirmatory aspects of the environment, which in turn increase physiological arousal. This process often escapes top-down regulation due to the experiential urgency that it engenders.

In responding to a threat, real or perceived, the activation of "survival mode" includes the activation of anger structures. Anger schemas are integrated mental representations about environment behavior relationships entailing rules governing threatening situations. For example, rules pertaining to personal protection, response to injustice, challenges to self-worth, and justified retaliation are part of anger schemas, the activation of which includes conjoined arousal and behavioral control information. Because people with PTSD are "primed" to identify threat, they often engage "survival mode" more rapidly. The spreading activation of threat schemas consequently strongly potentiates anger. Conversely, the activation of anger structures can serve to activate the full "survival mode." Importantly, inhibitory controls on aggression can be overridden by the conjoined activation of the hostile appraisal and the heightened arousal.

The linking of anger to survival carries several implications about its activation in PTSD: (1) Its onset carries a coping response urgency that preempts alternative appraisals of the triggering event and considerations of alternative action plans; (2) it engages cognitive processes that dispose or bias the system toward confirmation of the expectation of threat; (3) the association of anger with survival leads to its activation in response to minimal cues; (4) the strong arousal and the peremptory nature of the threat schemas suppress inhibitory controls of aggressive behavior; and (5) threat–anger responses are organized as a positive feedback loop; the more threat is perceived, the more anger and aggression. Conversely, the more anger and aggression, the greater the readiness to perceive the presence of a threat. This self-confirming vicious cycle can be interrupted early in its activation by the detection of disconfirming evidence, including consideration of mitigating circumstances (e.g., such as lack of hostile intent or by trained self-monitoring that permits reframing the episode). However, there is an activation level at which the system triggers into "survival mode" and becomes far more difficult to regulate after the mode shift. Because of the tendency to engage "survival mode" more readily, PTSD patients are more likely to become angry.

Put succinctly, the anger system is viewed as having three major domains (cognition, arousal, and behavior) which are interrelated in activation and inhibition, and it is intrinsically connected to the threat system, with its associated fear and avoidance responses. Anger regulation is affected by traumatic experi-ence, which resets activation and inhibition patterns in accordance with perceived threat, and by the shift into "survival mode" functioning. Patients with PTSD readily shift into "survival mode," and, as part of the peremptoriness of that shift, there is substantial loss of self-monitoring. The context-inappropriate cognitive distortions, which tend to confirm the presence of threat and lead to the defensive activation of anger and aggression, have for that person a powerful subjective quality of immediacy and validity. A fuller presentation of this conceptual frame-work can be found in Chemtob, Novaco, Hamada, Gross, and Smith (1997).

Anger dyscontrol is among the most challenging of clinical problems, par-ticularly when it is conjoined with impulsive, aggressive behavior. High-intensity anger combined with diminished inhibitory control is alarming and worrisome. Hence, the occurrence of anger in the context of combat-related PTSD has provoked particular concern about treatment needs and treatment delivery sys-tems. Clinical concerns about anger, however, are not restricted to its potential to activate violent behavior. Riggs et al. (1992), in their study of female crime victims, called for effective treatment of anger, which they viewed as impeding psycholog-ical adjustment following trauma, and they speculated that anger during exposure sessions may reduce the efficacy of anxiety treatment.

Because certain clinical populations (e.g., institutionalized psychiatric pa-tients, as well as combat veterans) have had long-standing problems with anger, typically compounded by comorbid substance abuse, instability in employment and personal relationships, and physical health problems, psychotherapeutic treatment of their anger difficulties encounters considerable obstacles. Remedia-tion of anger in such treatment-resistant groups would also sound an optimistic note for anger interventions with other difficult to treat patients, and we have some good news later in that regard.

SPECIAL CHALLENGES IN TREATING ANGRY CLIENTS

Uncontrolled anger, being too easily transformed into destructive aggression, beck-ons for therapeutic intervention to restore or improve self-regulation. However, the treatment of anger presents a number of special challenges to clinicians and to health care institutions, as the delivery of "anger management" services is less than straightforward. Horowitz and Solomon (1975) described the person with delayed stress syndrome as typically suspicious, easily frustrated, and feeling as though he or she will lose control over hostile impulses. Chronically angry patients are not only treatment resistant, but treating them is also problematic because of their readiness to become angry during therapy and toward the therapist.

Angry people are often fiercely resistant to anger treatment. Because anger can mobilize one's psychological resources, energizing behaviors that take correc-tive action, the capacity for anger is needed as a survival mechanism. In a world where the significance of the individual is diminished by bureaucracy, anger is a fortification for a sense of worth. Proposing "anger management" could be viewed disparagingly as an insidious strategy to stifle the individual human personality or to constrain the will to determine one's own destiny. Anger provides for personal resilience. It is a guardian of self-esteem, it potentiates the ability to redress grievances, and it can boost determination to overcome obstacles to happiness and aspirations.

In effect, people can remain attached to anger, because it is so very functional. Dislodging the attachment to anger is a matter of helping the person to see that chronic anger has costs that outweigh the functions that it has been serving. Achieving this hinges on the therapeutic relationship. However, there are a number of refractory impediments to establishing that relationship, as special difficulties arise in the treatment of anger that can thwart or derail the therapeutic process. These challenges or difficulties peculiar to anger treatment are clinician safety, the low frustration tolerance of clients, the instrumentality of anger and aggression, and the resource impoverishment of clients.

Clinician Safety

A prevalent issue for the clinician is personal danger. Indeed, PTSD has been found to be a consequence of patient violence on clinical staff (Caldwell, 1992). Needless to say, it is unsettling for therapists and counselors to work with persons who have explosive tendencies. In cases where there has been a history of violent behavior, the clinician's concern is easily aroused by the client's expressions of anger and by descriptions of anger experiences accompanied by aggressive impulses. It is imperative that the therapist be at ease with client anger expressed in narrative accounts or in direct personal communication in the therapy room or on the ward. Precautions for personal safety should always be in place, particularly in conjunction with treating mentally disordered patients who have been previously violent.

While, on the one hand, anger imparts a sense of mastery, on the other, it can signify that one is out of control. When it attains levels of intense arousal, it can be profoundly troubling to the person having the anger experience. Because of its intrinsic connection to the threat system, strong anger, and its implied loss of control, is anxiety engendering for the client. The admixture of fear can intensify rage reactions. To forestall a spreading activation, the therapist must provide a sense of control and in many ways serve as a role model for how to handle anger experiences. Thus, it is imperative that the therapist not be unduly alarmed by exposure to anger. Remaining calm not only provides a counterbalancing reassurance, it prevents emitting cues that might be read as threat signals in the confirmation-biased perception of the client. Even with regard to anger communications that are relatively low in explosiveness, if the therapist becomes uneasy, the troubled individual might well wonder whether it is safe or the least bit useful to reveal matters of deep personal significance to someone who becomes unsettled upon hearing the disclosures. When clients sense that their psychological realities alarm the therapist, the helping process is undermined, because their sense of safety is compromised by the therapist's alarm.

Some clients may indeed test the therapist's acceptance of them by describing angry feelings, hostile fantasies, and violent behavior. Distrust often takes the form of anger reactions; hence, composure on the part of the therapist is imperative for enhancing the therapeutic relationship, as well as for clinician safety. Treatment of angry clients requires the mastery of anxiety about assaultive risk. This requires sharpened awareness, safe arrangement of physical surroundings, training in personal protection, and having a security response to crisis.

Low Frustration Tolerance

Persons who are prone to provocation are inherently impatient. Like other types of clients, they are often ambivalent and have poorly defined or unrealistic goals for the course of therapy. They may thus become frustrated when desired treatment effects are not quickly forthcoming. As their frustration mounts, they become inclined to disengage from therapy, the impulse for which may be activated by relatively minor events in their regular life or in conjunction with receiving treatment. Because angry people, by their own long-standing behavior, have raised the probability of exposure to aversive events, the therapist should be prepared for such occasions of client frustration and demoralization.

It is imperative that the clinician exercise good coping skills when faced with client expressions of frustration, viewing this as a manifestation of the clinical problem and to not "take it personally." Rather than making undue personal attributions about the client's reactions, the therapist can utilize the manifest crisis as an opportunity to teach anger coping skills. Instead of merely providing reassurance and attempting redirection, the client's frustration and impatience can be engaged and explored, thereby teaching how to communicate about anger and how to deal with conflict. Beyond the ordinary inertia impeding change, angry patients can feel hopeless about ever being different, particularly if they have been recurrently institutionalized.

Given the impatient disposition of clients with anger problems, it is advantageous for a treatment program to be clearly defined and structured, so as to minimize the frustration that can result from vague expectations regarding treatment. Moreover, the proneness to frustration and impatience that are intrinsic to the problem constellation also dictates that treatment studies be thoughtfully designed with control group conditions that do not activate anger responses.

Instrumentality

Like habitual aggressive behavior, chronic anger is an obstinate problem by virtue of its instrumentality. Anger has considerable value in dealing with aversive situations, particularly as it imparts a sense of mastery or control. One can overcome constraints and dispatch unwanted others by becoming angry and acting aggressively. Persons who are so disposed are reluctant to relinquish this sense of effectiveness. The propensity for anger reflects a combative orientation in responding to situations of threat and hardship, which is not easily surrendered as a learned style of coping. This has important implications for the clinician's presentation of anger treatment and for maintaining a sense of safety.

If the presentation of "anger control" therapy suggests to clients that their sense of effectance will be jeopardized ("robbed of their power"), then the leverage for treatment is easily undermined. Learning anger control skills must be seen to mean enhancement of effectiveness in handling provocation. Very importantly, "anger control" must be approached in a preventive sense and in an arousal-regulatory sense, as well as with regard to enhancing overt behavioral skills. Clients must learn to ask themselves, not only "What should I do when I get angry," but "How can I not get angry in the first place, and if I do get angry, how can I keep the anger at a moderate level of intensity?" They can be helped to see that, whatever they want to accomplish that is lasting and meaningful, uncontrolled anger does not increase its likelihood of attainment. The costs of unregulated anger are the keystone for therapeutic change.

That anger episodes can be used to coerce desired behavior is sometimes understood in terms of "secondary gain," which we conceptualize as attempts to gain adaptive advantage from disability. With respect to anger, "secondary gain" involves the recognition, conscious or unconscious, that one can manipulate one's own anger state to get others to do what one wants. The key aspects of using anger dysregulation for advantage is to manipulate the fear of aggression, so as to induce others to yield ground. In the context of treatment, therapeutic effectiveness in addressing this special difficulty hinges on the clinician safety theme, as well as management of the countertranferences that angry patients provoke. The latter issue highlights the importance of having procedures for case supervision.

Resource Impoverishment

A fourth impediment to treatment is that clients with problems of anger and aggression have deficiencies in cognitive, social, and economic resources. Persons institutionalized for mental disorder, developmental disabilities, or criminal behavior are often of low socioeconomic status (SES) and have few resources to overcome their anger difficulties, and as we noted at the outset, combat veterans with PTSD have had significant postwar adjustment difficulties in the realms of employment, family, and health. Several dysfunctional reciprocities between anger/aggression and resource variables exacerbate treatment difficulties.

Eruptions of anger are not conducive to job stability. Reciprocally, unstable employment raises the risk of anger and aggression by increasing aversive experiences and other motives for aggression, as well as by diminishing aggresssion-neutralizing influences. Economic hardships are frustrative conditions that activate anger and aggression. In a large sample study in three U.S. metropolitan areas, job loss was found to increase the risk of violent behavior by a sixfold ratio, controlling for age, alcohol disorder, other psychiatric disorder, gender, race, household SES, and previous violent behavior (Catalano, Dooley, Novaco, Wilson, & Hough, 1993). Violent behavior, during that investigation's 18-month study interval, increased the likelihood of job loss by a fifteenfold ratio, controlling for the above covariates. In a subsequent study involving a time-series analysis of regional economic data, communitywide job loss was found to affect the rate of psychiatric hospital civil commitments for behavior dangerous to others, controlling for autocorrelation and other types of commitments (Catalano, Novaco, & McConnell, 1997). This suggests a need for therapist sensitivity and advocacy regarding client employment issues.

Clearly, diminished economic resources aggravate anger difficulties, but in addition to the aversiveness associated with economic strain, anger dyscontrol negatively impacts important social relationships, especially marital and family support systems. Male Vietnam War veterans with PTSD, compared to theater veterans without PTSD, have been found to have severe family adjustment problems, including three times the rate of family violence, by both the veteran and the spouse/partner (Jordan et al., 1992). Those investigators also found that the spouses or partners of the veterans with PTSD reported high levels of nonspecific distress, and about half "felt on the verge of a nervous breakdown" (p. 923). Moreover, their children had a significantly greater likelihood of having clinical-range behavior problems. Trauma, anger, and violence not only diminish family support, but they also add additional stressful aggravations.

The economic and social resource deficits of aggression-prone populations are exacerbated by their lack of cognitive skills. The third reciprocity here is between intellectual functioning and aggressive behavior. Huesmann, Eron, and Yarmel (1988) have shown that aggressive behavior in childhood interferes with the development of intellectual functioning and is predictive of poorer intellectual achievement in adulthood, and that low intelligence makes the learning of aggressive response more likely. More generally, persons with clinical problems of anger and aggression often have cognitive skill deficits in areas fundamental to implementing cognitive-behavioral treatment. They frequently need help in elementary matters, such as identifying emotion, differentiating types and degrees of emotion, and recording self-observations, which are the foundation of self-regulatory procedures, such as self-monitoring. However, limitations in cognitive skills need not disqualify application of a cognitive-behavioral approach to anger disorder, as Benson, Rice, and Miranti (1986) and Black and Novaco (1993) have successfully applied cognitive-behavioral therapy anger treatment to mentally handicapped patients.

ASSESSMENT OF ANGER

Anger is a subjective emotion, and it is therefore very appropriate that anger has been assessed primarily by self-report procedures. However, the assessment of anger in a clinical context is highly reactive. Because of a variety of negative connotations and anticipated consequences of having a "high anger" designation, people will mask their anger reactions or their anger disposition on self-report assessments, whether it be on psychometric scales or on interviews. Clients with anger problems tend not to be at all forthcoming in self-disclosure, having a highly suspicious, distrusting mind-set. Thus, the interpretation of anger scores on self-report scales must be done cautiously. Establishing trust and confidentiality will maximize the validity of anger self-report measures. This issue is particularly salient with regard to forensic patients and others in secure settings, as well as when health, employment, or disability benefits might be affected by anger status.

Bearing in mind that anger can be assessed through a variety of clinical rating procedures, including interview and behavioral observation approaches, we here restrict our presentation to psychometric assessment of anger and to a few scales that we have found to be useful with regard to anger in the context of PTSD.

Two psychometric instruments for assessing anger by patient self-report are (1) the Spielberger State–Trait Anger Expression Inventory (STAXI; Spielberger, 1991) and (2) the Novaco Anger Scale (NAS; Novaco, 1994a). The STAXI includes measures of state anger, trait anger, and anger expression. The trait anger scale has subscales of angry temperament and angry reaction; the anger expression scale has subscales of anger-in, anger-out, and anger control. The STAXI has had extensive development and validation with adolescent and adult samples, from both normal populations and clinical populations with physical health problems (Spielberger, 1991). The STAXI combines the State–Trait Anger Inventory (STAI; Spielberger, 1988a) with the Anger Expression Scale (AX; Spielberger, 1988b).

The NAS has cognitive, arousal, and behavioral domain scales as components of its anger disposition measure. The NAS was developed and validated for use with mentally disordered and normal populations. In studies with psychiatric patients in California state hospitals (Novaco, 1994a), it was found to have an internal reliability of .95 and a test–retest reliability of .84, and to be significantly related to a number of anger and aggressive behavior criteria evaluated in concurrent, retrospective, and prospective analyses, which also included comparative anger measures. The concurrent correlation of the NAS scale with the Spielberger Trait Anger Scale was found to be .84; and its predictive correlation with Spielberger State Anger was found to be .36 at 2 weeks, .43 at 1 month, and .46 at 2 months with 151 patients in the analyses. As the NAS has theoretically specified subscales, it was designed to be an improvement over the Novaco Provocation Inventory (NPI; Novaco, 1975, 1988). The latter measure, previously 80 items in length, has now been condensed to a 25-item scale, which measures anger reactions to hypothetical situations.

In PTSD research, the combined STAI and AX scales were used in the study of female crime victims by Riggs et al. (1992) and that of Vietnam War veterans by Lasko et al. (1994), both of which examined anger in PTSD and non-PTSD groups. The AX has been used in the laboratory study of anger, impulsivity, and PTSD by Chemtob et al. (1994), which also used the NPI. In the PTSD anger treatment study by Chemtob, Novaco, Hamada, and Gross (1997), the AX and the NAS were used. Pertinent to differentiating PTSD from non-PTSD groups, Riggs et al. found that State Anger and Anger-In were significant, Lasko et al. found all STAXI subscales to be significant, and Chemtob et al. (1994) found the AX and the NPI to be significant. The NAS has not yet been reported for a PTSD differentiating study, but we are presently engaged in that regard. A more extended discussion of anger measures pertinent to cognitive-behavioral treatment of anger can be found in Novaco (1994b).

Another potentially valuable index of anger are five items on the Mississippi Scale for Combat-Related Posttraumatic Stress Disorder (Keane, Caddell, & Taylor, 1988). These items, with their scale numbers in parentheses, are as follows: "If someone pushes me too far, I am likely to become violent" (3); "The people who know me best are afraid of me" (5); "I am frightened by my urges" (23); "I am an easygoing, even-tempered person" (27); and "I lose my cool and explode over minor everyday things" (31). We have found this set of anger/aggression items to have a high degree of internal consistency ($r = .87$) in a sample of 142 veterans referred for clinical services.[1] We have found this set of items, computed as an index, to be very significantly related to the AX and NAS measures.

ANGER TREATMENT AND PTSD

Given the far-ranging negative impact of anger problems, the dearth of research on anger treatment for PTSD patients is lamentable. Treatment intervention studies for PTSD have not been focused on, or even prioritized, anger as an outcome criterion. For example, Foa, Rothbaum, Riggs, and Murdock (1991) successfully treated female crime victims for PTSD with cognitive-behavioral interventions, but anger was not a specified treatment target in that study and was not part of the measurement protocol. Yet that patient population has been found to have significant anger in conjunction with PTSD (Riggs et al., 1992). Similarly,

---

[1]These five items are noted by Lasko et al. (1994) as being "aggression-related items" (p. 375), although they did not report separate analysis of them. We had already isolated this set of items as a subscale in our own research and computed the five-item total as an anger index with 77 patients in spring 1993. We are presently preparing an empirical report of the relationship of anger to PTSD based on our work with multiple samples of veterans.

in a PTSD treatment study with female sexual assault victims, Resick and Schnicke (1992) introduced their study making the point that PTSD is much more than a fear-based disorder and that intrusive memories and avoidance might be activated by strong affects other than fear. In that context, they assert that "crime victims often report experiencing anger" (p. 749). Curiously then, they did not describe any of their cognitive processing therapy as addressing anger, nor did they give any report of an anger measure, despite using the Symptom Checklist 90 (SCL-90) as a dependent variable and this scale having a hostility subscale. Research on male violence victims as well ignores anger in assessing PTSD symptoms, as did Burton, Foy, Bwanausi, Johnson, and Moore (1994) in their study of male juvenile offenders.

The scant attention given to anger treatment with PTSD populations may be a function of the strong priority given to fear and depression in conceptualizing PTSD symptomotology. However, the various obstacles to treating anger discussed earlier may also be significant in diverting focus. Given the range of impediments to doing therapy with seriously angry patients, our recent study with Vietnam War combat veterans having severe PTSD and severe anger offers an optimistic note for the efficacy of anger treatment. As the patients in our Vietnam War veteran study were very treatment-resistant, the results have implications for efficacy in treating the anger problems of other traumatized populations.

Despite the documented association between anger and combat-related PTSD, and despite the importance of treating the anger component of PTSD, there had been no empirically validated approach to anger treatment for this disorder. The project utilized a cognitive-behavioral intervention for anger that had been demonstrated to be effective with other clinical populations in research involving experimental, multiple baseline, and case study designs (Novaco, 1975, 1994b). In an important addition to the preexisting protocol (Novaco, 1983), we focused on the patients' cognitive schemas related to combat experience, threat, survival, and trauma as these structures affected their daily lives.

The treatment of anger remains a relatively neglected topic in clinical research, especially with seriously disturbed patients. Vietnam War combat veterans with PTSD most certainly fall into that latter category. The studies by Chemtob et al. (1994) and by Lasko et al. (1994) showed the heightened anger associated with Vietnam combat PTSD patients and called attention to the importance of anger control skills. These men are often remarkably treatment resistant and are additionally problematic because of their readiness to become angry during treatment and toward the therapist. Thus, our controlled study (Chemtob, Novaco, Hamada, & Gross, 1997) was an important step in advancing treatment implementation.

The cognitive-behavioral treatment of anger began with Novaco (1975) in an experimental study with an outpatient population. In that initial project, the anger treatment principally involved cognitive therapy and relaxation training applied in conjunction with graduated exposure to provocation. A treatment components and control group design was used, and the combined anger treatment resulted in a significantly greater reduction in anger on multiple measures in multiple provocation modes, compared to a self-monitoring, attention control condition, and to the cognitive and relaxation component conditions.

The anger treatment was subsequently reconceptualized and developed further in terms of a stress inoculation framework (Meichenbaum, 1975), which emphasized cognitive-behavioral coping skills. The stress framework served to broaden the conceptualization of anger as a clinical problem and facilitated the presentation of the treatment as the learning of coping skills. Also, Meichenbaum's three-phase approach of cognitive preparation, skill acquisition, and application practice provided useful rubrics for the development of treatment components. The central components of the anger treatment were then constructed as cognitive restructuring, arousal reduction, and behavioral coping skills, and were successfully applied to a hospitalized patient with severe anger problems (Novaco, 1977a) and to police officers (Novaco, 1977b; Sarason, Johnson, Berberich, & Siegel, 1979). The training of therapists in the use of the treatment method was also experimentally validated in a controlled study with probation counselors (Novaco, 1980).

This stress inoculation approach to anger management has been evaluated with diverse clinical populations. Several experimental studies of this approach with institutionalized juvenile delinquents obtained significant treatment effects (Schlichter & Horan, 1981; Saylor, Benson, & Einhaus, 1985; Feindler, Marriott, & Iwata, 1984), and Feindler and Ecton (1986) developed some new treatment elements, including social skills training components. Other experimental studies of anger treatment based on the Novaco approach, using control and comparison groups, include Benson et al. (1986) with mentally retarded adults, Stermac (1983) with forensic patients, Moon and Eisler (1986) with college students, and Hazaleus and Deffenbacher (1986) with college students. Subsequent work by Deffenbacher gave explicit attention to arousal reduction in treating recruited college student clients (Deffenbacher, 1988; Deffenbacher, Story, Brandon, Hogg, & Hazaleus, 1988; Deffenbacher, Story, Stark, Hogg, & Brandon, 1987).

A number of case studies and multiple baseline design studies involving a variety of serious clinical disorders have provided further support for the efficacy of cognitive-behavioral interventions based on this anger treatment procedure. Successful treatment results have been reported by Nomellini and Katz (1983) with child-abusing parents, by Bistline and Frieden (1984) with a chronically aggressive man, by Spirito, Finch, Smith, and Cooley (1981) with an emotionally disturbed boy, by Lira, Carne, and Masri (1983) with a brain-damaged patient, by Black and Novaco (1993) with a mentally handicapped man, and by both Bornstein, Weisser, and Balleweg (1985) and Howells (1989) with institutionalized forensic patients. Recently, Renwick, Black, Ramm, and Novaco (1997) achieved significant treatment gains with very angry and assaultive psychiatric patients with serious mental disorder in a maximum security hospital.

This cognitive-behavioral approach to anger treatment involves the following key components: (1) client education about anger, stress, and aggression; (2) self-monitoring of anger frequency, intensity, and situational triggers; (3) construction of a personal anger provocation hierarchy, created from the self-monitoring data and used for the practice and testing of coping skills; (4) arousal reduction techniques of progressive muscle relaxation, breathing-focused relaxation, and guided imagery training; (5) cognitive restructuring by altering attentional focus, modifying appraisals, and using self-instruction; (6) training behavioral coping in communication and respectful assertiveness as modeled and rehearsed with the therapist; and (7) practicing the cognitive, arousal regulatory, and behavioral coping skills while visualizing and role-playing progressively more intense, anger-arousing scenes from the personal hierarchies.

Provocation is simulated in the therapeutic context by imagination and role play of anger incidents from the life of the client, as directed by the therapist. This is a graduated exposure based on a hierarchy of anger incidents produced by the collaborative work of client and therapist. This graduated, hierarchical exposure, done in conjunction with the teaching of coping skills, is the basis for the "inoculation" metaphor and is most central to the "stress inoculation" approach (cf. Meichenbaum, 1985).

This stress inoculation approach to anger control was the foundation of the specialized anger therapy implemented in our controlled treatment trial with Vietnam War veterans, which was conducted through the Hawaii VA, in collaboration with Roger Hamada, Doug Gross, and Gary Smith. Importantly, the anger treatment protocol was augmented by therapeutic derivations of the cognitive action model of PTSD and the concept of "survival mode" functioning discussed earlier. Centrally, in "survival mode," a person responds with context-inappropriate cognitive distortions that tend to confirm the presence of threat and lead to the defensive activation of anger and aggression. The shift into that mode of functioning is accompanied by a substantial loss of self-monitoring.

In augmenting the anger treatment protocol, therapists educated patients about the phase-shift into survival mode that occurs in PTSD and enabled them to recognize the phase shift dynamic and the automatic anger activation. Patients were helped to see that their anger was once functional as part of a survival response and was a legitimate attempt to adapt to that past survival context. With supportive guidance, they can then identify the present context inappropriate aspects of survival mode functioning and the dysfunctionality of the conjoined anger and aggression. The associated loss of self-monitoring can then be remedied.

Essential to reinstituting regulatory controls for anger and aggression is treating the central self-monitoring deficits. In that regard, the clinician helps the patient to (1) monitor the cognitions that he or she typically experiences when threatened and which induce anger episodes; (2) identify signs of arousal, including its intensity, duration, and lability in response to the perception of danger or threat; (3) recognize the role that anger reactions play, both as responses to sensing danger and as behaviors that create danger for others, thus escalating the threat potential of a situation; and (4) distinguish impulsive actions from more controlled responses. The cognitive, arousal, and behavioral domains of anger are thus segmented for self-monitoring.

Anger has been commonly understood by patients and nonpatients, as being a "passion" by which one is "gripped," "seized," or "torn" (Averill, 1982), suggesting a loss of control. High intensity anger is patently distressing. Putting anger in a survival context and segmenting its domains of activation facilitate the development of regulatory skills, as its meaning is clarified and its intrinsic goals are validated. Instead of viewing anger as a mysterious force that takes charge of the personality, the client is given conceptual tools to make sense of his or her experience, to focus change efforts into partitioned subdomains of anger, and to gauge therapeutic progress more meaningfully and realistically. The client is able to work on focused, goal-limited objectives, rather than on a global "anger problem" that can otherwise seem impenetrable and insolvable. This, then, provides a safeguard against the problem of frustration and demoralization discussed earlier as an obstacle to anger treatment. Correspondingly, the segmenting of anger domains enables the therapist to track therapeutic progress with greater sensitivity to change.

The cognitive distortions linked to threat perceptions and highly automatized anger have a powerful immediacy and validity. For war veterans with PTSD, the perceptual frame of reference is the combat environment, hence "what is" and "what was" are confused. Their day-to-day functioning occurs with a high degree of self-protectedness and reactivity. Life's hassles, insufficient resources, and postwar government administrative bureaucracy reinforce that reactivity. It is in this context that one encounters the continuance of threat perceptions and anger-engendering cognitions, such as "I'm expendable," "I'm a problem to them," "I can't let my guard down," "Anyone could be the enemy," and "If I screw-up, somebody dies." Being very much stuck in a self-protective mode, their cognitions are replete with dichotomous and polarized thinking (good–bad; friend–enemy). Even when the anger is disguised as flippancy or inappropriate laughter, it is not far from the surface and can be readily uncovered.

Anger is intrinsically infused with the theme of justification, and this is compounded for Vietnam veterans due to the well-known circumstances of the war. Indeed, anger became a core theme in group identity and in social cohesion connected to the traumatic experience, and it is fair to say that one risked group rejection by not sharing in justified beliefs of persecution and victimization. Anger expanded to intense moral indignation of group members against diffusely constituted "others"—saying, in effect, " 'They' are responsible for my actions," and, therefore, " 'They' can be discounted," and " 'They' betrayed me and abandoned me, and now I am entitled to exoneration and compensation." This strongly justified moral posture serves to entrench anger. Moreover, as "they" can be discounted, one does not need to be concerned about "their" needs, desires, or worth. Hence, the fixation in the self-protective mode presents a formidable barrier to the role-taking perspective that is essential to anger regulation. Self-absorption, defensiveness, and preoccupation with threat run counter to empathic understanding when faced with an aversive experience. Rather than disappointment, one gets anger provocation.

Cognitive restructuring efforts must be grounded in the trust and safety of the therapeutic relationship. The "survival mode" concept provides a meaningful connection between the troublesome current anger eruptions and the originating traumatic exposure, which then facilitates consideration of alternative constructions of contemporary events, arousal modulation, and context-appropriate modes of responding. However, this is far from being a smooth road. For example, efforts to promote a shift to being empathic may import a confrontation with the trauma of have killed people, and resistance might then emerge (e.g., "If they don't care about me, why should I care about them?"). As a safeguard to ensure trust and promote therapeutic alliance, our recent controlled treatment trial used clinicians who were experienced therapists and also had extensive combat experience in Vietnam. Yet even this did not always help, as one veteran angrily denounced his therapist, who had been frequently in combat in Vietnam, saying, "Anyone knows that officers cannot be trusted." One can here see the refractoriness of anger-engendering schemas and the formidable obstacles to treatment engagement. Nevertheless, the project, which we next describe briefly, achieved significant treatment gains.

HAWAII VA TREATMENT STUDY

As the anger therapy is understood to be a treatment adjunct to routine psychological and medical care, the Chemtob, Novaco, Hamada, and Gross (1977) study randomly assigned patients to either (1) routine clinical care only, or (2) routine clinical care plus the specialized anger treatment, implemented over 12 sessions. The routine clinical care control condition consisted of an amalgam of treatments typically provided at veterans' centers and VA mental health clinics. These heterogeneous treatments consisted of psychiatric consultation, medication, and supportive psychological interventions, such as eclectic individual counseling, substance-abuse groups, and support/rap groups. Regarding the various psychological supportive interventions, each patient in the control group received at least two of these services, and several patients also received systematic desensitization addressing PTSD symptoms. Fifteen patients completed the assessment and treatment protocol, with 8 patients in the anger treatment condition and seven in the routine clinical care condition. In addition to pre- and posttreatment assessments, we conducted an 18-month follow-up for both treatment completers and dropouts.

The patients in the study had severe PTSD, reflected in their average Mississippi Scale score ($M = 130.3$; $SD = 13.5$), which exceeded by several standard deviations the cutoff score of 89.0 used in the National Vietnam Veteran Readjustment Study (Kulka et al., 1990) to discriminate combat-related PTSD. They were also significantly higher on this index than 170 consecutive admissions to a specialized Hawaii VA PTSD outpatient clinic ($M = 118.6$, $SD = 23.7$). The study participants were also an extremely angry group, as evidenced by their NAS scores ($M = 112.7$; $SD = 15.8$), which are substantially higher than California State Hospital civil commitment and forensic inpatients ($M = 90.1$; $SD = 18.2$) and also significantly higher than the PTSD clinic sample ($M = 97.6$; $SD = 20.7$).

Recognizing anger's multidimensionality, we measured (1) anger disposition, assessing trait-like aspects of anger responding, (2) anger reactions, pertaining to the impact of situational provocation, and (3) anger control, reflecting the capacity for anger regulation. Compared to the routine clinical care treatment condition and controlling for pretreatment scores, we obtained significant anger treatment group effects on multiple self-report measures of anger reactions and anger control at posttreatment, and the significant differences in anger control were maintained at 18-month follow-up. We also found in covariance analyses on posttreatment Clinician-Administered PTSD Scale (CAPS) indices that traumatic reexperiencing, in frequency and intensity, was significantly lower for patients in the anger treatment condition in contrast with the control group, and a similar effect was obtained for state anxiety. However, we did not find any significant anger treatment effects on physiological measures of anger reactions obtained in conjunction with imaginal provocations, nor did we find differential treatment group effects on anger disposition measures, although post hoc analyses did find a significant reduction from pretest to posttest in AX scores and NAS Cognitive scores for the anger treatment group. Overall, we found modest but noteworthy treatment gains for the anger treatment.

The size of our treatment groups is an obvious limitation of the study in evaluating its internal validity and generalizability. However, the routine clinical care condition represented a conservative control group, as it represented real treatment for PTSD, and we used conservative analyses and demonstrated strong effect sizes. An important cause for caution, though, is the high dropout rate that we experienced. Thirteen of the 28 patients who began treatment dropped out, representing an attrition rate of 46.4%. Reassuringly, treatment completers did not differ on age or education, nor on Mississippi or NAS scores, from treatment refusers or from treatment noncompleters, and we did not have differential dropout rates between treatment conditions.

In considering the attrition in our study, we compared the rate to that found in other studies. Riggs et al. (1992) studied anger in crime victims, taking measurements on two occasions 1 month apart. These investigators experienced a 26% dropout rate from one testing to the next in a sample scoring one standard deviation below ours in anger severity. Dropout rates in controlled treatment studies (including inpatient samples, as well as psychopharmacological studies) of combat-related PTSD, as reviewed by Solomon, Gerrity, and Muff (1992), range from 25% with inpatients to 46% with outpatients. Our participants exhibited levels of PTSD symptomatology consistent with those of inpatients, and their retention was made more difficult by their outpatient status and by their extreme anger. Thus, our attrition rate was not unusual.

IMPLICATIONS AND FUTURE DIRECTIONS

Controlled studies of anger treatment have been done primarily with college students and with outpatients in college clinics. Our patients were severely angry, even when compared to incarcerated, violent forensic inpatients, This treatment population was extremely difficult to maintain and evaluate in a treatment outcome study context. Vietnam veterans with PTSD often experience substantial distrust of research, perceiving such efforts as exploitative, akin to their perception of exploitation during military service. The level of dropout that we experienced is likely to be characteristic of this severely disordered population.

We were well aware of the problem of treatment resistance regarding our patient population and constructed procedures intended to mitigate it. For example, we used experienced Vietnam veterans as therapists. We provided reminders of appointments, sought to establish therapeutic alliances with significant others, coordinated our treatment closely with other providers, and designed our treatment protocol to provide for primary care concurrent with our adjunctive treatment. These steps kept our dropout rates within the upper range experienced by other investigators with less severe PTSD samples, but it obviously did not resolve the problem of obtaining treatment engagement.

These issues also raise important questions with respect to the generalizability of our findings on anger treatment to similar patients outside the resources of a research project to other, less severely afflicted Vietnam veterans with PTSD, to persons with combat-related PTSD from other wars, or to other violence-related trauma. While questions about generalizability can only be resolved by further research, our clinical impression is that downward extensions of the protocol to other traumatized populations should prove fruitful.

Given that residual anger is commonly found among those who have experienced trauma and that this anger is associated with very problematic complications in personal adjustment, systematic investigation of anger assessment and anger treatment for PTSD ought to be undertaken. The nature of the relationship between PTSD and its symptom clusters to component dimensions of anger (e.g., cognitive, arousal, and behavioral) remains to be examined. However, by showing that patients with severe anger and severe PTSD can be helped to increase their anger regulatory abilities, our findings are clearly encouraging for continued work with such populations and with other PTSD patients having great needs for clinical care. We believe that we have taken a worthwhile first step.

REFERENCES

Averill, J. (1982). *Anger and aggression: An essay on emotion.* New York: Springer-Verlag.

Bandura, A. (1973). *Aggression: A social learning analysis.* Englewood Cliffs, NJ: Prentice-Hall.

Bandura, A. (1983). Psychological mechanisms of aggression. In R. G. Geen & E. I. Donnerstein (Eds.), *Aggression: Theoretical and empirical reviews* (Vol. 1, pp. 1–40). New York: Academic Press.

Benson, B.A., Rice, C.J., & Miranti, S.V. (1986). Effects of anger management training with mentally retarded adults in group treatment. *Journal of Consulting and Clinical Psychology, 54,* 728–729.

Berkowitz, L. (1990). On the formation and regulation of anger and aggression. *American Psychologist, 45,* 494–503.

Berkowitz, L. (1993). *Aggression: Its causes, consequences, and control.* New York: McGraw-Hill.

Bistline, J. L., & Frieden, F. P. (1984). Anger control: A case study of a stress inoculation treatment for a chronic aggressive patient. *Cognitive Therapy and Research, 8,* 551–556.

Black, L., & Novaco, R. W. (1993). Treatment of anger with a developmentally handicapped man. In R. A. Wells & V. J. Giannetti (Eds.), *Casebook of brief psychotherapies* (pp. 143–158). New York: Plenum.

Blum, M. D., Kelley, E. M., Meyer, K., Carlson, C. R., & Hodson, L. (1984). An assessment of the treatment needs of Vietnam-era veterans. *Hospital and Community Psychiatry, 35,* 691–696.

Bornstein, P. H., Weisser, C. E., & Balleweg, B. J. (1985). Anger and violent behavior. In M. Hersen & A. S. Bellack (Eds.), *Handbook of clinical behavior therapy with adults* (pp. 603–629). New York: Plenum.

Boulanger, G. (1986). Violence and Vietnam veterans. In G. Boulanger & C. Kadushin (Eds.), *The Vietnam veteran redefined: Fact and fiction* (pp. 79–90). Hillsdale, NJ: Erlbaum.

Burton, D., Foy, D., Bwanausi, C., Johnson, J., & Moore, L. (1994). The relationship between traumatic exposure, family dysfunction, and post-traumatic stress symptoms in male juvenile offenders. *Journal of Traumatic Stress, 7,* 83–93.

Byrne, C. A., & Riggs, D. S. (1996). The cycle of trauma: Relationship aggression in male veterans with symptoms of posttraumatic stress disorder. *Violence and Victims, 11,* 213–225.

Caldwell, M. F. (1992). Incidence of PTSD among staff victims of patient violence. *Hospital and Community Psychiatry, 43,* 838–839.

Carroll, E. M., Rueger, D. B., Foy, D. W. & Donahoe, C. P., Jr. (1985). Vietnam combat veterans with posttraumatic stress disorder: Analysis of marital and cohabiting adjustment. *Journal of Abnormal Psychology, 94,* 329–337.

Cascardi, M., O'Leary, K. D., Lawrence, E. E., & Schlee, K. A. (1995). Characteristics of women physically abused by their spouses and who seek treatment regarding marital conflict. *Journal of Consulting and Clinical Psychology, 63,* 616–623.

Catalano, R., Dooley, D., Novaco, R. W., Wilson, G., & Hough, R. (1993). Using ECA survey data to examine the effect of job layoffs on violent behavior. *Hospital and Community Psychiatry, 44,* 874–879.

Catalano, R., Novaco, R., & McConnell, W. (1997). A model of the net effect of job loss on violence. *Journal of Personality and Social Psychology, 72,* 1440–1447.

Chemtob, C. M., Hamada, R. S., Roitblat, H. L. & Muraoka, M. Y. (1994). Anger, impulsivity and anger control in combat-related posttraumatic stress disorder. *Journal of Consulting and Clinical Psychology, 62,* 827–832.

Chemtob, C. M., Novaco, R. W., Hamada, R. S., Gross, D. M., & Smith, G. (1997). Anger regulatory deficits in combat-related post-traumatic stress disorder. *Journal of Traumatic Stress, 10,* 17–36.

Chemtob, C. M., Novaco, R. W., Hamada, R. S., & Gross, D. M. (1997). Cognitive-behavioral treatment for severe anger in post-traumatic stress disorder. *Journal of Consulting and Clinical Psychology, 65,* 184–189.

Chemtob, C. M., Roitblat, H. L., Hamada, R. S., Carlson, J. G., & Twentyman, C. T. (1988). A cognitive action theory of post-traumatic stress disorder. *Journal of Anxiety Disorders, 2,* 253–275.

DeFazio, V. J. (1978). Dynamic perspectives on the nature and effects of combat stress. In C. R. Figley (Ed.), *Stress disorders among Vietnam veterans: Theory research and treatment* (pp. 23–42). New York: Brunner/Mazel.

DeFazio, V. J., Rustin, S., & Diamond, A. (1975). Symptom development in Vietnam era veterans. *American Journal of Orthopsychiatry, 45,* 158–163.

Deffenbacher, J. L. (1988). Cognitive-relaxation and social skills treatments of anger: A year later. *Journal of Counseling Psychology, 35,* 234–236.

Deffenbacher, J. L., Story, D. A., Brandon, A. D. Hogg, J. A., & Hazaleus, S. L. (1988). Cognitive and cognitive-relaxation treatments of anger. *Cognitive Therapy and Research, 12,* 167–184.

Deffenbacher, J. L., Story, D. A., Stark, R. S., Hogg, J. A., & Brandon, A. D. (1987). Cognitive-relaxation and social skills interventions in treatment of general anger. *Journal of Counseling Psychology, 34,* 171–176.

Feindler, E. L., & Ecton, R. B. (1986). *Adolescent anger control: Cognitive therapy techniques.* New York: Pergamon.

Feindler, E. L., Marriott, S. A., & Iwata, M. (1984). Group anger control training for junior high school delinquents. *Cognitive Therapy and Research, 8,* 299–311.

Figley, C. R. (1978). *Stress disorders among Vietnam veterans: Theory research and treatment.* New York: Brunner/Mazel.

Figley, C. R., & Eisenhart, W. (1975). *Contrasts between combat/noncombat Vietnam veterans regarding selective indices of interpersonal adjustment.* Paper presented at the annual meeting of the American Sociological Association, San Francisco.

Foa, E. B., Rothbaum, B. O., Riggs, D. S., & Murdock, T. B. (1991). Treatment of posttraumatic stress disorder in rape victims: A comparison between cognitive-behavioral procedures and counseling. *Journal of Consulting and Clinical Psychology, 59,* 715–723.

Grinker, R. R., & Spiegel, J. P. (1945). *Men under stress.* Philadelphia: Blackington.

Hazaleus, S. L., & Deffenbacher, J. L. (1986). Relaxation and cognitive treatments of anger. *Journal of Consulting and Clinical Psychology, 54,* 222–226.

Houskamp, B. M., & Foy, D. W. (1991). The assessment of posttraumatic stress disorder in battered women. *Journal of Interpersonal Violence, 6,* 367–375.

Horowitz, M. J., & Solomon, G. F. (1975). A prediction of delayed stress response syndromes in Vietnam veterans. *Journal of Social Issues, 31,* 67–80.

Howells, K. (1989). Anger-management methods in relation to the prevention of violent behaviour. In J. Archer & K. Browne (Eds.), *Human aggression: Naturalistic approaches* (pp. 153–181). London: Routledge.

Huesmann, L. R., Eron, L. D., Yarmel, P. W. (1987). Intellectual functioning and aggression. *Journal of Personality and Social Psychology, 52,* 232–240.

Jordan, B. K., Marmar, C. R., Fairbank, J. A., Schlenger, W. E., Kulka, R. A., Hough, R. L., & Weiss, D. S. (1992). Problems in families of male Vietnam veterans with posttraumatic stress disorders. *Journal of Consulting and Clinical Psychology, 60,* 916–926.

Kardiner, A., & Spiegel, H. (1947). *War stress and neurotic illness.* New York: Paul B. Hoeber.

Keane, T. M., Caddell, J. M., & Taylor, K. L. (1988). Mississippi Scale for Combat-Related Posttraumatic Stress Disorder: Three studies in reliability and validity. *Journal of Consulting and Clinical Psychology, 56,* 85–90.

Knight, J. A., Keane, T. M., Fairbank, J. A., Caddell, J. M., & Zimering, R. T. (1984). *Empirical validation of DSM-III criteria for posttraumatic stress disorder.* Paper presented at the 18th Annual Meeting of the Association for Advancement of Behavior Therapy, Philadelphia.

Konecni, V. J. (1975). The mediation of aggressive behavior: Arousal level versus anger and cognitive labeling. *Journal of Personality and Social Psychology, 32,* 706–712.

Krupnick, J., & Horowitz, M. J. (1981). Stress responses syndromes: Recurrent themes. *Archives of General Psychiatry, 38,* 428–435.

Kubany, E. S., Gino, A., Denny, N. R., & Torigoe, R. Y. (1994). Relationship of cynical hostility and PTSD among Vietnam veterans. *Journal of Traumatic Stress, 7,* 21–31.

Kulka, R. A., Schlenger, W. D., Fairbank, J. A., Hough, R. L., Jordan, B. K., Marmar, C. R., & Weiss, D. S. (1988). *Executive summary: Contractual report of findings from the national Vietnam veterans readjustment study.* Triangle Park, NC: Research Triangle Institute.

Kulka, R. A., Shlenger, W. E., Fairbank, J. A., Hough, R. L., Jordan, B. K., Marmar, C. R., & Weiss, D. S. (1990). *Trauma and the Vietnam War generation.* New York: Brunner/Mazel.

Kulka, R. A., Schlenger, W. E., Fairbank, J. A., Hough, R. L., Jordan, B. K., Marmar, C. R., & Weiss, D. S. (1990). *Trauma and the Vietnam War generation: Report of findings from the National Vietnam Veterans Readjustment Study.* New York: Brunner/Mazel.

Lasko, N. B., Gurvits, T. V., Kuhne, A. A., Orr, S. P., & Pitman, R. K. (1994). Aggression and its correlates in Vietnam veterans with and without chronic posttraumatic stress disorder. *Comprehensive Psychiatry, 35,* 373–381.

Laufer, K. S., Yager, T., Frey-Wouters, E. & Donnellan, J. (1981). *Legacies of Vietnam: Comparative adjustment of veterans and their peers: Vol. 3. Post-war trauma: Social and psychological problems of Vietnam veterans in the aftermath of the Vietnam war.* New York: Center for Policy Research.

Lindemann, E. (1944). Symptomology and management of acute grief. *American Journal of Psychiatry, 101,* 141–148.

Lira, F. T., Carne, Q., & Masri, A. M. (1983). Treatment of anger and impulsivity in a brain damaged patient: A case study applying stress inoculation training. *Clinical Neuropsychiatry, 4,* 149–160.

Meichenbaum, D. (1975). A self-instructional approach to stress management: A proposal for stress inoculation. In C. Spielberger & I. Sarason (Eds.), *Stress and anxiety* (Vol. 2, pp. 237–263). New York: Wiley.

Meichenbaum, D. (1985). *Stress inoculation training.* New York: Pergamon.

Moon, J. R., & Eisler, R. M. (1983). Anger control: An experimental comparison of three behavioral treatments. *Behavior Therapy, 14,* 493–503.

Nomellini, S., & Katz, R. C. (1983). Effects of anger control training on abusive parents. *Cognitive Therapy and Research, 7,* 57–68.

Novaco, R. W. (1975). *Anger control: The development and evaluation of an experimental treatment.* Lexington, MA: D. C. Heath.

Novaco, R. W. (1976). The functions and regulation of the arousal of anger. *American Journal of Psychiatry, 133,* 1124–1128.

Novaco, R. W. (1977a). Stress inoculation: A cognitive therapy for anger and its application to a case of depression. *Journal of Consulting and Clinical Psychology, 45,* 600–608.

Novaco, R. W. (1977b). A stress inoculation approach to anger management in the training of law enforcement officers. *American Journal of Community Psychology, 5,* 327–346.

Novaco, R. W. (1980). The training of probation counselors for anger problems. *Journal of Counseling Psychology, 27,* 385–390.

Novaco, R. W. (1983). *Stress inoculation therapy for anger control: A manual for therapists.* Unpublished manuscript, University of California, Irvine.

Novaco, R. W. (1986). Anger as a clinical and social problem. In R. Blanchard & C. Blanchard (Eds.), *Advances in the study of aggression* (Vol. 2, pp. 1–67). New York: Academic Press.

Novaco, R. W. (1988). Novaco Provocation Inventory. In M. Hersen & A. S. Bellack (Eds.), *Dictionary of behavioral assessment techniques* (pp. 315–317). New York: Pergamon Press.

Novaco, R. W. (1994a). Anger as a risk factor for violence among the mentally disordered. In J. Monahan & H. Steadman (Eds.), *Violence and mental disorder: Developments in risk assessment* (pp. 21–59). Chicago: University of Chicago Press.

Novaco, R. W. (1994b). Clinical problems of anger and its assessment and regulation through a stress coping skills approach. In W. O'Donohue & L. Krasner (Eds.), *Handbook of psychological skills training: Clinical techniques and applications* (pp. 320–338). Boston: Allyn & Bacon.

Renwick, S., Black, L., Ramm, M., & Novaco, R. W. (1997). Anger treatment with forensic hospital patients. *Legal and Criminological Psychology, 2,* 103–116.

Resick, P. A., & Schnicke, M. K. (1992). Cognitive processing therapy for sexual assault victims. *Journal of Consulting and Clinical Psychology, 60,* 748–756.

Resnick, H. S., Kilpatrick, D. G., Dansky, B. S., Saunders, B. E., & Best, C. L. (1993). Prevalence of civilian trauma and posttraumatic stress disorder in a representative national sample of women. *Journal of Consulting and Clinical Psychology, 61,* 984–991.

Resnick, H. S., Kilpatrick, D. G., & Lipovsky, J. A. (1991). Assessment of rape-related posttraumatic stress disorder: Stressor and symptom dimensions. *Psychological Assessment: A Journal of Consulting and Clinical Psychology, 3,* 561–572.

Riggs, D. S., Dancu, C. V., Gershuny, B. S. Greenberg, D., & Foa, E. B. (1992). Anger and post-traumatic stress disorder in female crime victims. *Journal of Traumatic Stress, 5,* 613–625.

Rodriguez, N., Ryan, S. W., Kemp, H. V., & Foy, D. W. (1997). Posttraumatic stress disorder in adult female survivors of childhood sexual abuse: A comparison study. *Journal of Consulting and Clinical Psychology, 65,* 53–59.

Sarason, I. G., Johnson, J. H., Berberich, J. P., & Siegel, J. M. (1979). Helping police officers to cope with stress: A cognitive-behavioral approach. *American Journal of Community Psychology, 7,* 593–603.

Saunders, D. G. (1994). Posttraumatic stress symptoms profiles of battered women: A comparison of survivors in two settings. *Violence and Victims, 9,* 31–44.

Saylor, C. F., Benson, B. A., & Einhaus, L. (1985). Evaluation of an anger management program for aggressive boys in residential treatment. *Journal of Child and Adolescent Psychotherapy, 2,* 5–15.

Schlichter, K. L., & Horan, J. J. (1981). Effects of stress inoculation on the anger and aggression management skills of institutionalized delinquents. *Cognitive Therapy and Research, 5,* 359–365.

Scurfield, R. M., Corker, T. M., & Gongla, P. A. (1984). Three post-Vietnam "rap/therapy" groups: An analysis. *Group, 8,* 3–21.

Silver, S. M., & Iocono, C. U. (1984). Factor-analytic support for DSM-III's post-traumatic stress disorder for Vietnam veterans. *Journal of Clinical Psychology, 54,* 5–14.

Solomon, S. D., Gerrity, E. T., & Muff, A. M. (1992). Efficacy of treatments for posttraumatic stress disorder. *Journal of the American Medical Association, 268,* 633–638.

Spielberger, C. D. (1991). *State–Trait Anger Expression Inventory: Revised research edition.* Odessa, FL: Psychological Assessment Resources.

Spielberger, C. D. (1988a). State–Trait Anger Scale. In M. Hersen & A. S. Bellack (Eds.), *Dictionary of behavioral assessment techniques* (pp. 446–448). New York: Pergamon.

Spielberger, C. D. (1988b). Anger Expression Scale. In M. Hersen & A. S. Bellack (Eds.), *Dictionary of behavioral assessment techniques* (pp. 27–29). New York: Pergamon.

Spielberger, C. D., Johnson, E. H., Russell, S. F., Crane, R. J., Jacobs, G. A., & Worden, T. J. (1985). The experience and expression of anger: Construction and validation of an Anger Expression Scale. In M. A. Chesney & R. H. Rosenman (Eds.), *Anger and hostility in cardiovascular and behavioral disorders* (pp. 5–30). New York: Hemisphere/McGraw-Hill.

Spirito, A., Finch, A. J., Smith, T. L., & Cooley, W. H. (1981). Stress inoculation for anger and anxiety control: A case study with an emotionally disturbed boy. *Journal of Clinical Child Psychology, 10,* 67–70.

Spitzer, R. L., Williams, J. B. W., Gibbon, M., & First, M. B. (1988). *Structured Clinical Interview for DSM-III-R—Nonpatient/Outpatient* (SCID-NP/OP, 6/1/88 Version). New York: New York State Psychiatric Institute.

Spitzer, R. L., Williams, J. B. W., Gibbon, M., & First, M. B. (1989). *Structured Clinical Interview for DSM-III-R—Personality Disorders* (SCID-II, 9/1/89 Version). New York: New York State Psychiatric Institute.

Stermac, L. E. (1986). Anger control treatment for forensic patients. *Journal of Interpersonal Violence, 1,* 446–457.

Stouffer, S. (1949). *The American soldier: Combat and its aftermath.* Princeton, NJ: Princeton University Press.

van der Kolk, B. A., Boyd, H., Krystal, J., & Greenberg, M. (1984). Post-traumatic stress disorder as a biologically based disorder: Implications of the animal model of inescapable shock. In B. A. van der Kolk (Ed.), *Post-traumatic stress disorder: Psychological and biological sequelae* (pp. 123–134). Washington, DC: American Psychiatric Association Press.

Warren, R., & McLellarn, R. W. (1982). Systemic desensitization as a treatment for maladaptive anger and aggression: A review. *Psychological Reports, 50,* 1095–1102.

Watson, C. G., Plemel, D., DeMotts, J., Howard, M. T., Tuorila, J., Moog, R., Thomas, D., & Anderson, D. (1994). A comparison of four PTSD measures' convergent validities in Vietnam Veterans. *Journal of Traumatic Stress 7,* 75–82.

Zillmann, D. (1979). *Hostility and aggression.* Hillsdale, NJ: Erlbaum.

Dissociative Behavior

AMY W. WAGNER
MARSHA M. LINEHAN

While it is virtually commonplace and definitely expected to see a chapter on "dissociation" in a book focusing on trauma, the appearance of "dissociation" in a behavioral text is far less conventional. The concept of "dissociation" has historically been discussed by psychoanalytic and psychodynamic theorists, and behavioral conceptuatizations are virtually absent in the literature. Nonetheless, few contemporary behaviorists would deny the existence of dissociative phenomena or the significance of dissociative behavior and experiences in the treatment of many clients. Instead, many behaviorists tend to rely on the existing formulations of "dissociation," and treatments from these formulations vary considerably. It is the premise of this chapter that while the existing theories have greatly advanced our understanding of dissociative phenomena, these theories also make assumptions about the factors that cause and maintain such experiences that may be erroneous, and more importantly, may greatly affect treatment outcome. This chapter provides a comprehensive behavioral conceptualization of dissociative phenomena and applies this conceptualization to a description of a behavioral approach to the assessment and treatment of dissociative behavior. The focus of this chapter is on the conceptualization and treatment of dissociative behavior specifically, rather than diagnosable dissociative disorders, although the principles have applicability to dissociative phenomena across diagnostic categories. As a substantial proportion of individuals with borderline personality disorder (BPD) present with dissociative behavior, the treatment approach proposed draws primarily from Linehan's (1993a) cognitive-behavioral therapy for BPD, dialectical behavior therapy. First, a description of dissociative behavior is reviewed and epidemiological data are presented.

OVERVIEW AND EPIDEMIOLOGY
OF DISSOCIATIVE PHENOMENA

The concept of dissociative behavior was first proposed by Piere Janet, in 1889, to describe his observation that ideas and behaviors could be separated from consciousness, especially under stressful conditions (*desagregations psychologiques*; Hilgard, 1992). Since then, attention to dissociative phenomena has had a variable course, with interest decreasing dramatically from the 1920s to the 1950s due to such factors as Freud's recanting of the seduction theory, and increasing again in the 1970s and 1980s, largely related to increased attention to childhood abuse (Ross, 1996). While the occurrence of dissociative phenomena is now widely accepted, contemporary descriptions of dissociative behavior vary considerably, and there have been few efforts to examine these empirically (Cardeña, 1994; Ray, 1996). DSM-IV (American Psychiatric Association, 1994) defines dissociation as "a disruption in the usually integrated functions of consciousness, memory, identity, or perception of the environment" (p. 477). Terms commonly used to describe dissociative experiences include "depersonalization," which refers to a wide range of experiences in which one feels detached from current perceptions, actions, emotions, or thoughts; "derealization," which involves having the experience that one's surroundings are unreal or not quite real; "amnesia," referring to partial or complete loss of memory for either past experiences (that one would normally remember) or current experiences or actions; and "absorption," that is, becoming so involved in a particular task that one loses track of time or surrounding activities (Cardeña, 1994). In addition, most descriptions of dissociation include problems with *identity* or the *self* as related to these experiences.

Dissociative behaviors can occur sporadically, in certain situations or under certain conditions, or more chronically and frequently and in combination with other types of dissociative behaviors. The DSM-IV has identified five discrete dissociative *disorders* to account for the occurrence of severe and chronic dissociative behaviors that lead to significant distress or impairment in functioning (including dissociative amnesia, dissociative fugue, dissociative identity disorder (formally multiple personality disorder), depersonalization disorder, and dissociative disorder not otherwise specified). In contrast, individual dissociative behaviors have been found to occur in nonclinical populations and to co-occur with other DSM-IV diagnoses. Unfortunately, the term "dissociation" is typically used to describe both the array of individual behaviors and the constellations of behaviors labeled as dissociative disorders. This practice is partly based on the common assumption that dissociative behaviors occur on a continuum of increasing severity and share common underlying etiologies (e.g., Ross, 1985; Braun, 1986). Recent research, however, does not support the continuum theory, and instead suggests that the behaviors of individuals with diagnosable dissociative disorders are qualitatively different than the behaviors of those without such diagnoses (e.g., Waller, Putnam, & Carlson, 1996). In addition, the factors that lead to and maintain dissociative behavior may vary considerably across diagnostic categories. We propose that the overinclusive use of the term "dissociation" to date is particularly problematic for assessment and treatment, as it implies a reified construct dependent on etiology and independent of context. For the remainder of this chapter, we use the term "dissociative behavior" (and "dissociative phenomena") to refer to individual behaviors, and the term "disorder" to refer to the diagnostic categories labeled as dissociative in the DSM-IV. This chapter focuses primarily on dissociative behavior.

Investigations on the epidemiology of dissociative phenomena are based predominantly on the continuum conceptualization of dissociation; therefore, prevalence data are reported in terms such as "mild" or "moderate" rates of occurrence rather than specifying information on specific dissociative behaviors. Of the studies that do examine specific behaviors, some types of dissociative experiences appear to be common in the general population. Behaviors related to *absorption* are most commonly reported in the general population, with one large-scale study finding that 29% of the sample endorsed experiencing absorption-related behaviors at least 30% of the time (Ross, Joshi, & Currie, 1990). Higher rates of absorption-related experiences have been reported for college populations (Ray & Faith, 1995). In contrast, *amnesic* experiences are the least commonly endorsed dissociative experience (Vanderlinden, Van Dyck, Vandereycken, & Vertommen, 1993). Ross and colleagues (1990) found that only 1.5% of the sample had amnesic-type experiences more than 30% of the time. Among clinical populations and psychiatric inpatients, rates of dissociative behaviors are reportedly higher than in the general population (e.g., Quimby & Putnam, 1991; Ross, Anderson, Fleisher, & Norton, 1992), however, again, these data are typically reported as summary scores of the construct "dissociation" rather than prevalence of individual dissociative behaviors. In studies of general psychiatric inpatients, it is reported that 15–23% score in the "extreme range" on measures of dissociation (Chu & Dill, 1990; Saxe et al., 1993). In general, information on the prevalence of specific dissociative behaviors in clinical populations is largely unavailable.

In addition to the dissociative disorders, dissociative phenomena frequently co-occur with other DSM-IV diagnoses. Dissociative behavior is a defining criterion for posttraumatic stress disorder (PTSD; including inability to remember important parts of the trauma, feelings of detachment, and numbing of affect), borderline personality disorder (BPD; simply referred to as "dissociative symptoms" in DSM-IV), acute stress disorder (including affective numbing, reduction of awareness, derealization, depersonalization, and amnesia), and somatization disorder (including amnesia), and there appears to be high comorbidity between these diagnoses and the dissociative disorders. For example, among a sample of inpatients diagnosed with a dissociative disorder, Saxe and colleagues (1993) found that 90% also met criteria for PTSD and 71% met criteria for BPD.

Furthermore, number and severity of dissociative behaviors have been positively related to the frequency of PTSD (Bremner et al., 1992; van IJzendoorn & Schuengel, 1996) and BPD criteria (Modestin, Gerhard, Junghan, & Erni, 1996; Shearer, 1994; Zweig-Frank, Paris, & Guzder, 1994). Based on existing studies, Ross (1996) estimates that 38–70% of individuals diagnoses with dissociative identity disorder also meet criteria for BPD. The comorbidity between dissociative behavior, PTSD, and BPD may be related to common predisposing factors as described later.

A few studies have examined the relations between dissociative behavior and demographic factors. Consistently, scores on summary measures of dissociative behaviors have been negatively related to age (more frequent and severe dissociative behaviors are reported among younger respondents), but unrelated to socioeconomic status or education (Modestin et al., 1996; Ross et al., 1990; Vanderlinden et al., 1993). Regarding gender, no differences have been found for rates of dissociative behaviors between men and women in the general population (Ross et al., 1990; Vanderlinden et al., 1993). In a meta-analysis of studies using a common (continuum) measure of dissociative behaviors, including both clinical and nonclinical samples, gender was similarly unrelated to dissociative behaviors (van IJzendoorn & Schuengel, 1996). Among the dissociative disorders, however, more women than men receive these diagnoses (American Psychiatric Association, 1994). Finally, there are some tentative data that suggest the prevalence and phenomenology of dissociative-like behavior may differ across certain cultural groups (Kulka et al., 1990; Lewis-Fernandez, 1994; Modestin et al., 1996). Similarly, the degree to which dissociative behavior is viewed as "pathological" appears to vary by culture, thus likely influencing the detectability of such behavior among certain cultural groups (Krippner, 1994; Lewis-Fernandez, 1994).

THEORETICAL ORIENTATION

As mentioned initially, the majority of existing conceptualizations of dissociation are psychodynamic in orientation. Historically, behaviorists have not attended to dissociative phenomena, since they are largely inaccessible to public observation and assessment must primarily rely on subjective report. This emphasis on publicly observable behavior, largely held by *methodological* behaviorists, has gradually been replaced by the views of *radical* behaviorists. Currently, thoughts, emotions, and physiological processes are all viewed behaviorally as types of behavior, worthy of study and important in treatment. Therefore, dissociative behaviors are entirely within the domain of behavioral research and treatment. The primary difference between behavioral conceptualizations of internal experiences, including dissociative behavior and psychodynamic conceptualizations, is that behaviorists do not view internal experiences as *entities,* nor do they infer motivations or drives to account for their occurrence. Instead, internal experiences are described in terms of behavior (e.g., remembering as opposed to memory), and the occurrence of internal experiences is accounted for by thorough assessments, based on learning theory. Although a comprehensive behavioral description and formulation of dissociation has not been fully articulated by behaviorists, behavioral conceptualizations do exist for many of the psychological processes involved in dissociation, such as unconscious processes (including memory processes), and notions of the self. These will briefly be described next.

The Unconscious and Awareness

A behavioral conceptualization of the "unconscious" simply refers to those processes (involving oneself) of which one is not aware. For example, Bower (1990) makes a distinction between two types of awareness: the first type, "$aware_1$," includes those experiences and beliefs that one is able to talk about or communicate to another. The second type, "$aware_2$," manifests in one's behavior, in such a way that it would be clear to an outside observer that one was "taking account of" a belief or experience, even if the person is not able to report it. Bower describes unconscious processes as those "bodily and psychological events of which we are not $aware_1$" (p. 212).

Bower further asserts that infants do not have $awareness_1$, although they may demonstrate $awareness_2$. He states that children can *learn* many types of $awareness_1$, that is, how to talk about their internal states, by feedback and modeling from caretakers. This occurs, for example, when parents infer and label a child's internal experience (e.g., a child loses her doll and cries and the parent says, "You're sad you lost your doll"; Kohlenberg & Tsai, 1991). This description of awareness encompasses other domains in addition to emotional experiences, including physiological processes and the factors that elicit and maintain behaviors and reactions, such as conditioned associations between stimuli and processes of reinforcement and punishment. For example, a woman may be fearful when approaching closets, and therefore avoid closets, without having any understanding of why she feels and behaves this way. In reality, this may be because closets were associated with punishment when she was a child, but she may not be $aware_1$ of this association.

In behavioral theory, experiences may be unconscious (out of awareness) for a number of reasons. For example, the experience may be completely unobservable and not available for external feedback (e.g., liver functioning). In addition, the environment may chronically give erroneous feedback about internal states (e.g., a parent tells a boy there is nothing to cry about when he's upset). Similarly, the environment may not attend to internal states (e.g., parents who ignore a child when he or she is upset), or label variables that control internal states (e.g., parents who deny that family problems are occurring). Furthermore, one may be punished for attending to the experience or reinforced for not attending to the experience. Punishment for attending to the experience or reinforcement for not attending to it can come from the external environment (a parent yells at a child for talking about family problems), or from one's own emotional reactions (a girl becomes highly anxious whenever she thinks of a trauma, and the anxiety decreases when she distracts).

This brief discussion allows for a behavioral conceptualization of several behaviors classified as dissociative. For example, *amnesia* for past experiences can be understood as lack of awareness$_2$, resulting from any of the experiences described earlier. Similarly, the variety of conditions under which awareness$_2$ develops or fails to develop could explain the phenomenon of selective amnesia. One could further speculate that the experiences of *depersonalization* and *derealization* are partly related to lack of awareness$_2$ of internal states. For example, if in a situation that can be cognitively appraised as stressful or upsetting, one is unable to identify emotional reactions to the situation, one may feel a lack of connection with one's body (*depersonalization*) or, alternatively, with the situation (*derealization*). Similarly, lack of awareness$_2$ of factors eliciting an emotional reaction (i.e., having an emotional experience without the ability to identify situational causes) could lead to feelings of depersonalization or derealization. Thus, dissociation may be related to failures to develop fully awareness$_2$, and suggests that the environments that fail to teach awareness$_2$, such as those described earlier, may be related to the development of dissociation.

Memory/Remembering

As mentioned, behaviorists refer to the process of remembering rather than memory as an entity. According to Kohlenberg and Tsai (1991), "Remembering is the behavioral process of seeing, hearing, touching, and tasting of stimuli that are not present" (p. 81). Remembering can happen in two ways. First, remembering can occur when one comes into contact with stimuli associated with the original event; this is based on the idea that remembering is "respondently conditioned seeing" (or hearing, touching, etc.; Kohlenberg and Tsai, 1991). Bower (1990) similarly argues that "memories are simply dispositions that can be actualized in certain circumstances and not in others; they are like 'responses' waiting for the right stimulus to release them" (p. 222). Second, remembering can also occur through operant conditioning and is thus viewed as "operant seeing"; that is, remembering is a result of past and present reinforcement for visualizing past experiences.

Kohlenberg and Tsai (1991) assert that forgetting can occur when one has been punished or has not been reinforced for these visualizations. This can lead to selective forgetting or amnesia for events. Bower (1990) suggests two additional ways that forgetting can occur. First, one may not have attended to the event initially, because one was punished for attending to the event, because one was not positively reinforced for attending to the event, or, conversely, because one was negatively reinforced for diverting attention from the event (e.g., experienced fear reduction); therefore, the material was never learned. In addition, forgetting may happen when one learns new associations to the same cues. For example, if as a child, a woman was locked in a closet by her mother one time, and she subsequently played in the closet several times, the closet may become associated with the emotions and images related to playing, and the memory of the original experience may never be elicited.

This discussion has implications for the conceptualization of *amnesia*, especially of distal experiences, and accounts for the experience of "selective amnesia," that is, amnesia for some experiences during a specific time period but not all. As in the account of unconscious processes, this conceptualization also implicates both punishment and negative reinforcement in the development of amnesia and suggests that certain types of environments are related to the development of dissociative behavior.

The Self

Again, instead of discussing the "self" as an entity or structure, behaviorists focus on processes or activities of the person or self-referent behaviors. Skinner (1953, 1957) was the first to provide an analysis of the "self" in behavioral terms. His views were elaborated by Kohlenberg and Tsai (1991), who discuss the notion of "sense of self" and how this develops. According to Kohlenberg and Tsai (1991), a sense of self is the experience of internal (private) stimuli associated with "I X" responses, where "X" is any verb related to beliefs, desires, and experience (such as "I think," "I want," "I see"). Further, the degree to which "I X" responses are under the control of private stimuli (e.g., physical sensations, thoughts, images) as opposed to public stimuli (e.g., someone else's stated desires) defines the strength of sense of self.

Kohlenberg and Tsai (1991) describe how one develops a sense of self. In brief, they propose that infants are born with little or no sense of self. In non-pathological environments, children develop a sense of self through the feedback they receive from caretakers, that is, through consistent reinforcement for these types of "I X" statements. Initially, this occurs with experiences that consist of both public and private stimuli (such as "I see," where the object can be seen by both the child and the caretaker). Over time, children learn to use these statements to describe experiences that cannot be observed by others, such as an event seen when no one else is present, an image, a physical sensation, or a desire. To the extent then that caretakers can reinforce these experiences, "I X" responses will come under the control of private stimuli (such as physical sensations) and will be less under the control of public stimuli.

Kohlenberg and Tsai (1991) propose that "problems of the self" can be attributed to the degree of private control of "I X" responses. In severe disturbances of the self, such as in BPD and dissociative identity disorder, they suggest that a large number of "I X" responses are under the control of public stimuli.

When a large number of "I X" responses are under the control of public stimuli, the person's experience of self changes according to the views and expectations of others. This can develop from caretakers who are extremely inconsistent or absent in their reactions to public stimuli, or who fail to reinforce (or who punish) private control of the child's responses (i.e., expressions about private experiences). Although problems in the self can develop in the absence of traumatic experiences, Kohlenberg and Tsai suggest that trauma can contribute to extreme problems with the self. This is particularly likely when trauma occurs during early development, when the child's sense of self is not primarily under the control of private stimuli, and when imaginary play is common. Under these circumstances, the child is motivated to avoid the emotions associated with the trauma and may more easily experience him- or herself as absent, removed or different (i.e., dissociated), or as a different person (i.e. dissociative identity disorder).

To summarize, we have briefly reviewed behavioral conceptualizations of three processes that have been implicated in dissociative behavior: unconscious processing, remembering, and the sense of self. In each review, consistent external (public) reinforcement for communication of private experiences was described as necessary in the normal development of these processes. Consistent lack of positive reinforcement or punishment for communication of private experiences can lead to disruptions in the development of these processes. Furthermore, negative reinforcement (generally in the form of reductions in negative affect) was implicated in the maintenance of these disruptions. Other dissociative experiences, including derealization and depersonalization, were hypothesized to result from similar processes. Therefore, we propose that the development and maintenance of dissociative behavior in general can be understood in large part according to these behavioral principles. In addition, as described later, research on both the biological and cognitive correlates of extreme stress contribute further to a behavioral understanding of the development and maintenance of dissociative behavior. The implication here is that certain types of environmental experiences, including highly stressful or traumatic experiences, are related to dissociative phenomena. Relevant research related to this conceptualization is briefly reviewed next.

DESCRIPTION OF EMPIRICAL RESEARCH

Development and Maintenance of Dissociative Phenomena

Research to date implicates three primary pathways to the development of dissociative phenomena: (1) brain disorder, resulting from injury or temporal lobe dysfunction; (2) substance use; and (3) extreme stress or trauma. Regarding brain disorder, temporal lobe epilepsy has been most frequently associated with the experience of dissociative experiences, including depersonalization, derealization, and amnesia (Devinsky, Putnam, Grafman, Bromfield, & Theodore, 1989; Mesulam, 1981). In addition, brain lesions in certain areas, in particular the hippocampus and amygdala, have been shown to result in dissociations between emotional responding and declarative knowledge (Bechara et al., 1995). These studies suggest that some dissociative experiences develop directly from, and are maintained by, neurochemical and neuroanatomical dysfunctions in the brain. Treatment of such behaviors would therefore be limited to neurochemical or neuroanatomical interventions (e.g., medications or surgery). Regarding substance use, it has been found that a variety of psychoactive and neurotoxic drugs, including alcohol, barbiturates, benzodiazepines, cannabinoids, serotonergic hallucinogens, general anesthetics, and others, can induce such dissociative experiences as depersonalization, derealization, amnesia, fugue states, and impairments in one's sense of self (Good, 1989; Krystal, Bennett, Bremner, Southwick, & Charney, 1996). Thus some dissociative experiences develop from and are maintained by the use of these substances. Therefore, treatment of dissociative experiences that develop from use of these substances would focus on disuse or attenuation of these substances. Finally, a large body of research suggests strong associations between traumatic or highly stressful experiences and dissociative behavior. We propose that the development and maintenance of dissociative experiences that relate to traumatic experiences can be largely understood through behavioral principles and thus are highly amenable to behavioral treatment. Therefore, the research relating trauma to dissociative experiences is described in some detail. Research relating dissociative phenomena to traumatic experiences has focused on the particular traumatic events that correlate with dissociative experiences, the biological correlates of extreme stress or trauma, and the cognitive effects of extreme stress or trauma.

Traumatic Events

The associations between reports of *childhood* trauma (including sexual trauma, physical trauma, emotional trauma, witnessing violence, and neglect) and dissociative experiences in both childhood and adulthood have been widely studied. Here, it has been consistently found that reports of dissociative experiences are related to reports of childhood physical trauma and/or sexual trauma specifically, for psychiatric inpatients (e.g., Chu & Dill, 1990; Sanders & Giolas, 1991; Saxe et al., 1993), outpatients (e.g., Keaney & Farley, 1996; Lipschitz, Kaplan, Sorkenn, Chorney, & Asnis, 1996), and nonclinical samples (e.g., Briere & Runtz, 1988). Furthermore, higher rates of dissociative experiences have been found among people who report multiple types of childhood trauma (e.g., Chu & Dill; 1990; Zlotnick et al., 1994), more severe childhood trauma (Ensink & Van Otterloo, 1989; Kirby, Chu, & Dill, 1993), multiple perpetrators (e.g., Ensink & Van Otterloo, 1989; Zlotnick et al., 1994), longer duration of trauma (e.g., Kirby et al., 1993), and early onset of trauma (Ensink & Van Otterloo, 1989; Kirby et al., 1993;

van der Kolk, van der Hart, & Marmar, 1996). Studies also link higher rates of dissociative behavior to reports of childhood sexual trauma specifically, compared to (and controlling for) other types of childhood trauma (e.g., Keaney & Farley, 1996; Vanderlinden, Van der Hart, & Varga, 1996; Zlotnick et al., 1994), suggesting that aspects of childhood sexual trauma or the environment in which it occurs are particularly related to the development of dissociative experiences.

Dissociative experiences are not limited to individuals who report childhood traumas, as research has demonstrated relations between reports of dissociative phenomena and traumas that occur in adulthood as well. Specifically, a number of studies document heightened dissociative experiences among victims of adulthood *assault,* including both physical and sexual assault (Briere & Runtz, 1989; Burgess & Holmstrom, 1976). Furthermore, there is some evidence that sexual assault in particular may lead to more dissociative behavior over time compared to physical assault (Dancu, Riggs, Hearst-Ikeda, Shoyer, & Foa, 1996). Increased rates of dissociative experiences have also been found for individuals exposed to combat and war atrocities, such as in the Vietnam War (e.g., Branscombe, 1991; Bremner et al., 1992; Marmar et al., 1994) and Cambodia (e.g., Carlson & Rosser-Hogan, 1991). In addition, heightened levels of dissociative experiences have been reported by victims of natural disasters, such as earthquakes (e.g., Cardeña & Spiegel, 1993), fires (e.g., McFarlane, 1986), and severe accidents (e.g., Noyes & Kletti, 1977; Noyes, Hoenk, Kuperman, & Slymen, 1977). Two studies have examined rates of dissociative phenomena among individuals who report both childhood and adulthood traumas. Here, it has been found that individuals who report both childhood and adulthood traumas report more dissociative behavior compared to individuals who report either childhood or adulthood trauma alone (Dancu et al., 1996; Lipschitz et al., 1996). Finally, an interesting recent finding is that the reporting of having dissociative experiences at the time of the trauma is a strong predictor of subsequent dissociative experiences (Shalev, Peri, Caneti, & Schreiber, 1996; van der Kolk, 1996b).

Although research clearly supports a strong relationship between traumatic experiences and dissociative experiences, direct causal explanations for the association between trauma and dissociative behavior are unwarranted at this time for several reasons (see Tillman, Nash, & Lerner, 1994, for a good review of this issue). First, many of the studies reported here, and virtually all of the studies on childhood trauma, rely on retrospective reports of trauma, often with no corroborating evidence. Thus, there exists the real possibility that aspects of the trauma will be misremembered; that is, the trauma could be reported when it did not occur, remembered differently than it actually occurred (Loftus, 1993), or denied when it did occur. Second, the majority of studies use cross-sectional designs, and information about pretrauma functioning is rarely obtained. It is possible that a tendency to dissociate precedes some cases of trauma and could in fact be a risk factor for some types of trauma. Third, assessment of both trauma and dissociative experiences occurs primarily by self-report, which can be influenced by memory as well as other factors such as demand effects, lying, and so on. Fourth, the definitions and measurement of both trauma and dissociative behavior vary considerably between studies, thus limiting the generalizability between studies. Finally, it is important to note that a large percentage of individuals who have experienced trauma do not report elevated rates of dissociative behavior, and many people who do dissociate deny traumatic experiences. Thus, other factors likely contribute to the development of dissociative behavior in addition to traumatic experiences.

In particular, it has been suggested that the environment in which trauma typically occurs may be more important in the development of dissociative behavior than trauma itself, especially in cases of childhood trauma (Cole, Alexander, & Anderson, 1996; Tillman et al., 1994). As described earlier, the manner in which caregivers interact with children and give feedback about their internal states are hypothesized to have direct relevance to the development of awareness, memory, and the formation of a sense of self. Similarly, Cole et al. (1996) argue that self-awareness and integration (conceptualized as the opposite of dissociation) develop through the ability to use self-referent language (such as "me" or "I"), the ability to label internal emotional states, the ability to conceptualize multiple aspects of the world and oneself, and the ability to utilize self-soothing strategies, which are typically taught directly from caregivers. Environments that fail to foster these abilities may or may not be abusive in nature. In reference to the etiology of BPD, for example, Linehan (1993a) has used the term "invalidating environment," to describe environments that fail to foster or that punish children's communications about their emotional experience, and she further notes that although environments in which trauma occurs can be highly invalidating, invalidating environments can occur in the absence of overt trauma. Therefore, Linehan postulates that severely invalidating environments contribute to the development and the dissociative behavior characteristic of BPD.

Biological Processes

Recent research on the neurobiological correlates and effects of extreme stress and PTSD suggests possible biological explanations for dissociative phenomena related to highly stressful experiences. For example, studies have found extreme stress to be related to changes in the output of certain brain neurohormones (such as the glucocorticoids) and physical changes in certain brain structures (such as the hippocampus) (van der Kolk, 1996a). Recent studies have similarly found decreased hippocampal volumes among individuals with PTSD (Bremner et al., 1995; Pitman, Shenton, & Gurvitz, 1995). These biological processes have been found to correspond to such experiences as analgesia (or "numbing"), problems consolidating memories, and dissociations between cognitive and emotional processing (Pitman, van der Kolk, Orr, & Greenberg, 1990; van der Kolk, Greenberg, Orr, & Pitman, 1989). Although a thorough description of this research is beyond the scope of this chapter (see Friedman, Charney, & Deutch, 1995, for more in-depth coverage of this topic), it should be stressed that biological processes are implicated in the occurrence and maintenance of some dissociative behavior and may further predispose individuals to have dissociative experiences.

Cognitive Processes

Research has identified cognitive processes associated with severe stress, which also inform our conceptualization of dissociative behavior. For example, there is evidence that under extreme stress, one's attention narrows and focuses on certain aspects of an experience to the exclusion others (e.g., Christianson & Loftus, 1991). This can occur automatically, without the person's conscious intent, or it can be a purposeful strategy to cope with a stressful situation. Furthermore, a large body of research on state-dependent learning indicates that material is more likely to be remembered when retrieval mood matches the mood in which it was originally learned (Blaney, 1986). This corresponds to our previous behavioral description of memory; that is, remembering is enhanced when stimuli occur in the present that are similar to stimuli that were present when the original event occurred (cf. Kohlenberg & Tsai, 1991). Others have proposed that certain dissociative behavior (such as amnesia), as well as DID, may be related to state-dependent learning (Braun, 1988a; Putnam, 1989a).

Although not directly involved in the development of dissociative behavior, there are likely other cognitive processes that contribute to the maintenance of dissociative behavior. For example, Foa and Hearst-Ikeda (1996) and Resick and Schnicke (1993) note that individuals who have experienced trauma often make faulty assumptions about the world and themselves (e.g., believing the world to be more dangerous than it is and themselves to be more incompetent than they are). It is easy to see how such beliefs could lead to heightened emotionality in general and increase the chances that dissociative behaviors would occur among individuals predisposed to such experiences. Indeed, Fine (1993) asserts that cognitive errors contribute directly to the maintenance of dissociative identity disorder and are the primary obstacle in effective treatment.

BEHAVIORAL CONCEPTUALIZATION
OF DISSOCIATIVE PHENOMENA

To summarize the review at this point in relation to traumatic experiences, dissociative behavior can be understood to develop from the combined influences of the experience of extreme and prolonged stress or trauma plus environments that fail to reinforce or that punish communications about negative affect. The origin of the extreme stress or trauma can be experiences in childhood, such as physical trauma, sexual trauma, severe neglect, and severe invalidation, as well as adulthood, such as assault, combat experiences, and natural disasters. We have already provided examples of ways in which caretakers of children can fail to reinforce or punish communications of negative affect. For individuals with adulthood traumas, this can occur in a number of ways including communications from the assailant (e.g., "I'll hurt you if you ever tell anyone"), limitations characteristic of the situation (e.g., lack of support for extended periods of time in combat situations), or characteristics of the individual (e.g., preexisting difficulties labeling internal states, a tendency to distract and/or withdraw from others under extreme stress, a tendency to feel shame or be self-critical in reaction to extreme stress). The experience of stress may be heightened by a biological vulnerability to reactivity to stress, thus accounting for individual differences in reactions to similar experiences.

Based on this summary, we assert that the primary *function* of dissociative phenomena is the regulation of exposure to cues related to traumatic experiences. Therefore, dissociative behavior that occurs at the time of the trauma may function to regulate exposure to aspects of the trauma as it is occurring, and dissociation after the trauma may function to regulate exposure to cues associated with the trauma. Current cues can range from obvious reminders of the trauma (e.g., loud noises, certain smells, a similar-appearing man) to "higher-order" associations to the trauma (i.e., cues that became associated with the primary cues, such as intimacy, crowded places, weather conditions) to emotions associated with the trauma (e.g., fear, anger, shame). Furthermore, we propose that a secondary function of dissociative phenomena is the regulation of exposure to cues to negative affect more generally, regardless of whether the affect is associated with traumatic experiences. Most likely, dissociative behavior of this type is operant, perhaps learned in the context of traumatic experiences and generalized to other situations. Others have similarly conceptualized dissociative behavior as avoidance of emotions (e.g., Foa & Hearst-Ikeda, 1996; Foa & Riggs, 1993; Horowitz, 1986) and as a "phobia of memory" (van der Kolk et al., 1996); however, our conceptualization is broader and includes nonemotional cues and cues not directly related to traumatic memories. It should be stressed that this does not mean dissociative behavior is consciously used as a means to avoid such cues, although at times this may be the case. Finally, factors implicated in the maintenance of dissociative behavior include biological processes, cognitive processes, and skills deficits. In addition, behavioral principles such as classical and operant conditioning and modeling can account for the occurrence and maintenance of dissociative phenomena in many cases.

Although dissociative behavior can be an effective means of regulating exposure to trauma cues (and indeed, the common view is that dissociative behavior at the time of trauma is adaptive; e.g., Putnam, 1989b), it can also be distressing to experience, can disrupt interpersonal and occupational functioning, and is often related to a number of dysfuntional behaviors, such as physical aggression, shoplifting, eating disorders, and parasuicidal behavior, as well as revictimization (e.g., Brodsky, Cloitre, & Dulit, 1995; Demitrack, Putnam, Brewerton, Brandt, & Gold, 1990; Ross & Norton, 1989; van der Kolk, Perry, & Herman, 1991). Dissociative behavior is thus an important target of treatment, and this conceptualization directly informs behavioral treatment of dissociative behavior; that is, effective treatment of dissociative behavior would necessitate decreasing the availability of trauma cues, regulating emotional responses to trauma cues and negative affect more generally, and changing the associated value of trauma cues. The applicability of aspects of Linehan's dialectical behavioral therapy (DBT) to these treatment goals is described in the next section.

CLINICAL APPLICATIONS

Assessment Instruments for Dissociative Behavior

A number of self-report questionnaires exist for the assessment of dissociation. The most commonly used measures include the Dissociative Experiences Scale (DES; Bernstein & Putnam, 1986), the Perceptual Alterations Scale (PAS; Sanders, 1986), the Stanford Acute Stress Reaction Questionnaire (SASRQ; Cardeña, Classen, & Spiegel, 1991), the Peritraumatic Dissociation Experiences Questionnaire (PDEQ; Marmar & Weiss, 1990), and the Questionnaire of Experiences of Dissociation (QED; Riley, 1988). Of these, the DES, PAS, and QED measure the presence and frequency of current dissociative behavior, while the SASRQ and the PDEQ-RV measure dissociative phenomena that occurred during and immediately after a specified trauma. These instruments assess dissociative behavior rather than dissociative diagnoses, although they frequently are used as screening instruments for dissociative disorders.

The DES is the most frequently used and studied self-report instrument. This 28-item scale assesses problems with memory, attention, identity, and perception, and yields three subscales according to factor-analytic studies of this measure (Carlson & Putnam, 1993; Ross, Joshi, & Currie, 1990, 1991): absorption–imaginative involvement (behaviors such as becoming so involved in an activity that one becomes unaware of external events), activities of dissociated states (behaviors such as finding oneself in an unfamiliar place but unaware how one got there), and depersonalization–derealization (behaviors such as not feeling real, feeling that other people are unreal). The DES has demonstrated good reliability and validity among inpatient and outpatient samples (Bernstein & Putnam, 1986; Carlson & Armstrong, 1994; Lowenstein & Putnam, 1988). It instructs respondents to answer the questions for times when they were not under the influence of drugs and alcohol, and it has been able to discriminate populations with dissociative disorders from those with temporal lobe epilepsy (Lowenstein & Putnam, 1988).

The two most widely used interviews for dissociative behavior include the

Dissociative Disorders Interview Schedule (DDIS; Ross et al., 1989) and the Structured Clinical Interview for DSM-IV Dissociative Disorders (SCID-D; Steinberg, 1993, 1994). The DDIS is a 133-item structured interview designed to assess the presence of DSM-III-R dissociative disorders, as well as major depression, BPD, and somatization disorders (there is an unpublished DSM-IV version that can be obtained from the authors). The format is simple, "yes–no," which makes training and administration of the measure fairly easy. The full interview takes approximately 40 minutes to complete. Studies on the psychometric properties of the DDIS have found mixed results, with some indicating good interrater reliability and sensitivity (Ross, Heber, Norton, & Anderson, 1989) and others showing less favorable properties (Ross et al., 1989). Steinberg (1996) notes several limitations of the DDIS, including its highly structured format, which includes only one item for each DSM criterion and may lead to underdiagnoses of these disorders. In addition, Steinberg questions the applicability of the DDIS to chemically dependent populations.

This SCID-D is a 250-item structured interview designed to assess the presence of both dissociative behaviors and DSM-IV dissociative disorders. It can take from 10 to 90 minutes to complete, depending on the degree of dissociative experiences endorsed, and requires high degree of clinical knowledge and training to administer reliably. In a number of studies, the SCID-D has demonstrated good to excellent reliability and discriminant validity (e.g., Boon & Draijer, 1991; Steinberg, 1996).

Treatment of Dissociative Behavior

Although much has been written about the treatment of dissociative behavior and disorders, we were unable to find any controlled, randomly assigned outcome studies evaluating pharmacotherapy or psychotherapy for dissociative phenomena in the literature, including cognitive-behavioral treatments (for select case studies of cognitive-behavioral approaches to the treatment of dissociative disorders, see Caddy, 1985; Kohlenberg, 1973; Price & Hess, 1979). Furthermore, descriptions of treatment approaches that have been published primarily focus on treatment of dissociative identity disorder rather than dissociative behavior specifically (for descriptions of common treatments of dissociative identity disorder see Braun, 1989b; Kluft, 1996; Putnam, 1989b; and Fine, 1993). The absence of treatment approaches for dissociative behavior specifically is noteworthy. We speculate that this is in part due to the common "continuum" conceptualization of dissociative behavior and the assumption that all dissociative behavior is related to a common underlying pathology. In the case of psychodynamical formulations, for example, it is assumed that dissociative phenomena are *defense mechanisms,* utilized to defend against emotions and memories related to traumatic experiences (e.g., Braun, 1989b). Therefore, the focus of treatment of specific dissociative behavior in psychodynamical treatments is similar to the focus of dissociative disorders, and generally involves "accessing" and discussing traumatic memories. The inattention to treatment of dissociative behavior can also be attributed to traditional behavioral approaches to treatment, which have typically downplayed the significance of "private" experiences and experiences attributed to unconscious processes. As mentioned earlier, however, contemporary behaviorists do attend to private experiences as well as unconscious processing. Based on our conceptualization, we propose that aspects of Linehan's DBT may be particularly applicable to the treatment of dissociative behavior related to traumatic experiences.

Dialectical Behavioral Therapy

DBT is a cognitive-behavioral therapy, developed originally for the treatment of BPD. Studies have shown DBT to be more effective than "therapy as usual" in the treatment of many of the dysfunctional behaviors of BPD (Linehan, Armstrong, Suarez, Allmon, & Heard, 1991; Linehan, Tutek, Heard, & Armstrong, 1994). In the complete, standard DBT model, therapy is divided into discrete stages. Stage 1 aims to reduce suicidal behaviors, form and maintain a strong therapeutic relationship, and change behaviors and circumstances that interfere with achieving a good quality of life (e.g., problems with finances, housing, relationships, substance abuse, etc.). Behaviors are addressed in a hierarchical manner in each session, in that life-threatening behaviors take precedence, followed by therapy-interfering behaviors and then quality-of-life behaviors. Dissociative behavior is commonly addressed as a quality of life problem, but may also be addressed if it interferes with the process of therapy, or is directly related to suicidal behavior. Most of what has been published on DBT pertains to Stage 1, including Linehan's treatment outcome studies. Stage 2 focuses on processing past traumatic and invalidating experiences; thus, such experiences do not become the focus in DBT until behavioral and social stability and connection to the therapist have been established. In Stage 3 DBT, increasing self-respect and working toward any remaining goals are the primary targets.

Interventions in DBT are guided in large part by behavioral theory and the theory of dialectics. Although a full discussion of dialectics is beyond the scope of this chapter (see Linehan, 1993a), in brief, a dialectical philosophy refers to both a worldview on the nature of reality, as well as a process of change in therapy (Koerner & Linehan, 1997). Reality is viewed as interrelated (similar to systems perspectives), comprised of opposing forces (thesis–antithesis), and always changing, rather than static. Change in therapy occurs through the synthesis of opposing forces. The overarching dialectical tension in DBT is between accepting the client where he or she is and pushing for change. Thus, in addition to the change-oriented procedures characteristic of traditional behavior therapies, DBT also utilizes strategies for promoting and achieving acceptance. The balance of acceptance and change in psychotherapy has been discussed by others as well (e.g., Hayes, Jacobson, Follette, & Dougher, 1994). In addition, Linehan's theory of the etiology of BPD influences the ultimate goal of DBT, to increase emotion regulation ability and decrease dysfunctional behaviors. This is similar to our goal for the treatment of dissociative behavior, to increase tolerance for and regulation of emotional responses to cues of traumatic experiences. This is accomplished in DBT through the theory-guided use of various "strategies," as well as the teaching of specific behavioral skills (Linehan, 1993a, 1993b).

Our behavioral approach to the treatment of dissociative behavior draws primarily from DBT. Although the effectiveness of DBT for the treatment of dissociative behavior specifically has not yet been evaluated, based on our behavioral conceptualization, we propose that aspects of this treatment may be effective for treatment of dissociative behavior. It should be stressed that we are only overviewing select strategies and skills of DBT (rather than the treatment as a whole) and discuss the applicability of these techniques to the treatment of specific dissociative behaviors (as opposed to dissociative disorders). We next discuss the use of behavioral analyses, as used in DBT, to the assessment of dissociative behavior, and the use of select DBT strategies and behavioral skills for the three primary goals in the behavioral treatment of dissociative behavior discussed previously: (1) reduction of the availability of cues to traumatic experiences, (2) regulation of emotional responses to such cues and to negative affect more generally, and (3) change of the associated value of trauma cues. For a full discussion of DBT see Linehan (1993a, 1993b).

Behavioral Analysis of Dissociative Behavior

A comprehensive assessment of dissociative behavior is recommended in order to gather information on the likely etiology of the behavior (i.e., brain disorder, substance abuse, or traumatic experiences), the topography of the behavior (i.e., the type, frequency, and duration of the behavior), and on the factors that precede, follow, and maintain the behavior. As discussed, we present a treatment approach for dissociative behavior related to traumatic experiences only. In order to ascertain that dissociative behavior is related to traumatic experiences, a thorough history of the client's alcohol, drug, and medication use, and history of head injuries should be obtained. If epilepsy is suspected, an ictal EEG is recommended; however, it should be noted that some epileptic activity cannot be detected with surface EEG (Williamson, 1993). Information on the topography of the dissociative behavior can be obtained in part from standard self-report questionnaires and interviews such as those listed earlier, as well as by direct questioning. Finally, a *behavioral analysis* is used to obtain a thorough account of the events, cognitions, and emotions that precede and follow the dissociative behavior, in order to understand the factors that elicit and maintain it. A behavioral analysis is essential to determine the most effective points and procedures for intervention, and is described next.

The first step in a behavioral analysis is to get a precise and detailed description of the dissociative behavior. A client simply stating "I dissociated" is insufficient, especially in the early stages of treatment. Instead, a client should be questioned in such a way that a detailed description of the experience is obtained (e.g., "I felt numb," "I felt as if things were unreal, like I was looking down a tunnel," "I felt separate from my body, like I was watching myself from the ceiling," "I blacked out and I can't member what happened," "I felt spacey"). Information should also be obtained on the frequency and duration of the behavior. Some examples of questions useful for eliciting this type of information include "What do you mean by that exactly?" "Describe for me what you experienced." "How long did the feeling last?" "How many times did that happen last week?" "Did you have any thoughts at the time?" "Did you have any feelings at the time? What were they? How strong were they, on a scale of 1 to 100?" As a therapist, one should take the role of a naive observer, assuming nothing about the behavior, especially early in treatment. Over time, when the nature of a client's dissociative behavior is understood, this questioning can be shortened considerably.

In the next step, a *chain analysis* of the sequence of events preceding and following the dissociative episode is obtained in order to identify possible cues and precipitating events, as well as factors that may be reinforcing the behavior or punishing desired behavior. First, information is gathered about events prior to the dissociative behavior, including the client's thoughts, emotions, somatic sensations, actions, and images, as well as environmental circumstances. Next, similar information is gathered about internal and external events following the dissociative behavior, that is, information about the effect the dissociative behavior had on the client's thoughts, emotions and behaviors, and on the environment. Questions useful for beginning the chain analysis include "When did you first start dissociating?" "What set that off?" "What was going on at the moment you started dissociating?" For a client who has difficulty remembering the onset of the behavior, it can be helpful to pick a point in time near the behavior, for example, "Walk me through your evening from the moment you got home from work." To track the chain of events, it can be helpful to ask questions such as "What happened next?" or "How did you get from feeling angry to dissociating?" The consequences to look for are those that may be maintaining, strengthening, or increasing the behavior, including decreases in negative affect or reinforcing responses from the environment. Remember, the goal is to find out how the dissociative behavior is functioning, what is maintaining it, and what is preventing more desirable behavior from occurring. The approach is to gather as much detailed information as possible.

The following is a segment of a behavioral analysis of dissociative behavior conducted by the second author with a client she had been seeing for a year. The (composite) client is a 30-year-old, divorced, Caucasian woman, with a current diagnosis of BPD. She has a history of severe sexual abuse by her uncle, beginning in early childhood and continuing through adolescence, and physical abuse by both parents. She also has an extensive history of parasuicidal behavior beginning in childhood (including overdosing and cutting) and several near-lethal suicide attempts. She reports that during the abuse by her uncle and parents, she would imagine herself in the corner of the room, watching herself, and that she rarely felt pain until after it was over (indicating that dissociation began in early childhood). The dissociative episode had occurred at the end of the preceding week's therapy session. While in the middle of a difficult conversation, the client had stopped talking completely and stared into space. She was completely unresponsive to the therapist for the remainder of the session. The therapist is conducting a behavioral analysis on the preceding week's episode of dissociation.

THERAPIST: Okay, we have a lot of work to do, Mary.

CLIENT: I know, too much, I didn't want to come in because it seemed too heavy.

THERAPIST: Hmm, well, what we have to do is talk about last session.

CLIENT: That's going to be a problem, I don't remember that much of it.

THERAPIST: Well, we have to work on it. . . . So, what happened last time?

CLIENT: I don't know, I really don't. I went somewhere. I don't even know where I went.

THERAPIST: Okay, what do you remember about last session.

CLIENT: I don't.

(It is typical in a behavioral analysis of dissociative behavior for the client to initially have difficulty reconstructing the chain of events. Compared to other target behaviors, the behavioral analyses of dissociative behavior generally requires more input and/or hypothesis testing from the therapist. This is, of course, easier to do if the dissociative behavior occurred in session and is one of the reasons DBT places emphasis on analysis of in-session behavior.)

THERAPIST: Okay, we had been talking about me going to Europe . . .

(Alternatively, the therapist could have asked, "What is the last thing you remember us discussing?")

CLIENT: . . . Right . . .

THERAPIST: So, what do you remember thinking then?

CLIENT: I don't know . . .

THERAPIST: . . . try. This is really important, that we figure this out.

CLIENT: I don't know. . . . I just can't believe you're going out of town again, and to Europe!

THERAPIST: Were you thinking that last session?

CLIENT: Yeah.

THERAPIST: So what do you think you were feeling?

CLIENT: Just frustrated that this is happening again.

THERAPIST: Hmm, so, you were mad at me? Do you think you dissociated after you started feeling angry?

CLIENT: Not really angry . . . more like scared.

(Here the therapist offered a hypothesis, it did not completely fit for the client, and the behavioral analysis continues.)

THERAPIST: That's interesting, what do you think you were scared about? Scared that I might not come back?

CLIENT: Yeah . . . no, more like scared that if I really need you while you're gone, you won't be there for me.

THERAPIST: How strong was the feeling of fear?

CLIENT: I don't know, about a 50, I guess.

THERAPIST: So it's as if the thought of me not being here lead to a strong feeling of fear, and you withdrew?

CLIENT: Yeah, I think so.

During a chain analysis, the therapist is looking to identify both the factors related to the current episode of dissociation and options for alternative responses. As discussed earlier in our behavioral conceptualization, dissociative behavior can be viewed as functioning to regulate exposure to cues related to traumatic experiences and to negative affect more generally. In this case, the client was exposed to the feeling of fear, which is likely an emotion associated with her childhood traumas. The part of the conversation related to the therapist leaving town seemed to elicit the dissociative behavior. The next step in the behavioral analysis is to formulate hypotheses about the factors that are maintaining the dissociative behavior, based on the behavioral conceptualization. In this case, this behavioral analysis (and others) revealed that the client had several thoughts that led to the experience of intense fear (e.g., "I might fall apart if I need you and you're not here"). As had been typical for her in the past, the dissociative behavior was apparently a conditioned response to the feeling of fear. Based on our conceptualization of dissociative behavior (including the biological research on trauma), it can be further hypothesized that this client has heightened reactivity to fear stimuli and that the dissociative behavior was functioning as avoidance of fear specifically. Furthermore, the client lacked skills for regulating emotions in alternative ways. The primary goals of the behavioral analysis are to help clients notice functional patterns between internal and external events and dissociative behavior, and to determine points for behavior change. In this case, the client may benefit from cognitive restructuring, emotion regulation skills, or exposure to the feeling of fear (emotion regulation skills and exposure are discussed later).

Treatment of Dissociative Phenomena in DBT

Decreasing the Availability of Cues to Traumatic Experiences

Given our conceptualization of dissociative phenomena as functioning to avoid cues related to traumatic experiences, the first target for treatment is the actual reduction of such cues. This is accomplished in several ways in DBT. First, discussion and processing of the traumatic experiences is avoided until Stage 2 DBT. Instead, clients are oriented to the behavioral rationale for the stages approach to treatment, and in Stage 1 DBT, work toward establishing stability and connection to the therapist first. While an assessment of such experiences is warranted at the commencement of Stage 1, detailed and prolonged discussions are avoided. Second, clients are encouraged to get out of situations that are currently traumatic and to avoid situations or activities that provide chronic cues to past traumatic experiences. This could include domestically violent situations, living in violent neighborhoods, any relationship that is conflictual or otherwise provides cues to traumatic experiences, reading material or movies related to the traumatic experiences, being in physical locations that provide cues to traumatic experiences, and so on. An assessment of such situations would of course be required initially in order to determine what should be avoided. Third, clients are taught specific skills to cope with and avoid cues to traumatic experiences. Know as "crisis survival strategies" in DBT (Linehan, 1993b), these include common techniques such as distracting with other activities, engaging in activities which elicit "opposite emotions," "pushing" the situation away by leaving it or blocking thoughts, engaging in self-soothing activities (e.g., comforting and nurturing oneself using the various senses), and skills for improving the moment (e.g., using imagery, relaxation, taking brief "vacations"). Finally, avoidance of traumatic cues in DBT can be accomplished through a strategy labeled "environmental intervention." This refers to interventions by the therapist on behalf of the client, conducted when the outcome is essential and the client does not have the capability or power to achieve the outcome. In the case of cue reduction, this might involve removing the client from a harmful situation, pursuing alternate housing opportunities, hospitalizing a client, and so on. Although the main goal of DBT is to help clients solve their own problems, at times environmental interventions are necessary (see Linehan, 1993a, for guidelines for effective implementation of this strategy).

*Regulation of Emotional Responses to Traumatic Cues
and Negative Affect in General*

Unfortunately, the majority of cues to traumatic experiences are typically ubiqui-
tous in the lives of severely traumatized individuals, and thus are difficult to
completely eliminate without causing extreme environmental and activity restric-
tions. Therefore, the second target we propose for the treatment of dissociative
behavior is the regulation of emotional responses to traumatic cues and negative
affect more generally. To this end, DBT utilizes two primary interventions: (1)
teaching of skills targeting *mindfulness* and *emotion regulation,* and (2) exposure
to *present* cues to traumatic experiences and *present* emotions.

In DBT, *mindfulness skills* are derived from Zen philosophy and are compatible with both Western and Eastern meditative practices. The primary goal of
mindfulness skills is to *cultivate awareness* of internal and external experiences.
Such awareness is critical to the ability to identify internal and external precipitants to one's reactions and to the ability to tolerate and regulate emotional
experiences. Specifically, clients are taught the skills of *observing, describing,* and
participating. Observing is drawing one's attention to external events, emotions,
thoughts, or other behavioral responses, without trying to avoid, push away, or
cling to what is observed. *Describing* refers to labeling what is observed objectively, and without evaluations or judgments. Finally, *participating* refers to experiencing with awareness and without self-consciousness. To aid the acquisition of
each of these skills, clients are also taught the importance of having a nonjudg-
mental stance (dropping evaluations and interpretations), of doing things "one-
mindfully" (one thing at a time), and being "effective" (doing what works).
Through the use of mindfulness skills, clients begin to learn that all experiences,
including negative emotions, are impermanent and tolerable. Mindfulness skills
are also fundamental to some emotion regulation skills in DBT.

Emotion regulation skills consist of several techniques aimed at increasing
clients' understanding and awareness of emotions, reducing vulnerability to emotions, and changing emotions (Linehan, 1993b). First, clients are taught how to
identify and label emotions. This is done by educating clients about the nature
and function of emotions, typical words used for labeling emotions, and physical
correlates of emotions. Clients are taught to observe and describe events that
prompt emotions, their interpretations of events, their physical sensations, and
their behaviors that express the emotions. Second, clients are taught to reduce
their vulnerability to emotions, by attending to their physical health and engaging
in activities that promote feelings of mastery. Third, emotion regulation is enhanced by increasing positive experiences. Clients are taught to increase short-
term, positive experiences, formulate and work toward long-term goals, and
increase mindfulness of positive experiences. Next, mindfulness of painful emotions is directly addressed. The idea here is that exposure to emotions without
judgments or other negative consequences will lead to a natural lessening of the

emotions. Finally, clients are taught how to regulate their emotions by changing the behavioral–expressive components of their emotions. This requires the ability to observe the "action urge" associated with an emotion and to act in a way that is inconsistent with this urge (e.g., for depression, getting active as opposed to withdrawing).

In Stage 1 DBT, *exposure* strategies are also used to decrease emotional responses to traumatic cues and increase tolerance to current negative emotions, toward the goal of treating dissociative behavior. The use of exposure is based on the theory that dissociative behavior is maintained by avoidance of cues to traumatic experiences (or negative affect more generally), and that this avoidance can be either an operant or a respondent behavior. As used by others (e.g., Foa & Rothbaum, 1998; Resick & Schnicke, 1993), the basic principles in exposure in DBT are the following: (1) Present stimuli that elicit the emotion; (2) ensure that the affective response is not reinforced (there is corrective information); (3) block escape responses and other forms of avoidance; and (4) enhance the client's sense of control. Exposure is said to "work" when there is a reduction in the emotion or sustained attention to the cue without the client resorting to dissociative behavior or an alternative (dysfunctional) avoidant behavior. It should be stressed that in Stage 1 DBT, exposure is to *present* cues to past traumatic experiences (e.g., loud noises, men, anger, shame), as opposed to past traumatic memories specifically. In addition, exposure procedures are typically used *informally* during Stage 1, that is, there is no formal protocol for implementing these procedures across a series of sessions and the exposure is generally for shorter periods of time, compared to Stage 2.

There are several applications of informal exposure toward the treatment of dissociative behavior in Stage 1 DBT. First, exposure can be used on an "as needed" basis when the results of the behavioral analysis suggest that the dissociative behavior functions as avoidance of cues to traumatic experiences or avoidance of negative affect more generally. For example, it may be determined in a behavioral analysis that a male client dissociates whenever he feels extreme anger. The intervention might then be to expose the client to the emotion of anger. In this case, exposure can be conceptualized as a "solution" or discrete treatment intervention. In addition, informal use of exposure can occur during the course of a behavioral analysis of dissociative behavior; that is, in the process of reporting the events, thoughts, and emotions that lead up to the dissociative behavior, it is likely that the client will begin experiencing some of the cues (including emotions) that she experiences at the time she originally dissociated. Therefore, the behavioral analysis itself functions as exposure to the original cues. Furthermore, exposure can occur simply in coming to therapy, in forming a relationship with the therapist, and in the learning and enactment of new skills. For a number of clients, the process of disclosing personal information and reporting on behavior can produce a number of emotions that may be cues that elicit dissociative behavior. Likewise, the process of forming a strong therapeutic relationship can lead to emotions such as fear or shame that may be related to dissociative behavior (Kohlenberg & Tsai, 1991; see Kohlenberg & Tsai, Chapter 12, in this volume). In the learning of new skills, clients are asked to approach situations that elicit emotions in order to try new behavior. The point here is that a number of situations in therapy can function as exposure to cues to dissociative behavior, providing the therapist is aware of the situations as they relate to the client's dissociative behavior. In addition, the effective use of informal exposure requires attention to the principles of exposure mentioned earlier and described more fully below.

Change the Associated Value of the Cues to Traumatic Experiences

For many clients, dissociative behavior persists in some contexts even after they have increased their ability to regulate emotional responses to traumatic cues and negative emotions. This is likely to be the case for clients whose dissociative behavior is related to more direct cues to past traumatic experiences (such as memories of past traumas), and for clients who experience more direct cues (e.g., clients with "reexperiencing" symptoms, characteristic of PTSD) . Changing the associated value of the cue to traumatic experiences is therefore the third target for treatment of dissociative behavior. Based on the assumption that many dissociative behaviors are learned responses to traumatic cues, and that these cues are related to past traumas but that many (if not most) are not harmful in isolation of these associations, *exposure* is again used in DBT to change these associations. Although informal use of exposure to present cues, as described earlier, at times serves to change the associated value of the cues, this is more fully accomplished by the formal use of exposure to the actual traumatic experiences, typical of Stage 2 DBT. It is important to remember here that some dissociative behavior might be related to experiences that might not appear "traumatic" but are experienced as traumatic by the individual (e.g., verbal invalidation); formal exposure would be advocated in these cases as well. We next describe the guidelines for achieving effective exposure (see Foa & Rothbaum, 1998 and Resick & Schnicke, 1993, for specific strategies for implementing formal exposure).

Presenting Stimuli That Elicit the Emotion. This refers to the process of presenting clients with the events, thoughts, memories, or emotions that elicit the emotion related to the traumatic experience and the dissociative behavior. Although dissociative behavior can occur in response to both nonemotional and emotional cues related to the traumatic experience, the process of exposure inevitably elicits some emotion (typically anxiety is evoked in the presence of nonemotional cues). The idea here is that the presence of the emotion signifies that the focus is on target. This can be accomplished *imaginally,* by having the client think about a particular scenario associated with the traumatic experiences and dissociative behavior, or "live" (*in vivo*), by having the client engage in an activity that elicits the emotion related to the dissociative behavior. *Imaginal* exposure is typically less arousing for clients and can be a useful starting point for exposure. *In vivo* exposure can occur both out of the therapy office (through a behavioral "homework assignment") or in the therapy session. Since dissociative behavior can occur so seemingly automatically, use of in-session emotional reactions can be particularly effective for exposure treatment of dissociative behavior. For this reason, it is essential that therapists are alert to the occurrence of emotions during session that are related to dissociative behavior.

Nonreinforced Exposure. An essential component of effective exposure is that the emotional reaction is not reinforced. In regard to traumatic experiences and dissociative behavior, there must be some new learning or "corrective information" about the experience or emotional reaction prior to dissociative behavior (or other escape behavior) occurring (e.g., learning that one can tolerate the memory or emotions longer than believed, habituating to the emotion, having the realization that the trauma is not occurring now). New learning is more likely to occur by carefully designing the exposure and graduating the intensity and length of the exposure, so that the client is not overwhelmed. A number of different emotions may be elicited through exposure, including fear, anxiety, anger, sadness, shame, and guilt, as well as emotions *about* these emotions (e.g., fear of feeling angry). The approach to exposure would differ to some extent depending on the eliciting emotion. For example, if a client was dissociating in response to feelings of fear of "losing control," it would be important that the exposure was designed so that the client felt in control and was able to leave the session feeling relatively calm. If shame was an elicitor of dissociation, the therapist should be alert to the client's feelings of shame and take care to validate, as oppose to censure, communications that feel shameful.

Block Avoidance. The most common obstacle to effective exposure is avoidance of emotional experiencing, and it is essential that therapists block these forms of avoidance during exposure. Of course, dissociative behavior itself is a primary means of avoidance. The occurrence of dissociative behavior may be obvious, but often it is not. Be alert to silences, averted eye gaze, and other signs that the client may be "spacing out." On the other hand, caution should be taken not to assume that these behaviors signify dissociative behavior—always assess! Other common forms of avoidance include missing sessions, not doing homework assignments, refusing to participate in behavioral analyses, and diverting the conversation. Less obvious (but effective) means of avoidance include secondary emotions (e.g., shame about anger, fear of fear). If exposure is focusing on the primary emotion, the secondary emotions should be blocked. Similarly, judgments about emotions or oneself can function as avoidance. For example, a client may berate him- or herself for feeling very sad about a loss. This judgment is likely inhibiting the experience of loss and should be blocked. Blocking avoidance can usually be accomplished by drawing attention to the avoidance and by pulling the client's attention back to the exposure. Finally, helping clients to change their body posture can block avoidance. This can be done through relaxation and by changing postures, and expressions related to secondary emotions (e.g., sitting up strait to block the feeling of shame).

Enhance Control. Given that dissociative behavior often occurs in response to events or emotions that are appraised as uncontrollable, an important part of exposure treatment is increasing clients' perceived ability to control events and emotions. This can be accomplished by giving clients some control over how session time is used, including when the exposure will occur, and allowing clients to control the pace and intensity of exposure if they are feeling overwhelmed. In addition, a client's sense of control can be greatly aided by discussing with the client ahead of time the rationale and procedures of exposure and designed interventions with the client's input.

Continue until the Exposure Works. The length of an exposure intervention can vary tremendously. The essential criterion for exposure is that there is some reduction in affect without the client resorting to dissociative or other dysfunctional behavior. With the more informal uses of exposure described earlier, this could be a few minutes or less. When exposure is being used as a specific treatment intervention, and when the focus is past traumatic experiences, this could take several minutes to an hour, over several weeks or months. Typically, for clients with dissociative behavior, exposure can be embedded in a session, allowing ample time for the client to achieve a calmer emotional state before leaving the session. Occasionally, a session can be lengthened slightly to enable the reduction in affect to occur. Reductions in affect are typically tracked with verbal reports of intensity, such as using a "1–100" rating scale, or by simply observing the client's behavior, or by asking directly if the emotions have lessened. Knowing when to stop exposure requires a thorough understanding of a client's emotional response and where the behavior is on a shaping curve.

Before concluding this section, it should be stressed that the coexistence of traumatic experiences and dissociative behavior does not determine that the dissociative behavior is a learned response to a traumatic cue—this must always be assessed! It is quite possible that dissociative behavior is occurring in response to other types of cues or because of another etiology. Therefore, exposure to the traumatic experience toward the goal of changing the associated value of the cue may not always be necessary or warranted. Furthermore, it would rarely be a goal of this treatment to put effort into "accessing" forgotten past traumatic experiences, even if these experiences could be validated by an objective source. While we hold the assumption that current dissociative behavior often functions to regulate exposure to cues related to past traumas, we also hold that the inability to remember past traumatic experiences may be due to a number of factors, including not learning the material in the first place. Indeed, recent theories on information processing propose models by which experiences (including traumatic experiences) may not be processed initially in sufficient depth to ever be recalled (see Barnard & Teasdale, 1991; Greenwald, 1997).

Common Treatment Obstacles

How do you know whether to expose to present cues or past traumas? This is a frequently asked question, that can refer to the treatment of a number of dysfunctional behaviors, including dissociative behavior. In our experience, treatment should focus primarily on present cues when the client would not be able to effectively modulate emotional reactions to discussions of past traumatic experiences. This may be due to skills deficits, vulnerability factors, or environmental circumstances, any of which could lead to severe emotion dysregulation in the presence of discussions of past traumas. When a client appears able to modulate such reactions, exposure to past traumatic experiences is recommended *in addition to* exposure to present cues. However, therapy is rarely linear; instead, the focus of therapy often goes back and forth between exposure and emotion regulation and crisis survival strategies as the need for additional assistance regulating affect arises. There is one exception to this guideline: when a traumatic experience occurs *during the course of therapy* with a dissociative client. In this case, it is recommended that exposure to the traumatic event commence immediately in order to prevent the development of a severe stress reaction or PTSD. In some cases, hospitalization may be necessary to ensure the client's safety under these conditions, if emotion regulation abilities are lacking.

How do you determine whether to work on avoiding traumatic cues or exposing to traumatic cues? Similar to the previous answer, exposure to traumatic cues is recommended to *follow* the acquisition of emotion tolerance and regulation ability. Toward this objective, avoidance and reduction of traumatic cues are suggested as the initial target, in order to achieve decreases in overall emotional arousal, which can in turn facilitate the learning of new skills. In addition, the focus of cue reduction is primarily on cues that occur outside of the therapy session, while in session, clients are gradually taught to tolerate exposure to cues as described earlier. The goals are to prevent clients from becoming overwhelmed by exposure to traumatic cues and to develop flexibility and control over the exposure process.

How do you know whether to treat the dissociation or other dysfunctional behaviors? Typically, clients with dissociative behavior present with additional dysfunctional behaviors, including parasuicidal behavior, substance abuse, eating disorders, relationship problems, and so on. The decision of "what to treat first" can be complicated by both the number of additional problems as well as the fluctuating importance and urgency that clients place on these problems from week to week [labeled by Linehan (1993a) the "crisis of the week" phenomenon]. In DBT, this question is answered by structuring the sessions according to a predetermined hierarchy of therapy targets. As mentioned earlier, life-threatening behaviors take precedence over all other behaviors, such that if any parasuicidal behavior occurred in the previous week, this would be the primary focus of the session. Next, behaviors that threaten the course of therapy (such as missing or coming late to appointments, not complying with treatment tasks, etc.), take priority if no life-threatening behaviors occurred. Dissociative behavior would fall on the hierarchy next, along with other behaviors that threaten the ability to have a good quality of life, including such behaviors as substance abuse and eating disorders. The specific focus of the session would be based on which behavior was evaluated as most threatening to achieving a good quality of life, as well as the functional relationship of the behaviors to one another (e.g., if dissociative behavior followed and seemed related to substance abuse, the substance abuse would take precedence). Despite the hierarchy, however, several behaviors often become treated simultaneously. A common example is parasuicidal behavior that only occurs when the client is experiencing feelings of depersonalization. In this case, dissociative behavior would be treated as part of the treatment of parasuicidal behavior.

Difficulty finding precipitants; dissociative behavior comes "out of the blue." At times during a behavioral analysis of dissociative behavior, a client will be unable to identify any precipitating events, thoughts, or emotions, and will instead report that it came "out of the blue" or, alternatively, that he or she woke up in a dissociated state. It can be helpful in these situations to refer to the behavioral conceptualization and be clear (to yourself and to your client) that all behavior comes from somewhere, that it is just a matter of figuring out the precipitants, and regardless of whether you can figure it out or not, there *is* a precipitant. This framework is especially important for clients to adopt, in order to encourage constant evaluation and analysis of their own behavior. During a behavioral analysis, it can also be helpful to continue questioning despite "I don't know" responses from the client. Gentle prodding can be useful here, such as "I know you don't, but try to remember." Finally, it is important to remember that, often, several behavioral analyses are required before patterns become evident. As an example, the first author had a client who frequently reported simultaneous panic attacks with dissociative behavior; however, the client could not identify any precipitating event for either. Over time, it became clear that the client was having classic panic attacks (related to physiological cues), and that the feeling of panic itself was a cue to past traumatic experiences, and thus was eliciting the dissociative behavior. It was only after several behavioral analyses that this pattern emerged.

Client is reluctant to "give up" dissociative behavior. It is not uncommon for clients to express reluctance to give up dissociative behavior, since in many respects it appears to "work" as a problem-solving technique and emotion regulation strategy. It can be helpful here to discuss with clients the ways in which dissociative behavior causes problems in their lives (e.g., feeling disconnected from others, missing appointments, engaging in harmful behaviors), as well as proposing a treatment with more effective ways of achieving the same goals (e.g., emotion regulation skills). We have further found it helpful to stress with clients that our goal is not to eliminate dissociative behavior, but instead to increase their control over the use of the behavior.

SUMMARY

Although behaviorists have acknowledged the significance of dissociative phenomena in the treatment of individuals with traumatic experiences for years, only recently have behavioral accounts of the processes involved in dissociative phenomena been articulated. Based on this literature, as well as recent findings on the biological and cognitive effects of trauma, the current chapter provided a comprehensive behavioral conceptualization of dissociative behavior. It was asserted that the primary function of dissociative behavior is the regulation of exposure to cues related to traumatic experiences. Based on this formulation, a behavioral treatment was proposed, focusing on decreasing the availability of cues related to traumatic experiences, regulating emotional responses to trauma-related cues, and changing the associated value of such cues. Specific aspects of Linehan's dialectical behavioral therapy, particularly applicable to these treatment objectives, were discussed in detail. Although data are not yet available to support this behavioral conceptualization, or the use of DBT to the treatment of dissociative behavior, this chapter provides a theoretical basis to begin such investigations.

REFERENCES

American Psychiatric Association. (1994). *Diagnostic and statistical manual of mental disorders* (4th ed.). Washington, DC: Author.

Barnard, P. J., & Teasdale, J. D. (1991). Interacting cognitive subsystems: A systemic approach to cognitive-affective interaction and change. *Cognition and Emotion, 5,* 1–39.

Bechara, A., Tranel, D., Damasio, H., Adolphs, R., Rockland, C., & Damasio, A. R. (1995). Double dissociation of conditioning and declarative knowledge relative to the amygdala and hippocampus in humans. *Science, 269,* 1115–1118.

Berstein, E. M., & Putnam, F. W. (1986). Development, reliability and validity of a dissociation scale. *Journal of Nervous and Mental Disease, 174,* 727–734.

Blaney, P. H. (1986). Affect and memory: A review. *Psychological Bulletin, 99,* 229–246.

Boon, S., & Draijer, N. (1991). Diagnosing dissociative disorders in the Netherlands: A pilot study with the Structured Clinical Interview for the DSM-III-R Dissociative Disorders. *American Journal of Psychiatry, 148,* 458–462.

Bower, G. H. (1990). Awareness, the unconscious, and repression: An experimental psychologist's perspective. In J. L. Singer (Ed.), *Repression and dissociation* (pp. 209–231). Chicago: University of Chicago Press.

Branscombe, L. B. (1991). Dissociation in combat-related post-traumatic stress disorder. *Dissociation, 4,* 13–20.

Braun, B. G. (1986). Issues in the psychotherapy of multiple personality disorder. In B. G. Braun (Ed.), *Treatment of multiple personality disorder* (pp. 1–28). Washington, DC: American Psychiatric Association Press.

Braun, B. G. (1988a). The BASK model of dissociation. *Dissociation, 1,* 4–23.

Braun, B. G. (1988b). The BASK model of dissociation: Part II. Treatment. *Dissociation, 1,* 16–23.

Bremner, J. D., Randall, P., Scott, T. M., Bronen, R. A., Seibyl, J. P., Southwick, S. M., Delaney, R. C., McCarthy, G., Charney, D. S., & Innis, R. B. (1995). MRI-based measurement of hippocampal volume in combat-related posttraumatic stress disorder. *American Journal of Psychiatry, 152,* 973–981.

Bremner, J. D., Southwick, S., Brett, E., Fontana, A., Rosenheck, R., & Charney, D. (1992). Dissociation and posttraumatic stress disorder in Vietnam combat veterans. *American Journal of Psychiatry, 149,* 328–332.

Brodsky, B. S., Cloitre, M., & Dulit, R. A. (1995). Relationship of dissociation to self-mutilation and childhood abuse in borderline personality disorder. *American Journal of Psychiatry, 152,* 1788–1792.

Burgess, A. W., & Holmstrom, L. L. (1976). Coping behavior of the rape victim. *American Journal of Psychiatry, 133,* 413–418.

Caddy, G. R. (1985). Cognitive behavior therapy in the treatment of multiple personality disorder. *Behavior Modification, 9,* 267–292.

Cardeña, E. (1994). The domain of dissociation. In J. Lynn & J. W. Rhue (Eds.), *Dissociation: Clinical and theoretical perspectives* (pp. 15–31). New York: Guilford Press.

Cardeña, E., Classen, D., & Spiegel, D. (1991). *Stanford Acute Stress Reaction Questionnaire.* Stanford, CA: Stanford University Medical School.

Cardeña, E., & Spiegel, D. (1993). Dissociative reactions to the Bay Area earthquake. *American Journal of Psychiatry, 150,* 474–478.

Carlson, E. B., & Armstrong, J. (1994). The diagnosis and assessment of dissociative disorders. In S. J. Lynn & J. W. Rhue (Eds.), *Dissociation: Clinical and theoretical perspectives* (pp. 159–174). New York: Guilford Press.

Carlson, E. B., & Putnam, F. (1993). An update on the Dissociative Experiences Scale. *Dissociation, 6,* 16–27.

Carlson, E. B., & Rosser-Hogan, R. (1991). Trauma experiences, posttraumatic stress, dissociation, and depression in Cambodian refugees. *American Journal of Psychiatry, 148,* 1548–1551.

Christianson, S. A., & Loftus, E. F. (1991). Remembering emotional events: The fate of detailed information. *Cognition and Emotion, 5,* 81–108.

Chu, J. A., & Dill, D. L. (1990). Dissociative symptoms in relation to childhood physical and sexual abuse. *American Journal of Psychiatry, 147,* 887–892.

Cole, P. M., Alexander, P. C., & Anderson, C. L. (1996). Dissociation in typical and atypical development: Examples from father–daughter incest. In L. K. Michelson & W. J. Ray

(Eds.), *Handbook of dissociation: Theoretical, empirical, and clinical perspectives* (pp. 69–89). New York: Plenum.

Dancu, C. V., Riggs, D. S., Hearst-Ikeda, D., Shoyer, B. G., & Foa, E. B. (1996). Dissociative experiences and posttraumatic stress disorder among female victims of criminal assault and rape. *Journal of Traumatic Stress, 9,* 253–267.

Demitrack, M. A., Putnam, F. W., Brewerton, T. D., Brandt, H. A., & Gold, P. W. (1990). Relation of clinical variables to dissociative phenomena in eating disorders. *American Journal of Psychiatry, 147,* 1184–1188.

Devinsky, O., Putnam, F., Grafman, J., Bromfield, E., & Theodore, W. H. (1989). Dissociative states and epilepsy. *Neurology, 39,* 835–840.

Ensink, B. J., & Van Otterloo, D. (1989). A validation of the DES in the Netherlands. *Dissociation, 2,* 221–223.

Fine, C. G. (1993). A tactical integrationalist perspective on the treatment of multiple personality disorder. In R. P. Kluft & C. G. Fine (Eds.), *Clinical perspective on multiple personality disorder* (pp. 135–153). Washington, DC: American Psychiatric Association Press.

Foa, E. B., & Hearst-Ikeda, D. (1996). Emotional dissociation in response to trauma. In L. K. Michelson & W. J. Ray (Eds.), *Handbook of dissociation: Theoretical, empirical, and clinical perspectives* (pp. 207–224). New York: Plenum.

Foa, E. B., & Riggs, D. S. (1993). Post-traumatic stress disorder in rape victims. In J. Oldham, M. B. Riba, & A. Tasman (Eds.), *American Psychiatric Press review of psychiatry* (Vol. 12, pp. 273–303). Washington, DC: American Psychiatric Association Press.

Foa, E. B., & Rothbaum, B. O. (1998). *Treating the trauma of rape: Cognitive-behavioral therapy for PTSD.* New York: Guilford Press.

Friedman, M. J., Charney, D. S., & Deutch, A. Y. (1995). *Neurobiological and clinical consequences of stress: From normal adaptation to posttraumatic stress disorder.* Philadelphia: Lippincott/Raven.

Good, M. I. (1989). Substance-induced dissociative disorders and psychiatric nosology. *Journal of Clinical Psychopharmacology, 9,* 88–93.

Greewald, A. G. (1997). Self-knowledge and self-deception: Further considerations. In M. S. Myslobodsky (Ed.), *The mythomanias: The nature of deception and self-deception* (pp. 51–71). Mahwah, NJ: Erlbaum.

Hayes, S. C., Jacobson, N. S., Follette, V. M., & Dougher, M. J. (1994). *Acceptance and change: Content and context in psychotherapy.* Reno, NV: Context Press.

Hilgard, E. R. (1992). Dissociation and theories of hypnosis. In E. Fromm & M. R. Nash (Eds.), *Contemporary hypnosis research* (pp. 69–101). New York: Guilford Press.

Horowitz, M. J. (1986). *Stress-response syndromes* (2nd ed.). Northvale, NJ: Aronson.

Keaney, J. C., & Farley, M. (1996). Dissociation in an outpatient sample of women reporting childhood sexual abuse. *Psychological Reports, 78,* 59–65.

Kirby, J. S., Chu, J. A., & Dill, D. L. (1993). Correlates of dissociative symptomatology in patients with physical and sexual abuse histories. *Comprehensive Psychiatry, 34,* 258–263.

Kluft, R. P. (1996). Treating the traumatic memories of patients with dissociative identity disorder. *American Journal of Psychiatry, 153,* 103–110.

Koerner, K., & Linehan, M. M. (1997). Integrative therapy for borderline personality disorder: Dialectical behavior therapy. In Norcross & Goldfried (Eds.), *Handbook of integrative psychotherapy* (pp. 433–459). New York: Basic Books.

Kohlenberg, R. J. (1973). Behavioristic approach to multiple personality disorder: A case study. *Behavior Therapy, 4,* 137–140.

Kohlenberg, R. J., & Tsai, M. (1991). *Functional analytic psychotherapy.* New York: Plenum.

Krippner, S. (1994). Cross-cultural treatment perspectives on dissociative disorders. In S. J. Lynn & J. W. Rhue (Eds.), *Dissociation: Clinical and theoretical perspectives* (pp. 338–361). New York: Guilford Press.

Krystal, J. H., Bennett, A., Bremner, D., Southwick, S. M., & Charney, D. S. (1996). Recent developments in the neurobiology of dissociation. In L. K. Michelson & W. J. Ray (Eds.), *Handbook of dissociation: Theoretical, empirical, and clinical perspectives* (pp. 163–190). New York: Plenum.

Kulka, R. A., Schlenger, W. E., Fairbank, J. A., Hough, R. L., Jordan, B. K., & Marmar, C. R. (1990). *Trauma and the Vietnam War generation: Report of findings from the National Vietnam Veterans Readjustment Study.* New York: Brunner/Mazel.

Lewis-Fernandez, R. (1994). Culture and dissociation: A comparison of *Ataque de Nervios* among Puerto Ricans and possession syndrome in India. In D. Spiegel (Ed.), *Dissociation* (pp. 123–167). Washington, DC: American Psychiatric Association Press.

Linehan, M. M. (1993a). *Cognitive-behavioral treatment of borderline personality disorder.* New York: Guilford Press.

Linehan, M. M. (1993b). *Skills training manual for treating borderline personality disorder.* New York: Guilford Press.

Linehan, M. M., Armstrong, H. E., Suarez, A., Allmon, D., & Heard, H. L. (1991). Cognitive-behavioral treatment of chronically parasuicidal borderline patients. *Archives of General Psychiatry, 48,* 1060–1064.

Linehan, M. M., Tutek, D. A., Heard, H. L., & Armstrong, H. E. (1994). Interpersonal outcome of cognitive-behavioral treatment for chronically suicidal borderline patients. *American Journal of Psychiatry, 15,* 1771–1776.

Lipschitz, D. S., Kaplan, M. L., Sorkenn, J., Chorney, P., & Asnis, G. M. (1996). Childhood abuse, adult assault, and dissociation. *Comprehensive Psychiatry, 37,* 261–266.

Loewenstein, R. J., & Putnam, F. W. (1988). A comparison study of dissociative symptoms in patients with complex partial seizures, MPD, and posttraumatic stress disorder. *Dissociation, 1,* 17–23.

Loftus, E. F. (1993). The reality of repressed memories. *American Psychologist, 48,* 518–537.

Marmar, C. R., & Weiss, D. S. (1990). *Peritraumatic Dissociative Experiences Questionnaire—Subject Version.* Unpublished scale. San Francisco: San Francisco Medical School.

Marmar, C. R., Weiss, D. S., Schlenger, W. E., Fairbank, J. A., Jordan, B. K., Kulka, R. A., & Hough, R. L. (1994). Peritraumatic dissociation and posttraumatic stress in male Vietnam theater veterans. *American Journal of Psychiatry, 151,* 902–907.

McFarlane, A. C. (1986). Posttraumatic morbidity of a disaster: A study of cases presenting for psychiatric treatment. *Journal of Nervous and Mental Disease, 174,* 4–14.

Mesulam, (1981). Dissociative states with abnormal temporal lobe EEG. *Archives of Neurology, 38,* 176–181.

Modestin, J., Gerhard, E., Junghan, M., & Erni, T. (1996). Dissociative experiences and dissociative disorders in acute psychiatric inpatients. *Comprehensive Psychiatry, 37,* 355–361.

Noyes, Jr., R., Hoenk, P. R., Kuperman, S., & Slymen, D. J. (1977). Depersonalization in accident victims and psychiatric patients. *Journal of Nervous Disorder and Mental Disease, 164,* 401–407.

Noyes, Jr., R., & Kletti, R. (1977). Depersonalization in the face of life-threatening danger: A description. *Psychiatry, 39,* 19–27.

Pitman, R. K., Shenton, M. E., & Gurvitz, T. V. (1995, November). *Reduced hippocampal volume in magnetic resonance imaging in chronic post-traumatic stress disorder.* Paper presented at the 11th annual meeting of the International Society for Traumatic Stress Studies, Boston, MA.

Pitman, R. K., van der Kolk, B. A., Orr, S. P., & Greenberg, M. S. (1990). Naloxone reversible stress induced analgesia in post traumatic stress disorder. *Archives of General Psychiatry, 47,* 541–547.

Price, J., & Hess, N. C. (1979). Behavior therapy as precipitant and treatment in a case of dual personality. *Australian and New Zealand Journal of Psychiatry, 13,* 63–66.

Putnam, F. W. (1989a). Pierre Janet and modern views of dissociation. *Journal of Traumatic Stress, 2,* 413–429.

Putnam, F. W. (1989b). *Diagnosis and treatment of multiple personality disorder.* New York: Guilford Press.

Quimby, L. G., & Putnam, E. W. (1991). Dissociative symptoms and aggression in a state mental hospital. *Dissociation, 4,* 21–24.

Ray, W. J. (1996). Dissociation in normal populations. In L. K. Michelson & W. J. Ray (Eds.), *Handbook of dissociation: Theoretical, empirical, and clinical perspectives* (pp. 51–66). New York: Plenum.

Ray, W., & Faith, M. (1995). Dissociative experiences in a college age population: Follow-up with 1190 subjects. *Personality and Individual Differences, 18,* 223–230.

Ray, W. J. (1996). Dissociation of normal populations. In L. K. Michelson & W. J. Ray (Eds.), *Handbook of dissociation: Theoretical, empirical, and clinical perspectives* (pp. 51–66). New York: Plenum.

Resick, P. A., & Schnicke, M. K. (1993). *Cognitive processing therapy for rape victims: A treatment manual.* Newbury Park, CA: Sage.

Riley, K. (1988). Measurement of dissociation. *Journal of Nervous and Mental Disease, 176,* 449–450.

Ross, C. A. (1985). DSM-III: Problems in diagnosing partial forms of multiple personality disorder. *Journal of the Royal Society of Medicine, 75,* 933–936.

Ross, C. A. (1996). History, phenomenology, and epidemiology of dissociation. In L. K. Michelson & W. J. Ray (Eds.), *Handbook of dissociation: Theoretical, empirical, and clinical perspectives* (pp. 3–24). New York: Plenum.

Ross, C. A., Anderson, G., Fleisher, W. P., & Norton, G. R. (1992). Dissociative experiences among psychiatric inpatients. *General Hospital Psychiatry, 14,* 350–354.

Ross, C. A., Heber, S., Norton, G. R., & Anderson, G. (1989). Differences between multiple personality disorder and other diagnostic groups on structured interview. *Journal of Nervous and Mental Disease, 177,* 487–491.

Ross, C. A., Heber, S., Norton, G. R., Anderson, D., Anderson, G., & Barchet, P. (1989). The dissociative disorders interview schedule: A structured interview. *Dissociation: Progress in the Dissociative Disorders, 2,* 169–189.

Ross, C. A., Joshi, S., & Currie, R. (1990). Dissociative experiences in the general population. *American Journal of Psychiatry, 147,* 1547–1552.

Ross, C. A., Joshi, S., & Currie, R. (1991). Dissociative experiences in the general population: A factor analysis. *Hospital and Community Psychiatry, 42,* 297–301.

Ross, C. A., & Norton, G. R. (1989). Suicide and parasuicide in multiple personality disorder. *Psychiatry, 52,* 365–371.

Sanders, B. (1986). The Perceptual Alterations Scale: A scale measuring dissociation. *American Journal of Clinical Hypnosis, 29,* 95–102.

Sanders, B., & Giolas, M. H. (1991). Dissociation and childhood trauma in psychologically disturbed adolescents. *American Journal of Psychiatry, 148,* 50–54.

Saxe, G. N., van der Kolk, B. A., Berkowitz, R., Chinman, G., Hall, K., Lieberg, G., & Schwartz, J. (1993). Dissociative disorders in psychiatric inpatients. *American Journal of Psychiatry, 150,* 1037–1042.

Shalev, A. P., Peri, T., Caneti, L., & Schreiber, S. (1996). Predictors of PTSD in injured trauma survivors: A prospective study. *American Journal of Psychiatry, 153,* 219–225.

Shearer, S. L. (1994). Dissociative phenomena in women with borderline personality disorder. *American Journal of Psychiatry, 151,* 1324–1328.

Skinner, B. F. (1953). *Science and human behavior.* New York: Macmillan.

Skinner, B. F. (1957). *Verbal behavior.* New York: Appleton–Century–Crofts.

Steinberg, M. (1993). *Structured Clinical Interview for DSM-IV Dissociative Disorders (SCID-D).* Washington, DC: American Psychiatric Association Press.

Steinberg, M. (1994). *Structured Clinical Interview for DSM-IV Dissociative Disorders— Revised (SCID-D-R).* Washington, DC: American Psychiatric Association Press.

Steinberg, M. (1996). The psychological assessment of dissociation. In L. K. Michelson & W. J. Ray (Eds.), *Handbook of dissociation: Theoretical, empirical, and clinical perspectives* (pp. 251–267). New York: Plenum.

Tillman, J. G., Nash, M. R., & Lerner, P. M. (1994). Does trauma cause dissociative pathology? In S. J. Lynn & J. W. Rhue (Eds.), *Dissociation: Clinical and theoretical perspectives* (pp. 395–414). New York: Guilford Press.

van der Kolk. (1996a). The body keeps the score: Approaches to the psychobiology of posttraumatic stress disorder. In B. A. van der Kolk, A. C. McFarlane, & L. Weisaeth (Eds.), *Traumatic stress: The effects of overwhelming experience on mind, body, and society* (pp. 215–241). New York: Guilford Press.

van der Kolk. (1996b). Trauma and memory. In B. A. van der Kolk, A. C. McFarlane, & L. Weisaeth (Eds.), *Traumatic stress: The effects of overwhelming experience on mind, body, and society* (pp. 279–302). New York: Guilford Press.

van der Kolk, B. A., Greenberg, M. S., Orr, S. P., & Pitman, R. K. (1989). Endogenous opioids and stress induced analgesia in post traumatic stress disorder. *Psychopharmacology Bulletin, 25,* 108–112.

van der Kolk, B. A., Perry, J. C., & Herman, J. L. (1991). Childhood origins of self-destructive behavior. *American Journal of Psychiatry, 148,* 1665–1671.

van der Kolk, B. A., van der Hart, O., & Marmar, C. R. (1996). Dissociation and information processing in posttraumatic stress disorder. In B. A. van der Kolk, A. C. McFarlane, & L. Weisaeth (Eds.), *Traumatic stress: The effects of overwhelming experience on mind, body, and society* (pp. 303–327). New York: Guilford Press.

Vanderlinden, J., Van der Hart, O., & Varga, K. (1996). European studies of dissociation. In L. K. Michelson & W. J. Ray (Eds.), *Handbook of dissociation: Theoretical, empirical, and clinical perspectives* (pp. 25–49). New York: Plenum.

Vanderlinden, J., Van Dyck, R., Vandereycken, W., & Vertommen, H. (1993). Trauma and psychological (dys)functioning in the general population of the Netherlands. *Hospital and Community Psychiatry, 44,* 786–788.

Van IJzendoorn, M. H., & Schuengel, C. (1996). The measurement of dissociation in normal and clinical populations: Meta-analytic validation of the Dissociative Experiences Scale (DES). *Clinical Psychology Review, 16,* 365–382.

Waller, N. G., Putnam, F. W., & Carlson, E. B. (1996). Types of dissociation and dissociative types: A taxometric analysis of dissociative experiences. *Psychological Methods, 1,* 300–321.

Williamson, P. D. (1993). Psychogenic non-epileptic seizures and frontal seizures: Diagnostic considerations. In A. J. Rowan & J. R. Gates (Eds.), *Non-epileptic seizures* (pp. 55–72). Boston: Butterworth-Heinemann.

Zlotnick, C., Begin, A., Shea, T. M., Pearlstein, T., Simpson, E., & Costello, E. (1994). The relationship between characteristics of sexual abuse and dissociative experiences. *Comprehensive Psychiatry, 35,* 465–470.

Zweig-Frank, H., Paris, J., & Guzder, J. (1994). Psychological risk factors for dissociation and self-mutilation in female patients with borderline personality disorder. *Canadian Journal of Psychiatry, 39,* 259–264.

Assessment and Treatment of Concurrent Posttraumatic Stress Disorder and Substance Abuse

JOSEF I. RUZEK
MELISSA A. POLUSNY
FRANCIS R. ABUEG

The trauma survivor is often a consumer of alcohol and other drugs, and understanding the frequently observed concurrence of substance abuse and posttraumatic stress disorder (PTSD) has important implications for clinical practice. Ongoing substance abuse limits trauma survivors' abilities to activate adaptive coping repertoires, mobilize social support, and engage in trauma-focused treatments. Substance-abusing individuals are also particularly vulnerable to experiencing victimization and other traumatic events while intoxicated. Moreover, posttraumatic symptomatology may be associated with poorer substance-abuse treatment outcomes and earlier relapse. In this chapter, we summarize the empirical literature on the interactions between trauma exposure, PTSD, and substance-abuse problems. Aspects of a model for understanding the relationship between these psychological phenomena are reviewed. Finally, we propose a set of clinical guidelines for the assessment and treatment of individuals with concurrent PTSD and substance abuse. Case material from our clinical work with two clients is provided to illustrate several of these guidelines.

TRAUMA EXPOSURE, PTSD, AND SUBSTANCE ABUSE

There is a growing body of empirical literature investigating the link between exposure to traumatic events and substance-abuse problems (for reviews, see Kofoed, Friedman, & Peck, 1993; Brown & Wolfe, 1994; Polusny & Follette, 1995;

Stewart, 1996). Researchers have found that development of alcohol and other drug problems is associated with childhood sexual abuse (CSA; Briere & Runtz, 1987; Burnam et al., 1988; Miller, Downs, & Testa, 1993; Boyd, 1993; Wilsnack, Vogeltanz, Klassen, & Harris, 1997) and physical abuse (e.g., Widom, 1993). Higher rates of substance-abuse problems have been reported among battered women compared to women from the general population (Kantor & Straus, 1989; Miller & Downs, 1993), and studies investigating survivors of disasters suggest a link between exposure and substance abuse (Gleser, Green, & Winget, 1981; Adams & Adams, 1984; Green, Grace, & Gleser, 1985). Findings from the literature on combat have been inconsistent; a correlation between combat exposure and increased levels of substance use has been reported in many studies (e.g., Branchey, Davis, & Lieber, 1984; Yager, Laufer, & Gallops, 1984; Green, Grace, Lindy, Gleser, & Leonard, 1990; Kulka et al., 1990; Cottler, Compton, Mager, Spitznagel, & Janca, 1992; Reifman & Windle, 1996), but there have also been many results unsupportive of such a relationship (e.g., Laufer, Yager, Frey-Wouters, & Donnellan, 1981; Helzer, 1984; Centers for Disease Control, 1988; Kulka et al., 1990; Boscarino, 1995).

A great deal of research has also investigated the comorbidity of PTSD and substance abuse (Brown & Wolfe, 1994; Najavits, Weiss, & Shaw, 1997; Stewart, 1996). Among male veterans seeking treatment for combat-related PTSD, high rates of lifetime alcohol disorders (ranging from 47% to 77%) and lifetime drug abuse/dependence (from 25% to 54%) have been documented (e.g., Escobar et al., 1983; Sierles, Chen, McFarland, & Taylor, 1983; Davidson, Swartz, Storck, Krishman, & Hammett, 1985; Sierles, Chen, Messing, Besyner, & Taylor, 1986; Keane, Gerardi, Lyons, & Wolfe, 1988; Davidson, Kudler, Saunders, & Smith, 1990; Keane & Wolfe, 1990; Roszell, McFall, & Malas, 1991; Fontana, Rosenheck, Spencer, & Gray, 1995). Similarly, an extensive literature has documented high rates of PTSD among male veterans seeking substance-abuse treatment (e.g., Hyer, Leach, Boudewyns, & Davis, 1991; McFall, Mackay, & Donovan, 1991; Triffleman, Marmar, Delucchi, & Ronfeldt, 1995). For example, Triffleman et al. (1995) found that 40% of substance-abusing inpatient veterans had a lifetime history of combat-related PTSD, 58% had a lifetime history of PTSD due to combat or other traumatic exposure, and 38% had current PTSD. High rates of PTSD have also been documented among women with substance-abuse problems (Fullilove et al., 1993; Brown, Recupero, & Stout, 1995; Najavits et al., 1998; Dansky, Saladin, Brady, Kilpatrick, & Resnick, 1995). Conversely, rates of substance abuse in samples of women presenting with PTSD are also high (Breslau, Davis, Andreski, & Peterson, 1991). Generally, research indicates a strong relationship between PTSD and substance abuse among both males and females. For example, in a community sample, Kessler, Sonnega, Bromet, Hughes, and Nelson (1995) found that 52% of male subjects with PTSD were also diagnosed with alcohol abuse or dependence, compared to 34% of those without PTSD. Thirty-five percent of men with PTSD met criteria for drug abuse and dependence compared to 15% of men without PTSD. For women, 28% of subjects diagnosed with PTSD also reported alcohol abuse or dependence compared to 14% of women without PTSD. Twenty-seven percent of women with PTSD met criteria for drug abuse or dependence diagnoses compared with 8% of women without PTSD.

Finally, several studies have compared the *relative* impact of trauma exposure and PTSD on substance use and abuse among male veterans (Streimer, Cosstick, & Tennant, 1985; Boman, 1986; Solomon, 1993; McFall, Mackay, & Donovan, 1992; Triffleman et al., 1995). Overall, these studies have suggested that PTSD is a stronger predictor of substance abuse than trauma exposure. For example, Solomon (1993) investigated the effects of combat exposure and PTSD on self-reported changes in alcohol and drug consumption among Israeli veterans. Veterans who developed PTSD were more likely to report increasing their alcohol and cigarette consumption as well as initiating new medication use, compared to combat participants with no diagnosed PTSD and noncombat controls; combat exposure had no significant impact on substance-use patterns.

THEORETICAL MODELS FOR UNDERSTANDING THE PTSD–SUBSTANCE ABUSE RELATIONSHIP

The relationship between trauma exposure, PTSD symptomatology, and substance abuse is complex. In order to develop a framework for guiding clinical practice, we briefly outline aspects of a cognitive-behavioral model for conceptualizing the frequently observed links between these psychological phenomena.

Operant Learning Theory, Escape/Avoidance, and Self-Medication

Consistent with behavioral models of substance abuse, alcohol and drug use are seen as operant behaviors, established and maintained by the pharmacological, cognitive–emotional, social, and environmental consequences contingent upon them. Especially important is the process in which substance use is negatively reinforced when it is followed by escape from aversive stimuli (Wulfert, Greenway, & Dougher, 1996). Clinicians often assume that trauma survivors drink or use drugs in order to reduce distressing PTSD symptoms, an idea that is consistent with the proposition that substance abuse among trauma survivors may represent attempts at avoidance of abuse-specific memories and affective responses characteristic of PTSD (e.g., Briere, 1992; Follette, 1994; Polusny & Follette, 1995; Root, 1989). Polusny and Follette (1995) conceptualized substance abuse among CSA survivors as a form of emotional avoidance that has been defined as "the unwillingness to experience unpleasant internal events, such as, thoughts, memories, and affective states associated with an abuse history, and subsequent attempts to reduce, numb, or alleviate these negatively self-evaluated internal experiences" (p. 158).

In addition to reducing negative stimuli, alcohol and drug use by trauma survivors may be maintained, in part, by positive consequences of consumption; that is, substance use may temporarily strengthen sense of control, increase social confidence, provide access to social contacts, and, especially, enhance positive affect or other desired forms of emotional experience. For example, Briere (1992) suggested that the acute effects of drugs and alcohol may provide individuals with an opportunity to express painful emotions such as sadness and rage. McFall et al. (1992) similarly noted that "PTSD patients with pronounced avoidance/numbing symptoms may rely more on drug abuse to induce sensations that are otherwise blunted" (p. 361).

The self-medication hypothesis outlined here is consistent with more general explanations of substance abuse, which hypothesize that alcohol and other drugs are consumed in order to reduce tension (Cappell & Greeley, 1987) or anxiety (Wilson, 1988). Although an extensive body of research investigating these more general hypotheses has produced inconclusive findings, there is a dearth of empirical data bearing directly on the functions of alcohol and drug ingestion in relation to PTSD symptomatology. Few studies have attempted to test aspects of the self-medication hypothesis among individuals diagnosed with PTSD (Saladin, Brady, Dansky, & Kilpatrick, 1995; Bremner, Southwick, Darnell, & Charney, 1996).

Classical Conditioning, Trauma Cues, and Substance Abuse

According to classical conditioning theories of relapse (e.g., Rohsenow, Childress, Monti, Niaura, & Abrams, 1990), stimuli that reliably precede administration of alcohol or drugs may come to elicit a variety of possible substance-related conditioned responses: alcohol and drug urges or "cravings," other physiological changes such as increased salivation and heart rate, thoughts about alcohol and drugs, negative affective states, or withdrawal symptoms. Stimuli that may elicit these involuntary or "automatic" responses include places, people, times of day, drug paraphernalia, sights and smells associated with alcohol or drugs, and negative emotions. Exposure to these learned "triggers" and the conditioned emotional and physical responses elicited by them increases the likelihood of alcohol or other drug consumption. Because substance-abusing individuals with PTSD often drink or use in the presence of traumatic reminders, memories, or PTSD symptoms, these trauma-related stimuli may also come to elicit urges to drink or use substances.

Recently, researchers have begun to investigate reactivity to various types of classically conditioned cues among individuals with PTSD and substance-use disorders (Peirce et al., 1996; Meisler & Cooney, 1996). For example, Peirce et al. (1996) studied a sample of women in methadone maintenance treatment. Subjective reactivity to drug, neutral, and sexual assault cues was compared in subjects with and without sexual assault-related PTSD. Women with PTSD reported increased negative emotion, reduced positive emotion, and greater symptoms of opiate withdrawal following exposure to both sexual assault and drug cues. Women without PTSD did not show emotional reactivity to either type of cue. These findings suggest that hyperresponsivity to emotionally significant stimuli may increase risk for relapse.

Strengthened Reinforcer Value of Substance Abuse among Trauma Survivors

Increased levels of subjective distress, greater intensity of response to common alcohol and drug cues, and fears about emotional experiencing may operate to raise the "reinforcer value" of substances that are expected to produce anxiolytic effects. Learning theory suggests that, like deprivation, satiation, and other physiological processes, aversive stimuli can be seen as "establishing operations" that influence how effectively other stimuli (e.g., alcohol and drugs) may operate as reinforcers (Wulfert et al., 1996; Michael, 1994).

There is a growing body of research that suggests that substance abusers with trauma histories or PTSD experience higher levels of subjective distress and other problems than substance abusers without PTSD (e.g., Schaefer, Sobieraj, & Hollyfield, 1988; Rounsaville, Weissman, Wilber, & Kleber, 1982; Van Kampen, Watson, Tilleskjor, Kucala, & Vassar, 1986; Villagomez, Meyer, Lin, & Brown, 1995). For instance, compared with women who abuse substances but do not meet diagnostic criteria for PTSD, female PTSD substance abusers report greater psychopathology, substance-abuse problems, dissociation, and behaviors associated with borderline personality disorder (Brady, Killeen, Saladin, Dansky, & Becker, 1994; Najavits, Weiss, & Liese, 1996; Ouimette, Wolfe, & Chrestman, 1996; Saladin et al., 1995). Trauma exposure, and PTSD in particular, may exacerbate negative emotional responses to many ostensibly non-trauma-related relapse precipitants described in the general alcohol and drug literature, such as interpersonal conflict, physical pain, sexual and emotional intimacy, failure experiences, and so on. Because many of these precipitants may also function as trauma reminders, they may activate intense emotional responses. Such responses may be very difficult to manage with current coping repertoires, and, consequently, the subjective potency of alcohol or other substances as coping tools may be strengthened.

Many clinicians and researchers have noted that trauma survivors appear to have great difficulty in tolerating strong emotions. Ansorge, Litz, and Orsillo (1996) hypothesized that individuals with PTSD have dysfunctional attitudes about emotion (e.g., "feelings like grief and fear are unacceptable and uncontrollable") which impede constructive efforts at "mood repair" and interfere with emotion processing. Similarly, some research has suggested that individuals with

PTSD may experience heightened anxiety sensitivity (Taylor, Koch, & McNally, 1992), which has been defined as fear of the consequences of anxiety symptoms. Research has recently linked anxiety sensitivity to higher levels of alcohol consumption (Stewart, Peterson, & Pihl, 1995) and greater use of alcohol to cope (Stewart & Zeitlin, 1995).

Environmental Changes and Impairment of Effective Coping

The development of PTSD and substance-abuse problems often brings in their wake a series of environmental changes that make the tasks of coping and behavior change increasingly difficult. Both problems are often associated with conflict with significant others, difficulties in maintaining job performance, impairment of concentration and short-term memory, diminished social support, and health problems. These stressors introduce additional challenges for coping repertoires already taxed by trauma symptoms, and create more aversive situations that may prompt efforts at chemical escape.

Problems associated with PTSD, including difficulties in self-monitoring and labeling of emotions ("alexithymia," e.g., Hyer, Woods, Summers, Boudewyns, & Harrison, 1990), heightened sense of guilt and shame (Kubany, Chapter 6, this volume), deficits in interpersonal trust (Serafin & Follette, Chapter 13, this volume), and excessive use of avoidance coping (Roth & Newman, 1991) may interfere with efforts at adaptive coping.

CLINICAL GUIDELINES FOR THE ASSESSMENT AND TREATMENT OF THE SUBSTANCE-ABUSING TRAUMA SURVIVOR

General Considerations in Treating Addictions in the Presence of PTSD

Regardless of theoretical orientation, there are several practical concerns relevant to the treatment of concurrent PTSD and substance abuse. First, a stable period of abstinence from abused substances should precede trauma-specific interventions. Daniels and Scurfield (1992) argued that urine drug screens and breathalyzer tests should be routinely implemented at time of initiation of PTSD treatment, and that when a client cannot pass the screen, referral for substance-abuse treatment should be made prior to initiation of PTSD treatment. On the other hand, noting the difficulty in engaging patients with both PTSD and substance abuse in treatment, Reilly, Clark, Shopshire, Lewis, and Sorensen (1994) encouraged but did not require abstinence in a first treatment phase designed to engage and further assess dually diagnosed combat veterans. These practices are not necessarily incompatible. A practitioner or program may require that abstinence be demonstrated prior to systematic exploration of trauma-related issues, while continuing to work with a using or drinking client in order to increase motivation to abstain and engage him or her in treatment.

Second, severity of alcohol and/or drug abuse in the dually diagnosed patient has direct bearing on selection of treatment. The "career" substance abuser who has engaged in a drug-taking lifestyle for many years will require more intensive treatment than an individual with a less chronic problem. In cases where drug and alcohol problems have been chronic or severe, or caused multiple significant life problems, it may be advisable for many practitioners to refer the client for adjunctive, specialized substance-abuse treatment. In this way, he or she can encourage delivery of appropriately intensive care for substance abuse while continuing to address issues related to traumatization. Comprehensive interventions with long-term abusers appear to have promise and include residential treatment communities and community reinforcement approaches (Azrin, 1976; Smith & Meyers, 1995). For some clients in crisis, inpatient settings may facilitate the sense of perceived safety important to PTSD treatment (Herman, 1992; Resick & Schnicke, 1992). Whatever the approach, a clinician can take steps to supplement substance-abuse treatment by supporting participation in the substance-abuse program and dealing with trauma-related needs. Because most substance-abuse treatment programs provide little or no help for PTSD, this dual-treatment model may be helpful for the client. The main point here is not the necessity of referral, but rather the need to systematically address substance abuse in its own right. As Miller and Brown (1997) argued, "Assuming that psychologists have the requisite knowledge and therapeutic skills (e.g., empathy, training in cognitive-behavioral approaches), clients with substance abuse may have at least as good a chance for recovery when receiving integrated psychological treatment as when referred to specialist programs" (p. 1272).

A third general treatment consideration relates to the importance of acknowledging and addressing the multiple environmental influences on substance use. As Baer, Wolf, and Risley (1987) noted, the label "substance abuse" represents "complex classes of topographies serving complex functions involving many agents of reinforcement/punishment and stimulus control, all of whom interact to constitute and maintain the system as such" (p. 323). Interactions between posttrauma problems and substance use are similarly complex and multidetermined. The implication is that substance abuse is unlikely to yield to treatments that focus on one or two aspects of the problem and ignore the variety of behavioral influences and environmental contexts in which the traumatized person is embedded. Models of multisystemic therapy (Henggeler, Schoenwald, & Pickrel, 1995) have recently been developed that acknowledge this variety, and simultaneously (or in succession) target key behaviors and processes in several of the multiple systems in which clients participate: family, peer groups, school, workplace, neighborhood/community, and treatment environments. This multisystem-oriented thinking is consistent with the approach to functional analysis described in this chapter, in that it generally points to multiple influences on target behaviors that should be addressed in treatment if efforts at behavior change are to succeed.

Gender Issues Related to Trauma and Substance Abuse

A number of gender issues also have important implications for the assessment and treatment of individuals with concurrent PTSD and substance abuse. There is some evidence suggesting that the link between PTSD and substance abuse may be stronger among women than men (Gil-Rivas, Fiorentine, & Anglin, 1996; Najavits et al., 1997), a finding that may be influenced by the facts that women are more likely than men to experience sexual victimization (e.g., Finkelhor, 1994) and that women participating in outpatient drug abuse treatment are significantly more likely than male participants to report a history of sexual and physical abuse (Gil-Rivas, Fiorentine, & Anglin, 1996; Gil-Rivas, Fiorentine, Anglin, & Taylor, 1997). A number of researchers have found that women diagnosed with PTSD and substance abuse are more likely than women with PTSD only (Ouimette et al., 1996; Saladin et al., 1995) and women with substance abuse only (Brady et al., 1994; Brown, Stout, & Mueller, 1996) to report a history of sexual victimization.

It is important for clinicians to recognize that women with a history of CSA as well as women with substance-abuse problems are at risk for being victimized through adult sexual assault and physical partner violence (e.g., Kantor & Straus, 1989; Miller, 1990; Polusny & Follette, 1995; Wyatt, Guthrie, & Notgrass, 1992). Koss, Dinero, Seibel, and Cox (1988) found that more than 40% of sexual assault victims reported using alcohol prior to their assault. Higher rates of adult sexual victimization in alcohol-abusing women are consistent with findings from the social psychology literature suggesting that intoxicated women are viewed by others as more sexually available and more likely to engage in sexual activities (George, Gournie, & McAfee, 1988; Norris & Cubbins, 1992).

Treatment of concurrent PTSD and substance abuse may be further complicated by the presence of an Axis II disorder. While antisocial personality disorder is particularly prevalent among male veterans with substance-abuse problems and histories of childhood trauma (e.g., Krinsley, Young, Weathers, Brief, & Kelley, 1992), borderline personality disorder (BPD) has been associated with both substance abuse (Linehan & Dimeff, 1997) and childhood trauma among women (Linehan, 1993a; Polusny & Follette, 1995). Ouimette et al. (1996) found that women with concurrent PTSD and alcohol abuse reported more borderline personality traits compared to women with PTSD only and women with neither diagnosis. Linehan (1993a, 1993b) has developed an empirically validated, comprehensive behavioral treatment—dialectical behavior therapy (DBT)—for women who meet diagnostic criteria for BPD. Several authors have recently reported on the use of DBT in PTSD treatment programs (Errebo, 1996), and Linehan (1993c) reported that DBT may be an effective treatment for substance abusers who also meet criteria for BPD given the high rates of comorbidity for these two disorders. Preliminary findings on the efficacy of DBT with BPD substance abusers appear promising (Linehan, Schmidt, & Dimeff, 1996; see Wagner and Linehan, Chapter 8, this volume, for a discussion of the treatment of dissociative behaviors).

Importance of Systematic Screening

Data on the comorbidity of PTSD and substance-abuse disorders suggest both that the substance-use patterns of clients with trauma histories should be routinely assessed and that substance abusers should be routinely screened for trauma exposure and PTSD (e.g., Bollerud, 1990; Brown et al., 1995). Evidence suggests that PTSD is frequently underdiagnosed among individuals receiving treatment for substance abuse (Dansky, Roitzsch, Brady, & Saladin, 1997), and routine inquiry about traumatic experiences greatly increases the probability that they will be identified (e.g., Rohsenow, Corbett, & Devine, 1988). Clinicians should note that substance abuse may mask or suppress PTSD symptoms, causing some individuals to apparently fail to meet criteria for PTSD diagnosis (Hyer, McCranie, & Peralme, 1993).

Overview of Treatment "Tasks"

It may be helpful for the therapist to conceptualize treatment in terms of a number of basic tasks that include (1) performing an ongoing functional assessment; (2) developing a therapeutic relationship; (3) building motivation for various aspects of participation in treatment and agreeing treatment goals; (4) minimizing exposure to alcohol, drugs, and related cues; (5) modifying the social environment to support treatment goals; and (6) implementing relapse prevention methods and teaching skills for coping with risk situations.

Clinical Guidelines for Functional Assessment

One of the basic tenets of behavior therapy is the importance of conducting an idiographic assessment of the client's problem behaviors. Two primary goals of assessment are to identify targets for behavioral change and to understand the utility, functions, and contexts of behavior problems, that is, to perform a "functional analysis" of the target behaviors (Kanfer & Saslow, 1969). Haynes and O'Brien (1990) defined functional analysis as "the identification of important, controllable, causal functional relationships applicable to a set of target behaviors for an individual client" (p. 654). Behavioral therapists are most interested in identifying those controlling variables whose manipulation will result in clinically significant changes in target behaviors for an individual client (Haynes & O'Brien, 1990).

Classical functional analysis as described by Hayes and his colleagues (Hayes & Follette, 1992; Hayes, Follette, & Follette, 1995) consists of six steps, illustrated in Table 9.1, using the case of Debra:

> Debra, a 21-year-old, single, female undergraduate student presented in outpatient psychotherapy with symptoms of PTSD and dysthymia. Four months prior to entering therapy, Debra was sexually assaulted by a male acquaintance she had met at a party. After the assault, she was overwhelmed by feelings of guilt and shame. She blamed herself for the rape and believed that she could have prevented it from occurring. She experienced frequent distressing intrusive thoughts and nightmares about the assault, felt tense and anxious most of the time, and had difficulty sleeping. She became increasingly withdrawn and avoided social gatherings, because they reminded her of the event. After experiencing a flashback during a lecture, she stopped attending classes and became concerned about failing her classes.
>
> Debra's father was an alcoholic who began sexually molesting her at age 7. The sexual abuse continued until she was 13 years old, when she became fearful of becoming pregnant and told him to stop. Although there was no further sexual contact after this point, he continued to make inappropriate comments about her developing body.
>
> When Debra entered high school, she started socializing with a group of slightly older, troubled youths who often drank and experimented with other drugs. She started drinking and became sexually promiscuous. On the evening of her recent sexual assault, she became severely intoxicated and agreed to go to the home of a male acquaintance for coffee. She was unable to resist his pressure for sex and was forced by him to engage in sexual intercourse. After the sexual assault, she began reexperiencing flashbacks of being molested by her father as well as of the recent assault. Her drinking increased and she became increasingly depressed and withdrawn. She entered therapy after one of her instructors spoke with her about her declining academic performance and absenteeism.

In order to generate hypotheses about the controlling variables involved in Debra's presenting complaints, the therapist identified when and under what circumstances she engaged in sexual behavior, drank excessively, and experienced intrusive thoughts and symptoms of depression. The functional analysis also identified what happened *after* Debra engaged in these behaviors (e.g., alcohol intoxication reduced her intrusive thoughts).

Assessment of substance-abuse problems requires data on the quantity and frequency of the client's consumption, the extent of alcohol- and drug-related problems, and the severity of dependence. In order to conduct a broad assessment of substance-abuse issues and facilitate treatment planning, Miller, Westerberg, and Waldron (1995) recommended a number of comprehensive instruments and interviews. The Addiction Severity Index (McLellan et al., 1985), Alcohol Use Inventory (Horn, Wanberg, & Foster, 1987), and Comprehensive Drinker Profile

TABLE 9.1. Steps of a Classical Functional Analysis

Step	Clinical case example
1. Identify potentially relevant characteristics of the client, his or her behavior, and its contexts via broad assessment.	A clinical interview was conducted to gather information about Debra's current sexual assault, previous victimization experiences, current and past psychological functioning, patterns of substance use, interpersonal relationships, and academic performance.
2. Organize the information collected in step 1 into a preliminary analysis of the client's difficulties in terms of behavioral principles so as to identify important causal relationships that might be changed.	Data collected during the clinical interview with Debra suggested the following preliminary functional analysis: During childhood and adolescence, Debra developed emotional avoidance coping strategies (reading, studying, drinking) that served to reduce or eliminate her negative abuse-related private experiences. These negative thoughts and feelings were generalized to social situations and sexual activity in general. Consensual sexual activity in college elicited further abuse-related thoughts and feelings, and she subsequently used alcohol to numb her affective responses associated with sex. After experiencing the recent sexual assault, social situations became stimuli for assault-related intrusive thoughts and feelings. In order to reduce her intrusive symptoms, Debra began avoiding social situations and continued drinking. However, these behaviors resulted in greater symptoms of depression and decreased the likelihood of Debra attending her academic classes.
3. Gather additional information based on step 2, and finalize the conceptual analysis.	A number of assessment techniques were used in this step, including written self-report instruments (e.g., Impact of Events Scale, Beck Depression Inventory) and self-monitoring methods (e.g., mood and thought diaries, daily monitoring of the antecedents and consequences of specific drinking situations). Through daily self-monitoring, Debra identified a functional relationship between her PTSD symptoms, social anxiety, and excessive drinking.
4. Devise an intervention based on step 3.	An individualized cognitive-behavioral intervention was designed to enhance Debra's skills for coping with abuse-related private experiences and social anxiety. An acceptance-based behavioral intervention aimed at increasing her willingness to experience negative affect and thoughts was employed.
5. Implement treatment and assess change.	Ongoing assessment of Debra's progress was conducted.
6. If the outcome is unacceptable, recycle back to step 2 or 3.	

(Miller & Marlatt, 1984) are examples of such measures. The Inventory of Drinking Situations (Annis, Graham, & Davis, 1987) and Situational Confidence Questionnaire (Annis, 1987) may be useful in identifying targets for relapse prevention and can be modified to apply to substances other than alcohol. We advise readers unfamiliar with the alcohol assessment and treatment literature to consult Hester and Miller's (1995) *Handbook on Alcoholism Treatment Approaches.*

Using the Assessment Process to Guide Treatment

A basic principle of behavior therapy is the direct link between assessment and treatment. As treatment progresses, new information comes to light that suggests additional targets for intervention, new variables of importance for change, and new interventions. This is especially likely when the client is given homework assignments to record urges to drink or use, PTSD symptoms, or ongoing problematic situations (e.g., marital conflict, social pressure to drink or use drugs, or work stress). When clients self-monitor situations hypothesized to influence initiation of substance use, a clearer understanding of changes required for abstinence may result. As they attempt to comply with treatment recommendations, obstacles to change are often identified. For example, when a client begins to attend Alcoholics Anonymous (AA) or Narcotics Anonymous (NA) meetings, he or she may experience social anxiety, difficulties in making friends, problems with self-disclosure during meetings, and so on. These issues may need to be targeted in treatment in order to achieve larger strategies of change (e.g., support group affiliation and participation; see Satel, Becker, & Dan, 1993). Finally, ongoing assessment and outcome evaluation provide information regarding the effectiveness of therapeutic practices. Telephone follow-up and other forms of posttreatment information gathering provide clinicians and administrators with valuable information about the nature of treatment outcomes. Such information can be used to redesign interventions if needed. In the absence of such efforts, ineffective therapeutic practices may be perpetuated or effective ones discontinued.

Developing a Therapeutic Relationship

Evidence suggests that PTSD is often associated with interpersonal problems related to trust, anger, conflict with authority, and interpersonal fears. Because treatment is conducted in social contexts, these problems may disrupt aspects of treatment participation, including establishment of a therapeutic relationship (Zaslav, 1994) and effective utilization of group support. The confrontational style of some substance-abuse treatment environments may increase the likelihood of interpersonal conflict. For example, Nace (1988) noted stylistic differences between the traditional confrontational approach taken in most alcohol- and drug-treatment settings (especially those based on a 12-step treatment philosophy) and the careful attention to development of a therapeutic alliance among clinicians treating PTSD. Miller and Rollnick's (1991) approach to nonconfrontational motivation building in alcoholics may offer a useful alternative approach with substance abusers with PTSD; however, clinicians may need to prepare their traumatized clients to cope with standard practice in AA and NA.

Perceived interpersonal safety may be influenced by such factors as the gender mix of clients, the interviewing practices of clerical and clinical staff, and even the physical layout of the clinic. Kuhne, Nohner, and Baraga (1986) argued that opportunity for discussion of trauma-related issues should be provided separately from other therapeutic group activities, suggesting that substance-abuse treatment groups could be disrupted when individuals with PTSD attempt to discuss their traumatic experiences and PTSD symptoms. The same recommendation can be made in order to create a therapeutic environment that actively supports disclosure of traumatic experiences. Finally, Nace (1988) also suggested that because PTSD is often associated with intense feelings of guilt, shame, and mistrust, treatment should commence in an individual rather than a group setting, a recommendation that goes against the traditional substance-abuse and 12-step, group-centered treatment approach.

Therapeutic relationship issues were addressed during individual treatment of Raymond:

> Raymond was a 53-year-old African American veteran of the Korean War with 8 years of formal education. As soon as he turned 18, Raymond enlisted in the Army; within 2 years of joining, he was given orders to go to battle in Korea as an infantryman. He had direct contact with the enemy on numerous occasions and felt in danger for his life for weeks on end, but the most traumatic event in the field was witnessing hundreds of Koreans burn in the fires of Pusan. His unit was responsible for much of the bulldozing of the remains of that conflict. While serving in Korea, he learned to drink heavily to ease feelings of rage and helplessness.
>
> Within the first few months of his return home, Raymond began to have frequent nightmares. One night he awoke from a nightmare to find himself choking his wife, who he believed was the enemy. He promptly moved out of the house for fear of hurting her again and became increasingly dependent upon alcohol to ease his anxiety, medicate his chronic foot pain, and simply fall asleep. In 1980, after numerous struggles to quit on his own, Raymond discovered Alcoholics Anonymous and was able to stay sober for almost 3 years. However, he suffered a dramatic and severe relapse after hearing of the death of his mother. His wife learned of services offered by the Veterans Administration, where he was formally diagnosed with post-traumatic stress disorder.
>
> Early in therapy, a therapeutic relationship was begun through discussion of how overwhelming coming to the hospital can be. The therapist was able to ask if Raymond felt poorly understood, being a black man and dealing with doctors who were predominantly Caucasian or other races. These conversations were welcomed with surprise by Raymond and forged

a strong working alliance and solid foundation for further disclosures. In fact, Raymond admitted never attending formal medical checkups but only picking up his medications. More than 5 years earlier, he had an interaction with a physician who was curt with him; in an attempt to curb his building rage, he left in the middle of an examination. Since then, only in dire circumstances would he see a doctor face-to-face.

When this issue was tackled as part of treatment, assessment revealed boyhood exposure to at least one episode of racial victimization—the lynching of an uncle. The connections between problems in trusting others associated with past trauma, fear of authority, and current fears of working with health professionals were explicitly drawn for the patient. Small, manageable goals were set, which allowed him to be directly seen by at least three different specialists. Each successful contact with a doctor was framed as a success, a necessary precursor to the work to be done regarding his traumatic memories.

Building Motivation and Setting Goals

Early in treatment, it is important to assess and, if necessary, build motivation to change drinking or drug-use practices. Initial level of motivation may be relatively low because, often, persons seeking help for trauma-related problems are not also requesting help for substance abuse. In fact, many will see substance use as a helpful means of remedying their distress, sleep problems, and so on. To challenge this attitude, it is helpful for therapist and patient together to undertake a review of the benefits and drawbacks of alcohol/drug use. As the patient identifies drawbacks of drinking or using, the therapist can ask questions to help elaborate on these negative consequences. Similarly, he or she can help the patient consider the accuracy of expected benefits of use. During this review, the patient can be encouraged to compare the pros and cons that he or she has identified. Parts of this practice of reviewing the consequences of drinking or drug were applied during treatment with Raymond:

> Raymond was praised for recognizing the gravity of his current difficulties and seeking help from the Veterans Administration. A rationale for treatment was presented to him that first emphasized the costs of not pursuing therapy. He readily provided an array of negative consequences of his continued problems with PTSD and drinking: His health would decline; his isolation would deepen; he could be a potential threat to others or himself. He also identified and appreciated manifold reasons for stopping drinking: fewer potential adverse reactions with medications he was taking; increased control over anger, rage, and depression; and room in his life for more constructive activities that he once enjoyed, such as listening to music and reading.

The review of benefits and drawbacks of substance use sets the stage for commitment by the patient to make changes, and the setting of specific goals makes this commitment more concrete. Therefore, an important early treatment objective is to establish and agree upon alcohol- and drug-related goals. Goals related to all substances should be discussed, because it is not unusual for clients to endorse abstinence with regard to one substance or class of substances (e.g., "hard drugs") while intending to continue use of another (e.g., marijuana or alcohol).

Miller and Rollnick (1991) provide a very helpful extended discussion of motivation enhancement methods based on five broad principles: (1) Express empathy, (2) develop discrepancy, (3) avoid argumentation, (4) roll with resistance, and (5) support self-efficacy. For example, to develop discrepancy means to "create and amplify, in the client's mind, a discrepancy between present behavior and broader goals" (p. 56). These nonconfrontational methods are especially likely to be useful with persons with a history of traumatization, who, as noted earlier, are often slow to form strong therapeutic relationships. The methods are designed to minimize opportunity for client resistance and therapist–client conflict, and can be adapted to tackle various aspects of treatment-relevant motivation unrelated to alcohol or drug use. For example, motivation to make use of support groups may be low, due to mistrust of people, social anxiety, and low self-esteem; motivation to address traumatic memories and PTSD may be low among individuals involved in substance-abuse treatment.

Finally, motivation must also be maintained. Because withdrawal symptoms experienced during early abstinence may be associated with resurgence of traumatic memories, worsening PTSD symptoms, and, possibly, increased risk for suicidal thoughts or attempts (e.g., Daniels & Scurfield, 1992; Kosten & Krystal, 1988), the client should be supported closely through this period, prepared for possible short-term worsening of PTSD symptoms, and helped to develop strategies for managing symptoms and urges to drink or use.

Managing Exposure to Alcohol, Drugs, and Related Cues

Repeated exposure to substance-related cues places great demands on coping resources and may undermine achievement of sustained abstinence. Therefore, a general goal for most clients is to help them change their environment and lifestyle to minimize such exposure. Family and peers, occupation, recreation activities, and neighborhood are among the aspects of the environment that are especially likely to affect access to alcohol and drugs and urges to drink or use. They can sometimes be changed to reduce risk of relapse, a strategy that may be more useful than attempting to enhance coping in a very unfavorable environment.

It is important to remember that the process of exposure therapy or other trauma-focused therapeutic discussion itself provides multiple cues for drug and alcohol use. This is not necessarily problematic; in case studies, Black and Keane (1982) found a decrease in alcohol use following imaginal exposure to traumatic combat experiences in a World War II veteran with severe combat-related anxiety, and Keane and Kaloupek (1982) similarly observed reductions in alcohol use in a Vietnam veteran with PTSD treated with exposure to trauma memories. However, the possible utility of exposure treatment must be balanced against the possibility of precipitation of relapse (Pitman et al., 1991). As a current rule of thumb, most clinicians advise that a stable period of abstinence be required as a prerequisite to exposure therapy in clients with alcohol or other drug problems. However, the need to promote stable substance-abuse recovery prior to direct treatment of trauma-related problems must also be weighed against the likelihood that untreated PTSD and other trauma-related psychopathology may precipitate relapse in the meantime. In practice, the decision about when and if to initiate exposure therapy with this population requires clinical judgment informed by a comprehensive assessment of the client and careful discussion with him or her.

When exposure therapy is delivered, it is important that it encompass direct attention to alcohol and drug issues. Specifically, the clinician and client should closely monitor substance-use urges, structure ongoing substance-specific care, and plan for urge management. When a client reports an urge to drink or use during or immediately following in-session exposure, he or she should be encouraged to, verbally (1) acknowledge the urge, (2) think through the negative consequences of use, (3) decide on immediate coping responses, and (4) remember and reaffirm commitment to abstinence. In this way, the client can learn and practice a new style of coping with urges elicited by trauma-related memories and symptoms.

Modifying the Social Environment

Important steps for sobriety include assessing and possibly modifying interactions with significant others, addressing recurrent patterns of interpersonal conflict with specific individuals, reducing contact with heavy drinkers and drug users, increasing contact with abstainers and other positive models, and increasing participation in and engagement with support groups. Support groups may be especially helpful to the trauma survivor who has become socially isolated. For example, Vietnam veterans with chronic combat-related PTSD can find at AA or NA meetings a pool of potential companions or friends who can enable them to begin to reconnect with people and develop a social life. We recommend that practitioners assess for, and address in treatment, negative attitudes toward such groups, significant levels of social anxiety, and deficits in social skills.

Of great importance are relationships with significant others. Some studies have found that married substance abusers have better treatment outcomes than unmarried clients (Kosten, Jalali, Steidl, & Kleber, 1987; Rounsaville, Tierney, & Crits-Christoph, 1982), and that clients whose spouses choose to be involved with treatment of cocaine dependence use cocaine less (Higgins, Budney, Bickel, & Badger, 1994). Cognitive-behavioral couple therapy has been demonstrated to improve outcomes for individuals receiving treatment for alcohol problems (McCrady, Stout, Noel, Abrams, & Nelson, 1991; O'Farrell, Cutter, Choquette,

Floyd, & Bayog, 1992) and for other substance abuse (Fals-Stewart, Birchler, & O'Farrell, 1996). Sisson and Azrin (1986) developed tactics for use with the spouses of uncooperative alcoholics, teaching them to stop "enabling" substance use—to change the consequences of use—by removing positive reinforcement when the husbands were drinking as well as ceasing to protect them from negative consequences (e.g., stopping calling the workplace with excuses for Monday morning absenteeism).

Implementing Relapse Prevention Methods/Training Skills for Risk Situations

Given the mixed findings generated by the few empirical studies bearing on the question, it is currently unclear whether individuals with alcohol or drug problems who also suffer from PTSD are at heightened risk for relapse into substance use (Brown et al., 1996; Gil-Rivas et al., 1996, 1997; Ouimette, Ahrens, Moos, & Finney, 1997). However, the relapse prevention methods that have emerged from cognitive-behavioral approaches to addictive behaviors (Marlatt & Gordon, 1985; DeJong, 1994) may be usefully applied with this population.

Systematic study has enabled the identification of relapse antecedents or "triggers" that are commonly associated with return to substance use following periods of abstinence. Prevention of relapse is predicated on the notion that clients can be helped to identify their personal triggers and avoid them or learn to cope more effectively in their presence. Prominent among precipitating factors are negative emotions, which are thought to motivate escape in the form of drug use or alcohol consumption. Such emotion triggers are apt to be especially important among those with PTSD, for whom distress and emotions of fear, anger, and depression occur frequently and with intensity. Coping with such emotions may be especially difficult and require careful therapeutic attention. Moreover, in addition to the range of relapse precipitants commonly experienced by those recovering from substance abuse, persons with PTSD may also face problems related to the occurrence of PTSD symptoms themselves, because, as noted earlier, it is likely that much drug and alcohol use by these individuals occurs as an attempt at self-medication. The implication is that clinicians must assess the degree to which PTSD symptoms are associated with substance use, and, especially, for which particular symptoms this association holds. If a client can manage symptoms using other means—relaxation, positive forms of distraction, social support—then use of substances may decrease.

Cognitive-behavioral therapists devote considerable time to the training and practicing of new repertoires or skills for responding to risky situations and triggers, especially PTSD symptoms themselves. Fortunately, there is now a considerable literature available that focuses on skill-training technologies. For example, Monti, Abrams, Kadden, and Cooney (1989) published a manual describing procedures for group treatment of alcohol dependence. These authors identified a range of important interpersonal (e.g., starting conversations, giving criticism, receiving criticism, drink refusal, enhancing social support networks) and intrapersonal (e.g., managing thoughts about alcohol, problem solving, increasing pleasant activities, relaxation, anger management, and management of negative thinking) coping skills. Because learning coping skills requires time and motivation, it is not feasible to teach unlimited numbers of them. Therefore, client and clinician, informed by the results of an ongoing functional analysis, must work together to identify major impediments to sobriety and select skills necessary to replace alcohol or drug consumption. This matching of person, problem situations, and coping skills is part of the art of skills training.

It is important that efforts at training coping skills go beyond didactic instruction and discussion. This can be accomplished through in-session role-play exercises, therapist modeling, in-session assignments (e.g., telephoning a significant other to communicate positive feelings, calling a sponsor to ask for help, calling about a job opening), and real-world practice tasks. Between-session practice should usually be accompanied by a brief written record of the efforts, to be used to guide discussion at the following session. Most importantly, practice of crucial skills must be continued until the client has used them many times in a variety of situations, in order to increase the likelihood of continued use following termination of treatment.

Many high-risk situations also arise within the therapy session itself, during discussion of treatment issues or via the therapist–client relationship. Commonly, such situations include interpersonal conflict, interpersonal closeness, and fear or anger. They offer an opportunity for the treatment provider to observe client responses, to provide direct instruction and modeling of new skills (e.g., assertion, problem solving, time-out or cool down periods, positive self-talk, active listening, self-disclosure, relaxation, appropriate verbal expression of feelings) and to model appropriate coping. Real-world change often begins in the therapist's office.

Existing Cognitive-Behavioral Treatment Packages and Outcome Research

Abueg and Fairbank (1992) were the first to elaborate upon the Marlatt relapse prevention model (see Marlatt & Gordon, 1985) for application to the modification of substance abuse among those with concurrent PTSD and substance abuse. Parallel to their conceptual discussion has been the development of program descriptions and formal treatment manuals for trauma-relevant relapse prevention training (TRRPT; Abueg & Kriegler, 1990; Abueg et al., 1994; Seidel, Gusman, & Abueg, 1994). TRRPT includes a number of features designed to respond to the uniqueness of PTSD-related stressors. First and foremost, psychoeducation focuses on the interaction of anxiety related to trauma, symptoms of intrusion and avoidance, and the various phases of addiction from first exposure to regular use or abuse. Second, identification of idiosyncratic high-risk stressors—PTSD symptoms and themes—becomes grist for the mill in developing a thorough functional analysis related to alcohol cravings or urges. Third, the abstinence violation effect (AVE) is of special relevance for trauma victims, especially survivors of war, and receives greater emphasis. The AVE refers to the dissonance often generated in a recovering alcoholic when he or she takes a drink, a behavior incompatible with the goal of remaining "clean and sober." The guilt and negative self-labeling that arise in a chronic sufferer of PTSD are often intense and pervasive (e.g., the military combatant has learned that "mistakes are lethal"). Skills in dealing with failure experiences, such as that potentially correctable lapse, are central to the TRRPT model. Finally, skills-building with respect to averting or managing high-risk emotional states such as anger and rage, guilt, depression, and dissociation is critical to maintaining effects of these interventions.

Preliminary results using this integrative model are promising. In one inpatient study of veterans with chronic, combat-related PTSD, the experimental group receiving this treatment showed significantly higher rates of abstinence at 6-month follow-up than a usual-treatment control (Abueg & Fairbank, 1992; Abueg, Falcone, Dondershine, & Gusman, 1990). Although relapse rates tended to converge at 9-month and 1-year follow-ups, striking differences were observed at all follow-up periods among those who did drink: The subjects in the experimental condition drank significantly fewer drinks per day when compared to control subjects. Interim results of a more recent, randomized control trial with combat veteran outpatients (Abueg, Fairbank, Penk, & Gusman, 1995) not only replicated these improved relapse rates in the TRRPT group over usual treatment (and a process-group control) but also demonstrated improved PTSD outcomes as measured by hyperarousal and reexperiencing subscales of the Mississippi Scale for Combat-Related PTSD (Keane, Caddell, & Taylor, 1988).

Outcome research using a cognitive-behavioral approach to treat women with problems related to both PTSD and substance dependence has also begun to emerge. A treatment package developed by Najavits and her colleagues (see Najavits et al., 1996) is designed for clients exposed to childhood trauma or severe, violent, or repetitive abuse. Groups meet twice per week for 3 months. Abstinence is specified as the substance-related goal. Unlike the approach used with combat veterans, Najavits and her colleagues do not promote exploration of trauma histories via narrative accounts or exposure treatment; rather, they describe their method as an "early treatment" or "first stage" present-centered therapy for substance use and PTSD, which is organized around issues of safety and self-care. This seems especially appropriate given the recency of active substance abuse among their sample (to follow).

Following an individual, pregroup interview and an individual HIV counseling session, women participate in two introductory sessions focusing on psychoeducation and identification and usage of community treatment resources; seven "action skills" sessions, covering emotional grounding, structure/activity scheduling, development of a self-care action plan, learning to ask for help, identifying and fighting substance use and PTSD triggers, managing ambivalence, and review of active coping; six cognitive restructuring sessions, with an introduction to distortions that increase PTSD and substance-related symptoms, methods of "rethinking," getting out of "user thinking" and "victim thinking," practice in rethinking, advanced rethinking, and review; six sessions focusing on relationships, covering self-protection in relationships, practice in saying "no" to dangerous social situations, identification of negative communication patterns, rebuilding trust through effective communication, healthy relationship thinking, and review and role play of relationship skills; and three sessions of review and termination. The approach is noteworthy for its explicit attention to the design of an "accessible and engaging" therapy, and for its use of educational devices to encourage sustained learning in a population showing difficulties with concentration and memory (e.g., provision of written session summaries, testing for retention of knowledge).

Najavits, Weiss, Shaw, and Muenz (1998) provided this 24-session group treatment for 17 women meeting diagnostic criteria for both substance use and PTSD. All subjects reported active substance use within the last 30 days, and, in this study, all women reported five or more lifetime traumas, with initial trauma occurring early in childhood (mean age, 7 years); 94% reported sexual abuse, 88% physical abuse, and 71% criminal victimization. Results showed significant improvements in drug use (self-reported abstinence and drug-use severity) at posttreatment and 3-month follow-up. Alcohol use and PTSD symptoms improved by 3-month follow-up. Importantly, there was also a relatively low (33%) dropout rate and good rates of session attendance (67%) by individual members. These findings are encouraging, but the authors correctly note that current conclusions are speculative given small sample size and other methodological limitations (e.g., absence of a control group, short follow-up interval).

One important result of the increasing interest on the part of cognitive-behavioral psychologists in the connection between trauma and substance abuse is the development of manualized treatments, setting the occasion for both careful evaluation and dissemination to clinicians (Abueg et al., 1994; Najavits et al., 1996; Linehan & Dimeff, 1997).

FINAL COMMENTS

Substance abuse and posttraumatic problems are characterized by a variety of commonalities that lend themselves to a cognitive-behavioral treatment approach. As Meisler (in press) noted, PTSD and drug or alcohol problems are both associated with intrusive thoughts (about traumatic experiences and about alcohol and drugs), difficulties in management of physiological arousal, and an excessive use of avoidance coping strategies. These difficulties lend themselves to an array of well-developed cognitive-behavioral methods designed to accomplish arousal reduction, attentional control, and active problem solving. Najavits et al. (1996) similarly observed that both disorders are often accompanied by overwhelming negative affect, impairment in functional behaviors related to relationship initiation and maintenance, and high relapse rates. Again, cognitive-behavioral treatments have a strong tradition of teaching self-management of negative emotions, social and communication skills, and relapse prevention tactics. Given the clear association between trauma exposure, PTSD, and substance abuse, it is necessary for clinicians specializing in working with either traumatized individuals or those with alcohol and drug problems to become skilled at treating (or, at least, identifying and making a referral related to) the other accompanying disorder. This chapter has provided some guidelines for application of a cognitive-behavioral model to treatment of co-occurring substance use and PTSD, and outlined some of the major clinical considerations in the delivery of services to this important client population.

SUMMARY OF TREATMENT RECOMMENDATIONS

- Routinely assess substance-use patterns of clients with trauma histories.
- Routinely screen substance abusers for trauma exposure and PTSD.
- Design treatment interventions to address multiple social systems in which the problem behaviors are embedded: family, peer groups, work or school environments, and neighborhood/community context.
- A stable period of abstinence from abused substances should predate trauma-specific interventions.
- In cases where drug and alcohol problems have been chronic or severe, implement close substance-abuse monitoring during treatment.
- In cases where drug and alcohol problems have been chronic or severe, refer the client for specialized substance-abuse treatment.
- If assessment indicates that motivation to change is low, take concrete steps to strengthen motivation; use nonconfrontational, motivation-building approaches.
- Agree on specific treatment goals with regard to all substances.
- Identify motivational conditions, antecedents ("triggers"), and consequences associated with substance use and other target behaviors (functional analysis).
- Assign written self-monitoring of situations hypothesized to influence initiation of substance use.
- Change the physical and social environments to minimize access/exposure to alcohol/drugs and related cues, and increase exposure to "recovery cues."
- Involve significant others in the treatment process.
- Assess (intervene where indicated) for negative attitudes toward partici-

pation in support groups, as well as significant levels of social anxiety and deficits in social skills that may interfere with participation.

- Adapt trauma-related exposure therapy to include direct attention to alcohol and drug urges.
- Identify individual, high-risk situations and prepare the client to cope with them.
- Help clients learn and practice more effective ways of coping with PTSD symptoms.
- Supplement didactic instruction in coping skills with in-session role-play exercises, therapist modeling, in-session assignments, and assigned real-world practice.
- Use therapist–client relationship difficulties as opportunities to teach skills.
- Use telephone follow-up and other forms of posttreatment information gathering (e.g., questionnaires) to measure effectiveness of treatment.

REFERENCES

Abueg, F. R., & Fairbank, J. A. (1992). Behavioral treatment of co-occurring PTSD and substance abuse: A multidimensional stage model. In P. A. Saigh (Ed.), *Posttraumatic stress disorder: A behavioral approach to assessment and treatment*. Boston: Allyn & Bacon.

Abueg, F. R., Fairbank, J. A., Penk, W., & Gusman, F.D. (1995). Interim findings from a randomized controlled trial of trauma relevant relapse prevention training (TRRPT) in PTSD and alcoholism. In *Advances in treatment of PTSD and substance abuse*. Symposium conducted at the annual meeting of the International Society of Traumatic Stress Studies, Chicago.

Abueg, F. R., Falcone, H. S., Dondershine, H., & Gusman, F. D. (1990). *Preventing alcohol relapse in Vietnam veterans with PTSD: Treatment outcome with 9-month follow-up*. Paper presented at the annual meeting of the Association for the Advancement of Behavior Therapy, New York.

Abueg, F. R., & Kriegler, J. A. (1990). *A 12-session manual for treatment of Vietnam veterans with PTSD and alcoholism*. Menlo Park, CA: National Center for PTSD.

Abueg, F. R., Lang, A. J., Drescher, K.D., Ruzek, J. I., Aboudarham, J. F., & Sullivan, N. (1994). *Enhanced relapse prevention training for posttraumatic stress disorder and alcoholism: A treatment manual*. Menlo Park, CA: National Center for PTSD.

Adams, P. R., & Adams, G. R. (1984). Mount Saint Helens's ashfall: Evidence for a disaster stress reaction. *American Psychologist, 39*, 252–260.

Annis, H. M. (1987). *Situational Confidence Questionnaire (SCQ-39)*. Toronto, Canada: Addiction Research Foundation of Ontario.

Annis, H. M., Graham, J. M., & Davis, C. S. (1987). Inventory of Drinking Situations (IDS) user's guide. Toronto, Canada: Addiction Research Foundation of Ontario.

Ansorge, S., Litz, B. T., & Orsillo, S. M. (1996). Thinking about feelings: The role of meta-mood in post-traumatic stress disorder. *National Center for PTSD Clinical Quarterly, 6,* 38–41.

Azrin, N. H. (1976). Improvements in the community-reinforcement approach to alcoholism. *Behaviour Research and Therapy, 14,* 339–348.

Baer, D. M., Wolf, M. M., & Risley, T. R. (1987). Some still-current dimensions of applied behavior analysis. *Journal of Applied Behavior Analysis, 20,* 313–327.

Black, J. L., & Keane, T. M. (1982). Implosive therapy in the treatment of combat related fears in a World War II veteran. *Behavior Therapy, 13,* 163–165.

Bollerud, K. (1990). A model for the treatment of trauma-related syndromes among chemically dependent inpatient women. *Journal of Substance Abuse Treatment, 7,* 83–87.

Boman, B. (1986). Combat stress, posttraumatic stress disorder, and associated psychiatric disturbance. *Psychosomatics, 27,* 567–573.

Boscarino, J. A. (1995). Post-traumatic stress and associated disorders among Vietnam veterans: The significance of combat exposure and social support. *Journal of Traumatic Stress, 8,* 317–336.

Boyd, C. J. (1993). The antecedents of women's crack cocaine abuse: Family substance abuse, sexual abuse, depression, and illicit drug use. *Journal of Substance Abuse Treatment, 10,* 433–438.

Brady, K. T., Killeen, T., Saladin, M. E., Dansky, B., & Becker, S. (1994). Comorbid substance abuse and posttraumatic stress disorder. *American Journal on Addictions, 3,* 160–164.

Branchey, L., Davis, W., & Lieber, C. S. (1984). Alcoholism in Vietnam and Korea veterans: A long term follow-up. *Alcoholism: Clinical and Experimental Research, 8,* 572–575.

Bremner, J. D., Southwick, S. M., Darnell, A., & Charney, D. S. (1996). Chronic PTSD in Vietnam combat veterans: Course of illness and substance abuse. *American Journal of Psychiatry, 153,* 369–375.

Breslau, N., Davis, G. C., Peterson, E. L., & Schultz, L. (1997). Psychiatric sequelae of posttraumatic stress disorder in women. *Archives of General Psychiatry, 54,* 81–87.

Briere, J. (1992). *Child abuse trauma: Theory and treatment of the lasting effects.* Newbury Park, CA: Sage.

Briere, J., & Runtz, M. (1987). Post sexual abuse trauma: Data and implications for clinical practice. *Journal of Interpersonal Violence, 2,* 367–379.

Brown, P. J., Recupero, P. R., & Stout, R. L. (1995). PTSD substance abuse comorbidity and treatment utilization. *Addictive Behaviors, 20,* 251–254.

Brown, P. J., Stout, R. L., & Mueller, T. (1996). Posttraumatic stress disorder and substance abuse relapse among women: A pilot study. *Psychology of Addictive Behaviors, 10,* 124–128.

Brown, P. J., & Wolfe, J. (1994). Substance abuse and post-traumatic stress disorder comorbidity. *Drug and Alcohol Dependence, 35,* 51–59.

Burnam, M. A., Stein, J. A., Golding, J. M., Siegel, J. M., Sorenson, S. B., Forsythe, A. B., & Telles, C. A. (1988). Sexual assault and mental disorders in a community population. *Journal of Consulting and Clinical Psychology, 56,* 843–850.

Cappell, H., & Greeley, J. (1987). Alcohol and tension reduction: An update on research and theory. In H. T. Blane & K. E. Leonard (Eds.), *Psychological theories of drinking and alcoholism* (pp. 15–54). New York: Guilford Press.

Centers for Disease Control. (1988). Health status of Vietnam veterans: I. Psychosocial characteristics. *Journal of the American Medical Association, 259,* 2701–2707.

Cottler, L. B., Compton, W. M., III, Mager, D., Spitznagel, E. L., & Janca, A. (1992). Posttraumatic stress disorder among substance users from the general population. *American Journal of Psychiatry, 149,* 664–670.

Daniels, L. R., & Scurfield, R. M. (1992). War-related post-traumatic stress disorder, chemical addictions and non-chemical habituating behaviors. In M. B. Williams & J. F. Sommer (Eds.), *Handbook of post-traumatic therapy.* Westport, CT: Greenwood.

Dansky, B. S., Roitzsch, J. C., Brady, K. T., & Saladin, M. E. (1997). Posttraumatic stress disorder and substance abuse: Use of research in a clinical setting. *Journal of Traumatic Stress, 10,* 141–148.

Dansky, B. S., Saladin, M., Brady, K., Kilpatrick, D., & Resnick, H. (1995). Prevalence of victimization and posttraumatic stress disorder among women with substance use disorders: A comparison of telephone and in-person assessment samples. *International Journal of the Addictions, 30,* 1079–1099.

Davidson, J. R. T., Kudler, H. S., Saunders, W. B., & Smith, R. D. (1990). Symptom and comorbidity patterns in World War II and Vietnam veterans with posttraumatic stress disorder. *Comprehensive Psychiatry, 31,* 162–170.

Davidson, J. R. T., Swartz, M., Storck, M., Krishnan, R. R., & Hammett, E. (1985). A diagnostic and family study of posttraumatic stress disorder. *American Journal of Psychiatry, 142,* 90–93.

DeJong, W. (1994). Relapse prevention: An emerging technology for promoting long-term drug abstinence. *International Journal of the Addictions, 29,* 681–705.

Errebo, N. (1996). *Dialectical behavior therapy in three trauma treatment programs.* Workshop presented at the annual meeting of the International Society for Traumatic Stress Studies, San Francisco.

Escobar, J. I., Randolph, E. T., Puente, G., Spiwak, F., Asamen, J. K., Hill, M., & Hough, R. L. (1983). Post-traumatic stress disorder in Hispanic Vietnam veterans: Clinical phenomenology and sociocultural characteristics. *Journal of Nervous and Mental Disease, 171,* 585–596.

Fals-Stewart, W., Birchler, G. R., & O'Farrell, T. J. (1996). Behavioral couples therapy for male substance-abusing patients: Effects on relationship adjustment and drug-using behavior. *Journal of Consulting and Clinical Psychology, 64,* 959–972.

Finkelhor, D. (1994). Current information on the scope and nature of child sexual abuse. *Future of Children: Sexual Abuse of Children, 4,* 31–53.

Follette, V. M. (1994). Survivors of child sexual abuse: Treatment using a contextual analysis. In S. C. Hayes, N. S. Jacobson, V. M. Follette, & M. J. Dougher (Eds.), *Acceptance and change: Content and context in psychotherapy* (pp. 255–268). Reno, NV: Context Press.

Fontana, A., Rosenheck, R., Spencer, H., & Gray, S. (1995). *The long journey home IV: The fourth progress report on the Department of Veterans Affairs specialized PTSD programs.* West Haven, CT: Department of Veterans Affairs, Northeast Program Evaluation Center.

Fullilove, M. T., Fullilove, R. E., Smith, M., Winkler, K., Michael, C., Panzer, P. G., & Wallace, R. (1993). Violence, trauma, and post-traumatic stress disorder among women drug users. *Journal of Traumatic Stress, 6,* 533–543.

George, W. H., Gournie, S. J., & McAfee, M. P. (1988). Perceptions of post-drinking female sexuality: Effects of gender, beverage choice, and drink payment. *Journal of Applied Social Psychology, 18,* 1295–1317.

Gil-Rivas, V., Fiorentine, R., & Anglin, M. D. (1996). Sexual abuse, physical abuse, and posttraumatic stress disorder among women participating in outpatient drug abuse treatment. *Journal of Psychoactive Drugs, 28,* 95–102.

Gil-Rivas, V., Fiorentine, R., Anglin, M. D., & Taylor, E. (1997). Sexual and physical abuse: Do they compromise drug treatment outcomes? *Journal of Substance Abuse Treatment, 14,* 351–358.

Gleser, G. C., Green, B. L., & Winget, C. (1981). *Prolonged psychosocial effects of disaster: A study of Buffalo Creek.* New York: Academic Press.

Green, B. L., Grace, M. C., & Gleser, G. C. (1985). Identifying survivors at risk: Long-term impairment following the Beverly Hills Supper Club fire. *Journal of Consulting and Clinical Psychology, 53,* 672–678.

Green, B. L., Grace, M. C., Lindy, J. D., Gleser, G. C., & Leonard, A. (1990). Risk factors for posttraumatic stress disorder and other diagnoses in a general sample of Vietnam veterans. *American Journal of Psychiatry, 147,* 729–733.

Hayes, S. C., & Follette, W. C. (1992). Can functional analysis provide a substitute for syndromal classification? *Behavioral Assessment, 14,* 345–365.

Hayes, S. C., Follette, W. C., & Follette, V. M. (1995). Behavior therapy: A contextual approach. In A. S. Gurman & S. B. Messer (Eds.), *Essential psychotherapies: Theory and practice* (pp. 128–181). New York: Guilford Press.

Haynes, S. N., & O'Brien, W. H. (1990). Functional analysis in behavior therapy. *Clinical Psychology Review, 10,* 649–668.

Helzer, J. E. (1984). The impact of combat on later alcohol use by Vietnam veterans. *Journal of Psychoactive Drugs, 16,* 183–191.

Henggeler, S. W., Schoenwald, S. K., & Pickrel, S. G. (1995). Multisystemic therapy: Bridging the gap between university- and community-based treatment. *Journal of Consulting and Clinical Psychology, 63,* 709–717.

Herman, J. L. (1992). *Trauma and recovery.* New York: Basic Books.

Hester, R. K., & Miller, W. R. (1995). *Handbook of alcoholism treatment approaches* (2nd ed.). New York: Pergamon.

Higgins, S. T., Budney, A. J., Bickel, W. K., & Badger, G. J. (1994). Participation of significant others in outpatient behavioral treatment predicts greater cocaine abstinence. *American Journal of Drug and Alcohol Abuse, 20,* 47–56.

Horn, J., Wanberg, K., & Foster, F. (1987). Guide to the Alcohol Use Inventory. Minneapolis, Minnesota: National Computer Systems.

Hyer, L., Leach, P., Boudewyns, P. A., & Davis, H. (1991). Hidden PTSD in substance abuse inpatients among Vietnam veterans. *Journal of Substance Abuse Treatment, 8,* 213–219.

Hyer, L., McCranie, E., & Peralme, L. (1993). Dual diagnosis: PTSD and alcohol abuse. *National Center for Post-Traumatic Stress Disorder Clinical Newsletter, 3,* 1–10.

Hyer, L., Woods, M., Summers, M. N., Boudewyns, P., & Harrison, W. R. (1990). Alexithymia among Vietnam veterans with posttraumatic stress disorder. *Journal of Clinical Psychiatry, 51,* 243–247.

Kanfer, F. H., & Saslow, G. (1969). Behavioral diagnosis. In C. M. Franks (Ed.), *Behavior therapy: Appraisal and status* (pp. 417–444). New York: McGraw-Hill.

Kantor, G. K., & Straus, M. A. (1989). Substance abuse as a precipitant of wife abuse victimization. *American Journal of Drug and Alcohol Abuse, 15,* 173–189.

Keane, T. M., Caddell, J. M., & Taylor, K. L. (1988). Mississippi Scale for Combat-Related Posttraumatic Stress Disorder: Three studies in reliability and validity. *Journal of Consulting and Clinical Psychology, 56,* 85–90.

Keane, T. M., Gerardi, R. J., Lyons, J. A., & Wolfe, J. (1988). The interrelationship of substance abuse and posttraumatic stress disorder: Epidemiological and clinical considerations. In M. Galanter (Ed.), *Recent developments in alcoholism* (Vol. 6, pp. 27–48). New York: Plenum.

Keane, T. M., & Kaloupek, D. G. (1982). Imaginal flooding in the treatment of a post-traumatic stress disorder. *Journal of Consulting and Clinical Psychology, 50,* 138–140.

Keane, T. M., & Wolfe, J. (1990). Comorbidity in post-traumatic stress disorder: An analysis of community and clinical studies. *Journal of Applied Social Psychology, 20,* 1776–1788.

Kessler, R. C., Sonnega, A., Bromet, E., Hughes, M., & Nelson, C. B. (1995). Posttraumatic stress disorder in the National Comorbidity Survey. *Archives of General Psychiatry, 52,* 1048–1060.

Kofoed, L., Friedman, M. J., & Peck, R. (1993). Alcoholism and drug abuse in patients with PTSD. *Psychiatric Quarterly, 64,* 151–171.

Koss, M. P., Dinero, T. E., Seibel, C. A., & Cox, S. L. (1988). Stranger and acquaintance rape: Are there differences in the victim's experience? *Psychology of Women Quarterly, 12,* 1–24.

Kosten, T. R., Jalali, B., Steidl, J. H., & Kleber, H. D. (1987). Relationship of marital structure and interactions to opiate abuse relapse. *American Journal of Drug and Alcohol Abuse, 13,* 387–399.

Kosten, T. R., & Krystal, J. (1988). Biological mechanisms in posttraumatic stress disorder: Relevance for substance abuse. In M. Galanter (Ed.), *Recent developments in alcoholism* (Vol. 6, pp. 49–68). New York: Plenum.

Krinsley, K. E., Young, L. S., Weathers, F. W., Brief, D. J., & Kelley, J. M. (1992). *Behavioral correlates of childhood trauma in substance abusing men.* Paper presented at the annual meeting of the Association for Advancement of Behavior Therapy, Boston.

Kuhne, A., Nohner, W., & Baraga, E. (1986). Efficacy of chemical dependency treatment as a function of combat in Vietnam. *Journal of Substance Abuse Treatment, 3,* 191–194.

Kulka, R. A., Schlenger, W. E., Fairbank, J. A., Hough, R. L., Jordan, B. D., Marmar, C. R., & Weiss, D. S. (1990). *Trauma and the Vietnam War generation: Report of findings from the National Vietnam Veterans Readjustment Study.* New York: Brunner/Mazel.

Laufer, R. S., Yager, T., Frey-Wouters, E., & Donnellan, J. (1981). *Post-war trauma: Social and psychological problems of Vietnam veterans in the aftermath of the Vietnam War: Vol. 3. Final report to the Veterans Administration.* Washington, DC: U.S. Government Printing Office.

Linehan, M. M. (1993a). *Cognitive-behavioral treatment of borderline personality disorder.* New York: Guilford Press.

Linehan, M. M. (1993b). *Skills training manual for treating borderline personality disorder.* New York: Guilford Press.

Linehan, M. M. (1993c). Dialectical behavior therapy for treatment of borderline personality disorder: Implications for the treatment of substance abuse. In *Behavioral treatments for drug abuse and dependence* (National Institute on Drug Abuse, Monograph No. 137). Rockville, MD: National Institute on Drug Abuse.

Linehan, M. M., & Dimeff, L. A. (1997). *Dialectical behavior therapy manual of treatment interventions for drug abusers with borderline personality disorder.* Unpublished manuscript, Department of Psychology, University of Washington, Seattle, WA.

Linehan, M. M., Schmidt, H. III, & Dimeff, L. A. (1996). *Dialectical behavior therapy for substance abusers with borderline personality disorder: One year later.* Paper presented at the annual meeting of the Association for Advancement of Behavior Therapy, New York.

Marlatt, G. A., & Gordon, J. R. (1985). *Relapse prevention: Maintenance strategies in the treatment of addictive behaviors.* New York: Guilford Press.

McCrady, B. S., Stout, R. L., Noel, N. E., Abrams, D. B., & Nelson, H. F. (1991). Effectiveness of three types of spouse-involved behavioral alcoholism treatment. *British Journal of Addictions, 86,* 1415–1424.

McFall, M. E., Mackay, P. W., & Donovan, D. M. (1991). Combat-related PTSD and psychosocial adjustment problems among substance abusing veterans. *Journal of Nervous and Mental Disease, 197,* 33–37.

McFall, M. E., MacKay, P. W., & Donovan, D. M. (1992). Combat-related posttraumatic stress disorder and severity of substance abuse in Vietnam veterans. *Journal of Studies on Alcohol, 53,* 357–363.

McLellan, A. T., Luborsky, L., Cacciola, J., Griffith, J., McGahan, P., & O'Brien, C. P. (1985). *Guide to the Addiction Severity Index.* Washington, DC: U.S. Government Printing Office.

Meisler, A. W. (in press). Group treatment of PTSD and comorbid alcohol abuse. In B. H. Young & D. D. Blake (Eds.), *Group treatment for post-traumatic stress disorders: Conceptualization, themes, and processes.* Washington, DC: Taylor & Francis.

Meisler, A., & Cooney, N. L. (1996). *Trauma cues elicit desire for alcohol in combat veterans with PTSD and comorbid alcohol dependence.* Unpublished manuscript.

Michael, J. (1994). Establishing operations. *Behavior Analyst, 16,* 191–206.

Miller, B. A. (1990). The interrelationships between alcohol and drugs and family violence. *National Institute on Drug Abuse Research Monograph Series, 103,* 177–207.

Miller, B. A., & Downs, W. R. (1993). The impact of family violence on the use of alcohol by women [Special issue: Alcohol, aggression, and injury]. *Alcohol Health and Research World, 17,* 137–143.

Miller, B. A., Downs, W. R., & Testa, M. (1993). Interrelationships between victimization experiences and women's alcohol use. *Journal of Studies on Alcohol, 11,* 109–117.

Miller, W. R., & Brown, S. A. (1997). Why psychologists should treat alcohol and drug problems. *American Psychologist, 52,* 1269–1279.

Miller, W. R., & Marlatt, G. A. (1984). *Manual for the Comprehensive Drinker Profile.* Odessa, FL: Psychological Assessment Resources.

Miller, W. R., & Rollnick, S. (1991). *Motivational interviewing: Preparing people to change addictive behavior.* New York: Guilford Press.

Miller, W. R., Westerberg, V. S., & Waldron, H. B. (1995). Evaluating alcohol problems in adults and adolescents. In R. K. Hester & W. R. Miller (Eds.), *Handbook of alcoholism treatment approaches: Effective alternatives.* Boston, MA: Allyn & Bacon.

Monti, P. M., Abrams, D. B., Kadden, R. M., & Cooney, N. L. (1989). *Treating alcohol dependence: A coping skills training guide.* New York: Guilford Press.

Nace, E. P. (1988). Posttraumatic stress disorder and substance abuse: Clinical issues. In

M. Galanter (Ed.), *Recent developments in alcoholism* (Vol. 6, pp. 9–26). New York: Plenum.

Najavits, L. M., Gastfriend, D. R., Barber, J. P., Reif, S., Muenz, L. R., Blaine, J., Frank, A., Crits-Christoph, P., Thase, M., & Weiss, R. D. (1998). Cocaine dependence with and without posttraumatic stress disorder among subjects in the National Institute on Drug Abuse Collaborative Cocaine Treatment Study. *American Journal of Psychiatry, 155*(2), 214–219.

Najavits, L. M., Weiss, R. D., & Liese, B. S. (1996). Group cognitive-behavioral therapy for women with PTSD and substance use disorder. *Journal of Substance Abuse Treatment, 13,* 13–22.

Najavits, L. M., Weiss, R. D., & Shaw, S. R. (1997). The link between substance abuse and posttraumatic stress disorder in women: A research review. *American Journal on Addictions, 6,* 273–283.

Najavits, L. M., Weiss, R. D., Shaw, S. R., & Muenz, L. R. (1998). "Seeking safety": Outcome of a new cognitive-behavioral psychotherapy for women with posttraumatic stress disorder and substance dependence. *Journal of Traumatic Stress, 11,* 437–456.

Norris, J., & Cubbins, L. A. (1992). Dating, drinking, and rape: Effects of victim's and assailant's alcohol consumption on judgments of their behavior and traits. *Psychology of Women Quarterly, 16,* 179–191.

O'Farrell, T. J., Cutter, H. S. G., Choquette, K. A., Floyd, F. J., & Bayog, R. D. (1992). Behavioral marital therapy for male alcoholics: Marital and drinking adjustment during two years after treatment. *Behavior Therapy, 23,* 529–549.

Ouimette, P. C., Ahrens, C., Moos, R. H., & Finney, J. W. (1997). Posttraumatic stress disorder in substance abuse patients: Relationship to 1-year posttreatment outcomes. *Psychology of Addictive Behaviors, 11,* 34–47.

Ouimette, P. C., Wolfe, J., & Chrestman, K. R. (1996). Characteristics of posttraumatic stress disorder—alcohol abuse comorbidity in women. *Journal of Substance Abuse, 8,* 335–346.

Peirce, J. M., Brown, J. M., Long, P. J., Nixon, S. J., Borrell, G. K., & Holloway, F. A. (1996). *Comorbidity and subjective reactivity to meaningful cues in female methadone maintenance patients.* Paper presented at annual meeting of the Association for Advancement of Behavior Therapy, New York.

Pitman, R. K., Altman, B., Greenwald, E., Longpre, R. E., Macklin, M. L., Poire, R. E., & Steketee, G. S. (1991). Psychiatric complications during flooding therapy for posttraumatic stress disorder. *Journal of Clinical Psychiatry, 52,* 17–20.

Polusny, M. A., & Follette, V. M. (1995). Long-term correlates of child sexual abuse: Theory and review of the empirical literature. *Applied and Preventive Psychology, 4,* 143–166.

Reifman, A., & Windle, M. (1996). Vietnam combat exposure and recent drug use: A national study. *Journal of Traumatic Stress, 9,* 557–568.

Reilly, P. M., Clark, H. W., Shopshire, M. S., Lewis, E. W., & Sorensen, D.J. (1994). Anger management and temper control: Critical components of posttraumatic stress disorder and substance abuse treatment. *Journal of Psychoactive Drugs, 26,* 401–407.

Resick, P. A., & Schnicke, M. K. (1992). Cognitive processing therapy for sexual assault victims. *Journal of Consulting and Clinical Psychology, 60,* 748–756.

Rohsenow, D. J., Childress, A R., Monti, P. M., Niaura, R. S., & Abrams, D. B. (1990). Cue reactivity in addictive behaviors: Theoretical and treatment implications. *International Journal of the Addictions, 25,* 957–993.

Rohsenow, D. J., Corbett, R., & Devine, D. (1988). Molested as children: A hidden contribution to substance abuse? *Journal of Substance Abuse Treatment, 5,* 13–18.

Root, M. P. (1989). Treatment failures: The role of sexual victimization in women's addictive behavior. *American Journal of Orthopsychiatry, 59,* 542–549.

Roszell, D. K., McFall, M. E., & Malas, K. L. (1991). Frequency of symptoms and concurrent psychiatric disorder in Vietnam veterans with chronic PTSD. *Hospital and Community Psychiatry, 42,* 293–296.

Roth, S., & Newman, E. (1991). The process of coping with sexual trauma. *Journal of Traumatic Stress, 4,* 279–297.

Rounsaville, B. J., Tierney, T., & Crits-Christoph, K. (1982). Predictors of outcome of opiate addicts. *Comprehensive Psychiatry, 23,* 462–478.

Rounsaville, B. J., Weissman, M. M., Wilber, C. H., & Kleber, H. D. (1982). Pathways to opiate addiction: An evaluation of differing antecedents. *American Journal of Psychiatry, 141,* 437–446.

Saladin, M. E., Brady, K. T., Dansky, B. S., & Kilpatrick, D. G. (1995). Understanding comorbidity between PTSD and substance use disorders: Two preliminary investigations. *Addictive Behaviors, 20,* 643–655.

Satel, S. L., Becker, B. R., & Dan, E. (1993). Reducing obstacles to affiliation with Alcoholics Anonymous among veterans with PTSD and alcoholism. *Hospital and Community Psychiatry, 44,* 1061–1065.

Schaefer, M. R., Sobieraj, K., & Hollyfield, R. L. (1988). Prevalence of childhood physical abuse in adult male veteran alcoholics. *Child Abuse and Neglect, 12,* 141–149.

Seidel, R., Gusman, F. D., & Abueg, F. R. (1994). Theoretical and practical foundation of an inpatient program for treatment of PTSD and alcoholism. *Psychotherapy, 31,* 67–78.

Sierles, F. S., Chen, J., McFarland, R. E., & Taylor, M. A. (1983). Posttraumatic stress disorder and concurrent psychiatric illness: A preliminary report. *American Journal of Psychiatry, 140,* 1177–1179.

Sierles, F. S., Chen, J., Messing, M. L., Besyner, J. K., & Taylor, M. A. (1986). Concurrent psychiatric illness in non-Hispanic outpatients diagnosed as having posttraumatic stress disorder. *Journal of Nervous and Mental Disease, 174,* 171–173.

Sisson, R. W., & Azrin, N. H. (1986). Family-member involvement to initiate and promote treatment of problem drinkers. *Journal of Behavior Therapy and Experimental Psychiatry, 17,* 15–21.

Smith, J. E., & Meyers, R. J. (1995). The community reinforcement approach. In R. K. Hester & W. R. Miller (Eds.), *Handbook of alcoholism treatment approaches* (2nd ed., pp. 251–266). New York: Pergamon.

Solomon, Z. (1993). *Combat stress reaction: The enduring toll of war.* New York: Plenum.

Stewart, S. H. (1996). Alcohol abuse in individuals exposed to trauma: A critical review. *Psychological Bulletin, 120,* 83–112.

Stewart, S. H., Peterson, J. B., & Pihl, R. O. (1995). Anxiety sensitivity and self-reported alcohol consumption rates in university women. *Journal of Anxiety Disorders, 9,* 283–292.

Stewart, S. H., & Zeitlin, S. B. (1995). Anxiety sensitivity and alcohol use motives. *Journal of Anxiety Disorders, 9,* 229–240.

Streimer, J. H., Cosstick, J., & Tennant, C. (1985). The psychosocial adjustment of Australian Vietnam veterans. *American Journal of Psychiatry, 142,* 616–618.

Taylor, S., Koch, W. J., & McNally, R. J. (1992). How does anxiety sensitivity vary across the anxiety disorders? *Journal of Anxiety Disorders, 6,* 249–259.

Triffleman, E. G., Marmar, C. R., Delucchi, K. L., & Ronfeldt, H. (1995). Childhood trauma and posttraumatic stress disorder in substance abuse inpatients. *Journal of Nervous and Mental Disease, 183,* 172–176.

Van Kampen, M. Watson, C. G., Tilleskjor, B. A., Kucala, T., & Vassar, P. (1986). The definition of posttraumatic stress disorder in alcoholic Vietnam veterans: Are the DSM-III criteria necessary and sufficient? *Journal of Nervous and Mental Disease, 174,* 137–144.

Villagomez, R. E., Meyer, T. J., Lin, M. M., & Brown, L. S. (1995). Post-traumatic stress disorder among inner city methadone maintenance patients. *Journal of Substance Abuse Treatment, 12,* 253–257.

Widom, C. S. (1993). *Alcohol and interpersonal violence: Fostering multidisciplinary perspectives* [Child Abuse and Alcohol Use and Abuse, Monograph Series, No. 24]. Rockville, MD: National Institute on Alcoholism and Alcohol Abuse Research.

Wilsnack, S. C., Vogeltanz, N. D., Klassen, A. D., & Harris, T. R. (1997). Childhood sexual abuse and women's substance abuse: National survey findings. *Journal of Studies on Alcohol, 58,* 264–271.

Wilson, G. T. (1988). Alcohol and anxiety. *Behaviour Research and Therapy, 26,* 369–381.

Wulfert, E., Greenway, D. E., & Dougher, M. J. (1996). A logical functional analysis of reinforcement-based disorders: Alcoholism and pedophilia. *Journal of Consulting and Clinical Psychology, 64,* 1140–1151.

Wyatt, G. E., Guthrie, D., & Notgrass, C. M. (1992). Differential effects of women's child sexual abuse and subsequent sexual revictimization. *Journal of Consulting and Clinical Psychology, 60,* 167–173.

Yager, T., Laufer, R., & Gallops, M. (1984). Some problems associated with war experiences in men of the Vietnam generation. *Archives of General Psychiatry, 41,* 327–333.

Zaslav, M. R. (1994). Psychology of comorbid posttraumatic stress disorder and substance abuse: Lessons from combat veterans. *Journal of Psychoactive Drugs, 26,* 393–400.

Acceptance and Trauma Survivors
APPLIED ISSUES AND PROBLEMS

ROBYN D. WALSER
STEVEN C. HAYES

There is a tendency to equate trauma with extremely painful events, but the two are quite different. Not all painful events are traumatic. The death of a loved one may be extremely painful, yet going through such an experience may be meaningful, valued, or even sacred. When and how does psychological pain transform into trauma? This chapter is about a possible answer to that question and the treatment of trauma based on that answer.

The etymology of the words involved give us a clue about how to approach the issue. "Trauma" comes from a Latin root meaning "wound." Unlike mere pain, wounds involve injury and bodily harm. They produce scars. They take time—perhaps a long time—to heal. The words "injury" and "heal" provide other interesting clues. "Injury" comes from a word meaning "wrong," and "heal" comes from a word meaning "whole."

What we are dealing with psychologically when we are dealing with trauma is a sense of being broken, through a wrong: The person's wholeness has somehow been shattered by the injustice of an event. Trauma, in that sense, is a highly abstract and verbal event, not merely something that is extremely uncomfortable or aversive. Viewed this way, it takes a verbal organism to be traumatized, because for an event to be wrong or unjust in the eyes of a recipient, there must be a verbal response to it.

Verbal behavior can occur under virtually any context, unlike most other forms of behavior. Self-talk regarding a traumatic experience can be engaged in for a virtually unlimited period of time and in many settings. In addition, humans can respond to their own self-talk much as if responding to actual events (Hayes & Brownstein, 1986; Hayes, Kohlenberg, & Hayes, 1991). Thus, how a traumatic event is held verbally can have a great deal to do with how it is maintained and how it impacts other aspects of life.

There are many sources of evidence showing the importance of how victims of trauma talk to themselves about traumatic events. For instance, some of the factors that are thought to be important in the etiology of posttraumatic stress disorder (PTSD) include appraisals of the event as uncontrollable, unpredictable, and objectively dangerous. These types of constructed stimulus characteristics may be central in determining subsequent reactions to the traumatic event (Foa, Zinbarg, & Rothbaum, 1992). Furthermore, individuals often feel the need to explain unusual, unwanted, or unexpected events and make causal attributions following trauma (Weiner, 1985, 1986). The nature of the individual's explanation will often influence how he or she will respond to the event (Brewin, 1985, 1988; Shaver & Drown, 1986; Tennen & Affleck, 1990; Weiner, 1986).

In the present analysis, self-talk, and particularly self-evaluations, can play a critical role in moderating the damage caused directly by a traumatic event. Aversive events produce a variety of aversive private experiences: negative emotions, negative self-evaluations, painful memories, and so on. As these reactions are described, categorized, and evaluated, it is common for humans to begin to treat these reactions to aversive experiences as themselves aversive. In essence, humans can begin to attempt to regulate not only objective situations, but also historically produced private experiences.

Consider a trauma victim who believes that she is "broken" and that something is wrong with her because she was molested. She may begin to respond as if this very feeling is something that she cannot have, and may take various actions to get rid of the feeling itself. The problems with this course of action are that (1) if she has a feeling she "cannot have," then, in one sense, there is something wrong with her; (2) humans are very poor in deliberately eliminating automatic emotions and thoughts; and (3) many of the methods that can be used (e.g., avoidance of situations that trigger the thought or feeling) are themselves destructive. For example, the person may now need to avoid such things as sexual encounters or healthy intimate relationships because they will remind her of the abuse. On the surface, these avoidance maneuvers constitute attempts to free herself from being "broken," thus, becoming worthy again, or whole. Their effect, however, may be the exact opposite.

The avoidance or control of private or internal experience commonly seems to become the goal for many trauma survivors. The function of these avoidance maneuvers serves to relieve immediate encounters with private, naturally occurring, experiences such as sadness, anxiety, fear, thoughts of worthlessness, and painful memories. As part of this avoidance effort, however, whole parts of the trauma survivor's experience may be cut off. The very thing survivors are seeking, a sense of wholeness, can be lost in their efforts to avoid private experience (Follette, 1994; Hayes, 1987; Hayes, 1994, Hayes & Wilson, 1994; Hayes, Wilson, Gifford, Follette, & Strosahl, 1996).

EXPERIENTIAL AVOIDANCE

Many approaches to dealing with problems in living involve efforts to change our responses to negative events (Hayes, 1994). One of the main goals for persons in our culture is to "feel good." However, many of life's events do not create this feeling. Tragedies, deaths, and failings occur, and all too often, the short cuts to "feeling good" are done at the cost of healthy living. Many forms of pathology have been shown to be related to these attempted experiential shortcuts (see Hayes et al., 1996, for a review).

The experiential avoidance approach to understanding trauma centers on the impact of an unwillingness to experience certain negatively evaluated emotions, thoughts, bodily states, memories, behavioral predispositions, and other private events, and the behavioral distortions caused by efforts to avoid these private experiences (Hayes, 1987, 1994; Hayes & Wilson, 1994). In the experiential avoidance model, the emotional responses of sadness and anxiety, and the thoughts and memories themselves, are not pathological, whereas the attempts to avoid or eliminate these primary thoughts and emotions can become so (Hayes, 1994).

Steps taken to avoid experiential states may include directed thinking or rumination and worry as a way to distract oneself from current experience or cognitive material associated with emotional content (Wells & Matthews, 1994), numbing oneself to emotional responses or engaging in one type of emotional reaction as a way to avoid another (e.g., anger to avoid hurt or using distraction from emotion as a coping style); removal of oneself from situations and personal interactions that elicit certain negative thoughts or emotions; or responding to verbally constructed "negative" futures or pasts and their constructed contingencies (Hayes, 1994). Each of these actions, if excessively engaged in, may lead to the development of problematic behavior.

For instance, certain posttrauma consequences are similar across trauma populations (Trimble, 1981) and may be indicative of pathology. Avoidance and numbing are two of the more crucial aspects of these consequences (American Psychiatric Association, 1994). A victim of trauma may spend energy avoiding two types of stimuli: feelings and thoughts associated with the trauma, or activities that stimulate memories of the trauma (Shapiro & Dominiak, 1992). The pervasiveness of these types of avoidance and their role in trauma-related problems support the core conception of an experiential avoidance model.

Furthermore, the sequelae of traumatic experiences such as a childhood history of sexual abuse, disasters, and war experiences are related to avoidance strategies. For example, victims of childhood sexual abuse experience symptoms that include repression, denial, and distortion (Shapiro & Dominiak, 1992). Some of the long-term effects of childhood sexual abuse include behaviors that are avoidance oriented, such as self-harming behaviors that may be conceptualized as an escape from anxiety (Briere & Runtz, 1993; Browne & Finkelhor, 1986;

Polusny & Follette, 1995), dissociation and memory impairment (Anderson, Yasenik, & Ross, 1993; DiTomasso & Routh, 1993), substance abuse (Rodriguez, Ryan, & Foy, 1992), and eating disorders (Conners & Morse, 1993; Miller, McCluskey-Fawcett, & Irving, 1993).

Victims of disaster demonstrate similar traumatic responses across a variety of event types (Green, 1993). Some of these responses are more transient, but may last for months (Green & Lindy, 1994). Symptoms include depersonalization, derealization, a subjective sense of numbing or detachment, dissociative amnesia and a reduction in awareness, as well as avoidance of reminders, anxiety and arousal, and intrusive reexperiencing of the event (Green & Lindy, 1994). Other symptoms found to be present include time distortion, alterations in cognitions, and somatic sensations (Cardea & Spiegel, 1993).

Finally, war veterans also experience similar symptoms (Helzer, Robins, & Davis, 1976; Southwick, Yehuda, & Giller, 1991). In addition, many veterans experience somatization disorders (Omer, 1992), marital problems stemming from loss of emotion and intimacy or physical aggression (Carroll, Rueger, Foy, & Donahoe, 1985), anxiety, nightmares and difficulty in coping (Card, 1987; Fairbank, Hansen, & Fitterling, 1991), increased feelings of alienation (Egendorf, Laufer, & Sloan, 1981), and are more likely to commit suicide (Hendin & Haas, 1991; Sutter, 1986), which may be considered the ultimate act of avoidance.

EMPIRICAL RESEARCH AS IT RELATES TO EXPERIENTIAL AVOIDANCE AND ACCEPTANCE ISSUES

The degree to which experiential avoidance plays a role in PTSD and trauma-related problems can be illustrated further by incidence of comorbidity, by data-supported characteristics of experiential avoidance that are relevant to PTSD, and by theories and systems of psychotherapy. Each of these areas are briefly reviewed.

Comorbidity and PTSD

Studies have found that 62–80% of individuals diagnosed with PTSD also meet criteria for at least one other disorder (Davidson & Fairbank, 1993). Disorders which have been found to co-occur include anxiety (Blank, 1994; Davidson & Foa, 1991; Joseph, Williams, & Yule, 1995), depression (Beitchman, Zucker, Hood, DaCosta, Akman, & Cassavia, 1992; Joseph, Williams, & Yule, 1995; Polusny & Follette, 1995), dysthymia, obsessive–compulsive disorder, manic–depressive disorder (Blank, 1994; Helzer, Robins, & McEvoy, 1987), somatization disorders (Davidson & Fairbank, 1993) and eating disorders (Beckman & Bums, 1990; Conners & Morse, 1993). Each of these disorders has experiential avoidance components, and diagnostic criteria often reflect some aspect of each disorder that may be considered to be avoidance related, particularly when a functional assessment of the behavior is conducted. For instance, binge–purge eating (Briere & Runtz, 1993), compulsive behaviors (Briere & Runtz, 1993) and self-mutilation (Linehan, 1993) have been viewed as tension-reducing behavioral strategies and are often conceptualized as behavioral forms of emotional avoidance.

Co-occurring substance abuse also fits the model of experiential avoidance. When a client presents with PTSD, co-occurring problems can resemble attempts to medicate or escape certain feared emotions or private experiences. Substance abuse is a common problem for survivors of trauma (Browne & Finklehor, 1986; Herman, 1981; McFall, Mackay, & Donovan, 1991; Polusny & Follette, 1995; Schetky, 1990) and survivors often report that the substance numbs the traumatic memories (Root, 1989).

The notion that alcohol is used as an experiential avoidance strategy is further supported by research that shows that alcohol abusers drink primarily in situations involving negative emotional states (Marlatt & Gordon, 1985). Alcohol also has a tendency to decrease processing of self-relevant information; thus, persons who consume alcohol may be using it as a way to reduce contact with negative self-evaluation information (Stephens & Curtin, 1995). Given these research findings and other explanations for the use of substances, one consistent theme emerges: Substance use is viewed as a means to escape aversive bodily states, emotions, certain cognitions, and other private events.

Depression is frequently observed among victims of trauma (McGorry et al., 1991; Southwick et al., 1991). There is much overlap in symptom criteria between PTSD and depressive symptomatology (Brewin, Joseph, & Kuyken, 1993), and the function of depression symptoms can readily be couched as experiential avoidance issues. For instance, support for the relationship between control of private events as problematic is demonstrated in Beck's theory of dysfunctional assumptions. These particular assumptions were investigated in a sample of survivors of a ferry disaster. Williams, Hodgkinson, Joseph, and Yule (1995) developed a measure of negative attitudes to emotional expression (e.g., "You should always keep your feelings under control"). They predicted that positive endorsement would predict dysfunctional processing of traumatic experiences. The study concluded that the more the dysfunctional assumption was believed, the more the victims experienced symptoms of PTSD and generalized anxiety. Given these comorbid conditions and that individuals' perceptions of themselves and the world often change posttrauma, survivors may seek help, not because of the original trauma, but because of the disturbing nature of the symptoms posttrauma.

Data Supported Characteristics of Experiential Avoidance That Are Relevant to PTSD

It has been suggested that some avoidance may be important in terms of coping, but that too much emotional suppression (avoidance) may result in emotional numbness or in dissociation from cognitive and emotional material. The possible final result of avoidance or suppression will be the reoccurrence of intrusive trauma cognitions (Clark, Ball, & Pape, 1991; Wegner, Shortt, Blake, & Page, 1990); that is, there may be a paradoxical effect to escape or avoidance tactics.

Experiential avoidance or suppression and elimination of private experience and its role in the development and maintenance of psychopathology has recently come under investigation. Current research suggests that attempting to avoid or suppress unwanted negative thoughts, emotions, and memories, as a means to create psychological health, may actually contribute to a magnification of the negative emotional responses and thoughts, and to a longer period of experiencing those events (Cioffi & Holloway, 1993; Wegner & Zanakos, 1994).

The effects of active suppression or avoidance of unwanted private experience has been documented in many studies (Cioffi & Holloway, 1993; Clark et al., 1991; Kelly & Kahn, 1994; Muris, Merckelback, van den Hout, & de Jong, 1992; Salkovskis & Campbell, 1994; Wegner, 1994; Wegner, et al., 1990). The effects of long-term suppression have also been explored (Trinder & Salkovskis, 1994). These effects are generally consistent and are briefly explored here.

Thought suppression studies (Macrae, Bodenhousen, Milne, & Jetten, 1994; Wegner, 1994; Wegner, Schneider, Carter, & White, 1987) indicate that subjects have a difficult time suppressing the unwanted thought and mention the thought frequently during suppression conditions. Subjects also report a conscious, effortful search for anything but the thought; however, these efforts to distract fail. This may be due to an unusual sensitivity to the thought throughout periods of attempted suppression (Wegner, 1994). These findings support the notion that we are more likely to think of the very thing we would like to avoid.

Personally relevant intrusive thoughts, or unwanted thoughts that repeatedly come to mind (Edwards & Dickerson, 1987), such as recurring memories, images, evaluations, judgements, and so on have also been investigated (Rachman & Hodgson, 1980; Salkovskis & Harrison, 1982). For instance, Salkovskis and Campbell (1994) found that suppression or avoidance causes enhancement of personally relevant, negatively valenced intrusive thoughts. Trinder and Salkovskis (1994) found that subjects who were asked to suppress their negative intrusive thoughts experienced significantly more of those thoughts than subjects who were asked just to monitor their thoughts. In addition, the suppression group recorded significantly more discomfort with the negative intrusions than did subjects in the monitor only group: that is, efforts to suppress were significantly correlated with average discomfort across the rating period. The more subjects tried to suppress a thought, the more discomfort they experienced about the intrusion.

Although personally relevant intrusive thoughts are quite common and are thought to occur in about 80% of the population (Rachman & de Silva, 1978), they appear to be particularly problematic for survivors of trauma. The suppression of disclosure about disturbing events, such as past trauma, has been linked to both psychological and physiological problems (Pennebaker, Hughes, & O'Heeron, 1987; Pennebaker & O'Heeron, 1984). Riggs, Dancu, Gershuny, Greenberg, and Foa (1992) have found that female crime victims who "hold in" their anger experience more severe PTSD symptoms.

It makes sense that a trauma survivor would engage in behaviors to counteract or avoid traumatic thoughts and the emotions that may be associated with them, given the likely aversiveness of the traumatic event. Furthermore, there is considerable evidence that people attempt to suppress thoughts when they are traumatized (Pennebaker, & O'Heeron, 1984; Silver, Boon, & Stones, 1983), obsessed (Rachman & de Silva, 1978), anxious (Wegner et al., 1990), or depressed (Sutherland, Newman, & Rachman, 1982; Wenzlaff & Wegner, 1990). Efforts at control of one's mood, however, may paradoxically cause the mood to continue. They may also lead to the execution of many maladaptive behaviors, such as alcohol use or binge eating (Herman & Polivy, 1993).

Finally, recycling through a process of suppression with recurrence of emotion and thought countered by further attempts at suppression could well produce internal experience that is fairly robust (Wegner et al., 1990). Suppression of thought and emotion may be a part of the development of such disorders as PTSD, depression, anxiety, and panic. What individuals believe to be the antidote may actually be the venom that produces the very problem, further contributing to their distress. Individuals who use suppression may actually be generating an assortment of unwanted consequences and problems as a result of the strategy.

Theories and Systems of Psychotherapy

Either implicitly or explicitly, the concept of experiential avoidance in psychopathology and acceptance as a treatment approach has long been recognized in many psychotherapy traditions. For instance, psychoanalytic tradition emphasizes the need for individuals to recognize problems and to effectively and cognitively incorporate the responses to these problems. Otherwise, the cognitive and affective material will be repressed, only to emerge in some other form (Suls & Fletcher, 1985). Freud (1920/1966) underscored the importance of avoidance of private experience and defined the purpose of psychoanalysis as the lifting of repressions and making painful and threatening unconscious material available to conscious awareness.

Existential psychotherapists generally focus on avoidance involving fear of death (Yalom, 1980). In order to cope with fears of death, individuals erect defenses that are often based on denial. If these defenses are maladaptive, clinical syndromes may arise (Yalom, 1980). The general phenomenon of emotional avoidance has also been noted by Foa, Steketee, and Young (1984). They state that emotional avoidance is a common occurrence: "Unpleasant events are ignored, distorted, or forgotten" (p. 34). Gestalt therapists propose that unwanted emotion and avoidance of painful feelings are the heart of many psychological problems (Perls, Hefferline, & Goodman, 1951), and client-centered therapists suggest that "openness to experience" is the predominant goal of psychotherapy (Raskin & Rogers, 1989; Rogers, 1961). According to Frankl's (1984) logotherapy, the more fruitful approach to life involves focusing attention on, not away from, unwanted experience (Frankl, 1975). Kabat-Zinn (1990) explains that there is no escape from the human condition and that habitual avoidance of our problems will only cause them to multiply. The solution is a mindfulness to experience, a complete "owning" of each moment, whether it be good or bad.

Finally, recent recognition of experiential avoidance as a concept and functional diagnosis has increased among the behavioral therapy traditions (Hayes et al., 1996) and cognitive therapy traditions (Ellis, 1989; Neimeyer, 1993). Experiential avoidance is becoming more of a central theme for psychotherapeutic intervention. For instance, acceptance and commitment therapy (Hayes, 1987; Hayes & Wilson, 1994; Strosahl, 1991) and dialectical behavioral therapy (Linehan, 1993, 1994), both behaviorally based treatments, hold experiential acceptance as an essential aspect of psychotherapy. Modern cognitive approaches also appear to be shifting in a direction that is less interested in controlling negative feelings.

In sum, the concept of emotional avoidance offers organization to the functional analysis of trauma-related problems and lends coherence to understanding many of the sequelae of trauma. The work reviewed supplies supporting evidence that avoidance of private events may play an etiological role in the development and maintenance of PTSD and trauma-related problems. This approach, then, provides a framework for intervention with PTSD and trauma-related problems sufferers. It also suggests a treatment alternative: acceptance-based therapy.

ACCEPTANCE: THEORY AND INTERVENTION

Acceptance involves the conscious abandonment of a mental and emotional change agenda when change efforts do not work, and emotional and social willingness or an openness to one's own emotions and the experience of others (Hayes, 1994). Such acceptance applies to the domain of private subjective events and experiences, but not to overt behavior or changeable situations (Greenberg, 1994). Hayes (1994) defines acceptance as "experiencing events fully and without defense, as they are and not as what they say they are" (p. 30), or, more technically, as "making contact with the automatic or direct stimulus functions of events, without acting to reduce or manipulate those functions, and without acting on the basis solely of their derived or verbal functions" (p. 30). Defined in this way, acceptance is a situated action, and is a nondualistic concept (Dougher, 1994).

Continuum of Acceptance

It seems useful to think of acceptance as on a continuum (Hayes, 1994). At the lower level of the continuum are resignation and tolerance, which may be initial steps toward acceptance. Both resignation and tolerance are still based on a control agenda, but they represent the early signs of collapse of that agenda. The next level is the conscious abandonment of the change agenda when change efforts do not work. At an even higher level are emotional and social willingness or an openness to one's own emotions and the experience of others. The final level involves being more and more in the present, which requires defusing from the literal content of one's own self-talk.

Areas of Acceptance

There are also several areas of acceptance, including personal history, private events, overt behavior, sense of self, and acceptance of others (Hayes, 1994). In the remainder of this section, we provide a short summary of these areas, largely taken from Hayes's (1994) theory on acceptance.

With acceptance of personal history, the key issue is time. Time moves in one direction, thus our inability to return to a previous time and change our history. History is not subtractive, only additive. The difficult part about this reality is that some people have traumatic events that have occurred in their history, and these events may play a role in current situations. In addition, as a result of our ability to construct events verbally, we can compare ourselves to an ideal self and imagine that if our history had only been different, we might be able to become that ideal. However, the only thing we can do is build on our history; thus, efforts to remove history fail. A more successful place to live is a place in which the events of our history are important and valid, but do not need to change in order for us to live a meaningful life.

A second area of acceptance is that of private events. This includes thoughts, emotions, bodily sensations, and so on. Efforts to control these events often create the very event itself (as stated earlier). All humans have thoughts they do not want or emotions they do not like; however, just by virtue of having them does not mean that they are literally true or cannot be felt in order to be a healthy or a fulfilled human being. Acceptance in this area pertains to the ability to have the thought, emotion, and so on, experience it for what it is, a thought or emotion, and continue to live a valued life.

In terms of overt behavior, acceptance is not a tool to explain away problems or justify behavior. Its purpose is to harness the capacity for change, carrying private experience with you. There is nothing about acceptance of that kind that would lead to acceptance of maladaptive behavior.

The fourth area is sense of self. There are three aspects of the self that are important to this issue. First, the conceptualized self, which is created by our ability to interact verbally with ourselves and others. We can evaluate, explain, rationalize, and so on. This is what might be called, "self-as-content," a conceptualized self that we create verbally to make sense of ourselves, our history, and our behavior. A problematic issue occurs in this area when one holds the content of this conceptualized self to be literally true. If a person makes the comment, "I am messed up because I was abused as a child," the problem to be solved becomes unworkable because no other childhood will occur. Therefore, acceptance of the conceptualized self held literally is not desirable.

The second self is the self as a process of knowing. We know about ourselves and can respond to others about our feelings and reactions. This knowing is valuable in terms of socialization and civilization. Through a process of training, we can report when we are hungry or when we are in pain, and so on. We can categorize our own and others' behavior based on this process. When a person's training history needed to gain this kind of knowledge is deviant, then that person may not know how to behave with respect to the social environment. For instance, suppose a young boy is sexually abused and his reactions to the abuse are ignored, denied, or reinterpreted. This type of developmental history could set the stage for a person to be unable to know or report to others accurately what he or she is feeling. One can imagine other histories where the process of accurately being able to describe your feelings or to express them appropriately is inhibited. Given this, taking the content of one's verbalizations to be who one literally is may be inherently problematic.

The third sense of self is self-as-context. This is the self in which "I" is the place from which one responds verbally. It is the sense of one's own perspective or point of view. This self is consistent and is present at all times. If we ask you questions about yourself, you *always* answer from your perspective. The content of your answers will change; however, the context from which you answer does not.

It is not too difficult to help clients experience this sense of connection to self-as-context. Localizing past memories and events, and current situations easily puts the client in contact with this sense of "I." The only reasonable thing to do is to accept self-as-context, since much verbal behavior is based upon it and we cannot function effectively as nonverbal organisms. It is also this form of self that allows other forms of acceptance. If self-as-context is always present, other kinds of content may come and go, and a stable sense of "I" will still remain the same. Therefore, one may experience pain or horrible memories, but that does not make one literally those things. They too shall pass and new content will be present, but the sense of "I" will remain unchanged.

In summary, a therapeutic alternative to emotional avoidance is acceptance. Acceptance in each of the areas discussed earlier can create a new context from which the trauma survivor may view the world and the self. Trauma survivors, if willing to hold private events dispassionately, can make behavioral changes that are consistent with their values and goals. A willingness move in this sense does not mean that the survivor must "feel willing," but rather that he or she must "be willing."

An Example: Acceptance and Commitment Therapy (ACT)

ACT (said as one word, not as letters) is a behaviorally based treatment that focuses on acceptance and deliteralization methods (Hayes, 1987; Hayes, 1994, Kohlenberg, Hayes, & Tsai, 1993). There are five main goals of ACT (Hayes, McCurry, Afari, & Wilson, 1992) and several specific techniques that are used to promote psychological acceptance as an avenue to behavioral change (see Hayes, 1987; Hayes et al., 1992). We briefly review these goals because they help show how acceptance might be integrated into a treatment approach for trauma.

The first goal of ACT is *creative Hopelessness* (Hayes, et, 1992). This is a condition created in therapy in which clients see that they have tried everything to rid themselves of negative emotional content, that their situation is hopeless. Things that clients have tried usually include "more, better, and different"; that is, clients feel that if they had a different history (one without sexual abuse, disaster trauma, or war trauma), then their problems would be solved and they would no longer be in emotional turmoil; they would "feel" better. However, as they try these solutions over and over again, they may come to realize they need "more" solutions. With ACT, the solutions the client has been trying are viewed as part of the problem, thus the hopelessness of the situation. However, this hopelessness is viewed as a creative condition, as now fundamentally new approaches are possible. Metaphors are often used to demonstrate the client's situation:

THERAPIST: Here is a metaphor that will help you understand what I am saying. Imagine you are blindfolded and given a bag of tools and told to run through a large field. So there you are, living your life and running through the field. However, unknown to you, there are large holes in this field and sooner or later you fall in. Now remember you were blindfolded so you didn't fall in on purpose; it is not your fault that you fell in. You want to get out ,so you open your bag of tools and find that the only tool is a shovel. So you begin to dig. And you dig. But digging is the thing that makes holes. So you try other things, like figuring out exactly how you fell in the hole, but that doesn't help you get out. Even if you knew every step that you took to get into the hole, it wouldn't help you to get out. So you dig differently. You, dig fast, you dig slow. You take big scoops, and you take little scoops. And, you're still not out. Finally, you think you need to get a "really great shovel," and that is why you are here to see me. Maybe I have a gold-plated shovel. But I don't, and even if I did, I wouldn't use it. Shovels don't get people out of holes—they make them.

CLIENT: So what is the solution? Why should I even come here?

THERAPIST: I don't know, but it is not to help you dig your way out. Perhaps we should start with what your experience tells you. That what you have been doing hasn't been working. And what I am going to ask you to consider is that it can't work. Until you open up to that, you will never let go of the shovel because as far as you know, it's the only thing you've got. But until you let go of it, you have no room for anything else.

As a therapist working with trauma survivors, it is very important when working on this goal to take extra care that the client does not feel blamed. When clients are told that they are responsible for their "digging," it can easily be misunderstood as blame. It will be important to acknowledge that it is not the client's fault that he or she fell into the hole, and he or she is responding in the only way he or she knows how. Responsibility is couched as the "ability-to-respond," thus opening up opportunities to do things differently. In addition, the therapist should always operate from a place of compassion for clients' situations and the struggles they have been engaging in their lives.

Control of private events as the problem (Hayes et al., 1992) is the second goal of ACT therapy. Emotional and cognitive control are explored as barriers to successful solutions to clients' problems in living; that is, conscious, purposeful efforts to get rid of, escape, or avoid negative thoughts and feelings actually may be preventing clients from behaving in ways that are consistent with what they value, and may be exacerbating the very events they are trying to control. If a trauma survivor is trying to escape something, a specific memory, perhaps, then (1) that is what the client is doing rather than some other, more productive form of action, and (2) the memories are likely to increase in frequency and negative impact.

"I" as content versus "I" as context is the third goal (Hayes et al., 1992). In this phase of therapy, the goal is to create a place in which clients can come to see themselves as context rather than content and to defuse from the literal content of self-talk. It is from the position of "I" that clients, and all of us, struggle; that is, it is as if the words that a person says and the actual person become fused. For example, when thinking "I am bad," from the position of self-as-content, then that statement seems to become what one literally is, rather than just a thought about what one is. From this position, the client has to fight to not be "bad." Now, suppose that "I am bad" could be viewed as just a thought and the client did not have to adhere to the construction, but rather could deliteralize or become "de-fused" from the thought. In the ACT approach, this defusion is only likely from an experiential perspective in which "I" equates with an ongoing awareness. Much like a walking mediation, ACT attempts to establish a place from which abandonment of control is not threatening, because the private events are mere content, not "who you are."

In the ACT approach, many techniques are then used to deliteralize language. These include (1) imagery exercises in which thoughts are allowed to flow as leaves on streams, without being bought, believed, adopted or rejected; (2) repeating thoughts rapidly for dozens or hundreds of times; the word loses its meaning and allows the client to see it for what it is— a sound or thought; (3) use of imagery exercises that turn emotions and thoughts into objects to be viewed and inspected; private experiences are given shapes, sizes, colors, and so on; (4) metaphor is also used extensively.

Letting go of the struggle is the fourth goal of ACT (Hayes et al., 1992). The goal in this stage of therapy is to encourage the client to let go of the agenda of control. This is a willingness move; that is, the client is asked to be willing to have whatever thoughts, feelings, memories, or bodily sensations that might show up without having to gain control over them, but simply experience them for what they are. Private events are brought into the therapy room and dissembled into component pieces (thoughts, memories, feelings, etc.). The goal is not to gain control, but to experience without attempts to escape or modify. Many "willingness exercises" are used at this point and generally include use of imagery. When working with a trauma survivor in this phase, a great deal of emotional exposure is done.

The fifth goal of ACT is *making a commitment to action* and behavior change (Hayes et al., 1992). It is at this point in therapy that clients commit to actions that are specific to their chosen values and goals. Through the previous work, ACT establishes a discrimination between unworkable solutions to a problem (i.e., control and avoidance of emotions, etc.) and workable solutions (e.g., commitments to behavior change). The client can begin to lead a valued life and choose directions that support that life. In this phase of therapy with a trauma survivor, the issues turn from making room for one's own history to creating a valued life. For example, concrete steps to develop more productive relationships might be taken, while simultaneously watching to prevent needless struggles with private experiences that might arise.

ACT is still a young therapy, but there is growing evidence that this approach is helpful in several areas. Recently, for example, Strosahl, Hayes, Bergan, and Romano (1998) showed that training clinicians in ACT produced better overall clinical outcomes in a general clinical practice in a managed care setting. In addition, versions of ACT have been applied to trauma survivors (Follette, 1994) with some success.

Assessment of Experiential Avoidance

Interest in emotional avoidance and acceptance is relatively new, and empirically oriented psychologists are just beginning to study these concepts. For that reason, assessment instruments and strategies are just now being developed, and well-established instruments are few (Hayes et al., 1996). A number of instruments exist that assess various cognitive and emotional states; however, acceptance is rarely addressed. We review a few measures that are related to the concepts of emotional avoidance, and may be used in assessment with trauma survivors.

There is a significant relationship between coping styles and certain forms of symptomatology (Abramsom, Seligman, & Teasdale, 1978; Fondacaro & Moos, 1987), many of which are included in the diagnosis of PTSD. Styles of coping adopted by individuals are among the mediating factors for the subsequent development of problematic behavior following a stressful event.

The Ways of Coping Questionnaire (WOC; Folkman & Lazarus, 1988), a widely used research instrument for assessing coping strategies, and the Coping Inventory for Stressful Situations (CISS; Endler & Parker, 1990) are each useful instruments that tap into emotion-focused or avoidant strategies. They assess a wide range of thoughts and behaviors that individuals use to deal with stressful life experiences. Three dominant means of coping with stressful situations have been identified. These are task-oriented, emotion-oriented, (Folkman & Lazarus, 1988) and avoidance-oriented (Endler and Parker, 1994). Task-oriented coping refers to the attainment of problem resolution through conscious efforts to solve or modify the situation, and emotion-oriented coping is defined by a set of reactions, such as tension and anger, of a self-oriented nature that occur in response to a problematic event. Avoidance-oriented coping involves responses that have the effect of distracting or diverting the individual's attention away from the stressful situation (Turner, King, & Tremblay, 1992).

Use of the WOC in studies of sequelae of childhood sexual abuse (Leitenberg, Greenwald, & Cado, 1992) and substance abuse (McMahon, Kelly, & Kouzekanani (1993), have been found to be predictive of outcome and supportive of the emotional avoidance perspective. Although these findings are encouraging, the data are only correlational and not causal, and they do not directly assess clients reactions to their own emotion and thought.

Other instruments which more directly assess avoidance of cognition include the White Bear Inventory (WBSI; Wegner & Zanakos, 1994), the Depression Sensitivity Scale (DSS; Wegner & Zanakos, 1994), and the Automatic Thoughts Questionnaire (ATQ; Kendall & Hollon, 1980). The WBSI is a self-report questionnaire designed to assess thought suppression or an individual's reported level of desire or ability to successfully avoid a thought. The DSS is an inventory that assesses the degree to which individuals find negative thoughts (e.g., sadness, anger) disturbing, scary, or socially unacceptable. And the ATQ is a questionnaire that assesses a person's frequency of thoughts that have occurred over the past month. The ATQ taps into four aspects of automatic thoughts: personal maladjustment and desire for change, negative self-concepts and negative expectations, low self-esteem, and helplessness.

The Acceptance and Action Questionnaire (AAQ; Hayes, 1996) more directly assesses emotional avoidance and emotion-focused inaction. Psychometric properties are currently under development. However, the factor structure has been cross-validated, and recent validation efforts suggest that the AAQ predicts psychopathology fairly well. For instance, correlation with the Beck Depression Inventory is .66.

Finally, several of these assessment instruments may be used throughout therapy to track the client's progress. The AAQ, WBSI, and DSS are relatively short instruments that can be given on a regular basis. The client can also use a daily diary that tracks both emotional willingness and action as it relates to valued living. These can be tracked with simple Likert-type scales that assess each area.

One of the most important aspects of assessment from the ACT approach is to have clients list their values in the areas of family relations, employment, friendship/social relationships, spirituality, education, citizenship, physical well-being, and recreation. They should rank these and list specific actions and goals that pertain to the values in each area. This list guides both the clients and therapist in the direction of therapy and provides feedback as to the progress clients are making. It is an indicator to clients that they are living according to their values. It is also useful to identify barriers to those goals. These barriers are usually experiential-avoidance related and should be addressed in therapy.

Evaluation of Treatment

Evaluation of treatment should generally be based on two specific areas: (1) Changes on the paper and pencil measures that indicate a positive movement in direction (less experiential avoidance), and (2) Is the client doing what works and living according to what he or she values? You can track the clients' progress by assessing different areas pertaining to the clients' goals and the values he or she has with respect to those goals: a decrease in number of drinking days, reduction in self-harm, report of relationship improvement, steady employment, volunteer services, or a steady exercise program, for example. The key is action with private experience, rather than action after private experience has changed.

Common Treatment Obstacles and Possible Solutions

There are three areas in which therapists generally make mistakes when using acceptance-based approaches. First, and specifically with ACT therapy, it is very easy to get caught up in the content of what the client has to say, and therapy can be derailed when this happens. It is critical to maintain a focus on context. This can be done by asking the client to "notice" the content and the process on a frequent basis. The therapist should also take notice at those times, in the sense of being mindful of the ongoing process. This process helps create a sense of perspective on the content at issue.

A second issue that is particularly crucial in the treatment of trauma survivors pertains to nonacceptance–acceptance of history. We are not asking clients to accept what has happened to them in an overt behavioral sense. Rather, clients are being asked to embrace those aspects of themselves that they have been trying to cut off. It is not a move in which clients are asked to "like" their history, but a move to hold it for what it is—a memory or thought. That is, clients' histories can inform them rather than "drive" them. Finally, as stated before, acceptance of private events does not mean acceptance of behavior. Behavior that is harmful or unhealthy is not the kind of acceptance we mean. This distinction should be made clear to the client.

Third, the role of responsibility in therapy with trauma survivors needs careful focus. It is important to couch responsibility as "ability-to-respond," ability to take action. The therapist must be careful not to make the client feel blamed for the trauma when talking about responsibility. Furthermore, if the therapist is not operating from a place of compassion for the client's dilemma, the client can be easily made to feel "wrong" about trying to control his or her private experience. From an ACT standpoint, "right" and "wrong" are also seen as content and not necessarily useful for progress. Essentially, there is only one way for the therapist to participate honestly, and that is for the therapist to be experientially willing also.

Summary

We cannot remove our private experiences or histories, but by death (Hayes, 1994). The difficult part about this reality is that some people have traumatic events that have occurred in their history, and these events may play a role in current situations. In addition, as a result of our ability to construct events verbally, we can compare ourselves to an ideal self and imagine that if our history had only been different, we might be able to become that ideal (Hayes, 1994). Under these conditions, trauma survivors will often imagine that if their history were different, or if they could change their attitude about their history, they would not currently be experiencing PTSD or trauma-related problems. However, history is additive, and we can only build it from where we are at the moment, and simply having positive psychological reactions to negative experiences does not mean that a difficult psychological history will be removed (Hayes, 1994). The solution is building a positive history from this moment forward, *with* all of our past experiences in tow. It is a willingness to have all aspects of the self, including the "good" and the "bad." It is an acceptance of private events in conjunction with directed action. Under these conditions, the trauma survivor can begin to live a valued life with the history rather than living a life driven by the history.

REFERENCES

Abramsom, L. Y., Seligman, M. E. P., & Teasdale, J. (1978). Learned helplessness in humans: Critique and reformulation. *Journal of Abnormal Psychology, 87,* 49–74.

American Psychiatric Association. (1994). *Diagnostic and statistical manual of mental disorders* (4th ed.). Washington, DC: Author.

Anderson, G., Yasenik, L., & Ross, C. A. (1993). Dissociative experiences and disorders among women who identify themselves as sexual abuse survivors. *Child Abuse and Neglect, 17,* 677–686.

Beckman, K. A., & Burns, G. L. (1990). Relations of sexual abuse and bulimia in college women. *International Journal of Eating Disorders, 9,* 487–492.

Blank, A. S. (1994). Clinical detection, diagnosis, and differential diagnosis of post-traumatic stress disorder. *Psychiatric Clinics of North America, 17,*351–383.

Brewin, C. R. (1985). Depression and causal attributions: What is their relation? *Psychological Bulletin, 98,* 297–309.

Brewin, C. R. (1988). *Cognitive foundations of clinical psychology.* Hillsdale, NJ: Erlbaum.

Brewin, C. R., Joseph, S., & Kuyken, W. (1993, April). *PTSD and depression: what is their relationship?* Paper presented at a meeting on Traumatic Stress, Northern Ireland Branch of the British Psychological Society, Belfast.

Briere, J., & Runtz, M. (1993). Childhood sexual abuse: Long-term sequelae and implications for psychological assessment. [Special Issue: Research on treatment of adults sexually abused in childhood.] *Journal of Interpersonal Violence, 8,* 312–330.

Browne, A., & Finkelhor, D. (1986). Impact of child sexual abuse: A review of the research. *Psychological Bulletin, 99,* 66–77.

Card, J. J. (1987). Epidemiology of PTSD in a national cohort of Vietnam veterans. *Journal of Clinical Psychology, 43,* 6–17.

Cardea, E., & Spiegel, D. (1993). Dissociative reactions to the San Francisco Bay Area earthquake of 1989. *American Journal of Psychiatry, 150,* 474–478.

Carroll, E. M., Rueger, D. B., Foy, D. W., & Donahoe, C. P., Jr. (1985). Vietnam combat veterans with posttraumatic stress disorder: Analysis of marital and cohabitating adjustment. *Journal of Abnormal Psychology, 94,* 329"337.

Cioffi, D., & Holloway, J. (1993). Delayed costs of suppressed pain. *Journal of Personality and Social Psychology, 64,* 274–282.

Clark, D. M., Ball, S., & Pape, D. (1991). An experimental investigation of thought suppression. *Behaviour Research and Therapy, 29,* 253–257.

Conners, M. E , & Morse, W. (1993). Sexual abuse and eating disorders: A review. *International Journal of Eating Disorders, 13,* 1–11.

Davidson, J. R., & Fairbank, J. A. (1993). The epidemiology of posttraumatic stress disorder. In J. R. T. Davidson & E. B. Foa (Eds.), *Posttraumatic stress disorder: DSM-IV and beyond* (p. 147). Washington, DC: American Psychiatric Association Press.

Davidson, J. R., & Foa, E. B. (1991). Diagnostic issues in posttraumatic stress disorder: Considerations for the DSM-IV. *Journal of Abnormal Psychology, 100,* 346–355.

DiTomasso, M. J., & Routh, D. K. (1993). Recall of abuse in childhood and three measures of dissociation. *Child Abuse and Neglect, 17,* 477–485.

Dougher, M. J. (1994). The act of acceptance. In S. C. Hayes, N. S. Jacobson, V. M. Follette, & M. J. Dougher (Eds.), *Acceptance and change: Content and context in psychotherapy* (pp. 37–45). Reno, NV: Context Press.

Edwards, S., & Dickerson, M. (1987). Intrusive unwanted thoughts: A two-stage model of control. *British Journal of Medical Psychology, 60,* 317–328.

Ellis, A. (1989). Rational-emotive therapy. In R. J. Corsini & D. Wedding (Eds.), *Current psychotherapies* (4th ed. pp. 197–238). Itasca, IL: Peacock.

Endler, N. S., & Parker, J. D. (1990). Multidimensional assessment of coping: A critical evaluation. *Journal of Personality and Social Psychology, 58,* 844–854.

Endler, N. S., & Parker, D. A. (1994). Assessment of multidimensional coping: Task, emotion, and avoidance strategies. *Psychological Assessment, 6,* 50–60.

Fairbank, J. A., Hansen, D. J., & Fitterling, J. M. (1991). Patterns of appraisal and coping across different stressor conditions among former prisoners of war with and without posttraumatic stress disorder. *Journal of Consulting and Clinical Psychology, 59,* 274–281.

Foa, E. B., Steketee, G., & Young, M. C. (1984). Agoraphobia: Phenomenological aspects, associated characteristics, and theoretical considerations. *Clinical Psychology Review, 4,* 431–457.

Foa, E. B., Zinbarg, R., & Rothbaum, B. O. (1992). Uncontrollability and unpredictability in posttraumatic stress disorder: An animal model. *Psychological Bulletin, 112,* 218–238.

Folkman, S., & Lazarus, R. S. (1988). *Ways of Coping Questionnaire, Research Edition.* Washington, DC: Consulting Psychologists Press.

Follette, V. M. (1994). Acceptance and commitment in the treatment of incest survivors: A contextual approach. In S. C. Hayes, N. S. Jacobson, V. M. Follette, & M. Dougher, (Eds.), *Acceptance and change: Content and context in psychotherapy.* Reno, NV: Context Press.

Fondacaro, M. R., & Moos, R. H. (1987). Social support and Coping: A longitudinal analysis. *American Journal of Community Psychology, 15,* 653–673.

Frankl, V. E. (1975). Paradoxical intention and deflection. *Psychotherapy: Theory, Research and Practice, 12,* 226–237.

Frankl, V. E. (1984). *Man's search for meaning: Revised and updated.* New York: Washington Square Press.

Freud, S. (1966) *Introductory lectures on psychoanalysis.* New York: Norton. (Original published 1920)

Green, B. (1993). Identifying survivors at risk: Trauma and stressors across events, pp. 135–144. In J. P. Wilson & B. Raphael (Eds.), *International handbook of traumatic stress syndromes* (pp. 137–144). New York, Plenum.

Green, B., & Lindy, J. D. (1994). Post-traumatic stress disorder in victims of disaster. *Psychiatric Clinics of North America, 17,* 301–309.

Greenberg, L. (1994). Acceptance in experiential therapy. In S. C. Hayes, N. S. Jacobson, V. M. Follette, & M. J. Dougher (Eds.) *Acceptance and change: Content and context in psychotherapy (pp. 53–67). Reno: Context Press.*

Hayes, S. C. (1987). A contextual approach to therapeutic change. In N. S. Jacobson (Ed.), *Psychotherapists in clinical practice: Cognitive and behavioral perspectives* (pp. 327–387). New York: Guilford Press.

Hayes, S. C. (1994). Content, context, and the types of psychological acceptance. In S. C. Hayes, N. S. Jacobson, V. M. Follette, & M. J. Dougher (Eds.), *Acceptance and change: Content and context in psychotherapy* (pp. 13–32). Reno, NV: Context Press.

Hayes, S. C. (1996). *Acceptance and Action Questionnaire.* Reno, NV.

Hayes, S. C., & Brownstein, A. J. (1986). Mentalism, behavior–behavior relations, and a behavior analytic view of the purposes of science. *Behavior Analyst, 9, 175–190.*

Hayes, S. C., & Hayes, L. J. (1989). The verbal action of the listener as a basis for rule-governance. In S. C. Hayes (Ed.), *Rule-governed behavior: cognition, contingencies, and instructional control* (pp. 153–190). New York: Plenum.

Hayes, S. C., Kohlenberg, B. S., & Hayes, L. J. (1991). Transfer of consequential functions through simple and conditional equivalence classes. *Journal of Experimental Analysis of Behavior, 56,* 119–137.

Hayes, S. C., McCurry, S., Afari, N., & Wilson, K. G. (1992). *Acceptance and commitment therapy manual.* Unpublished manuscript.

Hayes, S. C., & Wilson, K. G. (1994). Acceptance and commitment therapy: Altering the verbal support for experiential avoidance. *Behavior Analyst, 17,* 289–203.

Hayes, S. C., Wilson, K. G., Gifford, E. V., Follette, V. M., & Strosahl, K. (1996). Experiential avoidance and behavioral disorders: A functional dimensional approach to diagnosis and treatment. *Journal of Consulting and Clinical Psychology, 64,* 1152–1168.

Helzer, J. E., Robins, L. N., & Davis, D. H. (1976). Depressive disorders in Vietnam returnees. *Journal of Mental and Nervous Disease, 163,* 177–185.

Helzer, J. E., Robins, L. N., & McEvoy, L. (1987). Post-traumatic stress disorder in the general population: Findings of the epidemiologic catchment area survey. *New England Journal of Medicine, 317,* 1630–1634.

Hendin, H., & Haas, A. P.(1991). Suicide and guilt as manifestations of PTSD in Vietnam combat veterans. *American Journal of Psychiatry, 148,* 586–591.

Herman, J. L. (1981). *Father–daughter incest.* Cambridge, MA: Harvard University Press.

Herman, C. P., & Polivy, J. (1993). Mental control of eating: Excitatory and inhibitory food thoughts. In D. M. Wegner & J. W. Pennebaker (Eds.), *Handbook of mental control* (pp. 491–505). Englewood Cliffs, NJ: Prentice-Hall.

Joseph, S., Williams, R., & Yule, W. (1995). Psychosocial perspectives on post-traumatic stress. *Clinical Psychology Review, 15,* 515–544.

Kabat-Zinn, J. (1990). *Full catastrophe living: Using the wisdom of your body and mind to face stress, pain and illness.* New York: Dell Publishing.

Kelly, A. E., & Kahn, J. H. (1994). Effects of suppression of personal intrusive thoughts. *Journal of Personality and Social Psychology, 66,* 998–1006.

Kendall, P. C., & Hollon, S. D. (1980). Cognitive self-statements in depression: Development of an Automatic Thoughts Questionnaire. *Cognitive Therapy and Research, 4,* 383–395.

Kohlenberg, R. J., Hayes, S. C., & Tsai, M. (1993). Radical behavioral psychotherapy: Two contemporary examples. *Clinical Psychology Review, 13,* 579–592.

Leitenberg, H., Greenwald, E., & Cado, S. (1992). A retrospective study of long-term methods of coping with having been sexually abused during childhood. *Child Abuse and Neglect, 16,* 399–407.

Linehan, M. M. (1993). *Cognitive-behavioral treatment of borderline personality disorder.* New York: Guilford Press.

Linehan, M. M. (1994). Acceptance and change: The central dialectic in psychotherapy. In S. C. Hayes, N. S. Jacobson, V. M. Follette, & M. J. Dougher (Eds.), *Acceptance and change: Content and context in psychotherapy* (pp. 73–86). Reno, NV: Context Press.

Macrae, C. N., Bodenhausen, G. V., Milne, A. B., & Jetten, J. (1994). Out of mind but back in sight: Stereotypes on the rebound. *Journal of Personality and Social Psychology, 67,* 808–817.

Marlatt, G. A., & Gordon, J. R. (Eds.) (1985). *Relapse prevention.* New York: Guilford Press.

McFall, M. E., Mackay, P. W., & Donovan, D. M. (1991). Combat-related PTSD and psychosocial adjustment problems among substance abusing veterans. *Journal of Nervous and Mental Disease, 179,* 33–38.

McGorry, P. D., Chanen, A., McCarthy, E., Van Riel, R., McKenzie, D., & Singh, B. S. (1991). Posttraumatic stress disorder following recent-onset psychosis: An unrecognized postpsychotic syndrome. *Journal of Nervous and Mental Disease, 179,* 253–258.

McMahon, R. C., Kelley, A., & Kouzekanani, K. (1993). Personality and coping styles in the prediction of dropout from treatment of cocaine abuse. *Journal of Personality Assessment, 61,* 147–155.

Miller, D. A. F., McCluskey-Fawcett, K., & Irving, L. M. (1993). The relationship between childhood sexual abuse and subsequent onset of bulimia nervosa. *Child Abuse and Neglect, 17,* 305–314.

Muris, P., Merckelback, H., van den Hout, M., & de Jong, P. (1992). Suppression of emotional and neutral material. *Behaviour Research and Therapy, 30,* 639–642.

Neimeyer, R. A. (1993). An appraisal of constructivist therapies. *Journal of Consulting and Clinical Psychology, 61,* 221–234.

Omer, R. J. (1992). Post-traumatic stress disorders and European war veterans. *British Journal of Clinical Psychology, 31,* 387–403.

Pennebaker, J. W., Hughes, C. F., & O'Heeron, R. C. (1987). The psychophysiology of confession: Linking inhibitory and psychosomatic processes. *Journal of Personality and Social Psychology, 52,* 781–793.

Pennebaker, J. W., & O'Heeron, R. C. (1984). Confiding in others and illness rate among spouses of suicide and accidental-death victims. *Journal of Abnormal Psychology, 93,* 473–476.

Perls, F. P., Hefferline, R. F., & Goodman, P. (1951). *Gestalt therapy.* New York: Julian Press.

Polusny, M. A., & Follette, V. M. (1995). Long-term correlates of child sexual abuse: Theory and review of the empirical literature. *Applied and Preventive Psychology, 4,* 143–166.

Rachman, S., & de Silva, P. (1978). Abnormal and normal obsessions. *Behaviour Research and Therapy, 16,* 233–248.

Rachman, S., & Hodgson, R. J. (1980). *Obsessions and compulsions.* Englewood Cliffs, NJ: Prentice-Hall.

Raskin, N. J., & Rogers, C. R. (1989). Person-centered therapy. In R. J. Corsini & D. Wedding (Eds.), *Current psychotherapies* (pp. 155–196). Itasca, IL: Peacock.

Riggs, D. S., Dancu, C. V., Gershuny, B. S., Greenberg, D., & Foa, E. B. (1992). Anger and posttraumatic stress disorder in female crime victims. *Journal of Traumatic Stress, 5,* 613–625.

Rodriguez, N., Ryan, S. W., & Foy, D. W. (1992, November). *Tension reduction and PTSD: Adult survivors of sexual abuse.* Paper presented at the annual meeting of the International Society for Traumatic Stress Studies, Los Angeles.

Rogers, C. A. (1961). *On becoming a person: A therapist's view of psychotherapy.* Boston: Houghton Mifflin.

Root, M. P. P. (1989). Treatment failures: The role of sexual victimization in women's addictive behavior. *American Journal of Orthopsychiatry, 59,* 542–549.

Salkovskis, P. M., & Campbell, P. (1994). Thought suppression induces intrusion in naturally occurring negative intrusive thoughts. *Behaviour Research and Therapy, 32,* 1–8.

Salkovskis, P. M., & Harrison, J. (1982). Abnormal and normal obsessions: A replication. *Behavior Research and Therapy, 22,* 549–552.

Schetky, D. H. (1990). A review of the literature on the long-term effects of child sexual abuse. In R. P. Kluft (Ed.), *Incest-related syndromes of adult psychopathology* (pp. 35–54). Washington, DC: American Psychiatric Association Press.

Shapiro, S., & Dominiak, G. M. (1992). *Sexual trauma and psychopathology: Clinical intervention with adult survivors.* New York: Lexington Books.

Shaver, K. G., & Drown, D. (1986). On causality, responsibility, and self-blame: A theoretical note. *Journal of Personality and Social Psychology, 50,* 697–702.

Silver, R. L., Boon, C., & Stones, M. H. (1983). Searching for meaning in misfortune: Making sense of incest. *Journal of Social Issues, 39,* 81–102.

Southwick, S. M., Yehuda, R., & Giller, E. L., Jr. (1991). Characterization of depression in war-related posttraumatic stress disorder. *American Journal of Psychiatry, 148,* 179–183.

Stephens, R. S., & Curtin, L. (1995). Alcohol and depression: Effects on mood and biased, processing of self-relevant information. *Psychology of Addictive Behaviors, 9,* 211–222.

Strosahl, K. (1991). Cognitive and behavioral treatment of the personality disordered patient. In C. Austad & B. Berman (Eds.), *Psychotherapy in managed health care: The optimal use of time and resources* (pp. 185–201). Washington, DC: American Psychological Association Press.

Strosahl, K. D., Hayes, S. C., Bergan, J., & Romano, P. (1998). Assessing the field effectiveness of Acceptance and Commitment Therapy: an example of the manipulated training research method. *Behavior Therapy, 29,* 35–64.

Suls, J., & Fletcher, B. (1985). The relative efficacy of avoidant and nonavoidant coping strategies: A meta-analysis. *Health Psychology, 4,* 249–288.

Sutherland, G., Newman, B., & Rachman, S. (1982). Experimental investigations of the relations between mood and intrusive unwanted cognitions. *British Journal of Medical Psychology, 55,* 127–138.

Sutter, J. (1986). Les neuroses traumatiques deguerre: Evolution des ides. *Psychiatrie Francais, 5,* 9–20.

Tennen, H., & Affleck, G. (1990). Blaming others for threatening events. *Psychological Bulletin, 107,* 209–232.

Trimble, M. R. (1981). *Post-traumatic neurosis.* Chichester, UK: Wiley.

Trinder, H.,& Salkovskis, P. M. (1994). Personally relevant intrusions outside the laboratory: Long-term suppression increases intrusion. *Behaviour Research and Therapy, 32,* 833–842.

Turner, R. A. King, P. R., & Tremblay, P. F. (1992). Coping styles and depression among psychiatric outpatients. *Personality and Individual Differences, 13,* 1145–1147.

Wegner, D. M. (1994). Ironic processes of mental control. *Psychological Review, 101,* 34–52.

Wegner, D. M., Schneider, D. J., Carter, S., III, & White, L. (1987). Paradoxical effects of thought suppression. *Journal of Personality and Social Psychology, 58,* 409–418.

Wegner, D. M., Shortt, J. W., Blake, A. W., & Page, M. S. (1990). The suppression of exciting thoughts. *Journal of Personality and Social Psychology, 58,* 409–418.

Wegner, D. M., & Zanakos, S. I. (1994). Chronic thought suppression. *Journal of Personality, 62,* 615–640.

Weiner, B. (1985). Spontaneous causal thinking. *Psychological Bulletin, 97,* 74–84.

Weiner, B. (1986). *An attributional theory of motivation and emotion.* New York: Springer Verlag.

Wells, A., & Matthews, G. (1994). *Attention and emotion: A clinical perspective.* Hillsdale, NJ: Erlbaum.

Wenzlaff, R. M., & Wegner, D. M. (1990). *How depressed individuals cope with unwanted thoughts.* Unpublished research data.

Williams, R. M., Hodgkinson, P., Joseph, S., & Yule, W. (1995). Attitudes to emotion, crisis support and distress 30 months after the capsize of a passenger ferry. *Crisis Intervention, 1,* 209–214.

Yalom, I. D. (1980). *Existential Psvchotherapy.* New York: Basic Books.

CHAPTER ELEVEN

Sexual Revictimization
RISK FACTORS AND PREVENTION

MARYLENE CLOITRE

Sexual assault is one of the most frequent types of trauma associated with the development of posttraumtic stress disorder (PTSD) (Norris, 1992) and is a highly prevalent event, with one out of every eight women experiencing a sexual assault some time in her life (National Victim Center and Crime Victims Research and Treatment Center, 1992). Of note however, sexual assault in adulthood is not evenly distributed across the female population. Rather, there are certain subgroups of women who are more at risk than others. One of the most robust risk factors for sexual assault is a history of childhood abuse. Women who have experienced childhood sexual abuse are 2.5 to 3.1 times more likely to experience a sexual assault in adulthood than those without an abuse history (Cloitre, Tardiff, Marzuk, Leon, & Potera, 1996; Wyatt, Guthrie, & Notgrass, 1992). A review of epidemiological data collected on the prevalence and types of sexual assault and abuse in a community sample has revealed that among women reporting a history of sexual assault, the majority (59%) report having been assaulted in both childhood and adulthood, with much smaller numbers reporting only one or the other form of assault (Wyatt et al., 1992).

These data indicate that retraumatized women make up the largest subgroup of sexually assaulted women. Given this, sexual assault research should have as a priority the identification of the psychological characteristics of women with a history of childhood sexual abuse that put them "at risk" for adult sexual assault. It is also important to begin developing prevention programs for at-risk women and adolescent girls that target and reduce these risk factors. This chapter reviews the available data on the potential assault risk factors among women with a history of childhood abuse. It also presents a developing model of retraumatization and an intervention designed to reduce risk for repeated sexual assaults.

THEORETICAL ORIENTATION:
A SOCIAL–DEVELOPMENTAL PERSPECTIVE

Whether an assault occurred in childhood or adulthood matters, as the impact of interpersonal violence first occurring in childhood may be qualitatively different from that occurring in adulthood. It has been suggested that understanding the sequelae of childhood sexual violence in terms of a posttraumatic stress disorder (PTSD) model underestimates the range of negative effects (Briere, 1992; Finkelhor, 1990; Herman, 1992; van der Kolk, Roth, Pelcovitz, & Mandel, 1993). Contemporary developmental theorists posit that abuse that takes place in childhood profoundly interferes with developmental tasks of that period, among which are included the critical development of affect regulation and interpersonal relatedness. The disruption of affect regulation skills and interpersonal relatedness are hypothesized to create risk for subsequent assault in various ways. Below are descriptions of developmental processes associated with affect regulation and interpersonal relatedness, the ways in which these processes are disrupted as a result of abuse, and the way in which these disruptions create risk for future assaults.

AFFECT REGULATION

The capacity to regulate internal states and behavioral responses to external stressors is a skill facilitated by caretakers. For example, children's excitement and/or fear of the new and unknown is moderated by parental soothing and guidance concerning appropriate approach and avoidance behaviors. In general, effective caretakers engage in behaviors that modulate the child's physiological state, providing a balance between soothing and stimulation (Bowlby, 1984; van der Kolk, 1987). Under these circumstances, children learn how to take care of themselves effectively and, alternatively, how to get help when they are distressed (van der Kolk, 1996).

Sexual abuse interferes with affect regulation development in two ways. First, the abuse itself directly contributes to affect regulation problems as it promotes chronic arousal. Second, the family environments of children who experience abuse provide little learning opportunity to develop affect regulation skills. Caregivers in such families often have affect regulation and impulse control problems themselves, such as affective disorders and alcoholism (Shearer, Peters, Quaytman, & Ogden; 1990). Thus, normal development is stymied because the individual is exposed to unusual amounts of arousal, and he or she has very little guidance for learning effective ways of coping with this or other forms of aroused state.

Risk Factors Related to Affect Dsyregulation

Evidence is accumulating that certain problems associated with affect regulation such as alexithymia and dissociation are risk factors for sexual assault (Cloitre, Scarvalone, & Difede, 1997). In addition, there is anecdotal evidence that affect dysregulation, defined as alternating experiences of emotional flooding and numbing, may also be a contributing risk factor. Last, use of alcohol and drugs, often reported as coping mechanisms intended to blunt painful or overwhelming affect, has been repeatedly demonstrated as a risk factor for sexual assault.

Alexithymia

Alexithymia refers to difficulties in identifying and labeling feeling states. This difficulty may have its source in chronic hyperarousal experiences in which the intensity of arousal may make it difficult to discriminate among feelings such as anger fear and anxiety. It is also possible that problems in appropriately labeling feelings are the result of poor or inaccurate teaching by caretakers who themselves have limited abilities in this regard, or who are motivated to mislabel a child's emotional states to normalize or deny abuse. Differentiating among feeling states is a skill that develops in childhood, and recent data suggest that childhood abuse may subvert this skill (Cicchetti & White, 1990). A recently completed study found that women whose first sexual assault occurred in childhood were more likely to be alexithymic than women who had been assaulted for the first time in adulthood, even when other additional traumatic events in adulthood, such as domestic violence, were taken into account (Cloitre et al., 1997).

Alexithymia may be especially implicated in acquaintance assaults. Difficulty identifying and labeling feeling states results in a diminished emotional vocabulary and affectively out-of-sync self-presentation, which may lead others to more easily minimize or actively disregard an alexithymic individual's "no." Perhaps equally important, such individuals may be less able to accurately read others' emotional cues (e.g., to distinguish anger that is appropriate vs. dangerous), thus diminishing their capacity to respond effectively in interpersonally threatening situations.

Dissociation

Dissociation has also been implicated as a risk factor for subsequent assault among individuals with childhood abuse. In the study described earlier, women with both adult and childhood sexual assaults were found to report dissociative experiences much more frequently than women who had been assaulted for the first time in adulthood and those who had never been assaulted (Cloitre et al., 1997).

Although there has been some controversy about the definition of dissociation, it is typically understood as an experience in which the individual is cognitively and emotionally removed from the current circumstance and has reduced or no available memory for it. The high level of dissociation among retraumatized women may make them frequently unaware of their environment and insensitive to potential risks of a particular environment. In addition, being in a dissociative state may make them look confused or distracted, marking them as "easy targets" to sexual and other predators. Last, poor recall of experiences and events occurring during a dissociative state may make an assaulted woman less likely to either reach out for help and/or less likely to be believed, both of which may reduce the likelihood of effecting any psychological, social, or legal intervention that can reduce risk for future events.

Emotional Flooding and Numbing

Emotional flooding and numbing have been anecdotally reported as potential risk factors for assault. Floods of fear, or the absence of such feelings in the face of threat triggers, can derail appropriate flight-or-fight responses. Women who have been repeatedly assaulted report overreaction to low-level threats and, alternatively, a lack of reaction or appropriate response to an event or trigger that indicates risk of assault. High-level triggers such as trespassing of physical boundaries (e.g., being touched at work, being approached on the street) or presence of a weapon may not generate a fear response strong enough or early enough to initiate protective action. A recent study found that the number of danger cues identified by objective raters in a single-event rape narrative was negatively correlated with the number of sexual assaults the victim had experienced, suggesting a relationship between poor risk recognition and a history of multiple assaults (Meadows, Jaycox, Webb, & Foa, 1996). A client remarked that her feelings of fear wildly alternated so much that she could never trust them to function as a guide for action. She said she had been physically abused so often as a child that her "danger sensor was smashed." More research is needed assessing the relationship between a history of repeated trauma and the capacity to have accurate subjective experiences of threat in order to determine a useful intervention for this potential problem.

Alcohol and Drug Use

Alcohol and drug use are well-known risk factors for sexual assault, especially among adolescents (Gidycz, Hanson, & Layman, 1995; Koss & Dinero, 1989; Greene, Navarro, & Gidycz, 1995; Muelenhard & Linton, 1987). In addition, drug and alcohol abuse are highly prevalent among individuals with childhood sexual abuse (Browne & Finkelhor, 1986, Polusny & Follette, 1995). These data suggest that alcohol and drug use may be factors that mediate revictimization: Women who have been abused as children are more likely to abuse substances, which, in turn, contributes to further risk for additional assaults. At least one prospective longitudinal study of a large sample of college students has found that while prior victimization is the most robust risk factor for future victimization, alcohol use by victims was consistently correlated with victimization incidents and sometimes predictive of future incidents (Greene et al., 1995).

INTERPERSONAL RELATEDNESS

A developmentally sensitive assessment of potential risk factors among individuals with a history of childhood sexual abuse cannot overlook the fact that abuse occurs during a time when a child is organizing templates or schemas for relating to others and identifying effective contingencies for accomplishing this goal. Obviously, templates of interpersonal relatedness for the child from an abusive family involve contingencies that, whatever their particulars, suggest that to be interpersonally engaged means to be abused, and that abuse is a way to be connected.

The strength and resilience of these potentially maladaptive interpersonal templates can be appreciated if understood from the tenets of an interpersonal schema model (Safran, 1990), which derives from attachment theory. Bowlby (1969) and others have suggested that there is a biologically wired-in propensity for maintaining relatedness to the available caretaker. This biological imperative has its basis in the enormous dependency of the young on the caretaker for basic survival-relevant activity such as provision of safety and sustenance. One way this attachment is organized and maintained is through the development of interpersonal schemas that provide information to the child about the conditions and circumstances under which relatednesss occurs, so that the child may utilize this information to facilitate attachment to the caretaker and thus maximize survival. Typically, simple behaviors such as proximity and vocal calls elicit protection from caretakers, and caretakers, in turn, receive intrinsic satisfaction from the provision of protection and safety to their offspring (Bowlby, 1969).

The interpersonal schema for attachment in abusive settings clearly deviates from this format. For example, in a physically assaultive home, proximity, a condition for care, may also elicit physical assault. Thus, care and physical assault become paired. In sexually abusive homes, proximity can elicit sexual activity and other inappropriate demands on children that far exceed their cognitive, physical, and emotional resources.

Because these schemas are assumed to be the templates for future behaviors, and because they are automatically activated, it is easy to see how negative patterns set down in childhood can guide the adult toward repeating activities that are maladaptive in adulthood. For example, a young woman from an abusive family who has developed the understanding that interpersonal relatedness is contingent on sexual behavior is more likely to accept sexual activity as a way of emotionally connecting to others whether she is interested in sex or not. In our clinic, we have seen that women from abused homes are relatively unlikely to see the exploitation of their physical, sexual, and emotional assets in exchange for the "care" provided in romantic or other relationships.

Interpersonal schema theory is valuable because it provides a non-victim-blaming way to understand repeated sexual assaults and abusive relationships experienced by individuals with histories of childhood abuse. The theory suggests that there is a predisposition to base attitudes and actions upon past experience and that the interpersonal belief system that emerges from these experiences has its basis in efforts to adapt effectively to the given environment for satisfaction of relational and survival needs.

For those whose lives have been comprised of positive experiences and loving interpersonal relationships, the automatic activation of interpersonal schemas does them no harm and, in fact, probably will enhance the probability of positive relationships. In contrast, those whose lives have been comprised of trauma and negative relationships have a burden to identify and must change the automatic schemas in order to protect themselves from the negative consequences of inadvertently repeating their own histories.

A recent study suggested that the tendency to "repeat" one's history via automatic application of interpersonal schemas is a behavior that is typical of both abused and nonabused individuals; the difference is in the contents and consequences of the schemas. We assessed the content and structure of interpersonal schemas of three groups of women: incest victims who had experienced a subsequent sexual assault, incest victims who had never been sexually assaulted in adulthood, and women who had never been assaulted or abused (Cloitre & Scarvalone, 1995). The interpersonal beliefs of the revictimized women were strongly negative and reflected the expectation of negative responses regardless of the person with whom they were interacting (e.g., mother, father, friend) or the particulars of the situation (e.g., competitive, cooperative). In contrast, never-assaulted women expected generally positive responses regardless of person or situation. Thus, both groups showed relatively "rigid" interpersonal expectations that differed only in valence (positive vs. negative) but not in range or flexibility. Incest survivors who had not been assaulted in adulthood differed from both of these groups. While women in this group held somewhat negative interpersonal beliefs, they showed more variable expectations of others, depending on the person and situation. Thus, the nonrevictimized women showed a greater range of interpersonal expectations, which suggests the presence of greater flexibility in their approach to interpersonal events.

Although the data are cross-sectional and causal inferences must be made with caution, we surmise that the characteristic of relatively high interpersonal flexibility among the subgroup of incest survivors may make them less at risk for abusive relationships or assaults, as they may be sensitive to opportunities for more positive relating and/or reworking of negative circumstances. Research is under way to identify the experiential factors that may contribute to interpersonal flexibility, such as the presence of role models outside of the abusive family system (e.g., teachers, strong peer friendships, aunts or uncles), positive therapy experiences, or the good fortune of having developed and sustained healthy intimate relationships in early adulthood.

PTSD AS A RISK FACTOR FOR RETRAUMATIZATION

Several epidemiological studies have found that after an individual has experienced one high-magnitude stressor, he or she is at risk for experiencing additional traumatic events over the lifespan (Breslau, Davis, Andreski, & Peterson, 1991; Kilpatrick, Saunders, Veronen, Best, & Von, 1987). Of even greater significance is the recent report that, at least among rape victims, the presence of PTSD, in and of itself, contributes to risk for repeated traumatization (National Victim Center and Crime Victims Research and Treatment Center, 1992). Given these findings, it becomes critical to determine whether individuals abused as children have PTSD related to the childhood abuse and/or assault.

There has been less than a complete consensus concerning the existence of a diagnostic category that adequately captures the range of symptoms associated with a history of childhood abuse. However, the accumulation of data indicates that PTSD is a salient, if not core, component of the complex of symptoms related to childhood sexual abuse (CSA). The DSM-IV field trials identified the prevalence of CSA-related PTSD as 74% in a combined community and clinical sample (Newman, personal communication, 1996). A study assessing a clinical sample of 47 women with CSA found that 69% had PTSD (Rowan, Foy, Rodriguez, & Ryan, 1994). In another clinical study of 26 women with a history of CSA, 73% were diagnosed with PTSD (O'Neill & Gupta, 1991). In our own clinical sample of 98 women with CSA, Structured Clinical Interview for DSM-III-R (SCID) assessments revealed that 73% had DSM-III-R PTSD and that PTSD, was the most prevalent Axis I disorder.

Given that PTSD has been identified as a risk factor for additional sexual assaults among rape victims, it is possible that PTSD associated with childhood sexual abuse may be associated with even greater risk for subsequent assault than PTSD related to adulthood rape. This is because individuals who have PTSD deriving from childhood abuse are at risk for a greater portion of their lifespan and the risk includes a period of life (childhood/adolescence) in which coping strategies for responding effectively to risk may be underdeveloped.

IMPLICATIONS FOR A TREATMENT MODEL

The model from which the treatment intervention described here is derived assumes that there are three categories of psychological risk factors for revictimization: (1) problems in affect regulation, (2) problems in interpersonal functioning, and (3) PTSD. The model also identifies two related sources of these problems. One derives from the abuse itself and its direct psychological sequelae such as disrupted thresholds for arousal and posttraumatic stress symptoms. The other is the familial or caretaking environment, which is frequently limited or highly maladaptive in providing a learning environment for the development of an effective repertoire of basic affect regulation and interpersonal skills. This assessment suggests that the reduction of risk for future assault will require a two-component intervention: one focused on skills training related to the development of affect regulation and interpersonal abilities and the second on the amelioration of the direct psychological sequelae of trauma such as posttraumatic stress and other symptoms.

A PROPOSED TREATMENT MODEL: SKILLS TRAINING IN AFFECT AND INTERPERSONAL REGULATION/PROLONGED EXPOSURE

The treatment model recommended for retraumatized women is a two-phase model in which the first phase of treatment focuses on skills training in affect and interpersonal regulation (STAIR). Training includes skills development in (1) identifying and labeling feeling states (especially feelings of threat), (2) tolerating distress and modulating negative affect, and (3) effectively negotiating difficult interpersonal situations that require varying blends of assertiveness and self-control. Cognitive-behavioral techniques used to meet these goals include monitoring and rating feeling states, positive imagery and self-statements, identifying and challenging maladaptive cognitions, and role plays that emphasize context-sensitive and flexible interpersonal responses. Treatment is organized into eight sessions, although the treatment can be lengthened depending on the client's needs.

The second phase of treatment is a modified eight-session prolonged exposure (PE) treatment adapted from Foa's treatment for rape-related PTSD (Foa, Rothbaum, Riggs, & Murdock, 1991). The goal of this phase is to engage in exposure to the trauma memory in order to resolve posttraumatic stress symptoms such as fearfulness, nightmares, and irritability.

In the two-module approach, the STAIR phase takes place first, so that the increased ability to regulate feeling states obtained from Phase 1 can be utilized to enhance the effectiveness of the PTSD-related exposure work of Phase 2. However, the modules can be used separately. In particular, the STAIR module can be used alone as a skills training/prevention program for individuals at risk for assault who do not suffer from significant PTSD symptoms.

ASSESSMENT

There is growing evidence that the psychological effects of trauma are cumulative (Follette, Polusny, Bechtle, & Naugle, 1996; Nishith, Mechanic, & Resick, 1997). Thus, it is important to obtain a thorough history of trauma across the lifespan, ranging from childhood physical, sexual, and emotional abuse to adult events, including exposures to natural or man-made disasters.

Assessment of PTSD can be effectively accomplished using the Clinician Administered PTSD Scale (CAPS), which includes separate frequency and intensity scales for PTSD symptoms and items that assess social and occupational functioning (Blake et al., 1995). In addition, the Structured Clinical Interview for DSM-IV (SCID; Spitzer, Williams, Gibbon, & First, 1994) is useful in assessing the entire range of Axis I and Axis II disorders. Of special diagnostic interest in this population is the presence of complex PTSD, which can be assessed using the Structured Interview for Disorders of Extreme Stress (SIDES; Pelcovitz et al., 1997). This clinician-administered instrument systematically assesses typical problems in affect regulation, somatization, dissociation, and problems in meaning systems concerning self and the world.

A good history of physical health should be obtained, since women with multiple traumas tend to have a relatively large number of health problems, some of which (e.g., sexually transmitted diseases) may impact on psychological and interpersonal issues that emerge during treatment. Self-report questionnaires, which may not be typical in general treatment settings, but which are useful for assessment of trauma-related problems and symptoms and can be used by both client and therapist during the course of treatment, include assessment of alexithymia (Toronto Alexithymia Scale; Taylor, Bagby, Ryan, Parker, & Doody, 1988), anger expression (State–Trait Anger Inventory; Spielberger, 1988), Negative Mood Regulation (Catanzaro & Mearns, 1990) and dissociative experiences (Dissociative Experiences Scale; Bernstein & Putnam, 1986). Last, use of self-report measures evaluating social support (e.g., Social Adjustment Scale; Weissman & Bothell, 1976), interpersonal skills (e.g., Inventory for Interpersonal Problems; Horowitz, Rosenberg, Baer, Ureno, & Villasenor, 1988) and coping skills (e.g., Coping Orientation to Problems Experienced; Scheir & Carver, 1985) will help identify strengths and characteristic responses to stressors, all of which will help shape treatment goals and activities.

A complete evaluation of a multiply traumatized woman is a lengthy and emotionally draining experience for the client. The client may be providing information about her history and level of functioning that she has never before revealed. While this can be painful, it is often a relief for the client to be provided with a coherent understanding of her symptom picture and to engage in a collaborative and supportive effort in organizing a plan for treatment.

GUIDELINES FOR SELECTION

Any individual who has experienced childhood sexual abuse and additional assaults in childhood or adulthood may be considered for this treatment. Assessment of role functioning, dissociation, alexithymia, interpersonal schemas, and posttraumatic stress symptomatology will help determine where the emphases in treatment should be placed. There are certain problems for which this treatment is not ideally suited and which require referral to alternative programs. These include active substance abuse, self-mutilation, high risk for suicide, and presence of a dissociative disorder. Individuals in domestic violence situations or battering relationships also need these problems directly and immediately addressed in programs developed specifically for these purposes. Last, it should be noted that women who have chronic mental illnesses such as schizophrenia and schizo–affective disorder are among the group of women most at risk for retraumatization (Cloitre et al., 1996). Often, these women have expressed concerns that traditional cognitive-behavioral programs are not geared toward them: They do not understand the material, nor do they share the same perspective. There are programs currently being developed for the chronically mentally ill with these issues in mind, and referral to this type of program would be ideal (Jonikas & Cook, 1994).

CLINICAL APPLICATION

The following case describes the situation of a multiply traumatized woman whose most significant symptom was avoidance of cognitive, emotional, and behavioral difficulties associated with her many traumas. Underlying her avoidant style in all of these domains was a sense of helplessness–hopelessness regarding her recovery from the consequences of her traumas and her ability to protect herself from future traumas. As treatment progressed, it became clear that she viewed herself as having one source of strength from which she derived great pride, and that was her ability to withstand the abuse of others. The client not only believed that she was "fated" for a life of trauma, but also she embraced it as a guiding principle in her life. This perspective had multiple functions: it provided a source of personal identity and stability in an otherwise chaotic life, a sense of control and mastery over herself and others, and a sense of meaning and purposefulness for herself.

The treatment focused on (1) identifying and counteracting her trauma-related emotional, cognitive, and behavioral avoidance activities; (2) identifying existing coping skills, which provided evidence that she was not as helpless–hopeless as she felt herself to be, and (3) providing motivation for her to "give up" her identity as a victim by identifying alternative interpersonal schemas and behaviors that would support connection to others and the development of healthy, nonabusive relationships. Once these tasks were set in motion, the emotional processing of the trauma via prolonged exposure to the trauma memories was initiated and successfully completed.

Case Description

Ms. F. came for evaluation of PTSD under the recommendation of her psychopharmacologist, whom she had been seeing for treatment of moderate to severe depression. Ms. F., 48 years old, spoke in a soft voice with a faint Hungarian accent and revealed herself to be a gentle and well-educated individual. Approximately 1 year earlier, Ms. F. had been raped by an intruder into her fiancé's apartment while he was away. Her recollection of the rape and the accompanying violent physical assault was vivid, although she had no memory of the several hours after the rape she had spent in a local emergency room. Following the rape, she had not been able to shake a growing conviction that the world was a dangerous place and that she was constitutionally unable to protect herself.

She had quit her job as a manager of a small art gallery because the presence of men alone in the store with her made her feel vulnerable and elicited frightening images of being attacked, raped, and tortured. She began feeling highly anxious and avoided situations that reminded her of the rape and in which she felt she might be attacked, particularly elevators, taxis, and empty streets. She retreated to the comfort and safety of her apartment but in the process lost connection with some of her friends, who, over the year, lost sympathy with her situation. She had also broken off her engagement because she believed her fiancé blamed her for the rape and had lost desire for her. She maintained her income by translating art history books, but her concentration had deteriorated to the point that she was unable to translate more than a paragraph a day. She had begun sleeping a lot to escape her preoccupation with her fears, and from exhaustion derived from the anxiety symptoms she experienced when she did venture out. Her sleep was fitful and punctuated with nightmares of violence.

Upon questioning, Ms. F. revealed a history of having been emotionally and physically abused by her mother throughout her childhood. She also reported that she had been born at the outset of World War II and had spent the first 5 years of her life exposed to "bombs, fire, deaths, and hysterical adults." At ages 5 through 8, she was sexually abused by a neighborhood man. The abuse ended when her family relocated. In her late teens, she came to the United States and began a successful career as a model, followed by graduate training and employment as an art historian, which she very much enjoyed. She had a few long-term and passionate romances but had left those relationships when discord or conflict developed and had never married or had children. She had experienced a rape previous to the rape for which she had come into treatment. The man had been a stranger who had assaulted her in the vestibule of her home. He was eventually identified as a serial rapist in the neighborhood and was convicted of rape and imprisoned. She had also experienced a mugging and a significant accident in which she broke her arm and leg, and for which she required extensive physical rehabilitation.

The most recent rape seemed to have crystallized negative beliefs about herself and the world that had otherwise lain dormant. She viewed the world as a dangerous place, believed that there was something about her that attracted violence, and was full of self-blame for the traumas and problems she had experienced, from the rapes to the failed relationships. She felt doomed to a life of accumulated traumas and expected that she would die a horrible, violent death. She had never been in individual psychotherapy. Shortly after the rape, she had entered a rape survivor group but had become extremely upset listening to the experiences of other rape victims and had left the group after the second session.

Treatment Overview: Setting the Interpersonal Frame

Regardless of the form of intervention applied in the treatment of the multiply traumatized woman, there is one unifying aspect of treatment, and that is the therapist–client alliance. Because clients with a history of childhood abuse may have negative responses to perceived authority figures, a first and perhaps continuing challenge throughout the treatment will be managing issues of power, control, and trust in the treatment process. The therapist must be aware that the client has little reason to expect good to come from those in positions of authority and that he or she is likely to react negatively to strongly didactic approaches to treatment. It is easy for client and therapist to "lock horns" on issues that threaten the client's sense of safety, such as changing comfortable but maladaptive behaviors. The therapist can step out of power struggles by simply presenting the alternatives to the client and letting the client select for him- or herself the treatment activity. Usually, the ultimate choice is between continuing in patterns of behavior that the client has already decided to reject and taking risks in doing new and frightening things. The client will need to decide for him- or herself what he or she wishes to do. In the case of Ms. F., it seemed wiser to have her use her keen intelligence to work through some of the conflicting issues herself and take responsibility for solving the problems at hand. For example, while Ms. F.'s avoidance behaviors made her feel somewhat safe, she realized they never made her feel free or happy. It was her choice to decide between feeling "safe" in the short run versus "free" in the long run. This process provided a more thorough analysis of the pros and cons of a choice point in treatment than the therapist might otherwise have obtained. It also instilled a sense of responsibility and mastery in the client and increased motivation for follow through on behavioral plans.

Phase I: Skills Training in Affective and Interpersonal Regulation

Affect Regulation

Skills training in this area involves (1) enhancing emotional awareness and (2) developing greater ability in modulating negative feelings and tolerating distress. In the first sessions, the client is introduced to self-monitoring of feelings of distress, including identifying triggering situations and the intensity and frequency of the distress. Clients are also taught how to label and identify different feeling states (e.g., happy, sad, mad). Although this exercise appears quite simple, it can be a revolutionary experience for individuals who, from early life, have avoided or never been guided in differentiating and labeling their own feeling states. Often these exercises provide validation of feelings that were previously ignored or unrecognized. Such exercises can also produce experiences of self-expansion on the client's part: a "filling out" of his or her emotional self that is validated by the therapist's interest in the client's reports, thoughts, and concerns.

The client is also quickly introduced to self-soothing and affect-regulation activities, so that as feelings emerge there is some ability to moderate or control them. These coping strategies include deep breathing, utilization of time-out (which can vary from 3 minutes to a weekend), and cognitive exercises such as thought stopping, shifting of attention, and positive imagery and self-statements. In addition, identification and countering of maladaptive cognitions are introduced in the context of inquiring about clients' fears around experiencing and expressing their feelings. Frequent beliefs that emerge are "I'll get out of control," "I'll hit someone," and "I'll become my abuser." Elaborating on and countering these beliefs help the client engage more readily and confidently in emotional experiencing.

New coping techniques are added every session, with demonstration and practice followed by "between-session" daily practice of each skill. Each session also includes review of the between-session work and additional practice focused on trouble spots.

In the fourth session, after the client has begun to develop some affect regulation skills, he or she is introduced the concept of allowing and accepting the experience of distress. There is significant psychoeducation on this point, since many find the concept of accepting pain somewhat counterintuitive. However, the goal is for the client to understand that some distress in life in unavoidable. This is particularly true for clients who will ultimately need to confront and assimilate the pain of their trauma histories. Other psychoeducational aspects of distress tolerance include the notions that distress is a part of the process of changing oneself, that in order to experience positive feelings, one must allow for negative feelings, and that the inability to accept unavoidable distress leads to increased pain and suffering.

Client and therapist review situations that the client finds distressing and review the pros and cons of tolerating each situation. For example, Ms. F. and her therapist reviewed the distress Ms. F. experienced with even the smallest of physical intimacies with her boyfriend. Being embraced by him made her feel nauseous and disgusted. Her sole desire in these moments was to jump out of the embrace. Client and therapist reviewed reasons why she might want to tolerate this experience, which included her desire to connect with someone who seemed to understand her history and genuinely liked her and, more generally, to be able to have positive reactions to touch and physical contact.

Client and therapist should identify and practice coping techniques to assist in distress tolerance. These can include titrating the duration of the experience, deep-breathing exercises, self-statements such as "I can bear this for a little while," or temporarily leaving the upsetting situation and finding a soothing alternative activity (e.g., resting, taking a walk, washing hands and face).

Interventions for Affective Regulation Treatment Obstacles

The program described thus far is composed of relatively standard cognitive-behavioral techniques. The demonstration and practice of these techniques will pose little difficulty for the therapist. More challenging is coping with the client's desire to avoid feelings and his or her lack of confidence and sense of mastery in the process. These difficulties are often bound up with the client's history of abuse and his or her family–social learning experiences. The therapist will need to find ways to maintain the client's motivation and to introduce coping skills in ways that have value and meaning to a person with chronic and early life trauma. Listed below are four interventions for coping with avoidance and "sense of mastery" problems.

1. *Provide a historical frame for avoidant behaviors.* The retraumatized individual may believe that in using avoidance strategies she is behaving in ways that will be physically and emotionally protective. This may be because the coping strategies she uses, such as emotional numbing, denial, and acceptance of abuse, were actually adaptive under the circumstances of inescapable and chronic abuse. Because such strategies have worked in the past, their current application may give the client a sense of mastery, whereas the application of new strategies may engender anxiety. In addition, these strategies may be deeply entrenched, because their use may extend as far back as childhood, and the client may have the belief that they are the best and only coping strategies available to her.

One way to reduce anxiety and rigidity about coping strategies is to first point out the effectiveness of the client's coping strategies as they applied to past situations. The client has, after all, managed to survive through a series of traumas or escape from a chronically traumatizing environment. Pointing out the client's basic success will establish the fact that the client has the capacity and resources to cope with difficult situations. With this reassurance in mind, the client may be more able to begin contemplating both the frightening and wonderful view that she is no longer in the chronically abusive situation and that she needs to change coping strategies to adapt to a changed or changing life context.

2. *Provide psychoeducation about negative consequences of avoidance.* Clients with trauma histories who avoid their feelings also often avoid thinking about their avoidance. It is useful to draw out explicitly the burdens of avoidance, a consideration which the client may have given little focused attention. It is useful to review the fact that although avoidance appears to give a person control in the short run (e.g., immediate reduction in symptoms), he or she is really out of control with regard to long-term goals. For example, Ms. F. avoided many situations—cars, elevators, downtown areas, and certain park areas. While this

activity provided her with immediate relief from her anxiety, her life began faltering, especially her search for a job, because there were so many places to which she would not travel for interviews. Furthermore, avoidance limited her life experience, including pleasurable activities and feelings. Despite the fact that avoidance seemed to provide Ms. F. with brief emotional respites, she experienced almost chronic anxiety and fear, with little room for other feelings. She had few experiences with which to counter the powerful images and feelings that were associated with her catastrophic predictions of what were to happen if she ventured out. Her emotional experiencing became a uniform and rather exhausting blend of fear, anxiety, and depression. For many individuals abused as children, avoiding feelings and engaging in a limited set of prescribed behaviors were among the few coping strategies available in a chronically abusive home. Therapist and client need to review ways in which these behaviors ultimately create a prison in adulthood.

3. *Assess coping skills.* In order to help the client leave behind familiar but maladaptive coping strategies, it is extremely useful to identify coping skills that are currently effective and others that, with some adaptation, can be put to good use. Client and therapist should systematically review the coping strategies the client currently uses to deal with difficult feelings and situations. The Negative Mood Regulation self-report instrument (Cantanzaro & Mearns, 1990) is one measure that can be used to assess baseline coping skills. This measure rates how strongly a client believes him- or herself capable of engaging in a particular coping strategy (e.g., "Telling myself it will pass will help calm me down").

Sometimes clients cannot report any coping strategies that they view positively. Often, however, the client does have some good coping skills—they are simply undiscernible from within a negative or abusive life context. The therapist can help the client "translate" skills used in negative life circumstance for healthier purposes. For example, a recovered heroin addict was reminded that she had always been able to "hustle" enough money together to satisfy her addiction. She did, in fact, have a very good "sales person" personality and was very likable. Her therapist was able to help her view these behaviors as skills that could aid her in finding satisfactory employment in a people-oriented setting. Successful transition of behaviors from one life circumstance to another can provide a sense of continuity in self-identity and speed the process of skills enhancement. In the case of Ms. F., it was noted that she was well able to identify and monitor the mood of a potentially threatening person. This was an activity she had practiced extensively in childhood in order to manage and subdue her mother's irritability and reduce the risk of a beating. This interpersonal sensitivity was identified as a skill ready for "translation" to current circumstances. Her ability to detect the pleasure-displeasure of others was keen. The reorganization of this skill required disconnecting her monitoring skills from the automatic behavior of acquiescence to the source of threat. Client and therapist were able to identify a few alternative behaviors that would better protect her from danger.

4. *Use standard cognitive-behavioral techniques with sensitivity to client's history.* Standard cognitive-behavioral interventions such as identifying and correcting faulty thinking patterns (e.g., exaggerating the probabilities of a negative emotional event) are a valuable component in reducing avoidance. The countering of maladaptive beliefs can be facilitated by framing them realistically in the context of a life history of abuse. For example, Ms. F. identified the following: "There is something vulnerable about me. My anxiety might attract someone to harm me. I've been assaulted before. That means I am likely to be assaulted again." Ms. F.'s thinking had some basis in facts. Her history did indicate increased risk for future assaults. She might have been correct that her anxiety might be one of several cues that indicated that she was an "easy target" to potential perpetrators. Nevertheless, as treatment progressed, accurate and effective alternative thoughts included "I am not as easy a target as a few months ago" and "I am in better control of my anxiety." These types of statements should be reinforced with evidence. For example, Ms. F.'s treatment work led to improvement in her ability to assess more versus less dangerous situations. A decrease in hypervigilance led to a better sense of reality and better apportioning of her attention to actual threats.

Skills Training in Interpersonal Functioning

The second part of the treatment flows directly from the skills training in affect regulation, which serves as a foundation for the development of more adaptive interpersonal behaviors. One "transition session" is devoted to discussion about the tendency for individuals with affect regulation problems to engage in excessively confrontational and/or avoidant behaviors when dealing with interpersonal conflict (see Linehan, 1993).In addition, clients are invited to consider ways in which the feelings they experience in some settings have little to do with the interpersonal demands and goals of the situation and more to do with the presence of emotional triggers associated with their abuse. The client and therapist practice together making distinctions between feelings and interpersonal goals and develop a hierarchy of situations in which the client's interpersonal goals are disrupted by certain feeling states (e.g., anger, sense of rejection) and ways that the client can maintain focus on the interpersonal goals.

The general aim of this section of skills training is to help clients meet their interpersonal goals more effectively. Because the treatment is brief, these goals may be somewhat limited. However, goals such as becoming more assertive in current relationships or reducing emotional turbulence when working through conflicts may be met. Therapist and client can also monitor emerging relationships to ensure that abusive interpersonal patterns are not being repeated.

Problems with assertiveness and conflict resolution are often related to poor skills in these areas. The client has extensive experience interacting with abusive carefigures. Thus, the client's behavioral repertoire is likely to be heavily generated from internalized interpersonal schemas related to victim—abuser roles. The victim role tends to present the self as unquestioning, undeserving, fearful, and groveling. The abuser role tends to be bullying, inconsiderate of the needs of others, and operating from ultimatums. Neither of these roles is an appropriate or effective starting point for successful assertive behavior or conflict resolution. Client and therapist can role-play specific scenarios to provide "practice" experiences in doing things differently. Such scenarios can include a job interview, asking for a raise, or expressing preferences for what to do on a Friday night out with a friend. The goal is to identify the client's goals and feelings, and practice how they can be expressed in words and actions. Often the therapist can help the client find the right language and explore with the client the feelings he or she experienced in the role play (e.g., feeling scared, strange, or "fake") and identify and challenge the activation of maladaptive cognitions during the role play (e.g., "I don't deserve a raise").

For example, Ms. F. really did not want to go to a party given by a friend because he had been bullying her. Client and therapist role-played a phone conversation with this friend, in which the client stated she would not be attending the party. The client role-played herself and the therapist role played the bullying friend. The client's initial role play immediately placed her into a position where she was overly apologetic, defensive, and whining in tone. The therapist reversed this role play, explaining to the friend in a sensitive but unapologetic manner that she would not be able to attend the party but would want to meet with the friend at another time when they could spend some private time together. The client oriented herself to this language and tone, and practiced in an effective way. The role play was also useful because it facilitated identification and processing of conflicting beliefs about herself (e.g., "I have a right to be treated well by my friend and should be able to talk with him about this" vs. "I am being selfish. Although he is a bully, he really needs me").

Two additional types of role-play activities are included in the STAIR module. The first concerns situations in which the client's feelings tend to be counter to and overwhelm his or her interpersonal goals. Often, the client with an abuse history is easily distressed or angered in an interpersonal conflict. General coaching and role play is completed so that the client learns to allow interpersonal situations to be guided by the goals of the interaction (e.g., obtaining from boss a preferred vacation time) rather than an emerging feeling state (e.g., anger at boss for exploiting and overworking him or her). Frequently, intensive work is required in this area and skills training in affect regulation is critical in moving forward in this area. Clients need to learn how to use self-soothing skills and appropriate cognitive reframing skills in order to maintain focus on and achieve an interpersonal goal.

Secondly, clients with an abuse history often have difficulty trusting their judgment and evaluating the appropriate level of assertiveness in a situation. Because they tend to have limited and rigid schemas, they may assess a situation in such a way that results in their taking on a stance that is either too passive (the victim role) or too controlling (the abuser role), and in which the particulars of the situation are not well attended to. It is useful for the client and therapist to review situations in which the client may have been either too controlling or too assertive and learn to modify his or her behavior. This review highlights the importance of context: Who, what, and where determine the appropriate action and reaction. Next, the client is asked to engage in multiple role plays involving particular interpersonal conflict, where the therapist plays a different significant other each time (e.g., client's boss, spouse, child, and mother). These role plays provide material for discussion of the fact that different assumptions, attitudes, language, and behavior occur with different people, even when the goals are quite similar. The role plays are also intended to (1) contribute to the construction of a variety of new interpersonal schemas, especially as they relate to person- and situation-specific differences and (2) provide clients with an opportunity to enhance their self-experience (i.e., understand themselves as persons who can be flexible in behaviors and attitudes).

Obstacles in Interpersonal Skills Training

Facilitating change in interpersonal behavior is one of the greatest challenges in treatment of multiply victimized individuals. This goal is difficult because the client's schemas and negative beliefs about self were organized early in life and thus are deeply rooted and integrated in his or her personal history. Furthermore, many of the abusive and negative events such individuals have experienced began in childhood and have been encoded from a "just-world" perspective. Clients frequently assume that among the reasons they were treated badly was that they were bad. Thus, the therapist and client are confronted with two difficulties: The client experiences him- or herself as essentially "bad" and any significant change in his or her approach to relationships will mean an involved reorganization of self that frequently triggers deep existential anxiety. Ms. F., for example, did not believe that she could develop healthy relationships because she viewed herself as an essentially bad person. She was convinced that "if I try to be with others who don't abuse me, they don't want me or don't accept me." More problematic, still, was her own comfortable identification with victim–abuser relationships: "My only strength is in understanding and accepting people whose inner turmoil leads them to be abusive."

Interventions for Obstacles in Maladaptive Interpersonal Functioning

1. *Identifying sources of and challenging beliefs concerning "self-as-bad."* The sources of this belief are often not easily identified and take empathy, openness, and systematic inquiry to discover. Ms. F., for example, believed that she was bad for letting herself be abused as a child. This belief was maintained because of the

distorted, unrealistic expectations she held concerning her own autonomy and mastery as a child. Review of the dependence of children on adults for basic survival needs, as well as their relatively underdeveloped resources in cognitive and emotional domains, was helpful in revising this view. Of greatest impact, however, was engaging in "homework" to watch neighborhood children approximately the same age as she was (between 5 and 8 years) when she was abused. Watching them play and interact with adults provided very concrete and realistic information about the significant levels of dependency and trust children exhibited toward adults.

The second source of Ms. F.'s belief in "self-as-bad" derived from being told she was bad by her mother and other family members. This belief was challenged in a straightforward fashion by asking Ms. F. to assess the quality and soundness of her mother's judgment and by searching for alternative sources of information: What bad things had she done lately? Had she ever done anything good? Positive responses in this area provided a small but accumulating foundation of "evidence" for the creation of positive self-regard, which was reinforced by the therapist.

2. *Reapportioning the locus of blame.* Blame and guilt are reactions that women abused as children share with those who have been assaulted in adulthood. Trauma survivors of either childhood or adulthood sexual violence frequently muse over the extent to which they "contributed" to the experience and what they might have done differently. However, although women raped in adulthood often believe they contributed to or could have averted the assault in some way, they rarely assume the perpetrator to be blameless. In contrast, those abused as children often "protect" or avoid designating any blame to the caretaker, even into adulthood. This is partially related to the distorted and inordinate expectations that adults carry in retrospect about their own childhood behaviors. But it is also related to the fact that the perpetrator of the assault was a caretaker and expected to provide love, concern for, and protection of the child. Recognition of the caretaker's failure in this regard often engenders a great sense of loss and betrayal. It is often much greater than that which is also reported by survivors of rape and other interpersonal trauma in which there are fewer expectations of interpersonal regard. In the language of interpersonal schema theory, the survivor of childhood abuse is confronted with the fact that the ordinary contingencies for obtaining protection from a carefigure, which are considered a biological given or "birthright," did not occur for them.

Placing the locus of responsibility and blame on the carefigure is an important component of the treatment. The survivor's assumption of blame often functions to protect the past and current relationship with the abusive caretaker. Maintaining the stability of this relationship may have some perceived value, such as avoiding disruption to the larger family system. However, it also keeps intact a maladaptive schema. This, in turn, places the client at risk for using such a schema in the development of future relationships. For example, if the victim does not recognize that it was wrong for her caretaker to provide care contingent upon sexual favors, then she is at risk for finding this contingency acceptable in future relationships. She will have reasons "at the ready" for finding such behavior acceptable (e.g., "He can't help himself").

3. *Careful planning of gradual transitions to healthier interpersonal functioning.* The skills training module includes a substantial amount of role playing of difficult interpersonal situations. This is intended to help clients create or expand a behavioral repertoire that will help them avoid high risk situations and create opportunities for successful interactions and relationships. However, many therapists note that individuals with repeated traumas have difficulty entering and staying in nonabusive relationships and that progress in treatment is often followed by relapse into abusive relationships and behaviors. One reason for this difficulty is simply the large number of behavioral and cognitive changes required by individuals as they move out of abuse schemas and begin identifying and experimenting with healthier interpersonal behaviors. These changes entail a reorganization of their sense of self, and in this reorganizational period, clients are in an emotionally fragile state. Unexpected stressors that occur when clients enter a new relationship or job situation may overwhelm them. They may literally not know what to say, do, or feel in these new situations. Some clients report losing sight of what they want and who they think they are. In this state, it is easy for clients to fall back into abusive relationships and behaviors, not because they feel good, but because they are familiar, predictable, and controllable, all of which brings relief from what is nothing less than an existential crisis.

In order to reduce the anxiety associated with the transition to healthier functioning, the therapist and client should slowly titrate and carefully target specific changes in behaviors and lifestyle. It is important for the client to experiment with new situations and new people, but this should be done in a way that maximizes success in these ventures: task demands should match the client's abilities and readiness. Last, relapses are likely to occur. The therapist and client should think ahead about when or under what types of situations relapses are most likely to occur and have a relapse response plan ready.

Phase II: Emotional Processing of Trauma Memories

Once the eight sessions of skills training are completed, the client moves directly to the second phase of treatment: the processing of the trauma memories. Although a therapist may wish to add a couple more skills training sessions for clients who seem to need further training, it is best to move on to the memory processing despite clients' trepidation about being "ready" for the work. Delay in moving to the second phase of treatment reinforces avoidance behaviors as well as clients' generally unfounded belief that they are not capable of mastering their affect-laden memories. Skills may not seem completely solidified, and that is to be expected. Review and practice of skills are included in every session of the processing phase. Difficulties that clients have in processing their memories can be titrated by the depth and detail of the memories. It is expected that the narrative work will involve increased elaboration across time to more strongly negatively valence material.

We have adapted Foa's Prolonged Exposure treatment for rape-related PTSD (Foa et al., 1991) for use among women with a history of childhood abuse. It complements the skills training work of Phase I with very little redundancy in tasks. It should be noted, however, that current data indicate that at least two treatments for rape-related PTSD (Foa et al., 1991; Resick & Schnicke, 1992) are of equal effectiveness in the resolution of the PTSD diagnosis (Resick, Nishith, & Astin, 1996). It remains to be seen whether one treatment is more effective than the other in the resolution of PTSD symptoms experience by women with chronic trauma histories.

Phase 2 of the treatment begins with the development of a hierarchy of abuse-related trauma memories ranked by the level of distress they induce. The following sessions involve 45 minutes of imaginal exposure work followed by practice of coping skills, including refining those used in association with the exposure completed during the session. The therapist begins imaginal exposure using the most distressing sexual-abuse memory the client feels she can tolerate. The client describes the episode of abuse in the present tense, including visual and somatosensory detail, attempting to elicit a significant level of distress and to sustain the exposure for the allotted time, or until reported distress level declines. The therapist makes encouraging and directive remarks to the client during this effort (e.g., "You are doing fine, stay with the image"). A tape is made of the narrative and the client is encouraged to listen to the tape at least once a day. As the client habituates to the initial memory, she is encouraged to describe the events in greater detail and to focus more on her emotional response to the image. As habituation occurs, additional memories are incorporated into the exposure exercises and new exposures are constructed. The therapist and client may also include focus on habituation to emotional "hot spots" in patient's memory.

Presented next is a pair of excerpts from Ms. F.'s narrative, which shows an increased ability to focus on details and difficult emotions.

Early narrative:

"He pushed me on my knees with his penis in front of my face. He shoved it into my mouth. He came in my mouth. The taste was so disgusting and revolting. I pushed it noiselessly out of my mouth. It ran down my chin and onto my thighs. I felt every drop as if it was the most horrendously disgusting hated drop of horror and wrongness. To be forced to start an intimate moment with that hated face felt incredibly humiliating. He said: 'That wasn't so bad, was it?' "

Later narrative:

"He made me kneel, put himself in front of me, opened his fly and pushed his penis into my mouth. Why did I open my mouth? Out of fear? I felt so revolted, disgusted, sickened by the feel of this thick disgusting sausage in my mouth and in such a humiliating position. Every second was like an eternity. He finally came. I almost swallowed it out of natural reflex. But I caught myself in time. The drops oozed down my chin and dropped onto my thighs. Each one burning revulsion. I could have hurt him. Why didn't I? When finished he said, 'Now that was not so bad, was it?' "

The second narrative clearly includes not only greater details of her subjective experience but also an array of feelings including fear, shame, anger, and aggression. These feelings, especially fear and anger, were emotions that Ms. F. feared would overwhelm her (via a panic attack, crying jag, sense of disintegration, or assaulting someone) if she were to get close to them. Repeated exposure to these emotions in the sessions was followed by discussions of how it felt to experience them and skills she had to moderate them. The realization that she could handle these feelings significantly improved her day-to-day functioning by allowing her to engage in activities and situations that might elicit such feelings. She traveled more and she was less frightened of confronting situations that might involve interpersonal discord.

Obstacles to and Interventions for Completion of Prolonged Exposure

Typical obstacles encountered in processing trauma memories are avoidance of narrative work (e.g., not doing out-of-session narrative activity) and the absence of emotional engagement during trauma-processing activity. The introduction of the STAIR component of treatment is intended to ameliorate these difficulties. Skills training helps the client be more emotionally engaged and aware during the processing work and have greater ability to tolerate the distress associated with trauma processing.

During the actual processing work, the therapist should provide encouragement to the client and validate the client's skill and ability to process the trauma. The goal of this treatment component is to reduce PTSD symptoms. Perhaps equally important is the contribution that successful processing of the trauma will make to the client's sense of personal mastery and control. The traumatic memory and associated feelings are likely to have dominated the emotional life of the client with PTSD. The review and controlled experiencing of these memories reverses this relationship: the individual takes ownership of the memory rather than the memory of the trauma driving life decisions of the individual.

Termination and Follow-Up Care

Termination of treatment can be difficult, because it is often clear to both therapist and client that more work could be done. However, often significant gains have been made in PTSD symptoms, depression, and role functioning. The final session is devoted to reviewing the client's experience with the treatment and identifying progress and future goals with referrals appropriate to those goals. In addition, the client should be encouraged to call in to the therapist as needed. Such situations may include experiences where there are new stressors creating exacerbation of symptoms or when the client may be presented with a "choice point" or life decision. These phone calls can be viewed as "booster" sessions that reinforce established skills, guide the application of establish skills to new circumstances, or provide support in tough decisions and emotional transitions. The client's awareness of the availability of continued care is reassuring and is likely to keep him or her from panicking into a relapse of maladaptive behaviors (e.g., substance abuse). Often, a single session can prevent derailment into a spiral of decreased functioning and the need for reentering an extended therapy. The availability of follow-up care also sends the message that both therapist and client are aware that the recovery from trauma is a journey that will not be completed when therapy ends but continues for an unspecified time.

Ms. F. wrote a summary of her progress a couple of weeks after her treatment ended, identifying where changes had been made, and where she thought work remained to be done. She remains in contact with our clinic as she set about keeping her home, providing employment for herself, and making new relationships.

> "Before I came to treatment, the violent incidences of my life were very present in mind, body, and soul. Those incidences are now a less integral part of who I am. I hope it stays that way. I still feel 'danger everywhere' but it is less intense. I feel safer. Emotions are steadier. The fears of fear feelings have vanished! It is a tremendous relief.
>
> "It is wonderful to have new guidelines for relationships. I've learned how to protect myself in knowing how to assess others' trustworthiness, their negative judgments of me, and their reactions to my requests. These guidelines give me a sense of control and help me feel less vulnerable. Unfortunately, I can hold these standards to new people but cannot yet apply them to my [past abusers].
>
> "I still have self-doubt on all fronts and criticize myself excessively. I have thought about my past relationships and found to my great surprise that I was not entirely responsible for their failure. I am relieved to know that it is a human responsibility not to hurt some one, and that everyone is accountable for their actions. I have learnt that I am more than other people's reactions to me.
>
> "The ever-intrusive thought of meeting death by violence has moved farther to the background, being replaced by hope for the future. There actually appear thoughts of the possibility of nice things happening—a mere glimpse but a revelation nonetheless.
>
> "I realize that I will have to continue to work on all this, so that my fears continue to diminish. Unfortunately, I have a problem trusting myself with accomplishing anything. Maybe this is the next thing I need to work on."

FUTURE DIRECTIONS

The two-phase STAIR/PE treatment described here has been implemented with 7 women with histories of multiple trauma who were designated as "at risk" for future assaults because of the presence of high levels of alexithymia, dissociation, and problems with interpersonal functioning. Preliminary results were encouraging. Compared to 7 women wait-listed for treatment, who showed very little change on the following symptom targets, women who participated in the STAIR/PE treatment showed a 58% drop in rates of PTSD as well as significant reductions in alexithymia, dissociation, difficulty with anger regulation (inhibition and expression), and interpersonal oversensitivity (e.g., easily hurt or angered in interpersonal situations). While perceptions of social support improved, there were no significant changes in interpersonal functioning, at least as measured by self-report from the Inventory of Interpersonal Problems (Horowitz et al., 1988). Improvement in interpersonal functioning may require more "practice," as it may involve significant change in established relationships and the development of new relationships. The women will be followed for 6- and 12-month assessments to determine if interpersonal changes occur in the months following end of treatment. Future research is focused on refining the treatment and on assessing treatment outcome in a larger sample using a randomized trial design.

REFERENCES

Bernstein, E. M., & Putnam, F. (1986). Development, reliability and validity of a dissociation scale. *Journal of Nervous and Mental Disease, 174*, 727–735.

Blake, D. D., Weather, F. W., Nagy, L. M., Kaloupek, D. G., Gusman, F. D., Charney, D. S., & Keane, T. M. (1995). The development of a clinician-administered PTSD scale. *Journal of Traumatic Stress, 8*, 75–90.

Bowlby, J. (1969). *Attachment and loss* (Vol. 1). New York: Basic Books.

Bowlby, J. (1984). Violence in the family as a disorder of the attachment and caregiving systems. *American Journal of Psychoanalysis, 44*, 9–27.

Breslau, N., Davis, G. C., Andreski, P., & Peterson, E. (1991). Traumatic events and posttraumatic stress disorder in an urban population of young adults. *Archives of General Psychiatry, 48*, 216–222.

Briere, J. N. (1992). *Child abuse trauma: Theory and treatment of the lasting effects.* Newbury Park, CA: Sage.

Browne, A., & Finkelhor, D. (1986). Impact of child sexual abuse: A review of the research. *Psychological Bulletin, 99*, 66–77.

Cantanzaro, S. J., & Mearns, J. (1990). Measuring generalized expectancies for negative mood regulation: Initial scale development and implications. *Journal of Personality Assessment, 54*, 546–563.

Cicchetti, D., & White, J. (1990). Emotion and developmental psychopathology. In N.

Stein, B. Leventhal, & T. Trebasso (Eds.), *Psychological and biological approaches to emotion* (pp. 359–382). Hillsdale, NJ: Erlbaum.

Cloitre, M., & Scarvalone, P. (1995, May). Understanding sexual revictimization among incest survivors: An interpersonal schema approach. In M. Cloitre (Chair), *Interpersonal and Self-Functioning among Treatment-Seeking Incest Survivors.* Symposium conducted at the meeting of the Society for Psychotherapy Research, Vancouver, BC.

Cloitre, M., Scarvalone, P., & Difede, J. (1997). Post-traumatic stress disorder, self and interpersonal dysfunction among sexually revictimized women. *Journal of Traumatic Stress, 10,* 435–450.

Cloitre, M., Tardiff, K., Marzuk, P. M., Leon, A. C., & Potera, L. (1996). Childhood abuse and subsequent sexual assault among female inpatients. *Journal of Traumatic Stress, 9,* 473–482.

Finkelhor, D. (1990). Early and long-term effects of child sexual abuse: An update. *Professional Psychology: Research and Practice, 21,* 325–330.

Foa, E. B., Rothbaum, B. O., Riggs, D. S., & Murdock, T. B. (1991). Treatment of posttraumatic stress disorder in rape victims: A comparison between cognitive-behavioral procedures and counseling. *Journal of Consulting and Clinical Psychology, 60,* 715–723.

Follette, V. M., Polusny, M. A., Bechtle, A. E., & Naugle, A. E. (1996). Cumulative trauma: The impact of child sexual abuse, adult sexual assault, and spouse abuse. *Journal of Traumatic Stress, 9*(1), 25–35.

Gidycz, C. A., Hanson, K. & Layman, M. J. (1995). A prospective analyses of the relationship among sexual assault experiences: An extension of prior findings. *Psychology of Women Quarterly, 19,* 5–29.

Greene, D. M., Navarro, R. L., & Gidycz, C. A. (1995). *Secondary prevention of sexual victimization based on a prospective protective and risk factors.* Poster presented at the meeting of the Association for Advancement of Behavior Therapy, Washington, DC.

Herman, J. L. (1992). *Trauma and recovery.* New York: Basic Books.

Horowitz, L. M., Rosenberg, S. E., Baer, B. A., Ureno, G., & Villasenor, V. S. (1988). Inventory of interpersonal problems: Psychometric properties and clinical applications. *Journal of Consulting and Clinical Psychology, 56,* 885–892.

Jonikas, J. A., & Cook, J. A. (1994). *Safe, secure and street smart: Empowering women with mental illness to achieve greater independence in the community.* Chicago: Thresholds Research and Training Center.

Kilpatrick, D. G., Saunders, B. E., Veronen, L. J., Best, C. L., & Von, J. M. (1987). Criminal victimization: Lifetime prevalence, reporting to police, and psychological impact. *Crime and Delinquency, 33,* 479–489.

Koss, M. P., & Dinero, T. E. (1989). Discriminant analysis of risk factors for sexual victimization among a national sample of college women. *Journal of Consulting and Clinical Psychology, 57,* 242–250.

Linehan, M. M. (1993). *Cognitive-behavioral treatment of borderline personality disorder.* New York: Guilford Press.

Meadows, E., Jaycox, L. H., Webb, S., & Foa, E. B. (1996). Risk recognition in narratives of rape experiences. In S. M. Orsillo & L. Roemer (Chairs), *The use of narrative methodologies to explore cognitive and emotional dimensions among women with post-traumatic stress disorder.* Symposium conducted at the meeting of the Association for Advancement of Behavior Therapy, New York, NY.

Muelenhard, C. L., & Linton, M. A. (1987). Date rape and sexual aggression in dating situations: Incidence and risk factors. *Journal of Consulting and Clinical Psychology, 34,* 186–196.

National Victim Center and Crime Victims Research and Treatment Center. (1992). *Rape in America: A report to the nation.* National Victim Center and Crime Victims Research and Treatment Center. Arlington, VA.

Nishith, P., Mechanic, M., & Resick, P. (1997). Childhood sexual and physical abuse as predictors of adult sexual and physical revictimization in a sample of female crime victims. In M. Cloitre (Chair), *Sexual revictimization of women: Risk factors and prevention strategies.* Symposium conducted at the meeting of the Association for Advancement of Behavior Therapy, Miami, FL.

Norris, F. H. (1992). Epidemiology of trauma: Frequency and impact of different potentially traumatic events on different demographic groups. *Journal of Consulting and Clinical Psychology, 60,* 409–418.

O'Neill, K., & Gupta, K. (1991). Post-traumatic stress disorder in women who were victims of childhood sexual abuse. *Irish Journal of Psychological Medicine, 8,* 1224–1227.

Pelcovitz, D., van der Kolk, B., Roth, S., Mandel, F., Kaplan, S., & Resick, P. (1997). Development of a criteria set and a structured interview for disorders of extreme stress (SIDES). *Journal of Traumatic Stress, 10*(1), 3–16.

Polusny, M. A., & Follette, V. M. (1995). Long term correlates of child sexual abuse: Theory and review of the empirical literature. *Applied and Preventive Psychology: Current Scientific Perspectives, 4,* 143–166.

Resick, P. A., Nishith, P., & Astin, M. C. (1996, November). Results of an outcome study comparing cognitive processing therapy and prolonged exposure. In P. Resick (Chair), *Treating sexual assault/sexual abuse pathology: Recent findings.* Symposium conducted at the meeting of the Association for Advancement of Behavior Therapy, New York, NY.

Resick, P. A., & Schnicke, M. K. (1992). Cognitive processing therapy for sexual assault victims. *Journal of Consulting and Clinical Psychology, 60,* 748–756.

Rowan, A. B., Foy, D. W., Rodriquez, N., & Ryan, S. (1994). Posttraumatic stress disorder in a clinical sample of adults sexually abused as children. *Child Abuse and Neglect, 182,* 145–150.

Safran, J. D. (1990). Towards a refinement of cognitive therapy interpersonal theory: I. Theory. *Clinical Psychology, 56,* 5–8.

Scheir, M. F., & Carver, C. S. (1985). Optimism, coping and health: And implications of generalized outcome expectancies. *Health Psychology, 4,* 219–247.

Shearer, S. L., Peters, C. P., Quaytman, M. S., & Ogden, R. L. (1990). Frequency and correlates of childhood sexual and physical female borderline inpatients. *American Journal of Psychiatry, 147,* 214–216.

Spielberger, C. D. (1988). Manual for the state–trait anger expression inventory. In M. Hersen & A. S. Bellack (Eds.), *Dictionary of behavioral assessment techniques* (pp. 446–448). New York: Pergamon Press.

Spitzer, R. L., Williams, J. B., Gibbon, M., & First, M. B. (1994). *Clinical Interview for DSM-IV—Patient Edition.* New York: New York State Psychiatric Institute, Biometrics Research Department.

Taylor, G. J., Bagby, R. M., Ryan, D. P., Parker, J. D. A., & Doody, D. P. (1988). Criterion validity of the Toronto Alexithymia Scale. *Psychosomatic Medicine, 50,* 500–509.

van der Kolk, B. A. (1987). The separation cry and the trauma response: Developmental issues in the psychobiology of attachment and separation. In B. A. van der Kolk (Ed.), *Psychological trauma* (pp. 31–62). Washington, DC: American Psychiatric Association Press.

van der Kolk, B. A. (1996). The complexity of adaption to trauma: Self- regulation, stimulus, discrimination, and characterological development. In B. A. van der Kolk, A. C. McFarlane, & L. Weisaeth (Eds.), *Traumatic stress: The effects of overwhelming experience on mind, body and society* (pp. 182–213). New York: Guilford Press.

van der Kolk, B. A., Roth, S., Pelcovitz, D., & Mandel, F. (1993). *Complex PTSD: Results of the PTSD field trials for DSM-IV*. Washington, DC: American Psychiatric Association Press.

Weissman, E., & Bothell, S. (1976). Assessment of patient social adjustment by patient self-report. *Archives of General Psychiatry, 33,* 1111–1115.

Wyatt, G., Guthrie, D., & Notgrass, C. M. (1992). Differential effects of women's child sexual abuse and subsequent sexual revictimization. *Journal of Consulting and Clinical Psychology, 60,* 167–173.

Healing Interpersonal Trauma with the Intimacy of the Therapeutic Relationship

ROBERT J. KOHLENBERG
MAVIS TSAI

"If bad relationships messed me up, then it follows that I need good relationships to help me heal. And this is a good relationship." This quote by one of our clients who suffered interpersonal trauma as a child at the hands of her parents captures the essence of the healing process. In this chapter, we delineate and explore the central issues faced by clinicians in treating the effects of psychological trauma:

1. What are the causes of the clinical effects of trauma?
2. What is the nature of these problems?
3. What are the differences between circumscribed posttraumatic stress disorder (PTSD) and elaborated PTSD?
4. How can the symptoms of elaborated PTSD be ameliorated?

In answering these questions, we rely on the theoretical perspective of functional analytic psychotherapy (FAP; Kohlenberg & Tsai, 1991), a therapy derived from radical behaviorism, in which a caring and intimate client–therapist relationship is the core of the therapeutic change process.

THE CAUSES OF THE CLINICAL EFFECTS OF TRAUMA

The most popular and well-known learning-based account of the effects of trauma and PTSD is Mowrer's (1960) two-factor theory. Although the theory has been around for long time, we believe that it has implications that have been overlooked for the treatment of certain types of interpersonal trauma. We begin with a brief review of Mower's theory.

The deleterious effects of trauma are the result of operant and respondent conditioning based on aversive stimuli that lead to problematic conditioned responses and avoidance. According to this two-factor theory, symptoms or problematic behavior come from two sources. First, as a result of pairing previously neutral stimuli with a highly aversive event, visceral, autonomic responses are now evoked by these stimuli. Let us use the example of a man who was badly injured in a car accident, and who now has panic attacks whenever he comes near cars. The visceral responses and increased autonomic arousal that this man experiences constitute the first set of problems. Then, because of this respondent conditioning, the client avoids exposure to evocative stimuli, or in the case of this example, cars. The second set of the client's symptoms is based on this avoidance, which would involve difficulties associated with no longer being able to drive (e.g., alienating his family and colleagues by no longer carrying his share of the load with tasks that require driving). Furthermore, the symptoms would persist because the avoidance prevents exposure to the evocative stimuli (e.g., cars) and does not allow extinction of panic. The avoidance would also interfere with the acquisition of more adaptive behavior (e.g., being able to drive again).

In this chapter, we extend the traditional two-factor theory to explain and treat the effects of repeated trauma. We believe the most severe and difficult-to-treat effects of trauma arise from such histories. Thus, we distinguish the relatively short-term effects of circumscribed trauma from the longer-term effects of repetitive trauma that occur over an extended period of time.

CIRCUMSCRIBED PTSD SYMPTOMS

To begin with, we examine the PTSD symptoms described in DSM-IV and relate those symptoms to our model. As will become clear, we are not suggesting that DSM-IV exhaustively defines the dimensions of trauma. DSM-IV does, however, represent a distillation of commonly accepted features of the phenomenon. The DSM-IV descriptions are based on observed effects of prototypical circumscribed trauma such as combat, rape, and threats to one's life. Thus, we consider the descriptions given in DSM-IV to be the short-term effects of circumscribed trauma. We begin our analysis by accounting for the major features of DSM-IV PTSD symptoms in terms of respondent conditioning and operant avoidance.

Persistent Symptoms of Increased Arousal

According to the respondent conditioning model, a traumatic stimulus (the unconditioned stimulus) elicits responses that are mediated by the autonomic nervous system. These responses are the same ones referred to as "increased arousal" in DSM-IV. Because of respondent conditioning, previously neutral stimuli now come to elicit conditioned responses (increased arousal). Thus, as a result of the conditioning, the likelihood increases that the client will run into stimuli that evoke increased arousal during daily life. Going back to the car accident example, the stimuli that might evoke increased arousal include stimuli involved at the time of the accident, such as stop signs, rainy conditions, and tire screeching noises. Furthermore, evidence suggests that increased arousal produces a flattened generalization gradient (Sokolov, 1963; Mednick, 1975); that is, as arousal is increased, an even wider range of stimuli will evoke conditioned responses (e.g., airplanes, trains, and all other forms of transportation). This spreading or spiraling of arousal after traumatic conditioning can be further aided by verbal mediation or stimulus equivalence (Dougher, Auguston, Markham, & Greenway, 1994). Thus, our behavioral model is consistent with DSM-IV's description of increased arousal.

Persistent Avoidance of Stimuli Associated with the Trauma

DSM-IV directly refers to avoidance as posited by the behavioral model and includes the avoidance of thoughts, feelings, places, people, social situations, and memories associated with the trauma.

Intrusive Recollections

Intrusive recollections appear to be difficult to explain using the avoidance model, because reexperiencing seems to involve the client approaching and experiencing as opposed to avoiding and being unaware. The stipulation by DSM-IV, however, that the reexperiencing must be "intrusive" (p. 428), is a key factor in our explanation. According to the *American Heritage Dictionary*, an *intrusive* reexperiencing is one that is "force(d) in inappropriately, especially without invitation, fitness, or permission." In this way, reexperiencing is not just a typical remembering or recollection. In order for the client describe the reexperiencing as intrusive, it must occur without any effort or activity or desire to remember the event. In fact, the client may even say that the reexperiencing occurred despite efforts to prevent such occurrences.

From our behavioral viewpoint, all behavior is evoked by prior stimulation and since reexperiencing is a type of behavior, it also is evoked by a prior stimulus. In the case of reexperiencing however, the client is not aware of the prior stimulus and is both surprised by the reexperiencing and finds it disruptive and distracting. Therefore, what needs to be explained is the client's lack of awareness of the prior stimulation that evokes the reexperiencing. Consistent with our hypothesis, we would say that an absence of awareness occurs because the conscious experiencing of the eliciting stimulus is avoided. In other words, reexperiencing and flashbacks simply are another manifestation of avoidance.

TREATMENT FOR CIRCUMSCRIBED PTSD

Exposure is the primary behavioral approach to treating the clients with problems resulting from trauma and is present in all forms of psychological treatment. The learning principle underlying exposure is extinction. Extinction occurs if the evocative stimulus is presented and then is not followed by an aversive stimulus. Thus, in clinical work, exposure involves presenting the evocative stimuli and making sure that the client does not avoid or escape. If the client avoids or escapes, the avoidance or escape is strengthened (reinforced), and there is no therapeutic progress. Even worse, the problem may be exacerbated.

There are three conditions, two necessary and one desirable, needed for successful exposure-based treatment. First, the evocative stimuli must be known and specifiable; that is, the clinician must know what the evocative stimuli are before a method for exposure can be devised. Second, the client must be cooperative; that is, clients must be willing to talk about the trauma and tolerate a certain amount of anxiety by agreeing to place themselves in the presence of the evocative stimuli. Finally, it is highly desirable that the evocative stimuli be presented *in vivo*.

Known Evocative Stimuli

In the typical behavioral therapy treatment, the evocative stimuli are easily specified, and thus the presentation of evocative stimuli and the blocking of avoidance are straightforward procedures. In order to facilitate the therapeutic blocking of avoidance (and obtaining the client's agreement to participate) the therapist may use graded situations (e.g., a hierarchy) in which the client agrees to remain in a related but less evocative stimulus situation. According to learning theory, extinction of the conditioned response to the less evocative situation will enable exposure to more evocative ones. Continuing with the car accident example, a hierarchy might involve behaviors ranging from looking at the client's car from a distance to driving in the same location in which the accident took place, at the same time of day under similar weather conditions.

A Cooperative Client

As stated earlier, avoidance is one of the sequelae of traumatic conditioning. If the client were truly avoidant, however, it would be impossible to do exposure treatment, because the client would avoid evocative stimuli. If forced to be physically present with the evocative stimuli, the client would use other forms of avoidance such as "not paying attention" or dissociation. In fact, complete avoidance could lead the client not to talk about or even remember the traumatic conditioning. In this latter case, the client might seek treatment for problems but would not attribute the symptoms to the trauma or focus on it. Thus, the "willingness" of the client to tolerate the anxiety and thereby to "remember " and talk about the trauma are necessary for a successful exposure treatment. Client cooperation in the therapeutic process by cognitive-behavioral therapists usually is treated as a technical problem that can be taken care of by such interactions as prior negotiation with the client, therapist encouragement, and social contingencies; that is, the therapist presents an exposure plan and obtains the client's agreement to place him- or herself in the evocative situation and to remain there until extinction takes place.

In Vivo Presentations of Evocative Stimuli

The effectiveness of exposure treatment is greatly enhanced if the evocative stimuli are presented *in vivo*. For example, if the stimuli associated with the original traumatic conditioning included the patient being alone on a dark street, exposure to these same actual stimuli will be more effective than talking about them or merely imagining them. As stated by Goldfried (1985), the *in vivo* presentation of evocative stimuli is "more powerful than imagined or described" presentations (p. 71).

ELABORATED PTSD SYMPTOMS

DSM-IV descriptions of PTSD symptoms were developed for problems resulting from circumscribed, physical trauma. The aversive stimuli involved, and the resultant symptoms for such trauma, are relatively easy to describe. Furthermore, the clients involved in such experiences are able to tolerate anxiety to the extent that they are aware of the traumatic conditioning, attribute their PTSD symptoms to the trauma, and seek treatment for these symptoms. Easily described, circumscribed stimuli and a client who is able to tolerate at least some anxiety facilitate the development of hierarchies and arrangement for the presentation of evocative stimuli as required for exposure types of treatment.

In the last 20 years, however, focus has increased on a less easily described trauma, one that is interpersonal and repeatedly occurring over an extended period of time, usually in childhood (Blake, Albano, & Keane, 1992). The physical, sexual, and emotional abuse of children entail such trauma. This type of trauma cannot be avoided by the victim and has more pervasive and long-negative lasting effects than circumscribed trauma. For example, Terr (1990) reports that circumscribed childhood trauma, such as a kidnapping or sniper attack, can produce specific symptoms that may last for a few years but eventually are resolved without lingering ill effects in adulthood. In contrast, repetitive

trauma over extended periods of time during childhood produces more pervasive symptoms that usually persist into adulthood (Herman, 1992; Herman,
Russell, & Trocki, 1986).

We refer to this type of repetitive trauma and its associated symptoms as
elaborated PTSD (EPTSD). Although EPTSD symptoms involve the same aversive
conditioning and avoidance behavior that accounts for DSM-IV PTSD symptoms, they are "elaborated" and more harmful because the trauma occurred with
greater frequency and duration at the hands of a trusted caretaker. In the next
section, we explore the longer-term deleterious effects of increased autonomic
arousal and avoidance resulting from repetitive, inescapable, aversive stimuli
involving a parent or other trusted adult.

Persistent Symptoms of Increased Arousal

Sustained increased arousal over long periods of time could be expected to
produce chronic physical symptoms (medical problems) and/or problems with
self-medication or chemical dependency. Herman (1992) reports that adults who
sustained sexual and physical abuse during childhood are likely to report such
symptoms. We are not saying that clients presenting with problems of chronic
headache, lower back pain, or chemical dependence uniformly have been abused
as children. According to the two-factor theory, however, for a given client, this
may be the case, and a treatment plan should be able to accommodate this
possibility.

Persistent Avoidance of Stimuli Associated with the Trauma

A child who is physically and sexually abused over an extended period of time is
motivated to escape and avoid. In contrast to a circumscribed trauma, the direct
avoidance of the aversive stimuli is unlikely, because the child cannot physically
escape or prevent the aversive stimuli. Since the abuser is usually a parent or
caretaker with whom it is necessary to maintain a relationship, the child is
dependent on the abuser and must live in the environment where the abuse
occurs. Thus, it would be adaptive for the child if the relationship to the abuser
while the abuse is taking place is isolated from the relationship the child has with
same person during other times. This type of perceptual rather than physical
avoidance can involve alterations in the "seeing" (perception) or remembering of
the event. For example, perceptual contact with features of the abuser, the abuse,
as well as associated internal stimuli are avoided. With a perceptual isolation of
the trauma, the child even can be loving or affectionate to the abuser most of the
time and thus receive the care, food, and shelter necessary for survival. If this
isolation did not happen, then the effects of the trauma would be more intrusive
in the daily life of the child (as is the case with short-term adult PTSD), and

preclude whatever caretaking might be available. Sometimes, a total perceptual avoidance of the abuser and the environment in which it takes place (complete amnesia[1]) is necessary for the child's survival.

The types of avoidance described here could have serious impact on the development of relationship skills involved in ordinary day-to-day social interactions as well as those required for intimate relationships. Additionally, the perceptual avoidance could affect the ability to experience, identify, and describe internal states. The inability to experience internal, private states is associated with the development of problems of the self and personality disorders (primarily borderline personality disorder) (Kohlenberg & Tsai, 1991 Chap. 6; Kohlenberg & Tsai, 1995). Finally, the ability to tolerate anxiety that is required for exposure-based treatment might also be affected.

FUNCTIONAL ANALYTICAL PSYCHOTHERAPY: AN IDEAL BEHAVIORAL THERAPY FOR ELABORATED PTSD

In theory, the treatment for EPTSD involves the same exposure-based procedures described for circumscribed PTSD; that is, the evocative stimuli need to be identified and described, clients must be willing to expose themselves to these stimuli and not avoid or escape from them, and the stimuli should be presented *in vivo*. Since EPTSD involves difficult-to-describe evocative stimuli, however, it is also difficult to devise an *in vivo* exposure treatment that will present the evocative stimuli and then block avoidance. Difficulty in specifying stimuli occurs when the client cannot remember the trauma, or its longer-term, delayed effects are diffuse and do not formally resemble the behavior that occurred during the trauma itself. For example, the behavior during the original classical conditioning might include the experience of pain, fear, and numbing out. The presenting problems as an adult might be avoidance of intimacy, not having a

---

[1]Given the notoriety of the "repressed memory controversy," a word is in order about our view of the issues. From our radical behavioral vantage point, we do not believe that there is such a thing as a "memory" that is stored in the mind. Instead, remembering is the behavioral process of seeing, hearing, smelling, touching, and tasting of stimuli that are not currently present in the environment. One implication of viewing memory as the behavior of remembering is that there is no *a priori* reason for not also accepting the possibility that repression, the behavior of forgetting, also can be developed. Some empirical support for our position is derived from the literature demonstrating that animals can be taught to forget (Maki, 1981). As behaviors, the strength and nature of both remembering and forgetting are the result of our histories. Our view is consistent with both the traditional view that a client may not be amnesic for early trauma (repression) as well as idea that memories may be implanted during therapy by a careless therapist. In either event, remembering can be therapeutic in that avoidance is reduced in the process. For a more complete discussion of this topic, see Kohlenberg and Tsai (1991, Chaps. 4 and 6).

sense of self, insomnia, or not trusting others. Furthermore, even if the evocative stimuli could be specified, such as "becoming comfortable and trusting in a close relationship," it would be unclear how to arrange for the *in-vivo* presentation of such stimuli in an exposure-based format; that is, obvious problems exist with an intervention consisting of the therapist instructing the client to "go out there and get into an intimate relationship and stay in it even if you do become extremely anxious or fearful" as required for exposure-based treatment. Even if the client did attempt to comply with such instructions, it is doubtful that the outcome would be therapeutic. The "other" in such an exposure-based treatment might not be patient enough to allow extinction to take place, and, at worst, might act in a punishing way that reinforces the original trauma.

Such problems can best be dealt with by using the therapeutic relationship as a source for *in-vivo* evocative stimuli and thus provide the opportunity to block avoidance. In addition, the treatment of EPTSD involves the establishment of building-in of interpersonal repertoires that were precluded by the early effects of the trauma and the establishment of private control required for emotional responding and development of self (Kohlenberg, & Tsai, 1991, 1995).

We believe that FAP can help to produce the conditions that would facilitate EPTSD. FAP is radically behaviorally informed treatment devised by Kohlenberg and Tsai (1991) to account theoretically for the dramatic and pervasive improvements shown by some clients when involved in intense client–therapist relationships, and to delineate the steps therapists can take to facilitate intense and curative relationships. The result is a treatment in which, in contrast to popular misconceptions about radical behaviorism, the client–therapist relationship is at the core of the change process. FAP theory indicates that, in general, the therapeutic process is facilitated by a caring, genuine, sensitive, and emotional client–therapist relationship. It is precisely this type of therapeutic relationship that has the potential for effective treatment of EPTSD. In the following sections, we describe how FAP provides guidelines for obtaining the type of therapeutic relationship that can (1) lead to identification of the evocative stimuli, (2) provide a venue for presentation of evocative stimuli while blocking avoidance to evocative stimuli, and (3) provide *in-vivo* opportunities to build in more adaptive repertoires that failed to develop due to traumatic early life conditions.

As described below, FAP is based on three types of client behavior that are clinically relevant, and five rules or guidelines for therapeutic technique. Client behaviors include daily-life problems that occur during the session, improvements that occur during the session, and interpretations of their own behavior. Therapist guidelines are rules or methods that are aimed at evoking, noticing, reinforcing, and interpreting the client's behavior. A detailed case example involving a client with EPTSD also is provided to illustrate FAP principles.

Clinically Relevant Behaviors

It is assumed that the EPTSD client will bring certain behavioral patterns into the therapist–client relationship. These fall into three types and are referred to as clinically relevant behaviors (CRBs).

CRB1: Client Problems That Occur in Session

CRB1s are related to the client's presenting problems, and should decrease in frequency during therapy. For example, clients who suffer from EPTSD and avoid relationships because they have been hurtful may exhibit these CRB1s: avoid eye contact, answer questions by talking at length in an unfocused and tangential manner, have one "crisis" after another and demand to be taken care of, get angry at the therapist for not having all the answers, and frequently complain that the world "shits" on them and that they get an unfair deal.

Client problems can also involve thinking, perceiving, feeling, seeing, and remembering that occur during the session. For example, problems known as "disturbances of the self" (see Kohlenberg & Tsai, 1991, for an extensive discussion on how such disturbances are acquired and treated), such as "not knowing who the real me is" and multiple personality disorder, are translated into behavioral terms (e.g., problems with stimulus control of the response "I") and conceptualized as CRB1.

CRB2: Client Improvements That Occur in Session

In the early stages of treatment, these behaviors typically are not observed or are of low strength. For example, consider a male sexual-abuse survivor who feels withdrawn and worthless. Possible CRB2s for him would include expressing his feelings about his abuse, talking about what the therapist does that brings up his feelings of worthlessness, and asking directly for what he needs.

CRB3: Client Interpretations of Behavior

CRB3 refers to clients' talking about their own behavior and what seems to cause it. It includes "reason giving" (Hayes, 1987; Zettle & Hayes, 1986) and "interpretations." The best CRB3s involve the observation and description of one's own behavior and its associated reinforcing, discriminative, and eliciting stimuli. Learning to describe functional connections can help in obtaining reinforcement in daily life. CRB3 includes descriptions of functional equivalence that indicate similarities between what happens in session and what happens in daily life. For example, Esther, age 41, had not been sexually intimate with anyone for over 15 years. After a course of FAP with Dr. Tsai, Esther became the lover of a man she met through church. Her CRB3 was, "The reason I'm in that intimate relationship is because you had been there for me. It's such a phenomenal change. If not for you, I wouldn't be there. With you it was the first safe place I had to talk about what I feel, to find reasons why it's desirable to be sexual. There was a period of time that I was more overtly attracted to you, and you were accepting of my feelings. I learned that it was better to be whole and feel my sexuality than to be armored and empty, and I practiced learning how to be direct with you."

Rules of Therapy

The FAP therapist is urged to follow five strategic rules of therapeutic technique: watch for CRBs, evoke CRBs, reinforce CRB2s, observe the potentially reinforcing effects of therapist behavior in relation to client CRBs, and give interpretations of variables that affect client CRB. Each rule is described in turn below.

Rule 1: Watch for CRBs

This rule forms the core of FAP. Our major hypothesis is that following this rule improves therapeutic outcome; that is, the more proficient a therapist is at observing CRBs, the better will be the outcome. It is also hypothesized that following Rule 1 will lead to increased intensity—stronger emotional reactions—between therapist and client.

From a theoretical viewpoint, the importance of Rule 1 can not be overemphasized. If this is the only rule that a therapist follows, it alone should promote a positive outcome. In other words, a therapist who is skilled at observing instances of clinically relevant behavior as they occur also is more likely to react naturally to these instances. Thus, a therapist following Rule 1 is more likely to naturally reinforce, punish, and extinguish client behaviors in ways that foster the development of behavior useful in daily life. Any technique that helps the therapist in the detection of CRB1 has a place in FAP. For example, FAP therapists interpret latent content of what the client says as a means to detect CRBs, although these interpretations are based on the principles of verbal behavior and not on unconscious drives (Kohlenberg & Tsai, 1993).

Rule 2: Evoke CRBs

The ideal client–therapist relationship evokes CRB1 and provides for the development of CRB2. Such a condition usually exists for the EPTSD client, since the effects of EPTSD produce problems with intimate relating, and the FAP therapist encourages trust, closeness, and the open expression of feelings. Such a structure often evokes the clients' conflicts and difficulties in forming and sustaining intimate relationships. FAP guidelines at times can lead therapists to disclose their own private feelings to the client (see Rule 3). These disclosures often consist of presentations of the evocative stimuli that are avoided as a result of ETPSD. For example, the therapist who says, "I really care about you," might evoke CRB1s (e.g., anxiety, avoidance, feelings of worthlessness) on the part of the client.

Clients' descriptions of what they want from therapy point to the importance of an evocative relationship. As one client stated, "Therapy is about building a loving relationship. If you can overcome your blocks with one person, you can go on to do it with others."

Rule 3: Reinforce CRB2s

It is generally advisable to avoid procedures that attempt to specify the form of therapist reaction in advance. Such specification happens when one attempts to conjure up a reinforcing reaction (e.g., phrases such as "That's terrific" or "Great") without relating it to the specific client–therapist history.

The ways that therapists can be more naturally reinforcing are examined in detail by Kohlenberg and Tsai (1991). One such way is for therapists to observe their spontaneous private reactions to client behavior. Such private reactions are accompanied by dispositions to act in ways that are naturally reinforcing.

To illustrate, consider an ETPSD client whose problems partly result from avoidance that has interfered with the acquisition of intimacy skills; that is, the repetitive early trauma prevented intimacy and the opportunity to be reinforced for and to learn relevant skills. Suppose that, at some point in therapy, this client behaves in a way that evokes the following private, spontaneous reactions in the therapist: (1) dispositions to act in intimate and caring ways, and (2) private reactions that correspond to "feeling close." Because these responses probably are not apparent to the client, the therapist could describe the private reactions by saying, "I feel especially close to you right now." Without such amplification, these important basic reactions would have little or no reinforcing effects on the client's behavior that evoked them (CRB2).

Rule 4: Observe the Potentially Reinforcing Effects of Therapist Behavior in Relation to Client CRBs

If therapists have been emitting behavior that they think is reinforcing, it would be important for them actually to observe whether they are in fact increasing, decreasing, or having no effect on a particular client behavior. Feedback of this type is needed to increase therapist effectiveness.

Rule 5: Give Interpretations of Variables That Affect Client Behavior

As is the case with most other therapies, Interpretations are an important part of FAP. As a general strategy, FAP therapists interpret client behavior in terms of learning histories and functional relationships. For example, a client, Angela, in treatment with Dr. Kohlenberg, stated that she did not have initiative or take risks, because whenever she even thinks about it, she feels like she does not "have a right to exist," and that she is "just so much trouble." Interpretations that were helpful to Angela emphasized that her feeling of not having the right to exist and her inability to take initiative were the result of her history of being punished by her mother for being assertive, confident, or for doing almost anything that called her mother's attention to her existence.

Case Example

The following case history illustrates many of the principles we have described.

Joanne was a bright, compassionate, and sensitive woman who came into therapy because she was troubled by constant anxiety and insomnia (hyper-arousal), recurring nightmares of rape, and waking, intrusive images of being raped by unknown persons (flashbacks) that she did not experience as "real memories" (intrusive recollections). She also avoided and had difficulty in close, intimate relationships (persistent avoidance of stimuli associated with the trauma). Although she suspected that when she was a child she had been sexually abused by her father, she had no specific memories of such abuse. She gradually improved in almost every aspect of her daily life over the 6 years that she was in treatment with Dr. Tsai. The following are some of the CRBs that occurred during treatment:

1. *Remembering and emotionally responding.* During Joanne's childhood, she experienced physical and emotional pain at the hands of someone who supposedly loved her, her father. Remembering and emotionally reacting to these events were not reinforced. Instead, forgetting and not emotionally reacting were functional, and she avoided stimuli that could evoke undesired, punished feeling. Her avoidance was pervasive, and in combination with the invalidating early experiences, she often felt devoid of a sense of self.

The way that Joanne avoided aversive states such as pain, terror, powerlessness, and rage, was by avoiding contact with evocative stimuli that evoked them. The major class of such stimuli was intimate relationships, which had in common many of the same evocative stimuli that were present in her relationship with her father and the associated early, repetitive, traumatic conditioning. As would be the case for most children, she initially loved her father and felt loved by him. She also was open, trusting, and vulnerable with him. Eventually, these were paired with aversive stimuli. For example, her father might have implicitly said, "Love me, trust me, I will not hurt you," which inevitably was followed by being hurt, rejected, exploited, abused. As a result of the trauma, she avoided feeling love and was not loving, open, trusting, or vulnerable in subsequent committed, close relationships. Correspondingly, she initially did not feel loved and was not trusting or vulnerable in the therapy relationship (CRB1s).

The primary therapeutic goal was to reduce generalized avoidance of the intimacy in the therapy relationship. This was done by persistent exposure to the therapist's caring and expectations for increased trust, openness, and vulnerability. Increased intimacy in the therapist–client relationship led to CRB2s of remembering extremely cruel sexual and physical abuse by her father, and experiencing the aversiveness and anguish associated with the remembered (and present) stimuli. Gradually, Joanne increased her contact with vivid recollections of physical and sexual torture by her father. The process was painful, but through gradual exposure, she learned that tolerating aversiveness could often be done in small steps and survived. The ability to tolerate aversiveness and have more complete contact led to improvement in her relationship to the therapist. This transferred to improved relationships in general in her daily life.

2. *Learning to ask for what she wants* (i.e., that her needs were important and deserved attention). As with almost all survivors of sexual abuse (Herman, 1992), Joanne was reinforced for giving her father what he wanted but was severely punished for "wanting" for herself. Thus she had poor contact with those private stimuli commonly known as "needs," and further, had little opportunity to develop a repertoire for asking or requesting others to act in ways that satisfied these needs. Currently, she experienced these as not being entitled to expect from others, frequently not knowing what she wanted, and on those occasions when she was in contact with wanting something from others, that this "wanting" was "bad." During therapy, Dr. Tsai encouraged her to "want" by attempting to reinforce any contact that Joanne had with desires concerning their relationship. I responded positively and gave her what she "wanted" as much as I could in such areas as topics discussed, the length and frequency of scheduled sessions, and her wish for more verbal reassurances from me. An important incident occurred about 4 months into her therapy, when she called me at 11:30 P.M. in the middle of a flashback. Joanne was panicked and shrieking. Since I recognized this call as a CRB2 in which she was contacting unpleasant state that she wanted me to help with, I asked Joanne if she wanted to meet for a session right then; she said "yes." Later, Joanne told me it was very difficult for her to say "yes" because of her past history of being rejected and otherwise punished in such circumstances, but she was terrified and really wanted me to be with her. When I responded to her need, "wanting" was reinforced. Subsequently, Joanne learned to ask me for extra sessions and telephone time when she needed them, and this behavior of stating her wants and needs generalized to other relationships. As the strength of these CRB2s increased, there was a corresponding change in her feelings about "wanting" being acceptable and her needs being important. Obviously, therapists and others cannot meet all of a client's needs, and Joanne and I had several discussions about how her needs were important even if I or someone else did not meet them, and it did not mean she was "bad" for having them. Toward the end of therapy, Joanne understood the importance of taking responsibility for getting her needs met and balancing her needs with the needs of those who were close to her.

3. *Trusting.* Because her father's reactions to her were erratic and unpredictable, Joanne was reinforced for anticipating and being hypervigilant for such behavior from significant others. She told me that it took 6 months of my always being on time for our appointments before she started believing that I would show up when I said I would. She stated, "I had all these fears—that you were going to think I was crazy, that you were going to hurt me, that my feelings were going to scare you away. Rather than simply reassuring me, your response was to have me check out if that's what I was experiencing from you. I'd say no and you'd say you have to trust your experience." I was also reliable in keeping my word, consistent in the views I expressed, and did not behave unpredictably. So Joanne gradually was less vigilant for an erratic action on my part (an important CRB2 in PTSDT, which in turn allowed our relationship to grow.

4. *Accepting love.* Throughout treatment, Joanne struggled with accepting my caring and positive regard. Initially, she seemed to ignore my comments about my caring for her and descriptions of what I liked about her; that is, she avoided these stimuli. Statements of caring were reexpressed (exposure) whenever the context was appropriate, and I gently attempted to block avoidance by asking her about what she heard me say and how she felt. Eventually, Joanne described a daily-life problem regarding her interpersonal relating. She said that deep inside, she felt like she did not know how to love or be loved. I questioned her more, wanting to know exactly what she meant so that it could be viewed in behavioral terms. Joanne had difficulty describing it. As an alternative to obtaining her description of events happening in daily life, I attempted to bring the behavior into the session. I asked her if she could accept my love at the moment, and she said "no," that she felt closed. Although it was a private process whose dimensions were difficult to describe, I judged that CRB1 was occurring at the moment, and this is what was said between her and me:

THERAPIST: How do you feel closed?

CLIENT: It feels like my heart is closed.

THERAPIST: Totally closed?

CLIENT: It's about 5% open.

THERAPIST: I'd like you to try to open it to 20% and take in my love for you.

CLIENT: It's about 25% open.

THERAPIST: Great! Can you do 40%?

This process was maintained, and Joanne reported being able to "open her heart" more and more. Here is her description of what she experienced during that session: "It took courage to open up and draw in the love. It was a shift in focus in my mind and in my body. Although I was aware of my fear and the terror and pain of my experiences with my father, I focused on what I was feeling from you in the present as opposed to my fears. I let both be true—that my father had abused me, but that you were a person with whom I could feel safe and feel loved. I kept thinking to myself, 'I want to be open to taking in love.' I hold tension in my muscles when I shut down, a lot in my chest, like that muscle gets frozen. So the physical feeling of opening is softening that muscle, breathing more deeply, feeling the breath in my body. It's like the sensation of a lens aperture opening in my heart."

It is unclear what behavioral processes were involved with "accepting love," but Joanne's description of what she experienced suggests some possibilities. Our interpretation is that her not being able to accept love was a specific, largely private behavior that distanced her and reduced the aversiveness of relating to her father. Given some of the features of her description, some of these responses probably had been specifically evoked by the sexual abuse. The same behavior also occurred in the session because our relationship had enough functional similarity to the prior relationship. Despite the aversiveness, she remained in contact with her feelings, her avoidance extinguished, her physical responses changed, and there was an accompanying feeling of "accepting love."

That session was a significant turning point for Joanne because she learned she had control over whether she let love in or not. This aided in her developing more positive self-regard, and subsequently, more intimate love relationships.

In conclusion, Joanne's treatment for EPTSD was highly successful because the closeness of therapeutic relationship (1) evoked mistrust, vulnerability and fear, aversive feelings stemming from her relationship with her father; (2) enhanced her willingness to stay and work through her avoidance of these aversive stimuli; and (3) involved the *in-vivo* pairing of positive visceral responses with behaviors that facilitate intimate relationships: trust, vulnerability desires for closeness, and acceptance of caring.

It is our strong bias that the most powerful treatment experiences make use of the clinically relevant behavior between therapist and the client. This is especially important when the client's main emotional wounds come from childhood abuse involving trusted adults whose tasks were to protect and to nurture. Such betrayal is among the deepest wounds that can be endured. Because the therapist–client relationship captures many essential elements of the parent–child relationship, it has great potential for both harm and healing. We hope that our discussion of the origins and treatment of interpersonal trauma will provide a clear conceptual system to aid those of you who have taken on the noble task of helping to heal the emotional scars of clients who were violated as children.

REFERENCES

American Heritage electronic dictionary. (1992). New York: Houghton Miffin.

Blake, D., Albano, A., & Keane, T. (1992). Twenty years of trauma: Psychological Abstracts through 1989. *Journal of Traumatic Stress, 5,* 477–484.

Dougher, M. J., Auguston, E., Markham, M. R., & Greenway, D. E. (1994). The transfer of respondent eliciting and extinction functions through stimulus equivalence classes. *Journal of the Experimental Analysis of Behavior, 62,* 331–351.

Goldfried, M. G. (1985). *In vivo* intervention or transference? In W. Dryden (Ed.), *Therapist's dilemmas* (pp. 71–94). London: Harper & Row.

Hayes, S. C. (1987). A contextual approach to therapeutic change. In N. S. Jacobson (Ed.), *Psychotherapists in clinical practice: Cognitive and behavioral perspectives* (pp. 327–387). New York: Guilford Press.

Herman, J. (1992). *Trauma and recovery.* New York: Basic Books.

Herman, J., Russell, D., & Trocki, K. (1986). Long-term effects of incestuous abuse in childhood. *American Journal of Psychiatry, 143,* 1293–1296.

Kohlenberg, R. J., & Tsai, M. (1991). *Functional analytic psychotherapy: Creating intense and curative therapeutic relationships.* New York: Plenum.

Kohlenberg, R. J. & Tsai, M. (1993). Hidden meaning: A behavioral approach. *Behavior Therapist, 16,* 80–82.

Kohlenberg, R. J., & Tsai, M. (1995). I speak, therefore I am: A behavioral approach to understanding the self. *Behavior Therapist, 18,* 113–116.

Maki, W. S. (1981). Directed forgetting in pigeons. *Animal Learning and Behavior, 8,* 567–574.

Mednick, S. A. (1975). Autonomic nervous system recovery and psychopathology. *Scandinavian Journal of Behaviour Therapy, 4,* 55–68.

Mowrer, O. H. (1960). *Learning theory and behavior.* New York: Wiley.

Sokolov, Y. N. (1963). *Perception and the conditioned reflex.* New York: Pergamon.

Terr, L. C. (1990). *Too scared to cry: Psychic trauma in childhood.* New York: HarperCollins.

Zettle, R. D., & Hayes, S. C. (1986). Dysfunctional control by client verbal behavior: The context of reason giving. *The Analysis of Verbal Behavior, 4,* 30–38.

CHAPTER THIRTEEN

Couples Surviving Trauma
ISSUES AND INTERVENTIONS

JILL SERAFIN COMPTON
VICTORIA M. FOLLETTE

The immediate and long-term psychological difficulties associated with traumatic life events have been well documented in recent years. However, research across trauma populations (e.g., combat veterans, victims of rape, and child sexual-abuse survivors) has focused largely on the intrapersonal aspects of posttrauma functioning. Trauma survivors often experience a range of negative internal experiences, including depression, anxiety, intrusive thoughts, rage, and shame (Keane & Wolfe, 1990; Polusny & Follette, 1995; Resick, 1993). These populations commonly engage in behavior patterns that may function to avoid, escape, or reduce painful experiences or reminders of the trauma (Briere, 1992; Follette, 1994; Foy, 1992). For example, higher rates of substance abuse, binge eating, suicidal ideation, and suicide attempts have been reported in survivor populations (Briere & Runtz, 1993; Conners & Morse, 1993; Kilpatrick, Edmunds, & Seymour, 1992; Lacoursiere, Godfrey, & Ruby, 1980). Although the constellations of symptoms vary widely among individuals, the long-term sequelae of combat trauma (Foy, 1992), rape (Rothbaum, Foa, Murdock, Riggs, & Walsh, 1992), and child sexual abuse (CSA; Lindberg & Distad, 1985) often warrant a diagnosis of posttraumatic stress disorder (PTSD).

Many studies have investigated the relationship between individual problems, including depression, anxiety, and substance-abuse disorders, and couple functioning (e.g., Biglan et al., 1985; Jacobson, Holtzworth-Munroe, & Schmaling, 1989). Findings suggest that individual distress may influence social and intimate functioning, and conversely, the quality and type of relationships established by couples may influence individual health and well-being. There are some data that support a similar relationship between these variables among trauma survivors. Although there are substantially fewer studies investigating the interpersonal correlates of trauma, evidence that survivors experience significant disruptions in social adjustment and intimacy processes has been well established. These difficulties are quite pronounced in the context of marital and couple relationships, and many survivors experience severe relationship distress (Briere, 1992; Jordan et al., 1992; Resick, 1993; Riggs, Byrne, Weathers, & Litz, 1998).

The focus of the current chapter is on the transaction that exists between the sequelae of trauma and couple satisfaction and functioning. Behavioral couple therapy approaches to treating relationship distress are presented and empirical findings related to couple functioning will be reviewed across the trauma literature. Finally, a contextual/behavioral paradigm is used to provide a set of clinical guidelines for treating survivors and their partners.

COUPLE FUNCTIONING AMONG TRAUMA SURVIVORS: A LITERATURE REVIEW

While combat, rape, and CSA traumas differ in many important topographical ways, the long-term psychological correlates of these events are often more similar than they are different (Dye & Roth, 1991). Evidence suggests that disruptions in interpersonal functioning are common in the aftermath of trauma, and many survivors experience difficulties in their primary relationships. Couples commonly report problems with global social and relationship adjustment, emotional expressiveness and intimacy, physical violence and revictimization, sexual relating, and individual distress. Empirical and clinical findings across trauma literatures are reviewed for each of these frequently identified problem areas. In general, it should be noted that the problems faced by survivors and their partners have been addressed frequently in the literature (e.g., Buttenheim & Levendosky, 1994; Carroll, Foy, Cannon, & Zwier, 1991; Figley, 1985; Follette, 1991; Follette & Pistorello, 1995; Johnson, 1989; Mio & Foster, 1991; Serafin, 1996); however, systematic research in this area has lagged behind investigations of intrapersonal correlates of traumatization. More extensive and rigorous research is needed to fully understand the type and extent of problems experienced by couples surviving trauma.

Social and Couple Adjustment among Trauma Survivors

There is substantial evidence to suggest that combat, rape, and CSA traumas are associated with significant disturbances in overall social adjustment, with survivor couple[1] relationships being characterized by dissatisfaction, turbulence, and con-

---

[1]The term "survivor couple" is used as shorthand to refer to couples in which one or both partners report a history of combat, rape, or child sexual-abuse trauma.

flict (Carroll, Rueger, Foy, & Donahue, 1985, Caroll et al., 1991; Finkelhor, Hotaling, Lewis, & Smith, 1989; Nadelson, 1989; Silver & Iacono, 1986). Separation and divorce rates are higher among couples affected by trauma (Pavalko & Elder, 1990; Riggs et al., 1998; Russell, 1986), and many survivors avoid dating and establishing intimate relationships altogether.

Traumatic life experiences appear to affect all levels of social functioning, including adjustment at work, parenting skills, and relationships with extended family members and friends (e.g., Cole & Woolger, 1989; Ellis, Atkeson, & Calhoun, 1981; Gold, 1986; Harter, Alexander, & Neimeyer, 1988; Jordan et al., 1992; Resick, Calhoun, Atekeson, & Ellis, 1981; Solomon & Mikulincer, 1992). Fear and distrust of others are common among survivor populations (Briere & Runtz, 1987; Kilpatrick & Veronen, 1984), and many survivors and their partners experience themselves as detached and relatively isolated from others (Card, 1987; Solomon et al., 1992; Verbosky & Ryan, 1988).

Emotional Expressiveness and Intimacy

Among veteran populations, high levels of combat involvement have been associated with difficulties in both identifying and experiencing emotions, and being emotionally close to others (Penk et al., 1981). Veterans diagnosed with PTSD report more difficulties with intimacy and sociability (Kulka et al., 1990; Riggs et al., 1998; Roberts et al., 1982), less self-disclosing and expressive behavior with their partners, and more difficulties adjusting to cohabiting relationships when compared to veterans without PTSD (Carroll et al., 1985).

Research investigating the couples affected by rape trauma suggest a similar pattern of emotional withdrawal, as these couples report relationship difficulties in areas such as understanding, commitment, emotional support, and communication (Miller, Williams, & Bernstein, 1982). Moreover, findings from a recent study comparing survivors of CSA and their partners to nonabused control couples indicate that survivor couples experience less relationship satisfaction, decreased emotional expressiveness, and more difficulties with emotional communication and feeling connected (Waltz, 1993).

Considerable overlap in findings across trauma literatures suggests that survivor couple relationships are marked by low levels of emotional engagement and intimate behavior. This pattern of survivor couple interactions is consistent with an experiential avoidance model often used to conceptualize the long-term sequelae of trauma (Briere, 1992; Follette, 1994; Polusny & Follette, 1995). Experiential avoidance is characterized as an unwillingness to experience painful thoughts, feelings, and memories associated with one's history (Hayes, 1987). This avoidance results in a variety of behavioral attempts (e.g., emotional withdrawal, substance abuse) to minimize, numb, or eliminate the experience of these negatively evaluated internal events. Thus, many topographically different behaviors are conceptualized as serving the same function.

Although experiential avoidance functions to provide some degree of immediate relief from what are perceived to be intolerable affective states, this coping strategy may be associated with poorer outcomes overall (Leitenberg, Greenwald, & Cado, 1992; Rodriguez, Ryan, & Foy, 1992). Many couples report conflict between partners over the level of closeness desired in their primary relationships, and this discrepancy is often a presenting complaint for couple therapy (Christensen, 1988; Christensen & Shenk, 1991). The level of closeness experienced during couple relationships has been identified as a significant factor for both individual well-being (Brown & Harris, 1978) and relationship satisfaction (Jacobson, Waldron, & Moore, 1980). Moreover, research has shown that a pattern of withdrawing from couple interactions predicts decreased relationship satisfaction over time (Gottman & Krokoff, 1989) and poorer responses to couple interventions overall (Hahlweg, Schindler, Revenstorf, & Brengelmann, 1984). Conversely, couple relationships characterized by high levels of expressiveness between partners have been associated with significantly better individual adjustment among partners of combat veterans (Solomon, Waysman, Avitzur, & Enoch, 1991).

Physical Violence and Revictimization

Physical violence has been noted as a commonly occurring problem within the couple relationships of trauma survivors. Findings suggest that both male- and female-initiated violence is more prevalent among couples with a PTSD-diagnosed veteran when compared to couples without a PTSD diagnosed veteran (Jordan et al., 1992). Although both partners may initiate violence, it should be noted that male-initiated violence tends to result in more negative outcomes when compared to female-initiated violence (Holtzworth-Munroe, Beatty, & Anglin, 1995). Thus, while male veterans tend to report significant levels of hostility and aggression toward their partners (Caroll et al., 1985), the occurrence or escalation of physical abuse within the relationship is a common presenting complaint for therapy among female partners (Verbosky & Ryan, 1988).

There is evidence to suggest that women who report a history of CSA trauma are more vulnerable to later physical and sexual assault in adult relationships (Briere & Runtz, 1987; Naugle, Follette, & Follette, 1995; Wyatt, Guthrie, & Notgrass, 1992; Wind & Silvern, 1992). For example, more than half (65%) of a sample of battered women presenting for services at domestic violence shelters reported having a CSA history (Follette, Polusny, Bechtle, & Naugle, 1996), and CSA survivors were found to be twice as likely to experience sexual assault in adulthood (Chu & Dill, 1990). Furthermore, findings suggest that multiple traumatic experiences are associated with increased levels of individual distress (Follette et al., 1996).

Sexual Relating

There is substantial evidence to suggest that rape and CSA trauma have significant and aversive effects on immediate and later sexual adjustment (e.g., see Browne & Finkelhor, 1986; Polusny & Follette, 1995; Resick, 1993, for reviews). Reduced sex drive and sexual activity have been noted among combat veterans (Williams, 1980). Findings suggest that survivors of sexual traumas experience a range of sexual problems, including decreased sexual satisfaction and desire, increased rates of sexual dysfunction, and a tendency to engage in multiple, short-term sexual relationships (Courtois, 1988; Ellis, Calhoun, & Atkeson, 1980; Jackson, Calhoun, Amick, Maddever, & Habif, 1990; Maltz & Holman, 1987). Moreover, for many survivors, communication about sexual issues is especially problematic. These women frequently find it difficult to communicate their sexual and contraceptive needs to their partners (Wyatt & Lyons-Rowe, 1990).

Gender Roles and Distribution of Responsibilities

The distribution of power and responsibilities between partners is also considered to be fundamental in couple relationships (Christensen, Jacobson, & Babcock, 1995), and may be quite problematic in couples when trauma is an issue. For example, preliminary evidence suggests that many female survivors of CSA trauma establish relationships with men characterized by more traditional gender and family roles (Serafin & Follette, 1996; Van Buskirk & Cole, 1983), and that male veterans often choose women who are extremely nurturing and self-sacrificing (Solomon, 1988). While traditional gender roles work well for many couples, assessment of the level of satisfaction and flexibility within these roles may be useful. Many survivors of trauma experience individual difficulties and dysregulation that is readily apparent to their partners, and the primary responsibilities within the home (e.g., household chores, child care, finances, etc.) may be distributed unevenly to shield the survivor from further stress and exhaustion. While this may be a necessary and kind gesture in the short term, many partners experience resentment and anger over time.

BEHAVIORAL APPROACHES TO COUPLE THERAPY

Traditional behavioral couple therapy (TBCT; Epstein & Baucom, 1988; Jacobson & Margolin, 1979; Stuart, 1980) approaches to the treatment of relationship distress have dominated the empirical literature over past decades, and outcome studies have repeatedly demonstrated the effectiveness of these interventions compared to control groups (Hahlweg & Markman, 1988). TBCT is based on social learning theory and utilizes principles of behavior therapy to treat relationship distress. From this perspective, relationship stability and satisfaction are determined by the relative frequency of positive and negative behavioral exchanges between partners (Jacobson & Holtzworth-Munroe, 1986).

Relationship distress is theorized to result from a variety of factors, including decreased reinforcement in the relationship, skills deficits, conflict between partners about desired levels of closeness and independence, and influences external to the relationship (Jacobson & Margolin, 1979). Interventions in TBCT consist primarily of change strategies to promote positive behavioral exchange, increased communication and problem-solving skills, contingency contracting, and overall compromise and accommodation between partners (Jacobson & Margolin, 1986).

Despite unequivocal support for TBCT as an effective treatment, recent attention has focused on why substantial numbers of couples do not experience clinically meaningful changes by the completion of therapy (Jacobson & Addis, 1993). Estimates indicate that only about half of all couples who participate in therapy are successfully treated, and nearly one-third of these couples experience a pattern of relationship deterioration over time (Hahlweg, Schindler, & Revenstorf, 1982; Jacobson, Schmaling, & Holtzworth-Munroe, 1987; Snyder, Wills, & Grady-Fletcher, 1991).

There are several reasons to believe that couple relationships affected by trauma may be among those not substantially benefiting from TCBT. For example, there is evidence to suggest that TBCT is less effective for couples experiencing more severe levels of relationship distress (Baucom & Hoffman, 1986). Couples are also less likely to benefit from treatment when their relationships are characterized by emotional disengagement and conflict avoidance (Gottman & Krokoff, 1989; Hahlweg et al., 1984), as well as by more traditional and rigid gender roles (Jacobson, Follette, & Pagel, 1986). Furthermore, when one partner is suffering from psychological difficulties, such as depression, couple therapy is less effective in remediation of relationship problems (although it is often effective in treating individual depression; Jacobson, Fruzzetti, Dobson, Whisman, & Hops, 1993). Thus, although TBCT can be considered among the best available treatments for relationship problems, there remains a significant need for improvement in this area.

Many explanations for the limitations of TBCT have been discussed in the literature and have direct implications for the treatment of couples surviving trauma. In a recent review, Jacobson and Addis (1993) criticize the application of TBCT to general clinical populations without considering the unique treatment needs of particular groups of couples. These authors suggest that more sophisticated strategies are needed to understand who benefits from TBCT and in what cases TBCT should be modified or is contraindicated. They recommend making use of theoretical and clinical data to tailor effective interventions for specific groups of couples, in this case, couples affected by trauma.

Jacobson and Holtzworth-Munroe (1986) argue that another limitation of TBCT approaches is that the focus of treatment is largely limited to current relationship problems and functioning, often to the exclusion of understanding the couple in context. Consequently, the individual treatment needs and relevant historical factors experienced by each partner have often been overlooked or inadequately addressed. These considerations are particularly important for couples recovering from trauma, as individual distress, pretrauma functioning, and the characteristics of traumatization often play key roles in relationship distress.

Finally, Jacobson and Christensen (1996) argue that TBCT's emphasis on change strategies to promote compromise between partners has proven insufficient for many couples. These authors suggest that acceptance strategies are an essential element of couple therapy, particularly when partners have irreconcilable differences and traditional problem-solving approaches are ineffective. They have recently integrated strategies designed to facilitate both behavioral change and partner acceptance into a new model of couple therapy, namely, integrative couple therapy (ICT; Jacobson & Christensen, 1996).

Many useful elements of TBCT have been incorporated into ICT, and many improvements have been made that suggest that ICT may be well suited for couple therapy with trauma survivors. First, although many survivors of trauma and their partners attempt (or hope) to minimize, disregard, or ignore the impact of the traumatic events on them, both as individuals and as a couple, this practice is often associated with poorer long-term functioning (Briere, 1992; Eldridge, 1991; Follette, 1994; Moss, Frank, & Anderson, 1990; Verbosky & Ryan, 1988; Winkel & Koppelaar, 1991). Thus, for couples surviving trauma, the balance between change and acceptance may be particularly salient for successful therapeutic outcomes. Second, case formulation in this new approach has been expanded to include an increasingly functional assessment of idiographic variables (Christensen et al., 1995; Jacobson & Christensen, 1996). Partners' individual distress and public behaviors are examined within both historical and current contexts, and couple interactions are assessed to identify important controlling variables that inform treatment (this will be discussed later in this chapter). Finally, pilot data appear quite positive for ICT, and preliminary evidence indicates that this approach may be effective for couples with partners experiencing individual distress (Koerner, Prince, & Jacobson, 1994).

It is important to note that ICT is consistent with other contemporary behavioral therapies (e.g., Hayes, 1994; Kohlenberg & Tsai, 1991; Linehan, 1993) in that both public (observable) and private (thoughts and feelings) behaviors are assessed and considered important. In fact, affective responses often guide assessment and subsequent interventions. For instance, an intense affective reaction is generally viewed as an indication that the therapist is identifying important controlling variables in the relationship (Christensen et al., 1995). Finally, although there are many theoretical reasons to be excited about ICT as a successful treatment for survivor couple populations, empirical support is clearly needed to evaluate under what circumstances this intervention is effective.

Partner Involvement and Recovery: A Case for Couple Therapy

The pervasive effects of traumatic events are experienced not only by the survivor him- or herself, but also secondary traumatization is often experienced by individuals who are closely affiliated with the survivor (Figley, 1983). Among the most likely to be affected are partners of survivors, who often report psychiatric symptoms, physical complaints, strong emotional reactions, as well as disruptions in their perceptions of safety and their ability to trust (Graber, 1991; Kulka et al., 1990; Silverman, 1978; Solomon et al., 1992).

Many of the symptoms associated with PTSD directly impact couple functioning and the lives of survivor partners. Intrusive recollections of the trauma commonly disrupt daily activities and may make it difficult for a couple to function normally. For instance, female partners of veterans commonly report being physically struck in the middle of the night by their partners who are experiencing nightmares (Verbosky & Ryan, 1988). Common symptoms noted in rape populations include anger, concentration problems, intrusive nightmares and images, and withdrawal from support networks (Atkeson, Calhoun, Resick, & Ellis, 1982; Kramer & Green, 1991). In the case of CSA, intrusive flashbacks and images occur frequently during sexual activity and may make it uncomfortable for partners to communicate their needs and sexual desires (Briere & Runtz, 1991, 1993; Gorcey, Santiago, & McCall-Perez, 1986; Maltz & Holman, 1987).

Just as survivors' psychological functioning has a considerable impact on the health and satisfaction of their partners, the behavior of significant others may play a key role in either mitigating or exacerbating the impact of past traumatic experiences. For instance, although female partners may make demands for veterans to be more open and expressive in their relationships, it is not uncommon for the same partners to behave in ways that punish new behavior and subsequently maintain distance and dependence in their relationships (Verbosky & Ryan, 1988). Although this is a new area of inquiry with trauma survivors, individual psychopathology and couple distress have been found to have a reciprocal relationship in other populations. Relationship functioning in couples with a symptomatic partner has been examined in the context of a variety of psychological problems, including individuals who have been diagnosed with depression, agoraphobia, substance abuse, schizophrenia, and eating disorders (e.g., Cerny, Barlow, Craske, & Himaldi, 1987; Hooley, Richters, Weintraub, & Neale, 1987; Jacobson et al., 1989, 1993; Van den Broucke & Vandereycken, 1988, 1989). Overall, research findings have been remarkably similar across couples with an identified patient. Couples with a psychologically impaired partner report increased levels of relationship distress, conflict, and negative affect when compared to control groups (Gotlib & McCabe, 1990). Couple factors play a significant role in the etiology, maintenance, and treatment of individual distress (i.e., depressive disorders; Coyne, 1976; Jacobson, Dobson, Fruzzetti, Schmaling, & Salusky, 1991; O'Leary & Beach, 1990; Paykel et al., 1969), and "normal" partners are likely to report psychological troubles as well (Gotlib & Whiffen, 1989). Finally, couples with a diagnosed partner frequently engage in mutual avoidance of relationship issues, because there is a tendency to focus on the identified patient's individual difficulties rather than on shared interaction patterns (Beach, Sandeen, & O'Leary, 1990).

Couple therapy approaches have been used successfully with many of these populations and appear to address individual problems *and* concurrent relationship distress with some success (Jacobson et al., 1989). Although research investigating the problems and therapeutic needs of trauma populations is in the early stages, findings suggest that a similar reciprocal relationship exists between couple functioning and individual distress. From their work with veterans, Solomon et al. (1992) conclude that family systems interventions are desirable in order both to prevent secondary trauma among female partners and children, and to improve individual functioning among veterans themselves. In the sexual trauma literature, poorer psychological functioning has been observed among females who did not feel supported by their spouses after a sexual assault, especially if they had expected their partners to be supportive (Moss et al., 1990). Moreover, findings from a treatment outcome study for women reporting a CSA history indicate that group therapy may not be as beneficial for married survivors, as they did not make gains as great as participants who were single (Follette, Alexander, & Follette, 1991). In combination with clinical experience, these findings have persuaded many scientists–practitioners in the field of trauma to agree on the importance of including both partners in treatment (Follette, 1991; Follette & Pistorello, 1995, Johnson, 1989, Mio & Foster, 1991; Serafin, 1996; Solomon et al., 1991; Verbosky & Ryan, 1988).

CLINICAL GUIDELINES FOR ASSESSMENT WITH COUPLES SURVIVING TRAUMA

The treatment outlined in this chapter is largely adapted from the ICT behavioral model, which is based on principles of learning theory to conceptualize and intervene with couples. This perspective builds on the TBCT model in that increased attention is given to understanding the primary controlling variables in couple interactions, rather than to solving the numerous problems derived from these variables (Christensen et al., 1995). This approach is consistent with traditional behavioral assessment procedures that emphasize functional rather than topographical assessment. In a functional analysis, the context of behavior is examined to identify important relationships between events that set the occasion for (stimulus conditions), and maintain (consequences) the behavior of interest.

The goal of assessment in ICT is to conceptualize conflict in each couple relationship in terms of "response classes," or behaviors that appear different at a topographical level but serve the same function in the relationship (Koerner et al., 1994). The focus is on recurrent themes in the relationship rather than on each specific complaint or instance. For example, a survivor of CSA might instigate an argument, go to sleep early, experience somatic symptoms, or threaten suicide to avoid sexual activity with her partner (topographically different behaviors that serve the same function; to avoid sex). Thus, the task is to identify when problem behaviors are likely to occur or be maintained in the relationship, given each partner's individual learning history (e.g., traumatic experiences, prior relationships, family variables, etc.) and the characteristics of each couple's current interaction patterns. The antecedents and consequences of each partner's behavior are examined in a chain-like fashion, as each partner's behavior provides the context for the other's behavior. This procedure helps to identify how individuals in a relationship are influenced by each other, as well as how variables outside the relationship affect the couple.

Assessment of Individual Factors

Trauma

There are many individual or intrapersonal factors that influence relationship satisfaction, interaction patterns, and overall couple functioning. Of course, traumatic life events are among the important factors to be assessed and are the focus of the current chapter. Couple therapists are advised to routinely assess for the presence of trauma during individual interviews conducted early in treatment, as many survivors are initially reluctant to discuss these events and their impact (particularly with their partners). Feelings of shame, guilt, and stigma commonly associated with a history of trauma also interfere with communication of these events, and many survivors avoid, minimize, or dodge discussion of these experiences with their partners and therapists. Questions should be asked in a direct and supportive manner to validate how important and difficult these issues may be for individuals and their relationship.

Once aware that a traumatic event has been experienced, it is important for the therapist to assess whether and in what ways this event (or set of events) has affected the individual. Given the variety and range of symptoms and difficulties commonly associated with trauma, there is no a priori reason to make assumptions about how a particular individual has been affected. Thus, thorough assessment procedures are particularly important in this area. There are many factors that may affect responses to trauma (see Briere, 1992; Koss & Harvey, 1991) and contextual variables, including pretrauma functioning, age at trauma, characteristics of the trauma, immediate responses, social supports, subsequent treatments, and current functioning, should be explored. Despite the potential value of this information to successful treatment, many survivors are understandably reluctant to be forthright about this information if they do not feel safe or emotionally connected with the therapist and/or their partner. Thus, assessment may be an ongoing process in which sensitive information is gathered over time in the context of developing therapeutic and couple relationships.

The extent and level of symptoms associated with a lifetime history of trauma should be assessed, and it may be useful to identify whether the survivor meets criteria for PTSD. The Trauma Symptom Inventory (TSI; Briere, 1995) is an efficient 100-item, self-report questionnaire that may provide information useful in couple interventions. The TSI is designed to measure posttraumatic symptoms, including both intrapersonal and interpersonal difficulties commonly associated with psychological trauma. An overall score is obtained and 10 clinical subscale scores, including anxious arousal, depression, anger/irritability, intrusive experiences, defensive avoidance, dissociation, sexual concerns, dysfunctional sexual behavior, impaired self-reference, and tension-reduction behavior are provided. If desired, structured diagnostic interviews are available for the assessment of PTSD, including the Clinician Administered PTSD Scale-Form 1 (CAPS-1; Blake et al., 1990) and the Anxiety Disorders Interview Schedule (ADIS; Blanchard, Gerardi, Kolb, & Barlow, 1996).

Depression and Suicide

There are several reasons to suggest that depressive symptoms are an important individual variable to assess among couples affected by trauma. Traumatic experiences have consistently been associated with increased rates of major depression, suicidal ideation, and suicide attempts across survivor populations (Keane & Wolf, 1990; Polusny & Follette, 1995; Resick, 1993). Alternatively, depression is a common individual problem associated with couple distress and dissatisfaction more generally. Evidence suggests that depression may negatively affect relationship satisfaction (e.g., Coyne, 1976), couple distress may increase risk for depression (e.g., Nelson & Beach, 1990), and couple interventions are often effective for treating individual depressive symptoms (e.g., Jacobson et al., 1991). Thus, routine assessment of depressive symptoms is indicated at all times when working with couples.

The Beck Depression Inventory (BDI; Beck, Rush, Shaw, & Emery, 1979) is a simple and readily available measure of the severity of depressive symptoms. The BDI can be administered at regular intervals throughout treatment to monitor changes in depressive symptoms. Moderate to high scores on the BDI (> 10) indicate a need for further assessment, including a thorough assessment of current suicidal ideation and intent. A detailed history of suicide threats and attempts, their antecedents and consequences, and the possible function(s) of these behaviors should be explored. These issues may be particularly salient when trauma occurs during childhood. An accumulating literature indicates that childhood sexual, physical, and emotional traumas are associated with the development of personality disorders (e.g., borderline personality disorder (BPD), antisocial personality disorder), for both men (Raczek, 1992) and women (Herman, Perry, &

van der Kolk, 1989). In these populations, suicide threats or attempts, self-injurious behavior, and admissions to the hospital may function in many ways. These problem behaviors commonly function for people to decrease emotional pain, to communicate or get their needs met in the relationship, or to avoid demands made by their partners. It is important to assess the precipitating circumstances (triggers) and consequences (both desired and undesired) for problem behaviors in the relationship, and to identify factors that maintain dysfunctional behavior patterns. In severe cases, individual therapy and skills training may be indicated before proceeding with couple interventions.

Substance Abuse

Like depression, substance abuse occurs at high rates among survivors of trauma (Briere, 1988; Kilpatrick et al., 1992; Lacoursiere et al., 1980) and may also be a common problem for their partners (Serafin & Follette, 1996). The extent and type of substance abuse should be assessed early in treatment, and relationship patterns revolving around drugs and alcohol should be identified. More specifically, substance use may serve to maintain a level of emotional distance in the relationship.

Common screening instruments for substance abuse include the Michigan Alcoholism Screening Test (MAST; Selzer, 1971), and the Minnesota Multiphasic Personality Inventory—2 (MMPI-2; Butcher, Dahlstrom, Graham, Tellegen, & Kaemmer, 1989), which may be useful in understanding substance use in relation to other problems affecting the individual's functioning. While severe substance-abuse issues may necessitate individual detoxification and treatment, there is substantial evidence that suggests couple interventions are both desirable and effective when substance use is an issue (Jacobson et al., 1989; McCrady & Epstein, 1995).

Medical Problems and Somatization

For many survivors of trauma, the traumatic event(s) themselves were characterized by severe physical trauma or bodily injury. For instance, many combat veterans and survivors of violent rape and other crimes experience long months spent in medical recovery, and many never fully return their pretrauma level of health or physical functioning. In addition to physical difficulties directly associated with the trauma, many survivors experience their health less favorably in general and use medical services at a higher rate than nontrauma controls (e.g., Koss, Koss, & Woodruff, 1990). Moreover, medical problems including pelvic and gynecological pain have been associated with CSA, particularly when the abuse was severe or violent (Briere & Runtz, 1988; Pribor & Dinwiddie, 1992; Walker, Katon, Harrop-Griffiths, Holm, Russo, & Hickok, 1988).

Medical and health problems may be salient individual factors during recovery from trauma. The Symptom Checklist 90—Revised (SCL-90-R; Derogatis, Lipman, & Covi, 1973) is a widely used and well-validated measure of global psychological distress that may be useful for identifying a variety of physical complaints in a short time period. Subjects rate how frequently they have experienced 90 symptoms or complaints during the previous month. It is important that therapists discuss physical limitations, ongoing medical conditions, and physical complaints with the couple, and make referrals for medical evaluations when necessary. Physical and psychological effects of health issues on sexual and reproductive functioning should be explored with the couple.

Individual Historical Factors

Many historical variables influence expectations for couple relationships, and discrepancies between partners can be the source of conflict. It is often useful to assess experiences with parents, observations of parental relationships and gender roles in the family, and the characteristics of relationships with previous partners, friends, and children in order to gain an understanding of the quality and type of intimate relationships experienced. When trauma is an important factor, significant relationships with others may have been delayed, disrupted, or avoided altogether. It is important to explore interpersonal skills, as the ability to communicate effectively (Jacobson & Margolin, 1979) and to be emotionally available (Greenberg & Johnson, 1988) have been identified as necessary for success in couple interventions. Thus, assessment should outline interpersonal functioning before, during, and following trauma when this information is available. Analysis of historical relationships may provide a useful context for explaining and challenging rigid gender roles or dysfunctional tolerance for being treated in abusive ways.

Individual Strengths

While the preceding discussion has outlined a variety of problem areas that may be particularly important for couples affected by trauma, it is important to note that there are a variety of individual strengths often associated with having experienced difficult and challenging events that may have impact on couple work in positive ways. Recent findings suggest that some survivors of CSA perceive that they have benefited from their traumatic experiences by being better able to protect themselves and their children, having an increased knowledge of CSA, and being made stronger by their experiences (McMillen, Zuravin, & Rideout, 1995). Many survivors of trauma report having compassion and caring for others that have been enhanced through their own misfortunes. Additionally, given the challenges and struggles associated with traumatic life events, many survivors have a willingness to admit to individual weaknesses and to seek support or treatment when it is appropriate to do so.

Assessment of Relationship Factors

Areas of Conflict and Relationship Satisfaction

While intrapersonal factors provide useful contextual information about current couple functioning, it is also essential to understand how the couple interacts and functions as a unit. At the onset of treatment, it is useful to gain an understanding of how the couple describes their current situation and problems. Some problems commonly experienced by survivor couples are diffuse and difficult to identify, such as emotional distancing and withdrawal. Other couples may present in response to domestic violence, violations of trust, stressful life events, or problems in sexual adjustment.

A quick self-report measure such as the Dyadic Adjustment Scale (DAS; Spanier, 1976) provides quantitative data about level of global relationship distress, areas of agreement and conflict, discrepancies between individual descriptions of relationship problems, and commitment to the relationship in general. In addition to the DAS, the Areas of Change Questionnaire (Margolin, Talovic, & Weinstein, 1983) may be an efficient means of understanding the amount and type of change partners hope to target during treatment. It is also useful for the therapist to take notice of areas within the relationship that are not problematic, that function well, or even provide pleasure for the couple.

Safety and Conflict Style

Violence is a relevant factor for about 50% of couples seeking conjoint therapy, and couple therapists are encouraged to routinely assess the occurrence and extent of these issues (Holtzworth-Munroe, Beatty, & Anglin, 1995). Physical, emotional, and sexual abuse may occur even more frequently among couples affected by trauma, and may or may not be identified as a presenting problem for therapy. It is absolutely essential that current and historical violence be assessed directly with this population, and that partners are given an opportunity to discuss these issues in private.

The Conflict Tactic Scale (CTS; Straus, 1979) is a popular self-report questionnaire used to screen for violent behaviors occurring in the relationship. The CTS provides preliminary information about the type and frequency of violent behavior and should be used in conjunction with a clinical interview to discern the context and function of this behavior in the relationship. Care should be taken to understand the sequence of events commonly experienced before, during, and after a violent episode. Partners should be encouraged to explore their motives or intentions when engaging in violent behavior. Violent behavior in intimate relationships can function in many ways, and the function of these behavior patterns will direct treatment. For instance, the functions of violence have been discussed in terms of self-defense, titration of intimacy, and for the sake of gaining control in the relationship (Paque, Serafin, Fruzzetti, & Weiss, 1996). Violence occurring in response to demands for closeness and time together might suggest a need to discuss issues of intimacy and independence in the relationship, whereas violence used to get one's way might indicate an alternative course of treatment. There is controversy regarding the best modality of therapy when violence is a primary problem in the relationship, and therapists are strongly cautioned to consider whether conjoint couple or individual treatments are most suitable.

It is not uncommon for couples to minimize the level of violence in their relationships and the impact this violence has on them as individuals. Many couples report that rage reactions alternate with periods of remorse (Carroll et al., 1991), and this expression of regret may make it more difficult for partners to address issues of violence and "rock the boat." For couples with childhood trauma, violent family histories are common and may provide a context in which this behavior appears to be normative. Therapists should be aware of this tendency and should avoid behavior that functions to collude with the couple to avoid dealing with violence issues in treatment. Domestic violence itself has been associated with PTSD symptoms among battered women (Houskamp & Foy, 1991) and should be conceptualized as a form a trauma in its own right.

Intimacy, Emotional Expression, and Interaction Patterns

Interpersonal trauma is certainly associated with disruptions in the development of trust and intimacy, and long-term couple relationships are clearly affected by these issues. Couple assessments should include analyses of emotional expression and levels of closeness between partners, including obtaining an understanding of how these relationship variables have evolved during the course of the couple being together. Levels of closeness and distance characterizing couple relationships are core relationship issues and commonly lead to conflict and discontent when discrepancies exist between partners (Christensen et al., 1995).

Two brief assessment measures may provide useful information about couple interaction patterns: (1) the Closeness and Independence Questionnaire (updated from the Relationship Issues Questionnaire; Christensen, 1988), provides data about the desire for more or less closeness or independence in the couple relationship; and (2) the Communication Patterns Questionnaire (Christensen, 1987) provides each partner's perceptions of constructive and destructive communication patterns characteristic of the relationship, including negotiating, blaming, demanding, withdrawing, and avoiding during conflict.

One common interaction pattern identified from questionnaire and interview data has been labeled "demand–withdraw" (Christensen & Heavey, 1990), or "engage–distance" (Fruzzetti & Jacobson, 1996; Fruzzetti & Serafin, 1995), and is associated with differences in desired levels of intimacy between partners. In this scenario, one partner's requests or demands for increased closeness and emotional sharing are met by the other partner's desire to withdraw and distance from the relationship. This interaction pattern has been associated with decreased relationship satisfaction and poor long-term relationship success (Christensen, 1988; Fruzzetti & Jacobson, 1988), and may be particularly common among therapy-seeking couples when trauma is a factor.

Research suggests that there is a strong correlation between traumatic life events and disruptions in the ability to be emotionally available (e.g., Penk et al., 1981; Miller et al., 1982; Waltz, 1993), and trauma survivors may seek partners with similar difficulties or expectations. Thus, partners may initially be attracted by a mutual desire to limit closeness and emotional expression in the relationship. Mutual disengagement of this sort has been associated with poor relationship adjustment over time (Gottman & Krokoff, 1989), and partners may eventually seek treatment precisely because this interaction pattern is not tenable. Unfortunately, it is likely that one partner may desire change in this area while the other desires to continue maintaining a comfortable distance, establishing a demand–withdraw or engage–distance interaction pattern. Alternatively, partners may sacrifice their own needs for closeness and intimacy as an initial method of caring for the trauma survivor who is unable to be emotionally present in the relationship (Rabin & Nardi, 1991). Over time, the partner may become increasingly unhappy in the relationship and begin to place increasingly higher demands on the partner, resulting in the demand–withdraw or engage–distance interaction pattern.

Sexual Functioning

Finally, sexual issues are among the most difficult areas for couples to discuss openly during the assessment phase of couple therapy. Sexual functioning is traditionally thought of as a private domain and is even more difficult to discuss when it is the source of long-standing difficulties, as it may be for survivor couples. However, it is important to gain knowledge about sexual functioning and satisfaction from both partners' perspectives, even when the trauma under consideration is not of a sexual nature. Sexual functioning goes hand in hand with intimacy more generally and may be affected directly (e.g., flashbacks of a rape experience) or indirectly (e.g., impacting trust) by a traumatic experience. One clinically relevant assessment device for sexual functioning is the Sexual History Form (LoPiccolo & Freidman, 1987), which provides an expedient and less intrusive alternative to interviewing. Couples respond privately to questions addressing levels of sexual satisfaction and desire, the frequency and duration of sex, and symptoms of sexual dysfunction.

Sexual activity requires a degree of vulnerability and openness, and survivors may experience increased levels of self-loathing or disgust during these times. Questions may arise about whether their partners could truly love them if they knew the whole story (e.g., the CSA survivor experienced physical pleasure during the abuse, the veteran raped several women in Vietnam), and dissociation or avoidance may be used to cope with these feelings. Like other areas of importance, sexual functioning before, during, and after the trauma should be assessed, and any strengths in this domain highlighted.

Selection of Couples for Treatment

Although relationship difficulties are among the most frequent problems identified by survivors of trauma, many survivors present for individual treatments rather than couple modalities. It is not uncommon, for instance, for survivors to request individual or group interventions despite their intention to address relationship difficulties in treatment (Pistorello & Follette, in press). Although interpersonal difficulties may be more apparent when survivors present for therapy with their partners, a routine and thorough assessment should be completed at the onset of therapy to identify which treatment modalities best suit the current needs of the survivor and/or couple.

Some survivors prefer to explore relationship issues in an individual therapy context. Many partners are willing to tolerate the survivor seeking help; however, it is common for survivors to report that their partners are reluctant or refuse to participate in treatment themselves. In these cases, it is important to ascertain whether relationship issues will be the primary focus of treatment or merely among several potential areas to be addressed. In the event that relationship improvements are the survivor's primary goal, it is important to inform the client that progress made in individual therapy may not generalize to the couple relationship (Follette et al., 1991), and may even have iatrogenic affects on the couple relationship (Brody & Farber, 1989).

Other survivors present for individual rather than couple therapy because they have not yet disclosed their trauma histories to their partners. While this type of secret may severely impact levels of intimacy in the relationship, survivors should seriously explore individual expectations and hesitancies related to disclosing this information prior to making the choice to disclose (Follette & Serafin, 1995). Furthermore, in this situation, it is crucial to provide partners with educational materials about CSA and the impact this trauma may have on significant other relationships. In other cases, survivors pursue individual treatment prior to presenting with their partners, or hope to alternate between individual and couple sessions. Many survivors report a need for an appropriate forum to sort out unpleasant and vivid details of the trauma (abuse histories, rape experiences, war atrocities, etc.) that their partners may find overwhelming. Although some clinicians report success alternating between roles as an individual and a couple therapist (Johnson, 1989), when intensive couple work is indicated, it may be more appropriate to refer the couple to another therapist. Finally, survivors may present for individual therapy to address relationship difficulties so severe that it may not be advisable to include their partners in treatment initially.

Pretreatment: Safety and Commitment

Prior to engaging in the thorough individual and couple assessment procedures described earlier, the therapist must first establish whether individuals are safe enough to proceed. For this reason, we recommend that each couple be considered in the pretreatment stage until potential for suicide, homicide, violence, child abuse or neglect, or any other issue of direct safety (e.g., drinking and driving, high-HIV-risk behavior) has been assessed and resolved. When safety issues are imminent, the issue should become the single and primary focus of treatment until it is resolved. Individual or group interventions might be necessary to address suicidal or homicidal intent, develop safety plans, improve anger management or parenting skills, or treat severe substance abuse. Of course, practitioners are reminded that proper reporting actions must be taken when safety issues overlap with legal and ethical obligations. Couple therapists may consider referring one or both partners to community resources to address individual issues, working with partners individually, or utilizing conjoint couple sessions to resolve safety issues prior to beginning couple therapy.

When safety issues are not relevant (or have been resolved), the focus of pretreatment shifts to the second priority in pretreatment: commitment to the relationship and the process of couple therapy. Thus, the second goal is to obtain a unilateral commitment from each partner (i.e., independent of the other's ability to commit) to actively engage couple therapy for some proscribed amount of time (e.g., 12 weeks, 6 months, etc.). Similar to other treatment strategies (Fruzzetti & Serafin, 1996; Linehan, 1993), a clear commitment to treatment is obtained by acknowledging the difficulties *and* benefits of the upcoming work, and highlighting any obstacles that may impact either partner's ability or willingness to remain committed over time. It is essential that the couple make commitments to maintain a safe and open therapeutic environment, and to be willing to address trauma-related issues in the service of enhancing the relationship and individual functioning. Of course, the ability to make commitments of this nature varies over time, and therapists are encouraged to accept successive approximations of committed behavior, especially any commitment to addressing those factors and issues that make it difficult to commit to treatment.

It is also important to discuss any obstacles that make it difficult for partners to be committed to working on their relationship during the time period identified, including reluctance to be vulnerable, fear of getting hurt, having "one foot out the door," an ongoing affair, not wanting to burden the partner by disclosing information about the trauma, and anything else that might be a problem for a particular couple. It is important to impress upon the partners that during this phase of treatment, they are merely being asked to consider what might hinder their ability to engage treatment in a committed way. They are not being asked to discuss these issues. It is important to establish a positive working relationship with the couple and a thorough assessment before engaging in treatment.

Treatment Strategies

After couples have completed pretreatment and assessment procedures have been used to identify areas of conflict, relationship themes, controlling variables, and areas of strength, the couple is ready to move into the treatment phase of therapy. Therapy consists of two primary goals: (1) to resolve relationship conflicts by facilitating individual change, and (2) to facilitate acceptance when individual change is not possible. Change and acceptance strategies are interwoven into treatment rather than occurring in a sequential manner, and should be emphasized more or less depending on the needs of the individual couple.

Change Strategies

Behavior exchange (BE) strategies have been a mainstay in behavioral couple therapy (Jacobson & Christensen, 1996; Jacobson & Holtzworth-Munroe, 1986) and are particularly useful when working with couples affected by trauma. BE strategies require partners to focus on individual behaviors that may contribute to relationship distress, and are used to increase the amount of positive reinforcement in the relationship. Although a variety of techniques can be used, the essence of BE is to ask couples to generate lists of behaviors that they could engage in that would be likely to function as reinforcers for their partner, and therefore, increase their partner's day-to-day relationship satisfaction. Eventually, couples are directed to engage in many of these behaviors and asked to notice when their partners are also engaging in behaviors expected to be reinforcing to them.

Trust is a primary difficulty for many couples coping with past traumas, and BE strategies are useful for encouraging partners to take calculated risks that facilitate and build trust over time. Since the context of BE strategies is characterized by minimal conflict, they are useful for encouraging survivor couples to work as a collaborative team rather than as the "survivor" and the "partner." It is important to note that couples that have been severely disengaged for the duration of their relationship may have difficulty identifying behaviors that will be reinforcing for their partners. Thus, it is important to predict that this may be a difficult task, which often takes time and skillful communication.

BE homework may continue throughout the therapy process; however, communication and problem-solving training should be added soon after a basic trust and collaborative set has been established. It is likely that the majority of survivor couples presenting for treatment will have significant skills deficits in these areas, as many survivors are not able to identify or negotiate their individual needs and limits. Couples are taught to use receptive and expressive communication skills, including learning and practicing basic listening skills (showing attention and interest), using "I" statements, paraphrasing, making constructive requests, and so on (Jacobson & Holtzworth-Munroe, 1986). Given that many individuals have experienced traumatic life events within their family environments, they often have significant histories of invalidation in which their private experience (e.g., needs, thoughts, feelings, selves) were minimized, ridiculed, disregarded, or rejected. Therefore, it may be necessary to teach skills such as mindfulness, distress tolerance, emotion regulation, and interpersonal effectiveness (Linehan, 1993), and to practice recognizing and engaging in validation within the relationship (Fruzzetti, 1996).

When working with survivors and their partners, it is particularly important to introduce topics of conflict in a gradual manner, with increasingly difficult issues being addressed as the corresponding individual skills are developing or established. Since many survivors and their partners have worked hard for years to avoid contacting internal experiences that are uncomfortable and painful, they are likely to use avoidance strategies when overwhelmed in treatment (e.g., when topics of conflict are introduced too quickly). It is important to monitor behaviors that might indicate experiential avoidance, including dissociation during session, drug and alcohol abuse, binge eating, abrupt topic changes, and so on. When avoidance behaviors are noticed, it is important to engage in a collaborative and objective analysis of the triggers for the problematic response, as well as the function that the behavior serves. The emphasis during the functional analysis should be on "understanding" rather than "blaming" the partner or couple for the behavior. It should be communicated that even the least skillful behavior is an understandable one given the person's learning history and/or the current characteristics of the relationship or session.

The reciprocal nature of communication should always be emphasized, exploring how one partner's communication and level of emotional availability affects the other. Videotaping couple interactions may be one way of isolating interaction patterns and has been found to be a useful tool for communicating about interaction patterns during couple sessions (Fruzzetti & Serafin, 1995). While viewing the taped interaction, it is important to alternate inquiries from partner to partner. It may be useful to identify particular moments in the interactions and to ask questions that challenge individuals to view their behavior in the context of the relationship. Queries might include asking partners: (1) to observe and describe their private experience; (2) to observe and describe their perception of their partner's private experience; (3) to notice under what circumstances their behavior (or that of their partner) is engaged, distant, or aversive; (4) to identify what their goals were and/or what they needed from their partner; and, (5) to identify alternative behaviors that might have been more effective in meeting their goals or getting their needs met. It is useful for therapists to express how they might have felt in the same conversation, to point out validating and invalidating responses, to notice positive behaviors (listening, not being defensive, being emotionally available), and to guide examination of the context and consequences for partner behaviors.

Acceptance Strategies

In conjunction with the change strategies of BE, communication, and problem solving, several other strategies should be used to facilitate acceptance and communication of acceptance for issues in the relationship that cannot be changed. Jacobson and Christensen (1996) identify several strategies for facilitating acceptance during couple interventions: (1) acceptance through empathetic joining around the problem; (2) turning the problem into an "it"; (3) acceptance through tolerance building; and (4) acceptance through self-care. In the following sections, each of these strategies is reviewed and its utility for treating trauma couple populations is explored.

The strategy of acceptance through empathetic joining around the problem attempts to facilitate acceptance by encouraging each partner's experience of the other's pain, without blame or accusations. The focus of treatment shifts from the content areas typically associated with recurrent conflicts to the theme or overarching source of that conflict. The theme is discussed in terms of common differences between partners (e.g., wanting more closeness and time together vs. wanting more independence), and each partner's perspective is validated as legitimate. Care is taken to attribute relationship distress to the problematic reactions to their differences, rather than the differences themselves. Thus, the therapist encourages the partners to identify, understand, and accept their differences as individuals, while changing the problematic ways each partner has tried to resolve these differences.

During this process, the therapist also promotes acceptance by helping the couple to work in a collaborative way by viewing the problem as a common "it," rather than as something one partner does to the other. This strategy may facilitate an understanding of the other's experience and perspective by creating a level of emotional distance from the problem. When working with survivor couples whose relationships are characterized by emotional distance and experiential avoidance, it is important to notice whether this strategy is merely one way of minimizing an important relationship issue that is difficult to discuss. It is important to distinguish between emotional distance from the problem (which facilitates understanding and closeness to the other) and emotional distance that merely adds to the problem.

The strategy of acceptance through tolerance building seeks to extinguish negative behavior patterns between partners by prescribing that couples engage in negative behavior when they would not typically do so. Through assignments that "ritualize" negative behaviors, it is hoped that partners will begin to understand their roles and vulnerabilities during conflict, as well as those of their partners. When using this technique with couples surviving trauma, it is important to distinguish between learning better to tolerate negative behavior (not the goal) and learning when and why partners react in the ways they typically do during conflict. In other words, by engaging in problem behavior patterns out of context, partners learn to identify the bodily sensations, feelings, and reactions that are often associated with their negative couple interactions. It is acceptance of the fact that partners affect each other, and what seems to be an automatic response is actually a complex interaction that can be explored and understood.

Acceptance through self-care is a strategy designed to help partners to identify individual needs not being met in the relationship, and skillfully to consider other avenues for getting those needs met. This strategy is particularly tricky when working with couples affected by trauma, as many survivors are unable to identify their needs or to ask their partner to meet them. Thus, this strategy should be toward the end of treatment, with a goal of problem-solving how a particular need will be met within or outside of the relationship.

Sexual Issues

Sexual issues will often be identified as targets for treatment when working with survivor couples, whether or not the traumatic experience was sexual in nature. While a subset of couples may present for therapy specifically to address sexual problems, many will not report sexual problems without prompting. The range of sexual problems will vary across couples and forms of trauma; however, problems with sexual relating are among the most troublesome effects of trauma on significant others. It is common for intimate partners to experience feelings of inadequacy and rejection because of survivors' dislike and reluctance for sexual intimacy or compulsive quest for sexual attention (Graber, 1991; Maltz & Holman, 1987). Survivor partners frequently complain of feeling sexually unfulfilled. Sexual problems such as difficulties achieving or maintaining an erection, decreased sexual desire, and impotence are common clinical complaints among male sexual partners of trauma survivors, and many traditional sexual therapy techniques may be helpful (Graber, 1991; Maltz & Holman, 1987).

It is important to note that sexual problems are typically intertwined with issues of intimacy and emotional expressiveness, and treatment should address each level of functioning. In some cases, low sexual desire on the part of the survivor may develop as a way of avoiding intolerable levels of closeness in the relationship. This phenomenon has been observed in other couples with sexual difficulties who report discrepant needs for closeness in their relationships (LoPiccolo & Friedman, 1987). For these couples, low sexual desire tends to be perceived by the sexually functional partner as rejection, and often results in withdrawing behaviors. This pattern may function to decrease closeness in survivor relationships, maintaining a level of intimacy acceptable to the survivor.

Like other painful topics, survivor couples may avoid communication about sexual issues, and open discussions about each partner's fears, feelings, desires, and difficulties is often quite therapeutic. However, sex is a difficult topic for couples to engage in, even when things are going fairly well, and should only be introduced with trauma survivors when communication skills are well established. It is important to discuss avoidance of sex, flashbacks, nightmares, and dissociation during sexual activity, and each partner's sexual preferences and dislikes. Efforts should be aimed at understanding what activities, settings, smells, and other aspects of the context for sex trigger emotional withdrawal or other sexual problems. Finally, a distinction should be made between simply engaging in sexual activity and being emotionally present during sexual activity, as this subtle difference clearly affects the quality of the sexual relationship.

COMMON TREATMENT OBSTACLES AND POSSIBLE SOLUTIONS

Many of the common obstacles encountered when treating couples affected by trauma have been discussed throughout the text, including strategies to address experiential avoidance and domestic violence. There are two salient issues that often arise within this population that have yet to be discussed: treating dual trauma couples and couples who blame relationship problems on the survivor.

Dual Trauma Couples

The special circumstance of dual trauma couples, or couples with two trauma survivors, is one that complicates couple therapy. While couples with one trauma survivor often rely on the stability of one partner or the other, dual trauma couples may find it difficult to support each other in times of stress (Balcom, 1996). Moreover, as one member of the couple struggles to cope with the trauma and make sense of the experiences, this process may trigger painful memories for the partner. Thus, reciprocal reexperiencing and repeated crises may severely disrupt the development of closeness, trust, and emotional connection within the relationship. In fact, a pattern of mutual withdrawal and disengagement is often expected, and many dual trauma couples choose each other precisely because neither individual wants to be challenged in ways that require emotional vulnerability. It will be important to identify dual trauma issues at the onset of treatment, and routinely to inquire about each partner's individual functioning. It may be necessary to refer partners for individual therapy concurrent with their couple interventions if they find it difficult to remain regulated.

Blaming the Survivor

In recent years, couple interventions have become increasingly identified for the treatment of many individual psychological problems. Unlike other disorders, such as depression and agoraphobia however, PTSD is not theorized to be caused by marital distress. There is always an identifiable traumatic event (or multiple events) that survivors and their partners can point to and assign blame. Thus, while many survivors seek conjoint couple therapy with their partners, it is not uncommon for partners to view their role in therapy as merely facilitating individual growth on the part of the survivor. Although often well-meaning, partners who view the survivor as the identified patient in couple therapy may attribute primary responsibility for relationship difficulties to the survivor or their trauma history (Follette, 1991; Verbosky & Ryan, 1988). This pattern of "benevolent blame" may perpetuate feelings of shame and stigmatization already experienced by many survivors, and can maintain or even exacerbate PTSD symptoms.

It is important that couples routinely be reminded that relationships are not a solitary activity, and that their problems are mutually determined and mutually resolved. This notion of "mutual responsibility" should be addressed directly throughout treatment, both verbally and behaviorally. Alternating the emphasis of treatment from one partner to the other, and from historical issues to current relationship problems, may facilitate increasingly collaborative interactions among couples (Follette & Pistorello, 1995). Moreover, this strategy may assist the therapist by ensuring a position of neutrality during couple therapy.

Evaluation of Treatment

Like all treatments, couple therapy with trauma survivors should be evaluated on an ongoing basis to test hypotheses about controlling variables, inform treatment planning, and ultimately provide information about when to continue, modify, or terminate treatment. Many of the assessment measures discussed throughout the current chapter are brief and sensitive to short term changes. Thus, it is both economical and reasonable to have couples complete repeated measures throughout the duration of treatment at regular intervals.

When using videotaped assessments of couple interactions, therapists have a record of interaction patterns over time and can refer back to previous sessions to rate change in the relationship. Feedback regarding areas that have changed or remained the same can be given to couples using previous videotapes, and may be a powerful intervention in their own right. Finally, it is important to discuss satisfaction with the process of therapy, the rate of change, and the impact it has had on both individuals and relationship distress. Therapists may find it useful to note that treatment often seems to make things worse before making it better. For couples exploring the effects of trauma on their relationship for the first time, the therapeutic process is likely to bring problems and difficulties to the forefront that had been overlooked or avoided in the past. One way of minimizing anxiety or premature termination of treatment is to predict that change may take more time than the couple expects, and that it is common to experience the relationship as worse off at times during the process. It may be useful to describe therapy as being like a glass of water with sand at the bottom. Treatment begins by observing and discussing issues that have been dormant (or festering) in the sand, subsequently mixing the sand and water together, and making the relationship seem more "cloudy" than it did before treatment. The goal of therapy is to become aware of what is in the sand, to change what can be changed, and finally, to guide the sand to settle and clear in ways that facilitate individual and relationship satisfaction.

REFERENCES

Atkeson, B. M., Calhoun, K. S., Resick, P. A., & Ellis, E. M. (1982). Victims of rape: Repeated assessment of depressive symptoms. *Journal of Consulting and Clinical Psychology, 50,* 96–102.

Balcom, D. (1996). The interpersonal dynamics and treatment of dual trauma couples. *Journal of Marital and Family Therapy, 22*(4), 431–442.

Baucom, D. H., & Hoffman, J. A. (1986). The effectiveness of marital therapy: Current status and application to the clinical setting. In N. S. Jacobson & A. S. Gurman (Eds.), *Clinical handbook of couple therapy* (pp. 597–620). New York: Guilford Press.

Beach, S. R. H., Sandeen, E. E., & O'Leary, K. D. (1990). *Depression in marriage: A model for etiology and treatment.* New York: Guilford Press.

Beck, A. T., Rush, A. J., Shaw, B. F., & Emery, G. (1979). *Cognitive therapy of depression.* New York: Guilford Press.

Biglan, A., Hops, H., Sherman, L., Friedman, L. S., Arthur, J., & Osteen, V. (1985). Problem solving interactions of depressed women and their husbands. *Behavior Therapy, 16,* 431–451.

Blake, D. D., Weathers, F. W., Nagy, L. M., Kaloupek, D. G., Klauminzer, G., Charney, & Keane, T. M. (1990). A clinician rating scale for assessing current and lifetime PTSD: The CAPS-1. *Behavior Therapist, 13,* 187–188.

Blanchard, E. B., Gerardi, R. J., Kolb, L. C., & Barlow, D. H. (1996). The utility of the anxiety disorders interview schedule (ADIS) in the diagnosis of post-traumatic stress disorder (PTSD) in Vietnam veterans. *Behaviour Research and Therapy, 24,* 577–580.

Briere, J. (1988). The long-term clinical correlates of childhood sexual victimization. *Annals of the New York Academy of Sciences, 528,* 327–334.

Briere, J. (1992). *Child abuse trauma: Theory and treatment of the lasting effects.* Newbury Park, CA: Sage.

Briere, J. (1995). *Trauma Symptom Inventory.* Odessa, FL: Psychological Assessment Resources.

Briere, J., & Runtz, M. (1987). Post sexual abuse trauma: Data and implications for clinical practice. *Journal of Interpersonal Violence, 2*(4), 367–379.

Briere, J., & Runtz, M. (1988). Symptomology associated with childhood sexual victimization in a non-clinical sample. *Child Abuse and Neglect, 12,* 51–59.

Briere, J., & Runtz, M. (1991). The long-term effects of sexual abuse: A review and synthesis. In J. Briere (Eds.), *Treating victims of child sexual abuse* (pp. 3–13). San Francisco: Jossey-Bass.

Briere, J., & Runtz, M. (1993). Childhood sexual abuse: Long-term sequelae and implications for psychological assessment. *Journal of Interpersonal Violence, 8,* 312–330.

Brody, E. M., & Farber, B. A. (1989). Effects of psychotherapy on significant others. *Professional Psychology Research and Practice, 20*(2), 116–122.

Brown, G. W., & Harris, T. O. (1978). *Social origins of depression: A study of psychiatric disorder in women.* New York: Free Press.

Browne, A., & Finkelhor, D. (1986). The impact of child sexual abuse: A review of the research. *Psychological Bulletin, 99,* 66–77.

Butcher, J. N., Dahlstrom, W. G., Graham, J. R., Tellegen, A., & Kaemmer, B. (1989). *Manual for the restandardized Minnesota Multiphasic Personality Inventory: MMPI-2.* Minneapolis: University of Minnesota Press.

Buttenheim, M., & Levendosky, A. (1994). Couples treatment for incest survivors. *Psychotherapy, 31,* 407–414.

Card, J. J. (1987). Epidemiology of PTSD in a national cohort of Vietnam veterans. *Journal of Clinical Psychology, 43,* 6–17.

Carroll, E. M., Foy, D. W., Cannon, B. J., & Zwier, G. (1991). Assessment issues involving the families of trauma victims. *Journal of Traumatic Stress Studies, 4,* 25–40.

Carroll, E. M., Rueger, D. B., Foy, D. W., & Donahue, C. P. (1985). Vietnam combat veterans with posttraumatic stress disorder: Analysis of marital and cohabiting adjustment. *Journal of Abnormal Psychology, 94*(3), 329–337.

Cerny, J. A., Barlow, D. H., Craske, M. G., & Hiladi, W. G. (1987). Couples treatment of agoraphobia: A two year follow-up. *Behavior Therapy, 18,* 401–415.

Christensen, A. (1988). Dysfunctional interaction patterns in couples. In P. Noller & M. A. Fitzpatrick (Eds.), *Perspectives on marital interaction* (pp. 31–52). Clevedon, Avon, UK: Multilingual Matters.

Christensen, A., & Heavey, C. L. (1990). Gender and social structure in the demand/withdraw pattern of marital conflict. *Journal of Personality and Social Psychology, 59,* 73–81.

Christensen, A., Jacobson, N. S., & Babcock, J. C. (1995). Integrative behavioral couple therapy. In N. S. Jacobson & A. S. Gurman (Eds.), *Clinical handbook of couple therapy* (pp. 31–63). New York: Guilford Press.

Christensen, A., & Shenk, J. L. (1991). Communication, conflict, and psychological distance in nondistressed, clinic, and divorcing couples. *Journal of Consulting and Clinical Psychology, 59*(3), 458–463.

Chu, J. A., & Dill, D. L. (1990). Dissociative symptoms in relation to childhood physical and sexual abuse. *American Journal of Psychiatry, 147,* 887–892.

Cole, P. M., & Woolger, C. (1989). Incest survivors: The relation of their perceptions of their parents and their own parenting attitudes. *Child Abuse and Neglect, 13,* 409–416.

Conners, M. E., & Morse, W. (1993). Sexual abuse and eating disorders: A review. *International Journal of Eating Disorders, 13,* 1–11.

Courtois, C. C. (1988). *Healing the incest wound: Adult survivors in therapy.* New York: Norton.

Coyne, J. C. (1976). Toward an interactional description of depression. *Psychiatry, 39,* 28–40.

Derogatis, L. R., Lipman, R. S., & Covi, L. (1973). SCL-90: An outpatient psychiatric rating scale—preliminary report. *Psychopharmocology Bulletin, 9,* 13–28.

Dye, E., & Roth, S. (1991). Psychotherapy with Vietnam veterans and rape and incest survivors. *Psychotherapy, 28*(1), 103–120.

Eldridge, G. D. (1991). Contextual issues in the assessment of post-traumatic stress disorder. *Journal of Traumatic Stress, 4*(1), 7–23.

Ellis, E. M., Atkeson, B. M., & Calhoun, K. S. (1981). An assessment of long-term reaction to rape. *Journal of Abnormal Psychology, 90,* 263–266.

Ellis, E. M., Calhoun, K. S., & Atkeson, B. M. (1980). Sexual dysfunctions in victims of rape: Victims may experience a loss of sexual arousal and frightening flashbacks even one year after the assault. *Women and Health, 5,* 39–47.

Epstein, N., & Baucom, D. H. (1988). *Cognitive-behavioral marital therapy.* New York: Brunner/Mazel.

Figley, C. R. (1983). Catastrophes: An overview of family reactions. In C. R. Figley & H. I. McCubbin (Eds.), *Stress and the family: Vol II. Coping with catastrophe* (pp. 3–20). New York: Brunner/Mazel.

Figley, C. R. (1985). *Trauma and its wake: The study and treatment of post-traumatic stress disorder.* New York: Brunner/Mazel.

Finkelhor, D., Hotaling, G. T., Lewis, I. A., & Smith, C. (1989). Sexual abuse and its relationship to later sexual satisfaction, marital status, religion, and attitudes. *Journal of Interpersonal Violence, 4,* 379–399.

Follette, V. M. (1991). Marital therapy for sexual abuse survivors. In J. Briere (Ed.), *Treating victims of child sexual abuse* (pp. 61–71). San Francisco: Jossey-Bass.

Follette, V. M. (1994). Survivors of child sexual abuse: Treatment using a contextual analysis. In S. C. Hayes, N. S. Jacobson, V. M. Follette, & M. J. Dougher (Eds.), *Acceptance and change: Content and context in psychotherapy* (pp. 255–268). Reno, NV: Context Press.

Follette, V. M., Alexander, P. C., & Follette, W. F. (1991). Individual predictors of outcome in group treatment for incest survivors. *Journal of Consulting and Clinical Psychology, 59*(1), 150–155.

Follette, V. M., & Pistorello, J. (1995). Couples therapy: When one partner has been sexually abused. In C. Classen (Eds.), *Treating women molested in childhood* (pp. 129–161). San Francisco: Jossey-Bass.

Follette, V. M., Polusny, M. M., Bechtle, A. E., & Naugle, A. E. (1996). Cumulative trauma effects: The impact of child sexual abuse, adult sexual assault, and spouse abuse. *Journal of Traumatic Stress, 9,* 15–25.

Follette, V. M., & Serafin, J. M. (1995, November). *Contextual couple therapy for child sexual abuse survivors.* Premeeting institute presented at the Annual Meeting of the International Society for Traumatic Stress Studies, Boston, MA.

Foy, D. W. (1992). Introduction and description of the disorder. In D. W. Foy (Ed.), *Treating PTSD: Cognitive-behavioral strategies.* New York: Guilford Press.

Fruzzetti, A. E. (1996). Causes and consequences: Individual distress in the context of couple interactions. *Journal of Consulting and Clinical Psychology, 64,* 1192–1201.

Fruzzetti, A. E., & Jacobson, N. S. (1988, November). *Factors affecting the dissolution of intimate (dating) relationships.* Paper presented at the annual meeting of the Association for the Advancement of Behavior Therapy, New York.

Fruzzetti, A. E., & Serafin, J. M. (1995, July). *A functional approach to observing couple intimacy and distancing processes.* Paper presented at the World Congress of Behavioural and Cognitive Therapies, Copenhagen, Denmark.

Gold, E. R. (1986). Long-term effects of sexual victimization in childhood: An attributional approach. *Journal of Consulting and Clinical Psychology, 54*(4), 471–475.

Gorcey, M., Santiago, J. M., & McCall-Perez, F. (1986). Psychological consequences for women sexually abused in childhood. *Social Psychiatry, 21,* 129–133.

Gotlib, I. H., & McCabe, S. B. (1990). Marriage and psychopathology. In F. D. Fincham & T. N. Bradbury (Eds.), *The psychology of marriage: Basic issues and applications* (pp. 227–257). New York: Guilford Press.

Gotlib, I. H., & Whiffen, V. E. (1989). Stress, coping, and marital satisfaction in couples with a depressed wife. *Canadian Journal of Behavioral Science, 21*(4), 401–418.

Gottman, J. M., & Krokoff, L. J. (1989). Marital interaction and satisfaction: A longitudinal view. *Journal of Consulting and Clinical Psychology, 57*(1), 47–52.

Graber, K. (1991). *Ghosts in the bedroom: A guide for partners of incest survivors.* Deerfield Beach, FL: Health Communications.

Greenberg, L. S., & Johnson, S. M. (1988). *Emotionally focused couples therapy.* New York: Wiley.

Hahlweg, K., & Markman, H. J. (1988). The effectiveness of behavioral marital therapy: Empirical status of behavioral techniques in preventing and alleviating marital distress. *Journal of Consulting and Clinical Psychology, 56,* 440–447.

Hahlweg, K., Schindler, L., & Revenstorf, D. (1982). Treatment of marital distress: Comparing formats and modalities. *Advances in Behavior Research and Therapy, 4,* 57–74.

Hahlweg, K., Schindler, L., Revenstorf, D., & Brengelmann, J. C. (1984). The Munich marital therapy study. In K. Hahlweg & N. S. Jacobson (Eds.), *Marital interaction: Analysis and modification.* New York: Guilford Press.

Harter, S. Alexander, P. C., & Neimeyer, R. A. (1988). Long-term effects of incestuous child abuse in college women: Social adjustment, social cognition, and family characteristics. *Journal of Consulting and Clinical Psychology, 56,* 5–8.

Hayes, S. C. (1987). A contextual approach to therapeutic change. In N. S. Jacobson (Ed.), *Psychotherapists in clinical practice: Cognitive and behavioral perspectives* (pp. 327–387). New York: Guilford Press.

Hayes, S. C. (1994). Content, context, and the types of psychological acceptance. In S. C. Hayes, N. S. Jacobson, V. M. Follette, & M. J. Dougher (Eds.), *Acceptance and change: Content and context in psychotherapy* (pp. 13–32). Reno, NV: Context Press.

Herman, J. L., Perry, J. C., & van der Kolk, B. A. (1989). Childhood trauma in borderline personality disorder. *American Journal of Psychiatry, 146,* 490–495.

Holtzworth-Munroe, A., Beatty, S. B., & Anglin, K. (1995). The assessment and treatment of marital violence: An introduction for the marital therapist. In N. S. Jacobson & A. S. Gurman (Eds.), *Clinical handbook of couple therapy* (pp. 316–339). New York: Guilford Press.

Hooley, J. M., Richters, J. E., Weintraub, S., & Neale, J. M. (1987). Psychopathology and marital distress: The positive side of positive symptoms. *Journal of Consulting and Clinical Psychology, 96*(1), 27–33.

Houskamp, B. M., & Foy, D. W. (1991). The assessment of posttraumatic stress disorder in battered women. *Journal of Interpersonal Violence, 6,* 367–375.

Jackson, J. L., Calhoun, K. S., Amick, A. E., Maddever, H. M., & Habif, V. L. (1990). Young adult women who report childhood intrafamilial sexual abuse: Subsequent adjustment. *Archives of Sexual Behavior, 19,* 211–221.

Jacobson, N. S., & Addis, M. E. (1993). Research on couples and couple therapy: What do we know? Where are we going? *Journal of Consulting and Clinical Psychology, 61*(1), 85–93.

Jacobson, N. S., & Christensen, A. (1996). *Integrative couple therapy: Promoting acceptance and change.* New York: Norton.

Jacobson, N. S., Dobson, K., Fruzzetti, A. E., Schmaling, K. B., & Salusky, S. (1991). Marital therapy as a treatment for depression. *Journal of Consulting and Clinical Psychology, 59,* 547–557.

Jacobson, N. S., Follette, W. C., Pagel, M. (1986). Predicting who will benefit from behavioral marital therapy. *Journal of Consulting and Clinical Psychology, 54,* 518–522.

Jacobson, N. S., Fruzzetti, A. E., Dobson, K., Whisman, M., & Hops, H. (1993). Couple therapy as a treatment for depression: II. The effects of relationship quality and therapy on depressive relapse. *Journal of Consulting and Clinical Psychology, 61*(3), 516–519.

Jacobson, N. S., & Holtzworth-Munroe, A. (1986). Marital therapy: A social learning–cognitive perspective. In N. S. Jacobson & A. S. Gurman (Eds.), *Clinical handbook of marital therapy* (pp. 29–70). New York: Guilford Press.

Jacobson, N. S., Holtzworth-Munroe, A., & Schmaling, K. B. (1989). Marital therapy and spouse involvement in the treatment of depression, agoraphobia, and alcoholism. *Journal of Consulting and Clinical Psychology, 57*(1), 5–10.

Jacobson, N. S., & Margolin, G. (1979). *Martial therapy: Strategies based on social learning and behavior exchange principles.* New York: Brunner/Mazel.

Jacobson, N. S., Schmaling, K. B., & Holtzworth-Munroe, A. (1987). Component analysis of behavioral marital therapy: Two-year follow-up and prediction of relapse. *Journal of Marital and Family Therapy, 13,* 187–195.

Jacobson, N. S., Waldron, H., & Moore, D. (1980). Toward a behavioral profile of marital distress. *Journal of Consulting and Clinical Psychology, 48,* 696–703.

Johnson, S. M. (1989). Integrating marital and individual therapy for incest survivors: A case study. *Psychotherapy, 26*(1), 96–103.

Jordan B. K., Marmar, C. R., Fairbank, J. A., Schlenger, W. E., Kulka, R. A., Hough, R. L., & Weiss, D. S. (1992). Problems in families of male Vietnam veterans with posttraumatic stress disorder. *Journal of Consulting and Clinical Psychology, 60*(6), 916–926.

Keane, T. M., & Wolfe, J. (1990). Comorbidity in post-traumatic stress disorder: An analysis of community and clinical studies. *Journal of Applied Social Psychology, 20,* 1776–1788.

Kilpatrick, D. G., Edmunds, C. N., & Seymour, A. K. (1992). *Rape in America: A report to the nation.* Arlington, VA: National Victim Center.

Kilpatrick, D. G., & Veronen, L. J. (1984, February). Treatment of fear and anxiety in victims of rape (Final report, Grant No. MH29602). Washington, DC: National Institute of Mental Health.

Koerner, K., Prince, S., & Jacobson, N. S. (1994). Enhancing the treatment and prevention of depression in women: The role of integrative behavioral couple therapy. *Behavior Therapy, 25,* 373–390.

Kohlenberg, R. J., & Tsai, M. (1991). *Functional analytic psychotherapy.* New York: Plenum.

Koss, M. P., & Harvey, M. R. (1991). *The rape victim: Clinical and community interventions* (2nd ed.). Newbury Park, CA: Sage.

Koss, M. P., Koss, P., & Woodruff, W. J. (1991). Deleterious effects of criminal victimization on women's health and medical utilization. *Archives of Internal Medicine, 151*(2), 342–347.

Kramer, T. L., & Green B. L. (1991). Posttraumatic stress disorder as an early response to sexual assault. *Journal of Interpersonal Violence, 6,* 160–173.

Kulka, R. A., Schlenger, W. E., Fairbank, J. A., Hough, R. L., Jordan, B. K., Marmar, C. R., & Weiss, D. S. (1990). *Trauma and the Vietnam War generation.* New York: Brunner/Mazel.

Lacoursiere, R. B., Godfrey, K. E., & Ruby, L. M. (1980). Traumatic neurosis in the etiology of alcoholism: Vietnam combat and other trauma. *American Journal of Psychiatry, 137*(8), 966–968.

Leitenberg, H., Greenwald, E., & Cado, S. (1992). A retrospective study of long-term methods of coping with having been sexually abused during childhood. *Child Abuse and Neglect, 16,* 399–407.

Lindberg, F. H., & Distad, L. J. (1985). Post-traumatic stress disorders in women who experienced childhood incest. *Child Abuse and Neglect, 9*(3), 329–334.

Linehan, M. M. (1993). *Cognitive-behavioral treatment of borderline personality disorder.* New York: Guilford Press.

LoPiccolo, J., & Friedman, J. M. (1987). Broad-spectrum treatment of low sexual desire: Integration of cognitive, behavioral and systemic therapy. In S. R. Leiblum & R. C. Rosen (Eds.), *Sexual desire disorders* (pp. 107–144). New York: Guilford Press.

Maltz, W., & Holman, B. (1987). *Incest and sexuality.* Lexington, MA: Lexington Books.

Margolin, G. Talovic, S., & Weinstein, C. D. (1983). Areas of Change Questionnaire: A practical approach to marital assessment. *Journal of Consulting and Clinical Psychology, 51,* 920–931.

McCrady, B. S., & Epstein, E. E. (1995). Marital therapy in the treatment of alcohol problems. In N. S. Jacobson & A. S. Gurman (Eds.), *Clinical handbook of couple therapy* (pp. 369–393). New York: Guilford Press.

McMillen, C., Zuravin, S., & Rideout, G. (1995). Perceived benefit from child sexual abuse. *Journal of Consulting and Clinical Psychology, 63*(6), 1037–1043.

Miller, W. R., Williams, M., & Bernstein, M. H. (1982). The effects of rape on marital and sexual adjustment. *American Journal of Family Therapy, 10,* 51–58.

Mio, J. S., & Foster, J. D. (1991). The effects of rape upon victims and families: Implications for a comprehensive family therapy. *American Journal of Family Therapy, 19*(2), 147–159.

Moss, M., Frank, E., & Anderson, B. (1990). The effects of marital status and partner support on rape trauma. *American Journal of Orthopsychiatry, 60*(3), 379–391.

Nadelson, C. C. (1989). Consequences of rape: Clinical and treatment aspects. *Psychotherapy and Psychosomatics, 51,* 187–192.

Naugle, A. E., Follette, W. C., & Follette, V. M. (1995, November). *Toward prevention of revictimization: A functional analytic model.* Paper presented at the annual meeting of the Association for Advancement of Behavior Therapy, Washington, DC.

Nelson, G. M., & Beach, S. R. H. (1990). Sequential interaction in depression: Effects of depressive behavior on spouse aggression. *Behavior Therapy, 21,* 167–182.

O'Leary, K. D., & Beach, S. R. (1990). Marital therapy: A viable treatment for depression and marital discord. *American Journal of Psychiatry, 147*(2), 183–186.

Paque, C. J., Serafin, J. M., Fruzzetti, A. E., & Weiss, S. A. (1996, May). *The function of aggression and violence in heterosexual and lesbian couples.* Paper presented at the annual meeting of the Association for Behavior Analysis, San Francisco.

Pavalko, E. K., & Elder, G. H. (1990). World War II and divorce: A life-course perspective. *American Journal of Sociology, 95*(5), 1213–1234.

Paykel, E. S., Myers, J. K., Dienelt, M. N., Klerman, G. L., Lindenthal, J. J., & Pepper, M. P. (1969). Life events and depression: A controlled study. *Archives of General Psychiatry, 21,* 753–760.

Penk, W. E., Robinowitz, R., Roberts, W. R., Patterson, E. T., Dolan, M. P., & Atkins, H.

G. (1981). Adjustment differences among male substance abusers varying in degree of combat experience in Vietnam. *Journal of Consulting and Clinical Psychology, 49*(3), 426–437.

Pistorello, J., & Follette, V. M. (in press). Child sexual abuse and couples relationships: Female survivors' reports in therapy groups. *Journal of Marital and Family Therapy.*

Polusny, M. A., & Follette, V. M. (1995). Long-term correlates of child sexual abuse: Theory and review of the empirical literature. *Applied and Preventive Psychology, 4,* 143–166.

Pribor, E. F., & Dinwiddie, S. H. (1992). Psychiatric correlates of incest in childhood. *American Journal of Psychiatry, 150,* 1507–1511.

Rabin, C., & Nardi, C. (1991). Treating post traumatic stress disorder couples: A psychoeducational approach. *Community Mental Health Journal, 27*(3), 209–224.

Raczek, S. W. (1992). Childhood abuse and personality disorders. *Journal of Personality Disorders, 6,* 109–116.

Resick, P. A. (1993). The psychological impact of rape. *Journal of Interpersonal Violence, 8*(2), 223–255.

Resick, P. A., Calhoun, K. S., Atkeson, B. M., & Ellis, E. M. (1981). Social adjustment in victims of sexual assault. *Journal of Consulting and Clinical Psychology, 49,* 705–712.

Riggs, D. S., Byrne, C. A., Weathers, F. W., & Litz, B. T. (1998). The quality of the intimate relationships of male Vietnam veterans: Problems associated with posttraumatic stress disorder. *Journal of Traumatic Stress, 11*(1), 87–101.

Roberts, W. R., Penk, W. E., Gearing, M. L., Robinowitz, R., Dolan, M. P., & Patterson, E. T. (1982). Interpersonal problems of Vietnam combat veterans with symptoms of posttraumatic stress disorder. *Journal of Abnormal Psychology, 91*(6), 444–450.

Rodriguez, N., Ryan, S. W., & Foy, D. W. (1992, November). *Tension reduction and PTSD: Adult survivors of sexual abuse.* Paper presented at the annual meeting of the International Society for Traumatic Stress Studies, Los Angeles.

Rothbaum, B. O., Foa, E. B., Murdock, T., Riggs, D. S., & Walsh, W. (1992). A prospective examination of post-traumatic stress disorder in rape victims. *Journal of Traumatic Stress, 5,* 455–475.

Russell, D. E. (1986). *The secret trauma: Incest in the lives of girls and women.* New York: Basic Books.

Selzer, M. L. (1971). The Michigan Alcoholism Screening Test: The quest for a new diagnostic instrument. *American Journal of Psychiatry, 127,* 1653–1658.

Serafin, J. M. (1996). Disrupted relationships and couple therapy: Treating female survivors of child sexual abuse and their partners. *PTSD Clinical Quarterly, 6*(2), 42–45.

Serafin, J. M., & Follette, V. M. (1996, November). *Female survivors of sexual trauma and their partners: Issues in couple functioning.* Paper presented at the annual meeting of the International Society for Traumatic Stress Studies, San Francisco.

Silver, S. M., & Iacono, C. (1986). Symptom groups and family patterns of Vietnam veterans with post-traumatic stress disorders. In C. R. Figley (Ed.), *Trauma and its wake* (pp. 78–96). New York: Brunner/Mazel.

Silverman, D. C. (1978). Sharing the crisis of rape: Counseling the mates and families of victims. *American Journal of Orthopsychiatry, 48,* 166–173.

Snyder, D. K., Wills, R. M., & Grady-Fletcher, A. (1991). Long-term effectiveness of behavioral versus insight-oriented marital therapy. *Journal of Consulting and Clinical Psychology, 59,* 138–141.

Solomon, Z. (1988). The effect of combat-related posttraumatic stress disorder on the family. *Psychiatry, 51,* 323–329.

Solomon, Z., & Mikulincer, M. (1992). Aftermaths of combat stress reactions: A three-year study. *British Journal of Clinical Psychiatry, 31,* 21–32.

Solomon, Z., Waysman, M., Avitzur, E., & Enoch, D. (1991). Psychiatric symptomatology among wives of soldiers following combat stress reaction: The role of the social network and marital relations. *Anxiety Research, 4,* 213–223.

Solomon, Z., Waysman, M., Levy, G., Fried, B., Mikulincer, M., Benbenishty, R., Florian, V., & Bleich, A. (1992). From front line to home front: A study of secondary traumatization. *Family Process, 31,* 289–302.

Spanier, G. (1976). Measuring dyadic adjustment: New scales for assessing the quality of marriage and similar dyads. *Journal of Marriage and the Family, 38,* 15–28.

Straus, M. A. (1979). Measuring intrafamily conflict and violence: The conflict tactics scales. *Journal of Marriage and the Family, 41,* 75–87.

Stuart, R. B. (1980). *Helping couples change: A social learning approach to marital therapy.* New York: Guilford Press.

Van Buskirk, S. S., & Cole, C. F. (1983). Characteristics of eight women seeking therapy for the effects of incest. *Psychotherapy: Theory, Research, and Practice, 20*(4), 503–514.

Van den Broucke, S., & Vandereycken, W. (1988). Anorexia and bulimia nervosa in married patients: A review. *Comprehensive Psychiatry, 29*(2), 165–173.

Van den Broucke, S., & Vandereycken, W. (1989). The marital relationship of patients with an eating disorder. *International Journal of Eating Disorders, 8*(5), 541–556.

Verbosky, S. J., & Ryan, D. A. (1988). Female partners of Vietnam veterans: Stress by proximity. *Issues in Mental Health Nursing, 9,* 95–104.

Walker, E., Katon, W. J., Harrop-Griffiths, J., Holm, L., Russo, J., & Hickok, L. R. (1988). Relationship of chronic pelvic pain to psychiatric diagnoses and childhood sexual abuse. *American Journal of Psychiatry, 145,* 75–80.

Waltz, J. (1993). *The long-term effects of childhood sexual abuse on women's relationships with partners.* Unpublished doctoral dissertation, University of Washington, Seattle.

Williams, J. P. (1980). *Posttraumatic stress disorders of the Vietnam veteran.* Cincinnati, OH: Disabled American Veterans.

Wind, T. W., & Silvern, L. (1992). Type and extent of child abuse as predictors of adult functioning. *Journal of Family Violence, 7,* 261–281.

Winkel, F. W., & Koppelaar, L. (1991). Rape victims' style of self-preservation and secondary victimization by the environment: An experiment. *Journal of Interpersonal Violence, 6*(1), 29–40.

Wyatt, G. E., Guthrie, D., & Notgrass, C. M. (1992). Differential effects of women's child sexual abuse and subsequent sexual revictimization. *Journal of Consulting and Clinical Psychology, 60*(2), 167–173.

Wyatt, G. E., & Lyons-Rowe, S. (1990). African American women's sexual satisfaction as a dimension of their sex roles. *Sex Roles, 22,* 509–524.

Wyatt, G. E., & Newcomb, M. (1990). Internal and external mediators of women's sexual abuse in childhood. *Journal of Consulting and Clinical Psychology, 58*(6), 758–767.

PART THREE

TRAUMA ACROSS
THE LIFESPAN

CHAPTER FOURTEEN

Trauma in Children

WILLIAM O'DONOHUE
MATTHEW FANETTI
ANN ELLIOTT

Children experience the same kinds of trauma as adults. They can be in serious automobile accidents, experience the horrors of war and natural disasters, and can be physically and sexually abused. Unfortunately for reviewers, the literature on many of these traumas is spotty and largely undeveloped, particularly regarding children. The most developed literature regarding trauma and children is the literature on child sexual abuse. In this chapter, we review the literature on child sexual abuse; and although the literature still leaves many matters unresolved, it is the most informative regarding trauma and children. Although one must exercise extreme care in extrapolating from this literature to other traumas, at least many *methodological* points have a significant degree of relevance to other traumas. Given the early stage of development in this field, it is the methodological points that are the most important. Finally, it is our contention that one cannot make global conclusions about "trauma in children," but rather one must look at the particulars to make more particular conclusions.

CHILD SEXUAL ABUSE

Although we know that some children are sexually abused, accurate figures of the incidence and prevalence of this problem are difficult to come by. Epidemiological studies suggest anywhere from 10% to 64% of females and from 3% to 25% of males experience some kind of unwanted sexual contact before the age of eighteen (see Salter, 1992, for a review). The obviously wide range of frequency estimates calls for some explanation. The methodological characteristics of the study probably have a significant influence on the wide range of reported frequency. Factors such as varying definitions of abuse, different dependent measures, and diverse sample characteristics can contribute to a significant amount of variability in the reported frequency.

It also is difficult to interpret the significance of these findings: Are these estimates reliable enough that they can be taken to indicate a very widespread social problem? Are there trends in these figures that suggest that sexual abuse is increasing? Or, on the other hand, are the figures sufficiently high as to suggest that within these figures there are a sizable number of false reports of sexual abuse? Are these high figures both cause and product of a moral panic, inflamed by the media seeking sensational stories? A better knowledge of the real incidence of this problem would not only aid in deciding among these interpretations, but it would also aid the clinician. However, identifying accurate incidence and prevalence figures is a very difficult task, as there are usually no valid markers for the event, and discerning what has happened when there are conflicting reports, or no report at all, is quite difficult. However, a knowledge of base rates is useful in forming a reasonable index of suspicion during diagnosis.

Furthermore, although we know that child sexual abuse can have clinically significant effects for the child, the exact nature of these effects, whether they cluster together in some syndrome, the extent to which problems emerge immediately or are delayed, and factors that mediate or buffer the effects of abuse are largely unknown. Because much of this critical information is missing, the clinician is not in a good position to predict the course of the sequelae of abuse. Moreover, to the extent that the treatment prescribed will depend upon the exact nature of the problems that emerge, and that the literature indicates that these sequelae are quite variable (Browne & Finkelhor, 1986; O'Donohue & Elliott, 1992b; Polusny & Follette, 1995), the clinician will need to develop fairly ideographic treatment plans for each sexually abused child. In this chapter, assessment of potential sequelae of abuse and of related abuse issues is reviewed.

Relatedly, we briefly review the extant treatment outcome literature on sexually abused children and make some tentative recommendations concerning treatment. The reader should be advised at the outset, however, that this literature is sparse, methodologically problematic, and gives no clear indication that effective treatments exist for this population. Some of these studies, however, point to some promising clinical strategies that certainly can decrease some of the vast amount of uncertainty that exists in this area. We turn next to a discussion of the assessment of the sexually abused child. We first discuss the difficult forensic issue of determining whether a child alleged to have been sexually abused has, in fact, been abused.

FORENSIC ASSESSMENT

Once again, we will use child sexual abuse as a model, but the same processes apply to the assessment of any child trauma that may involve litigation. Before engaging in any course of treatment with a child who is thought to have been sexually abused, it is imperative to determine to the best of the therapist's ability whether the child has actually been sexually abused. One must also acknowledge that legal or other institutional decisions regarding abuse status may or may not decide this issue for the clinician. For example, if the local child protective service has decided that a report is unfounded, the clinician can accept this conclusion or come to another conclusion. It is important to note that various institutions have their own standards of evidence, and while the clinician should know these and understand the nature of the evidence, the clinician is not bound by these external decisions, but must come to his or her own reasonable conclusion about this important question.

There are two very important functions for the assessment of a child who may have been sexually abused. The first is to determine whether on adult or older child is to be reported as a possible perpetrator. It is necessary to concretely determine that an abusive event occurred, as well as the details of any event, so that abuse perpetrators can be dealt with appropriately. Making an inaccurate conclusion at this point can be devastating to either an innocent, accused individual or to an abused child who may then be abused further. The next function of assessment is to determine whether abuse occurred in order to make decisions about the appropriateness of psychotherapy. Once again, inaccurate decisions can be deleterious to the child. Deciding that no abuse occurred, when in reality it did, can leave the child without the therapeutic opportunities to deal with some possibly difficult or confusing memories. Deciding that abuse did occur when in reality it did not, can also be deleterious to the child. If therapy progresses under the false presumption of sexual abuse, the child may begin to incorporate some of the very experiences that therapy should be designed to ameliorate. Therefore, it should be clear that the assessment of the occurrence of sexual abuse should be taken very seriously, and the dangers of drawing inaccurate conclusions should be thoroughly understood. There are some different assessment strategies available to professionals who wish to assess a child they suspect may have been sexually abused. We now critically examine these.

Statement Validity Analysis

Statement validity analysis (SVA) is based on the hypothesis that true and false reports by children will be different, both qualitatively and quantitatively (Undeutsch, 1989). According to SVA, this difference should allow an approximate determination of the veracity of the child's report by interviewing the child in a specific manner and observing the child's responses. For example, SVA is used to evaluate five possible hypotheses regarding the child's report:

1. The allegations are basically valid but the child has substituted a different person for the perpetrator.

2. The fundamental allegations are valid, but the child has invented or has been influenced to make additional allegations that are false.
3. The child has been influenced or pressured to make a completely false allegation to serve the needs of someone else.
4. The child has made a false allegation for personal motives of revenge, gain, or to help someone else.
5. The child has fantasized the allegations, possibly because of psychological problems. (Raskin & Esplin, 1992, p. 272)

These hypotheses are related to the details of the reported event. In addition, SVA is designed to make judgments about a number of variables related to the child's report, which may provide information about the veracity of that report (e.g., level of contextual embeddedness, consistency of responses, etc.).

SVA is then a hypothesis testing process; that is, there are a number of possible hypotheses regarding the child's report, and the methodology is designed to assess each hypothesis in order to rule it out, or not rule it out. While this is a worthwhile goal, SVA has theoretical problems that serve to make the results it provides difficult to interpret, the first of which is enumeration of possible hypotheses. In order for a hypothesis testing model to provide useful information about an assessment, *every plausible hypothesis must be identified* (O'Donohue & Fanetti, 1996). If rival hypotheses are not identified, then conclusions drawn in their absence may be invalid. In that case, no assessment was available to determine the impact of the missing hypothesis on the results. SVA enumerates only an incomplete set of rival hypotheses.

The next problem facing SVA is that the purported mission of the tool is to make conclusions about the actual veracity of the child's report. This however is outside the realm of this assessment. No professional has direct access to the truth. Usually, the only two individuals who experienced the event are the perpetrator and the victim. There is a substantial body of empirical literature that suggests that the memory of children can be altered by certain influential factors such as leading questions (Ceci & Liechtman, 1992), the perceived authority of the interviewer (Clarke-Stewart, Thompson, & Lepore, 1989), and the nature of the questioning (King & Yuille, 1987; Cohen & Harnick, 1980; Cole & Loftus, 1987; Dale, Loftus, & Rathburn, 1987; Davies, 1989; Peters, 1987; see Fanetti & O'Donohue, 1998a, for a review). There is little question that children's reports *can* be affected and distorted. SVA is not explicitly designed to control for these information-processing biasing influences, and it cannot be determined whether it actually contains one or more. Therefore, any statement about the "veracity" of the child's report must be weighed in the light of the problems of (1) being unable to directly assess the truth, and (2) being unable to rule out biasing affects brought on by SVA itself or by other contacts. A later section on the Sexual Abuse Structured Interview for Children (SASIC) discusses a different way to utilize a hypothesis testing model.

Investigatory Interviewing

Many professionals use assessment methodologies that are described in "guide-lines" (e.g., deYoung, 1992; Gardiner, 1992; White & Edelstein, 1991; Yuille, 1992) . Often, these interviews take on the role of investigation and collection of event details. In fact, they are often referred to as "investigatory interviews." These types of interviews may be useful for law enforcement officials because they emphasize the importance of specific details. Offense details are often needed by prosecutors to enter the judicial process. Additionally, when a child is able to provide very specific and elaborate details about an event, it may be intuitively easier to infer that the child must then have experienced an event. However, this is simply not true. Loftus has spent a large part of her career demonstrating that even adults *can* be made to remember very specific details of events that demonstrably did not happen. There is no evidence that children are somehow free of this capacity. In fact, there is notable research that suggests that children *are not* free from this problem (Goodman, Aman, & Hirschman, 1987; Goodman & Reed, 1986; King & Yuille, 1987; Marin, Guth, & Kovac, 1979; Saywitz, 1987).

These types of interviews have several major problems. The first is that the methods proposed in the guidelines are often based on principles not grounded in the empirical literature. The second problem is that there is usually no means to make sense of a sometimes very large, but extraneous to the interview process, body of information (e.g., medical evidence) gathered during these investigations for the purpose of determining whether abuse did or did not occur. The third problem is that there is no empirical evidence that these interviews can be administered reliably, or that the information produced is valid. It should be noted that child sexual abuse assessments are a measurement activity, and thus are subject to investigations regarding their psychometric properties. An absence of psychometric data should make a scientific practitioner reluctant to use the device, especially if there is a device available that is supported by empirical psychometric evaluation.

Unstructured Interviews

Probably the most frequently used form of assessment is the unstructured, infor-mal interview. Unlike the aforementioned strategies, these interviews are not usually guided by a formal standard approach, but may instead be based on experience and intuitive judgment. This approach, however, is also hindered by the problems of the previous interviews, and arguably more so. It is impossible to determine what these interviews look like, and a reasonable guess would be that there is no standard format. What is certain is that there is no empirical research that supports this approach.

Structured Interviews

There are methods to construct an interview that facilitate the analysis of its content and psychometric properties. In order to do this, the content of the interview must be well detailed, and the responses–questions available to the interviewer must be controlled. This is known as a structured interview. A new structured interview, the Sexual Abuse Structured Interview for Children (SASIC, Fanetti & O'Donohue, 1998b) has been designed to aid in assessing the occurrence of child sexual abuse utilizing an information-processing, hypothesis-testing approach. It should be noted from the outset, however, that the goal of this interview is to improve the interpretability of the child interview by eliminating biasing factors in the interview and assessing those that might have occurred before the interview. It is not to make a final determination (or the determination of the probability) that the child has been sexually abused. This final conclusion must be made utilizing all information (e.g., the statements of others, medical evidence, etc.).

The SASIC systematically avoids the pitfalls of previous assessment attempts in several ways. First, it is designed to assess the quality of the child's report with regard to the possibility of bias that may be introduced by various behaviors before and during the interview. Instead of making leaps of faith by talking about the *veracity* (which we can never know) of the child's report, the SASIC investigates the things (called potential biasing factors) that may change a child's memory–report. If a potential biasing factor is found to be *not present*, there is no way that the child's report can have been affected by it. Table 14.1 lists factors that are controlled for/assessed by the SASIC. To deal with the problem of unidentified rival hypotheses making the conclusions uninterpretable, the SASIC has sought to assess/control all the major sources of bias that can be reasonably thought to be influential in the acquisition of memory reports from children.

The SASIC also has a structured format that should allow very little deviation from the planned progression of the interview. Exact question wordings and decision trees are provided. This was done to allow the scientific evaluation of the psychometric properties. If the format is sufficiently structured, interviewers should be expected to administer the same questions given the same presentation. This is prerequisite for studies of reliability and validity.

CLINICAL ASSESSMENT

Empirical evidence to date suggests that individuals respond to childhood sexual victimization with a highly diverse and idiographic set of responses. Some have even contended that sexual interactions between a child and adult can have no detrimental effects, or possibly even have beneficial effects for the child (e.g., Henderson, 1983; Ramey, 1979; Sandfort, 1992). Others, however (e.g., Browne

TABLE 14.1. Factors Controlled for or Assessed by the SASIC (O'Donohue & Fanetti, 1996)

Past event-derived information-processing hypotheses

1. The child did not sense the abuse (e.g., the child was drugged).
2. The child misperceived and mis-encoded the event, the child assimilated an abusive experience into another schema (e.g., "playing a game" or misperceived and misencoded a nonabusive event into an abuse schema (e.g., a medically prescribed enema).
3. The child has experienced some storage problem (e.g., decay).
4. The child has experienced a retrieval problem (e.g., a lack of appropriate cues).
5. The child has confabulated different experiences (e.g., the child has combined his experience of a sex prevention program with his experience of having a normal bath).
6. Due to some unspecified processing problems, the child displays general deficits in recounting real from imagined events.
7. The child's report has been contaminated by some outside source (previous contact with another professional; e.g., retroactive interference from some previous interviews).
8. The amount of detail of the account (either absence or presence) can be explained by developmental information processing abilities.
9. The child's disclosure is inhibited because he or she was taught not to talk about "dirty things."

Assessment-derived information-processing hypotheses

1. The child did not understand her role in the interview, or the purpose of the interview and therefore her answers were distorted.
2. The child, due to rapport problems, was not comfortable and therefore did not answer in a full, accurate manner.
3. The child had some sort of externally derived motivation to distort answers (e.g., fear of threats, purpose miscommunicated by some adult).
4. The child felt as if he or she had no choice but to answer a certain way.
5. Child did not know that he or she could say, "I don't know" when he or she did not know.
6. The child answered in a certain way in an attempt to please an authority figure.
7. Child did not know the importance of stating the truth.
8. Child did not understand what it means to tell the truth.
9. The child failed to understand the question.
10. The child misspoke in his or her answer.
11. The question was leading.
12. The child's utterances were at times disconfirmed.
13. The interviewer differentially reinforced certain types of answers.
14. The questions were repetitive and therefore coercive.
15. The child changed responses to repeated questioning because she assumed that a repetition of the question meant that her initial response was incorrect.
16. There were aspects of the child's total response (e.g., body posture, facial expression) that gives a different interpretation to the child's answer.

Other

1. The child is lying (i.e., knowingly presenting some false information).
2. The child's psychological state that is similar or dissimilar to abuse sequelae has some other explanation.

& Finkelhor, 1986; Hoier, Inderbitzen-Pisaruk, & Shawchuck, 1987; Lipovsky & Kilpatrick; 1992; Polusny & Follette, 1995; Wolfe & Wolfe, 1988), report a wide variety of psychological and behavioral disturbances. In the assessment section of this chapter, we first provide a brief review of various initial and long-term effects of child sexual abuse frequently noted in the literature. This is followed by a description of three models that have been proposed to organize data concerning the effects of childhood sexual victimization. Next, we present a general model for assessing sexually abused children. Finally, we review several assessment devices that have undergone psychometric evaluation for use with sexually abused children.

Initial and Long-Term Effects of Child Sexual Abuse

In an extensive review of the literature concerning the initial and long-term effects of child sexual abuse, Browne and Finkelhor (1986) reported that the most commonly observed initial effect of sexual abuse in children is fear, which may be either abuse-specific or generalized (Conte & Schuerman, 1987). Similarly, anger and hostility (Tufts New England Medical Center, 1984), delinquency (Gruber & Jones, 1981), truancy and running away (e.g., Herman, 1981; Meiselman, 1978), guilt and shame (DeFrancis, 1969), depression (Anderson, Bach, & Griffith, 1981), sexual behavior problems (Friedrich, Beilke, & Urquiza, 1987; Tufts New England Medical Center, 1984), and sleep and eating disturbances (Anderson et al., 1981; Peters, 1987) have been noted in abuse victims as well. History of sexual abuse has also been associated with dissociative symptoms in children (Hoier et al., 1988; Deblinger, McLeer, Atkins, Ralphe, & Foa, 1989) as well as with symptoms of posttraumatic stress disorder (PTSD; McLeer, Deblinger, Atkins, Foa, & Ralphe, 1988; Wolfe, Gentile, & Wolfe, 1989; Wolfe, Gentile, Michienzi, Sas, & Wolfe, 1992).

Browne and Finkelhor (1986) also reviewed various long-term effects related to a history of child sexual abuse. Whereas fear was the most commonly reported initial effect of abuse, depression was cited as the most commonly reported adult symptom (e.g., Bagley & Ramsay, 1985; Peters, 1984; Sedney & Brooks, 1984). Additional longer-term effects of child abuse frequently cited in the literature include anxiety and difficulty sleeping (Briere, 1984; Sedney & Brooks, 1984), negative self-concept (Bagley & Ramsay, 1985), increased revictimization later in life (Fromuth, 1983; Russell, 1986), problems with sexual functioning (Becker, Skinner, Abel, & Cichon, 1986; Briere, 1984; Meiselman, 1978; Tsai, Feldman-Summers, & Edgar, 1979), prostitution (Silbert & Pines, 1981), promiscuity (Herman, 1981), substance abuse (Peters, 1984), and suicide attempts or suicidal ideation (Bagley & Ramsay, 1985; Briere, 1984; Briere & Runtz, 1986). History of child sexual abuse has also been associated with symptoms of PTSD in adults (Kilpatrick, Amick-McMullan, Best, Burke, & Saunders, 1986), as well as dissociative responses (Briere & Runtz, 1987; Putnam, Guroff, Silberman, Barban, &

Post, 1986). For more thorough reviews of responses associated with a history of sexual abuse, the reader is referred to Browne and Finkelhor (1986), Hoier et al., (1987), Lipovsky and Kilpatrick (1992), Walker, Bonner, and Kaufman (1988), Polusny and Follette, 1995, and Wolfe and Wolfe (1988).

Models to Account for Reactions to Child Sexual Abuse

As evidenced by this brief overview of the literature concerning initial and long-term effects of child sexual abuse, the resulting sequelae are quite variable. Two models have emerged to account for the diverse set of reactions to child sexual abuse. The first model suggests that many sequelae resulting from abuse can be conceptualized as a form of PTSD (e.g., Deblinger, McLeer, & Henry, 1990; McLeer et al., 1988; Wolfe et al., 1989). The second model, proposed by Finkelhor (1986, 1987), suggests that four trauma-causing factors lead to cognitive and emotional distortions that impact the child's adjustment. Although recognizing that responses to abuse are highly variable, these models attempt to organize the existing empirical data concerning the effects of childhood sexual abuse. After reviewing both of these models, we conclude with a discussion concerning how responses to sexual victimization are dependent upon the complex interaction of a large number of preabuse, abuse, and postabuse factors.

The PTSD Model

Wolfe and her colleagues (e.g., Wolfe & Gentile, 1992; Wolfe et al., 1989) proposed that the sequelae resulting from childhood sexual abuse often can be viewed within a PTSD formulation. This viewpoint is based upon three premises: (1) The sexual abuse of a child meets the definition for "trauma" as outlined in the *Diagnostic and Statistical Manual of Mental Disorders*; (2) clinical impressions suggest that many abused children demonstrate at least some symptoms characteristic of the diagnostic criteria for PTSD (e.g., intrusive thoughts, avoidance, numbing, and hyperarousal); and (3) three variables that mediate adult victims' responses to sexual abuse (i.e., severity of abuse, availability of social support, and attributional styles) also mediate the impact of other types of trauma such as rape and combat (Wolfe & Gentile, 1992). Given that PTSD has been observed in children exposed to traumatic events such as natural and human-made disasters, medical trauma, violent crimes, and war-related trauma (Lipovsky, 1991), it was reasonable to hypothesize that trauma induced by sexual abuse could precipitate PTSD as well. Consistent with this viewpoint, both clinical impressions and empirical evidence suggest that symptoms of PTSD (e.g., dissociative states, hyperarousal such as sleep disturbance, and generalized and abuse-specific fear) are commonly associated with a history of child sexual abuse (e.g., Kendall-Tackett, Williams, & Finkelhor, 1993).

Criticisms concerning the application of the PTSD model to sequelae associated with child sexual abuse have been raised. Several researchers (e.g., Briere & Runtz, 1987; Finkelhor, 1987, 1990; O'Donohue & Elliott, 1992b) have suggested that the PTSD perspective is too narrow to account for all sequelae associated with sexual abuse (e.g., self-blame, sexual problems, suicidality, substance abuse, revictimization). Additional criticisms suggest that the PTSD model (1) fails to emphasize the initial adaptive nature of symptomatic behaviors (Briere & Runtz, 1987), (2) fails to account for cognitive issues that result from the abuse (Finkelhor, 1990), (3) does not present a theory to explain symptom development (Finkelhor, 1987), (4) fails to take into account how abuse-related trauma may be different from other types of trauma (e.g., Finkelhor, 1987; O'Donohue & Elliott, 1992b), and (5) does not account for abuse victims who do not experience symptoms of PTSD (e.g., Kendall-Tackett et al., 1993). In recent years, several broader conceptualizations of trauma have been proposed that address some of the criticisms of the PTSD model (see Wolfe & Birt, 1997, for a review). For example, Terr (1991) proposed that different types of trauma (which she labeled Type 1 and Type 2) may result in distinctive symptomatology. Janoff-Bulman (1989) proposed a cognitive conceptualization of trauma that examines how a victim's expectations and attributional style are related to symptoms such as intrusive thoughts and depression. Additionally, Seligman's learned helplessness model (Seligman et al., 1984) has been utilized in an effort to improve our understanding of abuse-related symptomatology.

Wolfe and her colleagues have further elaborated the PTSD model using a cognitive-behavioral framework (e.g., Wolfe & Birt, 1995, 1997; Wolfe & Gentile, 1992). Specifically, they suggest that the severity of abuse (e.g., use of coercion/force) is related to the development of symptoms of PTSD. On the other hand, they suggest that the course of abuse (e.g., duration and frequency) is "thought to relate to dysfunctional cognitive processes and dysfunctional coping, as represented by the following: (1) a learned helplessness attributional style and depression; (2) dissociation; (3) excessive emotionality and passivity in coping with day-to-day and trauma-related stressors; and (4) excessive, poorly managed responses to anger-provoking situations" (Wolfe & Birt, 1997, p. 585). In summary, the PTSD conceptualization of abuse-related symptomatology is an evolving model that has served as a useful framework for understanding a variety of the sequelae associated with child sexual abuse.

The Traumagenic Model

A second model for organizing the data concerning the effects of sexual victimization was proposed by Finkelhor (1986, 1987) and is referred to as the traumagenic model. This is a theoretically derived model intended to specify how and why sexual victimization results in different types of trauma. Four trauma-causing factors (called traumagenic dynamics) purportedly distort various cognitive and emotional processes in children (e.g., self-concept). These traumagenic dynamics are (1) traumatic sexualization, (2) betrayal, (3) powerlessness, and (4) stigmatization. Several sequelae of sexual abuse are associated with each traumagenic factor.

Traumatic sexualization refers to the development of distorted views of sexual attitudes and feelings. Finkelhor (1986) suggests that children may learn that sexual behavior is a means of obtaining attention or privileges, and they therefore may become promiscuous or turn to prostitution. In addition, sexuality may become associated with fear, and this may have negative impact on a person's sexual functioning or ability to develop intimate relationships as an adult.

The second traumatic dynamic, betrayal, refers to the harm inflicted on a person by those on whom he or she depends or with whom he or she has a trusting relationship. Children may feel a sense of betrayal by the perpetrator, family members, the person to whom the disclosure was made, siblings, peers, the legal system, and so on. This dynamic may account for subsequent reactions to abuse, including depression, anger, hostility, isolation, problems with intimacy, and delinquency.

Powerlessness is the third traumagenic dynamic proposed in Finkelhor's model. This refers to the case in which the child's control over his or her life has been usurped either prior to, during, or following the abuse. For example, the child may feel powerless to prevent or terminate the abusive incident, to disclose the abuse for fear of detrimental consequences, to convince disbelieving adults, or to prevent the perpetrator from being incarcerated. Sequelae of abuse related to this dynamic include depression, suicidality, fear, running away, revictimization, and dissociation.

The fourth traumagenic dynamic proposed by Finkelhor (1986) is stigmatization. This factor consists of negative thoughts and feelings such as guilt and shame that the child may adopt as a result of the abuse. Stigmatization may be direct or indirect, as well as real or perceived. For example, a parent may inform the child that he or she was not to blame for the abuse. However, the child may nonetheless feel a sense of responsibility and guilt for having participated in the abuse and possibly for having experienced a sense of pleasure from the act itself. In addition to guilt or blame, traumatic stigmatization may result in substance abuse, decreased self-esteem, and feelings of isolation.

A variety of factors may affect the extent to which an abusive incident causes one or all of the traumagenic dynamics to occur in a given individual. For example, a child may be more likely to experience a sense of guilt if the abuser used subtle threats and warned that disclosure would result in breaking up the family, than if the abuser simply coaxed the child to participate. Finkelhor (1986) has reviewed how various initial and long-term effects of abuse can be accounted for by the traumagenic model. Although this model provides a theoretical means of conceptualizing the effects of child sexual abuse, its major limitation is that there is little empirical evidence evaluating its accuracy. This is especially a problem because it is unclear if there are four traumagenic dynamics as opposed to some other number, or if the numerous causal pathways alluded to in the model are accurate.

Heterogeneity of Responding

As indicated earlier, general consensus suggests that there does not appear to be a syndrome or "typical" response to child sexual abuse (e.g., Kendall-Tackett et al., 1993). Although some symptoms of abuse may occur with greater frequency than others, children's responses to victimization appear to be highly heterogeneous. Many researchers (e.g., O'Donohue & Elliott, 1992a; Wolfe & Birt, 1997) have suggested that the lack of homogeneous responding to abuse results from a set of complex interactions between preabuse factors (e.g., age of child, diatheses, family support), abuse factors (e.g., duration of abuse, relationship to perpetrator), and postabuse factors (e.g., the disclosure process, reactions of others, court involvement). Table 14.2 contains a fuller explication of such mediating factors.

O'Donohue and Elliott (1992a) have suggested that questions such as "How do children respond to sexual abuse?" appear to be based on the problematic assumptions that "children" and "sexual abuse" represent homogeneous categories. They suggest that the use of the term "sexual abuse" accurately reflects a wide range of behaviors such as single noncontact abuse by a stranger as well as multiple episodes of violent rape by a father. Similarly, the term "child" (as in child sexual abuse) may accurately refer to abuse of both an infant and a 17-year-old. Given the wide range of factors that may influence an individual's response to "child sexual abuse," the observed heterogeneity is not surprising. It seems reasonable to assume, for example, that a 6-year-old male who is repeatedly fondled by his father and disbelieved by his mother at disclosure might respond differently than a 12-year-old male who was fondled once by a teacher and has a supportive family that immediately and appropriately responds to the child's accusation. Recognition that children's responses to abuse are highly heterogeneous emphasizes the importance of thoroughly evaluating the wide range of possible responses to abuse.

Model for the Clinical Assessment of Sexually Abused Children

Both the PTSD and traumagenic models suggest various aspects of functioning that should be assessed as part of a thorough evaluation of a child victim of sexual abuse. Neither model, however, provides guidelines concerning how the actual assessment should be conducted. Given the apparent heterogeneity of individual responses to sexual victimization, an idiographic approach to assessment is recommended. Elsewhere we have proposed a three-phase model for the clinical assessment of sexually abused children (O'Donohue & Elliott, 1992a) that includes (1) advocacy and protection, (2) understanding the context in which the assessment takes place, and (3) psychological assessment of the child and the

TABLE 14.2. Possible Mediating Variables

Preabuse status	Abuse characteristics	Postabuse characteristics
Age of child (chronological, mental, developmental, at onset, at disclosure)	Type or nature of abuse (penetration, fondling)	Time since abuse
Cognitive maturity	Duration and frequency (chronic vs. single episode)	Time since disclosure
Gender of victim	Relationship to perpetrator	Telling versus not telling
Gender of perpetrator	Severity of abuse (force and aggression)	Parental, societal, and institutional responses to disclosure
Isolation	Degree of participation and consent by victim	Legal stress (court proceedings)
Psychopathology of victim and family	Gender of victim	Disposition of perpetrator
Attributional style	Gender of perpetrator	Denial by perpetrator
Coping skills	Age of perpetrator	Other family characteristics
Friendships	Tactics used (coercion, bribes, threats)	Stigma
	Number of perpetrators	
	Attributions concerning the abuse	

child's environment. This model, designed for conducting a comprehensive clinical assessment, is reviewed briefly.

During the advocacy and protection phase, the clinician must ensure that the child is in a safe environment and that his or her needs are being met. This requires assessment of issues such as whether physical placement and care are appropriate, medical factors have been assessed fully, emotional needs are being met, the child is at risk for revictimization, and the child is in need of legal representation.

The second phase of this model (O'Donohue & Elliott, 1992a) involves developing an understanding of the context in which the assessment is taking place. This includes assessing the disclosure process, the child's reaction to the assessment process, the legal status of the case, the nature and extent of the abuse, and factors related to the perpetrator and/or family members. This involves an ongoing process of assessment, since different issues may emerge at different points in time (e.g., the child may experience fear during the actual disclosure process, whereas guilt may emerge as the prominent difficulty following incarceration of the perpetrator). The third phase proposed in this model involves the psychological assessment of the child and the child's environment. Using a funneling approach (Hawkins, 1979; Linehan, 1977), broadband information concerning general problem areas is obtained using a variety of assessment methods that have been psychometrically evaluated and contain normative data for children. One such commonly used assessment device is the Child Behavior Checklist (Achenbach & Edelbrock, 1983). Wolfe and Gentile (1992) have suggested that global adjustment problems may not be identified early in the disclosure process, which therefore emphasizes the need for ongoing assessment. Interviews with relevant parties (e.g., the child, parents, siblings, teachers, social workers) will also be used to gather relevant information. O'Donohue and Elliott (1992a) also emphasize the importance of obtaining information from "multiple informants (child, parents, siblings, teachers), concerning multiple actors (child, siblings, parents), in diverse settings (home and school), by a variety of assessment methods (self-report, other-report, questionnaires, direct observation, role play, and interviews) and concerning a variety of times (e.g., preabuse, disclosure, treatment, posttreatment, follow-up)" (p. 115).

Once broadband information has been obtained, psychological assessment will proceed with interviews as well as a series of narrowband assessment devices designed to assess specific problem areas such as depression (e.g., Children's Depression Inventory; CDI; Kovacs, 1983). Since it is assumed that clinicians have a general knowledge of both broad- and narrowband assessment devices for children, they will not be reviewed here. The reader is referred to Wolfe and Gentile (1992) and Wolfe and Wolfe (1988) for useful reviews of this topic. As part of a thorough evaluation, children should also be evaluated with instruments designed specifically for the purpose of assessing victims of child sexual abuse. Although there is a paucity of assessment devices psychometrically evaluated for this purpose, several have emerged in the literature and are reviewed here.

ASSESSMENT DEVICES PSYCHOMETRICALLY EVALUATED FOR USE WITH SEXUALLY ABUSED CHILDREN

In the past 10 years, numerous assessment devices have been developed to aid clinicians and researchers in gathering information regarding sexual abuse in children. Although psychometrically sound assessment devices such as the Child Behavior Checklist (Achenbach & Edelbrock, 1983) had previously been used to assist clinicians in evaluating sexually abused children, their usefulness was limited by the fact that they could only provide information concerning general problem areas, rather than more detailed information concerning abuse-specific difficulties. Although a thorough review of assessment devices specifically designed for sexual abuse evaluation is beyond the scope of this chapter, the reader is referred to Wolfe and Birt (1997) for a more detailed coverage of this topic. They review assessment instruments specifically designed to assess PTSD, sexuality problems, other trauma-related symptoms (e.g., dissociative symptoms, attributional style), and mediators of sexual abuse sequelae (family relations and social support).

Wolfe and Birt (1997) review several assessment instruments designed to tap PTSD symptomatology. The Children's Impact of Traumatic Events Scale— Revised (CITES-R; Wolfe & Gentile, 1991) is a structured interview designed to assess children's perceptions and attributions concerning the impact of abuse.

The scale is intended for children between the ages of 8 and 16. The Trauma Symptom Checklist for Children (TSCC; Briere, 1996) is a 54-item instrument that yields six subscales (i.e., anger, anxiety, depression, dissociation, PTSD, and sexual concerns). This instrument can be used with children regardless of whether they have disclosed abuse. A third scale reviewed by Wolfe and Birt (1997), the Sexual Abuse Fear Evaluation scale (SAFE; Wolfe & Wolfe, 1986; Wolfe, Gentile, & Klink, 1988) contains 27 items designed to assess "sexual fears, fears related to the disclosure and investigation, and fears of revictimization" (Wolfe & Gentile, 1992, p. 34). The Feelings and Emotions Experienced during Sexual Abuse questionnaire (FEEDSA; Wolfe & Birt, 1995) was designed to assess children's emotional reactions to their sexual abuse. This 54-item questionnaire assesses negative emotions (e.g., anger), perceptions that the situation was uncontrollable, and dissociation during the abuse (e.g., feeling as if one left his or her body). Finally, Wolfe and her colleagues (Wolfe et al., 1989; Wolfe et al., 1992) also derived a PTSD subscale from the Child Behavior Checklist—Parent Report Form to assess PTSD symptoms in abused children. The scale currently contains 23 items that reflect three symptom domains associated with PTSD (i.e., reexperiencing, fears and avoidance, and hyperarousal).

Wolfe and Birt (1997) also review several assessment instruments designed to tap sexual problems in abused children. The Child Sexual Behavior Inventory (Friedrich, Grambsch, Damon, & Hewitt, 1993) is a 36-item measure completed by the child's primary female caregiver. It assesses (1) environmental influences that potentially affect sexual behavior (e.g., opportunity to bathe with adults), and (2) the type and frequency of sexualized behaviors occurring during the previous 6 months. Finally, Wolfe and Birt (1997) also suggest that sexual problems can be assessed using the Child Behavior Checklist sexual problems subscale (CBCL; Achenbach & Edelbrock, 1983), the CITES-R eroticization scale (Wolfe & Gentile, 1991), and by various art or play techniques.

Several assessment instruments have emerged to assess trauma-related sequelae such as dissociative symptoms and attributional style. For example, the Child Dissociative Checklist (CDC; Putnam, 1988) is designed to serve as a screening device to measure the severity of observable symptoms of dissociation in children. The Children's Attributional Style Questionnaire (KASTAN; Kaslow, Rehm, & Siegel, 1984) contains 48 items designed to assess whether children's attributions for positive and negative events are internal or external, global or specific, and stable or unstable. Finally, attributional style in sexually abused children can also be assessed using the CITES-R Attributional Issues Scales (Wolfe & Gentile, 1991). Based on the theory of learned helplessness, this instrument contains four scales designed to assess abuse-related attributions (e.g., self-blame/guilt, dangerous world, personal vulnerability, and empowerment).

Several questionnaires have emerged to assess mediators of sexual abuse sequelae. Wolfe and Birt (1997) cite the following four areas of family functioning that mediate abuse, "caregiver reactions to the abuse, caregiver mental health, warmth of parent–child interactions, and ability to adapt to the changes and stressors resulting from the sexual abuse disclosure" (p. 610). The Parent Impact Questionnaire (Wolfe, 1985) was designed to assess the reactions of caregivers to disclosure of abuse. The Impact of Event Scale (Horowitz, Wilner, & Alvarez, 1979) was designed to tap intrusive thoughts and avoidance regarding a traumatic event. The Parental Reaction to Incest Disclosure Scale (PRIDS; Everson, Hunter, Runyon, Edelsohn, & Coulter, 1989) assesses the reactions and support provided by parents following the disclosure of intrafamilial sexual abuse. The CITES-R Social Reaction Scales (Wolfe & Gentile, 1991) assess both social support and negative reactions from others. Finally, additional scales that may be useful for sexual abuse evaluations but that were not specifically designed for that purpose include the Symptom Checklist 90—Revised (Derogatis, 1977), the Family Adaptability and Cohesion Evaluation Scale II (FACES II; Olson, Bell, & Portner, 1982), and the Family Environment Scale (FES; Moos & Moos, 1986).

SUMMARY OF ASSESSMENT

In summary, clinical impressions and empirical evidence suggest that children's initial and long-term responses to child sexual abuse are highly diverse. We reviewed two models that have been proposed to account for this diverse set of reactions, as well as a general strategy for evaluating sexually abused children. Finally, we also reviewed numerous assessment devices that should aid clinicians in conducting a comprehensive and psychometrically sound assessment.

TREATMENT OF SEXUALLY ABUSED CHILDREN

In a recently published review of the treatment outcome literature with sexually abused children, O'Donohue and Elliott (1992b) found only 11 published studies. Four of these were single-subject designs, with only two of these using experimental single-subject designs. The group designs all had notable methodological weaknesses, such as no attempt to ascertain preabuse status to distinguish effects of abuse from preexisting problems, use of dependent measures of unknown or problematic psychometric properties, lack of blind raters, lack of placebo and spontaneous remission control groups, lack of random assignment to conditions, lack of a comprehensive assessment of the possible universe of sequelae and clinical problems, lack of follow-up assessments to determine maintenance of effects, lack of assessment of clinical rather than simply statistical significance, and no inclusions of steps to assure that treatment protocols were faithfully implemented.

This state of affairs is unfortunate for several reasons. First, if the epidemiological estimates are accurate (Salter, 1992), many children need therapy for abuse-related problems, but there is an unfortunate paucity of information indicating that there are effective interventions to help these children. In short, the ratio of the need and demand for knowledge versus what is actually known is undesirable. Second, since some of Freud's (1896) patients presented with complaints of sexual abuse, it can be argued that mental health professionals have known of this problem for nearly a century, but this information has produced very little treatment research in this time period.

Single-Subject Designs

Kolko (1986) conducted a case study of an 11-year-old boy who was admitted to an institution and placed on an inpatient unit for behavioral disturbances following his sexual abuse of a younger child (the boy was thought to have been sexually abused as well). He was having social problems, such as aggression toward adults and other children, and was often socially unengaged to the point of withdrawal. To deal with these largely social impairments, he was given social skills training to assist him in learning to deal with frustrations and anger in a nondestructive manner. This training was classic in that it contained such strategies as modeling and practice. The boy demonstrated general improvement in social functioning in proximal and long-term assessments. The main obstacle to the use of this study is that the results were not replicated, and it is unknown whether the findings can be thought to generalize to children other than the case study client.

Becker, Skinner, and Abel (1982) described a case study of a 4-year-old girl who was the victim of intrafamilial sexual abuse. The girl was experiencing disturbances in eating patterns to the extent that the child had lost 20% of her body weight at a point in life when she should have been gaining weight. In addition, she was experiencing sleep disturbances and phobic reactions. To deal with these symptoms, the authors utilized a behaviorally driven token economy (details not available), which would be administered by the mother under the supervision of the therapist. The authors report that the child experienced a reduction in phobic reactions and sleep disturbances, and an increase in food intake.

Once again, the study has several weaknesses. The mother was utilized as the primary assessor and therapist (without description or fidelity checks), so the authors must rely on her (unknown) accuracy in order to interpret the results. Also, there is no evidence that these finding will generalize to anyone other than this child–parent combination.

McNeill and Todd (1986) described a case study of a 5-year-old girl who had been sexually abused at a day care center. The girl had been experiencing behavioral disturbances such as verbal rumination and whining. To reduce the frequency of these behaviors, the therapist initiated a behavioral "differential reinforcement of other behaviors" strategy that was designed to replace the negative behaviors with more positive behaviors. Once again, the mother was utilized as both data collector and therapist. The authors reasoned that the treatment was successful because there was an immediate elimination of the problematic behaviors after the treatment was administered.

Hoier and Shawchuck (1987) described a case study of a brother–sister pair who were victims of intrafamilial sexual abuse. The young girl displayed behavioral disturbances including public masturbation and sexual aggression toward other children. To reduce the frequency of these behaviors, the therapists directed the foster mother to give the children directions about their behavior, help them practice positive behavior, and give them verbal reinforcements. Positive results were seen but then reversed when the children were given a court-ordered visit by the abusing parent. Eventually the children were referred for intensive therapy.

Although the authors seem to indicate that improvements prior to the parents visit can be attributed to the specific therapy, the design does not demonstrate this. In addition, this study is still limited by concerns about external validity and parental (foster) administration, without a clear description of the parental exact role/behavior.

Individual Therapy, Group Analysis Designs

Deblinger et al. (1990) described a study of the therapy of girls who had been sexually abused and were experiencing the symptoms of PTSD utilizing a multiple baseline control strategy. The treatment was designed to be completed by the child and the nonoffending parent. The parents underwent three "modules." The first was designed to give the parent education and coping skills, the second was designed to bolster the parents' parent–child communication abilities, and the third was designed to instruct the parent in therapeutic behavior management. The children also underwent three "modules." The first was designed to bolster the child's coping skills by education and modeling. The second was designed to utilize exposure to reduce anxiety related to abuse cognitions. The third was designed to help the child learn effective prevention strategies for future abuse.

While this study focused on girls who had been sexually abused, it is a step toward true clinical experimentation. The study uses a multiple baseline control and analyzes both statistical and clinical improvement, compared to controls. In addition, it includes a logical theoretical framework that can be used to understand and justify treatment decisions. However, while the focus on PTSD is favorable because it does not treat children who have been sexually abused as a homogenous category, it does limit the study's external validity to that population experiencing those symptoms.

Downing, Jenkins, and Henry (1988) described a nonexperimental study of 22 children who were sexually abused. The study consisted of a follow-up 1 year after treatment by one of four private practitioners. Two of these practitioners were "psychodynamic," in that they focused on disturbances of self within the child, and two were "reinforcement" therapists who both indicated that they worked mostly with the parents to help them structure a positive environment for the children. Outcome data were collected, but no assessment of pretreatment functioning was conducted (it was estimated based on parental report). While the behaviors displayed by children did not differ significantly between groups, parents in the reinforcement group seemed more optimistic about the prospects of the abuse not always affecting their children's behavior.

The problems with any conclusions from this study are extreme. The study lacks all semblance of a proper experimental design. Children were not assigned to treatment randomly, there was no pretreatment assessment, there were no control groups, there was not enough adequate detailing of the course of therapy, and there was no assurance that the therapist adhered to any format.

Group Therapy

Burke (1988) described a study in which 25 girls who had been sexually abused were given a short, group-oriented therapy designed to implement a social learning model to reinforce coping and prevention behaviors. Data and depression and anxiety related and not related to child sexual abuse were collected pre- and posttest, and were then compared to a *no-treatment* control. Results suggested that a social learning model can be useful in reducing the girls' symptoms of depression and child sexual abuse-related anxiety.

This study seems to be solid in that it utilizes a strong theoretical framework and assesses treatment effects using pre–post assessment and a no-treatment control group. However, it focuses on girls only, thus limiting its external validity.

Hoier, Inderbitzen-Pizaruk, and Shawchuck (1988) described a study that utilized a group-oriented approach to administer a cognitive-behavioral intervention to 3 boys and 15 girls who were experiencing either externalizing or internalizing behaviors. This intervention was designed to investigate illogical cognitions, reframe them, and rehearse social and coping skills. The description of the study provided insufficient information regarding assessment and analysis, nevertheless, the authors reported that the results suggested that the treatment was effective for reducing internalizing behaviors but not for externalizing behaviors.

Though inadequate descriptions of methodology and analysis are fundamental problems with this study, the experimenters did opt to use assessment devices that have demonstrated some fairly stable psychometric properties, (e.g., the CDI, CBCL, etc.). Once again, the sample of boys in the study was very small (i.e., 3); generalizing to that population continues to be a major problem.

Verleur, Hughes, and de Rois (1986) discussed a study of the treatment of adolescent girls who were sexually abused and were subsequently ordered by the court to live in a residential treatment facility. The study did not include information about the initial presenting problems. In addition, the authors described the therapy as "vaguely homogeneous group therapy," with a component dedicated to sexual education. It is impossible to determine exactly what occurred in therapy. In addition, no information was provided about any controls for possible threats to internal or external validity, except that a no-treatment control was included (but not adequately described.). Results suggested that both groups improved in self-ratings of self-esteem, but not differentially. However, the authors indicate that the treatment group's knowledge regarding sexually transmitted diseases, birth control, and so on was statistically significantly higher than the no-treatment control.

The limitations to this study are pronounced. The lack of description regarding the content of therapy makes it impossible for readers to replicate the study, and for clinicians to implement any positive findings. The lack of express controls for threats to internal or external validity make the results uninterpretable. The only difference between the groups was the treatment group's knowledge regarding sexual issues. This is fine, but should be expected, as the no-treatment control group was not exposed to that information. Finally, the two groups did not demonstrate a difference in ratings of self-esteem after treatment. Although flaws in the experimental design make all *conclusions* impossible, a that which cannot be ruled out is that treatment was ineffective. Also, perhaps the milieu of the facility was an active component. In this case, there would have been be no *real no-treatment* control.

Corder, Haizlip, and DeBoer (1990) described a pilot study of a treatment of 8 girls between the ages of 6 and 9 who had been sexually abused. These girls presented with symptoms such as depression, withdrawal, sleep problems, and nightmares. The group treatment was described as containing 20 sessions. These sessions were targeted mainly at reducing the risk of future victimization by teaching the children to understand sexual abuse, by increasing self-esteem and self-efficacy, and by teaching problem-solving skills, including acquiring help from the environment. The authors described a number of techniques to implement these treatment goals, including homework, coloring books, and so on. Treatment effects were assessed by subjective report of the parental figure in terms of the child's willingness to talk about the event and general remission of symptoms.

The authors included more information about their actual treatment than do most. However, the failure to use a control group or a psychometrically valid instrument to assess treatment effect is very unfortunate. While the authors claim that this was only a pilot study, this does not eliminate research design considerations. Even a pilot study can produce usable information if it is designed, controlled, and implemented well. This was not done. While these results are not usable, they are fairly well specified. We hope that further studies or replications of this treatment approach will be conducted utilizing stronger methodology.

CONCLUSIONS REGARDING TREATMENT

The treatment outcome literature provisionally supports a few preliminary conclusions. These are only tentative and await more and better designed research.

First, the sequelae of sexual abuse in children appear to be heterogenous. Although anxiety and depression have been the most frequent targets of treatment in these studies (e.g., Becker et al., 1982; Burke, 1988; Corder et al., 1990, Deblinger et al., 1990; Hoier et al., 1988; Kolko, 1986) and in general tend to occur concomitantly, problems such as aggression (Hoier & Shawchuck, 1987; Hoier et al., 1988; Kolko, 1986), self-injurious behavior (Becker et al., 1982), sexual acting out (Corder et al., 1990; Downing et al., 1988; Hoier & Shawchuck, 1987; Hoier et al., 1988), inappropriate speech (McNeill & Todd, 1986), nightmares and sleep disturbances (Becker et al., 1982; Corder et al., 1990; Downing et al., 1988; Hoier & Shawchuck, 1987), social withdrawal (Corder et al., 1990; Kolko, 1986), eating disturbances (Becker et al., 1982; Hoier & Shawchuck, 1987; Kolko, 1986), and enuresis (Downing et al., 1988) have also been the targets of treatment. Two caveats need to be kept in mind. First, with the exception of the Deblinger et al. (1990) study preabuse status was not systematically assessed and therefore some of these problems may have preexisted the abuse and therefore should not properly be regarded as the sequelae of abuse. Second, it is unclear the extent to which a comprehensive assessment of the child and the child's environment were conducted in many of these studies, and therefore these studies might have overlooked the existence of some additional problems. However, the heterogeneity of the problems addressed in these treatment outcome studies suggests that the sequelae of sexual abuse in children can be quite diverse. Thus, the clinician must guard against biases that a certain restricted class of problems results from abuse and conduct a comprehensive clinical assessment (O'Donohue & Elliott, 1992a).

Another preliminary conclusion is that this literature seems best to support the effectiveness of behavioral and cognitive-behavioral interventions with this population. This might partly be due to the fact that other therapy approaches have simply failed to conduct any sort of outcome research with this population. However, this is a significant failing and is worrisome since it is the authors' experience that much therapy that is actually delivered to these children derives from models (e.g., a social work model) that appear to have no experimental support.

It is also important to note that the treatment techniques used in the studies reviewed are the techniques that have been shown to be effective for treating similar symptoms that have been caused by factors other than sexual abuse. For example, Burke (1988) relied on Lewinsohn and Libet's (1972) treatment program for depression. This program was originally designed as a general treatment for depression and not designed for depression that is a sequela of sexual abuse. The strategy of viewing the sequelae of child sexual abuse as being treatable by modifications of standard treatments appears promising and in need of further evaluation.

Another important implication of the studies reviewed is that primary caretakers can be useful change agents (Becker et al., 1982; Hoier & Shawchuck, 1987;

Kolko, 1986). Furthermore, there is some evidence that suggests that significant others (e.g., parents) may suffer their own sequelae from the abuse and require separate treatment (Deblinger et al., 1990). Addressing the resultant or preexisting psychological problems of caretakers can not only be important for their well-being but also for the child's welfare, given the influential role these adults have in the child's life and in the child's recovery from the abuse. Moreover, training caretakers to help their children also may be useful in addressing sequelae that emerge only in the longer term.

Furthermore, a number of the studies reviewed contained a prevention component in their treatment packages. Prevention may be important for several reasons (O'Donohue & Elliott, 1992a). First, there is some evidence to suggest that sexually abused children are prone to revictimization (Fromuth, 1983). Second, it is possible that children can experience numerous indirect benefits from prevention training. For example, skills acquisition in this area possibly can result in reducing fear and increasing self-esteem. Third, several studies indicate that a significant number of convicted perpetrators report sexual victimization in their own childhood (e.g., Langevin, Handy, Day, & Russon, 1985). Although this finding should not be used to claim that most victims become abusers, it does suggest that early prevention intervention may be a worthwhile attempt to break this cycle of abuse.

Selection of Appropriate Treatment Strategies

The lack of empirical treatment outcome studies for children who have experienced trauma makes it difficult to recommend a specific course of action for any population other than sexually abused girls. However, a lack of empirical research does not mean that there is a lack of seemingly sound *theoretical* examinations of possible treatments.

We recommend that practitioners faced with sexually abused children follow Deblinger and Heflin's (1996) treatment manual. This book provides useful information on initiating therapy, coping skills training, exposure and affective processing, and educational components for the child; it includes coping skills, gradual exposure, and behavior management skills for the nonoffending parent, as well as joint parent–child sessions. For other childhood traumas, we recommend that researchers follow the lead of Deblinger and her colleagues and develop and test other manualized treatments.

GENERAL CONCLUSIONS

When historians of the future write about the history of mental health professionals' concern with children who have been traumatized, one curious fact that will be difficult to explain is that despite the profession's commitment to science, and despite the clear recognition for at least the last century that there are traumatized children, very little substantive research was conducted during the first 80 years or so of psychological research. However, this unfortunate trend is clearly changing. In the past few decades, clinicians' uncertainty has been reduced by a number of important research projects. We hope this trend accelerates for this important social problem.

REFERENCES

Achenbach, T. M., & Edelbrock, C. S. (1983). *Manual for the Child Behavior Checklist and Revised Child Behavior Profile.* Burlington: Department of Psychiatry, University of Vermont.

Anderson, S. C., Bach, C. M., & Griffith, S. (1981, April). *Psychosocial sequelae in intrafamilial victims of sexual assault and abuse.* Paper presented at the Third International Conference on Child Abuse and Neglect, Amsterdam, The Netherlands.

Bagley, C., & Ramsay, R. (1985, February). *Disrupted childhood and vulnerability to sexual assault: Long-term sequels with implications for counseling.* Paper presented at the Conference on Counseling the Sexual Abuse Survivor, Winnipeg, Canada.

Becker, J. V., Skinner, L. J., & Abel, G. G. (1982). Treatment of a four-year-old victim of incest. *American Journal of Family Therapy, 10,* 41–46.

Becker, J. V., Skinner, L. J., Abel, G. G., & Cichon, J. (1986). Level of postassault sexual functioning in rape and incest victims. *Archives of Sexual Behavior, 15,* 37–49.

Briere, J. (1984, April). *The effects of childhood sexual abuse on later psychological functioning: Defining a "post-sexual-abuse syndrome."* Paper presented at the Third National Conference on Sexual Victimization of Children, Washington, DC.

Briere, J. (1996). *Trauma Symptom Checklist for Children (TSCC): Professional manual.* Odessa, FL: Psychological Assessment Resources.

Briere, J., & Runtz, M. (1986). Suicidal thoughts and behaviors in former sexual abuse victims. *Canadian Journal of Behavioural Science, 18,* 413–423.

Briere, J., & Runtz, M. (1987). Post sexual abuse trauma: Data and implications for clinical practice. *Journal of Interpersonal Violence, 2,* 367–379.

Browne, A., & Finkelhor, D. (1986). Impact of child sexual abuse: A review of the research. *Psychological Bulletin, 99,* 66–77.

Burke, M. (1988). *Short-term group therapy for sexually abused girls: A learning theory based treatment for negative affect.* Unpublished doctoral dissertation, University of Georgia, Athens.

Ceci, S., & Liechtman, M. (1992). I know that you know that I know that you broke the toy: A brief report of recursive awareness among three-year olds. In S. Ceci, M. Liechtman, & M. Putnik (Eds.), *Social and cognitive factors in early deception* (pp. 30–52). New York: Macmillan.

Clarke-Stewart, A., Thompson, W., & Lepore, S. (1989, May 2). *Manipulating children's interpretations through interrogation.* Paper presented at the Biennial Meeting of the Society for Research on Child Development, Kansas City, MO.

Cohen, R., & Harnick, M. (1980). The susceptibility of child witnesses to suggestion. *Law and Human Behavior, 4*(3), 201–210.

Cole, C. B., & Loftus, E. F. (1987). The memory of children. In S. Ceci, M. Toglia, & D. Ross (Eds.), *Children's eyewitness memory* (pp. 178–208). New York: Springer-Verlag.

Conte, J. R., & Schuerman, J. R. (1987). The effects of sexual abuse on children: A multidimensional view. *Journal of Interpersonal Violence, 2*, 380–390.

Corder, B., Haizlip, T., & DeBoer, P. (1990). A pilot study for a structured, time limited therapy group for sexually abused pre-adolescent children. *Child Abuse and Neglect, 14*, 243–251.

Dale, P., Loftus, E., & Rathburn, L. (1978). The influence of the form of the question on the eyewitness testimony of preschool children. *Journal of Psycholinguistic Research, 7*(4), 269–277.

Davies, G. (1989). Children as witnesses. *Psychological Survey, 7*, 175–193.

Deblinger, E., & Heflin, A. H. (1996). *Treating sexually abused children and their nonoffending parents: A cognitive behavioral approach.* Thousand Oaks, CA: Sage.

Deblinger, E., McLeer, S. V., Atkins, M., Ralphe, D., & Foa, E. (1989). Post-traumatic stress in sexually abused children, physically abused, and non-abused children. *Child Abuse and Neglect: The International Journal, 13*, 403–408.

Deblinger, E., McLeer, S. V., & Henry, D. (1990). Cognitive behavioral treatment for sexually abused children suffering from post-traumatic stress: Preliminary findings. *Journal of the American Academy of Child and Adolescent Psychiatry, 29*, 747–752.

DeFrancis, V. (1969). *Protecting the child victim of sex crimes committed by adults.* Denver, CO: American Humane Association.

Derogatis, L. R. (1977). *The SCL-90-R: Administration and scoring procedures manual.* Baltimore: Clinical Psychometric Research.

deYoung, M. (1992) Credibility assessment during the sexual abuse evaluation. In W. O'Donohue & J. Geer (Eds.), *The sexual abuse of children: Clinical issues* (pp. 256–282). Hillsdale, NJ: Erlbaum.

Downing, J., Jenkins, S., & Henry, D. (1988). A comparison of psychodynamic and reinforcement treatment with sexually abused children. *Elementary School Guidance and Counseling, 22*, 291–298.

Everson, M. D., Hunter, W. M., Runyon, D. K., Edelsohn, G. A., & Coulter, M. L. (1989). Maternal support following disclosure of incest. *American Journal of Orthopsychiatry, 59*, 197–207.

Fanetti, M., & O'Donohue, W. (1998a). *The development of a new structured interview for child sexual abuse.* NIMH-Funded Research Grant No. 1R43MM57194-01.

Fanetti, M., & O'Donohue, W. (1998b). *Children's memory research: Relevance in assessment.* Manuscript in preparation.

Finkelhor, D. (1986). *A sourcebook on child sexual abuse.* Beverly Hills, CA. Sage.

Finkelhor, D. (1987). The trauma of child sexual abuse: Two models. *Journal of Interpersonal Violence, 2*, 348–366.

Finkelhor, D. (1990). Early and long-term effects of child sexual abuse: An update. *Professional Psychology: Research and Practice, 21*, 325–330.

Freud, S. (1896). *The aetiology of hysteria,* London: Hogarth.

Friedrich, W., Grambsch, P., Damon, L., & Hewitt, S. (1993). Child sexual behavior inventory: Normative and clinical comparisons. *Psychological Assessment, 4*(3), 303–311.

Friedrich, W. N., Beilke, R., & Urquiza, A. J. (1987). Children from sexually abusive families: A behavioral comparison. *Journal of Interpersonal Violence, 2*, 391–402.

Fromuth, M. E. (1983, August). *The long-term psychological impact of childhood sexual abuse.* Unpublished doctoral dissertation. Auburn University, Auburn, AL.

Gardiner, R. (1992). *True and false accusations of child sexual abuse.* New York: Creative Therapeutics.

Goodman, G., Aman, C., & Hirschman, J. (1987). Child sexual and physical abuse: Children's testimony. In S. Ceci, M. Toglia, & D. Ross (Eds.), *Children's eyewitness memory* (pp. 72–90). New York: Springer.

Goodman, G., & Reed, R. (1986). Age differences in eyewitness testimony. *Law and Human Behavior, 10*(4), 317–332.

Gruber, K. J., & Jones, R. J. (1981). Does sexual abuse lead to delinquent behavior: A critical look at the evidence. *Victimology: An International Journal, 6,* 85–91.

Hawkins, R. P. (1979). The functions of assessment: Implications for selection and development of devices for assessing repertoires in clinical, educational, and other settings. *Journal of Applied Behavior Analysis, 12,* 501–516.

Henderson, J. (1983). Is incest harmful? *Canadian Journal of Psychiatry, 28,* 34–39.

Herman, J. L. (1981). *Father–daughter incest.* Cambridge, MA: Harvard University Press.

Hoier, T., Inderbitzen-Pisaruk, H., & Shawchuck, C. (1988).*Short-term cognitive behavioral group treatment for victims of sexual abuse.* Unpublished manuscript, West Virginia University, Department of Psychology, Morgantown.

Hoier, T. S., & Shawchuck, C. (1987, December). *The natural history and treatment of behavioral problems in sexually abused children: A case study.* Paper presented at the Rivendell Conference, Memphis, TN.

Horowitz, M. J., Wilner, N., & Alvarez, W. (1979). Impact of Event Scale: A measure of psychosomatic stress. *Psychosomatic Medicine, 41,* 209–218.

Janoff-Bulman, R. (1989). Assumptive worlds and the stress of traumatic events: Applications of the schema construct. *Social Cognition, 7,* 113–136.

Kaslow, N., Rehm, L., & Siegel, A. (1984). Social-cognitive and cognitive correlates of depression in children. *Journal of Abnormal Child Psychology, 12,* 605–620.

Kendall-Tackett, K., Williams, L., & Finkelhor, D. (1993). Impact of sexual abuse on children: A review and synthesis of recent empirical studies. *Psychological Bulletin, 113*(1), 164–180.

Kilpatrick, D. G., Amick-McMullan, A., Best, C. L., Burke, M. M., & Saunders, B. E. (1986, May). *Impact of child sexual abuse: Recent research findings.* Paper presented at the Fourth National Conference on the Sexual Victimization of Children, New Orleans, LA.

King, M., & Yuille, J. (1987). Suggestibility and the child witness. In S. Ceci, M. Toglia, & D. Ross (Eds.), *Children's eyewitness memory* (pp. 102–129). New York: Springer.

Kolko, D. (1986). Social-cognitive skills training with a sexually abused and abusive child psychiatric inpatient: Training, generalization, and follow-up. *Journal of Family Violence, 1,* 149–165.

Kovacs, M. (1983, April). *The Children's Depression Inventory: A self-rated depression scale for school-aged youngsters.* Unpublished manuscript, University of Pittsburgh, Pittsburgh, PA.

Langevin, R., Handy, L., Day, D., & Russon, A. (1985). Are incestuous fathers pedophilic, aggressive, and alcoholic? In R. Langevin (Ed.), *Erotic preference, gender identity, and aggression* (pp. 161–179). Hillsdale, NJ: Erlbaum.

Lewinsohn, P., & Libet, J. (1972). Pleasant events, activity schedules, and depressions. *Journal of Abnormal Psychology, 79*(3), 291–295.

Linehan, M. M. (1977). Issues in behavioral interviewing. In J. D. Cone & R. P. Hawkins (Eds.), *Behavioral assessment: New directions for clinical psychology* (pp. 30–51). New York: Brunner/Mazel.

Lipovsky, J. A. (1991). Posttraumatic stress disorder in children. *Family Community Health, 14,* 42–51.

Lipovsky, J. A., & Kilpatrick, D. G. (1992). The child sexual abuse victim as an adult. In W. O'Donohue & J. Geer (Eds.), *The sexual abuse of children: Vol. 2. Clinical issues* (pp. 430–476). Hillsdale, NJ: Erlbaum.

Marin, B., Holes, D., Guth, M., & Kovac, P. (1979). The potential of children as eyewitnesses: A comparison of children and adults on eyewitness tasks. *Law and Human Behavior, 3,* 295–306.

McLeer, S., Deblinger, E., Atkins, M., Foa, E., & Ralphe, D. (1988). Post-traumatic stress disorder in sexually abused children. *Journal of the American Academy of Child and Adolescent Psychiatry, 27,* 650–654.

McNeill, J. W., & Todd, F. J. (1986). The operant treatment of excessive verbal ruminations and negative emotional arousal in a case of child molestation. *Child and Family Behavior Therapy, 8,* 61–69.

Meiselman, K. (1978). *Incest.* San Francisco: Jossey-Bass.

Moos, R. H., & Moos, B. S. (1986). *Family Environment Scale manual.* Palo Alto, CA: Consulting Psychologists Press.

O'Donohue, W. T., & Elliott, A. N. (1992a). A model for the clinical assessment of the sexually abused child. *Behavioral Assessment, 13,* 325–339.

O'Donohue, W. T., & Elliott, A. N. (1992b). Treatment of the sexually abused child: A review. *Journal of Clinical Child Psychology, 21,* 218–228.

O'Donohue, W., & Fanetti, M. (1996). Assessing the occurrence of child sexual abuse: An information processing, hypothesis testing approach. *Aggression and Violent Behavior, 1*(3), 269–281.

Olson, D., Bell, R., & Portner, J. (1982). *FACES II: Family Adaptability and Cohesion Evaluation Scales.* St. Paul: Faculty of Social Sciences, University of Minnesota.

Peters, D. (1987). The impact of naturally occurring stress on children's memory. In S. Ceci, M. Toglia, & D. Ross (Eds.), *Children's eyewitness memory.* New York: Springer.

Peters, S. D. (1984). *The relationship between childhood sexual victimization and adult depression among Afro-American and white women.* Unpublished doctoral dissertation, University of California, Los Angeles, CA.

Polusny, M. A., & Follette, V. M. (1995). Long-term correlates of child sexual abuse: Theory and empirical findings. *Applied and Preventive Psychology, 4,* 143–166.

Putnam, F. W. (1988). *Child Dissociative Checklist (Version 22).* Unpublished manuscript, National Institute of Mental Health, Washington, DC.

Putnam, F. W., Guroff, J. J., Silberman, E. K., Barban, L., & Post, R. M. (1986). The clinical phenomenology of multiple personality disorder: Review of 100 recent cases. *Journal of Clinical Psychiatry, 47,* 285–293.

Ramey, J. (1979). Dealing with the last taboo. *Siecus Report 7,* 1–2, 6–7.

Raskin, D., & Esplin, P. (1992). Statement validity assessment: Interview procedures and content analysis of children's statements of sexual abuse. *Behavioral Assessment, 13*(3), 265–291.

Reich, J. W., & Gutierres, S. E. (1979). Escape/aggression incidence in sexually abused juvenile delinquents. *Criminal Justice and Behavior, 6,* 239–243.

Russell, D. E. H. (1986). *The secret trauma: Incest in the lives of girls and women*. New York: Basic Books.

Salter, A. C. (1992). Epidemiology of child sexual abuse. In W. O'Donohue & J. Geer (Eds.), *The sexual abuse of children: Theory and research*. Hillsdale, NJ: Erlbaum.

Sandfort, T. G. M. (1992). The argument for adult–child sexual contact: A critical appraisal and new data. In W. O'Donohue & J. Geer (Eds.), *The sexual abuse of children: Vol. 1. Clinical issues* (pp. 38–48). Hillsdale, NJ: Erlbaum.

Saywitz, K. (1987). Children's testimony: Age-related patterns of memory errors. In S. Ceci, M. P. Toglia, & D. F. Ross (Eds.), *Children's eyewitness memory* (pp. 36–52). New York: Springer-Verlag.

Sedney, M. A., & Brooks, B. (1984). Factors associated with a history of childhood sexual experience in a nonclinical female population. *Journal of the American Academy of Child Psychiatry, 23*, 215–218.

Seligman, M., Peterson, C., Kaslow, N., Tanenbaum, R., Alloy, L., & Abramson, L. (1984). Attributional style and depressive symptoms among children. *Journal of Abnormal Psychology, 93*, 235–238.

Silbert, M. H., & Pines, A. M. (1981). Sexual child abuse as an antecedent to prostitution. *Child Abuse and Neglect, 5*, 407–411.

Terr, L. C. (1991). Childhood traumas: An outline and overview. *American Journal of Psychiatry, 148*, 10–20.

Tsai, M., Feldman-Summers, S., & Edgar, M. (1979). Childhood molestation: Variables related to differential impact of psychosexual functioning in adult women. *Journal of Abnormal Psychology, 88*, 407–417.

Tufts New England Medical Center, Division of Child Psychiatry. (1984). *Sexually exploited children: Service and research project*. Final report for the Office of Juvenile Justice and Delinquency Prevention. Washington, DC: U.S. Department of Justice.

Undeutsch, U. (1989). The development of statement reality analysis. In J. Yuille (Ed.), *Credibility assessment*. Dordrecht, The Netherlands: Kluwer Academic Publishers.

Verleur, D., Hughes, R., & de Rois, M. (1986). Enhancement of self-esteem among female adolescent incest victims: A controlled comparison. *Adolescence, 21*, 843–854.

Walker, C. E., Bonner, B. L., & Kaufman, K. L. (Eds.). (1988). *The physically and sexually abused child: Evaluation and treatment*. New York: Pergamon Press.

White, S., & Edelstein, B. (1991). Behavioral assessment and investigatory interviewing. *Behavioral Assessment, 13*, 245–264.

Wolfe, V. V. (1985). *Parent Impact Questionnaire*. Unpublished assessment instrument. Available from Vicky Veitch Wolfe, Ph.D., Department of Psychology, Children's Hospital of Western Ontario, 800 Commissioners Rd. E., London, Ontario, Canada N6A4G5.

Wolfe, V. V., & Birt, J. (1995). The psychological sequelae of child sexual abuse. In T. H. Ollendick & R. J. Prinz (Eds.), *Advances in clinical child psychology* (Vol. 17, pp. 233–263). New York: Plenum.

Wolfe, V. V., & Birt, J. (1997). Child sexual abuse. In E. J. Mash & L. G. Terdal (Eds.), *Assessment of childhood disorders* (3rd ed., pp. 569–623). New York: Guilford Press.

Wolfe, V. V., & Gentile, C. (1992). Psychological assessment of sexually abused children. In W. T. O'Donohue & J. H. Geer (Eds.), *The sexual abuse of children: Theory, research and therapy* (Vol. 2, pp. 143–187). Hillsdale, NJ: Erlbaum.

Wolfe, V. V., Gentile, C., & Klink, A. (1988). *Psychometric properties of the Sexual Abuse*

Fear Evaluation (SAFE). (Available from the authors at the Department of Psychology, University of Western Ontario, London, Ontario, Canada N6A 5C2.)

Wolfe, V. V., Gentile, C., Michienzi, T., Sas, L., & Wolfe, D. (1992). The Children's Impact of Traumatic Events Scale: A measure of post-sexual abuse PTSD symptoms. *Behavioral Assessment, 13,* 269–281.

Wolfe, V. V., Gentile, C., & Wolfe, D. A. (1989). The impact of sexual abuse on children: A PTSD formulation. *Behavior Therapy, 20,* 215–218.

Wolfe, V. V., & Wolfe, D. A. (1986). *The Sexual Abuse Fear Evaluation (SAFE):A subscale for the Fear Survey for Children—Revised.* Unpublished questionnaire, University of Western Ontario, London, Ontario.

Wolfe, V. V., & Wolfe, D. A. (1988). The sexually abused child.In E. J. Mash & L. G. Terdal (Eds.), *Behavioral assessment of childhood disorders* (2nd ed., pp. 670–714). New York: Guilford Press.

Wolfe, V. V., & Wolfe, D. A., Gentile, C., & Bourdeau, P. (1987). *History of Victimization Form.* Unpublished manuscript. (Available from the authors, Department of Psychology, University of Western Ontario, London, Ontario, Canada.)

Wolfe, V. V., Wolfe, D. A., & Larose, L. (1986). *The Children's Impact of Traumatic Events Scale (CITES).* (Available from the authors at the Department of Psychology, University of Western Ontario, London, Ontario, Canada N6A 5C2.)

Yates, A. (1982). Children eroticized by incest. *American Journal of Psychiatry, 139,* 482–485.

Yorukoglu, A., & Kemph, J. P. (1966). Children not severely damaged by incest with a parent. *Journal of the American Academy of Child Psychiatry, 5,* 111–124.

Yuille, J. (1992). *A protocol for interviewing children.* Unpublished manuscript.

Phenomenology and Treatment of Trauma in Later Life

LEE HYER
M. G. WOODS

After the first death, there is no other.
—DYLAN THOMAS

The study of trauma in older people, especially regarding the diagnostic syndrome posttraumatic stress disorder (PTSD), is fraught with problems related to developmental and lifespan issues. Uncontaminated facts are hard to come by. Some of the complications are related to the nature of trauma, to cohort issues, and, depending on when the trauma occurred, to the natural transition from acute to chronic status of the trauma. In almost imperceptible ways, older people adapt to meet the needs of life changes, and the close relationship of symptoms to the particular and complex experience of an individual across the lifespan can be lost when trauma occurred in the past (see van der Kolk, McFarlane, & Weisaeth, 1996).

It is at the interface of aging and trauma that we seek more simplicity. It is conventional to argue that the adjustment to trauma is a function of the individual (personality variables), considerations of the trauma itself, and the mediating influences of the recovery process (Green, 1991). As people age, trauma appears to have influence on their development, to disrupt expectancies and competencies, to jostle transition points, and to disturb normal biological maturation (Summers & Hyer, 1994). In effect, the person must adjust developmentally. Across the lifespan (as a result of trauma), it is unclear how this need to adjust has impact—whether trauma affects the course of development continuously or discontinuously, whether it proceeds in an additive fashion or has regressive phases, and whether treatment is advantageous or not (Bamberg, 1997). It seems, however, that if trauma causes disruptions in lifespan transitions its results can alter the acquisition and integration of developmental competencies (Pynoos, Steinberg, & Goenjian, 1996).

An understanding of adjustment problems of an older victim of trauma rests to some extent on knowing the chronological status and lifespan trajectory of events, and to some extent on a knowledge of psychiatric disorders. PTSD is not the only disorder specific to poor adjustment to trauma (Gurian & Miner, 1991). Nowhere is it more evident that one's adjustment to trauma can be more or less serious than full-blown PTSD than when one considers older people. That trauma is a risk factor for a later mental disorder seems to be accepted; that it represents an etiological factor is not corroborated (Maughan & Rutter, 1997). The myriad factors related to the parameters of abuse (nature of the trauma), the balancing of risk and resilient components, extant cognitive schemata, the social network, and predisposing factors interact to "produce" a response to trauma, most often one that results in adjustment (Paris, 1997). In fact, factors that initiate psychopathology are generally not the same as those that maintain its persistence into older age (Rutter & Maughan, 1997). Additionally, the traditional way to categorize trauma, the criteria for PTSD in the *Diagnostic and Statistical Manual of Mental Disorders*, fourth edition (DSM-IV; American Psychiatric Association, 1994), may not well serve the study of trauma (Green, 1991), especially not in older people (Summers & Hyer, 1994). With older people, Hyer and Summers (1995), among others, have argued that the DSM-IV formulation does not represent well how memories of fear create erroneous messages that then generalize to behavior in life.

Given that thinking in terms of PTSD will yield an imperfect picture of how trauma is adjusted to in later life, we address three issues. First, we consider age and its role in the trauma experience. We primarily address combat trauma, as many of the current older cohort of trauma sufferers (which is the one we work with) experienced trauma in World War II and the Korean War (Spiro, Schnurr, & Aldwin, 1994). Second, we look at treatment studies and psychotherapy as these apply to older people and trauma victims. Third, building on the first two issues, a model of treatment is provided. Fourth, we consider both the caregiver and assessment. We also provide a brief case.

WISDOM OF AGE

The experience of aging is perhaps best viewed as a series of confrontations with the self, one's body, one's physical skills, one's thoughts and memories, and one's worldviews. In this "developmental" understanding, adulthood is an ongoing dynamic process, a continuing evolution of existing psychic structures (Storant, 1994). Jung (1971) and Erikson (1975), two early purveyors of this position, argued that there is a continuing process of self-discovery and self-development that improves with age. The individual resolves internal and external realities and integrates opposing functions, and this marks the culmination of development. In effect, for the first time, a person now has in place more skillful ways for revising meaning than earlier in life. Alternative theoretical explanations are that aging involves (1) chronological maturation, (2) the unfolding of individual differences in the direction of integrity (Erikson, 1975), (3) a postformation stage of cognitive development in which appreciation of context becomes more natural (Rybash, Hoyer, & Roodin, 1986), (4) increasing emotional complexity (Schulz, 1982), (5) wisdom an expert knowledge system of the fundamental pragmatics of life (Baltes & Staudinger, 1993), and (6) gerotranscendence, a self-transcendent view with much life satisfaction (Tornstam, 1996).

In regards to stress Sherman (1981) outlined several aging-related components that become integrated: increased interiority, internal locus of control, passive mastery, reminiscence, and a self-orientation that seeks to set the past right (life review). Perhaps the most important of these is a natural retrospective focus that seeks to meld with present (and future) concerns to allow for self-changes. While resistance or foreclosure can and does occur in later life, it is less virulent than at other ages (Sherman, 1991).

Despite the fact that older people experience both minor (Ensel, 1991) and major (Summers & Hyer, 1994) negative life events, often are bothered by them (Falk, Hersen, & Van Hasselt, 1994; Tait & Silver, 1984), and underrepresent or alter (e.g., by somaticizing) problems (Hankin, Abueg, Gallagher-Thompson, & Laws, 1996) or have a more closed view of mental problems (Logsdon, 1995), older victims may find themselves less worse off as a result of current trauma than they would have been earlier in life. Older age may not be just a continuation of earlier ages, and it may not just be that one has more mature resilience in coping or improved relation to stress. It is the time in which to see life as it is (Baltes & Staudinger, 1993) and to appreciate universal and cosmic properties (Chinen, 1986). The last tasks of life—love, care, and wisdom—are different in kind (Erikson, 1975), and present themselves with the hope that a sense of integrity can be achieved.

COMBAT TRAUMA

Prevalence of PTSD in Veterans

The vast majority of our information on the influence of stress on older people involves war trauma (Ruskin & Talbott, 1996). As with all disorders, how prevalent lifetime PTSD is varies as a function of the sample assessed, the methods used, and the definition of trauma. Although prevalence rates are small in community samples of veterans (at times < 2%) (Hankin et al., 1996; Schnurr, Aldwin, Spiro, Stukel, & Keane, 1993; Spiro, Aldwin, Levenson, & Schnurr, 1993), for European groups, rates for lifetime PTSD can be high (Op den Velde et al., 1993). Among psychiatric inpatients who are veterans, rates are high, estimated from 50% to 67% with symptoms enduring over 40 years (Goldstein, van Kammen, Shelly, Miller, & van Kammen, 1987; Hovens et al., 1994; Rosen, Fields, Hand, Falsettie, & van Kammen, 1989; Zeiss & Dickman, 1989). The same applies for prisoners of war (POWs; Tennant, Goulston, & Dent, 1993). Rates of 18% (World War II) and 30% (Korea) have been also been noted for medical inpatients in VA medical centers: for veterans who never sought psychiatric treatment, the numbers were 9% (World War II) and 7% (Korea) for PTSD (Blake et al., 1990).

In another group, psychiatric outpatients, Garfein, Ronis, and Bates (1993) studied point prevalence of PTSD on a sample of 77,429 veterans who came in for outpatient VA mental health services during a 12-day period. Of the 22.3% who served in World War II and the 12.5% who served in Korea (the remainder served in other wars), 12% and 7.2%, respectively, had PTSD diagnoses. Based on 70% medical and 30% psychiatric outpatient clinic samples, Summers, Hyer, Boyd, and Boudewyns (1996) found prevalence rates to be 40.3% for PTSD. In that study, 50% of these veterans still had two or more avoidant or hyperarousal symptoms some 50 years after the traumatic events, and two-thirds had at least one arousal symptom. In general, prevalence rates appear lower for World War II and Korean samples than for Vietnam samples (Blake et al., 1990; Davidson, Kudler, Saunders, & Smith, 1990), but are still significant. And it is perhaps of some interest that rates of symptoms and adjustment problems, are higher for Korean than World War II veterans, although this is unexplained (Rosenheck & Fontana, 1994).

In summary, the residue of stress in the older cohort is experienced as similar to (Rosenheck & Fontana, 1994) or in positive and distinctive ways (Elder & Clipp, 1989; Elder, Shanahan, & Clipp, 1994; Lee, Vaillant, Torrey, & Elder, 1995), compared to that of younger cohorts in other wars. Aldwin, Levenson, and Spiro (1994) found that both positive and negative outcomes existed and, unlike in later war experiences, were mediated by the combat experience. In fact, it may even be argued that in the older cohort, military experience was developmental (Schnurr, 1997). Despite the clinical fact that there is a long history of negative consequences as a result of combat, as we just noted, PTSD prevalence rates in the older cohort are low. Many possible reasons exist: those without PTSD have outlived those who had it, differences in cohorts in the nature of war experience and in homecoming, unwillingness to admit psychiatric problems, and generally higher levels of adjustment than in Vietnam War veterans. In fact, we will never know the exact prevalence of PTSD in these older men, and there is no longitudinal data for whether they had it when they were younger. We must rely on retrospective accounts of their experiences. Over time, trauma-related problems may be reactivated when reminders of the war occur, perhaps also with the stress of certain events associated with aging, such as feelings of helplessness that sometimes accompany retirement and medical illness. But these events do not happen for everyone and for most are not stressful in such a way as to trigger traumatic memories (Schnurr, 1997).

Variables Moderating Severity of PTSD

The mixture of life transition process and trauma adjustment makes for an interesting interaction (Elder, & Caspi, 1990; McAdams, 1993). Five variables are especially important: (1) the presence of other stressors, (2) health status, (3) social support, (4) comorbidity, and (5) cognitive decline. First, older people are vulnerable to the effects of different stressors, many of which may exacerbate latent PTSD symptoms, even after years of being relatively asymptomatic. For some veterans, military trauma remains the most severe stressor throughout the lifetime; for many, however, other traumas are rated as more severe (Hyer & Summers, 1995). For those who have experienced significant trauma and have not dealt with it in the context of ongoing life, the struggle to contain painful memories can be considerable (Mazor, Gampel, Enright, & Orenstein, 1990) and the likelihood of there being other stressors (and presumably their influence) is high (Yehuda et al., 1995).

Second, compromised health status covaries with PTSD (Bremner, Southwick, & Charney, 1991). Physical illness and functional impairment increase the degree of stress experienced by these older veterans (Green, Epstein, Kruptnick, & Rowland, 1997), and there is reasonable evidence to suggest that self-reported health problems, morbidity, and service utilization increase after exposure to trauma (Schnurr, 1996). In fact, PTSD itself may be a mediator between trauma and physical health (Schnurr, 1996). It is probable that war trauma is sometimes associated with poorer health outcomes simply because of its relationship to PTSD problems. In this way, health-related behaviors, such as exercise or low use of alcohol, mediate the relationship between PTSD and health status. The impact of the poor application of health behaviors on self-reports of health negatively affect most psychiatric disorders in older people (Gatz, 1994; Haley, 1996).

Third, social support is important in the etiology of PTSD (Flannery, 1990; Barlow, 1988) and for adjustment at older ages. Social support seems to enhance the emotional processing necessary for the treatment of PTSD (Foa & Kozak, 1986). In fact, emotional support at the time of the trauma (or shortly thereafter) may be *the* primary protection against being more severely traumatized (van der Kolk & McFarlane, 1996). Social support is important at older ages, but it tends to decrease as relatives and friends die, move away, or become seriously ill or incapacitated (Gatz, 1994). In addition, the strains of living in unfamiliar ways may be as significant as losses. Adjusting to a state of widowhood stands at the top of that list (Gatz, 1994). The diagnosis and treatment planning of trauma are inadequate without information on social support.

Fourth, there may be psychiatric comorbidity with other mental disorders (Hyer & Stanger, 1997) though some disorders (e.g., substance abuse) are not as prevalent among this age group as with Vietnam veterans (Hyer & Associates, 1994). Depression can be a special problem in later life, as it is interactive with (Hyer & Stanger, 1997; Lee et al., 1995) or significantly related to (Foa & Kozak,

1986) PTSD. In fact, it has been argued that PTSD in later life may be an anxiety disorder with depression a necessary part (Stanger & Hyer, 1997). At later ages, too, extended grief related to depression may be an unavoidable part of trauma adjustment (Brandsma & Hyer, 1995).

Last, evidence now exists that cognitive decline is evident in the older cohort that has trauma problems (Bremner et al., 1993; Creamer, Burgess, & Pattison, 1992; Gurvits et al., 1993; Sutker, Wibstead, Galina, & Allain, 1991; Sutker, Bugg, & Allain, 1991; Thygesen, Hermann, & Willnger, 1970; Uddo, Vasterling, Brailey, & Sutker, 1993; Zalewsi, Thompson, & Gottesman, 1994). Older people normally experience cognitive decline that influences the processing of information. Relative to PTSD, Litz and Keane (1989) noted that cognitive processing changes may be found when more sophisticated, higher order neuropsychological instruments are used. Several biologically based studies, too, in both clinical and preclinical populations suggest that cognitive functions are important in the understanding of the interaction of psychological and biological factors as they relate to the etiology and expression of PTSD (Charney & Heninger, 1986). It is no surprise that a recent review of this area (Knight, 1997) and "clinical common sense" (Hyer & Associates, 1994) point to the presence of neuropsychological problems. Interestingly, the symptoms of cognitive decline, memory deficits, amnesia, and concentration problems relate in important ways to the PTSD construct. How neuropsychological status affects PTSD, however, is unknown.

We are, of course, talking in generalities and the variables that affect adjustment to trauma differ over time—those that are influential immediately after the trauma are different from those that are influential 30 or 50 years later (Schnurr & Aldwin, 1993). In fact, trajectories of the (mental) health of war trauma victims vary over the lifespan (Mellman, Randolph, Brawman-Mintzer, Flores, & Milanes, 1992). With regard to combat trauma, roughly 20% of victims are continuously troubled, 20% are entirely symptom-free, and the remainder experience intermittent symptoms (Hyer & Summers, 1995; Zeiss & Dickman, 1989). The most typical pattern is one of decline that involves a continuation of decreasingly serious lifelong problems, and not the sudden development of new disorders. Often, the symptom expression of trauma alters, at times remitting and at times becoming reactivated, as aging-related variables assert a greater influence. Sometimes reactivation of trauma does occur only in later life, but it is not modal. The state of such reactivation is usually at a subclinical level of seriousness (Summers & Hyer, 1994). Perhaps at periods of remission, the older victim practices "escapist" coping or "downwardly adjusts" (Suls, Marco, & Tobin, 1991) to cope in the real world. In this way, the conditioning model that argues for simple connections in learning appears applicable only to acute PTSD and does not apply to chronic patterns (Hobfoll et al., 1991). This does not apply to most older people then.

TREATMENT STUDIES

Treatment for Older People

Reviews of psychotherapy during later life indicate clearly and convincingly that it is effective (e.g., Gallagher-Thompson & Thompson, 1995; Gatz, 1994; Gatz, Popkin, Pino, & VandenBos, 1985; Knight, 1996) in a wide variety of pathological areas (see Zeiss & Steffen, in press), combined with medication (Thompson, Gallagher, Hanser, Gantz, & Steffen, 1991), or applied to difficult problems (Hanley-Peterson et al., 1990; Thompson, Gallagher, & Czirr, 1988). Often, the therapist may wish to make some adjustments to traditional therapeutic techniques when dealing with older clients, such as being more active or task focused, with a few clearly outlined goals, and using a psychoeducational model and collaborative approach (Zeiss & Steffen, in press). Often, too, the special psychological needs of the elderly (Pfeiffer & Busse, 1973) require distinctive themes (e.g., loss, increased dependency, existential approach of death), age-specific reactions (e.g., survivor guilt at having outlasted others), and "aging" therapy needs (e.g., symbolic gift giving, more limited goals, greater amount of positive benefit, as well as a slower pace and lack of termination).

While other forms of therapy (e.g., interpersonal) have been addressed in the literature, two forms have received the most attention: cognitive-behavioral therapy (CBT) and reminiscence. Neither is specific to trauma therapy, but both have much to offer. During the past 15 years, the use of CBT has proved effective with later life depression (Beutler et al., 1987; Gallagher & Thompson, 1981, 1982; Hyer et al., 1990; McCarthy, Katz, & Foa, 1991; Thompson, Gallagher, & Breckenridge, 1987) and anxiety (Scogin, Rickard, Keith, Wilson, & McElreath, 1992). The application of CBT is also responsible for the maintenance of treatment gains (Gallagher-Thompson, Hanley-Peterson, & Thompson, 1990).

Reminiscence therapy does not have the methodological rigor that CBT has. Nonetheless, it has a long history, being used almost exclusively with older people (Butler, 1963; Parker, 1995). Overall results of its efficacy are inconclusive (Parker, 1995) but show it to be enjoyable, natural, informative, often social, and to end in improved outcomes such as increased self-esteem (Kovach, 1990). In one study Sherman (1991) showed that older people change through an active process of reminiscing—a conscious attempt to pull together positive and negative experiences and feelings into a cohesive pattern. Victims responded best when they were engaged, when they had developed a reasonable level of experiencing of the memories in question (exploratory or elaborated experience), and when they had attained the level termed "life review reminiscing," in which the person brings older memories to life, and feels and experiences them in the "now," bolstered by the ongoing processing of information, or reconstruction.

PTSD Treatment

There are no carefully controlled studies of the treatment in trauma on older victims. In a much cited review paper on treatment studies of PTSD (in general) Solomon, Gerrity, and Muff (1992) identified only 11 outcome studies that utilized random assignment to treatment and control groups. Although none of these studies used older victims, the active therapeutic ingredients for the treatment of PTSD are of interest. They included systematic desensitization and cognitive-behavioral therapy (Frank et al., 1988; Resick & Schnicke, 1992), exposure therapy (Boudewyns & Hyer, 1990; Cooper & Clum, 1989; Foa, Rothbaum, Riggs, & Murdock, 1991; Keane, Fairbank, Caddell, & Zimering, 1989; Kilpatrick & Veronen, 1983), and several general factors, including support and skills training (Resick, Jordan, Girelli, Hutter, & Marhoefer-Dvorak, 1988). The combination also of anxiety management training (AMT) or stress inoculation training (SIT), along with prolonged exposure (Foa et al., 1994; Resick & Schnicke, 1992), constitutes the treatment of choice for PTSD. In a manual for the treatment of younger combat veterans, Smyth (1995) reframed ideas of the Foa group, endorsing the activation of a target memory while the autonomic nervous system is not stimulated beyond a moderate range (i.e., the person is relaxed) and the concomitant use of the assimilation process. These ingredients, along with the therapeutic relationship, constitute curative agents for trauma victims (Smyth, 1995).

These findings would apply to older trauma victims. Intensive exposure methods are not productive with older people, tending to increase the level of autonomic arousal, with adverse effects on cognitive performance (McFarlane & Yehuda, 1996). AMT and SIT do not do this: AMT seeks to manage the anxiety as it occurs, due less to fear activation and more to necessary coping tools, and SIT addresses the perception of control over and tolerance of traumatic memories and the belief (and tools) that one can cope. Gradual exposure is implied in both methods. AMT strives for a comfortable atmosphere, where the client feels in control.

Eye movement desensitization and reprocessing (EMDR) acts in a similar way. Despite critical reviews (e.g., Acierno, Hersen, Van Hasselt, Tremont, & Meuser, 1994), this procedure provides exposure (in doses) that targets state-specific information related to the trauma (see Boudewyns & Hyer, 1996) and also has applicability with older victims (Hyer, 1995). Like standard CBT, EMDR employs all treatment modalities—emotions, sensations, cognitions, images—to unearth trauma experienced by the client. Like AMT and SIT, EMDR provides both exposure and assimilation components. Unlike these other methods, EMDR is more active and guides the client when information is blocked (Hyer & Brandsma, 1997).

These treatment methods allow for several positive types of changes. The exposure is dosed at the direction of the client. Additionally, the autonomic nervous system is activated within a moderate range, and new and incongruent data are added. Anxiety then is managed within the treatment context of AMT (or SIT). Just as exposure is provided in a dosed way, altered cognitions or behavioral interventions are introduced when the naturalness of the intervention is not effective. The stuck story of the trauma is reframed or repaired, then, with considerable assistance from cognitions.

The assimilation techniques used in these methods are close to narrative procedures (Hyer & Associates, 1994). With trauma, information processing is compromised in order to maintain the status quo (Litz & Keane, 1989). There is some consensus that the more traumatic memory is simply disclosed (Pennebaker, 1989) and validated (Murray & Segal, 1994), the more improvement occurs. Importantly, improvement occurs the more perceptions of traumatic events are organized (Foa, Molnar, & Cashman, 1995), placed into explicit memory (van der Kolk & Fisler, 1995), elaborated (Harvey, Orbuch, Chivalisz, & Garwood, 1991; Sewell, 1996), moved (Shapiro, 1995), or retrieved as less summary and more positive (McNally, Lasko, Macklin, & Pitman, 1995). Interventions used with older people, as in reminiscence (expose the story, unearth obvious distortions, and foster alternative beliefs) or CBT (examine surface and core construals) challenge the cognitive distortions that are unique to trauma. In the narrative context, the therapeutic task is to repair the story and rewrite the biography of the person. At the least, the task is to organize the story and provide a context for discovery and healing.

What can we derive from all this? Modal PTSD is less a continuation of an acute stress response than a distinct state that develops according to a variety of factors of the individual and the cohort, in addition to the severity of the trauma. Older people develop more stable patterns of interaction (personality), and they have the advantage of the ability to rework earlier stories, now at later life, when a life review is more natural. It may actually be that the constellation of symptoms changes over the course of a lifetime and that older victims recapitulate their trauma at life-cycle points. The use of CBT/AMT and the methods applied to one's narrative of events are especially apt for trauma processing in older victims. After all, trauma healing is a continual retelling, a shifting from previous negative narratives to more positive ones (van der Kolk & Fisler, 1995). With the combination, then, of exposure (AMT + exposure) and assimilation (CBT + narrative), trauma codes can become habituated (desensitized) *and* assimilated (with corrective cognitive codes). In our previous book (Hyer & Associates, 1994) we described how trauma disrupts core schemas and the self becomes disorganized, preventing new information from being assimilated. Indeed, we argued that memories (resulting from trauma) can be exemplars of such disrupted schemas. These ideas were built on earlier work (e.g., Dye & Roth, 1991; Horowitz, 1986; Janoff-Bulman, 1989; McCann & Pearlman, 1990; Meichenbaum & Frizpatrick, 1991).

TREATMENT MODEL

We now present a model for therapy for older trauma victims. This is a treatment model for trauma victims using common behavioral principles applicable to older people (Table 15.1). It is intended to provide structure with flexibility: First treat perturbation, then coping/social supports, then issues specific to trauma. In trauma therapy, always, a balance is necessary between the individual's resiliency and exposure to the traumatic memory so as not exceed the therapeutic window (Briere, 1992). In time, we seek a total deconstruction of the trauma experience of the person, to finesse the ongoing conscious construction of meaning by forcing a dialectical change (components 1, 2, 3, and 4) and activating emotional schemes (components 5 and 6).

The treatment model has six parts (Table 15.2). First, the task is to stabilize symptoms, including the treatment of comorbid disorders and current stressors (including health). This is an important component in the treatment of older people (Gatz, 1994) and for trauma in particular (McFarlane & Yehuda, 1996). Symptoms must be treated first both because they are important by themselves, and because only by a reduction of symptoms can later components of care be provided (Cummings & Sayama, 1995). Often, only a 50% reduction in severity level of symptoms is required before continuing on as this indicates progress, results in less perturbation, and heightens expectations/compliance (Hyer & Stewart, in press). In the context of trauma with older people, depression is a special problem (Fry, 1983) and may require a focused dose of CBT or medication, or both (see Gallagher-Thompson & Thompson, 1995; Hyer & Stanger, 1997). As with EMDR outcomes (Shapiro, 1995), clinical depression reduces the ability to access memories in a therapeutic way.

The second treatment component involves the relationship itself. No other component of therapy is more accepted than this second treatment factor (Bugental, 1987). For some, this *is* therapy (Kahn, 1991). How does the therapist let the client know that he or she is making the best possible effort to understand the way the situation looks to the client (Yehuda et al., 1995)? This involves the infrastruc-

---

TABLE 15.1. Cognitive-Behavioral Principles for Older Trauma Victims

 1. Socialize (positive expectations) client into therapy.
 2. Be collaborative/get active (ensure pleasant events).
 3. Target successes (small wins).
 4. Go slow/use practice.
 5. Be repetitive (educate and normalize)/use Socratic methods.
 6. Use favorite CBT techniques (e.g., ABCs) for management.
 7. Assure (at least) one coping strategy learned before trauma work.
 8. Monitor work/be scientific (e.g., use Beck Depression Inventory weekly).
 9. Adapt to the limits of the client.
10. Use homework.

TABLE 15.2. Treatment Model

1. Stabilize symptoms: Treat comorbid disorders or stressors (including health).
2. Relationship building: Build trust, the ability to confront combat trauma with a trusted therapist. Respect the narcissistic alliance (what client needs to have stroked).
3. Attend to necessary aging-related treatment and education (normalization) factors. Assure social supports, daily coping, social skills, and treatment compliance.
4. If avoidance/other symptoms: Use tactics of personality style.
5. Build on clients' self-defining memories (SDMs): Foster a renarration of self with core memories (SDMs) that can generalize to current life situations. This core life story assists in the balance of the client's life.
6. If intrusions: Decondition trauma memories. Apply AMT or EMDR.

ture of treatment, the ability to balance the need to make the client feel supported with the need to have the therapy progress (Hyer & Associates, 1994). With regard to older victims, this task above all else requires socialization (Gallagher-Thompson & Thompson, 1996); with regard to trauma, the task involves insuring safety (Weiss, 1971), as well as eliciting the needed components of mindfulness of the therapeutic process, affect tolerance, and the ability to self-soothe (Hyer & Stewart, in press). Howard (1991), too, noted that this is best done by therapists who can join the core issues of clients' stories and provide the appropriate word repair. With regard to trauma, reflection and unconditional positive regard are rarely overused in an environment of dosed exposure. Turner, McFarlane, and van der Kolk (1995) write: "Much of the treatment of victims of trauma is intuitive. It depends on both a sensitive understanding of the unique issues that make every individual different from all others, and clinical knowledge about the accurate timing of appropriate interventions" (p. 539).

An important part of therapy involves a "socialization" period that needs to be repeated now and then (Gallagher-Thompson & Thompson, 1996). Preparation of the older client for therapy is the most important component of therapy (McNally et al., 1995), and it is the slow process of mutually determining treatment goals, as well as education about and commitment to the process that normalizes and places trauma in perspective. In effect, the relationship sets the stage for the work of trauma, which is the necessary invalidation process of the *effects* of trauma after the requisite validation of the *experience* of trauma. The relationship precedes the therapeutic flow: initially, respect for the stuck story with clinically curious queries, then a shift of meaning with "nudging" questions; eventually, a revision of the story with challenges or reintegration; and finally, behavior tasks (Summers & Hyer, 1994). Often, the therapeutic tasks are basic: keeping the trauma victim in treatment, being supportive during difficult periods, maintaining appropriate arousal levels, and, in general, assuring commitment to the goals of therapy. In this way, the relationship is both an epiphenomenon and the phenomenon of care (Kahn, 1991).

The third task of trauma therapy is to attend to aging-related and treatment factors, as well as lifestyle factors. Aging-related factors include social support, daily coping, and social skills, as well as treatment compliance. If the trauma was intense, and if the social support (and coping mechanisms) are inadequate following the trauma, the "total" resources of the victim (social roles, possessions, self- and worldviews, and energy) become depleted (Freedy, Shaw, Jarrell, & Masters, 1992). Therapeutically, the older person must come to know what to do and have sufficient internal (coping and social skills, as well as treatment compliance) and external (social supports) skills for producing change. A not insignificant amount of change is attainable by the therapist's explaining the reasons for treatment compliance as well as the importance of social support, coping, and skill building.

Lifestyle factors are also relevant. Even though age increases the risk of many diseases, those with worse lifestyle indicators are at greater risk. For older people, the behavioral risk factors most amenable to change are smoking, alcohol use, obesity, cholesterol level, Type A behavior patterns, job strain, psychosocial stress, and sexual behavior (Siegler, 1994). Modification of risk factors is worth the effort. Siegler (1994) writes: "It is not sufficient to consider the older person who comes to the developmental health psychologist for assistance from only one perspective. If one does so, important variables may be ignored" (p. 137).

The goal is to keep the older person committed to therapy (and with appropriate skills) and to living a balanced and reasonably healthy life. These issues are assessed and addressed early in treatment. Simply assessing the person's day-to-day activities, with a special focus on coping and social support, is often all that is required (Gallagher-Thompson & Thompson, 1996). Implied is encouraging an active stance toward life, where social skills are required, that must be applied continuously and is best done with a coping repertoire of great latitude (Hobfoll et al., 1991). In order for later narrative components of care to be effective, then, the self-management components must be in place.

The fourth task is more complicated to explain but is simple in intent: if avoidance symptoms predominate, treat the salient patterns of the client's personality style. The idea is that an analysis of personality is the best vehicle available to improve the outcomes of psychotherapy, to understand entrenched patterns of coping (Ruegg & Frances, 1995). Evidence exists that ingrained patterns of personality are more resistant to change in PTSD outpatients than in others (Fontana & Rosenheck, 1994; Frueh, Turner, Beidel, Mirabella, & Jones, 1996), and that a knowledge of these assists in treatment (e.g., Hoglend, 1996). If PTSD in older combat veterans is chronic and relapsing, a knowledge of personality is helpful in the understanding of the whole trauma response (Millon & Davis, 1995). A comprehensive awareness, then, of the structural integrity of personality (behaviors, thoughts, emotions, and interpersonal and biological patterns) serves the clinician well.

Few studies have assessed which patient characteristics interact positively or negatively with exposure treatment of PTSD. We have argued that treatment problems and probably treatment symptoms (the actual memory of trauma) are best *managed* by an awareness and use of personality (Hyer & Boyd, 1996; Hyer, McCranie, Boudewyns, & Sperr, 1996). In effect, the clinician needs to address personality issues *and* trauma issues (Horowitz et al., 1984; Hyer & Associates, 1994; Ulman & Brothers, 1988; McAdams, 1990). And use of personality data for later life problems is recommended for any Axis I disorder (Abrams & Horowitz, 1995; Costa, 1994). In the context of trauma, a careful understanding of the meaning of trauma and other symptoms—their functional value for the person—is acquired. A personality assessment and a developmental history (lifestyle) are important (Hyer & Associates, 1994). Salient interpersonal, cognitive, emotional, and behavioral domains for each personality pattern are isolated and treated (see Millon & Davis, 1995).

The last two components of the model center on memories. Both are applied after other issues are considered, and both can occur at the same time. The trauma memory represents atypical events that do not fit into prior schemas and are not narrativized (McFarlane & Yehuda, 1996). The therapeutic task is to cause this *implicit* memory (triggered by emotional states, interpersonal contexts, external stimuli, and language cues) to be *explicit* memory, placed into language in the form of a narrative (Siegel, 1995).

Component 5 represents the positive side of memory processing. It involves positive memories. Here, therapist works within existing life stories (positive ones) to help the client get new perspectives on current issues or to facilitate the integration of unresolved past events and choices. (Narrative therapists focus on changing or "rewriting" dysfunctional stories about the self.) The therapist highlights positive aspects of the individual's life story, focusing on the past exclusively. Study subjects who participated in this form of reminiscence experienced a reduction in anxiety and a positive change in appraisal of coping abilities and resources (see Rybarczyk & Bellg, 1997).

Often, self-defining memories (SDMs) are employed. These are blended summary/single events important to the self (Singer & Salovey, 1993). They are core representations of the self, complete with goals. Each person has a collection of autobiographical memories, a core set of "slides in the carousel" (Singer & Salovey, 1993), which are episodes in the person's life repeatedly considered and strung together to form a script or personality. In therapy, they can assist in the balance of life and can generalize to current life situations. In therapy (or life), too these memories can be used to understand personal meaning and assist in meeting present demands.

Despite the fact that no taxonomy of memories exists and that curative treatment components are unknown (McAdams, 1996), with this (positive) balance, the victim undergoes both current experiential processing and reflects on self-referential components of these stories. The victim tells of an important defining event other than the trauma. The therapist validates the stability of the self, emphasizes the client's agency, endorses positive actions, stimulates growth, as well as fosterisng several other features of self-referenced components or change (Hyer & Stewart, in press). This is almost always helpful, as it gives the person permission to evaluate the self differently, to see the self compassionately and more realistically.

The last component involves the trauma memory: desensitize trauma memories by the application of AMT or EMDR. Whichever used, the standard EMDR evaluation, pretherapy procedure for clients is emphasized (see Shapiro, 1995). This is an excellent and efficient method for acquiring data on the target memory, its intensity, negative and positive cognitions, emotions, salient sensations, and safety cues. After this, there are several sessions of a relaxation procedure that is eventually linked to trauma memories. This is initially learned so that the client can control the anxiety associated with the traumatic event. The steps of the relaxation procedure are audiotaped and the person is instructed to practice the procedure at least once a day (Hyer & Associates, 1994; Suinn, 1990). Older people tend to respond well to relaxation techniques.

Following this, standard AMT or EMDR is used. Both appear effective and can actually be used interchangeably, as both are similar. In both, the trauma memory is initially the target. In AMT, the desensitization process is applied (Suinn, 1990) with some modifications (Smyth, 1995). The principle alteration is to have the client initially target a scene that has already occurred and is at a moderate level of distress. As with psychiatric medications with older people, the therapist should start low (in target memory perturbation) and go slow (Gatz, 1994). Commonly, failure results in an underresponse, where avoidance may be occurring (here, the clinician becomes active finding out and targeting the cause), or in an overresponse (here, the therapist can do any number of AMT responses, usually backing up and finding a memory lower in intensity). Success must occur before more difficult issues can be addressed. Sessions are taped and used as homework.

EMDR is the other option. This method requires a set procedure, a process in which the client experiences the target at his or her own pace (see Shapiro, 1995). EMDR utilizes the power of treatment expectations, accesses associative networks unique for each person, uses the language of the client, utilizes traditional cognitive techniques, especially the identification of positive and negative cognitions, challenges evidence, and applies affect and necessary "here and now" experiencing of past targets (Hyer & Brandsma, 1997). In EMDR, the mixture of both experiencing and metacommunication on the client-governed content is paramount: the client experiences, then comments on the target.

Ultimately, for change to occur, the resulting narrative of client's life must be made coherent and understandable. It has been argued that transformation occurs only when the client's core schemas are challenged (Tedeschi & Calhoun, 1995). It has also been argued that this is unnecessary, a focus on "best moments" or positive experiences in life (one's core goals) is often all that is necessary for change (Nichols, 1991). This model attempts challenge and positive emphasis with steps 5 and 6.

FAMILY CAREGIVING AND ASSESSMENT

Aging, especially encumbered by the baggage of trauma problems, most often plays itself out in a family context (Hyer & Stewart, in press). Two trends, in particular, have been found regarding the effects of PTSD on the family or significant others of (male) war trauma victims. First, gerontological research has seen a dramatic increase recently in the area of family caregiving. Caregiving has even been labeled a "career" (Pearlin, 1992). Caring for a physically or mentally disabled elder has been linked to increased levels of anxiety and depression (Gallagher, Rose, Rivera, Lovett, & Thompson, 1989), a compromised immune (Kiecolt-Glaser, Dura, Speidher, Trask, & Glaser, 1991) or cardiovascular system (Vitaliano, Russo, Bailey, Young, & McCann, 1993), among other problems (see Zarit, 1996). Many studies have conducted cognitive and affective appraisals of caregivers, including how well they cope with having to give care (Cook, Aherns, & Pearson, 1995); how their personality traits affect and prepare them for caregiving (Hooker, Monahan, Shifren, & Hutchinson, 1992), as well as models for depression in caregivers (Zarit, 1996). In general, these studies suggest that caregivers are at risk, that social support is important for their mental and physical health, that marital happiness affects outcomes for the better, that containing stress is important because it can proliferate into the rest of life and cause secondary role strain (Pearlin, Mullan, Semple, & Skaff, 1990), and that there are several models of effective caregiving can be used in the treatment of beleaguered caregivers (see Zarit, 1996).

The second area involves the effects PTSD itself can have on those close to PTSD sufferers, particularly women close to them. Prevalence rates (of PTSD) are generally higher for females regardless of the stressor (Riggs, Rothbaum, & Foa, 1995) or age (Potts, 1994). Generally, this also applies for the variables of less education, lower socioeconomic status, or being members of a minority (Breslau, Davis, & Andreski, 1995). Age, however, tends to be a factor that increases resilience (Ullman, 1995; Ullman & Siegel, 1994). Treatment models and care paradigms have also been offered regarding women who have *themselves* experienced war situations (Wolfe, Mori, & Krygeris, 1994). But, regarding older veterans' wives and significant others, less is known. Women in long-term relationships with veterans suffering from PTSD do seem to commonly experience PTSD-like symptoms themselves (Nelson & Wright, 1996). This has been labeled secondary victimization (Waysman, Mikulincer, Weisenberg, & Solomon, 1993) and also applies to children of sufferers (Hyer & Associates, 1994).

It is clear that caregiving is not a unitary process, and that caregivers are very different from each other in the ways they cope (or fail to cope) with the demands of their role. The multivariate nature of caregiving, interventions, and their effects is just now unfolding. At the very least, one needs to assess the adequacy of the social support network, the nature of the care-receiver's disability, the previous and current coping history of the caregiver, intercurrent stressful life changes, and the caregiver's physical and mental health. Caregivers' subjective burden is typically viewed as the emotional cost of the illness to family members (e.g., feelings of embarrassment, resentment, and helplessness), while objective burden is defined as the disruption of the everyday family life of the ill person's relatives (e.g., financial burden, loss of free time, and conflict with neighbors or law enforcement officials) (Thompson & Doll, 1982). Both require therapeutic tending.

One helpful tactic to use with the families of older war-trauma veterans is provided by Zarit (1996). He recommends a combination of individual therapy with a primary caregiver, followed by family meetings as well as support groups. Interestingly, the presence of adult children often provides assistance in treatment, as children appear universally accepted and needed in later life (Hyer & Associates, 1994). The significance of the reciprocal impact of a psychiatric patient upon the family cannot be understated especially in later life. Older trauma victims play many roles: the angry distant one, the submissive and depressed one, the confused and dependent one, among others. The "social" aspect of the treatment involves fundamental changes in an individual's family and social identity, along with declines in role performance. A whole family treatment focus is requisite.

Assessment occurs early in treatment. In fact, an "assessment as treatment" model applies (Hyer & Stewart, in press). Where the validation of scales for assessing PTSD is concerned, older victims have not been included. Current "better" measures are scales anchored to the DSM. The CAPS-1, the Clinician-Administered PTSD Scale (Blake et al., 1995) has been validated with older veterans (Hyer, Summers, Boyd, Litaker, & Boudewyns, 1996). There are also several self-report measures with at least concurrent validation with older people (e.g., Impact of Events, Mississippi Scale for Combat-Related PTSD, MMPI-2 scales PK and PS) (Hyer, Summers, Braswell, & Boyd, 1995). Physiological reactions of older people also continue to be good indicators of trauma response (Hyer & Summers, 1995). All of these can be used.

Based on our treatment model, clinicians should consider several issues in the formation of a plan. Issue 1 involves information on PTSD (CAPS-1) and an assessment of comorbidity. Issue 2 involves the target trauma and intervening trauma. Having the tell the trauma story gives information on the basis of which the clinician will decide whether to do trauma work. In fact, measuring intervening trauma (both current and past) may be as or more important than the target trauma itself. The assessment of trauma across the lifespan with an older victim is a form of life review, rich with information. This is a lifeline, "when" PTSD problems expressed themselves. Issue 3 includes an assessment of the influencing factors of older age, such as coping, social support, and health. Issue 4 is positive memories or SDMs. Several are requested for treatment elaboration. Issue 5 involves a measure of personality. We have used measures developed by Millon (Hyer & Associates, 1994). Information on personality assists in the application of tactics and strategies of care, along with or independent of the trauma memory.

The decision to treat trauma is not a light one. The overall goal of PTSD therapy involves the emotional processing of the trauma memory (Foa, 1996). War-trauma clients often have five decades of poor adaptation and inadequate coping styles (e.g., internal, global, and stable). Evidence exists that exposure treatment can have a negative impact with some older folks (Brink, 1978; Shapiro, 1995). Our rule of thumb, however, is that if intrusive symptoms or painful responses are noted, if the client consents to trauma work, and if adequate ego skills and self-capacities (Hyer & Associates, 1994; McCann & Pearlman, 1990) are present, then AMT or EMDR can be applied. If, on the other hand, traumatic memories are largely fragmented, partially or completely unconscious, with low tolerance for being accessed, or, in general, an excessive level of daily intrusions or a reduced capacity/willingness to retrieve trauma is present, supportive measures, guided by procedures 1, 2, 3, 4 (see Table 15.3), are more appropriate.

We have used several rules of thumb to understand the processing of the trauma memory itself. We have pilot-tested many methods for narrative repair—active reminiscence (Sherman, 1991), renarration (Hermans & Hermans-Jansen, 1995), biographical grids (Neimeyer & Stewart, in press), time lines (Stewart, 1995), active therapeutic alteration of the story (Bornat, 1994), narrative organization (Foa et al., 1995), newer forms of exposure (e.g., Ochberg, 1996), isolated targets of self-repair (Wolfe, 1995), and transformation (Tedeschi & Calhoun, 1995), among others. In general, the more movement or

---

TABLE 15.3. Client Indicators for Trauma Work

1. *Task*
   Knows/accepts client role
   Collaborates; provides ongoing feedback to experience (e.g., SUDs levels)
   Adequate imagery and verbal skills

2. *Psychological mindedness*
   Ability and willingness to stay on task and struggle nondefensively

3. *Trauma memory*
   Determine if memories are whole or fragmented.
   Assess self-skills:
   　Tolerates frustration/pain
   　Not self-condemning
   　Able to use calming self-talk
   　Ability to place symptoms in perspective
   　Ability to cope outside of therapy
   　Able to be alone
   　Able to establish boundaries between self and others

4. *Success monitors*
   Reduces avoidance mechanism
   Less anxiety/pain within/across sessions
   Committed to procedure
   Future oriented/hope

elaboration of the trauma memory there is, the greater the success; the more practiced the older victim is in relaxation and imagery, the better the response (often, relaxation-based techniques alone have a desired effect); the less skilled the client is, the more the therapist becomes active (partializing memories, reframing negative stories, suggesting alternative coping, and challenging or changing stories); the more the client remains in the "now," experiencing the feared object, the more change occurs; and the less memories change suggests that "training" methods for memory recall have been successful. In addition to relaxation, simple imagery training and narrative elaboration training, where the client practices recall on safer memories with a specific rationale, which is to extend memory (e.g., using person, place, time, details, etc.) and to gain strategies for organizing memories.

THE CASE OF TI

Ti is a 66-year-old white male who has been in a supportive marriage for 45 years. He has three children, also supportive. He has a 10th-grade education and worked as a textile worker for a number of years, retiring in 1972 because of PTSD problems. It was during that year also that he abused alcohol (for approximately 1 year). Currently, he has no compromising medical problems but did have a "minor" heart attack some 5 years ago.

He was in Korea for 13 months, in combat. He is able to identify several combat experiences, all involving death. Ti noted that since his combat experience he had always had the PTSD problems, but his worst years were 1952 (the event), 1972 (his retirement), and 1994 (the onset of his recent treatment when he was treated as a psychiatric inpatient). He describes a typical day as one where he gets up early due to poor sleep habits, stays around the house pestering his wife, and tinkers in the yard. Again, his presenting symptoms are intrusive trauma memories, anger at himself, and hopelessness.

Test data (see Table 15.4) show that Ti has PTSD and is depressed (Mood scale and Hamilton Depression Scale) He has also experienced heavy combat. He has high scores on the anxiety scale of the (MCMI-II). On the MCMI-II also, he has a mixture of patterns of detachment (schizoid and avoidant) and instability of mood and interpersonal conflicts (passive–aggressive). In general, such patients are characterized by a fear of others (or mistrust), as well as some eccentricities. Unable to function independently, they must rely on others but resent it. In a general way, they are passive–dependent, often symptom overreporters. As a result of Ti's history and these data, it can be determined that he has PTSD, chronic and major affective disorder, recurrent Axis I diagnoses, and personality traits consistent with avoidant and passive–aggressive styles.

Treatment follows the model (Table 15.2). First, symptoms were stabilized. With Ti, the problem of depression was apparent and aggressively treated with an

TABLE 15.4. Test Data for Ti

SCID-PTSD and CAPS-1	PTSD (on both)
Mississippi Scale	154
Impact of Events	60 (I = 30 and A = 30)
Combat Exposure Scale	27
Geriatric Mood Scale	11/15 items depressed
Hamilton Depression Scale	26
Millon Clinical Multiaxial Inventory (MCMI-II)	Schizoid, avoidant, passive–aggressive; dysthymia and anxiety

antidepressant as well as a behavioral program that addressed negative cognitions and activity. He had already been involved in the behavioral program and had no outstanding current stressors. The second and third features of the model involved the treatment relationship and necessary treatment and education (normalization) factors, including the assurance of social supports, daily coping, and social skills and treatment compliance. He was easy to relate to despite the probable issues of trust due to his avoidant personality style. There was a slow validation time during which the therapist let him tell his story, and let him know that "I hear you," regardless of the illogical or gory parts of his story. His role as a client and his ability to take an observing ego position were also fostered, again in a slow Socratic process. The therapist also emphasized Ti's active role, and how important it was that he understand what PTSD is and how it affects his life. He was also given data that suggested that he was "bigger than his problem" and that now he was "allowing himself to experience change." This took three to five sessions.

Fourth, the focus moved to predominant symptoms exclusive of intrusions of traumatic memories. As with other, older individuals, Ti had organized his life around avoidance as well as other symptoms. He had detached (schizoid and avoidant) and ambivalent (passive–aggressive) styles. Regarding the overall strategy for a detached style, the goal was to enhance pleasure and reduce the expectation of pain as well as his clinging to others. For the passive–aggressive style, the goal was to diminish self–other conflict and stabilize erratically changing actions. With Ti, the therapist chose to develop behavioral and cognitive interventions that reduced his alienated self-image ("I am no good"), practice assertion skills (reducing his penchant for ambivalent clinging), and moderate his dysphoric moods. Miniexperiments were devised for these. He was also requested to monitor the influence of his mood and challenge this over time. These tasks were ongoing and took the better part of 20 sessions.

During the sessions in which the personality-based strategies and tactics were addressed, a life review was undertaken and the acquisition of a several SDMs, according to the fifth treatment feature, were obtained. With Ti, one SDM was an early memory of helping others and being assertive. In a constructivist way, Ti was asked to provide for himself a new reality, one that allowed for a reauthoring of his identity. So with the use of the personality styles assisting in the forming of new behaviors/cognitions/feelings, and the use of the SDM in the forming of a new self-reality, therapy moved along.

Finally, a course of EMDR was applied. Trauma work is done last. With Ti, six sessions of EMDR took place. Initially, he was taught to relax. Some therapy time also was devoted to the purpose of trauma work—"We will take this at your pace, you will not fall apart, you will not forget the event, and it will allow you to have a sense of mastery over it." Ti had several identified trauma memories. One was selected. He had a negative cognition, "I am the worst human being alive," and a positive one, "I did the best I could." He had an initial Subjective Units of Distress scale (SUDs) of 10 in his first session. His emotion was depression, and his expressed sensation was that of being chocked. He processed the memories, reducing his initial and ending SUDS over the six-treatment sessions. During the last session, he reached a SUDS of 2. He saw many elements of the trauma that he had forgotten and saw what he was doing to himself with self-blame and feelings of hopelessness. Hopelessness was targeted as a special problem. He lessened this emotion but never gave it up fully. This was reframed as ecological and necessary for him, as well as a form of self-caring. At the end of his sixth session, his Impact of Events was < 10 and his Hamilton Depression score was < 10. At the end of this part of the therapy, too, he had been sleeping better, responding to his wife well, and was going to become a volunteer (remember his SDM).

CONCLUSION

No particular model of PTSD is entirely accurate. Treatment of an older, traumatized individual is dictated by the individual's needs, paced according to the degree of involuntary intrusion of the trauma and the individual's capacities to deal with intense emotions. The same axioms of treatment apply as at other ages—the more extreme and the longer the duration of the stressor, the stronger the avoidance posttrauma, and the less resilient the person, the greater the chance for a poor response to trauma. By any definition, PTSD is mostly chronic in older people and has associated, now functionally autonomous, problems. Perhaps the most distinctive feature of PTSD as a brand of anxiety disorder is not the unique quality of its principal components (physiological arousal, cognitive processes, and avoidant coping strategies), but its excessiveness and persistence.

We have argued that where trauma is concerned, aging may be a blessing. Something happens as people grow older that is positive, which is that there is an increasing tolerance and willingness to "look again" at painful experiences. If in the process of decline (due to trauma), the person is impacted unduly at first by fearful and intrusive experiences and later accommodates poorly in the form of avoidance, the strengths we posit exist in later life may indeed assist in treatment.

The existential issues of trauma—loss, meaning making, accepting reality, achieving ego integrity—are conceptually close to those of aging, and the treatment of trauma may indeed meld most naturally with concerns of aging.

We have also advocated an integrated therapy with our model. The goal of trauma therapy is to be able to *jointly cooperate and solve problems in the observing and evaluating of experiences related to the trauma in the ongoing drama of the therapy.* With trauma, time seems to be stuck, no growth occurs. The wise clinician "treats" the trauma victim in later life, ready to manage the victim or to facilitate a change in the trauma itself, or both. Not surprisingly, with many older trauma victims, other issues of therapy are equally important to those of the trauma itself—a supportive social system, an empowered problem-solving focus, ability to cope in ongoing (and past) stress situations. With the older victim (in this model), clinicians are requested to be active. They are not asked, however, to take over control or to pass control on to outside parties (van der Kolk et al., 1996). Therapeutic activism involves the danger of accepting clients' helplessness as inevitable and of taking over control where clients need to learn to establish control themselves. Any quick fix mentality of earlier ages will not be appropriate here. Moore (1994) says: "Care of the soul observes the paradox whereby a muscled strong-willed pursuit of change can actually stand in the way of substantive transformation" (p. 19).

Regrettably, in this chapter we have ignored many "critical" questions. Research on the organization, decision rules, and the best examples of PTSD in later life have been left out. What really is PTSD in later life? If an older victim has a few intrusion and arousal symptoms, but no evident avoidant problems, what does that mean? We ourselves do not know what potentiates problems of the most common variety in the aging person, the appearance of PTSD symptoms after remitted periods. Do trauma symptoms occur as a result of age-related coping decline, recent stressful events, or is it just the nature of the disorder? Also, how are narratives defined—in terms of textual structures, social interactions, or cultural issues? Indeed, what is the best developmental framework for understanding the core issues of older people? And for simplicity, we have not brought up the issue of whether the DSM provides the best model for the categorization of a person who experiences trauma.

Perhaps this needs to be said, too: to the "knowing" clinician, the study of the response to trauma is really only an illusion, a Platonic form or an approximation of something that is both real and unspeakable, perhaps unknowable. Trauma symptoms represent only memory markers that capture moments of traumatic situations of helplessness, terror, horror, and utter ineffectiveness. The DSM creates order, but imperfect order and order that does not provide clear treatment rules. The value or meaning of a symptom in the context of PTSD for an older person ultimately needs a clinical ear. Therapy will always depend on the therapist and will always be something more than that which is objectively presented (Bugental, 1987).

REFERENCES

Abrams, R. C., & Horowitz, S. V. (1996). Personality disorders after age 50: A meta-analysis. *Journal of Personality Disorders, 10*(3), 271–281.

Acierno, R., Hersen, M., Van Hasselt, V. B., Tremont, G., & Meuser, K. T. (1994). Review of the validation and dissemination of eye-movement desensitization and reprocessing: A scientific and ethical dilemma. *Clinical Psychology Review, 14,* 287–299.

Aldwin, C. M., Levenson, M. R., & Spiro, A., III (1994). Vulnerability and resilience to combat exposure: Can stress have lifelong effects? *Psychology and Aging, 9,* 34–44.

Baltes, P. B., & Staudinger, U. M. (1993). The search for a psychology of wisdom. *Current Directions in Psychological Science, 2,* 75–80.

Bamberg, M. (1997). *Narrative development: Six approaches.* Hillsdale, NJ: Erlbaum.

Barlow, D. H. (1988). *Anxiety and its disorders: The nature and treatment of anxiety and panic.* New York: Guilford Press.

Beutler, L. E., Scogin, F., Kirkish, P., Schretlen, D., Corbishley, A., Hamblin, D., Meredith, K., Potter, R., Bamford, C. R., & Levenson, A. I. (1987). Group cognitive therapy and alprazolam in the treatment of depression in older adults. *Journal of Consulting and Clinical Psychology, 55,* 550–557.

Blake, D., Weathers, F., Nagy, L., Kaloupek, D., Gusman, F., Charney, D., & Keane, T. (1995). The development of the Clinician-Administered PTSD Scale. *Journal of Traumatic Stress, 8,* 75–90.

Blake, D. D., Weathers, F. W., Nagy, L. M., Kaloupek, D. G., Klauminzer, G., Charney, D. S., & Keane, T. M. (1990). A clinician rating scale for assessing current and lifetime PTSD: The CAPS-1. *Behavior Therapy, 13,* 187–188.

Bornat, J. (Ed.). (1994). *Reminiscence reviewed: Perspectives, evaluations, achievements.* Buckingham, UK: Open University Press.

Boudewyns, P., & Hyer, L. (1990). Changes in psychophysiological response to war memories among Vietnam veteran PTSD patients treated with direct therapeutic exposure. *Behavior Therapy, 21,* 63–87.

Boudewyns, P., & Hyer, L. (1996). Eye movement desensitization and reprocessing (EMDR) as treatment for post-traumatic stress disorder (PTSD). *Clinical Psychology and Psychotherapy, 3,* 185–195.

Brandsma, J., & Hyer, L. (1995). The treatment of grief in PTSD. *National Center for PTSD Clinical Quarterly, 5.*

Bremmer, J., Scott, T., Delanwy, R., Southwick, S., Mason, J., Johnson, D., Innis, R., McCarthy, G., & Charney, D. (1993). Deficits in short-term memory in posttraumatic stress disorder. *American Journal of Psychiatry, 150,* 1015–1019.

Bremner, J. D., Southwick, S. M., & Charney, D. S. (1991). Animal models for the neurobiology of trauma. *PTSD Research Quarterly, 2*(4), 1–3.

Breslau, N., & Davis, G. C. (1992). Posttraumatic stress disorder in an urban population of young adults: Risk factors for chronicity. *American Journal of Psychiatry, 149,* 671–675.

Breslau, N., Davis, G., & Andreski, P. (1995). Risk factors for PTSD-related traumatic events: A prospective analysis. *American Journal of Psychiatry, 152,* 529–535.

Briere, J. (1992). Methodological issues in the study of sexual abuse effects. *Journal of Consulting and Clinical Psychology, 60,* 196–203.

Brink, T. L. (1978). Geriatric rigidity and its psychotherapeutic implications. *Journal of the American Geriatrics Society, 26*(6), 274–277.

Bugental, J. (1987). *The art of the psychotherapist.* New York: Norton.

Butler, R. N. (1963). The life review: An interpretation of reminiscence in the aged. *Psychiatry, 26,* 65–76.

Charney, D. S., & Heninger, G. R. (1986). Abnormal regulation of noradrenergic function in panic disorder. *Archives of General Psychiatry, 43,* 1042–1058.

Chinen, A. (1986). Elder tales revised: Forms of transcendence in later life. *Journal of Transpersonal Psychology. 26,* 171–192.

Cook, J., Aherns, A., & Pearson, J. (1995). Attributions and depression in Alzheimer's disease caregivers. *Journal of Clinical Gerontology, 1,* 119–132.

Cooper, N. A., & Clum, G. A. (1989). Imaginal flooding as a supplementary treatment for PTSD in combat veterans: A controlled study. *Behavior Therapy, 20,* 381–391.

Costa, P. (1994). Personality continuity and the changes of adult life. In M. Storant & G. VandenBos (Eds.), *The adult years: Continuity and change* (pp. 41–78). Washington, DC: American Psychological Association Press.

Creamer, M., Burgess, P., & Pattison, P. (1992). Reaction to trauma: A cognitive-processing model. *Journal of Abnormal Psychology, 1,* 452–459.

Cummings, N., & Sayama, M. (1995). *Focused psychotherapy: A casebook of brief, intermittent psychotherapy throughout the life cycle.* New York: Brunner/Mazel.

Davidson, J., Kudler, H., Saunders, E., & Smith, R. (1990). Symptom and comoribidity patterns in World War II and Vietnam veterans with posttraumatic stress disorder. *Comparative Psychiatry, 31,* 162–170.

Dye, E., & Roth, S. (1991). Psychotherapy with Vietnam veterans and rape and incest survivors. *Psychotherapy, 28,* 103–120.

Elder, G. H., & Clipp, E. C. (1989). Combat experience and emotional health: Impairment and resilience in later life. *Journal of Personality, 57,* 311–341.

Elder, G. H., Shanahan, M. J., & Clipp, E. C. (1994). When war comes to men's lives: Life course patterns in family, work, and health. *Psychology and Aging, 9,* 5–16.

Elder, L., & Caspi, A. (1990). Studying lives in a changing society: Sociological and personological explanations. In A. Rabin, R. Zucker, R. Emmons, & S. Frank (Eds.), *Studying persons and lives* (pp. 201–247). New York: Springer.

Ensel, W. M. (1991). "Important" life events and depression among older adults: The role of psychological and social resources. *Journal of Aging and Health, 3,* 546–566.

Erikson, E. (1975). *Life history and the historical movement.* New York: Norton.

Falk, B., Hersen, M. H., & Van Hasselt, V. (1994). Assessment of post-traumatic stress disorder in older adults: A critical review. *Clinical Psychology Review, 14*(5), 383–415.

Flannery, R. B. (1990). Social support and psychological trauma: A methodological review. *Journal of Traumatic Stress, 3,* 593–612.

Foa, E. B. (1996). *Failure of emotional processing: Post-trauma psychopathology and its treatment.* Paper presented at the 104th Annual Convention of the American Psychological Association, Toronto.

Foa, E. B., Freund, B. F., Hembree, E., Dancu, C. V., Franklin, M. E., Perry, K. J., Riggs, D. S., & Molnar, C. (1994, November). *Efficacy of short term behavioral treatments of PTSD in sexual and nonsexual assault victims.* Paper presented at the annual meeting of the Association for Advancement of Behavior Therapy, San Diego, CA.

Foa, E. B., & Kozak, M. J. (1986). Treatment of anxiety disorders: Implications for psychopathology. In A. H. Tuma & J. Maser (Eds.), *Anxiety and the anxiety disorders* (pp. 421–452). Hillsdale, NJ: Erlbaum.

Foa, E. B., Molnar, C., & Cashman, L. (1995). Change in rape narratives during exposure therapy for posttraumatic stress disorder. *Journal of Traumatic Stress, 8*(4), 675–690.

Foa, E. B., Rothbaum, B. O., Riggs, D. S., & Murdock, T. B. (1991). Treatment of posttraumatic stress disorder in rape victims: A comparison between cognitive-behavioral procedures and counseling. *Journal of Consulting and Clinical Psychology, 59,* 712–715.

Fontana, A., & Rosenheck, R. (1994). A short form of the Mississippi Scale for measuring change in combat-related PTSD. *Journal of Traumatic Stress, 7*(3), 407–414.

Frank, E., Anderson, B., Stewart, B. D., Dancu, C., Hughes, C., & West, D. (1988). Efficacy of cognitive behavior therapy and systematic desensitization in the treatment of rape trauma. *Behavior Therapy, 19,* 403–420.

Freedy, J. R., Shaw, D. L., Jarrell, M. P. & Masters, C. R. (1992). Towards an understanding of the psychological impact of natural disasters: An application of the conservation resources stress model. *Journal of Traumatic Stress, 5,* 441–444.

Frueh, B. C., Turner, S. M., Beidel, D. C., Mirabella, R. F., & Jones, W. J. (1996). Trauma management therapy: A preliminary evaluation of a multicomponent behavioral treatment for chronic combat-related PTSD. *Behaviour Research and Therapy, 34*(7), 533–543.

Fry, P. S. (1983). Structured and unstructured reminiscence training and depression among the elderly. *Clinical Gerontology, 1,* 15–37.

Gallagher, D., Rose, J., Rivera, P., Lovett, S., & Thompson, L. (1989). Prevalence of depression in family caregivers. *Geronotologist, 29,* 449–456.

Gallagher, D., & Thompson, L. W. (1981). *Depression in the elderly: A behavioral treatment manual.* Los Angeles: USC Press.

Gallagher, D., & Thompson, L. W. (1982, August). *Elders maintenance of treatment benefits following individual psychotherapy for depression.* Results of a pilot study and preliminary data from an ongoing replication study. Paper presented at the annual meeting of the American Psychological Association, Washington, DC.

Gallagher-Thompson, D., Hanley-Peterson, P., & Thompson, L. W. (1990). Maintenance of gains versus relapse following brief psychotherapy for depression. *Journal of Consulting and Clinical Psychology, 58,* 371–374.

Gallagher-Thompson, D., & Thompson, L. W. (1995). Psychotherapy with older adults in theory and practice. In B. Bonger & L. Beutler (Eds.), *Comprehensive textbook of psychotherapy* (pp. 357–379). New York: Oxford University Press.

Gallagher-Thompson, D., & Thompson, L. W. (1996). Applying cognitive-behavioral therapy to the common psychological problems of later life. In S. H. Zarit & B. G. Knight (Eds.), *A guide to psychotherapy and aging* (pp. 61–82). Washington, DC: American Psychological Association Press.

Garfein, A. J., Ronis, D. L., & Bates, E. W. (1993). *Toward a case-mix planning model for the VA mental health outpatient system: Factors affecting diagnostic case-mix.* Ann Arbor, MI: Great Lakes Human Resources Research and Development Field Program.

Gatz, M. (1994). Application of assessment to therapy and intervention with older adults. In M. Storandt & G. R. VandenBos (Eds.), *Neuropsychological assessment of dementia and depression in older adults: A clinician's guide* (pp. 79–114). Washington, DC: American Psychological Association Press.

Gatz, M., Popkin, S., Pino, C., & VandenBos, G. (1985). Psychological interventions with older adults. In J. E. Birren & K. W. Schaie (Eds.), *Handbook of the psychology of aging* (2nd ed., pp. 755–788). New York: Van Nostrand Reinhold.

Goldstein, G., van Kammen, W., Shelly, C., Miller, D. J., & van Kammen, D. P. (1987). Survivors of imprisonment in the Pacific Theater during World War II. *American Journal of Psychiatry, 144,* 1210–1213.

Green, B. (1991). Evaluating the effects of disasters. *Psychological Assessment: A Journal of Consulting and Clinical Psychiatry, 3,* 538–546.

Green, B., Epstein, S., Kruptnick, J., & Rowland, J. (1997). Trauma and medical illness: Assessing trauma-related disorders in medical settings. In J. P. Wilson & T. Keane (Eds.), *Assessing psychological trauma and PTSD* (pp. 160–191). New York: Guilford Press.

Gurian, B., & Miner, J. (1991). Clinical presentation of consulting in the elderly. In C. Salzman & B. Lebowitz (Eds.), *Anxiety in the elderly: Treatment and research* (pp. 31–40). New York: Springer.

Gurvits, T., Lakso, N., Schachter, S., Kuhne, A., Orr, S. & Pitman, R. (1993). Neurological status of Vietnam veterans with chronic posttraumatic stress disorder. *Journal of Neuropsychiatry and Clinical Neurosciences, 5,* 183–188.

Haley, W. E. (1996). The medical context of psychotherapy with the elderly. In S. H. Zarit & B. G. Knight (Eds.), *A guide to psychotherapy and aging* (pp. 221–240). Washington, DC: American Psychological Association Press.

Hankin, C. S., Abueg, F. R., Gallagher-Thompson, D., & Laws, A. (1996). Dimensions of PTSD among older veterans seeking outpatient care: A pilot study. *Journal of Clinical Geropsychology, 2*(4), 239–246.

Hanley-Peterson, P., Futterman, A., Thompson, L., Zeiss, A. M., Gallagher, D. & Ironson, G. (1990). Endogenous depression and psychotherapy outcome in an elderly population [abstract]. *Gerontologist, 30,* 51A.

Harvey, J., Orbuch, T., Chivalisz, K., & Garwood, G. (1991). Coping with sexual assault: The roles of account making and confiding. *Journal of Traumatic Stress, 4,* 515–532.

Hermans, H. J. M., & Hermans-Jansen, E. (1995). *Self-narratives: The construction of meaning in psychotherapy.* New York: Guilford Press.

Hobfoll, S., Spielberger, C., Breznitz, S., Figley, C., Folkman, S., Lepper-Green, B., Meichenbaum, D., Milgram, A., Sandler, I., Sarason, I., & van der Kolk, B. (1991). War-related stress: Addressing the stress of war and other traumatic events. *American Psychologist, 46,* 848–855.

Hoglend, P. (1996). Analysis of transference in patients with personality disorders. *Journal of Personality Disorders, 10,* 122–132.

Hooker, K., Monahan, D., Shifren, K., & Hutchinson, C. (1992). Mental and physical health of spouse caregivers: The role of personality. *Psychological Aging, 3,* 367–375.

Horowitz, M. J. (1986). *Stress response syndromes.* New York: Aronson.

Horowitz, M. J., Marmar, C., Krupnick, J., Wilmer, N., Kaltreider, M., & Wallestein, R. (1984). *Personality styles and brief psychotherapy.* New York: Blair.

Hovens, J. E., van Der Ploeg, H. M., Klaarenbeek, M. T., Bramsen, I., Schreuder, J. H., & Rivero, V. V. (1994). The assessment of posttraumatic stress disorder with the Clinician Administered PTSD Scale: Dutch results. *Journal of Clinical Psychology, 50*(3), 325–336.

Howard, G. (1991). Culture tales: A narrative approach to thinking, cross-cultural psychology, and psychotherapy. *American Psychologist, 46,* 187–197.

Hyer, L. (1995). Use of EMDR in a "dementing" PTSD survivor. *Clinical Gerontologist, 16,* 70–74.

Hyer, L., & Associates. (1994). *Trauma victim: Theoretical issues and practical suggestions.* Muncie, IN: Accelerated Development Inc.

Hyer, L., & Boyd, S. (1996). Personality scales as predictors of older combat veterans with post-traumatic stress disorder. *Psychological Reports, 79,* 1040–1042.

Hyer, L., & Brandsma, J. (1997). EMDR minus eye movements equals good psychotherapy. *Journal of Traumatic Stress, 10,* 515–527.

Hyer, L., McCranie, E., Boudewyns, P., & Sperr, E. (1996). Modes of long-term coping with trauma memories: Relative use and associations with personality among Vietnam with chronic PTSD. *Journal of Traumatic Stress, 9,* 299–317.

Hyer, L., & Stanger, E. (1997). The interaction of posttraumatic stress disorder and depression among older combat veterans. *Psychological Reports, 80,* 785–786.

Hyer, L., & Stewart, A. (in press). *Treatment of trauma in later life: A model for care.* New York: Guilford Press.

Hyer, L., & Summers, M. (1995). An understanding of combat trauma at later life. Augusta, GA: VA Merit Review.

Hyer, L., Summers, M., Boyd, S., Litaker, M., & Boudewyns, P. (1996). Assessment of older combat veterans with the CAPS: Psychometric properties, correct classification ratios, and best items. *Journal of Traumatic Stress, 9,* 587–595.

Hyer, L., Summers, M., Braswell, L., & Boyd, S. (1995). Posttraumatic stress disorder: Silent problems among older combat veterans. *Psychotherapy, 32,* 348–365.

Hyer, L., Swanson, G., Lefkowitz, R., Hillesland, D., Davis, H., & Woods, M. (1990). The application of the cognitive behavioral model to two older stressor groups. *Clinical Gerontologist, 9*(3–4), 145–190.

Janoff-Bulman, R. (1989). Assumptive worlds and the stress of traumatic events: Application of the schema construct. *Social Cognition, 7,* 113–136.

Jung, C. G. (1971). The stages of life. In J. Campbell (Ed.), *The portable Jung.* New York: Viking Press.

Kahn, M. (1991). *Between therapist and client: The new relationship.* New York: Freeman.

Keane, T. M., Fairbank, J. A., Caddell, J. M., & Zimering, R. T. (1989). Implosive (flooding) therapy reduces symptoms of PTSD in Vietnam combat veterans. *Behavior Therapy, 20,* 245–260.

Kiecolt-Glaser, J. K., Dura, J., Speicher, C., Trask, O. J., & Glaser, R. (1991). Spousal caregivers of dementia victims: Longitudinal changes in immunity and health. *Psychosomatic Medicine, 53,* 345–362.

Kilpatrick, D. G., & Veronen, L. J. (1983). Treatment for rape-related problems: Crisis intervention is not enough. In L. H. Cohen, W. L. Claiborn, & G. A. Specter (Eds.), *Crisis intervention.* New York: Human Sciences Press.

Knight, B. G. (1996). *Psychotherapy with older adults* (2nd ed.). Newbury Park, CA: Sage.

Knight, J. A. (1997). Neuropsychological assessment in posttratumatic stress disorder. In J. P. Wilson & T. M. Keane (Eds.), *Assessing psychological trauma and PTSD* (pp. 448–492). New York: Guilford Press.

Kovach, C. (1990). Promise and problems in reminiscence research. *Journal of Gerontological Nursing, 16*(4), 10–14.

Lee, K. A., Vaillant, G. E., Torrey, W. C., & Elder, G. H. (1995). A 50-year prospective study of the psychological sequelae of World War II combat. *American Journal of Psychiatry, 152,* 516–522.

Litz, B. T., & Keane, T. M. (1989). Information processing in anxiety disorders: Application to the understanding of post-traumatic stress disorder. *Clinical Psychology Review, 9,* 243–257.

Logsdon, R. G. (1995). Psychopathology and treatment: Curriculum and research needs. In B. G. Knight, L. Terri, P. Wohlford, & J. Santos (Eds.), *Mental health services for older adults: Implications for training and practice in geropsychology* (pp. 41–51). Washington DC: American Psychological Association.

Maughan, B., & Rutter, M. (1997). Retrospective reporting of childhood and adult psychopathology. *Journal of Personality Disorders, 11,* 19–33.

Mazor, A., Gampel, Y., Enright, R. D., & Orenstein, R. (1990). Holocaust survivors: Coping with post-traumatic memories in childhood and 40 years later. *Journal of Traumatic Stress, 3,* 1–14.

McAdams, D. (1990). Unity and purpose in human lives: The emergency of identity as a life story. In I. Rabin, R. Zucker, R. Emmons, & S. Frank (Eds.), *Studying person and lives* (pp. 148–200). New York: Springer.

McAdams, D. P. (1993). *The stories we live by: Personal myths and the making of the self.* New York: Morrow.

McAdams, D. P. (1996). Personality, modernity, and the storied self: A contemporary framework for studying persons. *Psychological Inquiry, 7*(4), 295–321.

McCann, I., & Pearlman, L. (1990). *Psychological trauma and the adult survivor: Theory, therapy and transformation.* New York: Brunner/Mazel.

McCarthy, P., Katz, I., & Foa, E. (1991). Cognitive-behavioral treatment of anxiety in the elderly: A proposal model. In C. Saltzman & B. Lebowitz (Eds.), *Anxiety in the elderly: Treatment and research* (pp. 197–214). New York: Springer.

McFarlane, A. C., & Yehuda, R. (1996). Resilience, vulnerability, and the course of post-traumatic reactions. In B. A. van der Kolk, A. C. McFarlane, & L. Weisaeth (Eds.), *Traumatic stress: The effects of overwhelming experience on mind, body, and society* (pp. 155–181). New York: Guilford Press.

McNally, R. J., Lasko, N. B., Macklin, M. L., & Pitman, R. K. (1995). Autobiographical memory disturbance in combat-related posttraumatic stress disorder. *Behavior Research and Therapy, 33*(6), 619–630.

Meichenbaum, D., & Frizpatrick, D. (1991). A constructivist narrative perspective of stress and coping: Stress inoculation applications. In L. Goldberger & S. Breznitz (Eds.), *Handbook of stress.* New York: Free Press.

Mellman, T. A., Randolph, C. A., Brawman-Mintzer, O., Flores, L. P., & Milanes, F. J. (1992). Phenomenology and course of psychiatric disorders associated with combat-related posttraumatic stress disorder. *American Journal of Psychiatry, 149,* 1568–1574.

Millon, T., & Davis, R. (1995). *Disorders of personality: DSM-IV and beyond.* New York: Wiley.

Moore, T. (1994). *Care of the soul.* New York: Free Press.

Murray, E. J., & Segal, D. L. (1994). Emotional processing in vocal and written expression of feelings about traumatic experiences. *Journal of Traumatic Stress, 7,* 391–405.

Neimeyer, R. A., & Stewart, A. E. (in press). *Trauma, healing, and the narrative employment of loss.* University of Memphis Press.

Nelson, B. S., & Wright, D. W. (1996). Understanding and treating post-traumatic stress disorder symptoms in female partners of veterans with PTSD. *Journal of Marital and Family Therapy, 22,* 455–467.

Nichols, C. (1991). *Manual for the assessment of core goals.* Palo Alto, CA: Consulting Psychologists Press.

Ochberg, F. (1996). The counting method for ameliorating trauma memories. *Journal of Traumatic Stress, 9,* 873–881.

Op den Velde, W., Falger, P. R. J., Hovens, J. E., de Groen, J. H. M., Lasschuit, L. J., Duijn, H. V., & Schouten, E. G. W. (1993). Posttraumatic stress disorder in Dutch resistance veterans from World War II. In J. P. Wilson & B. Raphael (Eds.), *International handbook of traumatic stress syndromes* (pp. 219–230). New York: Plenum.

Paris, J. (1997). Introduction: Emotion and empiricism: Research on childhood trauma and adult psychopathology. *Journal of Personality Disorders, 11,* 1–4.

Parker, R. G. (1995). Reminiscence: A continuity theory framework. *Gerontologist, 35*(4), 515–525.

Pearlin, L. (1992). The career of caregivers. *Gerontologist, 32,* 647–648.

Pearlin, L. I., Mullan, J. T., Semple, S. J. & Skaff, M. M. (1990). Caregiving and the stress process: An overview of concepts and their measures. *Geronotologist, 30,* 583–594.

Pennebaker, J. W. (1989). Confession, inhibition, and disease. In L. Berkowitz (Ed.), *Advances in experimental social psychology* (Vol. 22, pp. 211–244). Orlando, FL: Academic Press.

Pfeiffer, E., & Busse, E. W. (1973). Mental disorder in later life: Affective disorders; paranoid, neurotic, and situational reactions. In E. W. Busse & E. Pfeiffer (Eds.), *Mental illness in later life* (pp. 107–144). Washington, DC: American Psychiatric Association Press.

Potts, M. K. (1994). Long-term effects of trauma: Post-traumatic stress amongcivilian internees of the Japanese during World War II. *Journal of Clinical Psychology, 50,* 681–698.

Pynoos, R. S., Steinberg, A. M., & Goenjian, A. (1996). Traumatic stress in childhood and adolescence: Recent developments and current controversies. In B. A. van der Kolk, A. C. McFarlane, & L. Weisaeth (Eds.), *Traumatic stress: The effects of overwhelming experience on mind, body, and society* (pp. 331–358). New York: Guilford Press.

Resick, P. A., & Schnicke, M. K. (1992). Cognitive processing therapy for sexual assault victims. *Journal of Consulting and Clinical Psychology, 60*(5), 748–756.

Riggs, D. S., Rothbaum, B. O., & Foa, E. B. (1995). A prospective examination of symptoms of posttraumatic stress disorder in victims of nonsexual assault. *Journal of Interpersonal Violence, 10,* 201–214.

Rosen, J., Fields, R. B., Hand, A. M., Falsettie, G., & van Kammen, D. P. (1989). Concurrent posttraumatic stress disorder in psychogeriatric patients. *Journal of Geriatric Psychiatry and Neurology, 3,* 65–69.

Rosenheck, R., & Fontana, A. (1994). Long-term sequelae of combat in World War II, Korea and Vietnam: A comparative study. In R. J. Ursano, B. G. McCaughey, & C. S. Fullerton (Eds.), *Individual and community responses to trauma and disaster: The structure of human chaos* (pp. 330–359). Cambridge, UK: Cambridge University Press.

Ruegg, R., & Frances, A. (1995). New research in personality disorders. *Journal of Personality Disorders, 9*(1), 1–48.

Ruskin, P. E., & Talbott, J. A. (1996). *Aging and posttraumatic stress disorder.* Washington, DC: American Psychiatric Association Press.

Rutter, M., & Maughan, B. (1997). Psychosocial adversities in childhood and adulthood. *Journal of Personality Disorders, 11,* 4–19.

Rybarczyk, B., & Bellg, A. (1997). *Listening to life stories: A new approach to stress intervention in health care.* New York: Springer.

Rybash, J. M., Hoyer, W. J., & Roodin, P. A. (1986). *Adult cognition and aging.* Elmsford, NY: Pergamon Press.

Schnurr, P. P. (1996). Trauma, PTSD, and physical health. *PTSD Research Quarterly, 7*(3), 1–3.

Schnurr, P. P. (September, 1997). *War trauma of WWII and Korean Veterans.* Presentation at the Readjustment Counseling Service Meeting, Nashua, NH.

Schnurr, P. P., & Aldwin, C. M. (1993). Military service: Long-term effects on adult development. In R. Kastenbaum (Ed.), *Encyclopedia of adult development* (pp. 351–356). Phoenix, AZ: Onyx.

Schnurr, P. P., Aldwin, C. M., Spiro, A., Stukel, T., & Keane, T. M. (1993). *A longitudinal study of PTSD symptoms in older veterans.* Poster Session for the Symposium on the Future of VA Mental Health Research, Department of Veterans Affairs Office of Research and Development and National Foundation for Brain Research, Washington, DC.

Schulz, R. (1982). Emotionality and aging: A theoretical and empirical analysis. *Journal of Gerontology, 37,* 42–51.

Scogin, F., Rickard, H. C., Keith, S., Wilson, J., & McElreath, L. (1992). Progressive and imaginal relaxation training for elderly persons with subjective anxiety. *Psychology and Aging, 7,* 419–424.

Sewell, K. (1996). Constructional risk factors for a post-traumatic stress response following a mass murder. *Journal of Constructivist Psychology, 9.*

Shapiro, F. (1995). *Eye movement desensitization and reprocessing: Basic principles, protocols, and procedures.* New York: Guilford Press.

Sherman, E. (1981). *Counseling the aged: An integrative approach.* New York: Free Press.

Sherman, E. (1991). *Reminiscence and the self in old age.* New York: Springer.

Siegel, D. J. (1995). Memory, trauma, and psychotherapy: A cognitive science view. *The Journal of Psychotherapy Practice and Research, 4*(2), 93–122.

Seigler, I. (1994). Developmental health psychology. In M. Storant & G. VandenBos (Eds.), *The adult years: Continuity and change* (115–143). Washington, DC: American Psychological Association Press.

Singer, J. A., & Salovey, P. (1993). *The remembered self: Emotion and memory in personality.* New York: Free Press.

Smyth, L. (1995). *Clinicians' manual for the cognitive-behavioral treatment of posttraumatic stress disorder.* Harve de Grace, MD: RTR.

Solomon, S., Gerrity, E. T., & Muff, A. M. (1992). Efficacy of treatments for posttraumatic stress disorder. *Journal of the American Medical Association, 268,* 633–638.

Spiro, A., Aldwin, C.M., Levenson, M.R., & Schnurr, P.P. (1993, November). *Combat-related PTSD among older veterans.* Poster session for the symposium on The Future of VA Mental Health Research and Development and National Foundation for Brain Research, Washington, DC.

Spiro, A., Schnurr, P., & Aldwin, C. (1994). Combat-related posttraumatic stress disorder symptoms in older men. *Psychology and Aging, 9*(1), 17–26.

Stanger, E., & Hyer, L. (1997). *PTSD and depression: The interaction and problems.* Poster presented at the annual meeting of the American Psychological Association, Chicago, IL.

Stewart, J. (1995). Reconstruction of the self: Life-span-oriented group psychotherapy. *Journal of Constructivist Psychology, 8,* 129–148.

Storant, M. (1994). General principles of assessment of older adults. In M. Storant & G. VandenBos (Eds.), *Neuropsychological assessment of dementia and depression in older adults: A clinician's guide* (pp. 7–32). Washington, DC: American Psychological Association.

Suinn, R. M. (1990). *Anxiety management training: A behavior therapy.* New York: Plenum.

Suls, J., Marco, C. A., & Tobin, S. (1991). The role of temporal comparison, social comparison, and direct appraisal in the elderly's self evaluations of health. *Journal of Applied Social Psychology, 21,* 1125–1144.

Summers, M., & Hyer, L. (1994). PTSD among the elderly. In L. Hyer (Ed.), *Trauma victim: Theoretical issues and practical suggestions* (pp. 633–671). Muncie, IN: Accelerated Development.

Summers, M. N., Hyer, L., Boyd, S., & Boudewyns, P. A. (1996). Diagnosis of later-life PTSD among elderly combat veterans. *Journal of Clinical Geropsychology, 2,* 103–117.

Sutker, P., Bugg, F. & Allain, A. (1991). Psychometric prediction of PTSD among POW survivors. *Journal of Consulting and Clinical Psychology, 3,* 105–110.

Sutker, P., Wibstead, D., Galina, Z., & Allain, A. (1991). Cognitive deficits and psychopathology among former prisoners of war and combat veterans of Korea. *American Journal of Psychiatry, 148,* 67–72.

Tait, R., & Silver, R. (1984, August). *Recovery: The long-term impact of stressful life experience.* Paper presented at the 92nd Annual Convention of the American Psychological Association, Toronto.

Tedeschi, R. G., & Calhoun, L. G. (1995). *Trauma and transformation growing in the aftermath of suffering.* Thousand Oaks, CA: Sage.

Tennant, C. C., Goulston, K., & Dent, O. (1993). Medical and psychiatric consequences of being a prisoner of war of the Japanese: An Australian follow-up study. In J. P. Wilson & B. Raphael (Eds.), *International handbook of traumatic stress syndromes* (pp. 231–240). New York: Plenum.

Thompson, E., & Doll, W. (1982). The burden of families coping with the mentally ill: An invisible crisis. *Family Relations, 31,* 379–388.

Thompson, L. W., Gallagher, D., & Breckenridge, J. S. (1987). Comparative effectiveness of psychotherapies for depressed elders. *Journal of Consulting and Clinical Psychology, 53,* 385–390.

Thompson, L. W., Gallagher, D., & Czirr, R. (1988). Personality disorder and outcome in the treatment of late-life depression. *Journal of Geriatric Psychiatry, 21,* 133–146.

Thompson, L. W., Gallagher, D., Hanser, S., Gantz, F., & Steffen, A. (1991, November). *Comparison of desipramine and cognitive/behavioral therapy in the treatment of late-life depression.* Paper presented at the meeting of Gerontological Society of America, San Francisco, CA.

Thygesen, P. Hermann, K., & Willnger, R. (1970). Concentration camp survivors in Denmark: Persecution, disease, disability, and compensation. *Danish Medical Bulletin, 17,* 65–105.

Tornstam, L. (1996). Gerotranscendence—A theory about maturing into old age. *Journal of Aging and Identity, 1*(1), 37–50.

Turner, S. W., McFarlane, A. C., & van der Kolk, B. A. (1995). The therapeutic environment and new explorations in the treatment of posttraumatic stress disorder. In B. A. van der Kolk, A. C. McFarlane, & L. Weisaeth (Eds.), *Traumatic stress: The effects of overwhelming experience on mind, body, and society* (pp. 537–558). New York: Guilford Press.

Uddo, M., Vasterling, J., Brailey, K., & Sutker, P. (1993). Memory and attention in posttraumatic stress disorder. *Journal of Psychopathology and Behavioral Assessment, 15,* 43–52.

Ulman, R. B., & Brothers, D. (1988). *The shattered self: A psychoanalytic study of trauma.* Hillsdale, NJ: Analytic Press.

Ullman, S. E. (1995). Adult trauma survivors and post-traumatic stress sequelae: An analysis of reexperiencing, avoidance, and arousal criteria. *Journal of Traumatic Stress, 8,* 179–188.

Ullman, S. E., & Siegel, J. M. (1994). Predictors of exposure to traumatic events and posttraumatic stress sequelae. *Journal of Community Psychology, 22,* 328–338.

van der Kolk, B. A., & Fisler, R. (1995). Dissociation and the fragmentary nature of traumatic memories: Overview and exploratory study. *Journal of Traumatic Stress, 8*(4), 505–525.

van der Kolk, B. A., & McFarlane, A. C. (1996). The black hole of trauma. In B. A. van der Kolk, A. C. McFarlane, & L. Weisaeth (Eds.), *Traumatic stress: The effects of overwhelming experience on mind, body, and society* (pp. 3–23). New York: Guilford Press.

van der Kolk, B. A., McFarlane, A. C., & Weisaeth, L. (Eds.). (1996). *Traumatic stress: The effects of overwhelming experience on mind, body, and society.* New York: Guilford Press.

Vitaliano, P. P., Russo, J., Bailey, S. L., Young, H. M., & McCann, B. S. (1993). Psychosocial factors associated with cardiovascular reactivity in older adults. *Psychosomatic Medicine, 55,* 164–177.

Waysman, M., Mikulincer, M., Weisenberg, M., & Solomon, Z. (1993). Secondary traumatization among wives of PTS casualities: A family typology. *Psychologia Israel Journal of Psychology, 3,* 166–179.

Weiss, J. (1971). The emergence of new themes: A contribution to the psychoanalytic theory of therapy. *International Journal of Psycho-Analysis, 52,* 459–467.

Wolfe, B. E. (1995). Self pathology and psychotherapy integration. *Journal of Psychotherapy Integration, 5*(4), 293–312.

Wolfe, J., Mori, D. & Krygeris, S. (1994). Treating trauma in special populations: Lessons from women veterans. *Psychotherapy, 32,* 87–93.

Yehuda, R., Kahana, B., Schmeidler, J., Southwick, S. M., Wilson, S., & Giller, E. L. (1995). Impact of cumulative lifetime trauma and recent stress on current posttraumatic stress disorder symptoms in Holocaust survivors. *American Journal of Psychiatry, 152,* 1815–1818.

Zalewsi, C., Thompson, W., & Gottesman, I. (1994). Comparison of neuropsychological test performance in PTSD, generalized anxiety disorder, and control Vietnam veterans. *Assessment, 1,* 133–142.

Zarit, S. (1996). Clinical interventions for family caregiving. In S. H. Zarit & B. G. Knight (Eds.), *A guide to psychotherapy and aging* (pp. 139–162). Washington, DC: American Psychological Association Press.

Zeiss, R. A., & Dickman, H. R. (1989). PTSD 40 years later: Incidence and person-situation correlates in former POWs. *Journal of Clinical Psychology, 45,* 80–87.

Zeiss, R. A., & Steffen, A. M. (in press). Interdisciplinary health care teams: The basic unit of geriatric care. In L. L. Carstensen, B. A. Edelstein, & L. Dornbrand (Eds.), *The handbook of clinical gerontology.* Newbury Park, CA: Sage.

Index